THE COLLECTIVE BARGAINING PROCESS

READINGS AND ANALYSIS

CONSULTING EDITOR IN MANAGEMENT

John M. Ivancevich
University of Houston

The Collective Bargaining Process

READINGS AND ANALYSIS

JEAN A. BADERSCHNEIDER

SCHOOL OF BUSINESS
UNIVERSITY OF KANSAS

RICHARD N. BLOCK

SCHOOL OF LABOR AND INDUSTRIAL RELATIONS
MICHIGAN STATE UNIVERSITY

JOHN A. FOSSUM

GRADUATE SCHOOL OF BUSINESS ADMINISTRATION
UNIVERSITY OF MICHIGAN

1983

BUSINESS PUBLICATIONS, INC.
PLANO, TEXAS 75075

ISBN 0-256-02752-8
Library of Congress Catalog Card No. 82–72757

Printed in the United States of America

1 2 3 4 5 6 7 8 9 0 K 0 9 8 7 6 5 4 3

Dedication

Mark
Marcia, Talia, and Jessica

Preface

In recent years industrial relations courses, particularly courses on collective bargaining and dispute settlement, have become an increasingly important and popular component of business school curricula. In teaching such courses we have discovered that business students are particularly concerned with the practical aspects of industrial relations. They have a special desire to understand the collective bargaining process in a way that prepares them for actual participation. To meet their concerns, course material must be drawn from a wide variety of practitioner, as well as academic, sources.

While industrial relations and collective bargaining have developed into academic disciplines, they have remained highly dependent upon a close alignment with practitioners. This alignment is necessary if researchers are to understand the numerous processes involved in industrial relations and collective bargaining and has resulted in a keen interest in the ability of researchers to address problems faced by practitioners. Since industrial relations and collective bargaining are academic disciplines that also deal with issues of important public policy concern, a great deal of evaluative research has evolved that focuses on the impact of specific policies. Consequently, research in these areas may be useful to both policymakers and policy-implementing practitioners.

This book of readings is designed to provide the diverse materials necessary to teach university-level collective bargaining in a manner that recognizes the special nature of business students and encourages a close and useful link between researchers and future practitioners. It blends classic descriptive materials, empirical research, and material written by and for practitioners. Our goal is to provide students with (1) a basic understanding of the field, (2) a familiarity with and an appreciation for how the results of research can be practically useful, and (3) background material that outlines the "nuts and bolts" operation of collective bargaining and its related processes.

The book focuses on the integration of traditional economic and newer behavioral approaches to collective bargaining. While it covers subject matter related to labor history and industrial relations theories, it emphasizes the collective process itself, i.e., inducements to unionization, inducements to strike, the issues in collective bargaining, collective bargaining power, and the union and management as organizations with internal constraints. The basic assumption of the book is that while business students must be exposed to historical antecedents to today's collective bargaining system, they are most interested in knowing as much about the modern collective bargaining process as possible and something about the modern labor union.

The readings are of several distinct types, including (1) descriptive analyses of major areas in collective bargaining, (2) edited versions of major research findings, (3) primary source material (e.g., excerpts from court cases and arbitration opinions), and (4) practitioner-oriented materials. In some areas where material is limited or outdated we have found it necessary to contribute our own text, analysis, and interpretation.

The research findings are taken from academic journals and are edited to reduce the complexity of empirical analysis. In each article we retain the discussion of the data base and the general overview of the methodology, but we shorten the statistical result sections. The statistical terms that remain are briefly defined in the Glossary of Statistical Terms at the end of the book. It should also be noted that the footnotes are edited in many of the articles; bibliographic footnotes are deleted while most explanatory footnotes are retained. The reader is encouraged to refer to the original articles to analyze the empirical results in more detail and to obtain a complete set of footnotes.

Our attempt throughout the book is to integrate institutional and behavioral material, research findings, and practitioner-oriented discussion. In so doing, this book of readings is intended to be an appropriate textbook supplement for the increasing number of collective bargaining/industrial relations courses being taught in business schools. It makes a wide variety of material available without the inconvenience and expense often associated with outside readings.

Our concern throughout the book is that the material be viewed as an integrated whole so that the reader understands all the facets of collective bargaining as well as how they interact with one another. To aid in this integration, we develop and use a model of the collective bargaining process to structure the presentation of materials. (This model is outlined in Chapter 1.) The model is premised on an open systems approach which recognizes the reciprocity of the component parts of a collective bargaining system and provides the basis for understanding the interrelation of the entire system. Each division within the book represents the various subsystems of activity in the larger system of collective bargaining.

As with the publication of most books of readings, we have numerous individuals and organizations to thank. They include: The American Assembly, The AFL–CIO, The Brookings Institution, The Bureau of National Affairs, Inc., U.S. Bureau of Labor Statistics, The Conference Board, Harper and Row, Inc., *Harvard Business Review*, Harvard University Press, Houghton-Mifflin Company, *University of Illinois Law Review, Industrial and Labor Relations Review, Industrial Relations, Industrial Relations Research Association, Journal of Applied Psychology, Journal of Labor Research, Journal of Political Economy*, Augustus M. Kelly, *Labor History*, Department of Labor–Labor-Management Services Administration, McGraw-Hill Book Company, Prentice-Hall Inc., Southern Illinois University Press, *Wisconsin Law Review*. We also wish to acknowledge the following individuals who assisted in the editing of the articles: Leslie F. Corbitt, Robert L. Heneman, Steven L. Premack—all Ph.D. candidates in Social Science/Labor and Industrial Relations at Michigan State University—and Loretta K. Conen, who is currently with the Bendix Corporation. Finally, we want to specifically acknowledge and thank the authors identified in the Contents. Each has contributed in some way to the development of the field of industrial relations and to our understanding of collective bargaining processes.

Jean A. Baderschneider
Richard N. Block
John A. Fossum

CROSS-REFERENCE TABLE I FOR RELATING THE MATERIALS IN THIS READER TO JOHN FOSSUM'S *LABOR RELATIONS:*
DEVELOPMENT, STRUCTURE, PROCESS, REV. ED. (PLANO, TEX.: BUSINESS PUBLICATIONS, 1982)

CHAPTERS IN FOSSUM'S *LABOR RELATIONS*	CHAPTERS IN *COLLECTIVE BARGAINING PROCESS: READINGS AND ANALYSIS*
Chap. 1—Introduction	Chap. 1—Introduction Chap. 2—Basic Concepts and Overview
Chap. 2—The Evolution of American Labor: I Chap. 3—The Evolution of American Labor: II	Chap. 3—History of Collective Bargaining in the U.S.
Chap. 4—Labor Law and Federal Agencies	Chap. 4—The Legal Framework
Chap. 5—Union Structure and Government	Chap. 5—Unions as Organizations and Institutions Chap. 7—Management as a Bargaining Organization
Chap. 6—Union Organizing Campaigns	Chap. 6—Determinants of Unionization
Chap. 7—Economic Issues in Bargaining Chap. 8—Noneconomic Bargaining Issues	Chap. 12—Bargaining Issues and Outcomes
Chap. 9—Bargaining Theory and Structure	Chap. 8—Bargaining Structure Chap. 9—Bargaining Power
Chap. 10—Contract Negotiations	Chap. 10—The Process of Bargaining
Chap. 11—Impasses and Their Resolution	Chap. 11—Industrial Conflicts and Impasse Resolution
Chap. 12—Union-Management Cooperation	Chap. 10—The Process of Bargaining
Chap. 13—Contract Administration Chap. 14—Grievance Arbitration	Chap. 13—Contract Administration
Chap. 15—Public Sector Labor Relations	Chap. 4—The Legal Framework—The Public Sector Chap. 10—The Process of Bargaining
Chap. 16—Health Care Organizations	————
Chap. 17—Labor and Equal Employment Opportunity	
Chap. 18—Challenges to Collective Bargaining	Chap. 14—Collective Bargaining and Public Policy in the 1980s

CROSS-REFERENCE TABLE II FOR RELATING THE MATERIALS IN THIS READER TO LABOR RELATIONS AND COLLECTIVE BARGAINING TEXTBOOKS

SELECTED TEXTBOOKS	PART I INTRODUCTION AND OVERVIEW OF INDUSTRIAL RELATIONS CONCEPTS	PART II THE HISTORICAL LEGAL ENVIRONMENT	PART III THE PARTIES/ ORGANIZATIONS TO BARGAINING	PART IV THE BARGAINING STRUCTURE AND BARGAINING POWER	PART V THE COLLECTIVE BARGAINING PROCESS AND OUTCOMES	PART VI THE POLICY FORMATION/ CHANGE PROCESS
Edwin F. Beal; Edward D. Wickersham; and Philip K. Kienast, *The Practice of Collective Bargaining,* 5th ed. (Homewood, Ill.: Richard D. Irwin, 1976).	Chap. 1	Chaps. 2, 5	Chaps. 3, 4, 14	Chap. 6	Chaps. 6, 7, 8, 9, 10, 11, 12, 13, 15, 16	
Neil W. Chamberlain; Donald E. Cullen; and David Lewin, *The Labor Sector,* 3d ed. (New York: McGraw-Hill, 1980).		Chap. 3	Chap. 4		Chaps. 5, 6, 7, 9	Chaps. 10, 11, 12
Neil W. Chamberlain and James W. Kuhn, *Collective Bargaining,* 2d ed. (New York: McGraw-Hill, 1965).		Chaps. 1, 2, 11	Chaps. 8, 9	Chaps. 7, 10	Chaps. 3, 4, 5, 6, 13, 15, 16	Chaps. 12, 14, 17

Thomas Kochan, *Collective Bargaining and Industrial Relations* (Homewood, Ill.: Richard D. Irwin, 1980).	Chaps. 1, 2	Chap. 3	Chaps. 5, 6, 7	Chap. 4	Chaps. 8, 9, 10, 11, 12, 14	Chaps. 13, 15, 16
Daniel Quinn Mills, *Labor-Management Relations* (New York: McGraw-Hill, 1982).	Chap. 1	Chaps. 2, 3, 4, 5, 8, 21	Chaps. 6, 7, 9	Chap. 19	Chaps. 10, 11, 12, 13, 14, 15, 16, 17, 18, 20, 22, 23	Chap. 25
Arthur A. Sloane and Fred Witney, *Labor Relations*, 3d ed. (Englewood Cliffs, N.J.: Prentice-Hall, 1977).	Chap. 1	Chaps. 2, 3	Chaps. 1, 4		Chaps. 5, 6, 7, 8, 9, 10	Chap. 11

Contents

INTRODUCTION AND OVERVIEW

PART ONE

INTRODUCTION AND
OVERVIEW

CHAPTER 1

Introduction

Labor relations in the United States is based on the tradition of "business unionism."[1] Business unionism refers to the economic orientation of American unions in establishing and pursuing their organizational goals within a capitalist economy. Business union efforts do not seek to reform or overthrow the prevailing system but are directed toward incremental gains possible within it. Collective bargaining is the primary means for achieving goals within a business union orientation since the goals are achieved through employment in a capitalistic economy.

THE COLLECTIVE BARGAINING COMPONENT

Within the U.S. system of industrial relations, collective bargaining is a key process. The relationship between collective bargaining and other components of the U.S. industrial relations system is outlined in Exhibit 1. The environment consists of the behavior of the labor force; current laws and procedures governing employment; and the interaction of employing organizations, individuals participating in the labor force, and clients or customers of employers. The parties/organizations to bargaining are the companies, public employers, unions, and associations involved in collective bargaining. The bargaining structure and bargaining power refer to the way in which bargaining is organized between the parties and the ability of the parties to influence each other toward preferred goals. The bargaining process is the method used to mobilize bargaining power to achieve preferred goals; the outcomes are the conditions of employment that result from this process. Finally, the policy formation process is the manner in which public opinion becomes implemented through legislative and administrative changes.

---

[1] The term *business unionism* has been used over the years by theorists and practitioners to refer to unions with pragmatic, economic goals as opposed to political or long-run reformist goals. The origin of this term is due in part to the pragmatic, business-like orientation Samuel Gompers, the first president of the American Federation of Labor, took in representing his workers. Gompers's orientation focused on the short-term and *continual* betterment of the conditions under which union members work.

EXHIBIT 1   THE U.S. SYSTEM OF INDUSTRIAL RELATIONS

THE COLLECTIVE BARGAINING PROCESS

A basic assumption of this book is that the collective bargaining process
and its outcomes are constantly changing and constantly interacting with
the other components of the system. As can be seen in Exhibit 1, the
environment within which industrial relations operates affects the parties,
the type of bargaining structure, and the level of power each party brings
to the table. In turn, they all affect the bargaining process and outcomes.
The nature of the process and the type and level of outcomes also become
determinants, affecting the nature of the parties themselves and/or the
nature of the environment through policy changes.

For example, as a product market within an industry expands geographically, a union operating within the industry may engage in efforts to
centralize bargaining (i.e., change the bargaining structure) so as to take
wages out of competition. In doing so, local unions may lose power resulting in a change in the national union's organizational structure. Centralization may alter the balance of bargaining power enabling the union to
achieve bargaining outcomes not previously possible, such as a pension
program. Difficulties in the operation of such a program may then necessitate the formation of public policy to regulate its operation (e.g., the
Employee Retirement Income Security Act of 1974) and the environment
for industrial relations changes. This environmental change may limit
one party's bargaining power through prohibiting certain previously permissible bargaining outcomes. Also, bargaining structures may change if
the law increases pension liabilities in multiemployer units if a failure
in one firm occurs.

While collective bargaining is a dynamic process, forces of stability
also operate within a system of industrial relations. Some benefit may
exist in maintaining a system with known characteristics, thus the tendencies toward change and stability serve as countervailing forces. For example, during a period of rapid and severe inflation, both unions and managements might be forced to settle within a particular range if both parties
want to avoid mandatory wage and price controls, thereby maintaining
the existing system. Had they settled outside this range, the policy formation process might react in a way that would signal changes in other

subsystems and would alter the future bargaining power of the parties to strike a bargain of their own choosing.

The component parts (subsystems) of an industrial relations system must be viewed as an integrated whole. The interrelationships between the components indicate the dynamic nature of the relationships between the bargaining process and outcomes and other significant components of the system. This interdependency highlights the importance of examining all the components of industrial relations and how they relate to one another if the collective bargaining process and outcomes are to be understood. Throughout this book we will explore the research and explanations offered by a variety of approaches concerning the role of collective bargaining within the industrial relations system.

A CONCEPTUAL FRAMEWORK FOR THE READINGS

The conceptual framework outlined in Exhibit 1 is used as the basis for organizing the material covered in this book. Each component of the industrial relations system represents a division within the material. In dealing with each of these components, we outline key issues and problems and how they affect the process and outcomes of collective bargaining. Throughout the material, the bargaining process and outcomes are the central concern of the parties involved in the overall system.

After a general overview and definition of collective bargaining, we begin in Part Two with the environment within which collective bargaining has developed. Included in this section is material on the historical and legal foundations for the American labor movement. The historical material outlines the traditions that have shaped our system and continue to constrain the nature of both the bargaining process and its outcomes. This material pictures American workers, their charateristics, values, and demands, and how these continue to affect the nature of collective bargaining. The legal material outlines the formal context within which collective bargaining operates. The legal foundations are closely tied to the historical tradition. They reflect the public's interest in the roles of management and labor organizations and give a good indication of the political context for collective bargaining.

Intuitively it is easy to conceptualize the historical and legal contexts as both causing changes in, and being changed by, the outcomes of the collective bargaining system. History determines the traditions upon which the system is based and the operation of that system may in turn change the traditions. Similarly, the nature of labor law constrains through rules which alter bargaining power. The results of changes in the system are compared with the current interests of legislators, and labor law policy is changed if comparisons between actual and desired outcomes indicate a discrepancy.

The role of the economic environment as a determinant of collective bargaining has been extensively examined.[2] Variables such as inflation, elasticities of demand in both product and labor markets, and industry concentration have been examined as possible determinants of bargaining outcomes. While the economic context is an important environmental component, it is not dealt with in a separate chapter. Instead, the nature and operation of the economic context of collective bargaining is examined in some manner in many sections of the book.

In Part Three, we focus on both the union and management as organizations with needs and constraints that directly affect the bargaining process and its outcomes. The characteristics and structure of these parties are a result of the environment within which they operate and are designed to maximize the achievement of the goals set by each party. Consequently, these characteristics not only affect the collective bargaining process and outcomes, but they change as a result of the outcomes. Any change that occurs is designed to minimize future losses or maximize future returns to each organization. The readings included in this section are designed not only to give the reader a view of unions and managements as organizations but also to emphasize the role of each as an organization responsive to individual workers and their decision to join or not to join a union.

The functioning of unions and managements as organizations is an important determinant of the strength the parties bring to the bargaining table. Thus, the organizational context of bargaining is tied directly to the nature of bargaining structure and the type and level of bargaining power each organization brings to bargaining.

Part Four deals with bargaining structure and bargaining power. While both are directly a function of the legal environment, the parties themselves have a direct impact on each by structuring the collective bargaining process (within the constraints of the law) in such a manner as to maximize the results of bargaining in their favor. Hence, depending upon the results of bargaining, each party may attempt to change the bargaining structure so as to constrain future bargaining results to levels it deems more appropriate. To do this they may change the degree of centralization in the bargaining process, the degree to which an informal pattern-setting/pattern-following scheme is followed, or a number of other characteristics of the bargaining structure. These changes may then affect the internal structure and organizational processes of both the union and management, particularly the decision-making processes of each organization.

Part Five deals with the bargaining process and outcomes. By examining the nature of the environment, the characteristics of the parties, and the structure and power of the parties, we set the stage for understanding both the process and substance of bargaining as well as the determinants

---

[2] Studies focusing on the economic environment as a determinant of collective bargaining include: Daniel J. B. Mitchell, "Union Wage Determination: Policy Implications and Outlook," *Brooking's Papers on Economic Activity*, 3 (1978), pp. 537–91; and Farrell E. Bloch and Mark S. Kuskin, "Wage Determination in the Union and Nonunion Sector," *Industrial and Labor Relations Review*, January 1978, pp. 183–92.

of bargaining outcomes. The substantive concerns deal with the nature of particular issues in negotiations (e.g., terms of employment, level of compensation, etc.), and the procedural concerns deal with the actual act of negotiating, how issues in dispute get settled (e.g., the use of impasse procedures, the formation of joint labor-management committees, etc.), and how the contract is implemented.

The bargaining process and its outcomes are both dependent and independent variables. They are a result of environmental and organizational/ structural factors *and* in turn determine changes in each of these factors. By examining the bargaining process and outcomes the importance of the interrelationship between components becomes very evident and the need for considering the impact of the environment in order to understand the overall operation and integration of the collective bargaining system is clearly demonstrated.

Part Six deals with the importance of the policy formation or policy change mechanism. The concept of policy adopted here refers to both publicly and privately formulated constraints. It includes legislation, administrative directives, or privately developed programs. These policy mechanisms have significant impact on the environment but also affect the parties directly by determining bargaining power. While they are not the only determinants of bargaining power (market, economic, technological, industrial, and other considerations affect the ultimate level of bargaining power), they are the most direct constraints on the parties because they determine the legitimation and limits of bargaining activities.

If one party in the system finds either the operation of the bargaining process or its outcomes unacceptable, it may seek to change the policy constraints so that future outcomes indicate a more socially acceptable distribution of power or more realistically reflect the existing power distribution. The parties advocating change may be labor, management, government, consumer groups, or social advocates, and the process of change may reflect attempts to "proportionally empower" a disenfranchised party or play out struggles involving "power politics."

Proportional empowerment refers to policy changes that equalize power between an individual, group, or institution and its adversary.[3] The changes are necessary because under existing terms there is a severe and *unjust* imbalance of power as determined by societal standards. We have seen examples of this throughout the middle 1900s as labor legislation changed from what was called a prolabor stance (represented by the Wagner Act of 1935) to a promanagement stance (represented by the Taft-Hartley Act of 1947). Power politics refers to the process whereby policy is thrust upon society by one party which has generated enough power to establish policy changes that are likely to result in more favorable bargaining outcomes. This has been the case with the success of powerful

[3] Proportional empowerment is defined in Gerald W. Cormick, *"Power, Strategy, and the Process of Community Conflict: A Theoretical Framework"* (Ph.D. dissertation, University of Michigan, 1971).

police and firefighter unions in achieving interest arbitration statutes in numerous states.

While the policy formation process is often viewed as a result of the outcomes of collective bargaining, it is our view that the potential for policy change forces the parties to consider the possible policy changes resulting from different settlements. Therefore, the *potential* for policy change affects the negotiations and the degree of "risk" associated with a given bargaining activity or outcome. The perceptions of the ability of any party to change policy is a direct component of bargaining power. Thus, we see policy changes occurring when society perceives an unfair power distribution or when one party gathers enough power to force policy changes that are closely related to the outcomes it desires. It is our view that the potential for such policy changes is an important dimension of the bargaining process.

The materials presented in Part Six provide the basis for understanding both the dynamics and stability of the collective bargaining system. For this reason, discussion of the policy formation process concludes our book.

VIEWS ON COLLECTIVE BARGAINING

Our concern throughout this book is to integrate descriptive, empirical, and practitioner-oriented materials. This integration is based on our belief that collective bargaining is an area where there must be a close link between researcher, practitioner, and policymaker. This link is necessary if the organizational, political, socioemotional, and attitudinal factors in bargaining are to be understood. In educating future practitioners, we want to encourage this link.

We have several other views concerning the American labor movement, collective bargaining, and constraints on the operation of the overall industrial relations system that may be important in understanding the presentation of materials in the following chapters. First, we believe that unions are institutions that serve a useful purpose in society. Whether this purpose is fulfilled directly by unions or by the operation of what has been called the *threat effect*[4] is debatable. However, we believe that the collectivization of labor power that unions represent balances the economic power of labor and capital, a balance that might not otherwise exist in a capitalistic society. At the same time we do not subscribe to either a prounion or promanagement ideology. We believe in the basic rights of both in a free market economy, but we do not believe, a priori, that either party is always justified in its actions.

Second, we do not subscribe to the belief that the labor movement is in a state of irreversible decline because it has been unable recently

---

[4] The threat effect operates where the wages of nonunion workers are increased by the unionization of others, i.e., wage increases in the unionized sector spill over to the nonunion sector because employers attempt to avoid unionization. Threats of unionism can therefore indirectly affect wages and other terms and conditions of employment of nonunion workers. See S. Rosen, "Trade Union Power, Threat Effects and the Extent of Organization," *Review of Economic Studies* 36 (1969), pp. 185–96, for an examination of threat effects.

to expand its membership. Instead, we see the labor movement in a period of transition, attempting to adjust to a labor force changing in terms of sex, occupational, industrial, and geographical distributions. We see unions caught in a classic organizational conflict between serving their present constituents and addressing the concerns of a more diverse group of potential members. Our view is that the labor movement is beginning to respond to the changing labor force—note recent union successes in organizing such groups as teachers and workers in health care.

Another view we hold is that the organizational/political nature of unions makes resort to total cooperation impossible, thereby limiting the nature of change occurring through the bargaining process. In recent years it has been argued that collective bargaining must become more "integrative" (i.e., problem solving in its approach) and less distributive (i.e., adversarial) if it is to survive in coming years.[5] Given the value placed on multilateral power bases and the competitive tradition in the United States, we do not see an end to confrontation-style bargaining. We may, however, see situations where a labor-management coalition makes sense to both on certain issues or for a temporary time period where both feel simultaneously threatened by the environment.

In the same vein, it has been argued that binding arbitration of collective bargaining disputes should replace the right to strike. While the verdict is not complete concerning the effectiveness of dispute resolution procedures as substitutes for the right to strike, we see resort to arbitration of bargaining disputes as realistic in only very unique situations where both labor and management are losing a great deal from exercising the right to strike.[6] Again, the organizational nature of the parties constrains the type of change that may occur in the bargaining process. Collective bargaining remains a power struggle and neither side is willing to cede the determination of an outcome to an outsider. Consequently, we do not see the end to "free" collective bargaining, i.e., collective bargaining buttressed by the right to strike.

While we see changes in the nature of the bargaining process being constrained by organizational characteristics, we do see indications that the substance of bargaining may shift in emphasis. Given recent declines in various sectors of the U.S. economy, we see job and income security as well as productivity becoming major bargaining issues. Given the interrelatedness of bargaining issues, these concerns are likely to affect the nature and level of settlements on other bargaining issues as well.

While the nature of the issues emphasized may change, the ideological premise of collective bargaining will not. The U.S. labor movement, with

---

[5] Both terms are developed by Richard E. Walton and Robert B. McKersie in *A Behavioral Theory of Labor Negotiations* (New York: McGraw-Hill, 1965).

[6] For example, arbitration was adopted in 1973 in the steel industry when the United Steelworkers of America and the 10 steel companies represented by the Coordinating Committee of Steel Companies negotiated the "Experimental Negotiating Agreement" (ENA) which substituted binding arbitration for the right to strike. The ENA was adopted because the boom-or-bust cycle of production that had resulted from the strike threat had resulted in adverse financial conditions for the companies and fluctuating employment trends for the employees.

its tradition of business unionism, is economically oriented and is not motivated by the goal of overthrowing society. While some have argued that recent defeats (most notably the defeat of the labor law reform bill in 1978) may force labor into a reformist mode, whereby acceptance of the capitalistic system is no longer central, we do not subscribe to such a view.[7] While the labor movement may become more involved in the elective process, its actions will surely be constrained to working within the system.

Finally, we ask readers to keep in mind several important questions as they read this material. As a society are we asking too much of collective bargaining? Has it become too easy to blame collective bargaining for the economic and industrial ills of the U.S. economy? Collective bargaining is viewed as a mechanism through which to increase the standard of living, but we ask that it do so without inflation. We ask that it contribute to rising productivity but yet much of our physical plant is antiquated. We ask unions to engage in "free" collective bargaining, but at the same time we ask them not to strike. We ask unions to respond to the interests of the majority of members but at the same time to avoid discriminating against minorities within their organizations. Such conflicting values make evaluation of the effectiveness of collective bargaining extremely difficult. Our own view is that while collective bargaining may not be the best process for handling employee relations, it should be judged fairly, understanding the many conflicting pressures on it.

---

[7] For a description of this arguement see Daniel Quinn Mills, "Flawed Victory in Labor Law Reform," *Harvard Business Review,* May–June 1979, pp. 92–102.

CHAPTER 2

Basic Concepts and Overview

The purpose of this chapter is to detail more specifically the concept of an industrial relations system, introduce the reader to the concept of collective bargaining, and provide a general description of collective bargaining as it exists in both the private and public sectors in the United States.

We begin with John Dunlop's paper which defines an industrial relations system and analyzes its component parts. He outlines the role of an industrial relations system within the overall industrial society and distinguishes it from the economic society. His analysis of the structure and characteristics of the industrial relations subsystem of industrial society defines more explicitly the components of the system used in this book and outlined in Chapter 1. The actors in Dunlop's system define the parties/organizations to bargaining; the contexts and ideology of the system describe various aspects of the environment that affect the parties, their power, and the nature of collective bargaining; and the establishment of rules generally defines the types of outcomes that result from the operation of an industrial relations system.

It should be noted that Dunlop's concept of ideology refers to the traditions of an industrial relations system as determined by its historical development. The ideology of the U.S. system is "business unionism." This ideology not only binds the system together but constrains the types of changes that occur within the system through the choice of bargaining structures the parties might use.

Jack Barbash's article outlines the general characteristics of American collective bargaining and the special characteristics of collective bargaining in specific U.S. industries. His article defines the operational characteristics of business unionism. It also shows how this concept results in variations in bargaining across industries by introducing case profiles of nine diverse industries that provide descriptive examples of labor-management problems that uniquely shape the process and outcomes of bargaining.

While the bulk of material covered in this book is concerned with private sector collective bargaining, the increasing strength of public sector unions and the importance of their operation in the overall system of industrial relations make it necessary to examine the special characteristics of public sector collective bargaining. The article by David Lewin summarizes recent changes in public sector labor relations and points out its unique characteristics that shape both the process and outcomes of collective bargaining.

INDUSTRIAL RELATIONS AND INDUSTRIAL SOCIETY

John T. Dunlop*

In primitive and agrarian societies the analogue of industrial relations problems arise—such as, who shall perform what work, what standards of discipline shall be applied at the work place, or how shall the fruits of labor be divided. These issues are typically handled within the extended family which is closely integrated into the society. In the plantation-slave society the corresponding problems are met by the political institutions that maintain slavery.[1] Thus, industrial-relations problems of a general type are not unique to modern industrial society. But industrial society, whatever its political form, creates a distinctive group of workers and managers. The relations among these workers and managers, and their organizations, are formally arranged in the industrial society outside the family and distinct from political institutions, although the family and political institutions may in fact be used to shape or control relations between managers and workers at the industrial work place.[2]

* * * * *

* Lamont University Professor, Harvard University. Reprinted from *Industrial Relations Systems* (Carbondale, Ill.: Southern Illinois University Press, 1958), pp. 3–18, © John T. Dunlop.

[1] W. Arthur Lewis, *The Theory of Economic Growth* (London: George Allen and Unwin, 1955), pp. 107–13.

[2] Clark Kerr, Frederick H. Harbison, John T. Dunlop, and Charles A. Myers, "The Labour Problem in Economic Development," *International Labour Review*, March 1955, pp. 223–35.

STRUCTURE OF AN INDUSTRIAL-RELATIONS SYSTEM

An industrial-relations system at any one time in its development is regarded as comprised of certain actors, certain contexts, an ideology which binds the industrial-relations system together, and a body of rules created to govern the actors at the work place and work community.

THE ACTORS IN A SYSTEM

The actors are: (1) a hierarchy of managers and their representatives in supervision, (2) a hierarchy of workers (nonmanagerial) and any spokesmen, and (3) specialized governmental agencies (and specialized private agencies created by the first two actors) concerned with workers, enterprises, and their relationships. These first two hierarchies are directly related to each other in that the managers have responsibilities at varying levels to issue instructions (manage), and the workers at each corresponding level have the duty to follow such instructions (work).

The hierarchy of workers does not necessarily imply formal organizations; they may be said to be "unorganized" in popular usage, but the fact is, that wherever they work together for any considerable period, at least an informal organization comes to be formulated among the workers with norms of conduct and attitudes toward the hierarchy of managers. In this sense workers in a continuing enterprise are never unorganized. The formal hierarchy of workers may be organized into several competing or complementary organizations, such as works councils, unions, and parties.

The hierarchy of managers need have no relationship to the ownership of the capital assets of the work place; the managers may be public or private or a mixture in varying proportions. In the United States, for instance, consider the diverse character of management organizations in the executive departments of the federal government, local fire departments, the navy yards, the Tennessee Valley Authority, municipal transit operations and local utilities, government-owned and privately operated atomic-energy plants, railroads and public utilities, and other private enterprises. The range of combinations is greater where governments own varying amounts of shares of an enterprise and where special developmental programs have been adopted. The management hierarchy in some cases may be contained within an extended or a narrow family, and its activities largely explained in terms of the family system of the society.

The specialized government agencies as actors may have functions in some industrial-relations systems so broad and decisive as to override the hierarchies of managers and workers on almost all matters. In other industrial-relations systems the role of the specialized governmental agencies, at least for many purposes, may be so minor or constricted as to permit consideration of the direct relationships between the two hierarchies without reference to governmental agencies, while in still other systems the worker hierarchy or even the managerial hierarchy may be assigned a relatively narrow role. But in every industrial-relations system these are the three actors.[3]

---

[3] The term *actor* may have the limitation that it conveys the unreality or pretense of the stage. But *participant* is too passive, and other terms are no more satisfactory. Actor is used in the sense of doer or reagent.

THE CONTEXTS OF A SYSTEM

The actors in an industrial-relations system interact in a setting which involves three sets of givens. These features of the environment of an industrial-relations system are determined by the larger society and its other subsystems and are not explained within an industrial-relations system. These contexts, however, are decisive in shaping the rules established by the actors in an industrial-relations system. The significant aspects of the environment[4] in which the actors interact are: (1) the technological characteristics of the work place and work community, (2) the market or budgetary constraints which impinge on the actors, and (3) the locus and distribution of power in the larger society.

The technological features of the workplace have very far reaching consequences for an industrial-relations system, influencing the form of management and employee organization, the problems posed for supervision, many of the features of the required labor force, and the potentialities of public regulation. The mere listing of a few different workplaces reveals something of the range of industrial-relations systems within an industrial society and the influence of the technological characteristics: airlines, coal mines, steel mills, press and wire services, beauty parlors, merchant shipping, textile plants, banks, and food chain stores, to mention only a few. The technological characteristics of the workplace, including the type of product or service created, go far to determine the size of the work force, its concentration in a narrow area or its diffusion, the duration of employment at one locale, the

---

[4] "There does always exist some organization of living matter whose function is to maintain itself in direct interaction with its environment. In the terminology of modern genetics, we may speak of this as the phenotypic system." Julian Huxley, "Evolution, Cultural and Biological," in *New Bottles For New Wine* (London: Chatto and Windus, 1957), p. 63.

stability of the same working group, the isolation of the workplace from urban areas, the proximity of work and living quarters, the contact with customers, the essentiality of the product to the health and safety or to the economic development of the community, the handling of money, the accident potential, the skill levels and education required, the proportions of various skills in the work force, and the possibilities of the employment of women and children. These and many other features of the technology of the workplace are significant to the type of managerial and worker hierarchies and government agencies that arise. They also pose very different types of problems for the actors and constrain the types of solutions to these problems that may be invented and applied. Significant differences among indusrial-relations systems are to be attributed to this facet of the environment, and, in turn, identical technological environments in quite different national societies may be regarded as exerting a strong tendency upon the actors (modified by other factors) to create quite similar sets of rules.

The market or budgetary constraints are a second feature of the environmental context which is fundamental to an industrial-relations system. These constraints often operate in the first instance directly upon the managerial hierarchy, but they necessarily condition all the actors in a particular system. The context may be a market for the output of the enterprise or a budgetary limitation or some combination of the two. The product market may vary in the degree and character of competition through the full spectrum from pure competition, monopolistic competition and product differentiation, to oligopoly and monopoly. A charitable institution or a nationalized plant is no less confronted by a financial restraint than a private business enterprise, and the harshness of the budgetary strictures which confront managements vary among nonmarket units in the

same way that degrees of competition vary among market-oriented enterprises. These constraints are no less operative in socialist than in capitalist countries. The relevant market or budgetary constraints may be local, national, or international depending on the industrial-relations system; the balance of payments constitutes the form of the market restraint for nationwide systems.

The product market or budget is a decisive factor in shaping the rules established by an industrial-relations system.[5] The history in the past generation of the textile and coal industries around the world is testimony to the formative influence of the market or budgetary influence on the operation of industrial-relations systems. The contrasts between industries sheltered or exposed to international competition is another illustration. The interdependence of wage and price fixing in public utilities gives a distinctive characteristic to these systems of industrial relations. The degrees of cost and price freedom in monopolistic industries permeate these industrial-relations systems. The market or budgetary context also indirectly influences the technology and other characteristics of the work place: the scale and size of operations and the seasonal and cyclical fluctuations in demand and employment. An industrial-relations system created and administered by its actors is adaptive to its market and budgetary constraints.

The locus and distribution of power[6] in the larger society, of which the particular industrial-relations complex is a subsystem, is a third analytical feature of the environmental context. The relative distribution of power among the actors in the larger society tends to a degree to be re-

[5] John T. Dunlop, *Wage Determination under Trade Unions* (New York: Macmillan, 1944), pp. 95–121.

[6] S. K. and B. M. Selekman, *Power and Morality in a Business Society* (New York: McGraw-Hill, 1956).

flected within the industrial-relations system; their prestige, position, and access to the ultimates of authority within the larger society shapes and constrains an industrial-relations system. At this juncture the concern is not with the distribution of power *within* the industrial-relations system, the relative bargaining powers among the actors, or their controls over the processes of interaction or rule setting. Rather the reference is to the distribution of power outside the industrial-relations system, which is given to that system. It is, of course, possible that the distribution of power within the industrial-relations system corresponds exactly to that within the contextual society. But that this need not be so is illustrated by numerous instances of conflict between economic power within an industrial-relations system and political power within a society, or by the tendency for an actor to seek to transfer a conflict to the political or economic arena in which his control over the situation is thought to be relatively greater. The general strike and French and Italian experience for a period after World War II particularly illustrate the point. The dominance of an army group, a traditional and dynastic family elite, a dictator, the church, a colonial administrator, a political party, or public opinion are types of power orientation in the larger society that tend to shape an industrial-relations system.

The distribution of power in the larger society does not directly determine the interaction of the actors in the industrial-relations system. Rather, it is a context which helps to structure the industrial-relations system itself. The function of one of the actors in the industrial-relations system, the specialized governmental agencies, is likely to be particularly influenced by the distribution of power in the larger society. Industrial-relations systems national in scope as different as those in contemporary Spain, Egypt, USSR, Yugosla-

via, and Sweden call attention to the distribution of power within the larger society. Industrial-relations systems of a lesser scope, such as those at the plant level, are also shaped by the distribution of power within the industrial-relations system which is exterior to the plant level. Thus, the industrial-relations system at a plant level which is part of a highly centralized industrywide arrangement is quite different from one which is decentralized to the plant level. The distribution of power in the society exterior to the industrial-relations system is regarded as given to that system and helps to shape its operations.

The full context of an industrial-relations system which is given for the three actors consists at a given time in the development of that system of (1) the technological and work-community environment, (2) the market or budgetary constraints, and (3) the distribution of power in the contextual society.

THE ESTABLISHMENT OF RULES

The actors in given contexts establish rules for the work place and the work community, including those governing the contacts among the actors in an industrial-relations system. This network or web of rules[7] consists of procedures for establishing rules, the substantive rules, and the procedures for deciding their application to particular situations. The establishment of these procedures and rules—the procedures are themselves rules—is the center of attention in an industrial-relations system. Just as the "satisfaction of wants" through the production and exchange of goods and services is the locus of analysis in the economic subsystem of society, so

---

[7] Clark Kerr and Abraham Siegel, "The Structuring of the Labor Force in Industrial Society: New Dimensions and New Questions," *Industrial and Labor Relations Review*, January 1955, pp. 163–64.

the establishment and administration of these rules is the major concern or output of the industrial-relations subsystem of industrial society. In the course of time the rules may be expected to be altered as a consequence of changes in the contexts and in the relative status of the actors. In a dynamic society the rules, including their administration, are under frequent review and change.

There is a wide range of procedures possible for the establishment and the administration of the rules. In general terms the following ideal types can be distinguished: the managerial hierarchy may have a relatively free hand uninhibited in any overt way by the other two actors; the specialized governmental agencies may have the dominant role without substantial participation of the managerial or worker hierarchies; the worker hierarchy may even carry the major role in rule fixing; the management and worker hierarchies in some relationships may set the rules together without substantial participation of any specialized governmental agency; finally, the three actors may all play a consequential role in rule setting and administration. The procedures and the authority for the making and the administration of the rules governing the work place and the work community is a critical and central feature of an industrial-relations system, distinguishing one system from another.

The actors who set the web of rules interact in the context of an industrial-relations system taken as a whole, but some of the rules will be more closely related to the technical and market or budgetary constraints, while other rules will be more directly related to the distribution of power in the larger society. Thus maritime safety rules are related primarily to the technology of ships, while rules defining the relative rights of officers and crew aboard ship are related primarily to the distribution of power in a larger society. But safety rules are also influenced to a degree by the distribution of power in the full community, and the obligations and rights of officers and crew aboard ship are clearly conditioned to a degree by the technical problems of running a ship. While the context is an interdependent whole, some rules are more dependent upon one feature of this context than others.

A vast universe of substantive rules is established by industrial-relations systems apart from procedures governing the establishment and the administration of these rules. In general, this expanse can be charted to include (1) rules governing compensation in all its forms, (2) the duties and performance expected from workers including rules of discipline for failure to achieve these standards, and (3) rules defining the rights and duties of workers, including new or laid-off workers, to particular positions or jobs. The actual content of these rules varies enormously among systems, particularly, as will be shown, as a consequence of the technological and market contexts of the systems.

One of the major problems of this inquiry is to determine the extent to which similar rules are developed in different industrial-relations systems with common technological contexts and similar market or budgetary constraints. The inquiry also seeks to isolate in systems otherwise similar the separate influence of the locus of power in the larger society, the form of organization of the actors, and their relationships upon the substantive rules. In general terms the rules, including the procedures for establishing and administering them, may be treated as the independent variable to be "explained" theoretically in terms of other characteristics of the industrial-relations system.

Whatever the specific content of rules and regardless of the distribution of authority among the actors in the setting of the rules, the detailed and technical nature of the rules required in the operation of an industrial society tends to create a special group of experts or professionals[8] within the hierarchies of the actors. This group within each hierarchy has the immediate responsibility for the establishment and the administration of the vast network of rules. The existence of job-evaluation plans, incentive or piece-rate systems, engineering time studies, pension plans, or many seniority arrangements is ample evidence of the role of experts or professionals in rule-making. Indeed, one of the major problems within the hierarchies of actors is the difficulty of communication and genuine understanding between such experts and the rest of the hierarchy. There may be on occasion a greater community of interests and understanding among such experts in different hierarchies than between them and the lay members of their own hierarchy.[9]

The experts tend to place the interaction among organizations of workers and managers and special governmental agencies on a more factual basis with careful technical studies made within each of the various hierarchies, or on a cooperative basis. These expert or professional ties on specialized issues tend to add to the stability of the system and to bind the actors closer together. The resort to a study by experts is an established method of reducing, at least for a period, tensions that arise among the actors.

The rules of the system may be expressed in a variety of forms: the regulations and policies of the management hierarchy; the laws of any worker hierarchy; the regulations, decrees, decisions, awards, or orders of governmental agencies; the rules and decisions of specialized agencies created by the management and worker hierarchies; collective-bargaining agreements, and the customs and traditions of the workplace and work community. In any particular system the rules may be incorporated in a number of these forms; they may be written, an oral tradition, or customary practice. But whatever form the rules may take, the industrial-relations system prescribes the rules of the workplace and work community, including the procedures for their establishment and administration.

THE IDEOLOGY OF AN INDUSTRIAL-RELATIONS SYSTEM

An industrial-relations system has been described so far in terms of actors who interact in a specified context and who in the process formulate a complex of rules at the workplace and work community. A further element is required to complete the analytical system: an ideology[10] or a set of ideas and beliefs commonly held by the actors that helps to bind or to integrate the system together as an entity. The ideology of the industrial-relations system is a body of common ideas that defines the role and place of each actor and that defines the ideas which each actor holds toward the place and function of the others in the system. The ideology or philosophy of a stable system involves a congruence or compatibility among these views and the rest of the system. Thus, in a community in which the managers hold a highly paternalistic view toward workers and the workers hold there is no function for managers, there would be no common ideology in which each actor provided a legitimate role for the other; the relationships within such a work community would be regarded as volatile, and no stability would likely

---

[8] The term *professional* does not mean a member of one of the generally recognized established professions with access by formal education.

[9] George W. Brooks, "Reflections on the Changing Character of American Labor Unions," *Proceedings of the Ninth Annual Meeting, Industrial Relations Research Association*, December 28 and 29, 1956, pp. 33–43.

[10] The term *shared understandings* has been suggested by Clark Kerr to characterize the English and American social scene. See Reinhard Bendix, *Work and Authority in Industry, Ideologies of Management in the Course of Industrialization* (New York: John Wiley & Sons, 1956), p. xii.

be achieved in the industrial-relations system. It is fruitful to distinguish disputes over the organization of an industrial-relations system or disputes that arise from basic inconsistencies in the system from disputes within an agreed or accepted framework.

Each of the actors in an industrial-relations system—managerial hierarchy, worker hierarchy, and specialized public agencies—may be said to have its own ideology.[11] An industrial-relations system requires that these ideologies be sufficiently compatible and consistent so as to permit a common set of ideas which recognize an acceptable role for each actor. Thus, in the industrial-relations system of Great Britain[12] the philosophy of "voluntarism" may be said in a general way to be common to all three actors; this accepted body of ideas defines the role for manager and worker hierarchies and defines their ideas toward each other within the system; it also prescribes the limited role for specialized public agencies. The ideologies which characterize the industrial-relations arrangements, for instance, of India[13] and the Soviet Union[14] are each different from the British.

The ideology of an industrial-relations system must be distinguished from the ideology of the larger society; but they can be expected to be similar or at least compatible in the developed industrial society. In the process of industrialization, however, there may be marked differences between the ideology (relevant to the role of managers, workers, and public agencies) of the actors within the industrial-relations system and other segments of the larger society which may even be dominant, such as the ideology of the traditional agricultural landholders. Nonetheless, the ideology of an industrial-relations system comes to bear a close relationship to the ideology of the particular industrial society of which it is a subsystem. Indeed, in the absence of a general consistency of the two ideologies, changes may be expected in the ideologies or in other facets of the industrial-relations system.

The term *ideology* may convey a more rationalized and formalized body of ideas than is intended. The actors in the system are often inclined to be pragmatic and may hold ideas that are to a degree inconsistent or lack precision. But hierarchies of managers and workers (when formally organized) and public agencies also tend to develop or adopt intellectuals, publicists, or other specialists concerned with articulating systematically and making some form of order out of the discrete ideas of the principal actors. These statements, preachments, and creeds tend to be reworked and reiterated, and in the process even a fairly explicit ideology may emerge. Each industrial-relations system contains its ideology or shared understandings.

---

[11] For a discussion of managerial ideologies see ibid.

[12] Allan Flanders and H. A. Clegg, eds., *The System of Industrial Relations in Great Britain* (Oxford: Basil Blackwell and Mott, Ltd., 1954), p. 260.

[13] Charles A. Myers, *Labor Problems in the Industrialization of India* (Cambridge, Mass., Harvard University Press, 1958).

[14] Issac Deutscher, *Soviet Trade Unions* (London: Royal Institute of International Affairs, 1950); Joseph S. Berliner, *Factory and Manager in the USSR* (Cambridge, Mass., Harvard University Press, 1957), pp. 25–44, 271–78.

COLLECTIVE BARGAINING: CONTEMPORARY AMERICAN EXPERIENCE—A COMMENTARY

Jack Barbash*

THE AMERICAN COLLECTIVE BARGAINING SYSTEM

Collective bargaining in the United States is a continuous process in which unions, as designated representatives of workers in specified units, and the appropriate public managements or private employers negotiate terms of employment. Collective bargaining is complemented by supporting activities like politics and public policy.

Unit describes the applicable employment territory—occupation, craft, department, multiplant, multiemployer, public jurisdiction, etc., or combinations thereof. The bargaining unit is commonly established by the National Labor Relations Board (NLRB) or a similar agency in a representation proceeding. Commonly, too, the unit established for representation is likely to change as the relationship evolves into negotiation.

The terms of employment about which the parties bargain are, fundamentally: (1) the price of labor, e.g., wages, supplements, methods of wage determination, wage structures; (2) the accompanying rules that define how the labor is to be utilized, including hours, work practices, job classifications, the effort input, etc.; (3) individual job rights, e.g., seniority,

discharge for cause; (4) the rights of union and management in the bargaining relationship; and (5) the methods of enforcement, interpretation, and administration of the agreement, including the resolution of grievances. In the most fundamental sense, the stakes of collective bargaining come to price and power.

Collective bargaining is normally coordinated with two complementary strategies. In internal bargaining, the sides bargain out their eventual position *within* their respective units before presentation at the bargaining table. In public employment, the union bargains politically with public administrators and politicians. Political bargaining is also involved as the parties seek to reenforce their collective bargaining interests through public policy enactments.

The union enforces its side of the bargaining through sanctions which, by promise of benefit, threat to withhold, rational persuasion (including public relations), and direct action, induce the other side to agree and compromise. The strike is the major union sanction—even if, as in the public sector, it is largely illegal. On occasion the strike is backed up by consumer boycotts—which is the organized withholding of product demand—and direct action or violence.

Withholding of employment is the employer's major sanction, known colloquially as "taking a strike." If the employer

* J. P. Bascom, Professor of Economics and Industrial Relations, University of Wisconsin. Reprinted from Gerald G. Somers, ed., *Collective Bargaining: Contemporary American Experience* (Madison, Wis.: IRRA, 1980), pp. 553–88.

initiates the withholding of employment, it is called a lockout. But not all sanctions are intended to disadvantage the other side. Standardization of labor costs, improving the employer's product market position (i.e., the union label), and conflict resolution on the shop floor (i.e., the grievance procedure) serve interests of both parties.

The negotiating table is figuratively and literally the forum in which the parties face each other in the making of the bargain. Negotiation, normally face-to-face or through mediation, allows the initially announced positions of the parties to be modified through continuous exchange of information and feedback. Negotiation is part of bargaining, but not all bargaining involves negotiation. That is to say, terms and sanctions can be communicated without face-to-face negotiation and without, of course, the instant feedback opportunities offered by face-to-face negotiation. Negotiation applies not only to the formal agreement, but also to subordinate bargains, including, most importantly, grievance processing.

Bargaining is of such scale and complexity that both sides require organizations to implement their representation. Organization, in turn, brings professionalization and bureaucracy. For the union this means that the traditional lay administration—that is, administration by members who are employed at other full-time jobs—tends to get displaced by full-time staff, particularly in the higher union bodies. For management, industrial relations requires expertness and is, in this respect, on a par with other management specializations.

Scale and complexity in their organizations make it necessary for the parties to bargain over the distribution of power *within* their respective organizations. Internal bargaining is most marked in public-sector management where the separation of powers inherent in constitutional government creates several, frequently competing voices, each purporting to speak in behalf of some segment of the employer-management interest. On the union side, internal bargaining is most marked in the industrial unions with their broad-based constituencies divided by skill, age, sex, and geography.

Management is normally the moving party in the direction of the enterprise. The union mostly reacts. In collective bargaining, these roles are reversed. Unions initiate and management reacts. But what the union initiates is modification of, or redress from, decisions first made by management. In this context, the union posture is defensive. Collective bargaining as a process thus involves a sequence of union demands and management responses. But employer initiatives are becoming more frequent, especially under cost pressures. There are atypical cases—perhaps the apparel industries come closest here—in which the union functions more positively, but these are special circumstances.

Collective bargaining is only one point, albeit a major point, along a continuum of diverse forms of joint dealing between workers and employers. At one end, the negation of joint dealing is management unilateralism where the right to make decisions is vested solely in management. At an interval along the way is human relations and its later variants. Human relations is still management-in-charge, but with greater awareness of the needs of the lower participants. Consultation, at still a further remove, is European usage and generally represents a type of formalized joint dealing in which the workers have a right to be informed, to question proposed management policies, and to get a response; but the eventual decision under consultation is made by management and is not contingent on a negotiated agreement with the workers' side. The American analogue is "meet and confer" found in several public-sector statutes.

In the collective bargaining type of joint dealing, decisions relating to the terms of employment—or more specifically, the price of labor and its attendant conditions—are contingent on negotiated agreement with an appropriate union. Codetermination—German in origin and setting—is, in its fullest development, the right of the workers' representatives to join with top management in the making of decisions in a predefined area, *whether in the employment area or not.* Industrial democracy generally means codecision making but, in the contemporary context, on (or at least close to) the shop floor. There are instances in collective bargaining which are very close to codetermination or industrial democracy, mostly in the public sector. (Codetermination, in practice, has been mostly confined to employment terms.)

Craft unionism tends to incorporate the major terms of employment in its own internal rules rather than in the collective bargaining agreement. It is close to workers' control in that power is substantially weighted toward the union side, but without the formidable workers' control ideology. Full-dress workers' control—syndicalism in an earlier time—is the negation of joint dealing, but on the workers' side, and exists nowhere as an established arrangement.

The major variations in collective bargaining are shaped by whether the bargaining relationship is (*a*) in a factory or nonfactory environment—in this collection, steel and electrical products contrasted with all of the others; (*b*) public or private—education, postal service, and government hospitals contrasted with the others; (*c*) the stage of negotiations, i.e., contract versus grievance negotiation; and (*d*) the stage of development of the relationship from confrontation to accommodation and possibly cooperation—perhaps agriculture contrasted to steel and airlines.

CASE PROFILES

In this section, the effort is made to convey the essence of the bargaining relationship, not really to summarize.

COAL

This is a bargaining relationship undergoing profound change and reeling under the impact. The new turmoil in the union began with the radically improved condition of the coal economy in the wake of the energy crisis. But the turmoil also reflects the jarring transition which the Mine Workers Union has had to make from John L. Lewis—one of the seminal and also one of the most authoritarian leaders in American trade unionism—to Tony Boyle's "corrupt kingdom" to Arnold Miller's attempt at coping with the forces unleashed by the collapse of the Lewis-Boyle tradition.

Lewis ran the Miners as a dictatorship, but its cutting edge was blunted by the Lewis charisma. Lewis innovated health insurance and pensions, not only for Miners but for the modern labor movement. At its high point, it looked as if the Miners' Welfare and Retirement Fund was on the verge of ushering in a new era for health care in Appalachia. But actuarial weaknesses caught up with Lewis's successors to make the welfare fund a major source of dissension. Lewis approved the mechanization which made U.S. coal mining among the most efficient in the world. But mechanization in a declining market also depopulated the mines and impoverished Appalachia.

Internally, the Boyle regime of corruption and murder led to Miller's revolution which the union is still trying to digest. From without, the union is very much threatened by a growing nonunion sector and rival unionism from the Operating Engineers in the western surface mines. Concentration and conglomeration are gradually but perceptibly altering the coal industry's market structure. Destructive competitive forces are no longer the critical circumstance they were in coal's past.

The power of the state, in one form or another, has touched the coal industry and its labor relations at every main point. The federal Coal Mine Safety Act, "the strongest single code of health and safety the country has ever known" regulates occupational health and safety. The emergency disputes provisions of Taft-Hartley have been the basis for four interventions, the latest in 1977. The Labor Management Reporting and Disclosure Act has been a major influence in the UMW internal struggles; the Employee Retirement Income Security Act (ERISA) is bringing about "a thoroughgoing change" in retirement funds.

Power in the coal bargaining structure has moved both up and down. On the up side is the negotiation of the key bituminous contract by one employer association instead of by three associations as was the case before 1950. But within the union, power has been moving downward since the heyday of John L. Lewis. From 1974 on, union negotiations have been carried on through a bargaining council which has grown accustomed to exercising its own judgment. Decentralization has come most of all from the rekindled spirit of insurgency among the younger generation of miners.

Straight-time or hourly earnings of coal miners are among "the highest earned by industrial workers in the nation—and quite possibly in the world." The critical bargaining issues have been health, pensions, mechanization, and the grievance-arbitration machinery. Lewis pioneered negotiated health care on an unprecedented but, as it turned out, unsustainable scale.

The union's mechanization policy permitted the operators to reduce their labor force to a level compatible with high efficiency at the same time that miners would be permitted (as Lewis said) to "maintain them[selves] and their families in comfort and with a provision for old age." It didn't quite work out that way. A workable grievance-arbitration mechanism which can command sufficient support from the rank and file to put an end to wildcats has yet to be achieved.

The Lewis era evolved from turmoil to stability. The stability watershed was the negotiation in 1950 of a national agreement. The renewal of struggle came in the 1970s and has dominated the industrial relations scene since then.

STEEL

In its evolution from combat to accommodation to intermittent collaboration, steel bargaining comes close to the maturity model that the philosophers of collective bargaining undoubtedly had in mind.

Steel, along with coal, autos, rubber, and electrical products, was in the vanguard of the industrial union revolution of the 1930s. The steel union was a spinoff from coal unionism, one might say. Even after the open break with Lewis, the Steelworkers under Philip Murray carried on the Mine Workers' tradition of strong and "highly centralized" national union leadership—but without repression.

Murray led the union in its militant period. Stability set in only with the accession of David J. McDonald in 1952. Several innovations bordering on (if not actually achieving) a modern approximation of "union-management cooperation" originated in his administration. But McDonald's personal leadership failed to take hold in the mills. His critics charged (and there were many in and out of the union) that his style was better suited to the executive's club than to the union hall or steel mill.

McDonald faced challenges several times until I. W. Abel eventually defeated him in 1965. Abel carried forward McDonald's "mutual trusteeship" in practice, if not in rhetoric or style. But Abel's roots as an honest-to-goodness steel worker, nevertheless, did not suppress the charge of elitism and efforts of challengers (unsuccessful) to unseat him on that ground.

Steel management has also undergone a major metamorphosis. From the turn of the 20th century on, no management fought unionism more resolutely. But from violent confrontation, steel management found its way to accommodation. Accommodation has meant the professionalization of industrial relations, a negotiated wage structure, and a willingness to innovate in grievance administration and strike substitutes. These are some of the most significant innovations in industrial union bargaining. Nor have steel workers' earnings suffered under accommodation. Earnings in the industry increased more per year than earnings of either automobile workers or all manufacturing workers during 1947–62.

Steel is one of the classic cases of government intervention. The strategic position of steel in the economy makes the industry particularly vulnerable to anti-inflation "jawboning" which goes back to the late 1950s. Even earlier it became clear, at least to steel management, that "Washington" was the invisible—sometimes not so invisible—participant at the bargaining table. Wage settlements turned on whether Washington would approve price increases. In 1962 steel provided the circumstances for President Kennedy's price crackdown.

Government intervention virtually forced the industry to recognize the union. Afterward, at one time or another, government resorted to almost every known form of intervention: mediation, fact-finding with and without recommendations, seizure, and injunction. The latest interven-

tion resulted in an antidiscrimination consent decree.

Steel has been a strike-prone industry from the early origins of unionism to the CIO organizing period, climaxed by the longest and last national strike in 1959. It is fitting for this industry to have pioneered an Experimental Negotiating Agreement (ENA) providing for new contract arbitration in lieu of striking. "Drastic action was necessary to quell steel imports in order to maintain a domestic market for American steel and prevent postsettlement layoffs and unemployment." The arbitration of a new contract in lieu of strike remains unused by the parties. They have been able to come to terms on their own. Nor has there been any replication of the ENA principle in other situations.

The accommodation style has not always been fully appreciated within the union ranks. Dissidents of one kind or another have denounced it at various times as elitism, bureaucracy, and proemployer. The steel experience raises the general question of whether collaboration can command general support over the long term.

Bargaining structure has also developed in the classic way from single-company bargaining "to what is in effect industry-wide bargaining." Structure's center of gravity is undergoing a downward pull as indicated by the more representative bargaining committees, the provision for local-issues strikes, and, as much as anything else, the heightened sensitivity of the leadership to what members will and won't take. The decentralization impulse runs through the vigorous efforts to expedite, simplify, and generally reform the grievance-arbitration process.

ELECTRICAL PRODUCTS

Up to the middle 1960s, electrical products is the situation that became noted for the successful efforts of General Electric to contain union penetration. Rival unionism, ideology, personality, and internal instability are some of the reasons why management was able to hold the unions in check.

The original union division was between the AFL's International Brotherhood of Electrical Workers (IBEW) and the CIO's United Electrical Workers (UE). The identification of UE leadership with the communist faction in the CIO led to the formation of the International Union of Electrical Workers (IUE) under the leadership of James Carey, and eventually to UE's severance from the CIO and to its displacement as the leading union in the industry. Carey's "boldness—or rashness—invective, and dramatic speechmaking" and his lack of "competence as an administrator" cast him as a continuously abrasive influence within the union and in a confrontation posture with management. Currently, foreign competition, the "massive" southern strategy of the industry, and "the mediocre performance of IUE and UE" are reordering union rankings; IBEW is now emerging as the leading union and "the most active organizer" even though it continues to lag behind IUE in the very large corporations.

GE set the tone of labor relations in electrical products, with Western Electric, Westinghouse, and RCA "play[ing] ancillary roles." Division within the union ranks made Boulwarism possible. In the NLRB's words, Boulwarism "denigrat[ed] give-and-take bargaining" and sought to "bypass the union and attempt[ed] to disparage its importance and usefulness in the eyes of its members. . . . The aim was to deal with the union through the employees, rather than with the employees through the union" and thereby decentralize bargaining to the local level. Later, coordinated bargaining (or "coalition bargaining," as GE preferred) tried to bring a measure of unity in the union ranks.

For a long time IUE's inability to win a strike vote undermined the credibility of its strike threats. "I owe GE a strike," Carey said in 1960. The strike that came may have been "the worst setback any union . . . received in a nationwide strike since World War II." The union disunity which brought about the 1960 disaster led to coordinated bargaining which, in turn, led to a strike "showdown" with GE. The "Great 1969–70 Strike," which lasted 101 days, brought about the "first fully negotiated contract in 20 years." GE and the locals found themselves as one against the national union in preferring strikes to grievance arbitration. The end of Boulwarism brought with it also "a grudging gradual acceptance of arbitration."

Since the Great Strike, as one union leader put it, "GE . . . entered the Twentieth Century." The adversary relationship prevails, but there is "no real bitterness or rancor." Altogether, "union-management relations at both plant and company levels have matured."

CONSTRUCTION

The construction industry typifies craft bargaining. Its distinguishing features are craft consciousness, multiunionism, casual employment, jurisdictional rivalry, weak employers, and employer association bargaining.

Many of the problems confronting bargaining in the industry intersect at one point or another with decentralization or "fragmentation" of bargaining and its "leap-frogging effect." Inflation of construction wage costs, the growing nonunion sector, and jurisdictional disputes arise out of competitive craft unionism and excessive localism. Most remedies, accordingly, involve doing something about bargaining structure. All proposed reforms—whether Construction Industry Stabilization Commission or wide-area bargaining or the Dunlop bill (which almost passed only to fail because of its link with the common situs issue)—in one way or another try to deal with fragmentation by moving union power upward.

The weakness of the contractors association, the employers' bargaining vehicle, feeds decentralization. Staffing is "sparse." Rapid turnover of personnel deprives the association of experienced negotiators. "Political turmoil" in the association is worse than in the union.

A construction strike puts "usually small and poorly capitalized" contractors in danger of contract cancellations. The union members, on the other hand, frequently are able to find other work during a strike.

Construction is one of the major strike-prone industries in the United States, and jurisdiction is a large source of these strikes. Some branches of the industry have, however, developed sophisticated alternatives to the strike. Of the longest standing are the Council of Industrial Relations of the Electrical Construction Industry and the Impartial Board for the Settlement of Jurisdictional Disputes. During the Nixon wage-price control era, a tripartite Construction Industry Stabilization Committee (1971–74) addressed itself to reform of the bargaining structure.

Federal and some state laws are actively involved in construction industrial relations. Federal efforts to reform bargaining structure have already been noted. Federal and state law regulates wages in public construction. Federal law prohibits jurisdictional strikes and the closed shop (not altogether successfully), restricts the secondary boycott with somewhat better results, and through affirmative action forces the recruitment, training, and hiring of larger numbers of minority employees.

The open-shop drive mounted by some of the largest firms in the industry is causing construction unions to reappraise their policies in a way that state intervention has been mostly unable to do. Construction unions are now stepping up organiz-

ing, liberalizing work rules, and permitting the coexistence of union and nonunion work in the same firm, all in an effort to recapture lost territory and prevent further attrition.

TRUCKING

Collective bargaining in trucking demonstrates the same general model of weak employers confronting a powerful union; only, unlike construction, the union interest is represented by one union instead of 20.

Like construction, the multiemployer bargaining association, rent by internal divisions, is no match for the union. Nor is the individual employer whose "slim financial resources" make him acutely vulnerable to strikes.

Bargaining consolidation received a powerful assist from Hoffa's empire building. But Hoffa's successor, Frank Fitzsimmons, has been unable to sustain the momentum, first, because he lacks Hoffa's personal appeal to the Teamster rank and file, and second, because of fissions among employers in the unionized sector.

The Trucking Employers, Inc. (TEI), as the employer instrumentality for collective bargaining, is marked by a high degree of internal tension. The pressure on the firms to go nonunion began to accelerate with the 1970 and subsequent negotiations which increased "even further the motivation of shippers to seek out nonunion or non-Teamster modes of transportation wherever possible."

Like construction, the Teamsters are facing an enlarging nonunion sector, the basic cause at work being "cumulative effects of . . . increases in labor costs" since 1970. Over the long run, deregulation, as the union sees it, would likely liberalize employee entry and further threaten the unionized sector.

By all accounts, racketeering and corruption permeate some sectors of the Teamster organization, notably in the central and southern areas, in a way that is not true of construction.

Government has intervened in a variety of ways to weaken Teamster power over employers and union recalcitrants with uneven effects. The Taft-Hartley prohibitions of the secondary boycott have probably made it more difficult for the union to move against nonunion truckers. But the closed-shop prohibition has been largely ineffectual. Much of the Landrum-Griffin Act was written against a legislative history of Teamster racketeering and internal repression. ERISA provisions have provided the leverage for wholesale investigation of Teamster pension funds for "mismanagement of investment, corruption, and kickbacks, questionable loans, tie-ins with organized crime, [and] excessive disqualifications of retirees." "Along with construction, the trucking industry is probably the most widely criticized for policies of discrimination against blacks and other minorities in hiring, assignment, transfer, and promotion."

Notably absent from agreements is the final arbitration step in the grievance procedure. What happens, in effect, is that the union sense of fairness prevails—which employers apparently prefer to costly arbitration with an overpowering union. "Since Hoffa's departure," employers feel "that decisions [have been] fair and equitable."

Prospects for reform from within the industry are not good. There is no strong tradition of union-management cooperation in this unbalanced power relationship to confront the industry's problems, although a new advisory committee has been established to make the attempt. So far, neither has government intervention materially altered the industrial relations condition.

AGRICULTURAL WORKERS

Bargaining in West Coast agriculture is just now emerging out of its primitive confrontation. By the signs of history, the Chicanos were not, on the face of it, the best material out of which to build a union that could survive in a hostile environment. Replacements from the "reserve army of the unemployed" across the border have always threatened the union's striking power. Denied legal protection generally available to workers, farm unions have had to face their tough employer antagonists alone.

But conditions changed. Somehow, a union and collective bargaining for farm workers has come to pass. It came to pass because their leader, César Chavez, was able to endow the dispute with a sense of mission so deeply felt as to overcome the feeling of powerlessness of this historically oppressed ethnic group. The cause—literally La Causa—attracted an auxiliary force in the churches, most significantly in the Roman Catholic Church, and university students. Indispensable to the maintenance of the organization as a going concern was the very substantial organizing and financial aid from the AFL–CIO, the United Auto Workers, and other unions.

Very early the United Farm Workers of America (UFWA) launched a consumer boycott against the products of struck employers. If the strike could not be effective, the national consumer boycott was. But the turning point in the union's fortunes came with the enactment of the California Agriculture Labor Relations Act (CALRA). The law established procedures to resolve the question of representation between the Farm Workers and the Teamsters, or alternatively no union. In the main, the Farm Workers won out. CALRA also protected the farm workers' rights of association, collective bargaining, and consumer boycott.

The termination of the bracero program helped UFWA, although the supply of farm labor continues to be augmented by the continuous flow of illegal aliens, with the union caught between ethnic loyalty and economics. Additionally, the new wave of social legislation—the Civil Rights Act, the Occupational Safety and Health Act (OSHA), and the extension of the Fair Labor Standards Act (FLSA) to larger farm operations—are bringing farm workers into the mainstream of labor legislation from which they had been traditionally excluded.

Although agreements have been signed, growing pains continue as the union evolves from movement to organization. The strains have shown up mainly in grievance handling and hiring-hall administration. For the long run, tensions in the relationship will come as technology replaces labor in the fields.

The two other agricultural organizations of importance are Local 142 of the International Longshoremen's and Warehousemen's Union (ILWU) in Hawaii and the Western Conference of Teamsters. Like the Farm Workers, Local 142's self-image is as a trade union and social movement. For many reasons, however, its organizing had easier sailing. Hawaii's sugar workers represent a more stable labor force and Hawaii represents a more favorable union environment for agricultural workers, including legal protection of the right to organize and bargain much earlier than in California. Hawaiian growers have not been resistant to agricultural unionism as have Californians. Perhaps because Local 142 is a kind of union conglomerate—actually a general workers' union with considerable economic and political power—most employers are loath to engage it in combat.

The Teamsters' importance in the fields derives from the fact that for the growers they represented a less worse alternative to the Farm Workers precisely because they were not a social movement. Although the benefits gained by Teamster groups were "roughly equivalent" to the UFWA, they did not insist on union-controlled hiring halls and, by contrast with UFWA, seemed "business-like and efficient." Eventually, UFWA victories in the CALRA elections brought about a jurisdictional treaty.

AIRLINES

The collective bargaining problems of the airlines flow from two sets of circumstances that surround the industry. It is a regulated industry and, until the present period, a technologically dynamic industry.

"CAB [and/or FAA] entered into and materially influenced every major aspect of airline personnel and industrial relations," including safety, merger displacement, employee qualifications, manning, subsidies, and dispute settlement. The airline unions have favored retention of CAB's "wide-ranging authority over air transportation." They fear that deregulation and the likely "liquidation of the CAB" will redistribute traffic among carriers and undoubtedly disturb the existing system of employee security and vested rights based on individual carrier seniority.

Collective bargaining is governed by the craft principle built into the Railway Labor Act (RLA), which is also the basic legislation for airlines labor relations. Single carrier bargaining remains the rule. Multicarrier bargaining poses too many complexities to be practical, aside from the fact that the unions are not pressing for it. In lieu of multicarrier bargaining, the carriers developed the now illegal Mutual Aid Pact (MAP). Multiunit bargaining occurs de facto when several units are represented by one union bargaining with a carrier over contracts with common expiration times. Union rivalry is common except in the pilot unit.

Following the Railway Labor Act pattern, grievances are handled through three-party boards, departing in this respect from the single-arbitrator system common elsewhere. It has its advantages, but it is a relatively elaborate, expensive, and slow process.

The emergency boards have been "relatively ineffective" in curbing strikes. Mandatory mediation has been a "positive contribution." Strikes have been "relatively infrequent," occurring on an average of four per year in the recent period. The Mutual Aid Pact strengthened carrier defenses against strikes, "increas[ing] the number of long strikes."

The airlines' technological evolution is epitomized in four waves of "aircraft innovation"—the Douglas DC-3, the Douglas DC-6, the Boeing turbojets (707), and the Boeing 747—each with its threat at the time to "the survival of the various crafts." But "the age of technological progress is over for the foreseeable future."

The era of optimism in the airline industry gave way to uncertainty in the 1970s, accompanied by fear that even some major carriers (notably Pan Am and Eastern) might not survive their cash crises. Cost reduction became a major management bargaining goal. But the late 1970s witnessed a dramatic resurgence of traffic and profits reenforced by the CAB's adoption of policies encouraging more competition.

The Pilots have found their "increment" pay system tactically superior, for bargaining purposes, to any direct demands for higher pay. Their goal of shorter hours was more effectively pursued through piecemeal change in rules than by open reductions in hours or by mileage limitations.

On balance, "collective bargaining has worked reasonably well." The RLA has "provided a suitable legislative framework." Professionalism has not deterred the Pilots from becoming a militant, hard-bargaining union indistinguishable in its basic strategies from other unions. The unions seem to have been uncommonly responsive to the more pessimistic prospects for the airlines, agreeing to postponement of pay increases, variable earnings, expe-

dited arbitration, and private fact-finding arbitration. The effects of prosperity and of deregulation on collective bargaining remain to be determined.

EDUCATION

The essential spirit of this relationship is the militancy and ardor with which teachers practice their unionism. This is all the more remarkable considering the nagging doubts that teachers voiced for a long time about the propriety of unions for professionals.

Two major unions are in the field. The strength of the American Federation of Teachers (AFT) is centered in the heavily urbanized areas and that of the National Education Association (NEA) affiliates "in the smaller cities and in suburban and rural areas." The two are indistinguishable as to union methods except that AFT puts a high value on permanent ties to the labor movement, while NEA does not. In fact, the issue of AFL–CIO affiliation seems to be the chief sticking point in the consummation of merger between AFT and NEA.

The road to bargaining in education has been marked by much introspection on the compatibility of professionals and unions. But once the union breakthrough occurred in the early 1960s, teachers shed their inhibitions and began to function pretty much like all other unions except in one vital respect inherent in their status as public employees. Like other *public* unions, education unions deal with their employers not only as management but—to put it summarily—as politicians or, alternately, as administrators responsible to politicians.

The employer in education bargaining could hardly be more different from the private-sector employer. There is not one education employer in any given situation, but many, depending on the terms being bargained. Accordingly, the education employer can be a school administrator, a lay board of education, a city council, a state legislature, or the voters in referendum. The employer in large-scale private-sector bargaining is also bureaucratized, to be sure, but the diverse manifestations that managements take are part of an integrated hierarchical system which will act as one at showdown time. Not so in the public sector; the union strategy is not only to bargain collectively, but to bargain *politically*—to play one face of management against the other as tactical advantage seems to dictate.

Bargaining operates within what is now an intricate legal framework. The state sets professional and civil service standards and establishes the rules by which the bargaining parties conduct themselves in union-management relations. Thus, labor relations law legitimates the bargaining relationship to begin with, and then goes on to fix the bargaining unit, the terms of recognition, the scope of bargaining, and methods of dispute settlement.

The law almost invariably bars the strike, but this is just as invariably disregarded. "Of all public employee groups, teachers appear to be most inclined to take bargaining issues to impasse and to strike." Strikes by teachers—or threats—have become "commonplace," especially in larger cities. In part, this is because strikes are likely to be less costly to teachers since lost time "is often recaptured through makeup days." Laws also commonly provide for fact-finding and other dispute-resolution procedures.

The bargaining structure is quite involved due to the fragmentation of employer authority. In another respect, the organization is simple and decentralized since multiemployer bargaining is rare. Many of the problems in bargaining stem from the inexperience of the participants who, with few exceptions, are still in the rudimentary stages of the bargaining relationship.

Unionized teachers bring an attitude,

it is not an exaggeration to say, of codetermination to the substance and enforcement of the agreement. "Teachers view conditions of employment as transcending mere matters of salaries, hours, fringe benefits, and a grievance procedure. The contract . . . becomes not only a constitution governing the working life of the teacher, but a document containing the educational philosophy of the district." This is hardly congenial to school administrators or to boards of education who are not prepared for this sharing of power.

Education bargaining, like all public-sector bargaining, is in a period of instability as education retrenches in reaction to rising costs, demographic changes, taxpayer "revolts," and citizen doubts about the educational process. The main effect of retrenchment is to put into question the lifetime job security that teachers thought they had acquired when they entered upon their public jobs. The militant phase is likely to be an extended one as teacher unions resist retrenchment and education management seeks to capitalize on this apparently favorable shift in the terms of power.

On balance, "bargaining has resulted in modest gains for teachers. . . . The greatest salary gains go to experienced teachers." Collective bargaining has also improved the teachers' working conditions. But teacher militancy seems to have raised a larger question: In whose interests is the public education system being run?

POSTAL SERVICE

The problems of collective bargaining in the Postal Service spring from these conditions: an immense public enterprise experimenting with more private-like management, particularly with how to meet costs without overpricing services; a network of unions stratified by craft and industrial as well as local and national interests; and a bargaining structure that attempts to give voice simultaneously to all of these diverse pressures.

Eighty-eight percent of Postal Service employees are in unions, which must be among the highest ratios anywhere in the public sector. But this high density is diffused among several craft unions and one semi-industrial union. The American Postal Workers Union is the semi-industrial union. It represents a merger of previously independent craft unions, but the merger has yet to be consummated in fact as well as in form. The three remaining craft unions are the Letter Carriers, Mail Handlers, and Rural Letter Carriers. All of the foregoing have bargaining rights. The National Alliance is mainly a civil rights gadfly in behalf of black postal workers, without consultative or bargaining rights. There are also three supervisory organizations, limited to consultation.

The Postal Service "is still the largest public employer and the most widespread organization" with a large headquarters and field labor relations staff, and title to match (Senior Assistant Postmaster General for Employee and Labor Relations, or SAPMGE&LR). The Service is governed by the "jointly bargained" Postal Reorganization Act and its law of labor relations by amendment to the National Labor Relations Act after years under Executive Order 10988. But the last and not infrequent resort is Congress, even on routine matters.

The NLRB has given its stamp of approval to "the existing bargaining structure comprised of occupational units on national lines" with some exceptions. Negotiations are carried on at three levels: nationally for the mail-processing employees and for each group of craft employees, locally at each installation. The union side is represented through a not entirely satisfactory approximation of "coordinated" bargaining, which broke down in the 1978 negotiations.

The first negotiations "quickly bogged down" due largely to intraorganizational problems and the sheer magnitude of the task. Until 1978 subsequent negotiations have gone more smoothly. Even so, the union tactic of using craft and local bargaining to improve on the national terms tends to entangle the negotiations. Efforts from topside to "defus[e]" local negotiations have been rebuffed down below with the charge that the national union leaderships are conspiring with management to cut down local power. Complicated structures produce complicated results. The 1975 agreement ran to 187 printed pages.

Enforcement of agreements also runs into difficulties. There is the problem of communicating the terms of the agreements to the vast constituency on both sides. Thirteen joint committees have been established to "administer the agreement and resolve differences." Not all committees have met. When they do meet, attendance is poor and the discussion agenda has "often been of little value." The grievance procedure provides for five basic steps capped by arbitration. The "high rate of grievance appeals," including those going to arbitration, is a major delaying factor.

The major issue in grievances is discipline, and in arbitration, work rules and work assignment. Work-assignment grievances carry "jurisdictional overtones" and have the effect of slowing down the Service's productivity campaigns. Management mostly wins in discipline cases. The courts are available to parties who do not have recourse to appeals mechanisms.

All things considered, there has been "little overt militancy." The 1978 dispute seemed to be leading inexorably to a strike, but the rhetoric proved to be stronger than the acts themselves. Withal, "postal employees have fared far better under collective bargaining to date than have federal Civil Service employees in the same period."

The expectation that collective bargaining would follow the classical private-sector model has not materialized. Political bargaining is still fundamental, and Congress is still very much a party to Postal Service bargaining. Collective bargaining is encountering all sorts of uncertainties: challenges to the postal monopoly, the changing postal technology, postal self-sufficiency, and the related question of federal subsidy.

HOSPITALS

The hospital is different. It dispenses perhaps the most public of all goods in the sense that, ideally, nobody should be denied access to quality care because of inability to pay. In fulfillment of this mission, government has become the most important "third-party" payer, thereby escalating hospital costs as to require public surveillance and containment.

In a very real sense, the hospital has become a public utility caught up in an intricate web of external regulation. Nor is management elsewhere so critically circumscribed in the exercise of authority *within* its organization.

The hospital was an almshouse and asylum—"places where the homeless and poverty stricken went to die." It is now a "multiphase center incorporating teaching and research as well as health-care services." Concurrently, the hospital has rapidly expanded the size of its plant, capital investment, and employment; public health care has shifted "from federal to state and local government, and nongovernment, not-for-profit hospitals have displaced investor-owned institutions." The hospital, in short, has evolved from philanthropy and charity into a business. Increasingly its staff and employees relate to it as a business institution.

The hospital labor force consists of "large numbers of high-wage, skilled workers at the upper end of the structure, equal numbers of low-wage low-skilled at the other end, and little in between." The upper end consists of professionals and quasi-

professionals insulated from the full authority of management. The lower end is "ghettoized" with " 'overrepresentation' " of the lowest paid ethnic minorities and women.

This is, hence, the classic segmented labor force with unionism likewise segmented. The dominating association is the guild-like physician corps. The physician, running true to guild form, is stratified into "apprentices" (interns), "journeymen" (residents), and "masters" (physicians). Whatever their legal status is finally determined to be, the residents and interns act like employees and form unions which, like all other unions, strike, bargain, and organize.

The nurses have drifted from sole reliance on a kind of nurses' guild, the American Nurses Association, and have transformed the state branches into virtual unions which, like those of the interns and residents, also bargain and strike. The ANA by this time is not alone in the field. Contesting the territory are the Service Employees, Retail Clerks, and Local 1199.

Dramatic change has also come at the lower end of the wage structure in the unionization of the nonprofessionals who make up about two thirds of the total hospital labor force. The forces behind unionization include increased demand and increased ability to pay, supportive federal and state legislation, militant unionism, and intensified civil rights awareness among the predominantly minority workforce. The marks of hospital unionism are rival unionism, craft and status separatism, and, unlike the other cases, the hospital situation has not produced a union national in scope with a primary mission in the field.

For all the recent activity, unionism and collective bargaining are unevenly distributed and very much a minority phenomenon. Urbanization and large-scale and federal control are good predictors of the presence of unions, as is location in a jurisdiction with supportive legislation. Thirty-four unions are active in representing hospital workers, but four "account for 75 percent of all hospital representation elections."

Unionization has not had the radical impact that most hospital managements feared. For one thing, most managements have learned how to keep unions out. If the union does get in, management has been able to more than hold its own. Strikes occur—many are illegal—but have been proportionately fewer than in industry generally. Somehow hospitals have learned how to cope, and strikes have not brought catastrophe in their wake, although short-of-catastrophe strikes raise serious problems, too.

* * * * *

THE ESSENCE OF THE PROBLEMS

In this final comment, I want to get at the essences of the problems that have been raised throughout this work. It is because the themes have recurred continually that I feel justified in disposing of them in a few words at the end. The large issues raised by this investigation appear to me to be:

1. How does collective bargaining adapt to adverse market conditions after a generation of virtually uninterrupted expansion? Can the parties reverse gear without major confrontations?

2. Are there necessary limits to state intervention in collective bargaining, or are the merits of intervention determined in each case by the nature of the objective?

3. As a special case of (2) above, how should the state intervene to minimize the inflationary effects of collective bargaining in the light of the demonstrated inefficiency of previous interventions to this end?

4. How should the question of bargaining structure be resolved as between the apparently conflicting values of self-determination, which favors decentralization, and economic stability, which seems to favor centralization?

5. What should be done about public-sector strikes which (a) disrupt or threaten public order and health, and (b) defy the law in a manner amounting to mass civil disobedience?

6. How should the problem of occupational health and safety be dealt with when enterprise economy and flexibility have to be measured against the value of life?

7. What should be done when racketeering and corruption infect a union, as seems to be the Teamster case?

These are *questions* in a real sense precisely because they raise "matter(s) or point(s) of uncertainty or difficulty"[1] which do not yield ready answers. At the vital center of all these questions is power. State intervention, either as a general proposition or in the instances of inflation, racketeering, public-sector strikes, and occupational health and safety, presents the problem of state power in a free society. Finally, power or, more exactly, forbearance in the use of power to avoid crisis confrontations is what's at stake in public-sector strikes and the shift in market positions.

It is of some interest that, if I have posed the questions validly, we are at bottom dealing here with political, and even ethical and moral, issues. The conventional wisdom in economics purports to know most of the solutions; it just doesn't know how to make the solutions work.

---

[1] *American College Dictionary* (New York: Random House, 1966), p. 993.

PUBLIC SECTOR LABOR RELATIONS

David Lewin*

Public sector labor relations in the United States are undergoing rapid and extensive change. In 1960, fewer than 1 in 10 public employees were organized. By 1972 (the latest year for which data are available), more than half of all federal civilian and full-time state and local government workers belonged to labor organizations, a membership rate almost twice that of private industry. Government represents the leading—indeed, virtually the only—sector of growth in the American labor movement. Three of the nation's largest labor organizations consist solely of public workers, and the recent membership gains of such well known private sector-based unions as the Teamsters and the Service Employees International Union (SEIU) have been recorded largely among government employees. The growing importance of the public sector to organized labor is further reflected in the creation, in 1974, of a public employees department within the AFL–CIO, only the seventh major department in that organization.[1]

Government employers have responded to employee organizational efforts by increasingly (if unwillingly) sharing decision-making authority over wages and working conditions. The federal government presently negotiates written agreements with a variety of labor organizations, though Congress still sets wage rates for military and most civilian employees.[2] In state and local government, where employment doubled over the 1960–75 period, collective bargaining or a variant thereof has been widely adopted.

* * * * *

The changing panorama of public sector labor relations, especially in state and local government, has attracted a considerable amount of scholarly interest and popular attention.

* * * * *

This voluminous literature is extraordinarily diverse, but some of its major themes and characteristics nevertheless are identifiable. Much of the writing, especially of the 1960s, is highly normative and prescriptive as exemplified in George W. Taylor's well-known essay, "Public Employment: Strikes or Procedures."[3] Taylor argued strongly for the regulation of public sector labor relations somewhat along the lines of private industry, but modified to include impasse resolution procedures in place of strikes. Taylor's

---

* Professor, Graduate School of Business, Columbia University. Reprinted from *Labor History*, 18, Winter 1977, pp. 133–44, © *Labor History*.

[1] U.S. Bureau of the Census, Census of Governments, 1972, Vol. 3, *Public Employment*, no. 3; *Management-Labor Relations in State and Local Governments* (Washington, D.C.: G.P.O., 1974); Joseph P. Goldberg, "Public Employee Developments in 1971," *Monthly Labor Review*, January 1972, pp. 56–66; U.S. Bureau of Labor Statistics, *Directory of National Unions and Employee Associations, 1973* (Washington, D.C.: G.P.O., 1974), *passim*.

[2] The framework for labor relations in the Federal Service is contained in the 1969 Federal Executive Order # 11491. Also see the Federal Salary Reform Act (1962) and the Federal Pay Comparability Act (1970) for pay setting guidelines in the federal government. Editors' note: In January 1979 the executive order was supplanted by the Federal Service Labor-Management Relations Statute.

[3] *Industrial and Labor Relations Review*, July 1967, pp. 617–36.

views, shared by many others, were instrumental in shaping the Public Employees' Fair Employment Law adopted by the New York State legislature in 1967 and, indirectly, the regulatory legislation of several other states.[4] The bulk of these statutes support the institutionalization of collective bargaining in government but, following Taylor, proceed from the premise that public sector labor relations differ generically from those in industry.[5]

Not surprisingly, this view is widely prevalent among public managers who use it as a rationale for opposing the sharing of decision-making authority with organized workers. However, it also has been forcefully promulgated by those academics, most notably Wellington & Winter, who believe that public employee unions are in an especially powerful position vis-à-vis their employers:

Market-imposed unemployment is an important restraint on unions in the private sector. But . . . no such restraint limits the demands of public employee unions. Because much government activity is and must be a monopoly, product competition, non-union or otherwise, does not exert a downward pressure on prices and wages.[6]

This opinion has received much popular support, particularly from those who purport to "explain" the financial and management plight of urban governments.[7] Essentially, it asserts that the wage elasticity of demand for labor in the public sector is totally (and uniformly) inelastic, and, thus, much smaller than in private industry. However, recent theoretical and empirical analyses of state and local government employment indicate that the elasticity of demand for public labor (1) is relatively but not totally inelastic, (2) differs substantially among various categories of public services, and (3) is quite similar to estimates of private sector demand elasticities.[8]

The "union power" thesis as applied to the governmental sector is further called into question by the findings of recent studies of union impacts on public sector wage rates. The "average" wage effect of unionism in government, according to these studies, is roughly on the order of 5 percent, a much smaller impact than is popularly supposed and smaller than the average union wage impact in private industry.[9] In education, which accounts for half of all nonfederal public workers, union wage impacts generally range between 1 and 4 percent, though occasion-

---

[4] Taylor was chairman of the New York State Governor's Committee on Public Employee Relations. The Committee's final report formed the basis of the Public Employees' Fair Employment Law, popularly known as the Taylor Act.

[5] An analysis of these alleged intersectoral differences is provided in David Lewin, "Public Employment Relations: Confronting the Issues," *Industrial Relations*, October 1973, pp. 309–21.

[6] Wellington and Winter, [*The Unions and The Cities* (Washington, D.C.: The Brookings Institution, 1971),] pp. 18–19. For fuller elaboration of this view in terms of public policy with regard to public employee strikes, see Wellington and Winter, "The Limits of Collective Bargaining in Public Employment," *Yale Law Journal*, June 1969, 1107–27. A contrasting perspective is offered in John F. Burton, Jr. and Charles Krider, "The Role and Consequences of Strikes by Public Employees," *Yale Law Journal*, January 1970, pp. 418–40.

[7] See, for example, Frederick O. R. Hayes, "Collective Bargaining and the Budget Director," in *Public Workers and Public Unions*, sponsored by the American Assembly, ed. Sam Zagoria (Englewood Cliffs, N.J.: Prentice-Hall, 1972), 89–100; John Chamberlain, "When Cops and Teachers Strike," *The Wall Street Journal*, October 22, 1975; and *Labor-Management Relations Service Newsletter*, October 1975, p. 1.

[8] Orley C. Ashenfelter and Ronald G. Ehrenberg, "The Demand for Labor in the Public Sector," in *Labor in the Public and Nonprofit Sectors*, ed. Daniel S. Hamermesh (Princeton, N.J.: Princeton University Press, 1975), pp. 55–78.

[9] The classic study of the private sector in this regard is H. Gregg Lewis, *Unionism and Relative Wages in the United States* (Chicago, Ill.: University of Chicago Press, 1963). For more recent evidence, see Leonard Weiss, "Concentration and Labor Earnings, *American Economic Review*, 56 (March 1966), pp. 96–117, and Michael Boskin, "Unions and Real Wages," *American Economic Review*, June 1972, pp. 466–72.

ally they are higher, while, in other functions, impacts range between + 6 and + 15 percent. Organized fire fighters apparently have the largest relative wage impact among public employee unions, having achieved this outcome as much or more through reductions in working hours as through salary increases. The sole study directly comparing wage impacts across a variety of blue and white collar occupations common to government and industry found but one case of a statistically significant differential between the two sectors, the value of "government ownership" in that instance being worth, at most, 12 percent.[10]

These wage impact studies do not, of course, fully resolve the issue of union power in the public sector. They have a variety of limitations, in particular the difficulty of fully controlling "spillover" effects and the inability to incorporate fringe benefits into the analysis. Nevertheless, their findings and the way in which they were achieved, that is through model building, hypotheses formulation, and systematic empirical verification, impose upon those who casually advocate the "union power" thesis in government the burden of more compellingly supporting their position.

If the ability of public employee unions to secure relative wage gains is more limited than is popularly supposed, then the wisdom of blanket antistrike laws and interest arbitration in the public sector also is called into question. Such laws, which recent analysis shows have little apparent impact on the incidence of strikes,[11] impute a "high" cost to public sector work stoppages. More precisely, they presume that the costs of strikes exceed the costs of settlements, even arbitrated ones. Yet

there is good reason to question this presumption in view of the absence of decision making accountability when third parties determine public labor agreements,[12] and the lack of incentives for the parties to bargain in all but the (sparingly used) final-offer approach to interest arbitration.[13] Recognition of the potential costliness of strike bars in the public sector may be spurred by the worsening financial condition of state and local governments; it already is partially reflected in several recently enacted state statutes that selectively permit public employee strikes.[14]

An additional shortcoming of the "union power" thesis with respect to the governmental sector is its deemphasis, even ignorance, of conditions that make for potentially diverse patterns of labor relations. For example, some unions are grievance oriented, concerned principally with deflecting or altering managerial directives, while others pursue an active voice in basic policy decisions, and still others seek control of the labor supply. Some public sector labor organizations represent a variety of blue-collar and white-collar workers, some but a single occupational group. Major differences exist among governments with respect to their services, control systems, organizational structures, and work force composition. These characteristics underscore the plausibility of a diversity model of public sector labor relations envisioning a multiple rather than singular pattern of bargaining outcomes. Such a model also suggests that the consequences of public sector bargaining will vary over time owing

[10] Daniel S. Hamermesh, "The Effect of Government Ownership on Union Wages," in Hamermesh, *Labor in Public Sector*, pp. 227–55.

[11] John F. Burton, Jr. and Charles E. Krider, "The Incidence of Strikes in Public Employment," in Hamermesh, *Labor in Public Sector*, pp. 135–77.

[12] On this point, see Raymond D. Horton, "Arbitrators, Arbitration and the Public Interest," *Industrial and Labor Relations Review*, July 1975, pp. 497–507.

[13] Peter Feuille, *Final Offer Arbitration: Concepts, Developments, Techniques* (Chicago, Ill.: International Personnel Management Association, Public Employee Relations Library, 1975); and Feuille, "Final Offer Arbitration and the Chilling Effect," *Industrial Relations*, October 1975, pp. 302–10.

[14] U.S. Department of Labor, *passim*. These states include Alaska, Hawaii, Minnesota, Montana, Pennsylvania and Vermont.

to changes in environmental conditions (e.g. intergovernmental revenue transfers, subcontracting and statutory provisions), a possibility that seems hardly ever to have been entertained by advocates of the "union power" thesis.[15]

While some of the supposedly unique characteristics of public sector labor relations have been debunked by recent analyses, others have been identified or affirmed. In particular, the presence of fractionalized, multiparty management in the governmental sector means that "a clear dichotomy between the employee and the management organization does not exist."[16] The result is multilateral rather than bilateral bargaining in the public sector, with the extent of multilateralism strongly related to the degree of intramanagement conflict. The multilateral bargaining model, which highlights the role of political variables in public sector labor relations and facilitates the integration of industrial relations with organizational behavior,[17] has been usefully applied to public education, police services, and most systematically, to fire protection.[18]

The fractionalized structure of govern-

mental management also has been identified as an important variable in public sector wage setting processes. Specifically, the political actors within these structures are guided in their wage decisions by the (perceived) voting behavior of particular interest groups. The larger and more cohesive these groups, the more likely are elected officials to be responsive to them. Such behavior helps to explain why blue-collar and lower level white-collar public employees are better paid, and why high-level professional, managerial, and executive personnel in government are more poorly paid than their private sector counterparts. Egalitarian pay structures are peculiarly characteristic of the public sector, and appear to antedate the growth of unionism in that sector.[19]

In their studies of public sector labor relations, moreover, researchers increasingly are emphasizing the analysis of nonwage impacts of unionism and collective bargaining. Thus, Begin has shown how public employee unions working through the grievance process spur city governments into management by policy;[20] Burton[21] and, more recently, Lewin[22] have delineated the ways in which municipal workers bring about shifts in the locus of labor relations responsibility in local gov-

[15] The diversity model of public sector labor relations is more fully developed in Raymond D. Horton, David Lewin, and James W. Kuhn, "Some Impacts of Collective Bargaining on Local Government: A Diversity Thesis," *Administration and Society*, February 1976, pp. 497–516.

[16] Thomas A. Kochan, "A Theory of Multilateral Collective Bargaining in City Governments," *Industrial and Labor Relations Review*, July 1974, p. 526.

[17] Thomas A. Kochan, George P. Huber and Larry L. Cummings, "Determinants of Intra-Organizational Conflict in Collective Bargaining in the Public Sector," *Administrative Science Quarterly*, March 1975, pp. 10–23.

[18] Kenneth McLennan and Michael H. Moskow, "Multilateral Bargaining in the Public Sector," *Proceedings of the Twenty-First Annual Winter Meeting of the Industrial Relations Research Association* (Madison, Wis.: IRRA, 1969), pp. 34–41; Peter Feuille, "Police Labor Relations and Multilateralism," *Proceedings of the Twenty-Sixth Annual Winter Meeting of the Industrial Relations Research Association* (Madison, Wis.: IRRA, 1974), pp. 170–77; and Kochan, "A Theory of Multilateral Collective Bargaining in City Governments," pp. 525–42.

[19] David Lewin, "Wage Determination in Local Government Employment" (Ph.D. diss., Univ. of California, Los Angeles, 1971); David Lewin, "Aspects of Wage Determination in Local Government Employment," *Public Administration Review*, (March/April 1974), pp. 149–55; Walter Fogel and David Lewin, "Wage Determination in the Public Sector," *Industrial and Labor Relations Review*, April 1974, pp. 410–31; and David Lewin, "The Prevailing Wage Principle and Public Wage Decisions," *Public Personnel Management*, November-December 1974, pp. 473–85.

[20] James P. Begin, "The Private Grievance Model in the Public Sector," *Industrial Relations*, February 1971, pp. 21–35.

[21] John F. Burton, Jr., "Local Government Bargaining and Management Structure," *Industrial Relations*, May 1972, pp. 123–40.

[22] David Lewin, "Local Government Labor Relations in Transition: The Case of Los Angeles," *Labor History*, Spring 1976, pp. 191–213.

ernments from the legislative to the executive branch; Derber and his colleagues have analyzed the influence of collective bargaining on public budgeting processes;[23] Lewin and Horton[24] have suggested a framework for analyzing the impacts of collective bargaining on the merit (civil service) system in government; Feuille and his associates[25] are investigating the potential for multiemployer bargaining in government; and Lewin, Kuhn and Horton[26] are studying the impacts of unions on manpower utilization and public management in major American municipalities.

More generally, Kochan and Wheeler,[27] and Gerhart,[28] have offered models of bargaining outcomes in public sector labor relations, models focusing heavily on nonwage issues. Indeed, the emerging impact analyses go beyond a concern for the consequences of bargaining per se, as reflected in Kochan's quantitative study of the correlates of state public sector labor

statutes,[29] Staudohar's qualitative exploration of the forces accounting for the emergence of Hawaii's public sector labor law,[30] and Weber's analysis of the role of law in supplanting management unilateralism with collective bargaining in local government.[31]

These studies, which utilize a variety of cross-sectional and longitudinal methodologies, implicitly suggest that wage impact analysis has been overemphasized and nonwage impacts underexamined in the study of public sector labor relations. The former are more amenable to quantification, measurement, and application of existing economic paradigms than the latter, but they exclude from consideration much of the substantive behavior and dynamics of public sector labor relations. A fuller assessment of the consequences of public employee unionism and collective bargaining will emerge only when nonwage impact studies are integrated with more narrowly oriented wage impact inquiries.[32]

To summarize, in only a short period of time, public sector labor relations have become an important arena of scholarly interest and intellectual inquiry. Anecdotal evidence, unsupported assertion, and loose generalization dominated the early writing on this subject, and continue to characterize some of the present literature. Increasingly, however, researchers are employing analytical frameworks and rigorous methodologies to systematically gather evidence about governmental labor rela-

[23] Milton Derber, Ken Jennings, Ian McAndrew and Martin Wagner, "Bargaining and Budget Making in Illinois Public Institutions," *Industrial and Labor Relations Review*, October 1973, pp. 49–62.

[24] David Lewin and Raymond D. Horton, "Evaluating the Impact of Collective Bargaining on the Merit System in Government," *The Arbitration Journal*, September 1975, pp. 199–211. Also see David Lewin, "Collective Bargaining Impacts on Personnel Administration in the American Public Sector," *Labor Law Journal*, July 1976, 426–36.

[25] Peter Feuille, Henry Juris, Ralph Jones, and Michael Jay Jedel, "Multiemployer Bargaining Among Local Governments" (Paper presented at 1976 Industrial Relations Research Association Meeting, Atlantic City, N.J., September, 1976).

[26] Lewin, Kuhn and Horton ["Some Impacts of Collective Bargaining on Local Government: A Diversity Thesis," *Administration and Society*,] pp. 497–516.

[27] Thomas A. Kochan and Hoyt N. Wheeler, "Municipal Collective Bargaining: A Model and Analysis of Bargaining Outcomes," *Industrial and Labor Relations Review*, October 1975.

[28] Paul F. Gerhart, "Determinants of Bargaining Outcomes in Local Government Labor Negotiations," *Industrial and Labor Relations Review*, April 1976, pp. 331–51.

[29] Thomas A. Kochan, "Correlates of State Public Employee Bargaining Laws," *Industrial Relations*, October 1973, pp. 322–37.

[30] Paul D. Staudohar, "The Emergence of Hawaii's Public Employment Law," *Industrial Relations*, October 1973, pp. 338–51.

[31] Arnold R. Weber, "Paradise Lost; Or Whatever Happened to the Chicago Social Workers?" *Industrial and Labor Relations Review*, April 1969, pp. 323–38.

[32] It is possible, of course, that such broader analyses would yield stronger support for the "union power" thesis than is observable from wage impact studies alone.

tions. These studies, initially focused on the measurement of union wage impacts, have broadened to include various non-wage issues, with collective bargaining conceptualized as an independent variable in some instances, and as a dependent variable in others.

Still, many aspects of public sector labor relations remain virtually unexplored. For example, the eruption and extension of unionism in government, a sector long considered unorganizable by saturationist interpreters of labor movement growth, has received only minimal attention.[33] The organization of substantial numbers of white-collar, professional, supervisory, and even some managerial employees in government appears especially provocative in terms of labor movement theory.[34] The possible extension of the Taft-Hartley Act to government employment or the promulgation of a federal collective bargaining or "minimum standards" law for public sector labor relations, have been popularly debated, but not subjected to dispassionate, scholarly analysis.[35] Similarly, the internal

dynamics of public sector labor organizations, in particular the extent to which they follow democratic processes, have yet to be investigated.[36]

It is worth noting, as well, that the findings and conclusions of recent studies of public sector labor relations are based on data obtained during a period of sustained expansion of the governmental sector of the economy. The continuation of this expansionary trend appears problematic, however, in view of the layoffs that are occurring in some large urban governments (most notably, New York City), and, more fundamentally, as the American citizenry reappraises its investments in public service.[37] Hence it seems likely that labor scholars will be afforded the opportunity of testing their observations about governmental labor relations against the phenomenon of cyclical changes in the economy of the public sector.

Finally, the study of governmental labor relations may be considered valuable not only in its own right, but also for the stim-

---

[33] The terms *eruption* and *extension* are due to Daniel Bell. See his discussion comments in *Labor and Trade Unionism*, edited by Walter Galenson and Seymour M. Lipset (New York: John Wiley & Sons, 1960), pp. 89–93. Saturationists contend that the labor movement will expand only if it permeates sectors or groups that historically have been resistant to organization, i.e., if it overcomes structural barriers. See William J. Moore and Robert J. Newman, "On the Prospects for American Trade Union Growth: A Cross Section Analysis," *The Review of Economics and Statistics*, November 1975, pp. 435–45.

[34] Unlike the Taft Hartley Act, public sector labor statutes exclude few personnel from organization and bargaining protections. White-collar and professional workers are more likely than others to pursue negotiations over a broad scope of issues, including basic management policies. See Archie Kleingartner, "Collective Bargaining Between Salaried Professionals and Public Sector Management," *Public Administration Review*, March-April 1973, pp. 165–72.

[35] See Thomas R. Colosi and Steven B. Rynecki, eds., *Federal Legislation for Public Sector Collective Bargaining* (Chicago, Ill.: The American Arbitration Association and the International Personnel Management Association, 1975). The "minimum standards" approach advocates a federal statute spelling out mini-

mum organization and bargaining rights for all public workers, but leaving to individual public jurisdictions decisions concerning the development of labor relations frameworks. Several bills providing one or another form of federal bargaining legislation for government employees, recently have been introduced into the House and Senate of the U.S. Congress, but none have yet been enacted into law.

[36] Indeed, only little attention presently is paid to the issue of union democracy, and nothing has been written on this subject in relation to public sector labor organizations. We simply do not know how these organizations compare with those in the private sector in terms of democratic practices or the factors affecting internal political processes.

[37] According to its Office of Management and Budget, New York City's municipal work force declined by more than 36,000 during 1975. The manpower reduction was achieved partly through attrition and partly (principally) by layoffs. In fiscal 1975, moreover, some 140,000 positions were eliminated by American state and local governments. The reductions were more than offset by growth in other parts of this sector, but the prospects for future expansion appear restricted, especially in view of declining federal aid to state and local governments. See Ralph Schlosstein, "State and Local Government Finances During Recession," *Challenge*, July-August 1975, pp. 47–50.

ulus that it provides to the reexamination of private sector labor relations. Many aspects of collective bargaining in industry which have been only cursorily explored, and others that have undergone important recent changes, appear susceptible to the application of models, concepts, and methodologies used to study public sector labor relations. The nonwage impacts of private sector unions are especially deserving of scrutiny. In any case, integration of knowledge about public and private sector union-management relations would contribute substantially to a broader understanding of the contemporary American industrial relations system.

PART TWO

THE ENVIRONMENT

CHAPTER 3

History of Collective Bargaining in the United States

The history of the labor movement in the United States must be placed in the context of this country's strongly individualistic culture. The United States, with its strong emphasis on the individual's right to do business, has never presented a particularly hospitable environment for the collective activities necessary for strong trade unionism, and this was especially true prior to the 1930s. As early as 1806, in the famous Philadelphia Cordwainers case, a combination of workers to raise their wages (a union) was found to be an unlawful conspiracy. By 1841, however, public pressure had forced a rethinking of this doctrine. In that year, the Supreme Court of Massachusetts, in the case of *Commonwealth* v. *Hunt* ruled that a combination of workers to raise wages was not, in and of itself, unlawful. Although the means (violence) or the ends (malicious destruction of someone's business) may be found to be unlawful, the mere combination was not.

Employers continued to find ways to combat unionism. Damage suits would make unions and their members liable for the loss of business to employers during strikes. Even more insidious, from the point of view of unions, or effective, from the point of view of employers, was the injunction. Obtained from a judge (any judge) at the beginning of the strike and picketing, on the grounds that the strike, if permitted to continue, would cause the employer irreparable harm, the injunction had the advantage of stopping the strike at its inception, using the sanction of placing the strikers in contempt of court if the picketing continued.

Although employer resistance combined with judicial hostility was (and, according to unions, still is) an important factor in inhibiting the growth of unionism, this by itself might not have been an insurmountable barrier if American workers and American culture were more hospitable to collective action. It is this inhospitality that is the subject of the reading in this section by labor theorist Selig Perlman in an excerpt from his *A Theory of the Labor Movement.*

Although Perlman's work was published in 1928, many of its insights into the American industrial relations system appear timeless, as even a cursory review of recent occurrences demonstrates. For example, the importance of private property was reemphasized in the debate over the proposed Labor Law Reform Act of 1977–1978. Much of the successful resistance to that bill seemed to coalesce around a provision which would have permitted unions the right to respond, on the employer's premises and time, to an employer's antiunion speech made to a captive audience speech on company time. Opponents argued that such a provision would constitute too great an infringement on the property rights of the employer.

Perlman's discussion of the difficulty that the American labor movement has had with staying organized provides insight into the reason why unions place so much emphasis on having union security provisions in collective bargaining agreements.

Yet, American workers have unionized. This was especially true of the eight-year period prior to World War II. In 1933, it is estimated that there were roughly 2.7 million union members in the United States. In 1941, union membership had increased to 10.2 million. As a percentage of the labor force, the increase was equally dramatic. In 1933, only 5.2 percent of the labor force could be considered union members. In 1941, this percentage had risen to 17.7 percent. If one looked at only employees in nonagricultural establishments, the respective percentages were 11.3 percent and 27.9 percent.

Clearly, this period involved a major alteration in the industrial relations system in the United States. The major characteristics of the system as we know it today took form at that time. This includes the unionization of the major manufacturing industries in the United States—automobiles, basic steel, rubber, and electrical equipment.

The agents of the change in the system were the unions and workers, two of the parties/organizations that comprise the system, and the economic and legal environments. Although scholars still have not agreed on the reasons for the sudden increase in the attractiveness of unions to workers, one can speculate that the massive unemployment of the depression must have suggested to workers that there was a basic conflict of interest between workers and employers. The labor movement, through the establishment of the unions that would eventually comprise the Congress of Industrial Organizations, became willing and capable of organizing unskilled workers on an industry-wide basis. In addition, the legal/political environment, with the passage of the Norris-LaGuardia, National Industrial Recovery, and National Labor Relations Acts, was far more hospitable to workers organizing unions than it had previously been.

A change of this magnitude could not be accomplished without substantial disruption. The second and third readings in this section attempt to provide a taste of what went on during the 1930s in industrial relations in the United States. The second reading, an excerpt from Walter Galenson's *The CIO Challenge to the AFL*, discusses the use of labor's most dramatic weapon, the sit-down strike, and its role in the attempt by the United Auto Workers to organize General Motors. The third reading, from Bernstein's *Turbulent Years*, briefly chronicles what was probably the major union organizing tragedy of the period, the Chicago Memorial Day Massacre of 1937.

LABOR AND CAPITALISM IN AMERICA[1]*

Selig Perlman

The most distinctive characteristic of the development of the labor movement in America has been . . . a perpetual struggle to keep the organization from going to pieces for want of inner cohesiveness. For, it has had to cope with two disruptive tendencies: First, American labor has always been prone—though far more in the past than now—to identify itself in outlook, interest, and action, with the great lower middle class, the farmers, the small manufacturers and business men—in a word, with the "producing classes" and their periodic "antimonopoly" campaigns. Second—and here is a tendency of a rising rather than diminishing potency—the American employer has, in general, been able to keep his employees contented with the conditions, determined by himself, on which they individually accepted employment. Both these tendencies have seriously hindered the efforts of trade unionism towards stability and solidarity. The first tendency proved inimical because the organized wage earners would periodically be drawn into the whirlpool of politics under the banner of the "antimonopoly" parties—so, under the American system of party politics, invariably suffering dissension, and ultimately disintegration. The second of the tendencies mentioned has balked unionism because the employer, wielding the initiative, has been able successfully to carry his own individualistic

competitive spirit into the ranks of his employees. Moreover, both factors making for disintegration go back to a common cause. For whether the labor organization has succumbed to the lure of a political reform movement aiming to shield the "small man" and the "man on the make" and has broken up in political dissension; or whether it has failed to get started because the individual laborer has accepted the incentive of a bonus wage and of a better opportunity for advancement within the framework of a nonunion bargain; the ultimate explanation, at all events, lies in the basic conditions of life in the American community—economic, political, ethnic, mental, and spiritual. Some of these are a heritage from the past, others of more recent origin, but all are closely interwoven with the present and the future of American labor.

THE BASIC CHARACTERISTICS OF THE AMERICAN COMMUNITY

1. THE STRENGTH OF THE INSTITUTION OF PRIVATE PROPERTY

A labor movement must, from its very nature, be an organized campaign against the rights of private property, even where it stops short of embracing a radical program seeking the elimination, gradual or abrupt, "constitutional" or violent, of the private entrepreneur. When this campaign takes the political and legislative route, it leads to the denial of the employer's right to absolute control of his productive property. It demands and secures regulatory re-

---

[1] See my *History of Trade Unionism in the United States* (Macmillan, 1922).

* Reprinted from Selig Perlman, *A Theory of the Labor Movement*, orig. ed. 1922 (New York: Augustus M. Kelly, 1966), pp. 154–76.

strictions which, under American constitutional practice, are within the province
of the police power vested in the states
and granted by specific authority to Congress; only they must, in every case, square
with "public purpose," as that term is interpreted in the last analysis by the United
States Supreme Court. When the same
campaign follows the economic route—the
route of unionism, strikes, boycotts, and
union "working rules"—the restrictions
on the rights of property are usually even
more thoroughgoing and far-reaching,
since unions are less amenable to judicial
control than are legislatures and Congress.
A third form of the labor movement seeks
to promote cooperative production and distribution, neither of which is practiced appreciably in this country. This cooperative
movement sets out to beat private capitalism by the methods of private business:
greater efficiency and superior competitive
power. To the advocates of the rights of
private property, this third mode of the
labor movement is the least offensive.

Because the labor movement in any
form is a campaign against the absolute
rights of private property, the extent to
which the institution of private property
is intrenched in the community in which
a labor movement operates is of overwhelming importance to it. In England,
the advent of industrial capitalism syn-
chronized with an agrarian revolution
which uprooted and set adrift hundreds
of thousands of her peasant yeomanry to
join the urban proletariat. Thus, eventually the urban capitalists in the fight for
their rights were denied the vital and valuable support which might have come from
a land-owning peasantry. England, therefore, permitted more drastic inroads into
property rights than France, where the
Great Revolution created peasant propri-
etors on a scale far vaster even than that
on which the contemporary English Enclosure movement destroyed them. The same
holds for newer countries. Property rights

are safer from infringement in Canada, settled by farming homesteaders, than in Aus-
tralia, where, until recently, the desirable
lands were owned in large holdings by capitalistic pastoralists.

The enormous strength of private property in America, at once obvious to any
observer[2] goes back to the all important
fact that, by and large, this country was
occupied and settled by laboring pioneers,
creating property for themselves as they
went along and holding it in small parcels.
This was the way not only of agriculture
but also of the mechanical trades and of
the larger scale industries. Thus, the harmony between the self-interest of the individual pursuing his private economic aim
and the general public interest proved a
real and lasting harmony in the American
colonies and states. . . .

The earnestness with which judges will
rush to stand between legislatures and
menaced property rights; the rigor of their
application of the injunction to keep
unionists and strikers from interfering
with those rights in their own way; the
ease with which a typically American middle class community may work itself up,
or be worked up, into an antiradical hysteria, when Soviet missionaries or syndicalist
agitators are rumored to be abroad in the
land; and the flocking to the election polls
of millions to vote for the "safe" candidate—all are of one piece, and are to be
explained by the way in which the American community originated and grew.

This social and economic conservatism,
bred in the American community from the
beginning, has been tested repeatedly by
sections of the American labor movement—now wittingly, now unwittingly,
and invariably the test has evoked the

---

[2] The utter disregard of the property rights of dis-
tillers, brewers, and others engaged in the drink traffic
resulted from the intensity of the moral passion
evoked—the historical heritage of puritanism. Had
private property been less entrenched than it is, the
property owning groups would have been more hesitant to remove even one stone of the arch.

same and identical reaction. It began in 1829, when the Workingman's Party of New York, moved by the desire to frighten employers lest they add to the recently won 10-hour day, officially endorsed the crude communistic "Equal Division" program of Thomas Skidmore.[3] A whole generation had to pass before the recollection of this brief indiscretion had faded from the public memory and ceased to plague the labor movement. Another such test of the public mind was the unplanned, but virtual anarchy of the destructive great railway strikes of 1877, from Baltimore to San Francisco. It was then that the judiciary, watching the paralysis which had seized the democratically chosen sheriffs and governors, and remembering well the Commune of Paris of 1871, resolved to insure society against a labor revolution by dint of the injunction, the outlawing of the boycott, and like measures. Nine years later, the Chicago "Anarchists," with a full-blown program of revolutionary syndicalism in all but the name itself, were made to feel the ferocious self-defense of a gigantically growing and self-satisfied community against those who would import the methods of the class struggle of Russia and of Spain. Still later, in the Pullman strike of 1894, the labor movement saw how the courts, the Federal Executive, and the ruling forces in the country could be counted on to act as one in crushing any real or fancied industrial rebellion. The treatment of the Industrial Workers of the World in the Western States, the anti-"Red" hysteria of 1919 and 1920, and the great godsend which the syndicalist past of William Z. Foster proved to the employers in defeating the great steel strike in 1919, which he led,—are of too recent occurrence to

necessitate detailed discussion. The state of Kansas, a representative American farming and midle-class community, furnishes perhaps the most telling illustration of the typical American reaction to industrial radicalism. That state, which was in 1912 a stamping ground for Roosevelt progressivism, just as it had been the heart of the "Populism" of the 90s showed no hesitancy in 1919 (when the coal miners' strike had endangered the comfort of its citizenry), at enacting a law depriving of the right to strike, labor in public utilities and in other industries supplying food, fuel, and clothing, which the law classed as public utilities for that purpose.

Briefly, if the century-long experience of American labor as an organized movement holds any great lesson at all, that lesson is that under no circumstances can labor here afford to arouse the fears of the great middle class for the safety of private property as a basic institution. Labor needs the support of public opinion, meaning the middle class, both rural and urban, in order to make headway with its program of curtailing, by legislation and by trade unionism, the abuses which attend the employer's unrestricted exercise of his property rights. But any suspicion that labor might harbor a design to do away altogether with private property, instead of merely regulating its use, immediately throws the public into an alliance with the anti-union employers. . . .

This is especially so because American organized labor lives in a potentially hostile environment. The American public has tolerated the labor movement, or has even aided it, as the miners were aided in their strike of 1902 against the anthracite coal combination. But a misstep can easily turn sympathy into hostility. Gompers' reiterated denunciations of communism in the disturbed years immediately following the Russian Revolution, which have been continued by his successor, seem to have been prompted at least

[3] Skidmore, a self-educated workman, published in 1829 a book entitled *The Rights of Men to Property: Being a Proposition to Make It Equal among the Adults of the Present Generation, and to Provide for its Equal Transmission to Every Individual of Each Succeeding Generation, on Arriving at the Age of Maturity.*

partly[4] by the realization of the ease with which the environment of the American labor movement may be turned into a hostile environment. And this same realization that in the American community labor is in a minority, and is facing a nation of property holders, actual or potential, is at the bottom of American labor's distrust of government authority which is so puzzling to Europeans. Experience has taught American labor leaders that, whatever may have been the avowed purpose when powers were extended to the government, and whatever may have been the express assurances given to labor that such powers would never be used against it, it is all in vain when a crisis breaks, like a threatened strike in a vital industry, and when the powers that be feel that with some stretching perhaps, the law might be applied to handle the situation. It is enough to recall that the Sherman Anti-Trust law was applied for the first time in the Debs case arising from the Pullman strike, and that the War-Time Lever Act, intended against food and other profiteers, was made the basis, one year after the Armistice, of an injunction against striking coal miners.

2. THE LACK OF A CLASS CONSCIOUSNESS IN AMERICAN LABOR

The overshadowing problem of the American labor movement has always been the problem of staying organized. No other labor movement has ever had to contend with the fragility so characteristic of American labor organizations. In the main, this fragility of the organization has come from the lack of class cohesiveness in American labor. That American unions have appreciated the full gravity of this problem, whether or not they have also consciously

connected it with a weak class cohesiveness, is shown by several practices, which they have carried to a much farther extent than unionists in other countries. It would seem as though through these practices they have tried to make up for the lack of a spontaneous class solidarity, upon which European unions could always reckon with certainty. These practices are ways of ruthlessly suppressing "dual" unions and "outlaw" strikes.

An *outlaw* strike is a strike by local groups, usually one or more local branches, undertaken without complying with the regular procedure prescribed in the constitution of the national union and against the wishes of the national officers. Such strikes are invariably defeated by the national officers themselves, who, if need be, and especially if a breach of a trade agreement with the employer is also involved, will not only expel the outlaws, but will even go to the extent of recruiting from among out-of-town members in sufficient numbers to fill the places of the strikers. In Great Britain, on the contrary, when national leaders have been thus defied by their own local branches, they have refused, to be sure, to put the strikers on the strike benefit rolls, but, on the other hand, they have never thought of visiting upon these "outlaws" anything like the reprisals employed in America. We find a similar contrast between England and America in regard to the treatment of dual unions. A *dual* union originates in the secession of a disaffected faction from an established union, or else it may arise as a brand new organization; in either case, it competes with the old union for membership in the same craft or industry. In America, dual unions are ruthlessly exterminated by the combined strength of all the unions in the American Federation of Labor. But British union leaders will view dual unionism with a complacency that seems utterly incomprehensible to American union officers. The American proce-

---

[4] Of course the policy of the communists, and, before them, of the socialists, of trying to capture the American Federation of Labor through the tactics of "boring from within," has been the constant factor accounting for this hostility.

dure, both in regard to outlaw strikes and dual unions, has often been decried as a bold and shameless manifestation of union "bureaucratism" and of boss-control. Much can be said in favor of this interpretation. Yet a different interpretation is equally in point. This ruthlessness, while making full allowance for the tyranny and ambition to rule by union bosses, is at the same time a device for self-protection hit upon by labor organizations operating under conditions in which everything and everybody seem engaged in a conspiracy to undermine their solidarity within. British unions, luckily for themselves, have their internal solidarity presented on a silver platter, as it were, by the very organization of the society in which they work. British society, with its hierarchy of classes, keeps labor together by pressure from the top. Accordingly, British workers act together in strikes, notwithstanding the rivalry between their unions. But the experience of American unionism has been that, with some few exceptions, easily explained,[5] whenever "radical" or merely impetuous local leaders defied their own union constitution with an "unauthorized" strike, or where factions have broken away to form a more "progressive" rival to the old union, the resulting fratricidal war, including mutual "scabbing" has always led to an all around defeat for labor, and to a total collapse of orgnization.

The cause of this lack of psychological cohesiveness in American labor is the absence, by and large, of a completely "settled" wage earning class. . . .

To be sure, the great mass of the wage earners in American industry today, unless they have come from the farm intending to return there with a part of their wages saved, will die wage earners. However, many of these do not stay in a given indus-

try for life, but keep moving from industry to industry and from locality to locality, in search for better working conditions. Moreover, the bright son of a machanic and factory hand, whether of native or immigrant parentage, need not despair, with the training which the public schools give him free of charge and with whatever else he may pick up, of finding his way to this or that one of the thousand and one selling "lines" which pay on the commission basis; or, if his ambition and his luck go hand in hand, of attaining to some one of the equally numerous kinds of small businesses; or, finally, of the many minor supervisory positions in the large manufacturing establishments, which are constantly on the lookout for persons in the ranks suitable for promotion. It is, therefore, a mistake to assume that with the exhaustion of the supply of free public land, the wage earner who is above the average in ambition and ability, or at least his children, if they are equally endowed (and the children's opportunities color the parents' attitude no less than do their own) have become cooped up for good in the class of factory operatives. For today, the alternative opportunities to bring a lowly factory hand are certainly more varied and entail less hardship than the old opportunity of homesteading in the West and "growing up with the country."

But, in a sense, the opportunity of the West has never ceased. In this vast country, several historical industrial stages are found existing side by side, though in demarcated areas. There is, therefore, the opportunity to migrate from older to newer and less developed sections, in which a person without much or any inherited property may still find the race for economic independence a free and open race. The difference between a section in the United States which is still underdeveloped economically and a similar one in a European country, is the difference between a navigable stream with some obsta-

---

[5] The organization of the Amalgamated Clothing Workers of America in 1914, a dual union to the United Garment Workers of America, is the outstanding illustration.

cles in its bed still waiting to be removed, and a stagnant pool without an outlet. In the former, opportunities are plentiful, multipliable by effort and only waiting to be exploited; in the latter, the few extant opportunities are jealously monopolized by their incumbents.

If the characteristically American fluidity of economic society has preserved and created opportunities for the nonpropertied individual of not much more than average ability, those with a higher ability and a gift for leadership have found their upward progression smoother still. Participation in political life in America has never been reserved to the upper classes, as until recently in England, nor to those with a higher education, as in France, but is open to all who can master the game. In the past, before the trade unions became stablized, capable of holding both their leaders and their membership, considerable leadership material drained away from labor into politics. However, at that time industry had not yet come to appreciate the "political" talent[6] of handling men as a valuable business asset. But in the present era of personnel management and industrial relations departments, of "welfare capitalism," and of efficiency by "inducement" and "leadership," there is room for that sort of talent, at least in the largest establishments. For the present, businessmen look to college-trained men to fill these positions. But it is not at all precluded that what otherwise might have been union leadership talent, is being drawn into this sort of activity.

Another cause of the lack of class-consciousness in American labor was the free gift of the ballot which came to labor at

an early date as a by-product of the Jeffersonian democratic movement. In other countries, where the labor movement started while the workingmen were still denied the franchise, there was in the last analysis no need of a theory of "surplus value" to convince them that they were a class apart and should therefore be class conscious. There ran a line like a red thread between the laboring class and the other classes. Not so, where that line is only an economic one. Such a line becomes blurred by the constant process of "osmosis" between one economic class and another, by fluctuations in relative bargaining power of employer and employee with changes in the business cycle, and by other changing conditions.

Next to the abundant economic opportunities available to wage earners in this country, and to their children, immigration has been the factor most guilty of the incohesiveness of American labor. To workers employed in a given industry, a new wave of immigrants, generally of a new nationality, meant a competitive menace to be fought off and to be kept out of that industry. For, by the worker's job consciousness, the strongest animosity was felt not for the employer who had initiated or stimulated the new immigrant wave, but for the immigrants who came and took the jobs away. When immigrants of a particular nationality acquired higher standards and began rebuilding the unions which they destroyed at their coming, then a new nationality would arrive to do unto the former what these had done unto the original membership. The restriction of immigration by the quota system has at last done away with this phenomenon, which formerly used to occur and recur with an inevitable regularity.

American labor remains the most heterogeneous laboring class in existence—ethnically, linguistically, religiously, and culturally. With a working class of such a composition, to make socialism or commu-

---

[6] In the bituminous coal industry, the operators began at an early date to employ ex-leaders of the miners as their "commissioners" in charge of labor relations under the agreement system with the union. These men, provided they did not practise trickery, never lost caste with the miners, any more than a member of the House of Commons does who "crosses the House."

nism the official *ism* of the movement, would mean, even if the other conditions permitted it, deliberately driving the Catholics, who are perhaps in the majority in the American Federation of Labor, out of the labor movement, since with them an irreconcilable opposition to socialism is a matter of religious principle. Consequently the only acceptable "consciousness" for American labor as a whole is a job consciousness, with a limited objective of wage and job control; which not at all hinders American unionism from being the most hard hitting unionism in any country. Individual unions may, however, adopt whatever consciousness they wish. Also the solidarity of American labor is a solidarity with a quickly diminishing potency as one passes from the craft group— which looks upon the jobs in the craft as its common property for which it is ready to fight long and bitterly—to the widening concentric circles of the related crafts, the industry, the American Federation of Labor, and the world labor movement.

3. THE INADEQUACY OF THE POLITICAL INSTRUMENT

The advocates of a political labor party for the United States are overlooking the fact that the political constitution of America actualizes the very "pluralist" principle which of late has become so fashionable among the younger political scientists. The American state has never been the "omnicompetent" state which these scientists abhor, because its written constitution and an ever-watchful judiciary have compelled it to treat as inviolate the autonomy of business and industry, which, though theoretically a sphere of liberty, practically are under "industrial government." The omnicompetent state has furthermore been prevented by a federal system which has broken up the political sovereignty into 49 disjointed pieces, setting going an eternal jealousy between the largest piece,

Congress, and the remaining 48. Futhermore, each of the 49 pieces has been divided into three members, two houses of the legislature and an independent executive, all of whom must agree in order to make a law. But then it is still open to the state supreme court to annul the law, and the state cannot even appeal to the supreme court, although it is open to the latter to annul national laws and state laws approved by state courts. Obviously, then, American governments are inherently inadequate as instruments of economic reform. However, the American situation has at least this merit, from the point of view of labor, that it does not disguise the weakness of government, in contrast with Europe, where labor, deluded by the theoretical omnicompetence of the state over industry, centered on capturing that instrument, but found it wanting in actual use.

It is to this situation, more than to anything else, that the stubborn "economism" of the American Federation of Labor must be traced. For economic action (strikes and boycotts) could never, notwithstanding court injunctions, be rendered as ineffectual as have been attempts at reform by legislation.

But not alone the inherent weakness of the state as an instrument of economic reform militates against placing reliance upon it. The prospects for success are diminished also by the now established mode of procedure for getting control of that instrument—namely, the American political party system, so essentially different from the European. It is indeed surprising that the guild socialists should have failed to notice how exellent a type-illustration the American political party is of their characteristic proposal for all industries—a self-governing guild of all workers, high and low, with the capitalistic entrepreneur eliminated. The pertinence of this illustration in no way suffers from the fact that in the American political industry there are two such guilds competing for the contract to govern, which is awarded periodically at elections, by the voters, who are the consumers of the commodity produced by these political guilds—government. Each of the two political producers' guilds—composed of brain workers (the bosses or leaders); of ordinary workers (the ward heelers); as well as of ultra-respectable figureheads—endeavors to guess in advance what assortment of political "goods" will please a majority of the consumers, and stocks up accordingly. Normally, there is a strong desire in each guild to try to hold the patronage of those "Customers" who have extended to it preference in the past, and to cultivate their buyers' good-will. Some of that patronage is held without an effort. Thus, with a number of customers, the good-will for one or the other producer guild has become so absolute that it is no longer the quality of the goods that matters, but solely the label on the goods. However, so far as the other and more "choicy" patrons are concerned, the "brain workers" of each guild must take care not to stock up on the wrong goods. Accordingly, when, after an election, they find that they have made a wrong guess, they not infrequently change the assortment of goods completely for the next election. This, however, happens much less frequently with the Republican guild than with its Democratic rival, because its customers are the "best people," the business men, to whom the rest look up as to connoisseurs in goods political. Another important wrinkle in the business of politics is that although these guilds are organized nationally, the managers of the local branches have practically unlimited discretion in the choice of the goods they wish to handle locally—so long as their way of managing the business has a favorable effect upon the all-important national deal. It has thus come about, by an accumulation of the effects of many alignments and bargains, both old and re-

cent, that each of the two rival guilds of political producers has developed a heterogeneous conglomerate of customers, some of whom by their own political prejudices are steady and "tied" customers; while others, on the contrary, are "independent" customers, necessitating political managers and bosses with a high grade of mental agility and great shrewdness. The upshot of the whole situation is that any third concern entering into the arena, such as a consumer-controlled labor party set up by the labor movement, is bound to encounter the deadly competition of the expertly managed producer-controlled old parties. These parties have the advantage that they are capable, if need be, of a flexibility of 180 percent in their platforms, with extraordinary dexterity at stealing the thunder of the new party. As they are out primarily to get from the voters the contract to run the government, like good business men, they are not rigid about consistency with their own past professions or actions. It is to this uncanny adaptability of the established American political parties, meeting with the weak group consciousness of American labor—weakest in regard to politics and political issues—that the uniform failure of American independent labor parties has been due.

To the labor movement, these realities of American politics have long been perfectly familiar. Ever since the advent of the first labor party, the Workingmen's Party of New York in 1829, labor has been learning through experience how slim are its chances in competition with the old political parties. Out of this experience there developed, as the choice, perhaps, of the lesser of two evils, a method of political collective bargaining between the organized labor movement and the leaders or bosses of the two old parties, which consists of trading off labor votes as payment for pledges made by regular party politicians to carry out, if elected to office, certain specific policies favored by labor. Under this arrangement, organized labor is nonpartisan, but throws its support to whichever party comes the nearest to accepting its demands, and "rewards its friends and punishes its enemies" on election day. This method is most effective when both parties are so matched that labor holds the balance of power. . . .

When a candidate so elected meets in Congress or in the state legislature others, whether Democrats or Republicans, who like himself were nominated and elected by labor votes, and upon whom the "yoke" of their respective party "bosses" sits with equal lightness, the result is a nonpartisan, labor-controlled bloc. However, in presidential nominations, where the convention system still rules despite the selection of the delegates by the primary system, the older method of "collective bargaining" on both sides—between labor and the political bosses—is still the only method.

3–2

THE GENERAL MOTORS STRIKE

Walter Galenson*

The strike called by the UAW against General Motors at the end of 1936 ranks as the most critical labor conflict of the 1930s. Up to this time, the UAW was a small, struggling organization, with great ambitions but few members. It emerged from the GM strike perhaps not yet a major power, but certainly a factor to be reckoned with in the industry. And it was able to capitalize upon its limited gains from the GM strike to consolidate its position into an impregnable one.

As a prelude to the General Motors strike, employees of the Bendix Corpora-

tion of South Bend, Indiana, manufacturers of automobile accessories, engaged in a sit-down strike on November 17, 1936. The sit-down strike was a relatively new device. It had been employed on a large scale by French metal workers in May, 1936, and while instances of sit-downs are to be found in the United States even prior to this date, it was the Rubber Workers who first used it as a regular instrument of union policy. Between March 27 and June 13, 1936, there were 19 known sit-down strikes in the Goodyear Akron plant alone, and one rubber concern in Akron reported having had over 50 quickie sit-down strikes lasting from several minutes to several hours. The Bendix local of the UAW had been rebuffed a number of times over a period of years in its attempt to be recognized as the bargaining agent for the workers in the plant. In none of the previous sit-downs had the workers re-

* Professor, New York State School of Industrial and Labor Relations, Cornell University. Reprinted by permission of the publishers from *The CIO Challenge to the AFL: A History of the Labor Movement, 1935–41* by Walter Galenson (Cambridge, Mass.: Harvard University Press, 1960), pp.134–50. Copyright © 1960 by the President and Fellows of Harvard College.

mained in the plant overnight, but the Bendix employees decided to remain until the company agreed to recognize the union. After staying in for nine days, the union won a contract calling for recognition as representative of its members, a bilateral grievance board, two-hours call-in pay, and a day's notice of layoffs.

On November 25, the day the Bendix strike was settled, workers in the Midland Steel Frame Company in Detroit sat down. This plant manufactured automobile frames for Chrysler and Lincoln, and within a few days, one Ford and five Chrysler assembly plants were shut down for lack of frames. At the end of a week, the company settled for a 10-cent-an-hour wage increase, seniority in layoff and rehiring, and time and a half for overtime, the most notable union victory to that date.

Another important preparatory strike occurred at the Kelsey-Hayes Wheel Company in Detroit during December. The workers remained in for five days, and the strike was called off sooner than it might otherwise have been to make way for General Motors. In this strike, Walter Reuther for the first time demonstrated his leadership capacities.

The General Motors strike was not the result of any strategic master plan. It began inauspiciously when, on November 18, workers at the Fisher Body plant in Atlanta sat down for a day in protest against the discharge of an employee for union activity. On December 15, employees of the Fisher Body plant in Kansas City sat down for the same reason, and forced the Chevrolet assembly plant in that city to close for lack of bodies. At UAW President Homer Martin's request, a conference was held between him and GM officials, which resulted in the following statement by William S. Knudsen, then executive vice president of General Motors:

A personal interview was granted Homer Martin, president of the United Automobile Workers, at which Mr. Martin presented various alleged discrimination cases and grievances outlined in his published telegram and letter. Mr. Martin was advised to take the various matters up with the plant manager or, if necessary, the general manager having jurisdiction in the location involved, this being in conformity with a corporation operating policy.

Following this rebuff to the union, the strike began in earnest. On December 28, a sit-down was commenced at the Fisher Body plant in Cleveland when the management postponed a conference with union representatives. The next day, the strike spread to the Fisher Body and Chevrolet plants in Flint, Michigan, which was to be the focus of events in the ensuing months. Actually, these strikes were premature. The top UAW leadership had planned no action until after January 1, 1937, when a Democratic administration under Governor Frank Murphy was installed in Lansing, the Michigan state capital. The workers at the Flint and Cleveland Fisher Body plants, key units in the General Motors system, jumped the gun in their impatience to have it out with the company. The importance of these plants has been described as follows:

These two plants were the major body manufacturing units of the corporation— "mother plants," according to GM terminology—being responsible for the fabrication of the greater portion of Chevrolet and other body parts which were then shipped in so-called knock down form to the assembly plants throughout the country. All the stampings for the national Chevy production were turned out in Cleveland. Fisher one [Flint] on the other hand manufactured irreplaceable parts for Buick, Oldsmobile, Pontiac, and Cadillac. In particular the great dies and enormous presses needed to stamp out the mammoth simplified units of the new "turret top" bodies were concentrated in the Cleveland and Flint body plants. Possibly three fourths or more of the corporation's production were consequently dependent on these two plants; an interlocking arrangement that was not unusual, moreover, in the highly specialized auto industry and especially among the leading corporations. There were perhaps a dozen other plants equally crucial to General Motors but in only the two designated was the union strong enough to halt production.

During the following week, employees of the Guide Lamp Company in Anderson, Indiana, the Fisher Body and Chevrolet plants in Norwood, Ohio, the Chevrolet transmission plant, the Chevrolet and Fisher Body plants in Janesville, Wisconsin, and the Cadillac assembly plant in Detroit, were all struck. Slowly the tieup continued to spread through the vast General Motors system, and by early February almost all the 200,000 GM employees were idle, with the weekly production of cars down to 1,500 from the mid-December peak of 53,000.

The first reaction of the GM management was one of shocked indignation. In reply to a letter from Homer Martin requesting a collective bargaining conference, Knudsen wrote:

Sit-down strikes are strikes. Such strikers are clearly trespassers and violators of the law of the land. We cannot have bona fide collective bargaining with sit-down strikers in illegal possession of plants. Collective bargaining cannot be justified if one party, having seized the plant, holds a gun at the other party's head.

In a prior interview, Knudsen reiterated his previously expressed position that all problems should be settled on a local basis with plant managers. "I cannot have all these matters come here," he said, "because that would concentrate too much authority in this office and I would be swamped." Martin retorted to this: "General Motors is an operating company, not a holding company. That is why we want a national conference. Policies are made here and cannot be changed by local or divisional representatives."

On January 2, 1937, upon the company's petition, Judge Edward Black of the Genesee County circuit court issued an injunction restraining the union from continuing to remain in the Flint plant, from picketing, and from interfering in any manner with those who wished to enter the plant to work. When the sheriff read the injunction to the Flint strikers and asked them to leave voluntarily, he was laughed out of the plant. A few days later it was discovered that Judge Black held a block of GM stock with a current market value of $219,900, which served to discredit his action and in effect rendered the injunction of no practical import.

On January 5, the company posted on all its bulletin boards a message from Alfred P. Sloan, Jr., its president, stating it to be the firm and unalterable position of General Motors "not [to] recognize any union as the sole bargaining agency for its workers, to the exclusion of all others. General Motors will continue to recognize, for the purpose of collective bargaining, the representatives of its workers, whether union or non union." It may be recalled that the National Labor Relations Act, which gave exclusive bargaining rights to the majority union, was in effect at the time, but the Supreme Court had not yet ruled upon it and there was widespread belief that it would be held unconstitutional.

As a condition for meeting with union representatives, GM insisted that the plants be evacuated. The union offered to do so, provided the company in turn would agree that all plants would remain closed, without movement of equipment or resumption of activities, until a national settlement was effected. This proviso was unacceptable to GM, and the first efforts at conciliation collapsed.

The corporation then turned to a frontal attack, and Flint, Michigan, became the center of the stage. More than 50,000 Flint workers were employed in GM plants, and a back-to-work movement was started under the sponsorship of the Flint Alliance, a new organization hastily formed in opposition to the UAW. The union claimed that the Alliance, the president of which was George Boysen, a former GM paymaster and at the time of the strike an independent business man, was company-sponsored, while industry pictured it as a spontaneous reaction on the part of loyal workers against a small minority of UAW strikers. On January 11, the heat in Fisher Body Plant No. 2 was shut off and attempts were made by the company police to prevent food from being carried into the plant. The sit-downers, faced with the possibility of being starved out, captured the plant gates from the company police to assure their source of food. At this point the city police attacked in an effort to recapture the plant gates. For hours the strikers battled the police, fighting clubs, tear gas, and riot guns with such improvised weapons as two-pound car door hinges and streams of water from fire hoses. The news of the riot spread, and the strikers were reinforced by thousands of supporters who poured into Flint. The battle ended with the strikers still in possession of the plant. Fourteen strikers suffered bullet wounds in this encounter, which became famous in union mythology as "The Battle of the Running Bulls."

At this juncture there might well have been a prelude to the bloody events of the Little Steel Strike half a year later. The city was in a state of civil war, with the sit-downers determined to resist any further attempts at eviction. To prevent further bloodshed, Governor Frank Murphy of Michigan despatched 1,500 National Guardsmen to Flint, with instructions to maintain the *status quo,* that is, to prevent attempts at forcible eviction of the strikers. He summoned union and company representatives to meet him in the state capital at Lansing, and on January 15, a truce was arranged: the strikers agreed to leave the plants on January 17, and negotiations were to begin the following day. Plants in Detroit and Anderson, Indiana, were evacuated, but shortly before the Flint strikers were scheduled to leave, the UAW learned that General Motors had sent telegrams to workers in the Cadillac and Fleetwood plants in Detroit directing them to report for work, and also had agreed to bargain with the Flint Alliance as well, and refused consequently to carry out any further plant evacuations. A few days later the company admitted that it had agreed to meet with representatives of the Flint Alliance, but asserted that since the UAW represented not more than 5 percent of its employees, "It would be the height of absurdity for it to try to represent the whole body of company workers." Besides, said the company, meetings with the Alliance had been scheduled for 9 a.m., while the UAW conferences were not to begin until 11 a.m., so that no conflict of scheduling was involved. The union learned about the intention of General Motors to bargain with the Flint Alliance through William Lawrence, then a reporter for the United Press, who had secured this information from Knudsen, and asked the union about its attitude toward the company's policy. It is likely that the evacuation of the plants would have been carried out on schedule if not for this piece of information.

General Motors declined to enter into negotiations, and the truce collapsed. Attempts at conciliation then shifted to Washington, where Sloan and Knudsen agreed to meet with Secretary of Labor Frances Perkins at her request, but refused to see John L. Lewis. The latter, angered, made the following statement to the press:

> For six months during the presidential campaign the economic royalists represented by General Motors and the Du Ponts contributed their money and used their energy to drive this administration from power. The administration asked labor to help repel this attack and labor gave it. The same economic

royalists now have their fangs in labor. The workers of this country expect the administration to help the strikers in every reasonable way.

Sloan, in his turn annoyed at the turn of events, left Washington for New York, and upon receipt of a letter from the secretary of labor requesting him to return, replied: "we sincerely regret to have to say that we must decline to negotiate further with the union while its representatives continue to hold our plants unlawfully. We cannot see our way clear, therefore, to accept your invitation."

At a press conference the next day, President Roosevelt expressed the view that Sloan's decision was a very unfortunate one, while Secretary Perkins went much further in her condemnation:

> an episode like this must make it clear to the American people why the workers have lost confidence in General Motors. I still think that General Motors have made a great mistake, perhaps the greatest mistake in their lives. The American people do not expect them to sulk in their tents because they feel the sit-down strike is illegal. There was a time when picketing was considered illegal, and before that strikes of any kind were illegal. The legality of the sit-down strike has yet to be determined.

Faced with this pressure, Sloan returned to Washington and met with the secretary of labor, but to no avail. The corporation then prepared to take the offensive once more on the industrial front.

The UAW, fearing that GM might succeed in reopening enough plants to commence production, decided to extend the area of the sit-down. Secret plans were laid to capture the strategic Chevrolet No. 4 plant in Flint, where motors were assembled. To draw police away, a detachment of men under Powers Hapgood and Roy Reuther made a feint at the nearby Chevrolet plant No. 9, thus permitting 400 workers to occupy Chevrolet No. 4 without difficulty.

General Motors responded by securing an injunction from Judge Paul V. Gadola ordering the Fisher Body plants evacuated by February 3. Thousands of union supporters swarmed into Flint from other automobile centers, determined to prevent the forcible eviction of the strikers. All windows were barricaded with metal sheets, and defense squads were organized as the 2,000 men now within the plant prepared to resist. The sheriff, however, declined to attempt enforcement of the injunction without assistance from the state, and Governor Murphy, anxious to avoid bloodshed, wired the sheriff to take no action pending further negotiations. He also prevented state troops, which had surrounded the plant, from taking any violent action. Thus the deadline passed quietly, and the union had won a significant victory.

The situation still remained explosive, however. Flint city authorities were reported to be arming vigilante groups. The chief of police was quoted as saying: "Unless John L. Lewis wants a repetition of the Herrin, Ill., massacres he had better call off his union men. The good citizens of Flint are getting pretty nearly out of hand. We are organizing fast and will have between 500 and 1,000 men ready for any emergency. At the direct request of President Roosevelt, Knudsen finally agreed to meet with Lewis. Following is Lewis' description of his reception upon his arrival in Detroit:

> It is a matter of public knowledge now that the Governor of this State read me a formal letter in writing demanding that this action [evacuation of the plants] be taken by me, and my reply to the Governor of the State when he read that letter, with the knowledge of the President of the United States—and the approval—was this: "I do not doubt your ability to call out your soldiers and shoot the members of our union out of those plants, but let me say that when you issue that order I shall leave this conference and

I shall enter one of those plants with my own people. And the militia will have the pleasure of shooting me out of the plants with them." The order was not executed.

Although the negotiations came perilously close to rupture on several occasions, Governor Murphy succeeded in bringing about a truce on February 11, 1937.

*　*　*　*　*

General Motors agreed to recognize the UAW as bargaining agent for its members only, a reduction of the original union demand of sole bargaining rights. Collective bargaining was to begin on February 16, and all court proceedings were to be withdrawn. To avoid a repetition of the incident which had ended the earlier truce, the corporation sent a letter to Murphy agreeing that for six months it would not bargain or enter into an agreement with any other union without securing his permission to do so. By this device, GM was spared the embarrassment of agreeing directly to bargain only with the UAW, while the latter was virtually assured of sole bargaining rights for at least six months. For its part, the UAW agreed to evacuate all GM plants which it was holding. The pertinent portion of the letter from Knudsen to Murphy read:

> We have been told that the UAW in justifying its demand for bargaining privilege states that they fear that without protection of some kind we might deliberately proceed to bargain with other organizations for the purpose of undermining the position of this particular union. We have said that we have no such intention. . . . As evidence of our intention to do all we can to hasten the resumption of work in our plants and to promote peace, we will not bargain with or enter into agreements with any other union or representative of employees of plants on strike in respect to such matters of general corporate policy, without submitting to you the facts of the situation and gaining from you the sanction of any such contemplated procedure as being justified by law, equity

or justice towards the groups of employes so represented.

Sloan paid handsome tribute to Murphy for his role in bringing about the settlement: "The corporation, its workers and the public are indebted to the Hon. Frank Murphy, assisted by Federal Conciliator James F. Dewey, for his untiring and conscientious efforts, as well as the fairness with which he has handled a most difficult situation. Only his efforts have made it possible to resume work at this time." The union, of course, was jubilant. A retrospective union evaluation of the significance of the strike had this to say about it: "The heads of the corporation were compelled, for the first time, to bargain with the spokesman of their employees, the officers of the UAW and the CIO. The end of the strike came on February 11, 1937, in a brilliant victory for the workers. . . . This was the greatest and most historic victory of the UAW. It broke the back of anti-unionism in the most powerful industry in the world." *A New York Times* correspondent who followed the events closely wrote a few months later that "By entirely stopping production of all General Motors cars in January and February and obtaining recognition in the first written and signed agreement on a national scale which that great citadel of the open shop had ever granted to a labor union, the CIO . . . opened the way for the remarkable upsurge in sentiment for union organization which is now going on in many sections of the country. . . . Since the General Motors settlement, the union has been spreading its organization rapidly in General Motors plants, which were weakly organized at the time of the strike."

*　*　*　*　*

THE SIT-DOWN STRIKE IN RETROSPECT

Scarcely any labor practice of the 1930s aroused as much animosity among employers, and public concern, as the sit-down strike, of which the General Motors strike was the most spectacular example. The sit-down strike trend, beginning late in 1936, rose to a peak in March 1937, when 170 such strikes, involving 167,000 workers, took place. In April, the month in which the Supreme Court upheld the constitutionality of the National Labor Relations Act, and in May, the number of strikes declined to 52 and 72 respectively. There was further tapering downward thereafter until by the end of the year the sit-down weapon had almost fallen into disuse.

The principal argument in favor of the sit down, from the labor standpoint, was its effectiveness. With a minimum of organization, it proved possible for small groups of determined men to shut down indefinitely huge plants, and by concentrating upon strategic producing units from the standpoint of the flow of materials, to spread paralysis to plants with no organization. Some of the advantages of this form of action in distinction to a "normal" strike have been well summed up by a communist leader who was active in the automobile industry:

Sit-down strikes give to the workers a greater feeling of strength and security because the strikers are inside the plants, in the solid confines of the factory, at the machines which are the sources of their livelihood, instead of away from the plant, moving around in "empty space," on the sidewalks surrounding the factories.

Sit-down strikes give to the workers greater sureness that there are no scabs within the plants and no production is being carried on and makes it difficult to run in scabs. . . .

The sit-down strike furthermore makes it difficult to resume operations even partially where scabs have gotten in because by holding down one section of the plant it is hard to begin operations.

The sit-down strike affords strikers greater possibility of defending themselves

against the violence of the police and company men. . . .

The sit-down strike makes for a greater discipline, group consciousness and comradeship among the strikers because of the very position in which they find themselves and thereby enhances the militancy and fighting spirit of the workers.

Finally, the sit-down strike arouses the widest sympathy and support among the working population because of the courage of the workers in taking "possession" of the factory and because of the self-sacrifice and hardship which such action entails.

From a moral point of view, UAW and other CIO leaders argued that the sit-down strike was merely a logical extension of the growth of worker property rights in their jobs. "Is it wrong," asked Wyndham Mortimer, a UAW vice-president, "for a worker to stay at his job? The laws of the state and nation recognize, in a hundred ways, that the worker has a definite claim upon his job; more fundamentally, it is recognized that every workman has a moral right to continue on his job unless some definite misconduct justifies his discharge. These sit-down strikers are staying at their work places; no one has a better right to be there than have these men themselves." Francis J. Gorman, then president of the United Textile Workers of America, was quoted in much the same vein: "A sit-down strike is clearly the most effective and least costly way for the worker to insure himself against encroachment on his 'property right' to his job by company-hired strikebreakers."

The national CIO, while somewhat more cautious than its young, enthusiastic affiliates, was inclined to take a pragmatic view of the sit-down, as evidenced by the following statement made by John Brophy, at the time organizational director of the CIO:

We do not condemn sit-down strikes per se. We consider that various kinds of labor activity will be used to promote organization of workers and establish collective bargaining. Sit-down strikes, under some of these conditions, may be a very necessary and useful weapon. In the formative and promotional stage of unionism in a certain type of industry, the sit-down strike has real value.

John L. Lewis took very much the same point of view: "The CIO stands for punctilious observance of contracts, but we are not losing any sleep about strikes where employers refuse to recognize the well-defined principles of collective bargaining. A CIO contract is adequate protection for any employer against sit-downs, lie-downs, or any other kind of strike."

Despite the fact that AFL unions were involved in 100 of the 477 sit-down strikes that occurred in 1937, the top AFL leadership disowned this strike technique from the first. In January 1937, the AFL Executive Council asked [AFL President] William Green to study the problem, and on March 28, he made public his findings, which read in part: "The sit-down strike has never been approved or supported by the American Federation of Labor because there is involved in its application grave implications detrimental to labor's interest. It must be disavowed by the thinking men and women of labor." He called the sit-down illegal and dangerous in the long run, and voiced the fear that its persistent use would result in the enactment of legislation inimical to the labor movement.

The press, business men, and legislators were with very few exceptions hostile to the sit-down strike. *The New York Times* condemned it as "a plain disregard of statutes forbidding the seizure of private property" and "essentially an act of lawlessness." The *Christian Science Monitor* said that it placed "confiscation and seizure above law." A group of Boston residents headed by A. Lawrence Lowell, president emeritus of Harvard University, wired Vice

President Garner on March 26, 1937, requesting that legislation be enacted to "establish the supremacy of constitutional government, law and order, national and state." Sit-down strikes were castigated in the following terms:

> Armed insurrection—defiance of law, order, and duly elected authority—is spreading like wild-fire. It is rapidly growing beyond control. . . . The issue is vital; it dwarfs any other issue now agitating the public mind; it attacks and undermines the very foundation of our political and social structure . . . freedom and liberty are at an end, government becomes a mockery, superseded by anarchy, mob rule, and ruthless dictatorship.

The governors of Virginia, Texas, Mississippi, New Jersey, Illinois and California announced that they would not tolerate sit-down strikes in their states. The United States Senate, after considerable debate, passed on April 7, 1937, a resolution condemning the sit-down strike as illegal and against public policy, although it coupled with this a condemnation of industrial espionage and violations of the National Labor Relations Act. Numerous anti-sit-down bills were introduced in state legislatures, and the State of Vermont enacted a law rendering a sit-down striker subject to imprisonment and heavy fine.

The courts were more directly involved than legislatures, and they almost uniformly declared sit downs illegal whenever called upon to enjoin strikers. On two separate occasions, as has already been noted, General Motors obtained equity injunctions, although in neither case was the order obeyed. The coup de grâce was eventually given the sit-down strike by the United States Supreme Court, which, in setting aside a National Labor Relations Board order that directed the Fansteel Metallurgical Corporation to reinstate sit-down strikers, declared: "It was an illegal seizure of the buildings in order to prevent their use by the employer in a lawful manner and thus, by acts of force and violence, to compel the employer to submit." The Court also held in this case that sit-down strikers, by their lawless conduct, forfeited all rights under the National Labor Relations Act. However, the sit down as a union weapon for all practical purposes had been abandoned a year prior to the Supreme Court decision.

In retrospect, the following may be said of the sit-down strike epidemic that occurred in 1937:

The strikes were clearly illegal, and there was little disposition on the part of anyone to take an opposite point of view. Although they would be unthinkable today, they were tolerated in 1937, and even received substantial public support, mainly because large segments of American industry refused to accept collective bargaining. Trade unions were the underdogs, and they were widely represented as merely attempting to secure in practice the rights that Congress had bestowed upon them as a matter of law. Senator Robert F. Wagner made this point forcibly in defending the sit-down strike in a Senate speech:

> The sit-down has been used only in protest against repeated violations of industrial liberties which Congress has recognized. The sit-down, even in the few cases where labor has used it effectively, has succeeded in winning for labor only such industrial liberties as both law and morals have long sanctioned. The sit-down has been provoked by the long-standing ruthless tactics of a few corporations who have hamstrung the National Labor Relations Board by invoking court actions . . .; who have openly banded together to defy this law of Congress quite independently of any Court action . . ; and who have systematically used spies and discharges and violence and terrorism to shatter the workers' liberties as defined by congress.

From an historical perspective, the sit-down era constituted an episode in the transition from one system of industrial relations to another; it hastened the replacement of untrammeled management prerogative in the disposition of labor by a system under which trade unions, as representatives of the workers, were to share in this function. It was perhaps inevitable that so violent a wrench with the past should have provoked management attitudes sharply antithetical to the new national labor policy. But by the same token, it is not surprising that industrial workers, having broken through on the legislative front, should seek to implement their hard won rights with whatever weapons were at hand, regardless of the law.

Despite all the public furor, the sit-down strike was actually a less costly weapon, in terms of human life and property, than, for example, the traditional form of labor strife as exemplified in the Little Steel strikes of 1937. No deaths were directly attributable to the sit-down strikes, despite their quasi-military character. One of the industry's trade journals had this to say of property damage, when the rash of stikes had run its course:

> Damage at automobile plants caused by sit-down strikers appears to have been confined largely to nonessential materials with production machinery found unhurt after evacuation, a survey now shows. The losses were not insignificant, however. An insurance adjuster has made a guess that the physical damage done to plants during all automobile plant strikes in Michigan would approximate $200,000. This is apart from losses due to deterioration of materials left outside plants.

There is no inherent reason for the sit-down strikes to have followed this relatively peaceful course. Most contemporary observers, however, credited Governor Frank Murphy with having averted what might have been a very unfortunate development in insisting upon negotiation rather than in employing force to evict the strikers.

The most important aspect of the sit-down strike was that it paved the way for rapid unionization of the automobile industry. John Brophy has testified to the fact that in November and December 1936, UAW attempts at mass meetings were generally failures; few workers stopped to listen to speeches that he and Philip Murray made at plant gates. It is impossible to ascertain what UAW membership was at the outset of the strikes, but certainly not more than a small fraction of the employees of General Motors had enlisted under its banner. Within six months of the beginning of the sit-down strikes, the UAW claimed a dues paying membership of 520,000, and the first stage of organization had been completed for the entire industry, with the exception of Ford. It is not at all unlikely that General Motors and other manufacturers could have resisted the UAW more successfully if the union had confined itself to more orthodox weapons.

THE AFTERMATH OF THE GENERAL MOTORS STRIKE

The truce of February 11, 1937, was the prelude to hard bargaining between General Motors and the UAW, resulting in a signed agreement more than a month later. The UAW was obliged to content itself with recognition as representative of its members only, and a promise that the speed-up would be studied to eliminate injustices. The union's demand that its shop steward system be recognized as part of the grievance machinery was denied, and instead a shop committee system was installed. The practical difference was that the contract provided for a maximum of nine committeemen for each plant, whereas there was a union shop steward for about every 25 members. Thus, the shop stewards did not gain the prestige they would have enjoyed as grievancemen. Nor was the union successful in securing

a reduced working week, the elimination of piecework, or a uniform minimum wage scale. Seniority in layoff and rehiring, an important union demand, was agreed to by the company, but with the proviso that married men were to be accorded preference when a permanent layoff was involved. There was no wage increase, the corporation having raised wages unilaterally while the strike was still on.

Following upon the General Motors settlement, the UAW turned its attention to the Chrysler Corporation, which in 1936 was the second largest producer in the industry. On March 8, after the corporation had refused to grant the union demand for sole bargaining rights, a strike was declared, and almost all the Chrysler plants were occupied. That sole bargaining was the principal issue involved was made clear by a corporation statement issued the following day:

> We have offered not only to continue to recognize the UAWA as the bargaining agent for its members in our plants, but also to work out with them shop rules which would enable union officers and stewards to function effectively for the employees whom they may represent. The union has rejected this. We offered to discuss modification of the existing seniority rules. . . . This the union has also rejected.

Nor did the union claim that Chrysler wages were below the general industrial level. The union strategy was simply to go a step beyond the General Motors degree of recognition: the sit down, it was felt, would quickly bring Chrysler to its knees.

But the union had failed to reckon with the mounting public clamor against the sit-down strike; the day when it could be used with impunity was already past. Governor Murphy lost no time getting Walter Chrysler and John L. Lewis together, and this time he made it clear to Lewis that he was prepared to use force to clear the plants. It was reported of the Lewis-Chrysler meetings that "the two men have been getting along famously at the conferences, amazing their colleagues by their amiability." On March 24, Lewis agreed to the evacuation of the plants, and in return the company agreed not to resume operations or to move machinery from the plants while collective bargaining was continuing. In the agreement reached on April 6, the UAW was recognized as the bargaining agent for its members only, but the company promised that it would not "aid, promote or finance any labor group which purports to engage in collective bargaining or make any agreement with any such group or organization for the purpose of undermining the union."

Although union offficials attempted to interpret this language as a virtual grant of exclusive representation rights, it obviously was not. A union partisan later said this of the agreement:

> The recognition for UAW members and the death of the Chrysler Company union system could have been obtained without a strike. It was not surprising that the Chrysler

sit-down strikers balked at leaving the plants when the settlement was brought to them. They had been told that the union would insist on obtaining sole recognition in a contract, as well as in practice.

Again, Governor Murphy played a major role in effecting the settlement. Walter Chrysler described him as "tireless, patient, and resourceful" and declared that "I have no hesitancy in saying he has done a great job."

Other major agreements were shortly secured, either with or without strikes. Hudson, Packard, Studebaker, Briggs, Murray Body, Motor Products, Timken-Detroit Axle, L. A. Young Spring and Wire, Bohn Aluminum, and numerous smaller plants were brought under union contract. In some cases, for example, Packard and Studebaker, sole recognition was achieved after NLRB elections. The only holdout was the Ford Motor Company, and here the union came up against an organizational problem which it was not able to solve until 1941.

Galenson's discussion of the sit-down strike and its aftermath call attention to [two] points. First, it should be noted that the GM sit-down strike was for *recognition* of the UAW. As such, the Union was asking that General Motors talk to it as the agent for its employees. Strikes over recognition, generally the most bitter, have all but disappeared with the advent of the procedures in the National Labor Relations Act for determining representation. Most strikes today are over the terms and conditions of employment to be included in a collective bargaining agreement.

Second, it is important to note the simplicity and crudeness of the agreement that resulted from the settlement of the sit-down strike as compared with the current UAW–GM agreement. Yet the shop committee system is still in existence with the Committee system incorporated in the grievance procedures. Piecework has been eliminated, and the 1982 agreement contained a uniform minimum wage scale. The 1982 agreement between GM and UAW, including contract language, appendixes, and letters and memoranda between the parties that they have chosen to incorporate into the agreement, is 434 pages. This is exclusive of local agreements negotiated at each GM plant. Needless to say, things have changed since 1937.

BREAKTHROUGH IN STEEL*

Irving Bernstein

The most important incident of the Little Steel strike and one of the great events of American labor history occurred on Memorial Day at Republic's South Chicago mill. This industrial site, occupying 274 acres of prairie within the city of Chicago, was located along Burley Avenue between 116th and 118th Streets, bounded on the west by the Calumet River and on the east by a barbed-wire fence along the Pennsylvania Railroad tracks. The main entrance was a large gate at Burley and 118th. To the north was a big, flat, empty field. The union's headquarters were five blocks north and one block east of the gate at a former tavern, Sam's Place, at Green Bay Avenue and 113th Street. Several dirt roads cut diagonally across the field from Green Bay below Sam's Place to Burley just north of 117th. Indiana Harbor, with its Inland and Sheet & Tube operations, lay only ten miles away.

The Chicago police had a long, notable, and dishonorable record of breaking strikes with force on behalf of employers in defiance of civil liberties. Secretary of the Interior Harold L. Ickes, himself a Chicagoan with considerable experience in these matters, wrote Senator La Follette on July 2, 1937:

I don't know whether any other city has a worse police force than Chicago but I doubt it. I have known something about it for a good many years and I have had two or three clashes with it over invasions of obvious civil rights. . . . The Augean stables emanated delicate perfume compared with some of the odors that have been redolent in this Department in the past. From the time of the Haymarket riots in Chicago, police always justified brutal invasions of civil rights by calling those whom they manhandled "anarchists."

The law of picketing, while currently uncertain, was in process of liberalization. On May 24, 1937, only two days before the Little Steel strike and six before Memorial Day, the Supreme Court had handed down the decision in the Senn case, holding that the 14th Amendment offered no bar to a state law permitting peaceful picketing. On March 31, 1937, Barnet Hodes, Chicago's Corporation Counsel, had notified the Commissioner of Police, "Our opinion . . . is . . . that the Police Department of the City of Chicago take no action to interfere with picketing when such picketing is conducted in a peaceable manner." On May 27, the newspapers carried a statement by Mayor Edward S. Kelly affirming the right to picket peacefully. From all this it is clear that SWOC[1] was legally permitted to picket before Republic's main gate at Burley and 118th, provided that the pickets conducted themselves peaceably.

Trouble, however, began even before the strike was officially called at 11 p.m. on Wednesday, May 26. Union workers started walking out during the afternoon and by the early evening several hundred were outside the gate. There were approxi-

* Reprinted from Irving Bernstein, *The Turbulent Years: A History of the American Worker, 1933–1941* (Boston: Sentry Edition, Houghton Mifflin, 1971), pp. 485–90. Copyright © 1969 by Irving Bernstein. Reprinted by permission of Houghton Mifflin Company.

[1] Steel Workers Organizing Committee.

mately 150 policemen inside. The strikers called those who continued to work and the police "scabs" and "finks," but attacked no one. The police summarily closed the area and arrested 23 individuals for unlawful assembly and disorderly conduct. That evening Captain John Prendergast established three police shifts, each with 90 patrolmen, 4 sergeants, and 2 lieutenants. On Friday he added a reserve detail of 38 men. Police headquarters were inside the gate; policemen were fed at company expense at its cafeteria; and Republic must have issued at least hatchet handles and gas, if not other arms, to the police.

In effect, the Chicago police had broken the picket line at the inception of the strike on Wednesday. The next day, when the union attempted to place pickets at the gate, the police ordered them to a spot two blocks away. Protests were filed downtown and on Friday SWOC was allowed five or six pickets at the gate. Late that afternoon the union people met at Sam's Place, decided to set up mass picketing, and began a march to the plant. The police intercepted them at Green Bay and 117th and a small riot occurred. The police fired three shots; several marchers and policemen were injured and six strikers were arrested. On Saturday the strikers were permitted restricted picketing at the gate.

By now the union was thoroughly confused and frustrated over the status of picketing at Republic; the Chicago police seemed to deny the law. While there is no reliable evidence, probably somewhere in the neighborhood of half of Republic's employees had struck. A picket line, therefore, was of decisive importance to the union to persuade the others to walk out. The fact that everyone was out without trouble in the much larger steel works in nearby Indiana Harbor must have stood as an example. SWOC, therefore, called a meeting for 3 p.m. on Sunday, Memorial Day, at Sam's Place to protest police restrictions on picketing. Learning of this on

Saturday evening, Captain James L. Mooney ordered both the day and swing shifts along with the reserve detail, a total of 264 policemen, to duty on Sunday afternoon.

Memorial Day was clear and warm in South Chicago. A large crowd, estimated between 1,000 and 2,500, gathered in midafternoon at Sam's Place. Most were strikers from Republic and workers from other nearby steel mills. There were a fair number of women and some children. Several outsiders, mainly drawn by curiosity, were also there: the writer Meyer Levin, who was to do a novel about the riot; the industrial relations secretary of the Council of Social Action of the Congregational Christian Churches, Frank W. McCulloch, who many years later was to become chairman of the NLRB; some ministers and divinity students; a social worker, Lupe Marshall; a part-time reporter for the *Chicago Daily News*, Ralph Beck; a Chicago surgeon, Dr. Lawrence Jacques, who had been asked by SWOC to come over in case there was need for medical care; and several teachers and students from a private school. Some of the workers and their wives were dressed in Sunday-best and observers noted "a holiday atmosphere."

A truck fitted with a public address system served as the speakers' platform. Joe R. Weber, a metalworker on the staff of SWOC, was chairman, so designated by John Riffe, the subregional director. Weber may have been a Communist. There were two speeches, one by Nicholas Fontecchio, former UMW official and now district director for SWOC, the other by Leo Krzycki of the Amalgamated Clothing Workers and SWOC. The burden of their remarks, in Krzycki's case enlivened by humor, was to support the union, including the right to picket peacefully. While they were critical of the police, neither advocated attacking either the police or the plant. As the meeting closed, someone in the audience moved to establish a mass picket line at the main gate. The motion carried by acclamation.

This motley throng, led by two young men carrying American flags, proceeded to walk down Green Bay Avenue to 114th Street and so onto the dirt roads leading to the mill. Their aspect, a policeman said, was that of "the Mexican Army." On the way a group split off and then returned to the main body. Several people carried placards that either denounced Republic's labor policy or asserted the right to picket. Some of the marchers, clearly a minority, picked up tree branches, ends of lumber, rocks, or pieces of pipe with which the field was littered. There is no evidence that anyone carried a gun. Several women were at the head of the line.

The police ranks moved forward to meet the marchers two blocks north of the gate at the approximate level of 116th Street. The two bodies joined across a 300-foot line of confrontation. Small groups of marchers engaged in conversation with policemen for several minutes. The substance of these discussions was identical: the marchers asked to be permitted to proceed to the gate in order to assert their right to picket peacefully and the police refused to allow them to advance any further.

According to Ralph Beck's testimony, which appears reliable, a marcher about 20 feet behind the line of confrontation threw a branch of a tree toward the police. Before it reached the peak of the arc, a policeman fired his revolver into the air and this was followed immediately by two more shots. Several marchers threw clubs and rocks. The police in the front ranks then fired their guns point blank (Beck estimated hearing 200 shots) and tossed tear-gas bombs directly into the crowd. Those marchers who were not dead or seriously wounded broke into full flight across the field. The police advanced, continuing to fire their guns and beating the fallen, now lying in tangled masses, with billies

and hatchet handles. Harry Harper, an employee of the Interlake Iron Corporation, who was there only because he was looking for his brother at his mother's insistence, described his view of the scene:

They charged like a bunch of demons. No one had a chance in the world. I was knocked down by the impact of the officers surging forward. I received a blow that struck me in the face. I went down. I tried to get up and blood was streaming out of my left eye. It also affected the right eye partially but I still had a little vision. I managed to run a little, covering my face with one hand. With the right eye I could see officers charging in a circle, shooting with revolvers—not up but right into the crowd—I realized the danger I was in. I feared I was going to be shot so I fell into a hole. Before I fell into this hole I saw people being mowed down, like with a scythe. . . . As I fell into this culvert there was a party lying there already. He said to me, "Help me, buddy. I am shot." And I said, "I am helpless. I cannot help you." I could not stay there much longer because just then a gas bomb fell into my face. It was choking me so I made one more attempt to go into the safety zone. But then I lost all sense of reasoning. . . .

The police seem to have become crazed with passion. Not only did they brutally attack the fallen; they dragged seriously wounded, unconscious men over the ground; they not only refused first aid themselves but interfered with Dr. Jacques; they piled severely injured people atop one another in patrol wagons. In at least one case, according to Dr. Jacques, death could have been prevented by prompt application of a tourniquet. "Wounded prisoners of war," the La Follette Committee observed, "might have expected and received greater solicitude."

Ten marchers were fatally shot. Seven received bullets in the back, three in the side. Thirty others, including one woman and three minors, were wounded by gunshot, nine of them, apparently, permanently disabled. Twenty-eight marchers received lacerations and contusions of the head, shoulders, and back requiring hospitalization and 25 to 30 others needed medical care. Thirty-five policemen reported injuries, none from gunfire and none fatal. Of this number, only three were hospitalized.

Those who died were: Hilding Anderson, aged 29; Alfred Causey, 43; Leo Francisco, 17; Earl Handley, 37; Otis Jones, 33; Sam P. Popovich, about 50; Kenneth Reed, 23; Joseph Rothmund, 48; Anthony Tagliori, 26; Lee Tisdale, 50. Six were residents of Chicago; Causey, Handley, Popovich, and Reed were from Indiana Harbor. Nine were white; Tisdale was a Negro. SWOC gave them a mass funeral on June 2 in Chicago.

Senator Elbert D. Thomas of Utah, who, as a member of the La Follette Committee, listened to a flood of testimony and examined a mountain of exhibits on this ghastly incident, drew the meaningful conclusions:

The encounter of May 30 should never have occurred. . . . It resulted in no gain for the state, or the property owners, or the laborers. No property was damaged, so the loss of life cannot be defended as having been in defense of property. Give to the strikers and to the police the benefit of every justification advanced by all witnesses for the affair and still the fight remains useless and without point. . . .

The use of police officers in such a way that they seem to be allied with either side of a labor dispute destroys their effectiveness as peace officers representing the public. The moment they are used in defense of a given group they are associated in the minds of the opposing group as partisans to the dispute. Therefore, their very presence in unusual numbers invites disorderly incidents which in turn magnify themselves into clashes that produce death and beatings. Riot duty is the most difficult task which even a well-disciplined soldier has to perform. Those not trained in this work should not be available to either owner or laborer for the taking of sides in a labor dispute.

The Memorial Day Massacre occurred in the midst of the "Little Steel" strike of 1937. This strike was, in actuality, an organizing campaign by the ancestor of the United Steelworkers of America, the Steel Workers Organizing Committee (SWOC) against the so-called Little Steel companies—Bethlehem, Republic, Youngstown Sheet and Tube, American Rolling Mill (Armco), National, Inland, and Jones and Laughlin. Big (U. S.) steel, had been successfully organized in early 1937. Although SWOC was able to organize J&L in 1937, the other companies were not successfully organized until World War II.

As noted, Irving Bernstein entitled his seminal work on the history of the American worker during the period 1933–41 *Turbulent Years.* This description is certainly fitting, during this period, American workers, the American labor movement, and the American industrial relations system experienced an upheaval unequaled, before or since, in its scope. This upheaval affected both the structure and size of the American labor movement.

The structure of the American labor movement in 1933 was not well suited to the unionization of the mass production industries. The American Federation of Labor was primarily an organization of craft unions, which lived by the principle of exclusive jurisdiction. In essence, this meant that each union could only organize workers in its own craft or jurisdiction. While such a situation might fit well in the construction industry, with its many distinct crafts and well-defined jobs, it was not appropriate for organizing the highly integrated mass production industries. Clearly, it was not only irrational but also contrary to the interests and desires of the workers to have the workers in a mass production industry divided up among several unions.

A minority of union leaders in the AFL, led by United Mine Workers President John L. Lewis saw this. After a rebuff by the AFL, Lewis and a group of fellow unionists formed the Committee for Industrial Organization (CIO) in November 1935. Although still ostensibly a dissident group within the AFL, the AFL in August 1936 suspended all of the unions that had affiliated with the CIO. Between February and May 1938, the AFL charters of all of the CIO unions were revoked.

Meanwhile, the CIO unions continued to support organizing drives in the mass production industries, and by August 1937, membership in CIO unions numbered 3.3 million, almost as high as the 50-year-old AFL. In November 1938, the CIO officially changed its name to the Congress of Industrial Organization. Thus, a rival labor federation had been established. The labor movement consisted of two federations until 1955, when the AFL and CIO merged to form the AFL–CIO.

CHAPTER 4

The Legal Framework

THE PRIVATE SECTOR

The current legal environment for the private sector collective bargaining system in the United States is determined by the National Labor Relations Act (NLRA). Originally enacted in 1935 (as the Wagner Act), it was amended by the Taft-Hartley Act in 1947. Important, but less sweeping revisions in the rights conferred by, and the coverage of, the NLRA occurred with the Landrum-Griffin amendments in 1959 and the Health Care Amendments in 1974. The latter amendments brought private, non-profit health care institutions under the jurisdiction of the Act.

The main purpose of the NLRA is the granting to employees the rights to self-organization and to engage, or to refrain from engaging, in concerted activity for the purpose of collective bargaining without fear of interference or reprisal by their employer or a union. The NLRA is administered by the National Labor Relations Board (NLRB) an administrative agency of the federal government. The purpose of having the rights under the act administered and enforced by an administrative agency rather than the courts is that an administrative agency provides consistency in the interpretation of the act and can apply its labor relations expertise in interpreting the broadly worded provisions of the act. The five members of the NLRB are appointed by the president with the advice and consent of the Senate. The terms are staggered, so that at least one vacancy occurs on the board every year.

The most important provisions of the act are those that deal with (1) representation and (2) enforcement. The representation provisions deal with the related questions of whether or not employees wish to be represented by a union, and if so, which employees and which union. The second set of provisions deals with enforcement of the employee rights under the NLRA, although employers and unions have some rights as well.

The main characteristic of the representation process is the principle of exclusive representation. This principle means that if a union is selected as the collective bargaining representative for a group of employees, no other union may represent that group of employees (unless that union is decertified), the union must represent all employees in that "unit," whether they are actually union members or not, and the employer must negotiate with that union and no other (unless that union is decertified). The two most important aspects of the representation process are the unit determination process and the representation election. The unit determination process, usually invoked only when the employer disputes the "appropriateness" of the unit requested by the union, makes a determination on which employees are to make the decision for or against representation. That decision is made through the representation election.

Through the creation of unfair labor practices, the NLRA attempts to guarantee to employees the right to self-organization and the right to engage in concerted activity without interference by either the employer or the union. Thus, employers are prohibited from discharging, disciplining, or otherwise adversely affecting an employee's employment status for the purpose of discouraging (or encouraging) union membership. In addition, in order to effectuate the rights of employees under the act, the board has permitted some compromise of the employer's property rights.

The cases illustrate some of the problem areas under the act. The excerpts from the *Edward G. Budd* and *Republic Aviation* cases present problems in the areas of discharge and discipline during an organizing campaign, and in the accommodation of employee property rights to the rights of employees to self-organization. The *Insurance Agents* and *American National Insurance* cases address problems that arise after a representative has been selected, i.e., the legality of tactics away from the bargaining table and the lawfulness of taking certain positions at the bargaining table.

Following that, excerpts from two broad-based studies of the NLRA are presented. Myron Roomkin and Richard N. Block analyze delay in the context of NLRB representation elections and Roomkin looks at the determinants of unfair labor practice charges.

Edward G. Budd Mfg. Co. v. National Labor Relations Board

United States Court of Appeals
Third Circuit, 1943
138 F.2d 86

On charges filed by International Union, United Automobile, Aircraft and Agricultural Workers of America, an affiliate of the Congress of Industrial Organizations, with the National Labor Relations Board, a complaint issued dated November 26, 1941, alleged that the petitioner was engaging in unfair labor practices . . . The complaint, . . . alleges that [Budd], in September 1933, created and foisted a labor organization, known as the Budd Employee Representation Association, upon its employees and thereafter contributed financial support to the Association and dominated its activities. The amended complaint also alleges that in July 1941, the petitioner discharged an employee, Walter Weigand, because of his activities on behalf of the union . . .

The board on June 10, 1942, issued its decision and order, requiring the disestablishment of the Association and the reinstatement of Weigand.

The case of Walter Weigand is extraordinary. If ever a workman deserved summary discharge it was he. He was under the influence of liquor while on duty. He came to work when he chose and he left the plant and his shift as he pleased. In fact, a foreman on one occasion was agreeably surprised to find Weigand at work and commented upon it. Weigand amiably stated that he was enjoying it. He brought a woman (apparently generally known as the "Duchess") to the rear of the plant yard and introduced some of the employees to her. He took another employee to visit her and when this man got too drunk to be able to go home, punched his time card for him and put him on the table in the representatives' meeting room in the plant in order to sleep off his intoxication. Weigand's immediate superiors demanded again and again that he be discharged, but each time higher officials intervened on Weigand's behalf because as was naively stated he was "a representative" [of the Association, an organization that was found to be unlawfully dominated by the employer]. . . .

In return for not working at the job for which he was hired, the [employer] gave him full pay and on five separate occasions raised his wages. One of these raises was general; that is to say, Weigand profited by a general wage increase throughout the plant, but the other four raises were given Weigand at times when other employees in the plant did not receive wage increases.

The [employer] contends that Weigand was discharged because of cumulative grievances against him. But about the time of the discharge it was suspected by some of the representatives that Weigand had joined the complaining CIO union. One of the representatives taxed him with this fact and Weigand offered to bet a hundred dollars that it could not be proved. On July 22, 1941, Weigand did disclose his union membership to the vice chairman

(Rattigan) of the Association and to another representative (Mullen) and apparently tried to persuade them to support the union. Weigand asserts that the next day he with Rattigan and Mullen, were seen talking to CIO organizer Reichwein on a street corner. The following day, according to Weigand's testimony, Mullen came to Weigand at the plant and stated that Weigand, Rattigan, and himself had been seen talking to Reichwein and that he, Mullen, had just had an interview with Personnel Director McIlvain and Plant Manager Mahan. . . . The following day Weigand was discharged. . . . [The] employer may discharge an employee for a good reason, a poor reason, or no reason at all so long as the provisions of the National Labor Relations Act are not violated.

It is, of course, a violation to discharge an employee because he has engaged in activities on behalf of a union. Conversely an employer may retain an employee for a good reason, a bad reason, or no reason at all and the reason is not a concern of the board. But it is certainly too great a strain on our credulity to assert, as does the petitioner, that Weigand was discharged for an accumulation of offenses. We think that he was discharged because his work on behalf of the CIO had become known to the plant manager. That ended his sinecure at the Budd plant. The board found that he was discharged because of his activities on behalf of the union. The record shows that the board's finding was based on sufficient evidence.

The order of the board will be enforced.

Even if one assumed (as did the judge in this case) that Weigand "deserved" to be discharged, Weigand's discharge was found to be an unfair labor practice because the evidence indicated that the reason he was discharged was *not* poor work performance or insubordination but his union activities. What evidence supported this finding? The timing of the discharge was considered: he was discharged not following his poor behavior on the job, but only after he was seen associating with the union. The employer's predischarge treatment of Weigand was also relevant—Weigand had been rewarded, not disciplined. Finally, he was a representative of the unlawfully dominated association.

Republic Aviation Corp. v. National Labor Relations Board

Supreme Court of the United States, 1945
324 U.S. 793

In the Republic Aviation Corporation case, the employer, a large and rapidly growing military aircraft manufacturer, adopted, well before any union activity at the plant, a general rule against soliciting which read as follows:

> Soliciting of any type cannot be permitted in the factory or offices.

The Republic plant was located in a built-up section of Suffolk County, New York. An employee persisted, after being warned of the rule, in soliciting union membership in the plant by passing out application cards to employees on his own time during lunch periods. The employee was discharged for infraction of the rule and, as the National Labor Relations Board found, without discrimination on the part of the employer toward union activity. . . .

The board determined that the promulgation and enforcement of the "no solicitation" rule violated . . . the National Labor Relations Act as it interfered with, restrained, and coerced employees in their rights . . . and [unlawfully] discriminated against the discharged employee. . . . As a consequence. . . . the board entered the usual cease and desist order and directed the reinstatement of the discharged employees with back pay and also the rescission of "the rule against solicitation in so far as it prohibits union activity and solicitation on company property during the employees' own time.". . .

In the case of Le Tourneau Company of Georgia, two employees were suspended two days each for distributing union literature or circulars on the employees' own time on company-owned and policed parking lots, adjacent to the company's fenced-in plant, in violation of a long standing and strictly enforced rule, adopted prior to union organization activity about the premises, which read as follows:

> In the future no Merchants, Concern, Company or Individual or Individuals will be permitted to distribute, post, or otherwise circulate handbills or posters, or any literature of any description on company property without first securing permission from the Personnel Department.

The rule was adopted to control littering and petty pilfering from parked autos by distributors. The board determined that there was no union bias or discrimination by the company in enforcing the rule. . . .

The board found that the application of the rule to the distribution of union literature by the employees on company property which resulted in the lay-offs was an unfair labor practice. . . . Cease and desist, and rule rescission orders, with directions to pay the employees for their lost time followed. . . .

These cases bring here for review the action of the National Labor Relations Board in working out an adjustment between the undisputed right of self-organization assured to employees under the

Wagner Act and the equally undisputed right of employers to maintain discipline in their establishments. Like so many others, these rights are not unlimited in the sense that they can be exercised without regard to any duty which the existence of rights in others may place upon employer or employee. Opportunity to organize and proper discipline are both essential elements in a balanced society.

The Wagner Act did not undertake the impossible task of specifying in precise and unmistakable language each incident which would constitute an unfair labor practice. On the contrary that act left to the board the work of applying the act's general prohibitory language in the light of the infinite combinations of events which might be charged as violative of its terms. Thus a "rigid scheme of remedies" is avoided and administrative flexibility within appropriate statutory limitations obtained to accomplish the dominant purpose of the legislation. . . . So far as we are here concerned that purpose is the right of employees to organize for mutual aid without employer interference. . . .

In the Republic Aviation Corporation case the evidence showed that the petitioner was in early 1943 a nonurban manufacturing establishment for military production which employed thousands. It was growing rapidly. Trains and automobiles gathered daily many employees for the plant from an area on Long Island, certainly larger than walking distance. The rule against solicitation was introduced in evidence and the circumstances of its violation by the dismissed employee after warning was detailed. . . .

No evidence was offered that any unusual conditions existed in labor relations, the plant location or otherwise to support any contention that conditions at this plant differed from those occurring normally at any other large establishment.

The Le Tourneau Company of Georgia case also is barren of special circumstances.

The evidence which was introduced tends to prove the simple facts heretofore set out as to the circumstances surrounding the discharge of the two employees for distributing union circulars.

These were the facts upon which the board reached its conclusions as to unfair labor practices. The Intermediate Report in the Republic Aviation case, . . . set out the reason why the rule against solicitation was considered inimical to the right of organization. "Thus, under the conditions obtaining in January 1943, the respondent's employees, working long hours in a plant engaged entirely in war production and expanding with extreme rapidity, were entirely deprived of their normal right to 'full freedom of association' in the plant on their own time, the very time and place uniquely appropriate and almost solely available to them therefor. The respondent's rule is therefore in clear derogation of the rights of its employees guaranteed by the act." This was approved by the board.

*   *   *   *   *

In the Le Tourneau Company case the discussion of the reasons underlying the findings was much more extended. We insert in the note below a quotation which shows the character of the boards opinion.[1]

_____

[1] "As the Circuit Court of Appeals for the Second Circuit has held, 'It is not every interference with property rights that is within the Fifth Amendment and . . . inconvenience or even some dislocation of property rights, may be necessary in order to safeguard the right to collective bargaining.' The board has frequently applied this principle in decisions involving varying sets of circumstances, where it has held that the employer's right to control his property does not permit him to deny access to his property to persons whose presence is necessary there to enable the employees effectively to exercise their right to self-organization and collective bargaining, and in those decisions which have reached the courts, the board's position has been sustained. Similarly, the board has held that, while it was 'within the province of an employer to promulgate and enforce a rule prohibiting union solicitation during working hours,' it

In the Republic Aviation case, [the employer] urges that irrespective of the validity of the rule against solicitation, its application in this instance did not violate [the act] because the rule was not discriminatorily applied against union solicitation but was impartially enforced against all solicitors. It seems clear, however that if a rule against solicitation is invalid as to union solicitation on the employer's premises during the employee's own time, a discharge because of violation of that rule [unlawfully] discriminates in that it dis-

courages membership in a labor organization.[3]

_____

[3] "The Act, of course, does not prevent an employer from making and enforcing reasonable rules covering the conduct of employees on company time. Working time is for work. It is therefore within the province of an employer to promulgate and enforce a rule prohibiting union solicitation during working hours. Such a rule must be presumed to be valid in the absence of evidence that it was adopted for a discriminatory purpose. It is no less true that time outside working hours, whether before or after work, or during luncheon or rest periods, is an employee's time to use as he wishes without unreasonable restraint, although the employee is on company property. It is therefore not within the province of an employer to promulgate and enforce a rule prohibiting union solicitation by an employee outside of working hours, although on company property. Such a rule must be presumed to be an unreasonable impediment to self-organization and therefore discriminatory in the absence of evidence that special circumstances make the rule necessary in order to maintain production or discipline."

_____

was 'not within the province of an employer to promulgate and enforce a rule prohibiting union solicitation by an employee outside of working hours, although on company property,' the latter restriction being deemed an unreasonable impediment to the exercise of the right to self-organization."

The issue in _Republic Aviation_, the conflict between employer property rights and employee rights of self-organization has been clarified in cases since Republic Aviation. Thus, for example, retail stores and health care institutions may ban employee solicitation on nonwork time in selling and patient care areas, respectively. Employers may give speeches to groups of employees (so-called captive audience speeches) on worktime. Employers need not permit nonemployee organizers access to the employer's premises unless the organizers have no other reasonable means to reach the employees.

National Labor Relations Board v. Insurance Agents' International Union

Supreme Court of the United States, 1960
361 U.S. 477

Mr. Justice Brennan delivered the opinion of the Court.

This case presents an important issue of the scope of the National Labor Relations Board's authority under . . . the National Labor Relations Act, which provides that "It shall be an unfair labor practice for a labor organization or its agents . . . to refuse to bargain collectively with an employer, provided it is the representative of his employees. . . ." The precise question is whether the Board may find that a union, which confers with an employer with the desire of reaching agreement on contract terms, has nevertheless refused to bargain collectively, thus violating that provision, solely and simply because during the negotiations it seeks to put economic pressure on the employer to yield to its bargaining demands by sponsoring on-the-job conduct designed to interfere with the carrying on of the employer's business.

Since 1949 the respondent Insurance Agents' International Union and the Prudential Insurance Company of America have negotiated collective bargaining agreements covering district agents employed by Prudential in 35 States and the District of Columbia. The principal duties of a Prudential district agent are to collect premiums and to solicit new business in an assigned locality known in the trade as his "debit." He has no fixed or regular working hours except that he must report at his district office two mornings a week and remain for two or three hours to deposit his collections, prepare and submit reports, and attend meetings to receive sales and other instructions. He is paid commissions on collections made and on new policies written; his only fixed compensation is a weekly payment of $4.50 intended primarily to cover his expenses.

In January 1956, Prudential and the union began the negotiation of a new contract to replace an agreement expiring in the following March. Bargaining was carried on continuously for six months before the terms of the new contract were agreed upon on July 17, 1956. It is not questioned that, if it stood alone, the record of negotiations would establish that the union conferred in good faith for the purpose and with the desire of reaching agreement with Prudential on a contract.

However, in April 1956, Prudential filed a . . . charge of refusal to bargain collectively against the union. The charge was based upon actions of the union and its members outside the conference room, occurring after the old contract expired in March. The union had announced in February that if agreement on the terms of the new contract was not reached when the old contract expired, the union members would then participate in a "Work Without a Contract" program—which meant that they would engage in certain planned, concerted on-the-job activities designed to harass the company. . . .

It was developed in the evidence that the union's harassing tactics involved activities by the member agents such as these: refusal for a time to solicit new business, and refusal (after the writing of new business was resumed) to comply with the company's reporting procedures; refusal to participate in the company's "May Policyholders' Month Campaign"; reporting late at district offices the days the agents were scheduled to attend them, and refusing to perform customary duties at the offices, instead engaging there in "sit-in mornings," "doing what comes naturally" and leaving at noon as a group; absenting themselves from special business conferences arranged by the company; picketing and distributing leaflets outside the various offices of the company on specified days and hours as directed by the union; distributing leaflets each day to policyholders and others and soliciting policyholders' signatures on petitions directed to the company; and presenting the signed policyholders' petitions to the company at its home office while simultaneously engaging in mass demonstrations there.

The hearing examiner filed a report recommending that the complaint be dismissed.

However, the board . . . rejected the trial examiner's recommendation, and entered a cease-and-desist order, . . . The Court of Appeals for the District of Columbia Circuit . . . set aside the board's order. We granted the board's petition for certiorari to review the important question presented. . . .

The policy of Congress [in enacting the National Labor Relations Act] is to impose a mutual duty upon the parties to confer in good faith with a desire to reach agreement, in the belief that such an approach from both sides of the table promotes the overall design of achieving industrial

peace. . . . Discussion conducted under that standard of good faith may narrow the issues, making the real demands of the parties clearer to each other, and perhaps to themselves, and may encourage an attitude of settlement through give and take. The mainstream of cases before the board and in the courts reviewing its orders, under the provisions fixing the duty to bargain collectively, is concerned with insuring that the parties approach the bargaining table with this attitude. But apart from this essential standard of conduct, Congress intended that the parties should have wide latitude in their negotiations, unrestricted by any governmental power to regulate the substantive solution of their differences. . . .

* * * * *

We believe that the board's approach in this case—unless it can be defended, . . . as resting on some unique character of the union tactics involved here—must be taken as proceeding from an erroneous view of collective bargaining. It must be realized that collective bargaining, under a system where the Government does not attempt to control the results of negotiations, cannot be equated with an academic collective search for truth—or even with what might be thought to be the ideal of one. The parties—even granting the modification of views that may come from a realization of economic interdependence—still proceed from contrary, and to an extent antagonistic, viewpoints and concepts of self-interest. The system has not reached the ideal of the philosophic notion that perfect understanding among people would lead to perfect agreement among them on values. The presence of economic weapons in reserve, and their actual exercise on occasion by the parties, is part and parcel of the system that the Wagner and Taft-Hartley Acts have recognized. Abstract logical analysis might find inconsistency between the command of the statute to negotiate toward an agreement in good faith and the legitimacy of the use of economic weapons, frequently having the most serious effect upon individual workers and productive enterprises, to induce one party to come to the terms desired by the other. But the truth of the matter is that at the present statutory stage of our national labor relations policy, the two factors—necessity for good-faith bargaining between parties, and the availability of economic pressure devices to each to make the other party incline to agree on one's terms—exist side by side. [George W. Taylor] recognizes this by describing economic force as "a prime motive power for agreements in free collective bargaining." Doubtless one factor influences the other; there may be less need to apply economic pressure if the areas of controversy have been defined through discussion; and at the same time, negotiation positions are apt to be weak or strong in accordance with the degree of economic power the parties possess. . . .

For similar reasons, we think the board's approach involves an intrusion into the substantive aspects of the bargaining process—unless there is some specific warrant for its condemnation of the precise tactics involved here. The limitations on board power . . . are exceeded, we hold, by inferring a lack of good faith not from any deficiencies of the union's performance at the bargaining table by reason of its attempted use of economic pressure, but solely and simply because tactics designed to exert economic pressure were employed during the course of the good-faith negotiations. Thus the board in the guise of determining good or bad faith in negotiations could regulate what economic weapons a party might summon to its aid. And if the board could regulate the choice of economic weapons that may be used as part of collective bargaining, it would be in a position to exercise considerable influence upon the substantive terms on which the parties

contract. As the parties' own devices became more limited, the government might have to enter even more directly into the negotiation of collective agreements. Our labor policy is not presently erected on a foundation of government control of the results of negotiations. . . . Nor does it contain a charter for the National Labor Relations Board to act at large in equalizing disparities of bargaining power between employer and union. . . .

The board contends that the distinction between a total strike and the conduct at [issue] is that a total strike is a concerted activity protected against employer interference . . . while the activity at [issue] is not a protected concerted activity. [For the sake of argument], we may agree . . . with the board that the employee conduct here was not a protected concerted activity. On this assumption the employer could have discharged or taken other appropriate disciplinary action against the employees participating in these "slowdown," "sit-in," and arguably unprotected disloyal tactics. . . . But surely that a union activity is not protected against disciplinary action does not mean that it constitutes a refusal to bargain in good faith.

* * * * *

The board contends that . . . these activities, as opposed to a "normal" strike, are [unlawful] because they offer maximum pressure on the employer at minimum economic cost to the union. One may doubt whether this was so here, but the matter does not turn on that. Surely it cannot be said that the only economic weapons consistent with good-faith bargaining are those which minimize the pressure on the other party or maximize the disadvantage to the party using them. The catalog of union and employer weapons that might thus fall under ban would be most extensive. . . . These distinctions . . . make clear to us that when the board moves in this area, . . . it is functioning as an arbiter of the sort of economic weapons the parties can use in seeking to gain acceptance of their bargaining demands. It has sought to introduce some standard of properly "balanced" bargaining power, or some new distinction of justifiable and unjustifiable, proper and "abusive" economic weapons into the collective bargaining duty imposed by the act. The board's assertion of power . . . allows it to sit in judgment upon every economic weapon the parties to a labor contract negotiation employ, judging it on the very general standard of that section, not drafted with reference to specific forms of economic pressure. We have expressed our belief that this amounts to the board's entrance into the substantive aspects of the bargaining process to an extent Congress has not countenanced.

The basic principle of the Insurance Agents case is that the parties to collective bargaining are permitted to use economic weapons in order to obtain a better bargain than they would have been able to obtain without using those weapons. Thus, unions may strike. Employers may presumably replace strikers or lock out their employees. The key restraint on employers are that they must not discriminate between strikers and nonstrikers, and they may not use an offer of permanent economic benefits as a weapon. Thus, an offer to pay accumulated vacation benefits only to employees who would abandon a strike has been found unlawful, as has discrimination among strikers in poststrike reinstatement. In short, from the point of view of an employer, power can be used to further a bargaining position vis-à-vis a union. It may not be used to discourage (or encourage) participation in that union. A manifestation of employer bargaining power is illustrated in the following case.

National Labor Relations Board v. American National Insurance Co.

Supreme Court of the United States, 1952
343 U.S. 395

Mr. Chief Justice Vinson delivered the opinion of the Court.

This case arises out of a complaint that [the employer, American National Insurance Company] refused to bargain collectively with the representatives of its employees as required under the National Labor Relations Act. . . .

The Office Employees International Union A. F. of L., Local No. 27, certified by the National Labor Relations Board as the exclusive bargaining representative of respondent's office employees, requested a meeting with [the employer] for the purpose of negotiating an agreement governing employment relations. At the first meetings, beginning on November 30, 1948, the union submitted a proposed contract covering wages, hours, promotions, vacations, and other provisions commonly found in collective bargaining agreements, including a clause establishing a procedure for settling grievances arising under the contract by successive appeals to management with ultimate resort to an arbitrator.

On January 10, 1949, following a recess for study of the union's contract proposals, respondent objected to the provisions calling for unlimited arbitration. To meet this objection, respondent proposed a so-called management functions clause listing matters such as promotions, discipline, and work scheduling as the responsibility of management and excluding such matters from arbitration. The union's representative took the position . . . that the union would not agree to such a clause so long as it covered matters subject to the duty to bargain collectively under the Labor Act.

Several further bargaining sessions were held without reaching agreement on the union's proposal or respondent's counterproposal to unlimited arbitration. As a result, the management functions clause was "by-passed" for bargaining on other terms of the union's contract proposal. On January 17, 1949, respondent stated in writing its agreement with some of the terms proposed by the union and, where there was disagreement, respondent offered counterproposals, including a clause entitled "Functions and Prerogatives of Management" along the lines suggested at the meeting of January 10th. The union objected to the portion of the clause providing:

The right to select and hire, to promote to a better position, to discharge, demote or discipline for cause, and to maintain discipline and efficiency of employees and to determine the schedules of work is recognized by both union and company as the proper responsibility and prerogative of management to be held and exercised by the company [and while an employee aggrieved by a decision of the employer, or] the union in his behalf, shall have the right to have such decision reviewed by top management officials of the company under the grievance machinery hereinafter set forth, it is further agreed that the final decision of the company made by such top management officials shall not be further reviewable by arbitration.

At this stage of the negotiations, [a complaint was filed against the employer] based on the union's charge that [the employer] had refused to bargain as required by the Labor Act and was thereby guilty of interferring with the rights of its employees guaranteed by Section 7 of the Act and of unfair labor practices. . . . While the proceeding was pending, negotiations between the union and respondent continued with the management functions clause remaining an obstacle to agreement. . . .

On May 19, 1949, a union representative offered a second contract proposal which included a management functions clause containing much of the language found in respondent's second counterproposal, quoted above, with the vital difference that questions arising under the union's proposed clause would be subject to arbitration as in the case of other grievances. Finally, on January 13, 1950, after the Trial Examiner had issued his report but before decision by the board, an agreement between the union and respondent was signed. The agreement contained a management functions clause that rendered nonarbitrable matters of discipline, work schedules, and other matters covered by the clause. The subject of promotions and demotions was deleted from the clause and made the subject of a special clause establishing a union-management committee to pass upon promotion matters.

[The question in this case is whether the employer's insistence on a "management functions" clause was an unlawful refusal to bargain under the act.]

First. The National Labor Relations Act is designed to promote industrial peace by encouraging the making of voluntary agreements governing relations between unions and employers. The act does not compel any agreement whatsoever between employees and employers. Nor does the act regulate the substantive terms governing wages, hours, and working conditions which are incorporated in an agreement. The theory of the act is that the making of voluntary labor agreements is encouraged by protecting employees' rights to organize for collective bargaining and by imposing on labor and management the mutual obligation to bargain collectively.

Enforcement of the obligation to bargain collectively is crucial to the statutory scheme. And, as has long been recognized, performance of the duty to bargain requires more than a willingness to enter upon a sterile discussion of union-management differences. Before the enactment of the National Labor Relations Act, it was held that the duty of an employer to bargain collectively required the employer "to negotiate in good faith with his employees' representatives; to match their proposals, if unacceptable, with counterproposals; and to make every reasonable effort to reach an agreement." The duty to bargain collectively, implicit in the Wagner Act as introduced in Congress, was made express by the insertion of the fifth employer unfair labor practice accompanied by an explanation of the purpose and meaning of the phrase "bargain collectively in a good faith effort to reach an agreement."

This understanding of the duty to bargain collectively has been accepted and applied throughout the administration of the Wagner Act by the National Labor Relations Board and the Courts of Appeal.

In 1947, the fear was expressed in Congress that the board "has gone very far, in the guise of determining whether or not employers had bargained in good faith, in setting itself up as the judge of what concessions an employer must make and of the proposals and counter-proposals that he may or may not make." Accordingly, the Hartley Bill, passed by the House, eliminated the good faith test and expressly provided that the duty to bargain collectively did not require submission of counterproposals. As amended in the Senate and passed as the Taft-Hartley Act, the good faith test of bargaining was retained. . . . [The amendment] contains the express provision that the obligation to bargain collectively does not compel either party to agree to a proposal or require the making of a concession.

Thus it is now apparent from the statute itself that the act does not encourage a party to engage in fruitless marathon discussions at the expense of frank statement and support of his position. And it is equally clear that the board may not, either directly or indirectly, compel concessions or otherwise sit in judgment upon the substantive terms of collective bargaining agreements.

Second. The board offers in support of the portion of its order before this Court a theory quite apart from the test of good faith bargaining prescribed in the act, a theory that respondent's bargaining for a management functions clause as a counterproposal to the Union's demand for unlimited arbitration was per se, a violation of the act.

Counsel for the Board [which had found a violation of the act] do not contend that a management functions clause covering some conditions of employment is an illegal contract term. As a matter of fact, a review of typical contract clauses collected for convenience in drafting labor agreements shows that management functions clauses similar in essential detail to the clause proposed by respondent have been included in contracts negotiated by national unions with many employers. . . . Without intimating any opinion as to the form of management functions clause proposed by respondent in this case or the desirability of including any such clause in a labor agreement, it is manifest that bargaining for management functions clauses is common collective bargaining practice. . . .

Conceding that there is nothing unlawful in including a management functions clause in a labor agreement, the Board would permit an employer to "propose" such a clause. But the Board would forbid bargaining for any such clause when the Union declines to accept the proposal, even where the clause is offered as a counterproposal to a Union demand for unlimited arbitration. Ignoring the nature of the Union's demand in this case, the board takes the position that employers subject to the act must agree to include in any labor agreement provisions establishing fixed standards for work schedules or any other condition of employment. An employer would be permitted to bargain as to the content of the standard so long as he agrees to freeze a standard into a contract. Bargaining for more flexible treatment of such matters would be denied employers even though the result may be contrary to common collective bargaining practice in the industry. The board was not empowered so to disrupt collective bargaining practices. On the contrary, the term "bargain collectively" as used in the act "has been considered to absorb and give

statutory approval to the philosophy of bargaining as worked out in the labor movement in the United States." . . .

Congress provided expressly that the Board should not pass upon the desirability of the substantive terms of labor agreements. Whether a contract should contain a clause fixing standards for such matters as work scheduling or should provide for more flexible treatment of such matters is an issue for determination across the bargaining table, not by the board. If the latter approach is agreed upon, the extent of union and management participation in the administration of such matters is itself a condition of employment to be settled by bargaining.

Accordingly, we reject the board's holding that bargaining for the management functions clause proposed by respondent was, per se, an unfair labor practice. Any fears the board may entertain that use of management functions clauses will lead to evasion of an employer's duty to bargain collectively as to "rates of pay, wages, hours, and conditions of employment" do not justify condemning all bargaining for management functions clauses covering any "condition of employment" as per se violations of the act. The duty to bargain collectively is to be enforced by application of the good faith bargaining standards of [the act] to the facts of each case rather than by prohibiting all employers in every industry from bargaining for management functions clauses altogether.

Third. The court below correctly applied the statutory standard of good faith bargaining to the facts of this case. It held that the evidence, viewed as a whole does not show that respondent refused to bargain in good faith by reason of its bargaining for a management functions clause as a counterproposal to the union's demand for unlimited arbitration.

The phrase *bargaining in good faith* has been the subject of extensive litigation under the National Labor Relations Act. The term *good faith* is, by definition, subjective, although some employer behavior, such as unilaterally changing terms and conditions of employment in the midst of negotiations have been found to be per se unlawful. In the main, however, the board must make an inference as to the employer's state of mind from the employer's outward behavior. A useful way of putting the issue in this case is as follows: Was the employer trying to reach an agreement with the union, albeit on the terms most favorable to the employer? Or, was the employer simply refusing to reach an agreement with the union, thereby denigrating the status of the union. The former would be lawful, the latter, unlawful.

4-1

CASE PROCESSING TIME AND THE OUTCOME OF REPRESENTATION ELECTIONS: SOME EMPIRICAL EVIDENCE

Myron Roomkin and Richard N. Block*

I. INTRODUCTION

Both the National Labor Relations Board (NLRB) and the parties involved are concerned with delays in the processing of representation cases. The NLRB's commitment to improving case processing speed has historically been anchored in the conviction that unnecessary delays are incompatible with the rights and obligations created by the National Labor Relations Act.

* * * * *

The use of delay as a strategic activity should not surprise those parties who have long contended that the union's chances for obtaining certification are reduced when the election is postponed. According to conventional wisdom, the passage of time makes it more difficult for the union to retain the loyalties of workers because delay gives employers added opportunity to dissuade employees and increases the likelihood of turnover in the work force. Although little published material provides convincing evidence that lawyers and other consultants advise their clients in representation proceedings to stall intentionally, the effectiveness of this tactic remains a widely accepted part of industrial relations folklore. Accordingly, persons in the labor movement are staunch advocates of improving the administration of the NLRB. Labor's efforts to enact the Labor Reform Act of 1977 and obtain so-

* Professor of Industrial Relations, Graduate School of Management, Northwestern University, and Associate Professor, School of Labor and Industrial Relations, Michigan State University. Reprinted from 1981 *Illinois Law Review*, 75, pp. 75–97. Copyright 1981 by The Board of Trustees of the University of Illinois, all rights reserved.

called speedy elections, as well as the strenuous resistance to that law by the business community, resulted in part from the parties' recognition that time had strategic importance in election cases.

The weight of empirical evidence supports the proposition that processing time is a determinant of election outcomes. One study found an average drop-off in union victories of 2.5 percent per month for elections taking six months or less during the 1962–1977 period. A second study that examined elections conducted between 1952 and 1972, estimated a 0.29 percent decrease in union victory percentages for every one day added to the median processing time for the median case. The board itself, in a 1946 analysis of consent elections in 1942, reported a drop in union victories with increases in case processing time. Anecdotes about employers who have stymied organizational efforts by protracting cases well beyond "normal or average" case processing time, moreover, support the findings of these systematic investigations. One study, however, was unable to document the relationship between outcomes and processing time after examining data for 1961, but the author pointed out the need for sophisticated statistical analysis and more detailed data on aspects of delay before rejecting this well established belief.

The recent availability of detailed administrative records of the NLRB in election cases, in the form of magnetic tapes, now allows closer study of election case processing and its relationship to the outcome of elections. By relying on official records, however, the amount of information on an election is limited to the data preserved by the board. But at the same time, because the official records preserve data on a case-by-case basis, researchers can analyze the record of each case separately. This article reports the results of disaggregated analysis of the board's election case processing based on these newly available

official records. Because of the high level of disaggregation, the analysis uncovered patterns in case processing time heretofore masked by the aggregate statistics reported by the board. Before discussing the results, however, this article summarizes the nature of case processing in representation cases and the origins of delay in those proceedings.

II. CASE PROCESSING PROCEDURES

*   *   *   *   *

The representation process . . . entails several steps. The filing of a petition initiates the representation case. Professional employees of the regional office then conduct an investigation. Thereafter, the board determines an appropriate unit for an election. That determination can be made without a formal hearing in a voluntary manner by the parties and ratified by the regional director or, following a hearing, by the regional director or the board on review. When the parties reach a voluntary agreement, they may operate under either a consent election agreement, which grants authority over any dispute to the regional director, or a stipulation for certification, which gives the board authority to settle disputes after the regional director writes an interim award. Once a regional director (or board) decision has been issued, a secret ballot election is conducted. . . .

In the period of our analysis (fiscal years 1973–1978), the overwhelming portion of elections took place in a relatively short time: 42 percent within one month of petition, 83 percent within two months, 92 percent within three months, and 94.5 percent within four months. To its credit, the board has achieved this record despite a dramatic increase in unfair labor practice cases. These cases compete with representation elections for the administrative resources of board professionals. The board's performance also has been achieved in the face of lagging growth in the number of professional employees relative to the agency's workload.

III.   SOURCES OF DELAY

A.   DELAY INDUCED BY THE PARTIES

Case processing time may be extended or shortened either before or after an election as a consequence of actions taken by one or both of the parties. Before an election a party may attempt to delay the election by filing unfair labor practice charges or by forcing the other party to file such charges, because the board generally will not proceed with an election if an unfair labor charge is pending. Should the charging party file a request to proceed, the board will go forward with the election, unless the pending charge involves an employer's refusal to bargain under section (8)(a)(5) or its assistance to another union under section (8)(a)(2).

The parties' decision to forego a consent election also affects case processing time. Of those cases requiring a hearing, some obviously take longer to dispose of because they pose novel issues, issues of agency jurisdiction, or issues of policy. Even an election case without these controversies, however, can become protracted when a hearing officer intervenes. A variety of problems may cause delay in the preelection stage. Parties' lawyers may fail to stipulate to uncontested facts, continuances by hearing officers may be needed, and delays may be encountered in the writing and filing of post-hearing briefs or the timely receipt of transcripts.[1] Admittedly, the total addition to the processing time of the case from these sources can be measured in days, not weeks or months. Rela-

tively small increments to case processing time, however, may have major consequences for the outcome of the subsequent election.

Once an election takes place, additional opportunities develop for extending the process. The parties may resort to the courts, or by refusing to bargain, prompt the other party to resort to the courts.[2] The parties may also delay the process by filing a objection concerning the conduct of the election.

B.   BOARD OR PARTY INDUCED DELAYS: SOME CORRELATIONAL RESULTS

Although one widely and long held theory of case processing time holds that the parties' actions and not the administrative apparatus or procedures of the NLRB cause the delays, several commentators dispute this claim. Their counter thesis maintains that the agency may be the source of its own fate because it can influence its intake through substantive decisions and procedures. . . .

[The results of a correlation analysis (not shown here) of data from fiscal years 1962–76 do not support the latter hypothesis. Rather, the results seem to confirm that delays are created mostly by the parties, not the administrative apparatus.]

* * * * *

IV.   THE CHARACTERISTICS OF DELAY

* * * * *

Table [1] reports the mean number of months from petition to election and election to closing, by selected characteristics compiled by the agency. The data are for

---

[1] If the board is requested to review the direction of an election, the region may still hold the election and impound the ballots pending the outcome of the board's decision.

[2] When an employer frivolously refuses to bargain with a majority union after an election, the board can order the employer to reimburse the NLRB for litigation expenses and the union for litigation and excess organizational expenses.

TABLE [1]   MEAN CASE PROCESSING TIME (MONTHS) OF SINGLE UNION REPRESENTATION CASES

| | *Fiscal years July 1972–September 1978* | | |
	NUMBER OF CASES IN WHICH AN ELECTION WAS HELD	NUMBER OF MONTHS PETITION TO ELECTION	NUMBER OF MONTHS ELECTION TO CLOSING
All cases	45,115	2.09	1.00
Outcomes of election			
Union win	20,835	1.93	1.00
Employer win	24,280	2.22	1.00
Type of election			
No hearing	37,277	1.79	0.96
Consent	5,009	1.48	0.71
Stipulated	32,268	1.84	1.00
Hearing	7,837	3.47	1.41
RD ordered	7,597	3.28	1.15
Bd. ordered	240	9.63	1.35
Expedited	23	0.91	1.18
Objecting party			
No objection	41,189	2.04	0.69
Employer	1,941	2.55	4.33
Union	1,973	2.49	3.87
Both	35	2.11	8.52
Type of unit			
Industrial	23,262	2.18	1.12
Craft	731	2.28	0.80
Departmental	1,634	2.07	0.90
Guard	49	2.31	1.00
Prof./Tech.	1,939	2.53	0.89
Prof./Tech. & Clerical	129	3.02	1.50
Truck Drivers	4,511	1.80	0.81
Office and Clerical	3,998	1.95	0.90
Other	8,864	1.90	0.85
Unit size (number of employees)			
1–10	12,636	1.75	0.70
11–20	9,450	1.88	0.91
21–30	5,476	2.03	0.99
31–40	3,577	2.12	1.06
41–50	2,469	2.16	1.11
51–60	1,749	2.26	1.09
61–70	1,358	2.32	1.02
71–80	1,055	2.37	1.17
81–90	857	2.35	1.22
91–100	683	2.49	1.13
101–150	2,201	2.62	1.43
151–200	1,145	2.64	1.41
201–250	643	3.07	1.35
251–300	395	2.70	2.19
301–400	577	3.16	1.56
401–500	272	3.54	1.89
501–750	274	3.33	1.90
751–1,000	127	3.59	2.73
1,001–2,000	107	4.12	2.78
2,001–3,000	18	5.11	1.45
3,001–4,000	3	2.67	0.56
4,001–5,000	2	3.00	3.50
5,001 +	1	2.00	0.00

all single-union elections closed between July 1, 1972 and September 30, 1978 or 81.5 percent of all closed representation cases. . . .

According to the table, failure of the parties to reach voluntary agreement on the unit and related matters extends the processing of cases noticeably. Nearly 100 percent more time or 1.6 additional months are needed on an average to hold an election if a case must go to a hearing before the regional director or the board. For elections that do not result in a pre-election hearing, stipulated cases take 50 percent longer to complete an election and 43 percent longer to be closed than consent cases.

Postelection objections, which were filed in approximately 10 percent of the studied cases, add an average of almost four months to a case. Cases in which employers file objections achieve administrative closure about one half of a month later than cases in which unions file objections.

In the different types of units represented in the studied cases, the processing of petitions and the conduct of elections take the same amount of time with two noticeable exceptions. Going from petition to election in professional-technical and professional-technical plus clerical units takes appreciably longer than it does in units of other varieties. This time lag, however, is expected because the act requires the board to conduct an election among professional employees before deciding that a unit containing both professionals and nonprofessionals is appropriate.

Of all the characteristics of cases compiled by the board's information system, election unit size evidences the strongest relationship with case processing time. Elapsed time from petition to close of an election undisputedly grows with increases in the number of workers eligible to vote in the election. Several plausible rationales explain the strength of this relationship.

First, election procedures for larger un-

TABLE [2]   UNIT SIZE BY TYPE OF ELECTION, JULY 1972–SEPTEMBER 1978

Consent	27.5 employees
Stipulated	57.5 employees
Regional director	67.7 employees
Board ordered	108.7 employees

its may be more likely to raise issues of board policy. Although this source of delay in larger units seems justifiable, only a minority of the cases reported in the table actually result in decisions by the board. This explanation, moreover, still fails to account for the consistent increase in case processing time as unit size increases among relatively small units (those with 100 or fewer employees). These smaller units rarely generate novel or controversial issues to the agency.

A second explanation may be that larger units are likely to entail more complex unit determination issues than smaller units, thus necessitating more time to resolve them. Some insight into this explanation may be obtained from Table [2] which presents data on average unit size by type of election. As can be seen, a strong positive relationship exists between the type of election and delay, and type of election and size. Clearly, the types of elections that entail more delay, those with a hearing or a right to appeal, also involve larger units.

Furthermore, although complex issues may be a concomitant of size, nothing suggests that a board or regional director hearing would, by itself, contribute to a resolution of those complex issues. If anything, negotiations between the parties, rather than a formal, adversary hearing before the regional director or the board would be more likely to result in a settlement of complex issues acceptable to all parties. While negotiations may occur in complex cases, one or both of the parties may still wish to retain the right to appeal to the regional director. Complexity per se, however, should not inevitably lead to an adversary proceeding.

A third explanation of the positive relationship between size and delay suggests that unit size, among other things, is a measure of employer size and the availability to the employer of resources to obtain delay. The data strongly imply that delay is related to the type of election held. Each type of election, starting with consent elections and ending with board ordered elections, entails a consistently greater employer investment in legal and other fees. Thus, larger employers may be better able than smaller employers to eschew voluntary settlements and seek a hearing. This explanation of the relationship between unit size and delay, while admittedly controversial, is quite plausible in view of the earlier evidence suggesting that the parties themselves can affect case processing speed.

Unit size may also determine union willingness to spend resources on organizing, with larger units constituting more important organizing goals. The difference between the union's available resources and management's would still favor employers, for two reasons. First, union resources must be spread across several organizing campaigns at one time, while the employer is free to concentrate its funds and human resources. Second, the employer cannot afford to lose the election even once, whereas the union can try again at a later time.

V. THE CONSEQUENCES OF DELAY

A. DELAY AND ELECTION OUTCOME

Despite substantial improvement in the administration of election cases, the speed with which elections are conducted remains a significant determinant of the outcome of a representation election. Of 45,115 single-union elections conducted between July 1972 and September 1978, the cases resulting in union victories (about 46 percent of the total) were

brought to election in approximately 1.9 months. In contrast, employer victories took roughly 2.2 months between petitions and election. Although this period of 10 days might be considered short, either absolutely or by any judicial standard of delay, . . . the difference in the two means is highly significant . . . , thus suggesting that the 10-day difference is not due to chance and is significantly related to the outcome of representation elections. This result, however, raises two issues. First, why should 10 days make a difference in the outcome of elections? Second, what are the characteristics of union election victories and losses that make such a relatively short period of time so important?

[Unreported data show that more] than 80 percent of all single-union representation elections during this period took place within two months, and more than 90 percent occurred within three months of petition. Thus, in more than 90 percent of all cases, this 10-day period is equivalent to at least a 10 percent increase in the time between petition and election as opposed to what this period might otherwise be. For the 80 percent of elections that occur within two months, this 10-day period amounts to at least a 16 percent increase in time between petition and election. Thus, if this 10-day period is placed not in the context of the relatively time-consuming adjudicatory process applicable to a decision in an unfair labor practice case, but in the context of the relatively short representation election process, 10 days is a significant period of time.

B. DELAY AND THE MARGIN OF VICTORY

Delay appears to affect not only the outcome of elections but also the size of the victory. . . . [We found that] on average, employer victory margins as measured here are smaller than union margins of victory. Whereas almost 26 percent of the votes cast would have had to switch to convert a union victory into an employer victory, only 16 percent of the votes cast would have had to change to convert an employer victor into a union victory. Employers, therefore, win the close contests.

These findings linking delay to outcome imply that delay affects elections the most when the outcome is in doubt and this class of contests generally result in a vote against unionization. The impact of delay on the margin of victory, however, is asymmetrical between union wins and employer wins. [We found that] unions' margin of victory consistently declines with delays of up to 12 months (comprising 98.85 prcent of all union victories). By comparison, the margin of an employer victory increases up to a delay of five months (equal to 95.4 percent of all employer victories). Delay tends to diminish the union's majority rather than the employer's majority.

Data . . . on the absolute numbers of voters who would have had to switch their votes in order to change the outcome of the elections provide further insight into the role of delay in the election process. Because of the relatively small size of the average bargaining unit (70.4 for employer wins, 39.4 for union wins), the absolute number of people who constitute the margin of victory is extremely small. For union wins, a change of only six votes would have altered the outcome. For employer wins, only 9 to 10 switched votes would have changed the outcome of the election. Thus, the marginal or swing component of an election tends to be small. Management's objective, seen in this light, could easily benefit from small increments to the time available between petition and election. An average added delay of 10 days, for example, is not enough time to alter the underlying sentiments of the work force, but could be profitably used by focusing on the workers at the margin. This delay may give employers greater opportunity to identify and influence the borderline voters.

C. DELAY AND VOTER PARTICIPATION

Public policy under the National Labor Relations Act has sought to provide individuals with an opportunity to secretly express their true sentiments once provided the necessary information on which to base a judgment. Public policy has also sought to guarantee that all workers entitled to vote are enfranchised and to preserve the legitimacy of the voting process. The focus, in short, has been on voters and voting. The fact that about 90 percent of all eligible voters actually voted—a percentage clearly greater than found in political elections—has been a source of pride to labor regulators and evidence that the focus of policy is proper and effective.

Yet [we found that] the portion of eligible employees casting a ballot tends to decline as more time elapses between the time of the petition and the election. Equally noteworthy is that as delay grows, turnout declines faster in union victories than in union defeats. This finding is surprising, for employers often claim that more time is needed to more completely communicate with workers. If anything, one might anticipate a stronger turnout if workers have been exposed to information for long periods. Given the relationships among delay, the likelihood of union victories, unit size, and the margin of victory, the discovery of lower voter turnout in longer elections complicates the story and suggests that nonvoting may not be the unbiased behavior that current policy considers it.

The number of nonvoters in absolute terms is large enough to potentially dilute the winner's plurality or even alter the outcome. On the highly liberal assumption that all nonvoters would vote against the winner, most of the employer victories in elections taking different amounts of time would remain with the employer but by pluralities ranging from .05 to 2.6 votes. Union victories, however, would be reversed in elections transpiring after three to four months. Thus, even though voter turnout is high from one perspective, nonvoting workers, although few in number, are of considerable potential importance to outcomes, especially to the unions.

Although new standards need not be promulgated to regulate nonvoting, more should be learned about who abstains, why they abstain, and how these abstentions vary with increments in election delay. While this article presents no answers, a few hypotheses seem apparent and should be explored.

First, some of the nonvoters probably represent normal employee attrition and turnover. . . . Newer employees would be less likely than more senior employees to have a preference with respect to unionization of their current employers. For this reason, nonvoting could be expected to increase with pre-election delays in case processing. But logically, this source of turnover should not fall unevenly on union-won elections and employer-won elections.

A second group of nonvoters are truly uninterested in the outcome of the campaign. Considering the significance of unionization, however, this group is unlikely to be very large or larger in union wins and smaller in employer wins.

A third reason that workers may not vote in representation elections is that they are averse to risk, and do not want to risk the enmity of either the employer (if they vote in favor of the union and the employer loses) or their fellow employees (if they vote in favor of the employer and the union loses). If these workers are in fact not disinterested in the outcome of the election, they still may vote only if they believe that their vote will have no effect on the outcome of the election.

The existence of these "free riders" de-

pends on two factors: (1) that the nonvoter can accurately predict the outcome of the election if he or she does not vote and (2) that the employer and/or fellow employees know the employee's sentiments toward unionization. The conditions most conducive for these factors are small units, in which all employees and the employer representative are familiar with each other on a daily basis and situations in which delays are encountered in the election process. Delay may give both the employer and fellow employees additional opportunities to break down the resistance of individual employees to revealing their otherwise secret preferences on unionization.

This third hypothesis is consistent with the findings that nonparticipation increases with delay faster in elections in which unions win over those in which employers win. Units are smaller in elections in which unions win than in elections in which unions lose. Thus, the asymmetry in the rate of growth in nonparticipation may not be due to the wins and losses per se, but rather to the size of the units associated with wins and losses.

This third hypothesis also suggests that nonvoting is an indirect consequence of delay, operating through the employee's aversion to risk. Alternatively, delay may affect nonvoting directly by creating uncertainty in the mind of the employee. An employee who is unsure about the benefits and cost of unionization may simply refuse to make a decision and not vote. Under such circumstances, the employer would benefit from nonvoting if the employees who nominally support change, as represented by the collective bargaining of the employment relationship, are also the ones most prone to uncertainty. This hypothesis that delay leads to uncertainty and nonvoting, and that nonvoting is likely to occur disproportionately among nominal union supporters, is consistent with the finding that delay decreases the margin of union victories and, although less so, increases the margin of employer victories.

This analysis, of course, is speculative. More than likely all four explanations, as well as others, are probably operating. Nonetheless, the evidence presented suggests nonvoting can have an impact on the outcome of representation elections. The board in its decisions may wish to account for the impact of the behavior of the parties on discouraging people from voting. . . .

VI. SUMMARY AND CONCLUSION

This paper has presented an overview of the characteristics of delay in NLRB representation elections. These data, although not without their limitations, suggest several points. First, delay in representation proceedings appears to be due more to the behavior of the parties than to board administrative inefficiencies in the processing of cases. Second, delay aids employers in that a longer period of time between petition and election appears to increase the likelihood of the employer winning. Third, the data suggest that "small" increases in case processing time are important. According to the estimate calculated here, a delay of approximately 10 days is significant in differentiating employer wins from employer losses.

Fourth, size appears to be a concomitant of delay. Cases in larger units take longer to process and are more likely to result in a hearing rather than in a voluntary settlement. The units in which unions win, moreover, are smaller than the units in which employers win. The inference is that unit size may be a proxy for the amount of resources the employer can invest in delay and increase its chances of winning.

Fifth, a small number of votes can have a great influence on the election. On the average, a switch of less than eight votes in all the elections would have changed the outcome. When one accounts for the nonvoters, the elections are even closer. Additionally, the data suggest that elections get closer, and nonparticipation increases, with delay. Although the reasons for this phenomenon are only speculative, they prompt questions on the assertion of employers that delay gives them time to present information to voters. More important, however, the small margins found in typical election yields some insight on how a "short" period of 10 days could have such a large impact on election outcomes.

In addition, the findings presented suggest two broader points. First, the results suggest that, while legally important, a preoccupation by the board, the parties, policymakers, and scholars on the election cases evidencing extreme delays can be misleading. Cases such as . . . *J.P. Stevens* have had great consequences for the substantive law. By focusing on these landmark cases, however, attention has been diverted from the trends in the more common representation cases, accounting for the great bulk of the board's representation case intake. Indeed, quantitative research techniques may possibly contribute to law in this area by identifying characteristics common to the majority of cases.

Second, in approaching the question of procedural delays, the board has adhered to the adage that "justice delayed is justice denied." In an adjudicatory proceeding, delay, while undesirable, is not thought to have an impact on the outcome of the case. . . .

This result, however, may not occur in NLRB representation elections. If delay results in the outcome of the election being different than it might otherwise be, then delay is a far more serious problem in the context of elections than in the context of adjudicatory decisions. If delay results in creating and employer win from what would otherwise be a union win, then the delay has resulted in a change in the substantive outcome of the process. To the extent that this delay is unnecessary or

results from a misuse of the board's processes, then the union may truly find itself

in a situation of "election delayed, election
denied."

4–2

A QUANTITATIVE STUDY OF UNFAIR LABOR PRACTICE CASES

Myron Roomkin*

To many students of industrial relations,
the growing number of unfair labor practice cases is a subtle but increasing threat
to the integrity of national labor policies.
. . . This paper presents a first attempt
to study unfair labor practice cases quanti-
tatively. This and other such studies may
help us identify the causes of unfair labor
practice cases and to expedite the processing of the board's expanding case load.

TRENDS IN UNFAIR LABOR PRACTICE CASES

Changes over time in several dimensions
of the NLRB's operation and case load are
evident from the data reported in Table
1.[1] The number of charges filed has in-

creased more than tenfold since fiscal year
(FY) 1948; in terms of the board's full
workload (mostly charge cases and petitions for elections), the proportion represented by charge filings has increased sev-
enfold. Yet, in spite of this rising case load,
the board has maintained a high proportion of closed charge cases to all cases on
docket—what is called "workload processing" in column 5.

Nonetheless, the board has been unable
to decrease substantially the time from
charge through complaint to adjudication.
The median amount of elapsed time from
filing to issuance of a complaint was 52
days in FY 1960, 57 in FY 1970, and 54
in FY 1975. Board decisions in the median
case took an additional 303 days in FY
1960, 266 days in FY 1970, and 278 in
FY 1975. (Considerably longer delays
would be likely if the median case were
reviewed by the federal courts.)

Most filed charges are settled or withdrawn before the board considers the case
or a complaint is issued. In FY 1978, for
instance, 37,152 charge cases were closed,
25 percent by private settlement or adjustment before issuance of an [administrative
law judge's] decision another 33 percent

* Professor of Industrial Relations, Graduate
School of Management, Northwestern University.
Reprinted in an abridged form, with permission, from
the *Industrial and Labor Relations Review*, 34, no.
2 (January 1981), pp. 245–56. © 1981 by Cornell
University. All rights reserved.

[1] Readers should keep in mind that a charge may
be disposed of by informal settlement before the issuance of an official complaint, by voluntary withdrawal by the parties themselves, or by dismissal if
no violation of law is found. In addition, it is important to note that the NLRB reviews the decisions
of its Administrative Law Judges (ALJs) and that the
board's decisions in turn may be reviewed by an appropriate United States Court of Appeals.

TABLE 1 SELECTED ASPECTS OF UNFAIR LABOR PRACTICE CASES FROM FISCAL YEARS 1948 THROUGH 1978

(1)	(2)	(3)	(4)	(5)	(6)
FISCAL YEAR	NUMBER OF CHARGE CASES FILED	CHARGE CASES AS PERCENT OF ALL FILINGS	MERIT FACTOR[a] AS PERCENT OF ALL FILINGS	PERCENT CHARGE CASES CLOSED (WORK LOAD PROCESSING[b])	TOTAL NUMBER OF BOARD EMPLOYEES[c]
1948	3,598	9.8	n.a.[d]	60.3	n.a.[d]
1949	5,314	20.5	n.a.	60.5	n.a.
1950	5,809	26.9	n.a.	63.4	n.a.
1951	5,261	23.6	n.a.	64.7	1402
1952	5,454	30.8	n.a.	63.7	1145
1953	5,469	37.1	n.a.	68.7	1345
1954	5,965	42.3	n.a.	69.1	1210
1955	6,171	46.1	n.a.	69.8	1149
1956	5,265	39.3	n.a.	70.8	1124
1957	5,506	41.2	n.a.	65.7	1172
1958	9,260	55.3	20.7	61.2	1145
1959	12,239	56.6	26.1	67.9	1475
1960	11,357	52.8	29.1	71.1	1715
1961	12,132	53.5	27.6	71.3	1812
1962	13,479	54.3	30.7	74.2	1857
1963	14,166	55.8	32.3	72.4	1982
1964	15,620	57.0	33.4	75.0	1992
1965	15,800	56.3	35.5	70.7	2096
1966	15,933	55.0	36.6	70.1	2216
1967	17,040	56.0	36.2	69.0	2263
1968	17,816	58.0	34.7	70.7	2342
1969	18,651	59.6	32.3	72.8	2297
1970	21,038	62.6	34.2	70.6	2206
1971	23,770	63.9	31.2	74.4	2152
1972	26,852	65.4	32.7	72.8	2261
1973	26,487	64.5	31.9	75.0	2368
1974	27,726	65.4	31.6	73.6	2397
1975	31,253	69.5	30.2	72.8	2376
1976	34,509	69.9	31.2	70.9	2474
1977[e]	47,028[f]	71.3[f]	32.8[f]	61.4[f]	2686
1978[e]	39,652	74.4	34.0	68.7	2821

[a] The proportion of all filed charges that, after investigation, are judged to have merit. Many cases found to have merit are adjusted or settled before a complaint is issued.

[b] Defined as the number of cases closed as a percentage of all cases placed on the docket.

[c] 1951–61 data are end-of-year totals; 1962–78 data are average employment for the fiscal year.

[d] n.a. = not available.

[e] Fiscal year ending September 30.

[f] Extended fiscal year, including transition quarter (July–September 1976) needed to change over to new schedule.

SOURCE: U.S. NLRB, *Annual Reports for Fiscal Years 1948–1978* (Washington, D.C.: G.P.O., pertinent years) and other data provided by the NLRB's Data Analysis Section.

by withdrawal before complaint, and 37 percent by dismissal.

Many of the cases settled beforehand would have warranted a complaint. These cases, plus those in which a complaint is actually issued, are said to "have merit." As shown in column 4 of Table 1, the merit factor (proportion of cases with merit) increased for the period FY 1958–1967, the first decade for which such determinations were made, when it settled onto a new plateau at 30 to 32 percent until FY 1976. It seems to be increasing, however, since then.

In recent years, over 50 percent of all charges have been filed by individual workers; at other times, union filings have been the most common. Charges brought by employers, however, have always been a relatively small portion of the board's annual work load, averaging about 15 percent since FY 1948 but falling to 10 percent in FY 1978.

Another significant trend in unfair labor practice cases has been an increase in the growing proportion of cases brought by individuals against unions. In FY 1948 these cases constituted approximately 8.2 percent of all charge cases; in the last few years they grew to more than 20 percent. This growth, which is partly a manifestation of general worker dissatisfaction with institutions, was given impetus by board rulings that made it an unfair labor practice for a union not to represent fairly and equally all workers in a unit.

Theory of Unfair Labor Practices

The National Labor Relations Act of 1935 (or Wagner Act) was predicated on a model of regulation, popular during the New Deal, that assumed that standards of conduct could be set, and disputes over these standards settled, by an administrative agency. The presumption was that the parties would follow the law and that disputes would be the exception, not the norm. It was also assumed, of course, that the activities of the NLRB, established by that act, would reduce, not cause, labor disputes. Such disputes are supposedly the product of the parties' attempts to adapt to changes in the environment and context of labor relations.

* * * * *

Consistent with this view, the NLRB seeks to minimize direct interference in the conduct of labor-management relations. It seeks to operate in unfair labor practice cases as a "public law enforcer." and not as either "a governmentally sponsored Robin Hood with a mission of aiding the weak and restraining the strong," or an investigative reporter searching for possible violations and more litigations.

Another source often held responsible for some of the agency's increased case load is the board's expanded industrial and occupational jurisdiction. Along with the expansion of employment in many covered industries, the number of employees and establishments under the board's jurisdiction has grown through statutory amendments, discretionary board acceptance of new sectors, and the failure of the board to adjust its dollar standards, used to assert or decline jurisdiction, to take inflation into account.

The notion that unfair labor practice cases are linked primarily to either environmental or jurisdictional changes may underemphasize, however, the role played by the board as a regulator of conduct. Experience suggests that the NLRB is in fact an active participant in the system. Like other regulatory agencies, the board adds to, or detracts from, the relative power of those parties it regulates. It does this by ruling on the tactics and goals of the parties in order to promote a balance of union-management power or to realize other goals of the National Labor Relations Act. Such involvement makes the board (and to some extent the courts) a determinant of conduct by the parties, both among themselves and toward the board. In this area of regulation, as in others, policy and behavior are best understood as a product of interactions among the regulator and the regulatees.

The board's principal impact on behavior has been through its decisions on the substantive rules of conduct. However, the board may have more subtle effects on the parties through its procedures and their administration. Suppose labor unions, employers, and individual workers judge the legitimacy of an adversary's conduct in terms of what the law actually protects as well as what they believe the law should protect. The subjective expectation is important because labor relations issues tend to have symbolic value. The gap between the expected and actual benefits of law may be greater where laws are interpreted frequently, as they are in labor relations, and where interpretations vary over the years, as they have in the development of labor law. Under ordinary circumstances, a party initiates a charge only when the expected benefits of pressing and perhaps winning the case outweigh the costs of filing the charge and seeing it through to completion. A great deal depends upon the perceived probability of ultimately winning one's case and the perceived relative importance of the issue. In this sense, the filing of an unfair labor practice charge bears a strong resemblance to the initiation of a civil suit.[2]

This approach is based on the belief that parties file charges to get favorable decisions. Recently, however, we have become more aware of another motivation, one less compatible with the effective operation of the NLRB. This might be called strategic motivation. The goal in these cases is to use the processes of the NLRB, not its decisional outcomes, for self-serving purposes. A charge might represent, for example, a means of achieving delay in formation of a union, commencement of bilateral negotiations, or harassment of one's opponent.

* * * * *

---

[2] Labor Board and court cases are only broadly analogous, however. For one thing, violators of the NLRA do not pay punitive damages when found in violation of the law. In fact, one of the weaknesses of the act has been the difficulty of enforcing board orders once they have been issued, a condition proposed statutory amendments may alter. Moreover, the pecuniary costs of litigation in labor cases are nearly all borne by the Labor Board, which investigates and prosecutes charges and, if necessary, appeals decisions to both the board and the federal courts.

THE VARIABLES

The arguments advanced above suggest that the volume of unfair labor practice cases . . . filed . . . , adjusted for expansion in the number of workers under the board's jurisdiction . . . , is [determined by] . . . changes in the volume of industrial relations activities that give rise to labor disputes; . . . [the] . . . economic environment; . . . [and] aspects of the board's operations that tend to encourage or discourage case filings. . . .

ACTIVITY VARIABLES. The research focused on the number of work stoppages in covered industries and the number of filed representation petitions as measures of the volume of labor-management activity, since both tend to be litigation-producing events. In pursuit of an election victory one of the participants is likely to engage in behavior considered unfair by the other. Indeed, public policy tends to encourage a losing party to file a charge as a means of voiding the election results.

Strikes or lockouts also contribute to the level of unfair labor practice. Under the law, an employer may hire permanent replacements in the event of an economic strike but may be directed to rehire unfair labor practice strikers.[3] Violence or coercive misconduct by a union may void these reinstatement rights and lead to charges by employers. Additionally, by filing a charge one party gains a symbolic advantage during a strike. The term itself, *unfair labor practice,* conjures up an image of impropriety and inequity and may dissuade some consumers from dealing with a struck employer or place the union in a bad light. A union may also derive some

---

[3] In fact, trade union training programs have been known to counsel union leaders to file charges in the event of a work stoppage, just as a precaution. Handbooks for management are also readily available and provide information on the legal rights of employers.

value from the way a pending charge serves to unite the rank-and-file and convince them of the difficult job facing their leaders.

ECONOMIC VARIABLES.   There is no specific guidance in the literature as to which economic factors influence filing rates and which do not. But if environmental forces are as significant as we believe them to be, then one might reasonably expect filing levels to be related to conventional labor market indicators. The economic variables examined here are the unemployment rate, the percentage change in the price level, the percentage change in the wage rate, and the percentage change in industrial output.

LITIGATION VARIABLES.   The model implies a positive relationship between the demand for board intervention and the likelihood of a charging party winning its case. Although data on the identity of winning parties—whether union, employer, or individual—at different levels of administrative or judicial review are scanty, three measures of the likelihood of winning can be identified. First [there] is the probability that the board will find a violation. . . .

A second measure [is] the political composition of the board. . . . Since conventional wisdom considers Democrats to be more prounion than Republicans, we anticipate higher filing rates by unions and lower filing rates by employers during periods of Democratic control.

A third variable . . . is the likelihood that a complaint . . . will be issued.

The model also predicts that demand for board services will decline as the cost of litigation rises. Since the board assumes nearly all costs of investigating and proving a case, the major cost is the time required to obtain a decision from the board. The longer it takes, commonly called delay, the longer the charging party must bear the burden of the practice in question. Two measures of delay are examined: . . . the amount of delay during the investigation of a charge up to and including the point at which a complaint is issued or denied, and . . . the time it takes the NLRB to hear and decide a case after a complaint has been issued.

If board procedures are being used primarily to settle disputes, not to obtain procedural advantage, delay will be viewed as a cost of litigation and will be negatively related to filings. A positive relationship would imply that delay was considered by the filing party to be beneficial.

RESULTS

The table in the appendix reports regression coefficients and related statistics when the model is [measured] . . . for fiscal years 1952–1975. . . . The dependent variable is the number of filings brought in [any single year]. . . . The measures of activity are [from the previous years], since strikes or elections may result from, as well as cause, unfair labor practices. Litigation variables are [from the previous year] to capture the [effect of expectations.] . . .

[The table] indicates that the variables in the model explain 94 percent of the variance in the total number of charges filed by all of the regulated parties. When all the variables are entered simultaneously, only 6 of the 12 [variables] achieve . . . the minimally acceptable level of significance. The measure of strike activity does not manifest a statistically significant [result] . . . , while the election is statistically significant. . . . An increase in the unemployment rate or rate of price change is positively [and significantly] related to the volume of filings. . . . Also positively [and significantly] related to filings . . . is the amount of postcomplaint delay. The board's political composition is another statistically significant determinant of subsequent filing levels in the aggregate. . . . Some economic factors, activity levels, and litigation factors influence the number of cases filed by both employers and unions.

Some variables appear to produce similar reactions by the parties and others produce different reactions. For example, both employers and unions file more charges as the number of elections increases. The strike variable in both equations surprisingly produces a negative coefficient but is only minimally significant in the equation representing union behavior. By implication, strikes do not contribute to the level of legal conflict in industrial relations and may even be a substitute for litigation. Both employers and unions also tend to file more charges during periods of high unemployment than low. Additionally, lagging industrial output tends to increase the volume of both employer and union cases, implying that industrial relations is practiced more aggressively when output rises slowly.

The more startling findings . . . pertain to the performance of the litigation variables. Unions are not influenced by the delays encountered in investigating charges and issuing complaints, while employers apparently decrease use of the board's services as precomplaint delays increase. After a complaint is issued, both employers and unions increase the number of charges they file in response to longer delays. Also noteworthy are (*a*) the absence in both equations of a statistically significant [result on] the opponent's violation rate and (*b*) the presence of a significant positive [result] on the likelihood of a complaint in only the equation representing union filing behavior.

Considering the highly competitive character of labor-management relations, one might suspect that a tendency by one actor to file a charge might prompt the responding party to file a charge in turn. Indeed, legal advocates often tell their clients to take "an offensive or aggressive defense" against a litigating adversary. At the very least, this sort of reactive use of the process gives the defending party the opportunity to bargain for the withdrawal of a charge pending against it.

In order to test this speculation, the [previous years] value of the responding party's filing behavior was added to the equation explaining the charging party's subsequent filing behavior . . . [The results, (omitted here) indicate that this variable] yields a significant positive [result] and brings about some changes in the statistical significance of a few variables. . . .

It was found, in addition, that the probability that one party would voluntarily withdraw a charge prior to the issuance of a complaint was [strongly related to] the probability that the other would voluntarily withdraw its charge. This implies that to some significant extent charges are being traded, whether or not they were motivated by bona fide causes.

By adding the adversary's behavior to the model, the violation rate variables are rendered . . . significant. The effects, however, are not identical in the two equations. Employers are encouraged to file cases when the board is more likely to rule against unions; however, unions are encouraged to file when the board is *less* prone to sustain a charge against employers. One plausible explanation is that employers more than unions see their violation rate as a deterrent. This explanation is consistent with the notion that the actors adhere to the substantive rulings of the Labor Board.

In the equations discussed so far, the political affiliation of Labor Board members is . . . significant . . . for union-initiated cases only. Under closer examination, however, there is no evidence that unions actually win more cases under Democratically-dominated boards. . . . This suggests quite strongly that the NLRB, to its credit, has found violations in an evenhanded fashion.

The discovered sensitivity of unions to political affiliations may be just a manifestation of the labor movement's long-term expectation about the sympathies of Democratic administrations. If so, the effect of politics will gradually decline as the administration of the law continues in an unbiased fashion. Alternatively, under Democratic majorities the board may be more likely to issue a new and significant ruling than under Republican majorities. Democratic majorities, therefore, bring forth more union cases in the anticipation of obtaining these new standards while neither encouraging nor discouraging employers to file.

Compared to the actions of employers and unions, the filing behavior of individuals is poorly understood. Whereas statistically significant coefficients were found in 9 of 11 variables in the equation representing cases brought by employers, no more than four of these variables achieve statistical significance in the equations representing the actions of individuals toward either unions or employers. . . .

In cases by individuals against employers, elections tend to increase the number of subsequent cases. One would expect this result, since many of the charges filed against employers during an organizing campaign are filed by individuals supposedly engaging in protected activities. The positive effect of [the unemployment rate] implies that workers are also more likely to seek the correction of an adverse working condition through litigation when opportunities decline for employment elsewhere. The . . . significant [results for] postcomplaint delay for charges brought by individuals against employers must be treated with suspicion. [In view of the lack of information individual employees would be expected to have, it is likely that this result] is capturing the actions of individuals working closely with unions during organizing drives.

The results representing charges filed by individuals against unions indicates that such cases are only influenced by wage and price changes. These regression results for individuals are consistent with the views of many observers and those of the board that such cases are the result of unfulfilled expectations against the union. A recent study by the general counsel of the NLRB found that the majority of cases filed by individuals tend to be filed by persons who lack sufficient information about what the NLRB can and cannot do.

CONCLUDING REMARKS

The analysis suggests that the propensity of employers and unions to file a charge is related not only to selected economic and activity variables, as might be anticipated, but it is also linked to aspects of the board's administration. Thus, contrary to the traditional view of the board, the regulator of labor-management behavior is not "beyond the drama" of behavior but may be one of the actors. Labor relations shares with other aspects of economic regulation the tendency for the behavior of the regulatees and that of the regulators to be closely interrelated, a condition that has come to be known as endogenization. That is, board activities feed back not only into the industrial practices of the parties but also into their propensity to litigate.

This paradigm implies, and statistics seem to confirm, that the board itself influences its case load, mostly by the speed with which it processes cases. Of course, no one would suggest encouraging delay as a means of limiting the board's case load. Public policy is correctly and firmly committed to the expeditious settlement of labor disputes. Instead, we should learn the impact on filing rates of speedier processing at different stages of the procedures or under different rules. This information could be used to evaluate the net contribution of a procedural change to overall regulatory effectiveness. For instance, speedier investigations will tend to contribute to the volume of employer cases, according to the regression analysis. Considering that employers file only a small share of the charges each year, improved precomplaint efficiency will probably not bring forth enough charges to tax board resources. But the same may not be true of postcomplaint delays. Results indicate that speedier adjudication at this stage will bring forth fewer cases from both unions and employers. Thus, postcomplaint reforms may work to encourage the voluntary settlement of disputes.

Quantitative analysis of unfair labor practice cases has been useful in questioning old notions about the decisional biases of the board. The board, it would appear, does not vote along prolabor or prounion lines when its aggregate voting record is considered. Nevertheless, unions tend to make greater use of the agency under periods of Democratic majorities. We have suggested that this may be the product of long-term expectations on the part of unions or the board's history of issuing significant new standards during Democratic administrations.

[This analysis must be treated as preliminary, however. Much more research needs to be done.]

APPENDIX

REGRESSION COEFFICIENTS AND RELATED STATISTICS FOR A MODEL OF UNFAIR LABOR PRACTICE FILINGS [LOG (F/E)] BY CHARGING AND RESPONDING PARTIES FOR FISCAL YEARS 1952–1975[a]

INDEPENDENT VARIABLE	EQ. 1A. ALL/ALL	Charging party/responding party			
		EQ. 1B. UNIONS/ EMPLOYERS	EQ. 1C. EMPLOYERS/ UNIONS	EQ. 1D. INDIVIDUALS/ EMPLOYERS	EQ. 1E. INDIVIDUALS/ UNIONS
$\log EI_{t-1}$	1.407 (5.189)‡	1.577 (6.977)‡	1.531 (5.319)‡	1.108 (2.013)†	−0.336 (−0.882)
$\log WS_{t-1}$	0.039 (−0.148)	−0.311 (−1.830)*	−0.018 (−0.046)	0.541 (1.598)	0.444 (1.590)
$\log \Delta O_t$	−0.049 (−1.547)	−0.063 (−2.914)‡	−0.108 (−2.529)†	−0.014 (−0.347)	0.023 (1.189)
$\log U_t$	0.823 (4.056)‡	0.659 (4.863)‡	1.222 (4.443)‡	1.001 (3.110)‡	0.101 (0.429)
$\log \Delta W_t$	0.012 (0.060)	0.068 (0.501)	−0.078 (−0.271)	−0.081 (−0.358)	−0.184 (−1.885)*
$\log \Delta P_t$	0.081 (2.310)†	0.041 (1.852)*	0.033 (0.600)	0.029 (0.717)	0.064 (3.463)‡
POL_{t-1}	0.181 (1.824)*	0.236 (3.826)‡	0.244 (1.461)	0.079 (0.521)	−0.130 (−1.153)
$\log DC_{t-1}$	−0.154 (−1.073)	0.022 (0.233)	−0.597 (−2.878)‡	−0.285 (−1.155)	0.120 (0.611)
$\log DBD_{t-1}$	1.116 (2.376)†	0.734 (2.433)†	1.486 (2.222)†	1.716 (2.625)‡	0.014 (0.041)
$\log COM_{t-1}^{(e+u)}$	0.190 (1.215)	—	—	—	—
$\log COM_t^{(e)}$	—	0.253 (2.607)‡	—	0.015 (0.081)	—
$\log COM_t^{(u)}$	—	—	−0.004 (−0.019)	—	−0.003 (−0.040)
$\log V_{t-1}^{(e+u)}$	0.239 (0.708)	—	—	—	—
$\log V_{t-1}^{(e)}$	—	−0.235 (−1.261)	—	0.519 (1.170)	—
$\log V_{t-1}^{(u)}$	—	—	0.856 (1.015)	—	0.093 (0.304)

		Changing party/responding party			
INDEPENDENT VARIABLE	EQ. 1A. ALL/ALL	EQ. 1B. UNIONS/ EMPLOYERS	EQ. 1C. EMPLOYERS/ UNIONS	EQ. 1D. INDIVIDUALS/ EMPLOYERS	EQ. 1E. INDIVIDUALS/ UNIONS
Constant	−20.191 (−4.608)‡	−18.613 (−5.499)‡	−25.244 (−5.656)‡	−26.581 (−3.868)‡	−3.522 (−0.696)
R^2	0.943	0.972	0.946	0.908	0.970
S.E.E.	0.153	0.101	0.204	0.211	0.129
D.W.	2.394	2.558	2.272	1.949	1.670

ᵃ Estimated through the Cochrane-Orcutt Iterative Technique.

* Significant at the .10 level.

† Significant at the .05 level.

‡ Significant at the .01 level.

DEFINITIONS AND SOURCES:

F is based on the Board's characterization of cases. Those against an employer are those designated CA by the Board and pertain to Sections 8(a)(I) through 8(a)(5) of the National Labor Relations Act. Cases against unions have been given the following designations: CB for alleged violation of Sections 8(b)(1)(A) to 8(b)(6); CC for alleged violations of 8(b)(4)(i) and subparts (A) through (C); CD for action pertinent to Section 8(b)(4)(i)(D); CP for alleged violations of Sections 8(b)(7)(A) through 8(b)(7)(C). CE, the so-called "Hot Cargo Cases," alleging violations of 8(e), were not considered because both the employer and union are defendants in such cases. Their omission is probably of little statistical consequence since they constitute a very small portion of each year's case load. Also not counted are those violations of the act only recently made part of the statute.

E is the number of nonsupervisory employees in private sector industries comprising the jurisdiction of the NLRB.

El is the number of filed election petitions.

WS is the number of private sector work stoppages reported in the *Survey of Current Business*.

ΔO is the percentage change in the index of private business sector output published by the Bureau of Labor Statistics.

U is the average unemployment rate and is calculated from the number of unemployed and labor-force members reported in various issues of the *Monthly Labor Review*.

ΔW is the percentage change in the average hourly earnings of employees in mining, manufacturing, construction, and wholesale and retail sales, weighted by employment in these industries.

ΔP is the percent change in the Consumer Price Index as reported in the *Monthly Labor Review*.

POL is a dummy variable set equal to one if a majority of NLRB members are appointed by a Democratic administration. Information on the timing of Board appointments is taken from various issues of the *Annual Report of the NLRB*.

DC is the median number of days from filing to complaint; DBD is the median number of days to a decision by the Board after a complaint has been issued.

$COM^{(e)}$, $COM^{(u)}$, $COM^{(e+u)}$ are the portion of the filings and pending cases against respondent that yield a complaint.

$V^{(e)}$, $V^{(u)}$ and $V^{(e+u)}$ are the portion of charges against employers, unions and both parties, respectively, sustained by the Board.

Data on the measures of V, DC, DBD, COM, and El have been provided by the Data Analysis Section of the NLRB.

THE PUBLIC SECTOR

Laws and other regulations defining the collective bargaining rights of public employees vary across jurisdictions (e.g., from state to state) and across employee groups (e.g., from teachers to sanitation workers). This variation is due to the efforts of various governing authorities to establish policies that balance the bargaining demands of public employees and the resistance of public employers to intrusion on their decision-making function. It is also due to the efforts of policymaking bodies to differentiate among employee groups according to the essentiality of the service each provides. (The unique characteristics of collective bargaining in the public sector are discussed by Lewin in Chapter 2.)

In the following article, B.V.H. Schneider examines the evolution of public sector legislation. Appendix Tables 1 through 4 summarize the diversity of state laws along several of the dimensions examined by Schneider.

4–3

PUBLIC-SECTOR LABOR LEGISLATION— AN EVOLUTIONARY ANALYSIS

B. V. H. Schneider*

A reading of the history of employer-employee relations in the public service shows a consistent thread of concern that collective bargaining as we know it in the private sector is irreconcilable with the nature of government. This concern has been expressed in a variety of specific ways over the years, but in general it says that the complete transplantation of traditional collective bargaining into the governmental process would impair the decision-making power of elected officials as they seek to represent the public interest.

Resistance to collective bargaining in the name of the public interest, however expressed, often represents little more than a simple reluctance of an employer

to share authority. Such a reaction is familiar in the private sector. But the problem is a larger one in the public sector. The political nature of government and its special relation to the public create a unique employment environment, one in which sovereignty and delegation of authority have been critical considerations in the creation of public-sector labor relations law.

Early thought on the subject concluded that such mechanisms as exclusive recognition, binding agreements, and the strike or lockout were not transferable from the private to the public sector. Ida Klaus reported in 1959 that many governmental units had permitted their employees freedom of association and had accorded some degree of recognition to organizations of employees in the determination of employment conditions, but *at no level* had any government adopted "a thoroughgoing and systematic code of labor relations

* Director, California Public Employee Relations Project, University of California-Berkeley. Reprinted from Benjamin Aaron, Joseph R. Grodin, and James L. Stern, eds., *Public Sector Bargaining*, IRRA Series (Washington, D.C.: BNA, 1979), pp. 191–223.

at all comparable in fundamental policy, basic guarantees and rights, and procedures for their enforcement, with those of prevailing labor-relations laws in the private sector."[1] Such a system was generally viewed as inconsistent with government's sovereign decision-making status.

Nonetheless, when it became impossible to prevent strikes or to ignore the demands of public workers for participation in the setting of their terms of employment, policymakers turned hesitantly to the private-sector model. At a loss for workable alternative policy instruments, they diluted, stretched, and bent the system in attempts to make it fit government needs and employee expectations in hundreds of public agencies and dozens of states. The result has been piecemeal adoption of traditional procedures.

The process has not been smooth or complete. The history of labor relations in the public sector is characterized by continuing tension between the drive for collective bargaining, interpreted as equity by public employees, and the resistance of government as it strives to protect and guarantee its right to make unfettered decisions. From this comes the overriding "labor relations problem" in the public sector: the need to separate or reconcile the sovereign authority of government and the bilateral authority inherent in the grant of collective bargaining rights.

Accommodation has been achieved in regard to many elements of traditional (i.e., private-sector-like) collective bargaining. In others, such as impasse resolution, the tension is unresolved, although the search for solution has been intense.

In no case has a law been adopted which reproduces the National Labor Relations Act, although many approximate it. . . .

---

[1] *Labor Relations in the Public Service: Exploration and Experiment*, 10 Syracuse L. Rev. 184 (1959).

[The questions that arise include:] What problems have arisen in the movement toward the private model? Which appear to have been solved? What problems remain? Using a broad brush, this chapter traces policy development on [several] major elements of collective bargaining—the right to bargain, impasse resolution, . . . and union security.

THE RIGHT TO BARGAIN

There was a time—spanning several decades before World War II—when even the act of joining or attempting to form a union for the purpose of self-protection was viewed with grave misgivings in many parts of the public sector. The right of public employees to associate might be constitutionally protected (although the law was not always clear on this), but such a right could not supersede the government employer's obligation to protect "the public interest." Although sovereign immunity had been delimited in other areas, government authority in labor relations was viewed as absolute. In the absence of law specific to the subject, governments were successful in claiming in the courts that collective bargaining would amount to an abrogation of governmental discretion, that organization of personnel and determination of pay and conditions were government functions, and that governmental functions might not be delegated. Bargaining, agreements, and/or force (strikes) would be "intolerable" invasions of the sovereign's absolute authority to act in the public interest.

But World War II and its aftermath brought dramatic changes in circumstances and attitudes. The demand for more government services, sharp increases in the numbers of public employees, and inflation led to the growth of more militant and durable public-employee organizations, a rash of more effective strikes than had ever been experienced before, and, coincidentally but importantly, a resurgence of interest in the reform of public personnel administration.[2]

PUBLIC POLICY AND THE STRIKE

. . . In 1947, eight states passed antistrike laws.[3] In the same year, the Taft-Hartley Act banned strikes in the federal service and made such action a possible felony. Penalties in the state laws tended to be stiff, ranging from termination and ineligibility for reemployment for 12 months, to fines and imprisonment, to definition of striking as a misdemeanor. New York's Condon-Wadlin Act required that rehired workers be placed on probation for five years and receive no pay increases for three years.

In spite of the harshness of the antistrike laws, a new trend was discernible. Some of the laws gave statutory recognition to the right of employees to communicate their views on employment conditions (Michigan, Ohio, Pennsylvania). Nebraska, in addition, created the industrial relations court to hear labor disputes and issue decisions regarding proprietary activities of the state. In Minnesota, public hospitals were covered by a law (1947) allowing for negotiations, exclusive representation, mediation, and binding arbitration in tradeoff for a strike prohibition.

By 1950, the limitations of antistrike laws had become apparent. Many local governments had established bargaining arrangements with unions. Strikes were settled and penalties were ignored as political bodies attempted to accommodate union aggressiveness and public demands for peace. An important straw in the wind

was a recommendation of the first Hoover Commission in 1949 that "the heads of departments and agencies should be required to provide for the positive participation of employees in the formulation and improvement of federal personnel policies and practices."[4]

COOPERATION IN THE PUBLIC INTEREST

Then, in the 50s, came the second major public policy breakthrough: laws which reconceptualized the "labor problem"—i.e., strikes—as solvable by structured systems of labor-management cooperation. . . .

Starting with Illinois and North Dakota in 1951, six states passed laws which supported formal bilateralism for some groups of employees.[5] Each established the rights of employees to join employee organizations. North Dakota and Minnesota placed an *obligation* on the employer to meet with representatives on employment problems. Illinois, New Hampshire, Wisconsin, and Alaska *authorized* employers to bargain collectively or to meet and confer. No law included a provision for exclusive representation or administrative machinery, although exclusive representation was practiced occasionally locally here and there and was standard practice in the Illinois state service.[6] At the other end of the spectrum were laws by which Alabama barred state employees from joining labor organizations and North Carolina prohibited police and fire employees from joining a national labor organization.

---

[2] O. Glenn Stahl, *Public Personnel Administration* (New York: Harper & Row, 1962), pp. 38–41.

[3] Michigan, Missouri, Nebraska, New York, Ohio, Pennsylvania, Texas, and Washington. Virginia led the way in 1946.

[4] Kenneth O. Warner and Mary L. Hennessy, *Public Management at the Bargaining Table.* (Chicago: Public Personnel Association, 1967), p. 398.

[5] Illinois and North Dakota (1951), New Hampshire (1955), Minnesota (1957), Wisconsin (1959), Alaska (1959).

[6] Richard C. McFadden, *Labor-Management Relations in the Illinois State Service* (Urbana: Institute of Labor and Industrial Relations, University of Illinois, 1954), pp. 18–21.

In the early 60s, California, Massachusetts, Oregon, and Rhode Island statutorily granted the right to organize. While California required all public employers to "meet and confer on request," Connecticut (municipal), Massachusetts (municipal), Oregon (municipal), and Rhode Island (police and fire) authorized "collective bargaining" on a permissive basis. No guidelines or standards were included.

BEGINNING OF COLLECTIVE BARGAINING

The stand that any form of bargaining in the public sector was impossible was crumbling in the face of experience and political expediency. General acceptance of the concept of a legal duty on the part of the employer to bargain in good faith was brought nearer by two events in 1962—federal Executive Order 10988 and a new law in Wisconsin.

Executive Order 10988, limited as its scope of bargaining was, had the effect of legitimatizing formal negotiating procedures, unit determination, exclusive recognition, and unfair-practice procedures in the public sector. The order also strongly emphasized participation for the good of the service. It wove together the objectives of the civil service cooperation principle with procedural elements of the NLRA. . . .

Of major importance in terms of impact was the adoption of exclusive representation and written agreements—steps toward the conventional private-sector bargaining model and away from the "government is different" syndrome which would have seemed inconceivable 10 years earlier. Some court decisions in the forties had held that it was an abuse of discretion for a public employer to grant exclusive recognition to an employee representative if all employees concerned were not supporters of the representative. This position was slowly abandoned when governments began to move past the view that bargaining involves an impermissible illegal delegation of authority and came to rest on the rationale that agreements are an exercise of discretion rather than a delegation of authority. Once written agreements were seen as a desirable, if not inevitable, consequence of formalized relationships, exclusive representation became a logical prerequisite to orderly procedure. The prerequisite was that "fair" representation be guaranteed, as it was in the executive order, by proof of majority support, by equal representation of all employees, and by assurance that individual representations could still be made to the employer.

The other public policy springboard of 1962 was the implementation of Wisconsin's pioneering law for municipal employees. It provided the sort of structure which the executive order did not—(1) a central administrative body, similar to the NLRB, to enforce and apply policies and procedures and (2) a means for resolving impasses (mediation and factfinding). Although exclusive representation was not specifically mentioned, the Wisconsin Employment Relations Board was mandated to hold elections and certify employee representatives, and employers were required to reduce agreements to writing in the case of negotiations with a majority representative.

NLRA STRUCTURE MINUS THE STRIKE

The years 1965–1967 brought a watershed in public-sector employment relations. Six more states—Connecticut, Delaware, Massachusetts, Michigan, Minnesota, and New York—moved by statute to a modified NLRA model, including a compulsion on the employer to bargain with certain groups of employees, machinery to administer and enforce procedures, and mediation–fact-finding mechanisms for the resolution of negotiations disputes. All included strike prohibitions.[7]

What were the reasons for this rush to an NLRA-type framework? Environmental conditions were of paramount importance. All seven states had influential labor movements and/or liberal political traditions, and a long history of public-sector employee organizations. Ad hoc bargaining arrangements had been developing steadily over the years. Perhaps the most critical factor of the time was the political-public realization that strikes were not a temporary postwar phenomenon or a condition which could be eradicated by law.[8] A statement of the American Federation of State, County, and Municipal Employees (AFSCME) in 1966 set forth the union's insistence on the right to strike as essential to free collective bargaining. In July 1967, the traditionally conservative NEA convention approved a policy statement that recognized strikes of NEA affiliates as likely to occur and worthy of support.[9] Clearly something more had to be done to counter the threat posed by the strike.

The situation in New York State in the mid-60s exemplifies the kind of process going on somewhat less dramatically elsewhere. A critical trigger was the notoriety given the New York City transit strike in January 1966, Governor Rockefeller's appointment of the Taylor Committee the same month, and the committee's subsequent findings.[10] The committee's terms of reference focused on the twin policy goals which had been evolving since World War II: "protecting the public against the disruption of vital public services, while at the same time protecting the rights of public employees."[11] The committee, in its final report, came to grips with sovereignty and described the word as "scarcely an apt term to apply to a system of representative democratic government, such as our own, which is responsive to the electorate. It is more realistic to inquire as to the manner in which public employees can participate in establishing their employment terms within the framework of our political democracy."[12] More importantly, the committee articulated the tradeoff which was to characterize public-sector legislation for the next few years: "It is elementary justice to assure public employees, who are stopped from using the strike, that they have the right to negotiate collectively."[13] The upshot was recommendations for procedures based loosely on the NLRA model, but adapted to public-sector differences—notably the substitution of mediation, fact-finding, and strike penalties for the right to strike.

By 1967, public policy in 21 states allowed participation of public employees in the determination of their pay and con-

---

[7] Eleven other states adopted provisions or amended existing statutes to allow or mandate bargaining for certain groups: Alabama, Florida, Maine, Missouri, Montana, Nebraska, Oregon, Rhode Island, Vermont, Washington, Wyoming.

[8] A total of 133 local government strikes were recorded in 1966. *Work Stoppages in Government, 1972*, BLS Report 434 (1974), p. 3.

[9] *90 Monthly Lab. Rev. III* (September 1967). Thirty public-school strikes occurred in 1966, the largest number ever recorded. See *90 Monthly Lab. Rev. 44* (August 1967).

[10] Other important influences were a New York City welfare workers' strike in 1965 which was ended by the use of mediation and fact-finding; the ignoring of Condon-Wadlin strike penalties following New York City teachers' strikes; the waiving by legislation of strike penalties in various instances, including the New York City transit strike. See *89 Monthly Lab. Rev. III-IV* (April 1966) and *90 Monthly Lab. Rev. 25* (December 1967).

[11] New York Governor's Committee (Taylor) on *Public Employee Relations, Final Report* (March 31, 1966), p. 9.

[12] Ibid. p. 15. (For an interesting example of the speed with which opinion changed on this subject, see *Railway Mail Assn.* v. *Murphy*, 44 N.Y. Supp. [2d] 601 [1943], which states in part, "To tolerate or recognize any combination of Civil Service employees of the Government as a labor organization or union is not only incompatible with the spirit of democracy, but inconsistent with every principle upon which our Government is founded.")

[13] Ibid. p. 20.

ditions of employment. Coverage of all public employees in a state was the exception, but coverage was slowly expanding and formal procedures and structures were increasingly common. The strike was still firmly rejected as incompatible with the nature of the government employer. Modified bargaining systems were intended to make the strike unnecessary, and mediation–fact-finding procedures were expected to evolve into an acceptable substitute.

IMPASSE RESOLUTION AND THE STRIKE

When the Taylor Committee contended that the strike was inappropriate in the public sector, it based this view on two points. First, the strike is incompatible with the orderly functioning of our democratic form of representative government, in which relative *political*, rather than economic, power is the final determinant. Second, while admitting that some public employees are in nonessential services and others are engaged in work comparable to that performed in the private sector, it concluded that "a differentiation between essential and nonessential governmental services would be the subject of such intense and never-ending controversy as to be administratively impossible."[14] It also dispensed with compulsory arbitration as an option: "There is serious doubt whether it would be legal because of the obligation of the designated executive heads of government departments or agencies not to delegate certain fiscal and other duties. Moreover, it is our opinion that such a course would be detrimental to the cause of developing effective collective negotiations."[15]

Pennsylvania proceeded to take a radically different line, moving directly from its 1947 no-strike statute to compulsory tripartite arbitration for police and fire fighters in 1968,[16] to a comprehensive law and a circumscribed right to strike for other public employees in 1970.[17] The commission that recommended the new approach stated: "Twenty years of experience [under a no-strike law] has taught us that such a policy is unreasonable and unenforceable, particularly when coupled with ineffective or nonexistent collective bargaining. It is based upon a philosophy that one may not strike against the sovereign. But today's sovereign is engaged not only in government but in a great variety of other activities. The consequences of a strike by a policeman are very different from those of a gardener in a public park."[18]

Apparently collective bargaining was an idea whose time had definitely come in Pennsylvania; the commission reported that it could recall no witness who opposed the concept.[19] Furthermore, "essentiality" as an insurmountable barrier to the right to strike was dismissed: "The collective bargaining process will be strengthened if this qualified right to strike is recognized. It will be some curb on the possible intransigence of an employer; and the limitations on the right to strike will serve notice on the employer that there are limits to the hardships that he can impose. . . . Strikes can only be effective so long as they have public support. . . . We look upon the limited and carefully defined right to strike

---

[14] Ibid. pp. 18–19.

[15] Ibid. p. 46.

[16] Preceded by a public referendum.

[17] Also covered by compulsory arbitration are prison and mental hospital guards and court employees. Voluntary arbitration is allowed other groups except on matters requiring legislation. Strikes are prohibited during statutory bargaining procedures (including mediation and fact-finding), and in the event they create a danger or threat to health, safety, or welfare. The power to determine the latter is vested in the courts, as is the authority to issue injunctions.

[18] Governor's Commission to Revise the Public Employee Law of Pennsylvania, Report and Recommendations (June 1968), p. 7.

[19] Ibid. p. 9.

as a safety valve that will in fact prevent strikes."[20]

The question which the New York committee and Pennsylvania commission attempted to deal with—given the limitations imposed by the governmental environment, how do you accommodate the pressure for finality in collective bargaining?—continues to absorb the parties, politicians, and public. More research has been carried on in this area than in any other in the field of public-sector labor relations. Legislative solutions, proposed and applied, have been imaginative and often daring.

Writing in 1967, only three years before passage of Pennsylvania's strike law, Andrew W. J. Thomson observed that no legislature "has yet permitted its employees to strike, and public opinion seems to indicate that such a development is not likely in the foreseeable future. The furthest that any legislative body has gone is to prohibit specifically only strikes which endanger the health, safety or welfare of the public as in Vermont. . . ."[21] A similar view was put forward by Ida Klaus who saw government as unyielding on the strike in part because of the unwillingness of the public to accept any action that would sanction strikes by public employees.[22] Both writers emphasized the difficulty of distinguishing between essential and nonessential services, the practical and philosophical point at which the New York and Pennsylvania legislatures chose to diverge, as noted above.

It is hardly surprising that heavy emphasis and high hopes were placed on mediation and fact-finding as procedural substitutes for strikes and lockouts. In 1973, Charles Rehmus reported that over 20 state statutes provided for fact-finding for some or all their public employees. He stated the reason for the attractiveness of the procedure: "If the issues in dispute and the recommendations for their resolution are clearly set forth and are well reasoned then the recommendations will be persuasive to all concerned."[23]

The problem with mediation and fact-finding, of course, is that they are not always persuasive, leaving the parties with the "finality" choices of an employer's unilateral action or an illegal employees' strike. In fact, it appears that only 16 states now provide for fact-finding as a last step for one or more groups. The trend has been toward mechanisms that will avoid the inequity connotations of a unilateral employer action and the antipublic interest considerations implicit in a strike.

THE RIGHT TO STRIKE

Given the historical aversion to the strike in the public sector, one of the most interesting developments over the 70s has been the statutory granting of this right in eight states.[24] The reasons seem to be basically those touched on by the Pennsylvania committee: a belief that bargaining will thereby be strengthened and a belief that true essentiality can be defined, and should be, to protect the interests of both public employees and the public. It is the latter objective which has most strongly marked these statutes. In no case is the right to strike unfettered. In all cases, a threat to the public health, safety, and/ or welfare triggers a "no-strike" mechanism. In all cases, certain prestrike impasse

[20] Ibid. pp. 13–14.

[21] Andrew W. J. Thomson, *Strikes and Strike Penalties in Public Employment* (Ithaca: New York State School of Industrial and Labor Relations, Cornell University, 1967), p. 8.

[22] Ida Klaus, *A Look Ahead*, in *Labor-Management Relations in the Public Service*, Part 6 (Honolulu: Industrial Relations Center, University of Hawaii, September 1968), pp. 775–76.

[23] Charles Rehmus, "The Fact Finder's Role," in *The Public Interest and the Role of the Neutral in Dispute Settlement* (Albany, N.Y.: Society of Professionals in Dispute Resolution, 1973), p. 37.

[24] Alaska (1974), Hawaii (1970), Minnesota (1975), Montana (1969), Oregon (1973), Pennsylvania (1970), Vermont (1967), Wisconsin (1977).

procedures must be complied with. Some of these involve the passage of considerable time. Others involve other kinds of devices to bring public pressure into the picture and to force harder bargaining. For example, after impasse, the new Wisconsin law requires each party to submit a single final offer, which becomes a public document; a public hearing must be held if five citizens request one; if *both* parties withdraw their final offers, the labor organization may strike after giving 10 days' notice unless a court finds that a strike would pose an imminent threat to public health or safety. Essentiality is doubly protected in five of these eight states by provision of compulsory arbitration for some group or groups of employees.[25]

THE TREND TOWARD COMPULSORY ARBITRATION

Far more marked than the trend toward strike rights has been the trend toward compulsory arbitration of bargaining impasses. In 1965, Maine and Wyoming provided compulsory arbitration for fire fighters. Two years later, Delaware allowed voluntary binding arbitration on all issues but wages, and Rhode Island, in education negotiations, had compulsory arbitration on all matters not involving the expenditure of money. In spite of a widely expressed concern of both employers and many AFL–CIO unions over the transfer of authority to third parties, by 1977, 18 states had laws including compulsory arbitration in some form for some group or groups of employees. All but two include police and fire fighters.[26] Eight of the 20 involve a variation on conventional arbitration, for example, last-best-offer by package or issue by issue, systems designed to shift responsibility for final terms to

the parties and away from the arbitrator, thereby extending the bargaining process.

The overriding expressed consideration in the passage of these laws has been the need to develop "peaceful" procedures for resolving impasses. This objective appears over and over again in statutory policy statements and in the arguments of proponents of compulsory arbitration. By shifting finality to a third party, compulsory arbitration is intended to create a substitute both for the strike and for employer unilateralism. At one stroke a sort of balance is created between the parties by divesting them of their ultimate weapons, equity is achieved by settling impasses through a quasi-judicial forum, and the public interest is protected in that we have real collective bargaining, no strikes, and fair awards.

Few would argue that we have achieved this ideal. Compulsory arbitration is challenged most often on three grounds: (1) it does not deter strikes, (2) it has a chilling effect on the bargaining process, and (3) it involves an unacceptable delegation of governmental authority.

Does it deter strikes? The evidence is inconclusive, although it appears that arbitration has reduced strikes in some states. Illegal strikes occur where they are illegal under all circumstances and where they are legal under some circumstances, without regard to the presence or absence of the arbitration option. Research on strikes has so far produced little evidence that public policy can be correlated with strike incidence. Environmental and structural factors peculiar to particular states appear to determine strike behavior.[27]

---

[25] The Hawaii, Montana, and Vermont laws do not include compulsory arbitration for any group.

[26] The exceptions are Maine (fire fighters only) and Wyoming (fire fighters only).

[27] John F. Burton, Jr., and Charles Krider, *The Role and Consequences of Strikes by Public Employees,* 79 Yale L.J. 418 (1970), and "The Incidence of Strikes in Public Employment," in *Labor in the Public and Nonprofit Sectors,* ed. Daniel S. Hamermesh (Princeton, N.J.: Princeton University Press, 1975); and contributions by James L. Perry and Jack E. Klauser in *Symposium: Public Sector Impasses,* 16 Ind. Rels. 273 (October 1977).

Does arbitration discourage true bargaining? The arguments on both sides of this proposition have been well-covered elsewhere.[28] Suffice it to say here that the trend in public-sector law toward arbitration suggests that "chill" is a factor that can be dealt with or lived with.

Far more important—because it goes to the heart of the public-sector employment-relations problem stated at the outset of this chapter—is the question of delegation of authority. So far nine state supreme courts have upheld compulsory arbitration statutes against claims that they improperly delegate legislative power, and two state supreme courts have declared such statutes unconstitutional.[29] The decisions upholding constitutionality have most often found that there is a public interest in preventing strikes, that illegal delegation does not occur when there are statutory provisions of explicit standards and guidelines for arbitrators and procedural safeguards in the form of court review, and that the power to tax has not been transferred in that an arbitration act is regulatory, and does not in itself impose a burden or charge.

*   *   *   *   *

The search for a satisfactory means of achieving finality goes on. Neither the strike nor compulsory arbitration is a comfortable theoretical fit, but arbitration has got the nod at the moment because, I would speculate, it is controllable in form

(it is "judicial," thereby satisfying an equity consideration) and it carries less emotional content than the strike.

New York's safety-service law was renewed last year despite a strong push by the governor for substitution of legislative review for binding awards. Massachusetts's law was renewed regardless of widely publicized charges of the Massachusetts League of Cities and Towns that use was excessive and that awards were running 14 percent higher than negotiated settlements. The New Jersey Study Commission, whose findings preceded the passage of a police-fire arbitration bill last year, found that "arbitration to compel finality, seems to be, at this time, the single position that would be acceptable to the most persons. . . ."[30] Wisconsin's extension of the arbitration option to all employees was described by one close participant as a result of prior lack of any feature in the law to resolve a dispute without recourse to work stoppages, plus a doubling of illegal strikes over the past five years.[31]

Currently, public discontent in California over illegal strikes among public school teachers has led to legislative examination of means by which such strikes might be eliminated. In Pennsylvania, similar dissatisfaction with the number of legal strikes is in part the reason for appointment of a governor's commission to study existing law. On the other hand, in New York, a senate research committee is studying the feasibility of moderating strike penalties.

Compulsory arbitration is seen by many as the best available instrument for maximizing the potentialities of the collective bargaining process and minimizing illegal

---

[28] See, for example, Robert G. Howlett, *Contract Negotiation Arbitration in the Public Sector,* 42 Cincinnati L. Rev. 47 (1973); Peter Feuille, *Final Offer Arbitration and the Chilling Effect,* 14 Ind. Rels. 302 (October 1975); James L. Stern et al., *Final Offer Arbitration* (Lexington, Mass: D. C. Heath, 1975), p. 182; Hoyt N. Wheeler, *How Compulsory Arbitration Affects Compromise Activity,* 17 Ind. Rels. 80 (February 1978).

[29] States where compulsory arbitration is held constitutional are Maine, Massachusetts, Michigan, Nebraska, New York, Rhode Island, Washington, Wyoming, Pennsylvania. States where compulsory arbitration is held unconstitutional are South Dakota and Utah.

[30] New Jersey Public Employer-Employee Relations Study Commission, Report to the Governor and the Legislature (February 2, 1976), p. 4.

[31] Gary R. Johnson, "Compulsory Binding Arbitration—Beyond the Crossroads," In *Public Sector Labor Relations: At the Crossroads* (Amherst: University of Massachusetts, 1977), p. 103.

strikes and employer unilateralism. In this sense, its proponents believe that compulsory arbitration is "in the public interest." Whether today's "best available instrument" is good enough to survive changing conceptions of the public interest is something else again. Continuing economic constraints, for example, may yet cause governments, management, employee organizations, and the public to reevaluate the professional neutral as the channel through which they choose to see final decisions made. The pendulum may then swing to greater experimentation with the legal strike. . . .

UNION SECURITY

Prior to the introduction of formal public-sector collective bargaining structures, the only form of union security was voluntary dues deduction. But once exclusive representation was accepted, with its companion obligation to represent all employees in a unit, union-security devices became a major employee-organization goal. One of the more interesting statutory developments of the 70s has been the rapid acceptance of union-security provisions, ranging from the fair-share service fee to, in a few cases, anything short of the closed shop.

The arguments presented in favor of union security are similar to those marshaled to support the transfer of other elements of traditional collective bargaining to the public sector, equity and stability: (1) as long as the exclusive representative must represent all employees in a unit equally, all employees should be obliged to pay their share of the cost of such services and (2) the goal of constructive collective bargaining and peaceful settlements is substantially forwarded when a union has the security that flows from support of its full unit constituency. These arguments are identical to those used to justify union security in the private sector. Although the issue has not been unat-

tended by controversy, it would appear that the private-sector position on union security has been widely accepted by the government employer.

Seventeen state statutes presently include provision for some form of union security (beyond voluntary dues deduction) for all or some groups of employees. Six states allow the union shop.[32] Two have maintenance-of-membership provisions.[33] Five provide for the agency shop,[34] while six provide for a service fee or fair-share arrangement.[35]

In the majority of cases, the union-security mechanism is a negotiable item, but there are some notable exceptions, where public policy has moved past the private-sector model and calls for the automatic grant of union security to an exclusive representative. This is presently the case in five states.[36] A variation on the mandatory requirement occurs in three states where union security is granted following a vote of unit members.[37]

With the exception of Vermont's (1969), all union-security statutory provisions were adopted in the 70s. However, local agreements on the subject became fairly common in some states before the enactment or amendment of laws. For example, in 1972 the Michigan Education Association stated that it had agency shops

---

[32] Alaska (all but teachers), Kentucky (fire fighters), Maine (higher education), Oregon (all), Vermont (municipal), Washington (all).

[33] California (state employees), Pennsylvania (all but police and fire fighters).

[34] California (public schools), Massachusetts (all), Michigan (all), Montana (all), Rhode Island (state employees).

[35] Connecticut (state employees), Hawaii (all), Minnesota (all), New York (all), Washington (state employees), Wisconsin (all).

[36] Connecticut (state), Hawaii (all), Minnesota (all; fair share not to exceed 85 percent of regular dues), New York (state), Rhode Island (state).

[37] A majority vote of unit members is required in Massachusetts (all) and Washington (state, higher education); in Wisconsin (state), the required margin is two-thirds of those voting.

in about half of its 530 contracts.[38] In 1969, union attorney I. J. Gromfine reported union shops in transit agreements in the cities of Chicago, Boston, Pittsburgh, St. Louis, and Memphis, among others; union-security agreements with public agencies in Michigan, New York, Missouri, Vermont, Indiana, and Illinois; union shops for police and fire department employees in Rhode Island and Connecticut.[39] In some cases, such as in Michigan, the topic was held to be within the scope of bargaining.[40] More often, such agreements were the result of local innovation, normally correlated with high proportions of membership. . . .

CONCLUSION

The trend of law and public opinion in the United States has been toward more egalitarian interpretations of how employees and management should function within labor relations systems. But in the public sector, unlike the private, the equity goal constantly has had to be reconciled with the need to maintain the sovereignty of government. The descriptive material above traces some of the successes and failures of the reconciliation process.

In a significant number of states, the duty to bargain, exclusive representation, binding agreements, and union-security arrangements are now viewed as acceptable means to labor peace rather than as unacceptable "invasions of government authority." A similar core of acceptance underlies those more rudimentary systems that merely compel the employer to meet and confer with majority representatives. The trend is unmistakably toward bilateral responsibility for pay, hours, and working conditions.

[38] 512 GERR E1 (July 16, 1973).
[39] At New York University's 22nd Conference on Labor. Reported in 304 GERR E9 (July 7, 1969).
[40] *Oakland County Sheriff, et al.*, 1968 MERC Op. 1.

This is not to suggest that all clashes with the sovereignty concept are likely to be resolved in due course. The nature of the conflict, rooted as it is in ideology, guarantees that the tension between sovereignty and bilateral authority can only be ameliorated, not eliminated. We will continue to see manifestations of the conflict whenever government's perceived need to have the last word intensifies (as is the case now regarding various scope issues, strikes, and compulsory arbitration).

Viewing public-sector labor relations in this manner points up the institutional barriers to full implementation of the traditional private-sector system, but fails to account for other factors influencing public-sector labor law. Economic conditions, for example, are of major importance. Following World War II, inflation, rising real incomes, the increased demand for government services and hence for government employees, and the improvement in private-sector pay and benefits relative to those in the public sector all contributed to militancy, public sympathy, and the subsequent passage of collective bargaining laws. Demands for "equal treatment" fell on fertile soil.

The enigmatic economic circumstances of recent years have had a different impact. Continued inflation, a relative decline in real incomes, unemployment, and concerns over public budgets have created an environment in which the demands of public employees are often greeted with public indifference, if not hostility. Where legislation has created a bilateral system of some kind, the public response appears to argue that public employees are as "equal" as they ought to be, at least for the time being. Where no statutory systems have been adopted (a handful of states mainly in the South and Southwest), economic pressures undoubtedly reinforce existing disinclination to experiment with increased labor rights.

Not only are public employees vulnerable in the area of labor relations legislation, their proximity to government makes them ready instruments (and targets) of wider public policy in times of general economic stress. For example, in spite of a highly sophisticated fair-comparison pay scheme, federal employees have been subjected to pay caps "in the national interest" and apparently will be again this year. Similar instances of government's response to public economic concerns abound at the local level.

One might speculate that these same economic factors, operating to alter public attitudes and political responses, account for current inactivity on the subject of a national public-sector labor law. *National League of Cities* v. *Usery*[41] destroyed con-

fidence that a national law could be declared constitutional under the commerce power, but it did not affect the possibility that Congress's taxing and spending powers could be used to require state compliance with national labor relations legislation.[42] The historical development of both public and private labor law suggests that the limbo in which a national public-sector law now resides may have more to do with attitudes of the moment than with loftier questions of constitutionality.

---

[42] See *City of Macon* v. *Marshall*, No. 77–155–Mac (October 28, 1977), 96 LRRM 2797, in which a federal district court ruled in a case arising under the Urban Mass Transportation Act that the federal government may condition the distribution of tax money to local governments on their meeting certain requirements, including the granting of collective bargaining rights to employees.

---

[41] *National League of Cities, et al.* v. *Usery, et al.*, 96 S. Ct. 2465, 426 U.S. 833 (June 24, 1976).

APPENDIX   SUMMARY OF STATE LAWS CONCERNING COLLECTIVE BARGAINING RIGHTS OF PUBLIC EMPLOYEES*

TABLE 1   BARGAINING PROVISIONS FOR TEACHERS

Statutes, executive orders, personnel policies, court decisions, and attorney general opinions

STATE	RECOGNITION	BARGAINING RIGHTS	IMPASSE PROCEDURES AND RIGHT TO STRIKE	UNION SECURITY
Alabama	N.P.	Consultation[a]	N.P./Prohibited	MDD
Alaska	Exclusive	Mutual duty	M,FF/N.P.	N.P.
Arizona	N.P.	Meet and confer	N.P./N.P.[b]	N.P.
Arkansas	N.P.	Permitted	N.P./Prohibited	N.P.
California	Exclusive	Mutual duty	M,FF/Prohibited	MDD; AG and MM permitted
Colorado	N.P.	Permitted	N.P./Prohibited	N.P.
Connecticut	Exclusive	Mutual duty	M,FOA-I/Prohibited	AG permitted
Delaware	Exclusive	Mutual duty	M,FF/Prohibited	MDD
D.C.	Exclusive	Mutual duty	M,FOA-P/Prohibited	MDD; AG permitted
Florida	Exclusive	Mutual duty	M,FF,L/Prohibited	MDD
Georgia	N.P.	Meet and confer	N.P./N.P.	N.P.
Hawaii	Exclusive	Mutual duty	M,FF,A-V/Permitted	MDD; AG mandatory
Idaho	Exclusive	Mutual duty	M,FF/Prohibited[c]	N.P.
Illinois	N.P.	Permitted	N.P./Prohibited	N.P.
Indiana	Exclusive	Mutual duty	M,FF,A-V/Prohibited	MDD; AG illegal
Iowa	Exclusive	Mutual duty	M,FF,FOA-I/Prohibited	N.P.
Kansas	Exclusive	Mutual duty	M,FF/Prohibited	N.P.
Kentucky	N.P.	Permitted	N.P./Prohibited	N.P.
Louisiana	Permitted	Permitted	N.P./N.P.	DD permitted
Maine	Exclusive	Mutual duty	M,FF,A[d]/Prohibited	N.P.
Maryland	Exclusive	Mutual duty	M,FF/Prohibited	N.P.
Massachusetts	Exclusive	Mutual duty	M,FF,A-V/Prohibited	MDD; AG permitted
Michigan	Exclusive	Mutual duty	M,FF/Prohibited	AG permitted

* Note: Tables 1–4 were compiled by the editors.

TABLE 1 (*concluded*)

STATE	RECOGNITION	BARGAINING RIGHTS	IMPASSE PROCEDURES AND RIGHT TO STRIKE	UNION SECURITY
Minnesota	Exclusive	Mutual duty	M,FOA-I-V/Permitted	MDD; AG permitted
Mississippi	N.P.	N.P.	N.P./N.P.	N.P.
Missouri	Prohibited	Meet and confer	N.P./N.P.	N.P.
Montana	Exclusive	Mutual duty	M,FF,A-V/Permitted	MDD
Nebraska	Exclusive	Meet and confer	FF,CIR*e*/N.P.	N.P.
Nevada	Exclusive	Mutual duty	M,FF,BFF/Prohibited	N.P.
New Hampshire	Exclusive	Mutual duty	M,FF,A-V*f*/Prohibited	N.P.
New Jersey	Exclusive	Mutual duty	M,FF,A-V/Prohibited	MDD; AG permitted
New Mexico	N.P.	Permitted	N.P./N.P.	N.P.
New York	Exclusive	Mutual duty	M,FF,A-V/Prohibited	MDD; AG permitted
North Carolina	N.P.	Prohibited	N.P./N.P.	N.P.
North Dakota	Exclusive	Mutual duty	M,FF/Prohibited	MDD
Ohio	Permitted	Permitted	N.P./Prohibited	AG permitted
Oklahoma	Exclusive*g*	Mutual duty	FF/Prohibited	N.P.
Oregon	Exclusive	Mutual duty	M,FF,A-V/Permitted	MDD; AG permitted
Pennsylvania	Exclusive	Mutual duty	M,FF,A-V/Permitted	MM permitted
Rhode Island	Exclusive	Mutual duty	M,A*d*/Prohibited	AG mandatory
South Carolina	N.P.	Permitted	N.P./Prohibited	N.P.
South Dakota	Exclusive	Mutual duty	M,FF/Prohibited	N.P.
Tennessee	Exclusive	Mutual duty	M,FF/Prohibited	DD permitted; MM unlawful
Texas	N.P.	Consultation	N.P./Prohibited	N.P.
Utah	N.P.	Permitted*h*	N.P./Prohibited	MDD
Vermont	Exclusive	Mutual duty	M,FF/N.P.	N.P.
Virginia	N.P.	Prohibited	N.P./Prohibited	N.P.
Washington	Exclusive	Mutual duty	M,FF/Prohibited	MDD; AG permitted; U prohibited
West Virginia	Permitted	Permitted	M-V,FF-V/N.P.	N.P.
Wisconsin	Exclusive	Mutual duty	M,FF,FOA-I/Permitted	MDD; AG permitted
Wyoming	Prohibited	Prohibited	N.P./N.P.	N.P.

Note: N.P. = no provision; MDD = mandatory dues deduction; M = mediation; FF = fact-finding or advisory arbitration; AG = agency shop; MM = maintenance of membership; FOA-I = final offer arbitration by issue; FOA-P = final offer arbitration by package; L = legislative action; A-V = conventional arbitration-voluntary; DD = dues deduction; A = mandatory conventional arbitration; BFF = binding fact-finding; U = union shop.

[a] Concerning rules and regulations related to school administration.

[b] Enjoinable if immediate and irreparable loss would have been suffered by the district.

[c] Teachers not granted right to strike even though strikes by teachers are not expressly prohibited by law.

[d] Binding on non-economic issues; advisory on economic issues.

[e] Action by commission of Industrial Relations (including M, FF, and A).

[f] Voluntary on non-cost items only.

[g] Individuals may enter into contracts with board, however.

[h] Salt Lake City has local ordinance.

SOURCE: U.S. Department of Labor, Labor-Management Services Administration, *Summary of Public Sector Labor Relations Policies* (Washington, D.C.: U.S. Government Printing Office, 1981).

TABLE 2 BARGAINING PROVISIONS FOR POLICE

STATE	RECOGNITION	BARGAINING RIGHTS	IMPASSE PROCEDURES AND RIGHT TO STRIKE	UNION SECURITY
Alabama	N.P.	N.P.	N.P./Prohibited	N.P.
Alaska	Exclusive	Mutual duty	M,A/Prohibited	MDD; AG and U permitted
Arizona	N.P.	Permitted	N.P./Prohibited	N.P.
Arkansas	N.P.	Permitted	N.P./Prohibited	N.P.
California	Exclusive	Meet and confer	M/Prohibited	N.P.
Colorado	N.P.	N.P.	N.P./Prohibited	N.P.
Connecticut	Exclusive	Mutual duty	M,FF,FOA-I/Prohibited	N.P.
Delaware	Exclusive	Mutual duty	DL,A-V/Prohibited	MDD
D.C.	Exclusive	Mutual duty	M,FOA-P/Prohibited	MDD; AG permitted

TABLE 2   (*concluded*)

STATE	RECOGNITION	BARGAINING RIGHTS	IMPASSE PROCEDURES AND RIGHT TO STRIKE	UNION SECURITY
Florida	Exclusive	Mutual duty	M,FF,L/Prohibited	MDD
Georgia	N.P.	Prohibited	N.P./N.P.	N.P.
Hawaii	Exclusive	Mutual duty	M,FF,A-V/Permitted[a]	MDD; AG mandatory
Idaho	N.P.	Prohibited	N.P./N.P.	N.P.
Illinois	N.P.	Permitted	N.P./Prohibited	N.P.
Indiana	N.P.	N.P.	LMC/N.P.	N.P.
Iowa	Exclusive	Mutual duty	M,FF,FOA-I/Prohibited	N.P.
Kansas	Exclusive	Meet and confer	M,FF,L/Prohibited	N.P.
Kentucky	N.P.	Mutual duty	N.P./Prohibited	N.P.
Louisiana	Permitted	Permitted	N.P./Prohibited	DD permitted
Maine	Exclusive	Mutual duty	M,FF,A[b]/Prohibited	AG illegal
Maryland	N.P.	N.P.	N.P./N.P.	N.P.
Massachusetts	Exclusive	Mutual duty	M,FF,FOA-I/Prohibited	N.P.
Michigan	Exclusive	Mutual duty	FOA-I[c]/Prohibited	N.P.
Minnesota	Exclusive	Mutual duty	M,FOA-I/Prohibited	MDD; AG permitted
Mississippi	N.P.	N.P.	N.P./N.P.	N.P.
Missouri	Exclusive	Meet and confer	N.P./Prohibited	N.P.
Montana	Exclusive	Mutual duty	M,FF,A-V/Permitted	MDD
Nebraska	Exclusive	Mutual duty	M,FF,A[d]/Prohibited	N.P.
Nevada	Exclusive	Mutual duty	M,FF,BFF/Prohibited	N.P.
New Hampshire	Exclusive	Mutual duty	M,FF,A-V[e]/Prohibited	N.P.
New Jersey	Exclusive	Mutual duty	M,FF,A/Prohibited	N.P.
New Mexico	N.P.	Permitted	N.P./N.P.	N.P.
New York[f]	Exclusive	Mutual duty	M,FF,A/Prohibited	MDD; AG permitted
North Carolina	N.P.	Prohibited	N.P./N.P.	N.P.
North Dakota	N.P.	N.P.	M,FF/Prohibited	N.P.
Ohio	Permitted	Permitted	N.P./Prohibited	DD permitted
Oklahoma	Exclusive	Meet and confer	FF/Prohibited	N.P.
Oregon	Exclusive	Mutual duty	M,FF,A/Prohibited	MDD; AG permitted
Pennsylvania	Exclusive	Mutual duty	A/N.P.	N.P.
Rhode Island	Exclusive	Mutual duty	A/Prohibited	N.P.
South Carolina	N.P.	Permitted	N.P./Prohibited	N.P.
South Dakota	Exclusive	Mutual duty	M,FF/Prohibited	N.P.
Tennessee	N.P.	Prohibited	N.P.[g]/N.P.	N.P.
Texas[h]	Exclusive	Mutual duty	M,A-V/Prohibited	N.P.
Utah[i]	N.P.	N.P.	N.P./Prohibited	MDD
Vermont	Exclusive	Mutual duty	M,FF,A-V/Prohibited	AG and U permitted
Virginia	N.P.	Prohibited	N.P./Prohibited	N.P.
Washington	Exclusive	Mutual duty	M,A/Prohibited	MDD
West Virginia	Permitted	Meet and confer	N.P./N.P.	N.P.
Wisconsin	Exclusive	Mutual duty	M,FF,FOA-I/Prohibited	MDD; AG permitted
Wyoming	Prohibited	Prohibited	N.P./N.P.	N.P.

Note: N.P. = no provision; M = mediation; A = mandatory conventional arbitration; MDD = mandatory dues deduction; AG = agency shop; U = union shop; FF = fact-finding; FOA-I = final offer arbitration by issue; DL = state department of labor; A-V = conventional arbitration-voluntary; FOA-P = final offer arbitration by package; L = legislative action; LMC = labor-management committee; DD = dues deduction; BFF = binding fact-finding.

[a] Enjoinable if strike is danger to public health or safety.

[b] Binding on non-economic issues; advisory on economic issues.

[c] Final offer on an issue-by-issue basis for economic issues; conventional for non-economic issues.

[d] Arbitration hearing held by the Commission of Industrial Relations (CIR).

[e] Non-cost items only.

[f] Separate statute for New York City.

[g] Arbitration ordinance in Memphis.

[h] By local option.

[i] Salt Lake City has local ordinance providing for collective bargaining for its employees.

SOURCE: U.S. Department of Labor, Labor-Management Services Administration, *Summary of Public Sector Labor Relations Policies* (Washington, D.C.: U.S. Government Printing Office, 1981).

TABLE 3   BARGAINING PROVISIONS FOR FIREFIGHTERS

STATE	RECOGNITION	BARGAINING RIGHTS	IMPASSE PROCEDURES AND RIGHT TO STRIKE	UNION SECURITY
Alabama	N.P.	Present proposals	N.P./Prohibited	N.P.
Alaska	Exclusive	Mutual duty	M,A/Prohibited	MDD; AG and U permitted
Arizona[a]	N.P.	Permitted	N.P./Prohibited	N.P.
Arkansas	N.P.	Permitted	N.P./Prohibited	N.P.
California	Exclusive	Meet and confer	M/Prohibited	N.P.
Colorado[b]	N.P.	N.P.	N.P./Prohibited	N.P.
Connecticut	Exclusive	Mutual duty	M,FF,FOA-I/Prohibited	N.P.
Delaware	Exclusive	Mutual duty	DL,A-V/Prohibited	MDD
D.C.	Exclusive	Mutual duty	M,FOA-P/Prohibited	MDD; AG permitted
Florida	Exclusive	Mutual duty	M,FF,L/Prohibited	MDD
Georgia	Exclusive	Meet and confer	FF/N.P.	N.P.
Hawaii	Exclusive	Mutual duty	M,FOA-P/Prohibited	MDD; AG mandatory
Idaho	Exclusive	Mutual duty	FF/Permitted	N.P.
Illinois	N.P.	Mutual duty	FF/Prohibited	N.P.
Indiana	N.P.	N.P.	LMC/N.P.	N.P.
Iowa	Exclusive	Mutual duty	M,FF,FOA-I/Prohibited	N.P.
Kansas	Exclusive	Meet and confer	M,FF,L/Prohibited	N.P.
Kentucky	Exclusive	Mutual duty	M,FF/Prohibited	MDD; U permitted
Louisiana	Permitted	Permitted	N.P./Prohibited	DD permitted
Maine	Exclusive	Mutual duty	M,FF,A[c]/Prohibited	AG illegal
Maryland	N.P.	N.P.	N.P./N.P.	N.P.
Massachusetts	Exclusive	Mutual duty	M,FF,FOA-I/Prohibited	N.P.
Michigan	Exclusive	Mutual duty	FOA-I[d]/Prohibited	N.P.
Minnesota	Exclusive	Mutual duty	M,FOA-I/Prohibited	MDD; AG permitted
Mississippi	N.P.	N.P.	N.P./N.P.	N.P.
Missouri	N.P.	N.P.	N.P./N.P.	N.P.
Montana	Exclusive	Mutual duty	M,FF,FOA-I/Prohibited	MDD
Nebraska	Exclusive	Mutual duty	M,FF,A[e]/Prohibited	N.P.
Nevada	Exclusive	Mutual duty	M,FF,FOA-P/Prohibited	N.P.
New Hampshire	Exclusive	Mutual duty	M,FF,A-V[f]/Prohibited	N.P.
New Jersey	Exclusive	Mutual duty	M,FF,A/Prohibited	N.P.
New Mexico	N.P.	Permitted	N.P./N.P.	N.P.
New York[g]	Exclusive	Mutual duty	M,FF,A/Prohibited	MDD; AG permitted
North Carolina	N.P.	Prohibited	N.P./N.P.	N.P.
North Dakota	N.P.	N.P.	M,FF/Prohibited	N.P.

TABLE 3 *(concluded)*

STATE	RECOGNITION	BARGAINING RIGHTS	IMPASSE PROCEDURES AND RIGHT TO STRIKE	UNION SECURITY
Ohio	Permitted	Permitted	N.P./Prohibited	DD permitted
Oklahoma	Exclusive	Meet and confer	FF/Prohibited	N.P.
Oregon	Exclusive	Mutual duty	M,FF,A/Prohibited	MDD; AG permitted
Pennsylvania	Exclusive	Mutual duty	A/N.P.	N.P.
Rhode Island	Exclusive	Mutual duty	A/Prohibited	N.P.
South Carolina	N.P.	Permitted	N.P./Prohibited	N.P.
South Dakota	Exclusive	Mutual duty	M,FF/Prohibited	N.P.
Tennessee	N.P.	Prohibited	N.P.[h]/N.P.	N.P.
Texas[i]	Exclusive	Mutual duty	M,A-V/Prohibited	N.P.
Utah[j]	N.P.	N.P.	N.P./Prohibited	MDD
Vermont	Exclusive	Mutual duty	M,FF,A-V/Prohibited	AG and U permitted
Virginia	N.P.	Prohibited	N.P./Prohibited	N.P.
Washington	Exclusive	Mutual duty	M,A/Prohibited	MDD
West Virginia	Permitted	Meet and confer	N.P./N.P.	N.P.
Wisconsin	Exclusive	Mutual duty	M,FF,FOA-I/Prohibited	MDD; AG permitted
Wyoming	Exclusive	Mutual duty	A/N.P.	N.P.

Note: N.P. = no provision; M = mediation; A = mandatory conventional arbitration; MDD = mandatory dues deduction; AG = agency shop; U = union shop; FF = fact-finding; FOA-I = final offer arbitration by issue; DL = state department of labor; A-V = conventional arbitration-voluntary; FOA-P = final offer arbitration by package; L = legislative action; LMC = labor-management committee; DD = dues deduction.

[a] Phoenix has local ordinance.

[b] Denver has local ordinance.

[c] Binding on noneconomic issues; advisory on economic issues.

[d] Final offer on an issue-by-issue basis for economic issues; conventional for noneconomic issues.

[e] Arbitration hearing held by Commission of Industrial Relations (CIR).

[f] Non-cost items only.

[g] Separate statute for New York City.

[h] FOA-P ordinance in Memphis.

[i] By local option.

[j] Salt Lake City has local ordinance providing for collective bargaining for its employees.

SOURCE: U.S. Department of Labor, Labor-Management Services Administration, *Summary of Public Sector Labor Relations Policies* (Washington: Government Printing Office, 1981).

TABLE 4 BARGAINING PROVISIONS FOR LOCAL EMPLOYEES

STATE	RECOGNITION	BARGAINING RIGHTS	IMPASSE PROCEDURES AND RIGHT TO STRIKE	UNION SECURITY
Alabama	N.P.	Prohibited	N.P./Prohibited	N.P.
Alaska	Exclusive	Mutual duty	M,A-V/Permitted	MDD; AG and U permitted
Arizona[a]	N.P.	Permitted	N.P./Prohibited	N.P.
Arkansas	N.P.	Permitted	N.P./Prohibited	N.P.
California	Exclusive	Meet and confer	M/Prohibited	N.P.
Colorado	N.P.	N.P.	N.P./Prohibited	N.P.
Connecticut	Exclusive	Mutual duty	M,FF,FOA-I/Prohibited	N.P.
Delaware	Exclusive	Mutual duty	DL,A-V/Prohibited	MDD
D.C.	Exclusive	Mutual duty	M,FOA-P/Prohibited	MDD; AG permitted
Florida	Exclusive	Mutual duty	M,FF,L/Prohibited	MDD
Georgia	N.P.	Prohibited	N.P./N.P.	N.P.
Hawaii	Exclusive	Mutual duty	M,FF,A-V/Permitted[a]	MDD; AG mandatory
Idaho	N.P.	Prohibited	N.P./N.P.	N.P.
Illinois	N.P.	Permitted	N.P./Prohibited	N.P.
Indiana	N.P.	N.P.	N.P./N.P.	N.P.
Iowa	Exclusive	Mutual duty	M,FF,FOA-I/Prohibited	N.P.
Kansas	Exclusive	Meet and confer	M,FF,L/Prohibited	N.P.
Kentucky	N.P.	Permitted	N.P./Prohibited	N.P.
Louisiana	Permitted	Permitted	N.P./Prohibited	DD permitted
Maine	Exclusive	Mutual duty	M,FF,A[b]/Prohibited	AG illegal
Maryland	N.P.	N.P.	N.P./N.P.	N.P.
Massachusetts	Exclusive	Mutual duty	M,FF,A-V/Prohibited	MDD; AG permitted
Michigan	Exclusive	Mutual duty	M,FF/Prohibited	AG permitted
Minnesota	Exclusive	Mutual duty	M,FOA-I/Permitted	MDD; AG permitted
Mississippi	N.P.	N.P.	N.P./N.P.	N.P.
Missouri	N.P.	N.P.	N.P./N.P.	N.P.
Montana	Exclusive	Mutual duty	M,FF,A-V/Permitted	MDD
Nebraska	Exclusive	Mutual duty	M,FF,A[c]/Prohibited	N.P.
Nevada	Exclusive	Mutual duty	M,FF,BFF/Prohibited	N.P.
New Hampshire	Exclusive	Mutual duty	M,FF,A-V[d]/Prohibited	N.P.
New Jersey	Exclusive	Mutual duty	M,FF,A-V/Prohibited	MDD; AG permitted
New Mexico	N.P.	Permitted	N.P./N.P.	N.P.
New York[e]	Exclusive	Mutual duty	M,FF,A-V/Prohibited	MDD; AG permitted

TABLE 4   (*concluded*)

STATE	RECOGNITION	BARGAINING RIGHTS	IMPASSE PROCEDURES AND RIGHT TO STRIKE	UNION SECURITY
North Carolina	N.P.	Prohibited	N.P./N.P.	N.P.
North Dakota	N.P.	N.P.	M,FF/Prohibited	N.P.
Ohio	Permitted	Permitted	N.P./Prohibited	DD permitted
Oklahoma	N.P.	N.P.	N.P./N.P.	N.P.
Oregon	Exclusive	Mutual duty	M,FF,A-V/Permitted	MDD; AG permitted
Pennsylvania	Exclusive	Mutual duty	M,FF,A-V/Permitted	MM permitted
Rhode Island	Exclusive	Mutual duty	M,A-V [b]/Prohibited	N.P.
South Carolina	N.P.	Permitted	N.P./Prohibited	N.P.
South Dakota	Exclusive	Mutual duty	M,FF/Prohibited	N.P.
Tennessee	N.P.	Prohibited	N.P. [f]/N.P.	N.P.
Texas	Prohibited	Prohibited	N.P./Prohibited	N.P.
Utah [g]	N.P.	N.P.	N.P./Prohibited	MDD
Vermont	Exclusive	Mutual duty	M,FF,A-V/Permitted	AG and U permitted
Virginia	N.P.	Prohibited	N.P./Prohibited	N.P.
Washington	Exclusive	Mutual duty	M/Prohibited	MDD
West Virginia	Permitted	Meet and confer	N.P./N.P.	N.P.
Wisconsin	Exclusive	Mutual duty	M,FF,FOA-I/Permitted	MDD; AG permitted
Wyoming	Prohibited	Prohibited	N.P./N.P.	N.P.

Note: N.P. = no provision; M = mediation; A-V = conventional arbitration-voluntary; MDD = mandatory dues deduction; AG = agency shop; U = union shop; FF = fact-finding; FOA-I = final offer arbitration by issue; DL = state department of labor; FOA-P = final offer arbitration by package; L = legislative action; DD = dues deduction; BFF = binding fact-finding; MM = maintenance of membership.

[a] Enjoinable if strike is danger to public health or safety.

[b] Binding on non-economic issues; advisory on economic issues.

[c] Arbitration hearing held by Commission of Industrial Relations (CIR).

[d] Non-cost items only.

[e] Separate statute for New York City.

[f] FOA-P ordinance in Memphis.

[g] Salt Lake City has local ordinance providing for collective bargaining for its employees.

SOURCE: U.S. Department of Labor, Labor-Management Services Administration, *Summary of Public Sector Labor Relations Policies* (Washington, D.C.: U.S. Government Printing Office, 1981).

PART THREE

THE PARTIES/ ORGANIZATIONS TO BARGAINING

CHAPTER 5

Unions as Organizations and Institutions

Labor unions are among the most enigmatic and misunderstood of American institutions. As organizations, they embody the conflict in American culture between a person's freedom of association and a persons right to act as an individual and to refuse to associate with others. In their role as collective bargaining agents for workers, unions find themselves in a conflict between freedom of association, the rights of an individual worker to associate with others and to freely contract with his or her employer, and the rights of an employer to exercise its property rights vis-à-vis its employees and a union that may represent or is seeking to represent its employees. Much of this conflict seems to result from two important and unique privileges that the legal environment of the system has granted unions. First, in certain circumstances, unions have the legal right to compel at least financial allegiance from workers. No other type of organization has been granted such a privilege.

Second, under an even broader set of circumstances, unions have the right to determine the employment contract for workers who are not even members of the union. This right, embodied in the principle of exclusive representation, gives the union the right not only to take a relatively small sum of money from workers in the form of dues and fees, but also gives to the union the right to participate in determining the sum total of the workers earnings on the job.

In theory, many of these union privileges are tempered by democratic processes in both the selection of the union as a collective bargaining agent (the subject of the previous section) and in the governance and administration of the union. Indeed, the most important aspect of trade unions is that, on the whole, they do provide what their members want from them: better terms and conditions of employment than could be obtained by the worker-members in the absence of a union. Freeman and Medoff, for example, found, based on a detailed review of the scholarly literature on the impact of unions on wages, that there is a wage premium of anywhere from 10 to 20 percent associated with unionism.[1]

This indicates an important point. Union members in the United States look to their unions to play but a limited role—the improvement of their terms and conditions of employment. Thus, the role of unions in the United States is for the most part, limited to the workplace. Although unions do engage in political activity, often as an arm of the Democratic Party, this activity is subordinate to, and funded separately from, their role as collective bargaining agents. The American labor movement then is job conscious rather than class conscious.

As George Strauss notes at the beginning of his paper, "democracy is an inevitable theme" of his work. The same may be said for this section of the paper. Unions have as their primary purpose the bringing of some measure of industrial democracy to the workplace. Their reason for existence in the United States is to provide workers with a voice as to their preferences for terms and conditions of employment. On a practical level, in order to determine the preferences of the workers, the union must be democratic. On a more philosophical level, one would not think that an undemocratic organization could provide industrial democracy.

This requirement for democracy must be tempered by the fact that if the union is going to be an effective agent in expressing the preferences of its members, it must be able to successfully use the ultimate union weapon—the strike. The successful use of that weapon requires some unity and coordination of action on the part of the members of the union. Such unity may be inconsistent with the requirements of union democracy and member choice.

This is the conflict found throughout this section—union democracy versus union strength. The article by Strauss focuses on the behaviorial aspects of unions and the informal aspects of union democracy. Strauss is asking why members participate in their union. Myron Roomkin looks at the manner in which the formal decision-making structures in the union affect the most noticeable aspect of union behavior—the strike. The next paper in the chapter is by Richard Block and examines an aspect of democracy by examining the extent to which unions respond to the needs of their membership in making a choice between allocating resources to servicing the present membership (administration) or to increasing the size of the union by recruiting new members (organizing). Finally, the structure of the labor movement is described in an excerpt from the *Directory of National Unions*.

---

[1] Richard B. Freeman and James L. Medoff, "The Impact of Collective Bargaining: Illusion or Reality," in *United States Industrial Relations, 1950–80: A Critical Assessment*, ed. Jack Stieber, Robert McKersie, and Daniel Quinn Mills (Madison, Wis.: Industrial Relations Research Association, forthcoming).

UNION GOVERNMENT IN THE UNITED STATES: RESEARCH PAST AND FUTURE

George Strauss*

This article seeks to accomplish two things: first, to review the research literature emphasizing behavioral, empirical work since 1960, and second to suggest specific questions for future study. . . .

I begin with . . . studies of union members' and leaders' attitudes and participation, move on to the local union, then look at various issues at the international level, and finally deal with measures and correlates of democracy, although democracy is an inevitable theme of the entire work. . . .

MEMBER ATTITUDES

During the [period 1945–1960], there were a series of studies of attitudes toward unions. For the most part these studies were concerned with three overlapping subjects: (1) member and nonmember attitudes toward unionism and collective bargaining generally, especially toward joining or voting for a union in a NLRB election; (2) member evaluations of particular aspects of their union's activities, for example, the willingness of their stewards to listen to their problems; and (3) preferences among alternative collective bargaining, political and social goals. . . .

SUPPORT FOR UNIONS AND COLLECTIVE BARGAINING. Many early studies were concerned primarily with the reasons workers gave for joining unions. . . .

Among the factors studied in relationship to attitudes toward unionism have been occupational differences, employer characteristics, demographic variables, and personal attitudes. Much recent interest has centered on the question of whether attitudes toward professionalism and unionism were positively or negatively [related], with special emphasis on the proposition that the easiest individuals to organize are those who aspire to, but have not quite reached professional status.

Had we a time machine, it would be nice to return to the 30s and compare the meaning of joining a union at that time with the meaning today. During the 30s, joining a union involved a highly charged act and frequently required considerable courage. Today unions are part of the establishment; most new members have no choice, being covered by union shop contracts. But I suspect that even among volunteer members, few view joining as an act of idealism or self-reaffirmation. Still, it would be worthwhile to contrast the probable variations in meanings of unionism as perceived by, for example, a fourth generation typographer, a temporary summer cargo handler forced to join the Teamsters, a newly organized Chicano farmworker, a young intern who joins a doctors' union to fight for better medical care, or a Serbian steelworker in Chicago's south side (where unions are key community institutions).

These differences deserve study, if for no other reason than that the attitudes and

* Professor, University of California-Berkeley. Reprinted from *Industrial Relations*, May 1977, pp. 215–42.

expectations that workers bring to their union help shape their behavior within it.

MEMBER ATTITUDES TOWARD THEIR UNIONS. Aside from attitudes toward unionism generally, how do members feel about their *own* unions? . . . Arnold Rosen and R. A. Rosen concluded that although most members were satisfied with most aspects of union life, few were happy about everything. Indeed, as Rose suggested, a member can be highly loyal to his union as such, yet critical of many of its aspects. Sayles and Strauss concluded that the nonactive majority of most unions (excluding exceptional cases, such as old-fashioned Jewish garment locals) look upon their union as "they" rather than "we" and feel somewhat ambivalent and hostile toward their leadership. Seidman et al. proposed a typology of members, spread along a continuum of loyalty and identification, with the "ideologically" oriented unionist at one end and the "unwilling" member at the other.

Earlier studies did not permit the systematic testing of interrelationships among attitudes. By the early 60s, numerous researchers were advocating the concept of dual loyalty (dual allegiance) which sought to explain the widely observed phenomenon that most union members express satisfaction with both union and management and that satisfaction with work is positively correlated with satisfaction with management. Indeed there is evidence that satisfaction with union and management is closely related to social integration with the occupational community.

Today the early dual loyalty studies seem unsophisticated. Even during the 50s, it was recognized that dual loyalty was most evident when union-management relationships were generally good. By now it is clear that satisfaction with a union is embedded in a complex network, including attitudes toward job, company, career prospects, etc. and that these are in part determined by such things as the respondent's age, sex, and race, the nature of his job, the community in which he lives, his personality, and the attitudes of his friends and role models. I would hypothesize that for many workers the union is a "hygiene," and that good stewards and good foremen are equally viewed as part of the "contextual environment" which helps reduce dissatisfaction.

PAYOFF FROM PARTICIPATION. A sense of occupational community is not enough, for there is no necessary reason why the life of this community should center on the union. For members to participate, they must feel that such action will result in some sort of payoff.[1] For instance, before they file a grievance they want to feel there is some chance of winning; before attending meetings they want to make sure there is some chance their voice will be heard. Thus the characteristics of the particular union and labor-management relationship make a difference. Other things being equal, participaton should be higher in small locals, in locals which are relatively autonomous from their internationals, and in unions which perform especially important functions, particularly those which operate hiring halls. Convenient meeting places, skilled leaders, well run meetings, and democratic procedures all combine to raise participation. Furthermore, members of occupational groups which have found that participation paid off in the past are more likely to participate in the future.

As expectancy theory predicts, personality affects the nature of the payoff desired. A distinction can be drawn between "hard core" activists, who attend meetings because of their interest in "internal union business" and sporadic attenders, whose

---

[1] In terms of "expectancy theory" a member will participate if he perceives that by participation he will achieve an objective, such as winning a grievance, meeting friends, or learning about matters of importance to him, which will satisfy a need important to him.

main concern relates to a specific grievance or collective bargaining issue. Similarly, William H. Form and H. Kirk Dansereau found that "social activists" were more active than those with economic interests. This view is consistent with Glick et al.'s findings that participation and satisfaction are related only for those with high decision-making needs, as well as with Spinrad's conclusion that high participants are "outgoing," "liking to deal with people," and "possessing high activity."[2]

CONSERVATIVE CAST. Taken as a whole these participation patterns seem to give unions a decidedly conservative cast. Union activists have high "stakes" in their present jobs and are well integrated into their occupational communities. In general, they are active not because of antagonism to management but because their activity satisfies important egoistic and social needs. Most studies suggest that high participators are no more antimanagement than are low participators.

UNION LEADERS

Particularly during the [1945–1960 period] there were numerous studies dealing with the backgrounds, careers, values, personalities, job problems, and aspirations of union leaders both paid and unpaid. . . . The cohort of leaders who became active during the 30s has now largely been replaced. The earlier generation was idealistic, militant, and its quick success meant that it never had to learn the apple-polishing skills required to work one's way up the bureaucratic ladder. In many unions the large concentration of leadership in a comparatively narrow age bracket created a classic personnel problem during the 50s

---

[2] Demographic factors also affect participation. Older members participate more actively, being less tied down by courtship and family activities. Participation differs among sex and ethnic groups and between rural and urban areas, in part reflecting cultural expectations as to its appropriateness.

and 60s. Few of these leaders died, reached retirement age, or were defeated in elections. At the same time union growth slowed precipitously. Thus there were few junior level openings which could be used to train replacements for the generation of the 30s when that generation reached retirement age. And in some unions an entire generation was skipped as men in their 30s replaced those retiring in their 60s.

This problem . . . was more serious in some unions than in others but has been almost unstudied. We have almost no information as to the replacement process or as to how the new generation differs from its predecessor. We know little about the new officers' careers, backgrounds, motivations for assuming union office, or how they differ from the rank and file. For example, there may well be some important differences among the leaders of various unions (and perhaps between generations) in attitudes toward the appropriate union political roles or the priority to be given to economic as opposed to noneconomic objectives, the latter ranging from job enrichment and workers' participation in management, to broader social objectives, such as full employment and national health insurance.

MOBILITY. Based on their observations, Sayles and Strauss concluded, as of 1953, that considerable numbers of local officers were suffering from blocked mobility. These were men (rarely women) who, except for the Depression, might have gone on to college and have entered management or the professions. For these men, union activity was in part a semiconscious reaction to the frustration of denied opportunities for status and achievement—and many of them were unusually militant.

Opportunities for working-class youth today to obtain education (either on a full-time basis or combined with work) are far better than they were during the Depression. "Employers have become more sophisticated in spotting promising workers for supervisory positions. As a result, while the job of union officials has grown more demanding, the pool of talent to fill these jobs seems to have diminished." On the other hand, even a college degree today may no longer guarantee a decent white-collar job. It would be useful to determine whether the educational level of the leadership has risen as fast as the work force. Possibly the present younger generation of union activists includes substantial numbers of at least partially college-trained men and women who once set their eyes on managerial or professional work. They may represent a new cohort of ambitious but frustrated workers for whom union activity provides a useful creative outlet. Equally important: to what extent do the ranks of the new leadership include ex-student radicals of the 60s?

PERSONALITY AND ROLE. Early attempts to describe what makes union officers tick . . . [characterized officers] as highly energetic, idealistic, and discontented. Leadership was viewed as satisfying their needs for status, power, and especially achievement and self-expression. Several attempts were made to classify officers in terms of their motivation and styles of leadership, categories determined primarily by the officers' adjustments to the pressures of protest versus accommodation and of democracy versus smooth administration. [Some work] . . . suggests that union leaders have even less confidence than do managers in the ability of those at lower levels and even less belief in the value of participative decision making. Hardly a strong background for democratic unionism!

UNION STAFFERS AS PROFESSIONALS? While the distinction between leaders of craft and industrial unions is undoubtedly less sharp today than it was in the 50s, that between full-time, paid "porkchoppers" (especially on the international payroll) and the unpaid local leaders may well have increased. The last 25 years have brought forth a new occupation (or quasi-

profession), that of union representative. The characteristics of this occupation—its recruitment, training and socialization, special interests, and "occupational myths"—certainly deserve attention.

Twenty-five years ago, a clear line could be drawn between what [could be] called intellectuals, educators, economists, lobbyists, and journalists—who were hired directly from outside the union—and line officers who had worked their way up from the rank and file. Legitimacy as a leader could be earned only through working in the shop, and college trained intellectuals were largely second-class citizens. . . . [Today] I would hypothesize that though the distinction between expert and line jobs continues, the differences between their incumbents has greatly declined. College and shop are no longer alternate routes of entry into union employment, and many officers today are graduates of both. College trained individuals (who may or may not be intellectuals) are increasingly moving into line positions. As of 1975, the president of the ILGWU and the two top officers of the ACW had law degrees.

As the above example illustrates, the needle trades unions which once recruited their officers largely from ideologically oriented Jewish pressers and cutters, now obtain part of their staff from outsiders with little or no industry experience. This pattern is occurring in other unions, even in the building trades. It seems obvious too that an increasing amount of job hopping is occurring between unions. The day when a defeated or discharged union representative returned to the shop may be largely over. All these developments contribute to a sense of identification with occupation rather than with a particular union.

Growing occupational identification also accentuates personnel problems. The staff man is a "man in the middle": no longer just a leader of the rank and file, he is also frequently excluded from the councils of the top brass. Thus he is required to defend and implement decisions he had little part in making. Junior staff salaries and fringe benefits are often low, and staffers typically lack job security, being completely dependent on their bosses. Furthermore, hardboiled top officers seldom make good supervisors: aggressiveness, use of threats, etc. may be appropriate for dealing with powerful employers, but not for handling relatively powerless subordinates. No wonder many staff representatives have organized formal and informal unions. While some top officials accepted these "unions within unions" in good faith, others reacted to them with all the ferocity of the most antediluvian employer. . . .

MINORITIES AND WOMEN

Minority and women's movements have been among the most significant social phenomena of the last 15 years. Indeed these movements have taken up many of the social energies once devoted to unionism. At the same time the proportion of union members who are women or members of new minority groups (blacks, Spanish-Americans, etc.) has increased rapidly with both women and minorities providing new sources for leadership. Despite these developments, there have been few studies of how the increased size and militancy of these groups has affected their role within the union's political life; instead the literature has focused on the discriminatory impacts of union policies, especially with regard to hiring halls and seniority.

MINORITIES. Irish (Patrick McGuire), Scotch (Phil Murray), Welsh (John L. Lewis), and Jews (Sam Gompers) all played an important role in labor's earlier days, and unions have traditionally provided a channel for minorities to win greater acceptance in our larger society. Victories in union elections paved the way

for victory in governmental elections, higher status in the community, and better treatment by the employer. But the path upward was never easy. Older minorities resisted the progress of newer ones, and even minorities of equal status struggled with each other. Even today political life in some locals center around rivalries among Poles, Italians, and Croatians. Thus black and Hispanic-American struggles for recognition fit into an older tradition.

Of the few studies of the new minorities in union life, Scott Greer's *Last Man In* may still be the most significant, even though based on the early 50s. Greer explains minority leadership and participation in 21 Los Angeles locals in terms of variations in proportional minority shares of local membership, the nature of minority jobs, and the structural characteristics of their unions (with opportunities for minorities being considerably greater in single-plant industrial unions).

Greer argues that economic and structural factors limit the ability of minority officers to make changes. The minority officer is a representative of both his race and his union, but if he is to retain his position, he must always remember that his union comes first. Consequently his function becomes that of channeling racial protests within union constraints. On the basis of a 1973 study, Lamm[3] concludes that while many minority leaders are "antiwhite" in their personal philosophy, in terms of their union activity they behave as unionists first; nevertheless, they are usually convinced they can serve union and racial ends simultaneously.

Writing in 1952, Kornhauser[4] observed that the typical minority route to office was through sponsorship by white leaders, that sponsored leaders played either "liai-

---

[3] Roger Lamm, "Black Leaders at the Local Level," *Industrial Relations*, 14 (May 1975), pp. 220–32.
[4] William Kornhauser, "The Negro Union Official: A Study of Sponsorship and Control," *American Journal of Sociology*, 56 (March 1952), pp. 443–52.

son" or "symbolic" (figurehead) roles, and that blacks obtained even this limited degree of recognition only when their numbers were large enough for them to play a crucial role in organizing campaigns, jurisdictional disputes, or union elections. Lamm finds that as of today minorities have developed significant power of their own and in combination with others, although sponsorship relationships continue "where the local is dispersed and no occupational community exists."

WOMEN. Women have been relatively inactive in unions and are underrepresented in leadership positions. There has been little research dealing with the impact on unions of the emerging new role for women in our society, with the major exception being Wertheimer and Nelson's[5] careful study of seven New York City locals. The authors compare reasons given by men and women for participation and nonparticipation, finding among the special reasons given by women for nonparticipation family demands, fear of having to assert oneself, and (for 10 percent of the sample) a belief that men are better than women in handling union affairs. Nevertheless, in the locals studied women filed grievances and attended meetings at least as actively as men, even though they were less likely to seek or be elected to office.

. . . The pioneering research of 25 years ago occurred before the advent of either civil rights or women's movements. [There is little knowledge as to how these movements and the resulting legislation have affected unions.]

THE LOCAL UNION

. . . At least four kinds of locals can be distinguished: plant, hall, craft, and white-collar-professional.

[5] Barbara M. Wertheimer and Anne H. Nelson, *Trade Union Women: A Study of Their Participation in New York City Locals* (New York: Praeger, 1975).

PLANT OR INDUSTRIAL LOCALS. These are centered in a single work location. Power tends to be divided among international officers, local officers, grievance committeemen, stewards, and the active rank and file. An industrial jurisprudence has developed which channels conflicts and protects members' rights. Considerable democracy is possible, with competing parties and contested elections frequently developing in large locals, and some measure of direct, participatory democracy in small ones. Meeting attendance may be low; nevertheless to some (and varying) extent those who do attend often act as unofficial departmental representatives. At the shop level, democracy operates through informal discussions as well as skillful use of grievance procedures and unofficial pressures, such as slowdowns. Even where there are multiplant contracts, the administration of the grievance procedure may permit considerable autonomy. The extent to which these locals are democratic is largely dependent on the growth of an occupational community—and this in turn on such factors as technology, plant layout, and local size.

CRAFT LOCALS. The typical craft local is characterized by a wide variety of work sites, but strong craft identification. The union plays a central part in the occupational community, especially in those locals where jobs are temporary, employment is handled through the union hall, and collective bargaining occurs locally. The business agent plays the key role; nevertheless, in many locals his freedom to exercise his power arbitrarily is greatly restricted by rank-and-file pressures. Although locals differ, hypothetically, the following factors may facilitate local democracy: small size (both geographically and in numbers); a low percentage of "travelling" members from other locals; high status (the highest status building trades, the electricians, may also be the most democratic); homogeneous craft skills (the heterogeneous Operating Engineers locals have a bad record on democracy and corruption); and weak control over the local labor and product markets (thus discouraging cozy relationships with management).

HALL LOCALS. These consist chiefly of unskilled workers (most in the service trades) who work in dispersed locations, often for a variety of employers. These members' low social status, weak individual bargaining positions, and widely scattered work locations all contribute to a weak sense of occupational community. Typically, leaders of these locals are in an impregnable political position and are rarely successfully challenged in elections. Their position is further strengthened in many locals by a requirement that jobs be obtained through the union hall.

Some hall locals are gigantic, e.g., Service Workers Local 32B in New York (with 40,000 members); they behave like small internationals, particularly since bargaining is conducted on a local level with the real internationals playing only an insignificant role. Their paid staff constitute a formidable bureaucracy by themselves.

Despite their secure position, leaders of such locals *sometimes* go to great lengths to keep communications channels open and to encourage membership commitment, as well as participation in a wide variety of activities. These efforts are motivated sometimes by political ideology, but also by the need to mobilize a core of stewards and active members who can police the contract and protect the union in a hostile environment. For purposes of mobilization, memberships of such locals are often divided into subunits, with some locals exerting great pressure to insure high turnout at subunit meetings. . . .

These meetings serve the purpose of communications, education, indoctrination, and to ratify the decisions of higher leadership, but do not make independent choices among alternatives. Thus high participation can be obtained despite the absence of democracy or an occupational community.

PROFESSIONAL WHITE-COLLAR LOCALS. The political dynamics of these unions have received little attention. Today such unions are concentrated among government employees and their membership has grown greatly. Better educated than blue-collar workers, these members are presumably more capable of running democratic unions and less willing to accept autocratic leadership. On the other hand, middle-class workers typically have numerous outlets for their social energies, and so they may look upon their union as purely a service agency, delegating decision making to the full-time staff.

Although specific types of locals have been studied, there is little research which compares locals of various types, size, and bargaining structure in terms of different membership attitudes, forms and levels of participation, formal and informal communications channels, and leadership patterns. . . . [T]hose individuals who obtain social and egoistic satisfaction from membership . . . [seem] to be a key to democracy and perhaps also for effective contract administration.

THE NATIONAL LEVEL

* * * * *

CONVENTIONS. Many of the case studies of individual unions describe the role of the convention in their particular union's political life. . . . One approach to conventions relates their structure and procedures to readily available "demographic" factors. Marcus, for example, finds that conventions meet more often in younger and smaller unions (and therefore suggests that these are more democratic). Convention rules also deserve study, especially those relating to the selection of committees, the control of the agenda, and the role of union staff. . . . Studies based on published convention proceedings may be misleading, since much of the convention's work takes place in committees, bars, and smoke filled rooms. . . .

LOCAL-NATIONAL RELATIONS. . . . These relations are governed formally by the union constitution (for instance with regard to the national union's power to impose trusteeships, to allocate strike funds, or to approve contracts); however, the national union's effective control depends on a variety of political and economic factors, especially the nature of collective bargaining. On the other hand, local unions (particularly large locals) may oppose officers politically, decline to support their bargaining objectives, refuse to go on strike, or even threaten to disaffiliate.

Recent years have seen powerful social, economic, and political forces working both for and against centralization. These include conglomerates, the growing governmental regulation of collective bargaining outcomes (e.g., in the equal employment area), technological change, experiments in job enrichment, and a variety of new bargaining structures (e.g., in steel). . . .

INTERMEDIATE BODIES. Some, but not all, unions have intermediate bodies—districts, joint boards, bargaining conferences [such as the UAW's General Motors Council] positioned between the national and local unions. Some are organized on the basis of geography, others by trade or industry. The existence of such bodies has been hypothesized to limit the power of national bodies, both by screening locals from national influence and by providing a base for those who wish to challenge the national leadership; on the other hand, intermediate bodies may also restrict the power of locals. [This could occur if the national union is involved in the selection of intermediate body officers, if the inter-mediate body must approve local actions, and if the local is required to affiliate with and provide substantial support for the intermediate body.] . . .

OFFICER TURNOVER AND ELECTION CLOSENESS. Turnover of officers and closeness of elections have commonly been used as measures of union democracy. Fear of defeat presumably makes officers more responsive to membership desires, while even replacement through death or voluntary retirement inhibits the growth of one-man rule.

Early studies merely gathered statistics, showing, for instance, that top national officers seldom faced opposition and were even more rarely defeated in elections. Replacement at the local level, however, occurred more frequently. More recent work has related turnover and election closeness with a variety of other factors. At the local level, turnover tends to be negatively correlated with officers' salaries, the age and size of the local, and the complexity of its organization. At the national level, as Edelstein and Warner[6] have amply demonstrated, election closeness is [related to] such factors as time between conventions. . . .

UNION FINANCES. Early studies of union dues, finances, and salaries were based on sketchy data. Beginning in the 60s the financial disclosure provisions of the Landrum-Griffin Act made available a vast amount of information. The few attempts to mine this lode generally fail to investigate possible regularities between financial data and other aspects of union life. It would be interesting to examine whether any systematic relationships exist among such variables as dues, officers' salaries, members' wages, rates of change of each, and union democracy (measured, for

---

[6] Jay David Edelstein and Malcom Warner, *Comparative Union Democracy: Opposition and Democracy in British and American Unions* (New York: Random House, 1976).

example, by election opposition). . . . For some research purposes, officer salaries may serve as a meaningful [measure of] ideological commitment. . . .

INTERUNION RELATIONS. Freeman and Brittain[7] [suggest] the possibility that interunion relations might well be studied in the same manner as interorganizational relations generally. Forms of interunion cooperation worth studying include not just mergers, but also no-raiding agreements, jurisdictional dispute settlement mechanisms, respect of other unions' picket lines, joint organizing drives, joint coordinating bodies (such as the building trades councils and the Industrial Union Department), and coordinated bargaining (as with G.E. or on an international basis with multinational firms). Other forms of interunion relations include city and state federations and the AFL–CIO itself. . . . [S]trategic alliances between "dependent unions," such as the Laborers and Retail Clerks, and more dominant unions [have been discussed] in which the dependent unions exchange various sorts of subservient behavior in return for the dominant union's economic support. . . .

DEMOCRACY

Implicitly or explicitly most studies of union government have been concerned with normative and descriptive questions relating to union democracy, and many have sought to discover the conditions under which Michel's "iron law of oligarchy" might or might not work.

Among the normative questions are the following: How democratic should unions be? Is democracy critical to their functioning, and, if so, should they be judged by the full standards of governmental (or even town-meeting) democracy, including

such protections as a bill of rights and independent judiciary? Or is internal democracy irrelevant, since the union's chief contribution to our larger democracy is that of a countervailing force to management? If so, effectiveness in its role requires it to maintain a disciplined, well-trained fighting force rather than to engage in factionalism and debate. Or should we adopt a middle ground positing that for a union to be strong it must respond to member pressures?

Another set of questions relates to how democracy is to be measured. One possible test is *legal*, in terms of constitutions, honest elections, regularly called meetings, and freedom for an opposition to develop. By this test low meeting attendance and lack of contested elections are not, in and of themselves, signs of lack of democracy. A second test is *behavioral*, focusing on institutionalized opposition, close elections, and high participation. Despite Lipset et al.,[8] close elections may not require an institutionalized opposition; and, as Cook[9] demonstrates, close elections and high participation rates need not occur simultaneously. Finally, there is the test of *responsiveness* and *control*. Do officers reflect the values of their members? Do they make an effort to find out what their members want? Do members feel that their officers are responsive to suggestions? Do they feel they have some "say about how things are decided"? According to the test of responsiveness (if not that of felt control), many benevolently autocratic hall locals (and possibly even the Teamsters) might qualify as democratic.

Much of the debate and research converges on two alternative approaches to union democracy, one informal, the other

---

[7] John Freeman and Jack Brittain, "Union Merger Process in Industrial Environment," *Industrial Relations*, 16, no. 2 (May 1977), pp. 173–85.

[8] Seymore Martin Lipset, Martin A. Trow, and James S. Coleman, *Union Democracy* (Garden City, New York: Anchor Books, 1956).

[9] Alice Cook, *Union Democracy: Practice and Ideal* (Ithaca, New York: Cornell University Press, 1963).

structural. The *informal* approach is concerned with the existence of (*a*) an occupational community with which a member can identify and in which he can participate and (*b*) a "middlemass" of active members who are politically and economically independent of the top leadership and who attend meetings, act as stewards, mobilize support for the union, but also keep the officers in line. (As an additional requirement for democracy, we might also ask that this middlemass represent the view of the rank and file, who themselves discuss important union issues, if not at the union meeting, then on the plant floor.)

The *structural* approach looks for formal arrangements which facilitate the development of power bases independent of the top leadership. Edelstein and Warner consider such features as the size and frequency of union conventions, the method of selecting executive board members (at large or to represent specific constituencies), and the existence of intermediate union bodies; all of these features have been found to be statistically related to closeness of elections. Additional [factors that may be important] include the percentage of union salaries going to personnel appointed by the president, constitutional requirements for rank-and-file ratification of contracts, and the practice of providing the opposition equal space in the union newspaper before elections.

The informal and structural approaches differ in some important ways. In explaining democracy the structural approach makes little allowance for collective bargaining arrangements, technology, characteristics of the membership, or a host of factors which other scholars have viewed as critical. On the other hand, the informal approach, which might well be useful in explaining the nature of union government in small and medium size locals, is less valuable in analyzing national unions or even large, amalgamated hall locals.

Actually the two approaches may be less inconsistent than they seem at first. Both require the existence of a middlemass with an independent power base. At the local level, this middlemass consists of the active, unpaid membership, and its power base is the occupational, shop level community. At the national level, it consists of key local officers (both paid and unpaid) as well as those regional and national staff representatives, who are not dependent on the top leadership. Structural arrangements may facilitate (but certainly not guarantee) the development of this middlemass, especially in national and large local unions. . . . For a strong middlemass to grow, internal organizational structure should be both consistent with collective bargaining structure and designed to permit the expression of occupational interests (although not to the extent of excessively threatening organizational solidarity). However, history and accident are also important here.

UNION STRUCTURE, INTERNAL CONTROL, AND STRIKE ACTIVITY

Myron Roomkin*

The objective of this paper is to relate internal structure of national unions to the collective bargaining activities of affiliated subordinate organizations, such as local unions. The linkage between the two is theorized to be in part the distribution of collective bargaining authority among levels of the union, most significantly, the amount of autonomy in collective bargaining enjoyed by subordinate bodies.[1] As an expression of this autonomy, we focus on the likelihood that a national union or one of its affiliated subordinate bodies will be involved in an authorized strike. Similarly, several measures of union structure are considered, which have been found in previous studies to represent the extent to which power is centralized at the level of the national union. [The] analysis . . . test[s] whether strikes are related to structure, using data for a large sample of national unions. The results, although exploratory, are broadly supportive of the hypothesis that strike activity by a national union or a subunit thereof is less likely as power becomes more centralized at the level of the national union.

* Professor of Industrial Relations, Graduate School of Management, Northwestern University. Reprinted in an abridged form, with permission, from the *Industrial and Labor Relations Review*, 29, no. 2 (January 1976), pp. 198–217. © 1976 by Cornell University. All rights reserved.

[1] Quite often unions maintain a second internal government concerned with day-to-day decision making and the internal administration of the union.

THE THEORY AND NATURE OF INTERNAL CONTROL

Within a national union, power to influence and participate in collective bargaining is distributed among the national and its subordinate bodies—locals and intermediate bodies—that comprise the organizational structure of the union. The extent to which this power is shared by subordinate organizations constitutes the amount of autonomy given to these units.[2] The obverse of autonomy, internal control, is used here to denote the degree to which the national leadership can control or interfere in the collective bargaining activities of its constituent organizations. It is a common mistake to think that subordinate unions are either completely autonomous or completely controlled from above. In reality, the amount of power given subunits and members within a union will vary from one national union to another.

When viewed historically, there has been a long-term decline in the amount of such autonomy reserved for subunits and a corresponding increase in the ability of nationals to control subunit bargaining behavior. Product market expansion and other changes in the industrial environ-

[2] In this respect, a union resembles a republic whose component governments (state and federal) have shared authorities and powers, along with different goals, interests, and constituencies. The issue of states' rights, for instance, is analogous to the issue of subordinate organization autonomy within unions.

ment motivated the formation of national organizations. In combining to form nationals, local unions took the first step in relinquishing their unfettered rights to develop their own collective bargaining policies. These rights were further reduced as additional changes in industry required subsequent consolidations of bargaining units and national organizations came to play dominant roles in the negotiation of multiplant and multiemployer contracts. Not surprisingly, another episode in this process is currently in evidence. Precipitated by a growth in conglomerate businesses, new forms of interunion cooperation and mergers among national unions are taking place. Such developments as these are likely to increase further the power of national unions at the expense of the locals. Thus, structural changes in unions, precipitated by changes in the economic environment, have altered the locus of power within unions.

According to the literature, sharing of power within a union produces internal tension and conflict among levels of the organization and their respective leaders. Subordinate bodies prefer sufficient autonomy and discretion to achieve collective bargaining settlements that meet the needs and desires of their constituents. The greater the control of the national over the collective bargaining activities of the subordinate body, the smaller is the freedom to deviate from settlements that are preferred by the national.

By contrast with its subordinate units, a national tends to be concerned about the well-being of the entire organization and all of its members. . . . Consequently, restrictions on the autonomy of subordinate bodies within the national union are likely to be seen by national leadership as one way to promote the welfare of the entire organization.

Bargaining structure, especially its degree of centralization as a reflection of product market size, is one factor conven-

tionally identified as a determinant of local autonomy. In national product markets, such as auto, steel, and rubber manufacturing, or where the national union is itself involved in bargaining, internal control is necessary to maintain credibility at the bargaining table. The national must convey to an employer that the negotiated settlement will be accepted by lower levels of the organization and by members employed at other companies. It may be necessary, at the same time, to give management the impression that the union is able to muster its full resources and present a united front. But internal control does more than just contribute to national union credibility in centralized bargaining situations. In seeking to establish comparable conditions throughout an industry, a national may rely upon the tactics of whipsawing and pattern setting, for which the ability to control subunits is an important precondition.

At the other extreme, in a localized product market, such as construction or retail sales, or where the national does not actually conduct negotiations, national control of subunits in collective bargaining is alleged to be less necessary, thus permitting a less centralized distribution of power.

Implicit in this treatment of autonomy is the right of a subordinate body to strike for its own interests. The national union prefers to control and limit strike activity by affiliates, that is, to use strikes selectively on behalf of the entire union's drive for better conditions of employment and to limit strikes not in the interest of the whole organization. National control over strikes is necessary to achieve objectives usually ascribed to unions: to take wages out of competition and to ensure that a common rule is maintained. Locals and other subordinate bodies are usually more interested in using the strike to obtain settlements more in line with local rank-and-file desires.

If, [other things equal] strikes by subunits of the national represent to some significant extent a behavioral manifestation of union autonomy and if, as argued, the amount of that autonomy varies among unions, then we might expect [aspects of structure that affect] autonomy to influence subordinate body strike activity within a national union. . . .

This suggests the following hypothesis: Other things being equal, *the likelihood of a subordinate unit within a national union participating in a strike is negatively related to the degree to which power is centralized at the level of the national union.*

SELECTED [ASPECTS] OF INTERNAL CONTROL

An empirical test of the hypothesis of this study requires the identification of quantifiable structural attributes of unions believed to capture or embody the internal distribution of power over collective bargaining decisions. Clearly the number of variables one could study in this connection is staggering. We have therefore selected the following five to reflect the relative degree of centralization within a union, albeit the last two are only direct measures: (1) the extent of national involvement in the conduct of collective bargaining by subordinate units; (2) the geographic scope of the product market as an indication of whether bargaining is localized or nonlocalized; (3) whether there are intermediate bodies between the locals and the national; (4) the frequency of national union conventions; and (5) the size of the national union. . . .

NATIONAL INVOLVEMENT IN SUBORDINATE BARGAINING.   Direct influence of the national union in subordinate negotiations may take several forms. In some unions, subordinate contract demands must receive national approval prior to negotiations. Many unions send national representatives to participate in, and sometimes direct, negotiations involving subordinate bodies. Settlements negotiated by subordinate bodies frequently require the approval of the national. One of the strongest sources of leverage the national can possess is the requirement that subordinate bodies receive national approval to call a strike. Subordinate units may be deterred from calling unauthorized strikes, because of the possibility that (*a*) they may be denied aid and assistance from the national, such as benefits from the strike fund or (*b*) they may risk disciplinary actions by the national, which could include being placed under trusteeship. . . . [T]his study will focus on requirements that subordinate bodies obtain from the national either prior approval to strike or postsettlement approval of contracts. . . .

[W]e anticipate that, other things held constant, a strike by a subordinate body is less likely to occur whether either prior approval to strike or postsettlement approval of contracts is required.

PRODUCT MARKET.   The nature of the product market influences the structure of bargaining, the structure of unions, and the degree of subordinate autonomy permitted. As the geographic scope of the market increases, broader bargaining units are required, thereby centralizing power within the national organization. Where the product market has remained localized, a greater degree of collective bargaining authority has been retained by lower levels in the union organizational hierarchy. Thus, according to our hypothesis, the likelihood of a subordinate body participating in a strike should decrease as the geographic scope of the product market increases. . . .

Building trades unions have, by and large, limited their jurisdiction to the construction industry. In addition, construction is a relatively localized industry, and bargaining in construction is conducted almost exclusively by local or intermediate union bodies. One would anticipate that subordinate bodies in building trades unions would have a higher incidence of strikes than nonbuilding trades unions because of the greater degree of autonomy permitted by the localization of bargaining. . . .

INTERMEDIATE BODIES. Several national unions are characterized by the existence of intermediate bodies between the local and the national levels that have collective bargaining responsibilities. Herbert Lahne calls such unions complex-structure organizations, whereas those not having intermediate bodies he calls simple-structure organizations. An intermediate union body could be responsible for: (1) coordinating bargaining among several locals; (2) actually negotiating contracts; or (3) processing local grievances.

The involvement of intermediate bodies in collective bargaining has implications for subordinate autonomy within unions. By the assignment of collective bargaining functions to intermediate bodies, power is distributed within the organization. In this sense, an intermediate body serves as a buffer or shield against complete national-level control over members. Furthermore, [Alice] Cook suggests that an intermediate body (one with bargaining responsibilities, for example) gives impetus to political self-government and subordinate independence.

Because the alleged contribution of the intermediate body to local autonomy may be balanced by the role some intermediates play in reducing the fragmentation of local bargaining, testing of the above hypothesis must include explicit controls for the scope of bargaining units. . . .

Therefore, we expect that once unit scope is held constant, nationals will have better control over collective bargaining activities of subordinate bodies if the nationals do not have intermediate bodies or do not assign to them collective bargaining responsibilities. Thus the incidence of strikes within the national organization is

likely to be greater for those unions that maintain active intermediate bodies. On the other hand, since building trades unions have traditionally developed intermediate bodies in order to control local fragmentation, it is also hypothesized that the incidence of strikes within the building trades unions is likely to be less for those unions that maintain active intermediate bodies.

THE FREQUENCY OF NATIONAL CONVENTIONS. The national convention is an important element in national-local relationships. Students of internal union affairs have long noted how conventions permit communication between leaders and members, give members an opportunity to influence policies directly (many of which involve shifts in the locus of power), serve as a court of final appeal against bureaucratic and administrative abuses, and allow members to review the performance of national leaders, since the tenure of leaders is usually coextensive with the interval between conventions.

Of the many characteristics of union conventions that are relevant to a discussion of internal control and the distribution of power, only the interval between conventions has received attention in prior empirical studies. One early attempt at comparing national unions suggests that the frequency of national conventions in unions is associated with their degree of centralization. . . . It is widely held, for instance, that union elections—usually held at conventions—give impetus to bargaining militancy. Challengers for elected office tend to accuse incumbents of insufficient militancy and, if elected, seek to fulfill election promises. Equally, incumbents often adopt militant bargaining positions if threatened by political opponents. Testing whether administrative centralization as reflected by convention frequency manifests itself in bargaining autonomy seems reasonable. We would expect that, holding other things constant, the likelihood of a strike by a national union or one of its subordinate bodies decreases as the interval between national conventions increases.

UNION SIZE. The size of the national union is another aspect of union structure that may be relevant to a discussion of internal control and centralization of authority. . . .

[It was] argued many years ago that large nationals tend to have a more heterogeneous membership than small ones. Such heterogeneity is likely to increase the diversity of membership interests, thereby increasing the amount of internal competition among groups of members and possibly producing dysfunctional consequences for the entire organization. In part to guard against such developments, nationals have become more centralized in their control of subordinate bargaining activities as their organizations have grown.

Limited empirical evidence suggests that size necessitates increased control within an organization. . . . In addition, a spate of studies has shown that membership participation in many types of organizations decreases with the size of the organization, and that low membership participation either leads to, or is caused by, strong centralization at the top of the organization. Holding other factors constant, size, as a measure of the relative degree of internal control within a national union, should be negatively related to the incidence of subordinate strikes across national unions.

MODEL, METHODOLOGY, AND DATA

For the purposes of this study, strike proneness is defined as the probability that a formal bargaining opportunity . . . involving an organizational component . . . belonging to a national union . . . results in a work stoppage. [Thus, the dependent variable is the number of strikes divided by opportunities where opportunities are represented by] contract expirations and within contract reopeners, excluding new or first contract negotiations. . . . [N]ot included [are] strikes conducted during a contract, many of which tend to be unauthorized. There are no readily accessible data by size of unit for new or first contract negotiations.

[The strike ratio is related to the following] variables discussed in the previous section:

NAC—the requirement that the contract . . . be approved by that national.

NAS—the requirement that the subordinate . . . obtain national . . . permission before striking. . . .

CON—the interval in years between national union conventions.

BLDG—if the national is officially classified as a building trades union.

[or]

JUDG—if the national is a building trades union *or* [emphasis in original] if it has been classified according to the author's judgment to face localized product markets. . . .

MEM—the number of members in [the] national union.

STR—[whether or not] an intermediate body is assigned collective bargaining responsibilities.

It is [expected] that [national contract approval requirements (NAC), national permission to strike requirements (NAS), greater time lapses between national conventions (CON), and the size of the national union (MEM) will be negatively related to the propensity to strike; while being a building trades union (BLDG) or operating in a localized product market (JUDG) and assignment of an intermediate body to collective bargaining activities (STR) will be positively related.]

Certainly, [these are not] all the factors known to influence strike activity. Conspicuously missing are the economic variables (wage increases, price increases, unemployment rates, and profits) on which collective bargaining outcomes will turn. Also absent are the often cited myriad of noneconomic determinants of strikes, including political considerations, inter- and intra-occupational comparisons, and other situational factors. Their omission here is not intended to deny their relevance. . . .

The sample in this study consists of 57 international unions. They were selected from the 72 national unions reporting more than 40,000 members in 1968. The 15 unions omitted possessed one of more of the following characteristics: (1) they had more than 25 percent of their membership employed in the public sector; (2) they either went out of existence or lost their identity through mergers with other unions during the 1968–70 period; or (3) their membership consisted primarily of railroad workers . . .

RESULTS

Table [1 in the Appendix] reports estimated regression coefficients and related statistics [for the dependent and independent variables] just described. . . .

[For the first model], equation 1*a* . . . , the sign of the regression coefficient on each variable used is as hypothesized, albeit most of these coefficients are not statistically significant at the . . . 5 percent [level]. Significant regression coefficients . . . are found [for the size of the] national union [MEM] . . . and [for] the convention interval [CON]. . . .

The poor performance of [the localized product market variable] JUDG stands in striking contrast to the performance of [the building trades union variable] BLDG. When substituted for JUDG in equation 1*b,* the BLDG . . . coefficient [is] statistically significant. . . .

One could argue, of course, that [the building trades union variable] is a much more accurate measure of unions facing a localized product market. . . . But . . .

the following explanation should also be considered.

Contrary to our hypothesis, localized product markets per se may not result in more autonomous subunits during bargaining. Instead, a local product market leads to locally dispersed bargaining units, which may or may not be given autonomy over collective bargaining matters. Among the building trades, for example, one finds both localized bargaining structure and a tradition of independent action. In looking for a reason why local unions in construction have preserved this autonomy, one should focus on the high degree of interdependence that exists among construction unions locally and the power of these unions vis-à-vis employers. The former condition makes local wage comparisons more compelling than intercity ones. The latter motivates the craft union to act when local comparisons are unfavorable.

While building trades unions have preserved considerable autonomy, many local and intermediate bodies of other unions have not, even though their respective product markets are also local in scope. It is partly for this reason that JUDG [localized product market], . . . does not perform well statistically. A few examples should be illustrative. In that portion of the printing industry not characterized by intercity competition by firms, the International Typographical Union (ITU) permits considerable local union autonomy in the negotiation of local economic provisions of contracts (wages, etc.), but closely supervises local negotiations over contract terms dealing with economic security (pensions, welfare, etc.). The ITU goes so far as to publish guidelines on economic security matters for the benefit of local negotiators.[3] In the local transit industry, the Amalgamated Transit Union endeavors to secure wage comparability across cit-

---

[3] The *ITU Book of Laws* also gives the national the clear authority to disappove any local contract not meeting these guidelines.

ies of comparable size, even though the product market is clearly local in scope. Local unions attempting to deviate significantly from their assigned pattern would be scrutinized closely by the national, and if necessary, the national would work to defeat such agreements.

The argument that localized product markets may be a necessary but not sufficient condition for local union autonomy is buttressed by equation 1d of Table [1]. [When the analysis is limited to only those 25 unions] classified as operating within local product markets, [the results improve substantially. The building trades variable] BLDG is significant . . . , with size [MEM] . . . , and convention frequency [CON] . . . also retaining the significance they displayed in equation 1a. There is also a significant negative coefficient . . . for whether the national requires prior approval for subordinate strikes [NAS]. Thus it appears that among local product market unions, building trade unions are more strike prone, and some national unions do exercise control over subordinate unit strike activity.

Because of errors of measurement, a finding of statistical insignificance for national approval of the contract (NAC) and national approval for subordinate strikes (NAS) does not necessarily vitiate the hypothesis concerning the strike-reducing consequences of national involvement in subordinate bargaining. In order to deal with these errors when we lack other sources of information, let us suppose that the probability of *actual* strike-reducing behavior by a national increases when its constitution mandates such behavior. Thus, a national might exercise controlling influences comparable to those mandated by rules elsewhere, even if it lacks a single constitutional requirement, but a union without rules has a lower probability of acting in such a manner. It is not that unreasonable to suggest, then, that the more a constitution has to say on the subject of national involvement, the greater the

probability a national will act in accordance with these rules. A two-rule union should exhibit a greater reduction in subordinate strike activity than any single-rule, or no-rule union. Under this hypothesis, an interaction variable, NAC·NAS, is added to the model. The results, as reported for equation 1c in Table [1 tend to support this hypothesis].

A variation of the model is estimated in equation 1e after all building trades unions are deleted from the sample. Such a specification appears justifiable in light of the building trades unions' unique qualities demonstrated in equations 1b and 1d. Regression coefficients in equation 1e are broadly similar in magnitude and statistical significance to their counterparts in equation 1b [lending further support to the findings that building trades unions with subordinate bodies in local product markets exhibit strike behavior that is markedly different from the strike behavior of other types of unions.] . . .

Finally, in equations 1f and 1g we take a closer look at the impact of union structure on the probability of subordinate strike activity. In equations 1a and 1b, STR (whether the union has or does not have an active intermediate body) fails to produce a significant regression coefficient when entered simultaneously with other variables in the equation. Its positive sign, however, is consistent with our hypothesis that simple-structure unions are less strike prone than complex-structure unions, due in part to the ability of national organizations to control locals directly without having to work through intermediate bodies. This hypothesis receives further support from the results of equations 1f and 1g. Equation 1f, estimated solely on data from simple-structure unions, [explains 30 percent of the variation in the strike ratio of simple-structure unions]. . . . The results in equation 1g, however, show that the [same variables explain only 3 percent of the variation in the strike ratio in complex-structure unions]. . . . This again suggests that mechanisms of control, represented here by the independent variables, are better suited for simple-structure unions in which the national constitutes the only higher level of union authority. Complex-structure unions, as previously suggested, appear to shield or buffer locals, giving them greater collective bargaining autonomy and making it more difficult to predict the likelihood of their participation in strikes. Of special interest [are the results for building trades unions] BLDG . . . [which give] modest support to the hypothesis that intermediate bodies tend to reduce autonomy among craftsmen's unions in construction.

CONCLUSION

The findings of this study are broadly consistent with our main hypothesis: centralization at the level of the national union reduces the likelihood that a subordinate unit will be involved in a strike. In the course of testing this hypothesis, the following relationships between structural characteristics of unions and the likelihood of subordinate strike activity were found at various levels of statistical significance and remain interesting subjects for future study.

1. Strikes by subordinate units seem to be less likely where the national union requires explicit approval of subordinate actions in collective bargaining.

2. The probability of a strike by subordinates shows evidence of being negatively related to the interval between national union conventions, which is used here as one proxy of the relative degree of centralization within national unions.

3. National unions appear to exhibit a negative relationship between the number of their members and the likelihood of subordinate unit strike actions. This, we argue, reflects the need in larger unions for more control due to membership heterogeneity.

4. We were unable to demonstrate that subordinate body strike proneness is higher in unions that operate in localized product markets than in those operating in geographically broader markets.

5. Still, craftsmen's unions in construction, also a localized industry, are more strike prone than other unions in the sample or other unions in localized markets. This, we argue, reflects in part the high degree of subordinate autonomy made possible by characteristics of the industrial relations system in the construction industry.

6. The presence of an intermediate body between locals and the national seems to alter the distribution of power within the union, probably making it more difficult for a national to control subordinate bodies. These complex-structure unions, therefore, have a higher degree of strike proneness among their subordinate units. There is indirect evidence that these intermediate bodies may tend to decrease local autonomy among craft unions in construction.

Finally, the present study emphasizes one dimension of an important public policy issue, that is, the tradeoff between centralization in industrial relations and the capacity of unions to represent the interests of their members. It has been suggested that membership interests could be better represented by reducing the degree of centralized decision making in unions through modifications in their internal structure. The nature of these modifications and whether or not they should be imposed on unions are issues that are beyond the scope of this inquiry. But in light of this study, we might expect some increase in the level of strike activity to accompany changes in union structure, as members exercise their newly granted autonomy. Increased industrial conflict in the form of officially authorized strikes will be, for both society and the unions, part of the costs of less centralized unions.

APPENDIX

TABLE [1] FACTORS INFLUENCING THE PROBABILITY OF SUBORDINATE BODY AND NATIONAL STRIKES (LOG [S'/O']) IN SELECTED NATIONAL UNIONS, 1968–70: ESTIMATED COEFFICIENTS AND RELATED STATISTICS[a,b]

SAMPLE	EQUATION NUMBER	INDEPENDENT VARIABLES								C	$\bar{R}^2$	SEE
		LOG(MEM$_{68}$)	STR	LOG(CON)	FUDG	BLDG	NAC	NAS	(NAC·NAS)			
All unions (N = 57)	1a	−.20† (.08)	.13 (.18)	−.46† (.19)	.10 (.18)	—	−.10 (.19)	−.13 (.28)	—	.84	.10	.65
	1b	−.23‡ (.08)	.07 (.16)	−.59‡ (.18)	—	.69‡ (.23)	−.14 (.17)	−.10 (.26)	—	1.78	.23	.61
	1c	−.22‡ (.08)	.13 (.16)	−.67‡ (.18)	—	.73‡ (.23)	−.93 (.66)	−.11 (.28)	−1.17* (.70)	1.67	.26	.59
Only local product market unions[c] (N = 25)	1d	−.36‡ (.09)	.02 (.18)	−.79‡ (.19)	—	.95‡ (.19)	−.07 (.18)	−.66† (.30)	—	3.22	.68	.40
Excluding building trades unions[d] (N = 48)	1e	−.22† (.09)	.09 (.19)	−.64‡ (.21)	—	—	−.19 (.20)	−.10 (.30)	—	1.09	.18	.65
Simple-structure unions[e] (N = 30)	1f	−.25† (.12)	—	−.76‡ (.24)	—	.86† (.38)	−.16 (.23)	−.16 (.38)	—	2.23	.30	.60
Complex-structure unions[f] (N = 27)	1g	−.20 (.13)	—	−.40 (.32)	—	.57* (.34)	−.08 (.31)	−.09 (.42)	—	1.37	.03	.69

[a] Estimated standard errors of the regression coefficients are in parentheses.

[b] R^2 is the adjusted coefficient of determination, SEE is the Standard Error of Estimate for the regression equation, and N is the number of unions in the sample.

[c] Includes unions for which FUDG = 1.

[d] Includes unions for which BLDG = 0.

[e] Includes unions for which STR = 0.

[f] Includes unions for which STR = 1.

* Significant at the 10 percent level.

† Significant at the 5 percent level.

‡ Significant at the 1 percent level.

UNION ORGANIZING AND THE ALLOCATION OF UNION RESOURCES

Richard N. Block*

In recent years, there has been a growing interest in the inability of unions in the private sector to increase their membership as fast as the private sector labor force is increasing. Between 1958 and 1978, the percentage of union members relative to the total labor force declined from 24.2 percent to 19.7 percent. Union membership as a percentage of employees in nonagricultural establishments also declined, from 33.2 percent to 23.6 percent.

While this decline has been variously attributed to the "cumbersome" procedures and "weak" remedies of the National Labor Relations Act, the increasing sophistication of management, and old union leadership with antiquated ideas about union organizing, this paper will make a different argument. It will be suggested that one of the main reasons that union membership as a percentage of the private labor force and employment has declined in recent years is because unions in the "traditional sectors" of manufacturing, mining, construction, and transportation—those sectors that account for almost 68 percent of union membership—have not placed a high priority on organizing. If unions are basically democratic organizations, then it is logical to think that the

reason that these unions have not placed an emphasis on organizing is because organizing new members may not be in the interests of the membership of the union.

This paper will attempt to show that for the large unions in the economy, the unions that have the resources to engage in large-scale organizing, this may indeed be the case. This paper will argue that as unions mature and increase the extent of their organizaton in their primary jurisdiction, the need of the membership for union-organizing services declines relative to their need for representation services. That fact, combined with the likelihood that the costs of organizing in highly organized jurisdictions will exceed the benefits from organizing, provides a substantial disincentive for unions to organize.

* * * * *

UNION TASKS

It will be argued here that the union has two main tasks to perform in order to maintain itself: recruitment and representation. It is these two tasks that account for the great bulk of the expenditures of the union's nonearmarked revenue.[1]

Recruitment. This is the process by which the union as an organization induces individuals to become affiliated with

* Associate professor, School of Labor and Industrial Relations, Michigan State University. Reprinted in an abridged form, with permission, from the *Industrial and Labor Relations Review*, 34, no. 1 (October 1980), pp. 101–13. © 1980 by Cornell University. All rights reserved.

[1] Union resources allocated to political activity must be collected and spent separately from monies acquired through and spent from general revenues.

it. It is the only way in which the union can grow. Generally, the union engages in recruitment in two kinds of situations: those in which workers do not have representation and those in which they do.[2]

Recruitment in the first type of situation is organizing, i.e., the attempt by a particular union to convince workers who do not presently have union representation to designate that union as their collective bargaining representative. In this country, the typical method of designation is through an election supervised by the National Labor Relations Board. The nature of the organizing process is such that it is costly for unions. Organizers must be hired, or the time of present employees (usually the international representatives) must be diverted to organizing and, therefore, away from other uses. In addition, leaflets and other literature must be printed and often distributed by mail, office space must be rented, and staff must be housed and fed. Finally, there are the legal costs involved with a representation election.

The second type of recruiting situation occurs in a unit in which the union already has representation rights. Two methods are used in this situation. When the union has a union security clause in the collective bargaining agreement, all employees in the unit must become union members or at least pay the union a service fee, usually equivalent to dues and fees.[3] Thus, for all practical purposes, the recruitment is done by the employer when it makes its hiring decision. When a union does not have a union shop clause in the agreement, it must sell itself to nonmembers who are in the unit. This is usually done by informal social pressure on the nonmembers, but sometimes through more aggressive actions as well.

For the purposes of this analysis, it will be useful to assume that the recruiting function of the union is completely synonymous with the organizing function. Given the prevalence of compulsory unionism clauses in collective bargaining agreements,[4] and in view of the legal obligations of unions to represent fairly all workers in the bargaining unit, it is unlikely that a great deal of recruiting resources are directed toward nonmembers in represented units.

Representation. This is the process by which the union provides services to its *present* membership. The representation process operates during both the negotiation of the contract and the term of the contract. During the negotiation of the contract, it encompasses such things as research on wages and benefits, expertise on matters of collective bargaining, and assessments of the bargaining strength of the two parties.

During the term of the contract the function of the union changes from one of exercising bargaining leverage to skillful administration of the agreement so as to permit the membership to obtain the greatest benefit from what has been negotiated. Thus, this function encompasses such activities as research on grievance and arbitration cases, providing representation to the local for negotiations with upper levels of the management hierarchy at higher steps of the grievance procedure, and possibly providing legal counsel during arbitration or NLRB hearings.

For purposes of this analysis, the func-

---

[2] A third method of recruitment is for one labor organization to induce another to merge or affiliate with it. This method of recruitment is sporadic, however, if it occurs at all, and does not account for a substantial portion of the average union's day-to-day expenditures.

[3] It is unclear whether an employee working under a union shop clause in a collective bargaining agreement must become a full union member in good standing, or whether that employee's obligation to the union extends only to paying dues and fees.

---

[4] In 1975, 75 percent of all collective bargaining agreements covering 1,000 workers or more had provisions for some form of compulsory unionism.

tion of representation may be thought of in two ways. First, it may be thought of as the services for which the member pays dues. This is because these are services delivered directly to the *present* membership. Second, it may be thought of as the criterion by which the union member judges the union leadership and makes decisions on whether to retain the present leadership in office. This is important, because if it is assumed that the two tasks of the union are recruitment-organization and representation-service, then it is also logical to assume that the resources of the union can be allocated to either of these two functions, but only to these two functions. It is to a model that determines how a union allocates its resources to the two tasks that we now turn.

A MODEL OF UNION BEHAVIOR

This section of the paper will set out a model from which it will be possible to derive implications for the related issues of union behavior and the manner in which the union allocates its resources. . . .

The membership welfare function. It is asserted that the union member wants two things from the union, (1) representation and bargaining power in the negotiations of the agreement and (2) representation and service in the administration of the agreement. With respect to negotiations, the employee-member wants better terms and conditions of employment than could be achieved in the absence of the union. The member believes that the terms and conditions of employment for which the union bargains will be greater the greater the bargaining power of the union. The key element in the union's bargaining power is the extent to which competitors of the employee's unit, both within the firm and outside the firm, are also represented by a union. Thus, at relatively low levels of unionization of competing units, the member will likely de-

mand that the union allocate a high percentage of its resources to organizing competing units so as to increase the bargaining power that can be exerted on the member's behalf.

As the competing units (those in the union's primary jurisdiction) become more unionized, the increment in the union's bargaining power for any increase in the extent of unionization after a threshold level will tend to decline. Thus, other things equal, as the extent of unionization in the union's primary jurisdiction increases, the membership will derive less benefit from a unit of organizing expenditures, and will insist that the union allocate greater percentages of resources away from organizing. . . .

The other main task of the union is administration, or representation and service during the term of the agreement. While administration can generally be offered at the same time as organizing services, under the assumption of limited resources it cannot be offered as effectively when the union is allocating a portion of its resources to organizing.

An international staff representative's time, for example, can either be used to handle grievances or to assist in organizing. To the extent the staff representative is organizing, the resolution of grievances may be delayed, making the quality of service available to the membership lower than it might otherwise be. Even if the unions's resource level was such that a full-time organizer could be hired, the membership could argue that those resources could be used instead to hire an additional staff representative and thus improve the available level of service.

[In the context of this model], at very low levels of union penetration, the membership has little to gain from union expenditures on representation and administration, as the union has very little bargaining power that it can exercise in order to gain favorable terms and conditions of employment for the membership.

As penetration (and presumably union power) increases, and the terms and conditions of employment improve, the member has more to gain from the administration function. Equally important, at higher levels of penetration, the increment to union power for any increase in union penetration declines. Therefore, [at higher levels of penetration] there should be membership pressure on the union leadership to allocate resources away from organizing and toward administration.

The leadership welfare function. The leadership of the union is assumed to have a two-part utility function. First, the union leader wants to stay in office and recognizes that to do so he or she must deliver a level of benefits acceptable to the members. The second [part of] the leader's utility function is the desire for increased prestige and income, a goal that can be achieved through a growth in the membership of the leader's union.[5] Growth, in turn, can be attained in either or both of two ways: through compulsory membership provisions and through organizing.

From the point of view of the union leadership, administering compulsory membership provisions is costless and risk free, but organizing involves both costs and risks. The costs of organizing have been discussed above; the risks result from the fact that there is no guarantee that the union will win any organizing campaign. From the point of view of the union leadership, then, the amount spent on organizing should be a function of the expected increase in union membership and the expected discounted dues receipts from the organizing campaign. These, in turn, should be a function of the probability of winning the representation election. If the probability of a union winning an election declines as the sector in which the election is taking place becomes more heavily organized, then, other things equal, the leadership will allocate fewer resources to organizing as the extent of union penetration in a sector increases.

The amount spent by the leadership on organizing is not just a function of these expected dues receipts, however. It is also a function of the welfare function of the membership with respect to the allocation of resources between organizing and administration. This, in turn, is determined by the extent of unionization in the sectors that compete with the union leader's constituency.

Thus, there appear to be two factors operating to keep organizing expenditures low when union penetration is high. First, the expected returns from a unit of organizing expenditures tend to decline as union penetration increases. Second, as union penetration increases, the membership demands that a larger percentage of the union's resources go to administration and a correspondingly smaller amount to organizing. . . .

. . . Thus, the simultaneous influence of both of these functions would appear to result in substantial disincentive for the union to engage in organizing when it has attained high levels of union penetration. The members do not want the union to organize, nor would organizing likely be economically feasible even if the members did want it.

This portion of the paper has attempted to analyze the relationship between union penetration and the manner in which the union allocates its resources between its organizing and administration functions. It was shown that, under the appropriate assumptions,, as union penetration increases, the membership has less need for organizing services than for administration services. Similarly, as penetration increases, organizing activities become less productive and more costly. Thus at high levels of union penetration, there are sub-

---

[5] Growth in leadership income, in a union context, refers to increases over previous salary levels within the same union, not to increases in leadership salaries relative to those in other unions. Variations across unions in the salaries of top-level leaders appear to have little relationship to union size.

stantial disincentives for the union to organize.

A TEST OF THE THEORY

Ideally, in order to test the theory described above, one would use as a dependent variable the percentages of union money expenditures and staff time allocated to organizing and to administration. Such data, however, are unavailable in published form and may not even be obtainable by direct survey methods, since unions may not keep such records. Data are available, however, on the number of National Labor Relations Board representation elections in which any individual union participated during the time period July 1972 to September 1978. By deflating these figures for a particular union by the number of members in that union, one should be able to obtain a measure of the extent to which that union allocates its resources to organizing. It seems reasonable to assume, that is, that the greater the number of elections per member for any individual union, the greater the percentage of resources (member dues) the union is allocating to organizing. The dependent variable, . . . in the analysis is . . . the number of single union nondecertification elections per 1,000 members in which [the union participated between July 1972 and September 1978].

Clearly, the independent variable of most interest would be one that captures the extent of union penetration in the union's primary jurisdiction. The variable used to measure this is . . . the percentage of all employees in [the] unions primary jurisdiction that were covered by collective bargaining agreements in 1972. In the sample used in this study, the mean value of [this variable] is 51.2 percent, much higher than the union penetration rate in the economy as a whole. This suggests that the industries in which representation

elections were held during the period studied tend to be more highly organized than the economy as a whole. [The membership of these unions would tend to have less need for organizing services than for administration services. Thus, a negative relationship between the number of NLRB representation elections per 1,000 workers and union penetration in the primary jurisdiction is expected.]

A second variable expected to have an effect on the extent to which unions would allocate resources to organizing is . . . the percentage of [the] union's membership in its primary jurisdiction. Other things equal, the greater the leadership's constituency in the primary jurisdiction, the more the leadership must respond to the needs of that particular constituency. In this case, given the relatively high degree of union penetration in the primary jurisdictions of the unions in this sample, [a negative relationship between the number of NLRB representation elections and the percentage of the union's membership in its primary jurisdiction is expected. The strongest negative relationship would be expected to] occur in cases where union penetration in the primary jurisdiction is high and where a high percentage of the union's membership is in that primary jurisdiction. [Regarding other influences on elections] it was hypothesized that . . . , unions in which a high percentage of agreements contain union security provisions are less likely to organize than those with a low percentage of such agreements, since the former may obtain membership growth via accretion in already organized units. . . . [On the other hand, there should be a positive relationship between elections and the change in employment in the union's primary jurisdiction, since,] other things equal, unions will be particularly interested in organizing new employees in their primary jurisdictions.

Measures of three other independent

variables . . . were designed to capture aspects of the union's internal governmental structure that are believed to affect leadership responsiveness. It has been argued that leaders will be more responsive to the membership in unions in which members of the international board are elected on a district rather than national basis, are full-time employees of the union, and are not dependent on the union president for their union jobs. . . . Among the unions in this sample . . . which tend to be in highly organized industries, more internal democracy would be expected to result in a lower allocation of resources to organizing, and hence fewer NLRB elections, than would be found in unions with less democracy.

THE RESULTS

[The results (presented in the Appendix) are generally consistent with expectations. The main variables of interest (the percentage of all employees in the union's primary jurisdiction covered by collective bargaining agreements and the percentage of the union's membership in its primary jurisdiction) were negatively related to the number of representation elections. In addition, an "interaction" term constructed by multiplying these two variables generated results that were negative and highly significant.] Taken together, these results indicate that high penetration by a union in its primary jurisdiction does have some dampening effect on the propensity of that union to organize, especially when the membership in the highly organized jurisdiction accounts for a high percentage of potential voters in the union.

Of the other variables analyzed, only . . . the change in employment in the union's primary jurisdiction, generated results that could be considered significant. . . . Unfortunately, for this sample and for this time period, the average em-

ployment change in a primary jurisdiction was a *decrease* of 280,000, and thus firm conclusions cannot be drawn about the allocation of a union's resources to organizing when employment *increases* in its primary jurisdiction. One might speculate that the positive association found between organizing and smaller decreases in employment implies that unions were responding to some partly offsetting increases in employment among the nonunion firms in the primary jurisdiction by trying to organize in those firms. Without data on the distribution of the employment change between the union and nonunion firms, however, there is no way of knowing whether that was indeed the case.

The other variables generated primarily insignificant results. [These results suggest] that union security agreements may not have a distinctive effect on the organizing decisions of unions, although they must be taken into account when examining the manner in which those decisions respond to changes in employment in the union's primary jurisdiction. . . .

[They also suggest] that internal union governmental structures may not have a great deal of effect on the manner in which unions respond to their members' interests vis-à-vis the allocation of the organization's resouces toward organizing. It should be observed, however, that organizing is only one of the ways in which the union leadership represents its constituency, and that these structural variables may perform better in predicting other union phenomena, such as internal election outcomes or leadership appointments. Alternatively, it may be that the size of the leadership's constituency with a particular interest is more important in determining the manner in which the leadership responds to the interests of that constituency than are the internal governmental structures through which the membership makes its decisions.

SUMMARY AND CONCLUSIONS

The . . . results presented here suggest that unions that have had success in organizing their primary jurisdictions organize less relative to the total availability of their resources than unions that have been less successful in organizing. They also suggest that the union leadership does respond to the interests of its membership, especially the interests of any group in the union with a substantial number of votes.

From a societal point of view, these results suggest that the labor movement in the United States may be caught in a con-tradiction of success and democracy. For many unions, success in organizing their primary jurisdictions has brought substantial resources with which to represent their membership. These unions are basically democratic institutions, however, and the interests of the membership may not be served by organizing. Thus, to the extent they have membership in highly organized industries, unions may not continue aggressively organizing. Union success, union democracy, and union growth through organizing may therefore be incompatible.

Appendix

FACTORS AFFECTING THE NUMBER OF REPRESENTATION ELECTIONS PER 1,000 UNION MEMBERS, INCLUDING UNION SECURITY PROVISIONS

$N = 65$ and t-values are in parentheses

INDEPENDENT VARIABLES	REGRESSION COEFFICIENTS											
P_u	−.019							−.021	−.021	−.021	−.021	−.020
	(1.42)							(1.60)	(1.53)	(1.4)	(1.57)	(1.47)
M_u	−.081		−.020*	−.021*	−.021*	−.021*	−.018					
	(1.61)		(1.76)	(1.83)	(1.81)	(1.80)	(1.58)					
I_u	−.179	−.111		−.375	−.543	−.349	−.219		.008	.276	−.006	−.072
	(0.31)	(0.20)		(0.66)	(1.00)	(0.60)	(0.38)		(0.04)	(0.48)	(0.01)	(0.13)
SF_u	.411	.397	.159		−.124	−.016	.272	.560		.216	.521	.470
	(0.65)	(0.64)	(0.28)		(0.22)	(0.03)	(0.46)	(0.95)		(0.37)	(0.89)	(0.82)
Sp_u	.349	.393	.364	.231		.346	.410	.574	.485		.515	.499
	(0.59)	(0.71)	(0.61)	(0.38)		(0.53)	(0.65)	(0.92)	(0.77)		(0.81)	(0.81)
N_u	.0004*	.0004*	.0004†	.0004*	.0004*		.0004†	.0004*	.0004*	.0004*		.0004*
	(1.88)	(1.88)	(2.38)	(2.27)	(2.24)		(2.03)	(1.90)	(1.94)	(1.92)		(1.88)
K_u	−.007	−.007	−.007	−.006	−.006	−.006		−.010	−.010	−.009	−.009	
	(0.84)	(0.86)	(0.80)	(0.75)	(0.75)	(0.77)		(1.20)	(1.21)	(1.05)	(1.11)	
Interaction Terms		P_u x M_u	P_u x I_u	P_u x SF_u	P_u x SP_u	P_u x N_u	P_u x K_u	M_u x I_u	M_u x SF_u	M_u x SP_u	M_u x N_u	M_u x K_u
		−.0003†	−.009	.003	−.0008	.000008*	−.0002	.001	.006	−.001	.000005*	−.0001†
		(2.32)	(0.96)	(0.3)	(0.06)	(1.83)	(1.30)	(.020)	(0.85)	(0.20)	(2.18)	(1.99)
R^2	.23	.23	.20	.20	.19	.17	.21	.19	.18	.18	.20	.22
$\bar{R}^2$	.12	.14	.11	.10	.09	.06	.11	.09	.09	.07	.10	.13
F	2.03	2.45	2.10	2.00	1.91	1.91	2.19	1.88	1.85	1.74	2.06	2.38

* Significant at .06 to .10 level.

† Significant at .02 to .05 level.

‡ Significant at or below .01 level.

Definition of independent variables:

P_u = the percentage of all employees in union u's primary jurisdiction that were covered by collective bargaining agreements in 1972.

M_u = the percentage of union u's membership in its primary jurisdiction.

I_u = a dummy variable that takes the value of 1 if the international executive board of union u is district-based, and zero otherwise.

SF_u = a dummy variable that takes the value of 1 if union u's constitution provides that members of the executive board will be full-time employees of the union, and zero otherwise.

SP_u = a dummy variable that takes the value of 1 if the full-time status of union u's board members is under the control of the president of the union, and zero otherwise.

N_u = the change in employment in union u's jurisdiction.

K_u = the percentage of union u's collective bargaining agreements that contain union or agency shop provisions.

STRUCTURE OF THE LABOR MOVEMENT*

A total of 196 organizations— 162 classified as unions and 34 as professional and state employee associations—are listed in this directory. Of the unions, 102 were AFL–CIO affiliates; 60 were unaffiliated.

THE AFL–CIO

The constitution of the American Federation of Labor and Congress of Industrial Organizations, adopted at its founding convention in 1955, established an organizational structure closely resembling that of the former AFL but vested more authority over affiliates in the new federation. The chief members of the federation continued to be national and international unions, trade and industrial departments, state and local bodies, and directly affiliated local unions (Exhibit 1).

The supreme governing body of the AFL–CIO is the biennial convention. Each union is entitled to convention representation according to the membership on which the per capita tax has been paid.[1]

Between conventions, the executive officers, assisted by the Executive Council and the General Board, direct the affairs of the AFL–CIO. In brief, the functions of the two top officers and of the two governing bodies are as follows:

Executive officers. The president, as chief executive officer, has authority to interpret the constitution between meetings of the Executive Council. He also

directs the staff of the federation. The secretary-treasurer is responsible for all financial matters.

Executive Council. The Executive Council, consisting of 33 vice presidents and the two executive officers, is the governing body between conventions. It must meet at least three times each year on request of the president. Responsibilities of the council include proposing and evaluating legislation of interest to the labor movement and safeguarding the federation from corrupt or communist influence. To achieve the latter, the council has the right to investigate any affiliate accused of wrongdoing and, upon completion of the investigation, make recommendations or give directions to the affiliate involved.

Furthermore, by a two-thirds vote, the Executive Council may suspend a union found guilty on charges of corruption or subversion. The council also is given the right to (1) conduct hearings on charges against a council member of malfeasance or maladministration and report to the convention recommending the appropiate action; (2) remove from office or refuse to seat, by two-thirds vote, any executive officer or council member found to be a member or follower of a subversive organization; (3) assist unions in organizing activities and charter new national and international unions not in jurisdictional conflict with existing ones; and (4) hear appeals in jurisdictional disputes.

General Board. This body consists of all 35 members of the Executive Council and a principal officer of each affiliated international and national union and de-

* Reprinted from U.S. Bureau of Labor Statistics, *Directory of National Unions and Employee Associations,* 1979.

[1] Nineteen cents a month.

EXHIBIT 1   STRUCTURE OF THE AFL–CIO

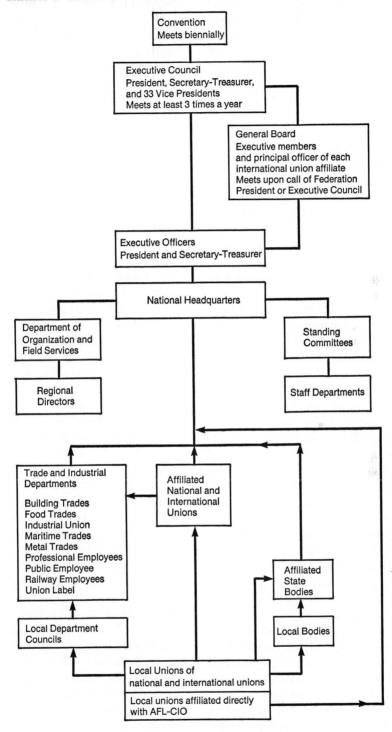

partment. The General Board acts on matters referred to it by the executive officers or the Executive Council. It meets upon call of the president. Unlike members of the Executive Council, General Board members vote as representatives of their unions; voting strength is based on per capita payments to the federation.

Standing committees and staff. The constitution authorizes the president to appoint standing committees to executive, legislative, political, educational, and other activities. These committees operate under the direction of the president and are subject to the authority of the Executive Council and the convention. Twelve standing committees are operating at present; staff departments are established as needed.

Department of Organization and Field Services. This department has the responsibility to help affiliates develop more effective organizing techniques, to provide assistance to state and local bodies, and to keep the regional directors and their staff informed of all major developments and policy decisions of the executive council. The director of the Department of Organization and Field Services is appointed by the president, subject to the approval of the Executive Council. The department has its own staff and other resources necessary to carry out its activities.

Trade and Industrial Departments. The 1979 AFL–CIO constitution provides for nine trade and industrial departments and others ". . . as may be established by the Executive Council or the Convention" (art. XI, sec. 1). Nine departments were in existence in 1979. Affiliation with departments is open to "all appropriate affiliated national and international unions and organizing committees." Affiliates are obligated to pay a department per capita tax which is determined by the number of members coming within their jurisdiction.

State and central bodies. Under the AFL–CIO constitutions, the Executive Council is authorized to establish central bodies on a city, state, or other regional basis, composed of locals of national unions, organizing committees, and directly affiliated local unions. In 1979 there were 51 state bodies, including one for Puerto Rico, and 744 local central bodies.

Organizing committees. The Executive Council has the authority to issue charters to groups not eligible for membership in national unions and to combine directly affiliated local unions into organizing committees. These committees have the same status as national unions, except that they are under control of the federation. At present, no organizing committees are in existence.

Directly affiliated local unions. When the federation was formed, local trade and federal labor unions (AFL) and local industrial unions (CIO) had a combined membership of 181,000. These local unions, having received charters from both federations, became directly affiliated local unions of the AFL–CIO; in June 1979 they claimed approximately 27,000 members. Under the constitution of the merged federation, the Executive Council of the AFL–CIO is responsible for issuing charters and controlling the affairs of these locals. The council also is under obligation at the request of the locals to combine them into national unions, organizing committees, or national councils where appropriate.

Jurisdictional problems. Former AFL and CIO affiliates joined the federation as fully autonomous unions and retained the same jurisdictional rights held before the merger. These principles are expressed as follows in article III, section 4, of the constitution: "The integrity of each . . . affiliate of this federation shall be maintained and preserved." Concepts of autonomy and jurisdictional rights are further supported in article III, section 7, which gives the Executive Council the right to issue charters to new organizations only if their jurisdiction does not conflict with that of present affiliates because "each affiliated national and international union is entitled to have its autonomy, integrity, and jurisdiction protected and preserved." With respect to craft versus industrial form of organization—the issue primarily responsible for the 1935 split—the constitution recognizes that "both craft and industrial unions are appropriate, equal, and necessary as methods of trade union organization . . ." (art. VIII, sec. 9). The constitution acknowledges the existence of overlapping jurisdictions which might invite conflict within the federation. Affiliates are urged to eliminate such problems "through the process of voluntary agreement or voluntary merger in consultation with the appropriate officials of the federation" (art. III, sec. 10).

Machinery to replace procedures previously provided for under the No-Raiding Agreement (art. III, sec. 4) was set up at the 1961 convention and incorporated into a new section of the constitution, article XXI, Settlement of Internal Disputes, effective January 1, 1962 (art. XX in the 1979 constitution). Under this article, affiliates are required to respect both the established collective bargaining and the work relationships of every other affiliate. In a dispute, the case first goes to a mediator chosen from a panel "composed of persons from within the labor movement" (art. XX, sec. 8). Should the mediator be unable to settle the dispute within 14 days, it is then referred to an impartial umpire selected from a panel "composed of prominent and respected persons . . ." (art. XX, sec. 9), for a decision which is effected five days after it has been handed down, unless an appeal has been filed. An appeal case is first referred to a subcommittee of the Executive Council, which can either dismiss it or submit it to the full Executive Council for a final decision. A variety of sanctions are provided against noncomplying unions, including loss of the right to invoke the dispute settlement machinery and possible suspension. The federation is further authorized to publicize the fact that a union has refused to comply with

a decision and that it can extend "every appropriate assistance and aid" (art. XX, sec. 15) to an aggrieved union.

A panel of impartial umpires and a panel of officers of international unions handle the mediation of internal disputes. All members of the federation's Executive Council serve on subcommittees which screen appeals and hear complaints of noncompliance.

According to the Executive Council's report to the AFL–CIO convention in 1979, a total of 1,960 cases had been filed through June 30, 1979, under the Internal Disputes Plan since its inception in 1962. Fifty-six percent (1,102) of the complaints were settled by mediation; only 27 were pending in mid-1979. Of the 831 to be decided by an impartial umpire, 826 were settled. Factfinding reports were filed in 21 cases; 5 cases were still pending in mid-1979. Only 25 decisions have not been complied with by the union and in these cases sanctions were imposed by the Executive Council. In 11 of these instances, compliance was eventually achieved.

COUNCILS

The Council of AFL–CIO Unions for Professional Employees, organized in March 1967, was granted department status in December 1977. This left the AFL–CIO without any councils for the first time since its inception in 1955.

RAILWAY LABOR EXECUTIVES' ASSOCIATION

This association is composed of the president of the Railway Employees' Department (AFL–CIO) and a major official from each of the 20 member labor unions, of which all but one are affiliated with the AFL–CIO. Nine of these unions have virtually all of their membership in the railroad industry; the remaining 11 are established principally in other industries.

The association is not a federation of

unions, but functions as a policymaking body on legislative and other matters of interest to railroad workers.

OTHER FEDERATIONS

Three organizations are listed which either act as a federation or have some characteristics of a federation, such as the issuance of charters to autonomous labor organizations and the maintenance of a formal affiliation among them. The Assembly of Governmental Employees (AGE), founded in 1952 as the National Conference of Independent Public Employee Organizations, is made up of 48 state, county, and local affiliated organizations. AGE is primarily concerned with establishing and maintaining the merit principle, although its affiliates have considerable autonomy on specific policy issues, including work stoppages. Part II lists the 27 AGE affiliates that engage in collective bargaining or representational activities. The second federation listed is the National Federation of Independent Unions (NFIU). Unions in the NFIU which negotiate agreements covering different employers in more than one state are included among the unaffiliated, or independent, unions discussed below. The third organization, the Telecommunications International Union, is an independent federation of 15 single-firm unions, each having members in only one state.

UNAFFILIATED OR INDEPENDENT UNIONS

A total of 66 national or international unions not affiliated with the AFL–CIO were known to the Bureau in 1978. All of the unaffiliated unions (other than those organizing government employees) reported agreements covering different employers in more than one state.[2] The com-

bined membership of these unions for 1978 was 4.8 million, and included members of long-established and well-known organizations such as the Brotherhood of Locomotive Engineers and the United Mine Workers of America. Approximately four fifths of the membership in unaffiliated national and international unions in 1978 were in unions once affiliated with the AFL–CIO or the former CIO. These include the United Automobile Workers[3] and expelled unions such as the International Brotherhood of Teamsters, the United Electrical Workers (UE), the Longshoremen's and Warehousemen's Union, and the Distributive Workers.

Unaffiliated local unions generally are confined to a single establishment, employer, or locality and therefore do not meet the bureau's definition of a national union used to compile this and previous directories. A 1977 Bureau of Labor Statistics survey showed about 332,000 members in 900 unaffiliated local unions. According to the bureau's finding, these local independent unions represented approximately 1.6 percent of the total 1978 union membership in the United States.

PROFESSIONAL AND STATE EMPLOYEE ASSOCIATIONS

Thirty-four associations known to be engaged in collective bargaining activities as of early 1980 are listed in part II. The membership series, which reflects 1978 data, indicates that these 34 associations had 2.6 million members.

---

[2] The requirement pertaining to collective bargaining agreements was waived for organizations of government workers. Since Executive Orders 10988

and 11491 were issued, the bureau has attempted to include federal unions holding exclusive bargaining rights. Organizations representing postal employees have been included. Some unaffiliated unions, interstate in scope, may have been omitted because of a lack of information about their existence or scope.

[3] Editors' note: The UAW reaffiliated with the AFL–CIO in 1981.

CHAPTER 6

Determinants of Unionization

Despite the importance of unions in the United States, researchers know surprisingly little about why workers voluntarily join unions. Many employees are required to join a union when they take a job with an employer that has signed a collective bargaining agreement containing a union security clause. In the typical case under a union shop provision, the employee must become a member of the union within a specified period of time (usually 30–60 days) or face termination. The problem for the researcher in this situation is that the decision to accept a job and the decision to join a union are, in essence, the same.

Where there is a collective agreement but no union security clause, employees may be covered by the agreement but not be members of the union. Some union security clauses, called *agency shop provisions*, provide that employees who do not wish to become "full" members of the union must pay the union a fee that is equal to dues. Therefore, these employees are paying for the representation services provided by the union without incurring the other obligations of union membership (such as compliance with the union's constitution and bylaws).

The only situation in which a researcher can observe an employee making a choice for or against union membership is when the employee votes for or against union representation in a National Labor Relations Board representation election. Even in this situation, an examination of why workers vote for or against a union is complicated by the fact that the election also occurs in the context of a campaign by both the employer and the union. The nature and impact of the election campaign must therefore be analyzed to determine the role it plays in the outcome of the election.

The readings in this section present several different ways of looking at the process of unionization and the decision to join a union. The paper by Roomkin and Juris provides insight into the extent to which economic and policy considerations affect the "win" rate for unions in NLRB elections. Two organization level views are presented by Farber and Saks and by Hamner and Smith. Farber and Saks look at individual voting behavior in 29 NLRB representation elections. Hamner and Smith ask a different question: What is the probability of union activity in units of an organization? Finally, Schrank takes a broader view and looks at the relationship between unionization and the nature of work.

UNIONS IN THE TRADITIONAL SECTORS: THE MID-LIFE PASSAGE OF THE LABOR MOVEMENT

Myron Roomkin and Hervey A. Juris*

If the modern era in industrial unionism began with the Wagner Act, the labor movement is over 40. Individuals turning 40 are said to evaluate their life goals and potential against their achievements, usually with depressing results.[1] Anthropomorphically, the modern labor movement at 40, especially in the so-called traditional sectors of railroads, construction, manufacturing, and mining, must face the same reality. The purpose of this paper is to document and discuss the status and near-term prospects of the manufacturing and construction sectors as they traverse this "Mid-Life Passage." Mining and railroads also have long been heavily unionized; but the product market position of these sectors, their centrality to economic activity, and the relative influence of unions in these two sectors began eroding many years ago. The actual or even potential erosion of union strength or influence is a relatively recent phenomenon in the manufacturing and construction sectors, the focus of our discussion.

* Professors of Industrial Relations, Graduate School of Management, Northwestern University. Reprinted from *Proceedings of the 31st Annual Meeting of the Industrial Relations Research Association*, August 29–31, 1978, Chicago, Ill., pp. 212–22.

[1] We have obviously borrowed the concept of life passage from the popular *Passages, Predictable Crises in Adult Life*, by Gail Sheehy.

MEMBERSHIP STATISTICS

For all of their limitations, the data on union membership unambiguously document an ebb in the percent of the work force affiliated with construction and manufacturing unions. As Table 1 shows, 1976 manufacturing union membership as a percent of total employment and of production worker employment (commonly called the union penetration rate) were at their lowest point over the 20-year period for which data are available (with the exception of 1966 for production workers). Even allowing for the fact that 1974 and 1976 were recession years, the decline in penetration is still evident. A similar trend, but at a less impressive rate of decay, is found in construction as documented in Table 2.

Much of this decline has been traced to product market or labor market shifts among organized businesses: companies have folded; plants have closed and either relocated abroad or shifted to the less organized South and West. Sometimes these organized firms have simply lost business to nonunion firms. This is especially true in the construction industry where the rise of nonunion firms in contract construction is widely known anecdotally, but has yet to be documented.

Declining membership has also been due to interindustry shifts in employment. Where manufacturing employment has

TABLE 1   REPORTED UNION MEMBERSHIP AND EMPLOYMENT IN
MANUFACTURING, 1956–76

YEAR	(1) UNION MEMBERS (000s)	(2) TOTAL EMPLOYMENT (000s)	(3) PRODUCTION WORKERS (000s)	(4) (1) AS PERCENT OF (2)	(5) (1) AS PERCENT OF (3)
1956	8,839	17,243	13,436	51.3	65.8
1958	8,359	15,945	11,997	52.4	69.7
1960	8,591	16,696	12,586	51.5	68.3
1962	8,050	16,853	12,488	47.8	64.5
1964	8,342	17,274	12,781	48.3	65.3
1966	8,769	19,214	14,297	45.6	61.3
1968	9,218	19,781	14,514	46.6	63.5
1970	9,173	19,349	14,020	47.4	65.4
1972	8,920	19,090	13,957	46.7	63.9
1974	9,144	20,016	14,607	45.7	62.6
1976	8,413	18,956	13,625	44.6	62.1

SOURCES: BLS *Bulletin* 1865, Tables 39 and 41 and *Handbook of Labor Statistics, 1975,*
as presented in Albert Rees, "The Size of Union Membership in Manufacturing in the 1980s,"
Conference.

grown it has been in newer high-technology industries not as easily organized as the older, heavy manufacturing industries. Particularly, we are referring to products such as computers, technical and scientific instruments, and some petrochemical products.

A third factor influencing membership statistics in manufacturing is the change in the occupational mix. Even though employment is growing, it is growing among the less easily organized white-collar segment. Consequently, union security clauses, which historically contributed to growth in union membership as production worker employment expanded, are decreasing in importance. These clauses were probably a major factor in the union growth in Table 1 during the years of the Vietnam war.

Finally, as discussed below, another factor leading to declining membership is the practice of employers'—even organized employers'—operating their new plants without unions. In construction, this has manifested itself in an open-shop move-

TABLE 2   REPORTED UNION MEMBERSHIP AND EMPLOYMENT IN CONTRACT
CONSTRUCTION, 1956–74

YEAR	(1) UNION MEMBERS (000s)	(2) TOTAL EMPLOYMENT (000s)	(3) PRODUCTION WORKERS (000s)	(4) (1) AS PERCENT OF (2)	(5) (1) AS PERCENT OF (3)
1956	2,123	2,999	2,613	70.8	81.2
1958	2,324	2,778	2,384	83.7	97.5
1960	2,271	2,885	2,459	78.7	92.4
1962	2,417	2,902	2,462	83.3	98.2
1964	2,323	3,050	2,597	76.2	89.4
1966	—	3,275	2,784	—	—
1968	2,541	3,306	2,786	76.9	91.2
1970	2,576	3,536	2,951	72.8	87.3
1972	2,752	3,831	3,166	71.8	86.9
1974	—	3,985	3,257	—	—

SOURCE: *Handbook of Labor Statistics, 1975.*

TABLE 3   VICTORY RATE AND UNIT SIZE IN MANUFACTURING AND CONSTRUCTION INDUSTRY CLOSED REPRESENTATION ELECTIONS, FISCAL YEARS 1956–76

FISCAL YEAR	PERCENT OF ALL CLOSED ELECTIONS		UNION VICTORY RATE*			ESTIMATED UNIT SIZE† IN MANUFACTURING		ESTIMATED UNIT SIZE† IN CONSTRUCTION	
	MANU-FACTUR-ING	CON-STRUC-TION	ALL	MANU-FACTUR-ING	CON-STRUC-TION	ALL ELEC-TIONS	UNION VIC-TORIES	ALL ELEC-TIONS	UNION VIC-TORIES
1956	69.9	0.1	65.3%	66.6%	82.6%	114.8	—	106.8	—
1957	69.4	1.2	62.2	61.4	69.1	108.9	—	51.3	—
1958	69.4	1.6	60.8	68.5	59.5	96.2	—	39.6	—
1959	64.1	2.1	62.8	63.0	86.6	94.9	—	77.2	—
1960	61.8	1.9	58.6	58.5	72.1	94.5	—	51.3	—
1961	58.8	2.4	56.1	57.0	63.4	81.7	—	31.0	—
1962	59.7	1.8	58.5	58.3	70.4	93.3	—	39.2	—
1963	58.2	1.9	78.4	57.0	54.6	72.8	—	47.1	—
1964	59.4	2.3	57.1	55.9	68.2	94.8	85.0	32.7	29.2
1965	58.5	2.7	60.2	61.0	67.3	95.3	96.8	47.9	46.7
1966	57.6	2.7	60.8	59.2	78.9	95.7	89.3	36.6	37.7
1967	55.1	2.7	59.0	57.3	67.7	108.4	95.7	33.0	32.1
1968	53.6	2.4	57.2	55.8	61.6	100.4	89.7	57.9	59.6
1969	55.5	2.4	54.6	53.1	51.6	106.4	99.5	34.2	34.3
1970	54.6	2.7	55.2	54.2	57.7	97.6	85.1	27.0	28.2
1971	51.7	2.2	53.2	51.7	65.4	90.7	73.6	36.2	35.7
1972	49.7	2.6	53.6	52.4	68.6	89.6	84.4	37.5	34.5
1973	49.5	2.3	51.1	49.5	54.5	79.8	65.2	34.3	41.3
1974	48.1	3.0	50.0	47.9	51.0	88.9	64.7	22.0	19.2
1975	43.6	2.4	48.2	46.2	46.9	91.0	61.4	36.3	27.1
1976	43.7	2.6	48.1	45.9	47.8	71.4	50.9	42.8	24.9

SOURCE: NLRB, *Annual Reports for Fiscal Years 1956–1976.*

* The victory rate is 100 times the number of closed elections won divided by the number of closed elections conducted.

† Estimated unit size is the average number of voters eligible to vote in the election.

ment in which it is alleged that unionized firms have created nonunion firms to compete with themselves—a practice called "double-breasting."

As the nonunionized segment gained in employment, the labor movement has found it increasingly difficult to organize the unorganized, even in these bedrock sectors. Table 3 shows that the union victory rate in manufacturing and construction representation elections has, with mild fluctuations, moved steadily downward since 1956. The decline in construction seems to have been steeper than in manufacturing. Exhibit 3 also shows that for the period [July] 1964 to [June] 1976, the average unit size of union representation victories is smaller than that of all elections held in these industries. Even

though the unit size as conventionally calculated is not a perfect proxy for new organizing (i.e., certifications and craft severance elections are included), it is patently clear that shrinking union membership in these sectors is strongly associated with failure at the polls, especially in the larger units.

THE SOURCES OF DECLINE

QUANTITATIVE

Despite 20 years of research, the causes of membership decline are still hotly debated between the followers of the saturationist school first advocated by Daniel Bell and the proponents of the historical school as enunciated by Irving Bernstein.

Saturationists believe that membership is a predictable function of known structural qualities in the economy; the historical school emphasizes the unpredictable character of union organizing. Reviewing the recent econometric literature, we find the following broad support for the saturationist position:

1. Union membership grows in periods of rising prices.

2. Unionization increases as employment levels increase.

3. Unionization increases as the unemployment rate increases.

4. Political climate may contribute to the growth of unions.

5. Some structural qualities of work and workers influence the propensity to organize.

6. It is not clear that public policy factors make a separate contribution to union growth or decline.

. . . As a further test of the determinants of union growth and as an opportunity to better explore the role of public policy, [we estimated a regression equation designed to predict the percentage of elections won by unions].

The dependent variable . . . is the percentage of union representation elections won by the union in a quarter. The independent economic variables are: . . . the percentage change in the index of industrial production in [the previous quarter], . . . the percentage change in real average hourly wages [in the previous quarter], adjusted for interindustry employment shifts; . . . the unemployment rate in [the previous quarter]; . . . the percentage change in the consumer price index in [the previous quarter]; and [a variable that captures the independent effect of the passage of time]. The following are considered policy factors: . . . [whether or not] the NLRB was politically dominated by democratic appointees [in the previous quar-

ter]; . . . [whether or not the election occurred] after the Landrum-Griffin Act 1959; . . . [whether or not the election occurred] after the AFL–CIO merger; . . . [whether or not the election occurred] after the 1961 order giving the regions of the NLRB authority over elections; and . . . the median number of days between the filing of an election petition and the conduct of an election [in the previous quarter]. . . .

[The results indicate that] the Landrum-Griffin Act, which made changes in the recognitional picketing rights of unions and focused public attention on administrative problems of unions, seems to have reduced the union success rate. Periods in which the board's majority is Democratic have a lower victory rate than periods in which Republican appointees control the board. This counterintuitive finding probably stems from the fact that unions do more organizing under Democratic regimes, thereby tackling units proportionately more difficult to organize. The negative [result for] . . . delay shows us why the labor movement was so desirous of speedier elections under the labor law reform bill [1977–78].[2] Only a part of election delay is attributable to NLRB administrative processes; the rest comes from the parties themselves. Clearly employers prefer lengthy campaigns which place a burden on the union to hold together a majority.

QUALITATIVE FACTORS

Econometric evidence is consistent with the "saturationist hypothesis," that is, that union win rates are influenced by identifiable (i.e., quantitative or struc-

---

[2 Among other things, this bill would have speeded up the NLRB's handling of unit determination cases and elections and would have increased the penalties on employers and unions that were found to have violated the National Labor Relations Act.]

tural) parameters and that lower win rates stem from the existence of unfavorable structural conditions. These studies do not, however, explain all of the recent interperiod variance in organizing. Qualitative factors must also be considered.

First, there has been increased management resistance to unionization in manufacturing and construction. Partially we may be witnessing the more visible resistance of the most antiunion employers now the focus of organizing campaigns in already heavily unionized sectors. This wave of resistance is consistent with the long-standing preference and ideology of American business to operate nonunion. In this regard, the bitter debate over labor law reform showed how little consensus we enjoy among labor and management on national labor policies. Management, for all the positive aspects of collective bargaining over the last 40 years and all the discussion of accommodation, still prefers philosophically to operate nonunion. They believe that they are entrepreneurs, and as the risk takers they want to retain control of the business.

Over these 40 years management has also become more sophisticated in understanding why workers organize and more aggressive within the framework of the law in getting their side of the story across to the employees. While it is true that in the past management has known why workers organize and has made attempts to eliminate the causes of labor unrest, these were usually ad hoc approaches. Today many managements continually monitor performance of first-line supervisors, wage levels in the community, and worker feelings in order to maintain a level of grievances below the critical mass necessary for the union to achieve a victory. Management knows what research has only recently documented, "a high relative wage lowers the probability that a worker will vote in favor of the union."

Second, the changing nature of the work force has slowed down union organizing. Women, the better educated, and younger workers have long been more difficult to organize.

Third, the rapid expansion in job rights through legislation has made it more difficult to organize workers. Simply put, the historical fear of the AFL against government involvement in employee relations was correct: public policy gives employees a free ride in areas where the union was the sole provider of benefits. Furthermore, this expansion in such programs as Equal Opportunity, Occupational Safety and Health, and pension plan security (ERISA), has contributed to employer resistance in two ways. Regulatory programs contribute to operating costs and curtail managerial discretion, underscoring the desirability of remaining nonunion and increasing the level of management sophistication in personnel practices, possibly alerting the small employer to this function for the first time.

REVERSING THE TREND?

Notwithstanding all the econometric evidence to the contrary, the historical school may yet prove a valid explanation of long-term developments in union membership. In the tradition of the historical school, Milton Derber points up that trade union membership has always spurted upward in economically or socially atypical periods: depression, war, or hyperinflation. By their nature, such events are highly unpredictable, as are such noncatastrophic developments capable of increasing union size as the growth of a new labor-intensive industry.

Should unionism in manufacturing reverse its downward decline, it will have to do so by organizing the white-collar and young professional workers, two groups representing a growing share of total manufacturing employment. In appealing to these workers, unions may be aided by two economic developments. First, there will be a labor market glut of highly educated persons age 25–44 over the next few years, reaching 50 percent of the labor force by 1990. The consequences, as Weber[3] has noted, will be more competition for available jobs and promotions, slower career growth, lower rates of increase in wages, and increased wage pressure from those 18 to 25. Second, we believe that employers have come to treat white-collar workers as variable costs. Whereas in earlier recessions, white-collar workers were inventoried and blue-collar workers laid off, more recent experience suggests that white-collar workers are no longer buffered from the vicissitudes of the business cycle. Taken together, these two forces could create the classic concerns of job insecurity and job consciousness among white-collar workers.

Some people believe that organizing would increase were the old-guard labor leaders replaced by a new breed. We disagree. Even in the 1920s, the failure of the labor movement to attract mass-production workers was due to the inherent nonappeal of the AFL to such workers, not a lack of organizing effort. The fact is union leaders follow membership preferences more than they shape them. By implication, in construction, because of the localized labor market and potential for job competition, rank-and-file unrest will be more likely to push leaders into aggressive organizing than in manufacturing where the rank and file are less likely to immediately see the connection between an unorganized jurisdiction and unemployment.

It has also been suggested that the goals of labor might change to meet the "new" needs of today's worker. Lodge and Henderson[4] have presented the most elaborate statement of this new ideology in their report for the Trilateral Commission. We, however, believe with Dunlop[5] and others that, despite a few notable and experimental approaches to industrial relations, the goals of the worker will remain very much what they have always been—economic welfare and job security.

IMPLICATIONS

Since bargaining power is still strongly related to [the extent of organization] and since [organization] is declining, we expect to see significant changes in the industrial relations systems in manufacturing and construction. Construction unions, for example, have been quite receptive to open as well as disguised wage reductions and productivity improvement programs. Manufacturing unions—if steel and automobiles are any indication—are moving toward the isolation of the internal labor market from outside forces, a process management seems willing to accept as long as newer plants can be made more productive. In short, the power relationship of labor and management in manufacturing and construction is finding a new level. We as observers should not lose perspective as this process works itself out.

The major point we would make is that the growth of unions is not a right chiseled in stone. The union as an institution evolved bacause individual workers needed a counterbalance to real and perceived mistreatment at the hands of management in the employment relationship. To the extent that management has cleaned up its act or workers perceive that management is behaving differently, workers may feel there is no need for this kind of protection. In a democratic society, unions are necessary, but they are not necessary to any given employment relation-

[3] Arnold R. Weber, "Casual Approach to Labor Supply May Haunt Business," *Wall Street Journal*, January 30, 1978, p. 12.

[4] George C. Lodge and Karen Henderson, "Changing Relationships among Labor, Business, and Government in U.S.," Working Paper prepared for Trilateral Commission, October 1977.

[5] John T. Dunlop, "Past and Future Tendencies in American Labor Organizations," *Daedalus*, 107, (Winter 1978), pp. 76–96.

ship unless the employees deem them necessary. Thus, we ought to be concerned that nothing in public policy undermines the potential for workers to form unions, if so motivated. Moreover, we should keep firmly in mind that what we are discussing here are the traditional sectors in which unions once thrived. For the trade union movement as a whole, looking across all sectors of the economy, the picture is not as gloomy. There are enough managers in the public sector and in the hospital and health services sector who are sufficiently less sophisticated than some of their manufacturing and construction counterparts to provide work for organizers far into the future.

In summary, if as amateur community social workers we could put the manufacturing and construction unions on the couch, we would say, "Face reality; adjust to your new environment and cope!"

6-2

WHY WORKERS WANT UNIONS: THE ROLE OF RELATIVE WAGES AND JOB CHARACTERISTICS

Henry S. Farber and Daniel H. Saks*

Why is it that some workers want unions to represent them and other workers do not? This question is basic to our understanding of union growth and behavior, and it is especially interesting in an era when private sector unionism in the United States has not been expanding.

Workers can join unions in a number of ways: for example, by electing a union to represent them at their current workplace; by joining an existing union in an open shop; and by taking jobs in a union shop. Unfortunately, the decision about the union is generally complicated by other potentially confounding decisions such as whether to be a "free rider" in an open shop and (for a new job) whether to participate in the "tied sale" of taking a job and joining a union.

* * * * *

Our study uses a unique set of voting and other data on 817 workers who participated in 29 union representation elections supervised by the National Labor Relations Board (NLRB) during the early 1970s. These data are used to estimate a model where workers vote for or against union representation depending on which alternative maximizes their expected utility from both the wage and the nonwage dimensions of their employment. Such data have three considerable advantages: First,

---

* Professors, Massachusetts Institute of Technology and Michigan State University. Reprinted from *Journal of Political Economy*, 88, no. 21 (1980), pp. 349–69 by permission of the University of Chicago Press. © 1980 by The University of Chicago.

since the workers voting are already employed, the union representation decision can be observed directly and is isolated from the employment decision. Second, there are data on enough workers in particular firms so that for the first time one can test hypotheses about the effect of relative intrafirm wages on a worker's desire for having union representation. Third, unlike the frequent analyses of union-status questions for individual workers, the worker's evaluation of the relative costs and benefits of the union is current and does not reflect the decision of someone who may have joined a union some years before under different circumstances.

In the next section a theoretical framework is developed which determines the individual decision to vote for a union in an NLRB representation election. This decision is hypothesized to be a function of current worker satisfaction with wage and nonwage aspects of a job in comparison with expectations about how a union would change these job aspects. . . . It is hypothesized that the impact of unionization on the wage of any individual, and hence on his or her likelihood of voting for union representation, is inversely related to the position of that individual in the . . . earnings distribution [within the firm]. . . .

I. A MODEL OF VOTE DETERMINATION

We are trying to understand the decision process of workers in a particular job who must choose whether or not they prefer their job to become a union job, that is, whether or not they would prefer that job to be covered by a collective bargaining agreement. If the expected utility from their job becoming a union job is higher than from it not becoming a union job, then they will vote for the union. Otherwise they will vote against the union. There are several important dimensions of

such a model: (1) the probabilities of holding various alternative jobs in the future; (2) [the preferences of the worker for] wage and job characteristics; and (3) tastes regarding unions which may vary systematically across subsets of the working population because of differences in background or differences in perceptions about what unions would do for particular subgroups. . . .

. . . The institutional literature . . . has concentrated on the standardization of rates of pay under collective bargaining agreements and the implicit reduction in the variance of intrafirm earnings associated with such a policy. . . . Where unions raise the average wage and impose a system of standard rates which tends to reduce the dispersion of earnings, . . . [w]orkers at the bottom will gain the largest wage advantage from unionization, and workers at the top will gain the least. Thus a worker's location within the firm's wage distribution is likely to be an important determinant of attitudes toward unionization.

The other major dimension of union behavior is modification of job characteristics, especially perceived arbitrariness on the part of supervisors. Collective bargaining imposes a "web of rules" on industrial relations. Slichter et al.'s[1] (1960) survey of collective bargaining agreements suggests the range of application of these rules: hiring, seniority, promotion, work scheduling, work assignment, etc. The issue is perhaps best illustrated by their discussion of disciplinary procedures.

Few areas of personnel policy have been more significantly affected by collective bargaining than management's administration of employee discipline. The origin of a union in many enterprises can be traced to a belief on the part of employees that the company

---

[1] Sumner Slichter, James J. Healy, and E. Robert Livernash, *The Impact of Collective Bargaining on Management* (Washington, D.C.: The Brookings Institution, 1960).

had been arbitrary, discriminatory, or capricious in meting out discipline. There have been foremen who acted like little czars in administering discipline and companies that imposed the most extremely personal rules upon employees. . . . Even where there was little evidence of such irresponsible behavior on the part of management, the union seeking to organize employees often impressed upon employees the protection offered by collective bargaining against unfair disciplinary treatment.

. . . Now obviously not everyone will benefit from the substitution of bureaucratic rules for personal rule. Only those who perceive that the current system operated against their interests and believe that a union will enforce what is to them a fairer system of industrial relations will favor a union. . . .

The difference between the utilities derived from the current job if it should become unionized and if it should remain nonunion . . . is a function of workers' expectations concerning the impact of unionization both on their wages and on the nonwage aspects of employment. It may also vary systematically with demographic characteristics which reflect differences in tastes for, or attitudes toward, unionization as well as systematic differences in the costs or benefits of unionization. [In order to estimate the model, we first constructed a variable which measures the position of the individual worker in the wage distribution of the firm. The expectation was that the worse off this individual was relative to fellow workers, other things equal, the more likely that person would be to vote in favor of a union.]

If individuals currently maintain a good relationship with their supervisors and if they feel that unions (in general) interfere with such good relationships, then they would have reason to feel that unionization of their current jobs would make them worse off. [Accordingly, we included

a variable which measured whether or not the worker expected] unionization to cause this sort of *relationship deterioration*. . . .

The second nonwage impact of unions is on fairness of treatment by supervisors. If individuals feel that supervisors in their company play favorites and if they feel that unions (in general) ensure fair treatment, then they would have reason to feel that unionization of their jobs would make them better off. [Therefore, we included a variable which measures whether or not the] individual . . . expects unionization to cause this sort of *improvement in fairness*. . . .

The final nonwage aspect of employment which is considered is the effect of unionization on the chances for advancement within the firm. Unions often make promotions within the nonsupervisory work force largely a function of seniority. This may work to the disadvantage of ambitious employees who feel that they will be promoted on their merits. [Included in the analysis was a variable which measures whether or not the individual] feels that there is a good chance that he or she will be promoted. . . . To the extent that unions actually reduce *promotion possibilities* for workers who expect promotions, . . . [such workers will be less likely, other things equal, to vote in favor of a union].

Demographic characteristics which may be systematically related to the vote and which are included are age, sex, race, education, and the urbanity of the environment where the individual was raised. The latter characteristic refers to whether the individual was raised in a large city, a small city, a suburb, or a rural area. [Finally, included were variables that took into account the individual's belief as to the difficulty of finding another job and the individual's dissatisfaction with the job security of his or her present job.]

II. THE DATA

The data were collected by J. G. Getman, S. B. Goldberg, and J. B. Herman for a study of unlawful campaigning and NLRB election outcomes.[2] The sample consists of a random selection of workers who participated in NLRB representation elections in 29 establishments between January 1972 and September 1973. Eighteen of the establishments, including 85.2 percent of the workers in the sample, were in manufacturing. . . . The rest were in transportation, wholesale trade, retail trade, and services. All of the plants were located in Illinois, Indiana, Iowa, Missouri, and Kentucky. The International Brotherhood of Teamsters participated in 10 of the 31 elections studied by Getman, Goldberg, and Herman. No other union participated in more than three elections.

The 29 elections involved 2,788 workers of whom 1,018 were interviewed both before the election to get basic information on characteristics and attitudes and after the election to determine how they voted. Individuals were deleted from the sample if they failed (or refused) to answer any of the questions relevant to this study. This resulted in a reduction in the sample to 817 individuals. . . .

The unions won eight of the 29 elections and lost 21. Of the 2,788 votes cast in the elections, 1,276 (45.8 percent) were cast for the union. This is compared to 385 (47.1 percent) pro-union votes from the 817 individuals in the sample used. . . .

There are a number of related factors

which restrict the sample to a rather special subgroup of the American labor force. The firms from which the workers were sampled are unusual. On the one hand, unless there was sufficient worker interest in having a union, no election would be held. On the other hand, if the preferences of the workers for union membership were clear enough then an employer might have agreed to bargain with a particular union without an election. Another factor is that firms which are already unionized (except in the rare case of a decertification drive) will not be represented among firms holding elections. In addition, the sample of firms was restricted because as Getman, Goldberg, and Herman explicitly state (p. 34), "the primary consideration in selecting elections was the likelihood of vigorous, possible unlawful campaigning."

Another problem is that the choice in the election is not actually of unionization versus nonunionization but of being represented by a *particular* union versus nonunionization. While unions are assumed to be homogeneous in this study, it may be true that an individual would join one union but not another. For example, if a particular union were thought to be corrupt then workers might prefer another union or even nonunion status to membership in the corrupt union. It is also true that different unions might have different effects on the job.

Despite these problems, the sample affords a unique opportunity to observe individuals explicitly stating their preference for union representation. On balance, it is likely that the effects of the selectivity biases are minor and that the results will be applicable to a wider class of workers than that contained in the sample.

III. RESULTS

. . . [The Appendix contains the results.] There are a number of striking implica-

---

[2] The authors wish to thank Julius G. Getman, Stephen B. Goldberg, and Jeanne B. Herman for making their data available. These data have been collected under grants from the National Science Foundation and the Russell Sage Foundation. See J. G. Getman, S. B. Goldberg, and J. B. Herman, *Union Representation Elections: Law and Reality* (New York: Russell Sage Foundation, 1976), for a detailed description of the construction of the sample and the data collection procedures.

tions of [these] results. . . . First, a worker's location within the earnings distribution of the potential bargaining unit played an important role in determining the vote. Second, the nonwage aspects of employment and unionization . . . had the hypothesized impact on the vote. Third, the individual characteristics . . . with the exception of race and age, seemed to have little relation to the vote. Fourth, tenure seemed to have no relationship with the vote. Finally, individuals who felt that it would be difficult to replace their current job had a greater (or lesser) probability of voting for the union as they were dissatisfied (or not dissatisfied) with their current job security. Each of the implications is discussed in turn.

EARNINGS AND UNIONIZATION

Unions generally raise the mean and lower the dispersion of the wage distribution within firms. As a result, it was hypothesized that workers at the lower end of the intrafirm earnings distribution would expect a larger increase in earnings from unionization and hence would be more likely to vote for the union than workers at the upper end of the earnings distribution. This hypothesis is supported by the result[s]. . . .

* * * * *

NONWAGE ASPECTS OF EMPLOYMENT AND UNIONIZATION

The three variables representing the effect of unionization on the nonwage aspects of employment . . . all had the hypothesized significant impact on the vote. If individuals felt that unionization would cause a deterioration of the currently satisfactory supervisory relationships . . . then they would be less likely to vote for unionization. If individuals felt that they were being treated unfairly and that unioniza-

tion could help this . . . then they would be more likely to vote for unionization. Finally, if individuals felt that the chances for promotion were good . . . then they would be less likely to vote for the union. This is interesting because it supports the view that ambitious workers who expect to get ahead find unions to be an inhibiting factor to their progress.

INDIVIDUAL CHARACTERISTICS AND THE VOTE

After controlling for the measurable aspects of union impact on wage and nonwage aspects of job satisfaction, there is little systematic relationship between preferences for union membership and individual characteristics. Sex, education, and the environment where raised do not have a significant impact on the vote, while race and age do affect the vote.

It has been suggested that women have traditionally been less likely to join unions because they were generally not permanently attached to the primary labor force. The fact that the women in the sample are all full-time employees implies that they do not fit that stereotypical mold. Further support for this contention is provided by the fact that [there is no relationship] between the sex [variable] and the . . . seniority variable. . . . Thus, women are no more likely to be low-seniority workers than men. For these reasons the lack of significance of the sex [variable] is not surprising. In fact it is probably true that females are more likely to vote for unions than males are, just because females are more likely to be located in the bottom part of the intrafirm earnings distributions. . . .

Blacks are significantly more likely to vote for union representation than nonblacks even after controlling for the measurable aspects of union impact on jobs. This suggests that blacks perceive that unions will provide more benefits to them than to similarly situated whites. One possibility is that blacks gain more than whites from the imposition of the quasi-legal framework for handling grievances that often accompanies unionization. Such a framework may be valuable in protecting blacks from certain aspects of discrimination on the job.

It was also found that older workers are significantly less likely to vote for union representation after controlling for the same factors. The latter result is in accord with views that older workers are more "conservative" and reluctant to join new organizations which will have an uncertain impact on their jobs.

SENIORITY AND THE PROBABILITY OF JOB RETENTION

Job seniority entered the model in a very specific way. It was hypothesized to affect the probability of retaining the job if the union won the election. . . . This probability in turn was used to weight any potential gains from unionization. It was found that seniority has little effect. . . . The . . . low-tenure . . . variables have signs opposite to what was expected, but they are not significantly different from zero.

JOB SECURITY AND THE VOTE

It was hypothesized that individuals who felt it would be difficult to replace their current job with an equivalent job might have mixed feelings about unionization. If they were dissatisfied with their current job security, then they might feel that the union would help and they would be more prone to vote for unionization. On the other hand, workers who in general expect that it would be difficult to replace their current job might worry that unionization would jeopardize their current job.

Both of these hypotheses receive some support from the results. . . . Taking the base group to be all individuals who do *not* feel that it would be difficult to replace their current jobs, those who feel that it would be difficult to replace their jobs and are not dissatisfied with their job security are significantly less likely to vote for unionization. . . . This suggests that these workers worry that unionization will jeopardize their jobs. Compared to the latter group, those who are both dissatisfied with security and would find it difficult to replace their jobs are significantly more likely to vote for unionization. . . . This suggests that fear of jeopardizing the current job is moderated by dissatisfaction with current job security. This may be due either to the fact that there is less security to jeopardize or to some expected help from unionization. Compared to the base group, the group of workers who would find it difficult to replace their jobs and who are dissatisfied with job security are more likely to vote for unionization. . . .

However, this is significantly greater than zero only at the 10 percent level. The major implication of these results is that fear of loss of a valued job is a significant factor in individual attitudes toward unionization.

IV. SUMMARY AND CONCLUSIONS

In this study a model of the determination of individual votes in NLRB representation elections based on the maximization of expected utility was developed. The model was estimated using data on how individuals voted in 29 elections.

There are four major implications of the results. First, individuals vote as if the effect of unionization on earnings is to raise average earnings and lower its dispersion. The conclusion is that the perceived earnings advantage of unionization is inversely related to the individual's position in the intrafirm earnings distribution.

Second, the explicitly measured individual perceptions of the impact of unionization on the nonmonetary aspects of the job are important determinants of the vote. The job dimensions considered include fairness of treatment by supervisors, general relationships with supervisors, and the likelihood of promotion.

Third, it was found that concern for the impact of unionization on job security is an important aspect of the unionization decision when workers felt that they could not easily replace the current job with an equivalent job.

Finally, it was found that after controlling for the effects of unionization on various aspects of the employment relationship, individual characteristics such as sex, education, and the environment where

raised have little relationship with the vote. The exceptions to this are race and age. Blacks were significantly more likely to vote for unionization, while older workers had a significantly lower probability of voting for unionization.

In conclusion, the data used in this study allowed us to estimate the parameters of a model of the rational worker who considers the major dimensions of unionization stressed in the institutional literature in making decisions about whether he or she wants to be represented by a union. Such a model seems to do quite well and offers a promising direction for future research on issues of union growth and behavior.

APPENDIX

TABLE 1   MAXIMUM LIKELIHOOD ESTIMATES OF PARAMETERS OF Z_i (Eq. [9])

COEFFICIENT OF:	SYMBOL	COEFFICIENT	ASYMPTOTIC STANDARD ERRORS
T_1 (SEN < 1)	α_1	.133	.205
T_2 (1 < SEN < 3)	α_2	.106	.226
Constant	γ_0	.0549	.214
DEV	γ_1	−.161	.049
$\dfrac{1}{\sigma_j}$	λ	−.207	.273
RDET	γ_2	−.607	.125
FIMP	γ_3	.747	.132
PRO	γ_4	−.453	.113
DIFF	γ_5	−.373	.115
DIFF * DS	γ_6	.594	.150
RACE (black = 1)	δ_1	.360	.150
SEX (female = 1)	δ_2	.0799	.109
ED_{HS}	δ_3	−.126	.114
ED_{COLL}	δ_4	−.0557	.154
SUB	δ_5	.204	.216
$CITY_{10-100k}$	δ_6	.190	.154
RURAL	δ_7	.120	.137
AGE_{25-44}	δ_8	−.154	.119
$AGE_{>44}$	δ_9	−.336	.150

Note.—Log likelihood = −416.53.

WORK ATTITUDES AS PREDICTORS OF UNIONIZATION ACTIVITY

W. Clay Hamner and Frank J. Smith*

This article attempts to extend our empirical knowledge of unionization efforts to see if the information gained from an attitude survey would have predicted the level of union activity that followed. Our general prediction is that attitudes expressing dissatisfaction with the work environment are good predictors of union activity. The prediction is based on the generally accepted assumption that when a unionization attempt is made, a work force that feels a high degree of dissatisfaction will be more likely to seek union representation than a work force that feels less dissatisfied.

The present study . . . examine[s] the attitudes toward work of employees in 250 naturally occurring settings prior to any history of unionization activity. Subsequently, unionization attempts were made in 125 of these settings. A predictive model of unionization activity based on the attitudes of these employees toward work was derived and [used] . . . to test our prediction.

METHOD

SAMPLE

In order to develop and test a predictive model of unionization, we looked at the attitudes and union activity of both a developmental sample and a cross-validation sample. The developmental sample consisted of 61,429 salaried employees from 188 units throughout the United States. In 94 of these units, some unionization activity had taken place shortly after the attitude survey had been administered. Data from a matched sample of employees from units in which no unionization activity had taken place were selected as a means of controlling for possible confounding factors. The two groups of units were matched on size and labor market similarities. . . .

The employees in these units performed a mixture of clerical, sales, and technical functions. All job levels below that of the managerial staff were involved in the study. However, only those units or subunits directly involved in the unionization activity or its matched equivalent were included in the data analysis. Examples of the types of subunits included are shipping and receiving, service, drivers, commissional sales, all nonsupervisory employees, and so forth. . . . The sample sizes within each unit ranged from 31 to 1,620, with an average size consisting of 325 employees.

The cross-validation sample consisted of 26,312 salaried employees from 62 units. Thirty-one units had a previous history of unionization activity, and 31 units had no such history. Again, the units were matched on labor market similarities and unit size as described above.

* Duke University and Sears, Roebuck and Company, Chicago. Reprinted from *Journal of Applied Psychology* 63, no. 4 (1978), pp. 415–21. Copyright 1978 by the American Psychological Association. Reprinted/adapted by permission of the publisher and author.

MEASURES

The attitude measures used were part of a larger organizational survey carried out among all members of the employees in these 250 units of a major corporation. In this study we examined 42 items from this larger survey that measured various aspects of work satisfaction. . . .

The eight scales derived from the 42 items included Supervision, Kind of Work, Amount of Work, Career Future, Security, Financial Reward, Physical Surroundings, and Company Identification. . . .

The level or severity of union contact ranged from 0 to 6 as follows:

0 = no union activity (125 total; 94 in the original sample and 31 in the cross-validation sample).

1 = hand billing of unit, which did not always involve any employee activity (33 total; 26 in the original sample and 7 in the cross-validation sample).

2 = card signing. Employees take affirmative action on behalf of union by signing authorization cards. (26 total; 20 in the original sample and 6 in the cross-validation sample).

3 = union meetings. Enough employees had signed authorization cards or expressed sympathy for the union to make it worthwhile for union to hold meetings to plan and initiate a serious organization attempt. (24 total; 18 in the original sample and 6 in the cross-validation sample).

4 = representation petition filed by union. At least 30 percent of the employees in the requested bargaining unit had signed authorization cards and a petition had been filed with the National Labor Relations Board. (20 total; 16 in the original samples and 4 in the cross-validation sample).

5 = union elections held and won by company. (10 total; 6 in the original sample and 4 in the cross-validation sample).

6 = union election held and won by the union. (12 total; 8 in the original sample and 4 in the cross-validation sample).

The severity of union contact at each level represents the highest degree of union activity, in most cases, all of the preceding degrees of severity of contact preceded in that unit.

PROCEDURE

The attitudinal data were collected 3–15 months prior to any unionization attempt as part of a triannual survey program. Data from the matched units were collected within 12 months of each other. The attitudinal data for the original 188-unit developmental sample were collected between 1971 and 1975. In 94 of these units some degree of unionization activity had taken place within 15 months after the survey was administered. In 94 of these units, no unionization activity had taken place through 1977. . . .

RESULTS

*   *   *   *   *

The unionization model contained items dealing with supervision . . . , co-workers . . . , career future . . . , company identification . . . , amount of work . . . , physical surroundings . . . , and kind of work. . . . It is interesting to note that 3 [of the items dealing with supervision and leadership, i]n combination, . . . explained a significant amount of variance in the model. . . . Overall, we could expect to explain approximately 30 percent of the variance in the level of unionization activity by examining the responses to these 13 attitude items.

*   *   *   *   *

In all cases, the units with no unionization activity were more satisfied than the units with unionization activity. . . . [T]his gives support to the power of these prior known attitudes in predicting the severity of future unionization attempts.

DISCUSSION

Whereas the situation studied was fortuitous in nature, it did present an opportunity to study unionization behavior that is normally not available for study, especially with more than one potential bargaining unit. Within the limitations of this setting, it does appear that job-related attitude items that measure the degree of dissatisfaction employees have with their work setting can predict the degree of success a union will have in gaining the support of a majority of a potential bargaining unit. . . .

The findings in this study give additional support to the findings of Getman, Goldberg, and Herman (1976), which showed that employees who were dissatisfied with working conditions were more likely to vote for union representation. Their findings also showed that those satisfied with working conditions supported the company in a union election.

The present results indicate that this organization had sufficient information from the triannual attitude survey to predict the relative degree of future union activity. Whereas attitude data are often collected by companies as means of determining areas of satisfaction and dis-

satisfaction among employees, rarely are those data used to predict job performance or future union activities. One reason that attitude surveys are seldom used by management to indicate needed action is that once unionization activities start, it is almost impossible to collect attitudinal information for fear of being charged with an unfair labor practice. Second, it is rare to find a real world setting with numerous criterion data points from which the validity of attitudes as predictors can be ascertained. The fortuitous nature of the setting was such that we could test the relationship of attitudes toward the working setting against future unionization activity levels in multiple work units. Additionally, attitudes of employees in this organization were ascertained on a scheduled basis, without regard to union activities.

These results not only show how attitudes can predict performance, but they also give support to the notion that attitude surveys could be used in a practical manner to allow management to make changes in the organizational setting that would reduce the perceived dissatisfaction with work. When these changes are not forthcoming, one would assume that the success of unionization would certainly be increased. Future research, measuring whether or not there is a reduction in unionization activity caused by changes in work practices resulting from attitude research, would be a logical next step to pursue.

APPENDIX

TABLE 1   SUMMARY OF THE CORRELATIONS, REGRESSION ANALYSIS, AND THE CROSS-VALIDATION ANALYSIS FOR THE RELATIONSHIP OF THE ITEMS FORMING THE ATTITUDE TOWARD WORK SCALE TO UNIONIZATION ACTIVITY

ITEM	INTERCORRELATIONS*													
	1	2	3	4	5	6	7	8	9	10	11	12	13	R†
1. The people who supervise me have (bad/good traits)	—	.43	.52	.93	.75	.72	.36	.61	.02	.22	.87	.59	.40	.24
2. The example my fellow employees set (greatly discourages greatly encourages me)		—	.78	.46	.57	.54	.57	.69	.23	.35	.62	.48	.67	.28
3. The way my future with the company looks to me now (hard work is worthless/very worthwhile)			—	.57	.67	.70	.61	.58	.47	.49	.72	.51	.79	.33
4. Do you ever have the feeling you would be better off working under different supervision? (almost always/never)				—	.77	.74	.40	.60	.14	.36	.90	.58	.50	.37
5. How does working for company influence your overall attitude toward your job? (very unfavorable/very favorable)					—	.61	.49	.75	.04	.24	.77	.60	.44	.39
6. How do you feel about the amount of work you are expected to do? (very dissatisfied/very satisfied)						—	.49	.46	.36	.37	.78	.14	.60	.42
7. How do your physical working conditions influence your overall attitude toward your job? (very unfavorable/very favorable)							—	.45	.14	.30	.50	.86	.49	.44
8. Work like mine (discourages/encourages me to do my best)								—	.07	.18	.65	.53	.40	.46
9. How does the amount of work you're expected to do influence your overall attitude toward your job? (very unfavorable/very favorable)									—	.00	.23	.00	.56	.49
10. In this department there is (a great deal of friction/no friction)										—	.70	.16	.70	.49
11. How does the way you are treated by those who supervise you influence your overall attitude toward the job? (very unfavorable/very favorable influence)											—	.51	.70	.51
12. For the work I do, my physical working conditions are (very poor/very good)												—	.35	.53
13. The supervision I receive is the kind that (greatly discourages me/greatly encourages me)													—	.55

Note. $n = 188 =$ units for the regression analysis. The sample consisted of 61,428 employees in these 188 units. $n = 62$ units in the cross-validation analysis. The sample consisted of 26,312 employees in these 62 units. Item scores range from 1 (bad) to 5 (good). Cross-validation r for 13-item regression model $= .42$, $p < .001$.

* $r > .18$, $p < .05$.

† Regression cumulative.

ARE UNIONS AN ANACHRONISM?

Robert Schrank*

Though at times it makes sense to be skeptical about forecasts—of the weather, the economy, politics, or the impact of technological change—some trends, if carefully observed, can give us a sense of where we are headed. In the case of the future of the labor movement, the changes in the labor market over the past 50 years and their impact on organized labor give some clues about how society will organize itself to get its work done.

Some of my evidence about the changes in the labor market grows out of my own 45 years of more or less steady employment—in factories, on construction work, and as a machinist, white collar worker, manager, administrator, teacher, and author. In the 1930s and 1940s, I spent some of the best years of my life in the labor movement, as an organizer and union official. They were years of crusading against what we in the unions thought were the worst kinds of industrial exploitation. Nothing compares to the euphoria of a crusade, and we had our share of it. And nothing motivates more powerfully than a crusade. The crusaders marched to "Solidarity Forever":

> *When the union inspiration*
> *Through the workers'*
> *Blood shall run*
> *There will be no power*
> *Any greater*
> *Anywhere beneath the sun. . . .*

* Project Specialist, Ford Foundation. Reprinted by permission of the *Harvard Business Review*. "Are Unions an Anachronism?" by Robert Schrank (September/October 1979). Copyright © 1979 by the President and Fellows of Harvard College; all rights reserved.

The unionizing crusades of the 1930s and 1940s succeeded in organizing the major basic industries—steel, auto, and rubber. Years of bitter strife between unions and employers followed, then years of slow but sure accommodation. The epitome of the adjustment was the joint union-employer committee in the steel industry that agreed on increases, which were then jointly passed along to the consumers. The interests of the union and the employers gradually merged.

The labor movement slowly but surely has lost its crusading spirit. Today the major "inspiration" running in labor's blood may be new ways to invest the pension funds. Although a few members of the United Automobile Workers still sing "Solidarity Forever," the major problems for the UAW, in solidarity with GM, Ford, and Chrysler, are what to do about the energy crisis, foreign imports, and government antipollution requirements.

I do not mean to criticize, merely to mark the end of an era. The crusade has accomplished its mission, the movement phase is over. It is no mean achievement that the major objectives of those organizing years have been met and some of the worst evils of the industrial workplace eradicated. It was an honor to participate in that good work, and I feel great about it.

But one has to stop now and wonder about the future of the labor movement. What great causes are left, what will its new song be? As with many other institutions, the labor movement is suffering from two serious problems that tend to reinforce each other. The first has to do with maturity that leads to bureaucratic arteriosclerosis. The second is the traumatic change in the labor market. I see the second problem as the more serious because it affects the raison d'être of the labor movement itself.

In this article, I want to look at those changes affecting labor—the end of the industrial era, the rise of the humane manager, the increase in technological development—and their impact on the unions. But first I want to look, for a moment, at the conditions the unions sprang from—their culture, spirit, crusade, and emotional appeal. Their origins were great and moved many of us.

DARK SATANIC MILLS

Although we call it a revolution, we seldom think of the industrialization of a country as a violent act. Yet the very term *revolution* certainly implies violence, and, in its violence against workers, industrialization was indeed a revolution. Before industrialization, the invention of the steam engine, and the factory, cottage industries, and the agrarian life employed most workers. Without in any way glorifying the agrarian, preindustrial cottage industry life in England, which was no bed of roses, I want to comment on one aspect of it that might seem romantic.

People had far greater control of their own work time. Enjoying advantages comparable to some modern-day professionals, farmers and field workers could decide when and how intensely to work. If "boozin' it up" at the Cheshire Pub was going great on Sunday, a farmer could sleep it off on Monday and Tuesday, then resume and continue work through the next Saturday and Sunday. One might call this an early application of flexitime.[1]

The evidence seems to be quite strong that people did not give up that life for the factory with any great enthusiasm. They had to be evangelized and taught that hard work would guarantee them a place in heaven. Along with St. Paul's and Calvin's religious efforts to inspire a work ethic, many other social forces conspired to drive people into the factories. The point is they did not go willingly. The enclosure acts in Great Britain toward the end of the 18th century, the erosion of guild sanctity with the hiring of cheap unskilled labor, and the increasing competition to which domestic workers were subjected all helped to recruit the earliest factory populations.[2]

When the factory workers could be recruited, they did not easily take to the work. They tended to work only until they had earned enough to tide their families over for a short while. Work attendance was extremely irregular; people would sometimes stay out of work and send for their wages at the week's end. When harvest time or a traditional festival came, they simply did not show up. It was common for annual labor turnover to equal 100 percent.

In the early part of the 19th century in America, the situation was similar. Workers who were being converted from an agricultural life joined with the waves of immigrants who brought their traditional working patterns from the old world. In 1817, a shipbuilder in Medford, Massachusetts, denied his men their grog privileges, and they all quit. Among cigarmakers and cobblers, it was common for one person to read aloud from the newspapers while the others worked. In the 1860s in Lowell, Massachusetts, a new set of work rules ordered the factory gates kept locked during working hours and, to further discourage the men from leaving, they

---

[1] See E. P. Thompson, *The Making of the English Working Class* (New York: Vintage, 1966), especially Part II; and E. P. Thompson, "Time, Work-Discipline, and Industrial Capitalism," *Past and Present*, 38 (1967).

[2] See Sidney Pollard, *The Genesis of Modern Management* (Cambridge, Mass.: Harvard University Press, 1966); and Thompson, *The Making of the English Working Class*, p. 234.

were not to take off their work clothes during the day. It caused a strike. The workers won.

For America's first managers, absenteeism and labor turnover were huge problems. In the years before World War I, it was not unusual for a tenth of the work force to be absent on a given day. Between 1905 and 1917, the majority of industrial workers changed jobs at least once every three years. And one out of three stayed at his job less than a year—often only for days or weeks. In 1914, at the Armour meat-packing plant in Chicago, for example, the average daily payroll numbered about 8,000. But to keep that number, the company had to hire that many during the course of the year. Surveys of textile mills, automobile plants, steel mills, clothing shops, and machine works showed labor turnover rates at least as high as the 100 percent reported at Armour.

People worked begrudgingly in the new industrial conditions. They chafed at the physical demands, repetitiveness of the work, inhuman discipline, and frightful working conditions. In 1913, when the Ford Motor Company first introduced the assembly line, it had a staggering turnover rate of 370 percent.[3]

Given these conditions plus low wages, early 20th century managers introduced extreme measures to get people to work hard. The great symbol of these disciplinary attempts was Jeremy Bentham's panopticon—a factory built like a five-pronged star in which one overseer standing at the center could observe every single worker. Factories in Great Britain and the United States had elaborate punishment and fining systems to enforce good work behavior. Following Frederick Taylor's lead, employers dealt with workers' reluctance to perform under those conditions

by breaking work processes down into ever simpler tasks.[4] The less complicated the task, the more women, children, ex-soldiers, vagrants, paupers, prisoners, and other unskilled laborers could perform it— at extremely low wages.

In general, these conditions formed the initial context for unionism. Workers in the dark satanic mills needed to protect themselves from the harsh disciplinary actions and the continuous wage-cutting schemes of their employers. If their skills were to retain value, the workers also needed to protect the integrity of their crafts from the deskilling activities of the industrial engineers.

A major effort of the early unionism of the guilds and Knights of Labor was to maintain craft skills in the face of mechanization. It was through his skill that a craftsman maintained at least a measure of control over the work tasks. The operative or production worker, as the nonskilled employee became known, was simply an extension of the machine—either feeding, adjusting, or unloading it. Instead of the craftsman, a machine was now doing the work.

The guilds and craft unions in the United States were influenced by the political debates that whorled around the events of the industrial revolution in Europe. Karl Marx and subsequent socialists made a valiant plea for turning the industrial revolution into a socialist one, thereby putting the means of production back into the hands of the workers. Socialists and radicals generally thought that if unions could be persuaded to see their struggle as one of power and control over the means of production, they could then constitute a strong revolutionary force.

Although at times radicals and socialists played significant roles in the U.S. labor movement, it is important to understand that they were never dominant. This is a

---

[3] See Herbert Gutman, *Work, Culture, and Society in Industrializing America: Essays in American Work-Class and Social History* (New York: Knopf, 1976), especially Part I; and Daniel Rodgers, *The Work Ethic in Industrial America: 1850–1920* (Chicago: University of Chicago Press, 1978).

[4] F. W. Taylor, *The Principles of Scientific Management* (New York: Harper & Row, 1911).

significant difference between U.S. and European unions. In Europe, the politics of the left with its class-based struggle has always been strongly represented within the unions, sometimes as groups within a union or in some places as separate organizations. While U.S. unions were not dominated by radical politics, the adversary relations between employers and workers that at times took on the character of a class struggle were very much a part of union tradition. The spirit, mission, and crusade that organized workers into unions in the United States were almost always based on the feeling of "us," the workers, against "them," the bosses.

This orientation fit in or was congruent with an American cultural myth growing out of our frontier heritage—"us," the cowboy good guys, against "them," the Indian bad guys. The workers were in "such a wonderful fight" against a clear-cut, easily identifiable enemy—the robber barons, the bosses, the owners, and their "lackeys." Although one can see that fight as a class struggle, it lacked the socialist or radical class consciousness of European workers that led to a far more political trade unionism. The political class consciousness of European unions has led to broader organizing capability than the more narrowly defined business unionism of the U.S. labor movement.

Though there are these significant differences between the U.S. and European labor movements, both have their roots in and are organically linked to the industrial revolution, the nature of industrial working conditions, and the problems involved in the intensification of production in industry. As the postindustrial era grows in Europe, the European unions will also find themselves deeply concerned over their future role.

In the United States, the economic consciousness of the worker, the cowboys-and-Indians tradition, and the frontier mentality created a trade unionism that was militant in organizing industry and

establishing an adversary position in that work setting, but it never went beyond that. The Samuel Gompers political strategy of "rewarding your friends and punishing your enemies" that continues to dominate the AFL–CIO is yet another expression of the frontier tradition applied to politics.

With some exceptions, the labor movement remains pretty much in that mold. The aging leadership of the AFL–CIO is simply a reflection of this tradition. An endless stream of articles has complained about George Meany, his aged coworkers, and their detriment to the "movement." But, continuing the cowboys-and-Indians analogy, Meany, back at the AFL–CIO ranch, *is* John Wayne, tall in his saddle. He's doing what the movement has always done. Only the objective circumstances have changed and made, if I may use the analogy again, the cowboy-and-Indian wars obsolete. The Indians are busy litigating land rights while the cowboys ride jeeps and helicopters to round up the herd. The frontier of "Stagecoach" has disappeared. What the labor movement needs now is a Woody Allen—not a John Wayne.

CHANGES IN THE LABOR MARKET

Because we are living in the postindustrial era, future problems for the unions are rooted in the radically changed labor market. Three dimensions of change have altered the context in which the unions operate. The first of these concerns the nature of management. The second involves the rapidity of technological development. The third centers on the startling occupational shift toward the service sector—or the arrival of postindustrial society.

AUTHORITY AT THE WORKPLACE

The structure of company ownership and the style of management during the past 50 years have changed so radically that it is now far more difficult to identify "the boss'' or the owner of the company. Is it a Carnegie, Grace, Morgan, 10,000 stockholders, or some conglomerate? Or, put another way, who benefits from the employees' labor? When I was a machinist, it did not take a complex analysis to figure out who was benefiting from my labor. Yet how many corporations are there today where the owner can be identified? Very few indeed. With its recent stock split it will be hard to tell IBM from the Bell Telephone Company. Employees no longer know who the bad guys are, but, more important, they are not sure if there are any.

In recent years, the fastest growing occupational category has been the government employee. But who owns government organizations? The taxpayers? As large corporate or nonprofit service sector workplaces define more and more of the labor market, the diffusion of ownership drastically alters the fundamental assumptions of labor relations. Who is the bad guy when a public union or hospital workers go on strike? Who is the bad guy in a giant corporation?

The success of Taylorism—scientific management—is now history. It was another profound defeat for the surviving skilled worker whose power lay in restricting detailed knowledge of a craft to those practicing it. Management made itself privy to guild secrets and took control of the work process through the rationalization and fragmentation of skills.

Taylorism, however, had another possibly more insidious effect. It introduced the impersonal authority of science into the labor process. Tasks and job assignments are now ''scientifically'' analyzed. Personnel departments, aptitude tests, and efficiency experts came into being. This was the first step in the process of obscuring authority in the workplace. Now it is not only unclear who owns the company, but also only a sophisticated analysis can unravel all the ways company and government procedures actually operate.

Another change in the nature of management, the wave of reforms known under the general heading of *human relations* management, has also contributed to the confusion of authority at the workplace. Under this rubric I include the developments that emerged from the experiments of Kurt Lewin and Elton Mayo, the participative management models of Douglas McGregor, the psychological development paradigms of Abraham Maslow and Carl Rogers, and to some extent the more recent programs of quality of work life innovators.

By educating managers in the techniques of leadership, employee motivation, effective communication, and worker morale, the human relations movement created a breed of managers with different attitudes from their predecessors who worked under the iron heel of the old robber barons and their lackeys. Managers do not have the same personal interest in exploiting people that owners did. Of course, a successful manager may get a promotion or a bonus, yet that is not the same as extracting greater wealth from the products of others' physical labor.

Humanistic management introduces a sense of cooperation into the workplace. It may be sincere or sometimes manipulative, but in either case it softens the adversary *feeling* at the workplace. With U.S. industry in a competitive battle with foreign manufacturers—and in many instances losing—employees find themselves as concerned as the managers over the very survival of the company. Taking for granted the idea that the corporation needs to make a profit to survive, employees find it difficult to know who the enemy is or in fact if there is one. If there is no enemy, or as Walt Kelly suggested in *Pogo*, ''it is us,'' then unions need a new and different role to play at the workplace.

TECHNOLOGICAL CHANGE

The second set of changes in the labor context has to do with the incredible pace of technological development. When I reflect on my own lifetime, I am boggled by the invention and diffusion of so many new things that we now just take for granted—to name a few, indoor plumbing, the refrigerator, the automobile and its highways, radios as common as paper clips, the airplane and the jetliner, television, computers, microcircuitry, solid-state circuitry, and space travel. When I was a child, these things were at best fantasies on the covers of *Popular Science* or *Popular Mechanics*. But they came into being so rapidly as a common part of our everyday lives that one doesn't tend to assimilate or question their full implications.

Technological change has undermined labor's traditional position in the manufacturing sector in two ways. First, as I have already indicated, it helped rob most workers of their special skill that was once their most important strength. When I was a machinist, the lathe I operated was an extension of my skills. This is no longer true. Today the same equipment can be numerically controlled by a computer that duplicates my skills by doing its own quality control and making corrections accordingly. The skill, as well as the job, has been automated. In the case of dirty, dumb, or dangerous work, automation may be a blessing. But as an old machinist who still cherishes his oak tool box with its many neat little drawers, I would consider it an insult to babysit a computer just in case a light should go out.

Second, as the advance of technology becomes more rapid, so does the pace at which industrial work becomes unskilled. The unskilled or semi-skill workers who follow in the wake of technological change do not have the same kind of bargaining power that their skilled fathers did. People can easily be trained on the job to do what is required to perform the industrial work that remains on the production floor. The technicians, computer programmers, and systems analysts who are replacing the craftsmen come out of a managerial mold that has no kinship to the cowboys-and-Indians trade unionism of the 1930s and 1940s.

The change in work technology has created a new kind of worker. Think of the industrial era as a time when men and women sweated over machines that became an extension of the body. The worker's physical self was involved in the work. Although the thumb and index finger that push a pencil are still parts of the body, they are indeed very small parts. In the postindustrial time, work has become more cerebral and abstract. The operator of a numerically controlled machine tool is the computer; the work is done by a computer programmer.

Because one cannot be physically exploited or overworked at a desk in the same way one could be at a blacksmith's anvil, the issues of exploitation or overwork become fuzzy and increasingly vague in today's workplace. Sweat running down one's face or an aching back caused by handling castings all day served as constant reminders that one was "worked" and that someone else was not working. Since the computerization or automation of manufacturing has made so much work abstract, so it has made the awareness of work classes—bosses and workers—more abstract. Also the worker himself or herself is more educated. The educated worker with the abstract job doesn't have a "High Noon" orientation; it is more likely "High Society."

A full-scale flight from blue-collar work is in progress. Increased education and a continuing denigration of manual work have raised people's gazes from the factory gate to the offices above. Some people may conceive of offices as white-collar factories, but I would warn the reader against minimizing the difference in status of the attaché case from that of the tin lunch bucket. The attaché case may still carry lunch or Alka-Seltzer, but it is an important symbol of having made it out of the factory.

THE SERVICE ECONOMY

The third dimension of change, and probably the strongest blow to the traditional adversary orientation of the labor movement, is the occupational shift from manufacturing to the service sector. Between 1900 and 1979, the white-collar sector has increased from 26 percent to 63 percent of the work force, while manual or blue-collar work has declined from 36 percent to 33 percent. The most dramatic decline in manual work has been in farming, where the work force went from 37 percent in 1900 to 3 percent in 1979. The data show that the bulk of society's employed people are now, and will increasingly be, involved in the service or non-manufacturing sector of the labor market.

Eli Ginzberg has pointed out that in 1977, 22.3 million professionals and managers constituted 25.6 percent of the labor force compared with 13.8 million in 1958. This means that since 1958 the number of professionals has increased by 97 percent and that of managers by 42 percent.[5] In 1947, manufacturing unions represented 41 percent of the total work force. In 1977, unions, still predominately in manufacturing, represented only 29 percent of the total work force.

One line of argument says that this shift toward the service sector is not all that significant since many service sector jobs are blue collar or manual. By a strict definition of the work tasks that may be correct, but in terms of the work environment the comparison does not hold. Blue-collar service workers do not work against the clock, and in many cases, such as IBM or Xerox machine service personnel, they appear as white-collar workers, attaché case and all.

What effect then do the explosion of the service sector and the decline of manu-

facturing have on unions and management? In order to answer that question, I will make a rough comparison of working conditions in the service sector to the manufacturing workplace where unions traditionally functioned. Even though not all workplaces in the service sector are the same, I believe it is possible to make some broad generalizations.

The major characteristic of work in the service sector is its abstract nature. It involves knowledge, or organization and communication of information, or an exchange of competence. Much of the work of the service sector is based on exchanges among people, or between people and paper, or between people and computers. The physical exertion—the use of the body and the fatigue that is part and parcel of traditional industrial work—is just not present.

When work is abstract, how does one determine what productivity is and, in turn, ways to intensify production? It may be possible to count how many insurance claims are processed daily, but how is productivity measured in a hospital, museum, advertising agency, corporate offices, retail sales, and, finally, in government—the fastest growing employer of them all? Wherever there is no discrete material product, productivity becomes a fuzzy concept. Managers wrestle daily with the problems of motivating white collar employees to higher productivity. Sometimes they try to turn the office into a factory, but the abstract nature of the work makes quality control impossible to ensure.

The white-collar worker deals with symbols—words, numbers, and formulas. How these symbols are produced determines the outcome of the work. The actual work is a mental activity. In contrast, a punch press, not the thought process of the operator, determines the shape of the metal it punches. Managers who understand this phenomenon have responded by giving these workers far greater control over their own work.

---

[5] Eli Ginzberg, "The Professionalization of the U.S. Labor Force," *Scientific American*, March 1979, p. 49.

I have suggested that a function of the union was to protect workers against the employer's extreme efforts to increase production at the workers' expense. Although office and service people may experience their managers' efforts to make them work harder as onerous, the experience is usually not enough to warrant their seeking protection against it. At the other extreme, in some workplaces such as the public sector, employees seem to have experienced no effort to increase productivity at all. In any event, in most postindustrial workplaces, it is unclear what "working harder" would in fact consist of.

The demarcation of class lines in service sector workplaces is never as clear as it was in the old factory. If the centers of power in a large manufacturing corporation are hard to identify, they are equally, if not more, hidden in service corporations.

In one department of a major New York bank, each employee has his or her own little cubby with a computer terminal. Everyone in the department feels important and has a sense of control vis-à-vis his or her terminal. Though power relationships throughout the organization seem vague at the point of control—that is, the terminal—it is quite clear who has power. In banks, insurance offices, or corporate headquarters such as this, everyone can dress nicely and have at least some modicum of freedom to move about. More often than not, the space will be nicely decorated, softly lit, and have piped-in music.

The impulse for traditional industrial unionization grew out of a raw kind of exploitation. In the postindustrial workplace atmosphere, union issues are far more subtle and conceptual (like the work itself) than the traditional labor movement is able to address or encompass. One simply cannot compare the physical discomfort one experiences sitting at a computer console with the overwhelming fatigue that comes from putting front wheels on a Chevy for eight hours. Also service em-

ployees do not turn out a defined product under pressure, such as 90 Vegas an hour. The nature of control these employees have is correspondingly diffuse, subtle, and unclear.

Issues of security, pay, and benefits arise in the service sector, but not the adversary life-or-death issues that the foundry or a Lawrence textile mill created. The new workplaces have managers, not bosses, who use feedback and support, not commands or wage reductions, as a way to achieve ends.

CAN THE UNIONS SURVIVE?

What does all this mean for the future of unions and management? The trends I have discussed are likely to become more evident and pervasive. We will continue to see automation eliminate many of the worst manual jobs. (By increasing its cost, Cesar Chavez may do more than any other factor to replace stoop labor in California with automatic picking machines.) Managers are not likely to turn back into bosses, and, for certain, the service sector is going to continue to expand. The question is, then, can the unions survive in a high technology, humane service economy?

Given that some traditional union issues, such as pay, security, and promotions, still exist in these workplaces, why haven't service workers responded more enthusiastically to union organizing efforts? Many of these workers think union members are tough, hard-hat manual laborers or auto workers picketing and singing "Solidarity Forever." This is not the image with which the white-collar service sector employee wants to identify. Many of them are the children of blue-collar workers who, with the full support of their parents, have run away from manual work. Modeling themselves after the white-collar class, this generation of employees prefers—or insists on—professional or managerial work.

In treating the work force as professionals, managers have muffled or completely diffused conflict around traditional issues. Prudential, Polaroid, or IBM not only have good pay and benefits often comparable to unionized companies but also pay attention to amenities like beautiful cafeterias, quiet workplaces, exercise rooms, and lounges—all of which mitigate the conflicts that once made unions so attractive.

Many of the newer electronics industries, such as IBM or Texas Instruments, have no unions. Managements in these companies have learned to make concessions to employees and to provide a pleasant work environment, creating conditions that do not lock them into an adversary relationship. The unions so far have been ineffective in the postindustrial era.

Many teachers and public workers unions representing the postindustrial world have struggled to carve out a place for themselves in the labor movement. But since the AFL–CIO remains under the pervasive influence of the unions, which are rooted deep in industrial soil, the service union grafts aren't taking, and the tree is dying.

With the exception of public workers the unionized sector of today's labor market (20 percent) tends to represent the old manufacturing industries. And although hospital staff and people who hold some of the worst jobs in the service sector have had some success in organizing, little unionizing progress has really occurred since the 1960s. Postindustrial-era employees—for example, the interns in New York City hospitals—organize only when threatened with unemployment. If job security in the service sector becomes threatened on any large scale, unionization could explode, but that does not form an optimistic platform on which to build the future of unions.

Similarly, if workers' demands are met by automatic cost-of-living increases every six months or year, what becomes of the traditional collective bargaining process? The labor movement will be faced with a dim future if it bases its activities primarily on past traditions. As the labor market continues to change, unions will represent an ever-declining part of the labor force.

If, as I have argued, postindustrial work is abstract and unionization is based primarily on the product manufacturing system, what, if any, is the role for unions in this new era? The picture is not altogether negative, since the postindustrial workplace does contain some areas where unions could be active.

One of the contradictions of postindustrial organizations is that while work tasks and products are totally new, the organization chart is a relic of the old industrial era. Though the new breed of managers does not adhere strictly to the old pyramidal structure or extreme division of labor, most organizations are formally designed that way and reflect implicit relationships of power and authority. Also, although they are far more subtle than they were, real issues relating to salaries, benefits, professional development, and autonomy arise in these workplaces as well.

Unions have resisted becoming involved in these issues on the ground that management manages and the union grieves, but if unions are to have a presence and impact in the postindustrial workplace, they need to begin to be involved in rethinking the concepts of management's prerogative and of how abstract work gets done. Union leaders need to appreciate the profoundly changed nature of work itself and the implications of that fact for the future of the labor movement.

For managers the postindustrial era can be seen as an opportunity to try out new behavior and new ways to solve problems. The new employee with higher educational credentials and expectations wants to be trusted, would like more responsibility, and does not want to be treated as a subordinate. Motivating this kind of employee to produce will require a managerial openness and a willingness to share authority.

But the benefits to both management and the unions of this approach can be enormous. At General Motors' Tarrytown plant joint union and management groups solved problems that neither could or were willing to solve on their own. If unions drop their traditional stance, then management must also.

For over a decade postindustrial workplace problems have been constantly, sometimes imperceptibly, growing. One example that I cite only for its typicality is a serious morale problem at AT&T over—guess what—worker discontent.[6]

---

[6] For a fuller discussion see "The Dissatisfaction at AT&T" *Business Week*, June 25, 1979, p. 91.

Twenty-five years ago the notion of worker discontent at AT&T would have been inconceivable. Now surprise at such a report is inconceivable.

What a challenge for both management and the union (the Communication Workers of America) to come up with new approaches to deal with the new discontents that are not related to wages, hours, or benefits but to the nitty-gritty of how the company gets its daily work done.

The company managers could see this problem as a real opportunity to test out new work arrangements based on extensive review of the problems, carried out with employee participation. And the union officials' new role would require thinking about how the union can more effectively represent the new worker.

Management as a Bargaining Organization

In the last two chapters we examined unions as institutions with unique organizational characteristics and goals. We now turn our attention to the special organizational characteristics that management brings to the bargaining relationship. These characteristics shape, in part, the bargaining structure and power that has an impact on both the process and outcomes of bargaining. Because of the requirement to bargain collectively, management must adapt to the bargaining process and as a result the process and its outcomes alter management practices and policies. To understand management as a bargaining organization, we must examine its constituencies, its structure for dealing with industrial relations, and its goals.

MANAGEMENT CONSTITUENCIES AND POLITICS

Neil Chamberlain and James Kuhn, in their overview of the politics of management, identify a number of competing interests that management must satisfy.[1] These interests include: (1) stockholders—management's first obligation remains directed towards its profit-making ability; (2) employees; (3) subgroups within management by function (e.g., finance, marketing, production, and public relations) and level (e.g., shop-level supervisors and middle level managers); and (4) other interlocking business groups which affect management's decisions (e.g., financial institutions, major customers, and suppliers).

The existence of competing interest groups means there are separate and overlapping political pressures on management, and its decision making must reflect this diversity of interest. These competing obligations have implications for the process of bargaining. To address each, management must build internal structures and processes that establish bargaining priorities based on reconciling the demands of its various constituencies. If these internal bargaining processes fail, management may have unclear

---

[1] Neil Chamberlain and James W. Kuhn, *Collective Bargaining* (New York: McGraw-Hill, 1967), pp. 210–32.

collective bargaining goals and/or a very irrational set of bargaining policies. Either way, its bargaining strength may be limited as unions make the most of its uncertain actions and lack of solidarity.

While it is not clear how the political nature of management affects the collective bargaining in any given relationship, the reader must note that the existence of competing political pressures is an important consideration in assessing management's policies and goals in industrial relations generally, and collective bargaining specifically.

MANAGEMENT STRUCTURE FOR INDUSTRIAL RELATIONS

The importance of the industrial relations function to the overall functioning of management and the need for internal consensus building has led to the development of organizational structures within management devoted specifically to the labor relations and collective bargaining functions. The first article in this chapter by Slichter, Healy, and Livernash outlines generally how management reorganizes in order to deal with unions and how such changes affect its policies and decision-making functions. While a given organization may vary in terms of its level and sophistication, general trends with regard to corporate organization for labor relations exist. The first Freedman article outlines these trends.

MANAGEMENT GOALS

Management goals concerning the industrial relations function are of two principal types: (1) goals concerning management's philosophy towards unions in general and (2) goals concerning management's objectives in actual negotiations. With regard to the former, management must decide whether remaining nonunion is an overriding concern. The Foulkes papers deal with the importance of this goal by analyzing management's motivation for remaining nonunion and by assessing the advantages and disadvantages of being nonunion. The second Freedman article deals with how management determines its targets/goals in bargaining. Freedman's analysis is based on a 1978 survey of 668 private-sector unionized firms concerning their labor relations practices.

7-1

ISSUES FOR MANAGEMENT IN INDUSTRIAL RELATIONS

Sumner Slichter, James J. Healy*, and Robert Livernash

DECISIONS INFLUENCING MANAGEMENT POLICIES TOWARD UNIONS AND COLLECTIVE BARGAINING

When employees want to deal with management through a union, the most fundamental question is how far management should be guided by definite policies. Every enterprise believes its actions to be guided by well-considered policies, whereas actually many policies are empty slogans that merely give the appearance of policy-guided action.

The conclusion that, in general, actions of management should be governed by policies does not exclude the possibility of some deliberate opportunism or experiment. Management is constantly being confronted with new and unusual situations, in which the wise choice may be to drift or to experiment. But there is a sharp contrast between drifting or experimenting for the purpose of developing policies, and opportunism that represents a failure to appreciate the need for policies. It is the latter sort of opportunism that has proved costly in many companies.

A second basic policy question is "How important are industrial relations policies relative to other policies?" Some managements never face up squarely to this ques-

* Professor, Harvard University. Reprinted from Sumner Slichter, James J. Healy, and Robert Livernash, *The Impact of Collective Bargaining on Management* (Washington, D.C.: The Brookings Institution, 1960), pp. 9–26. Copyright © 1960 by The Brookings Institution, Washington, D.C.

tion, and yet if the short-run interests of the business owners in sales and profits are balanced against their long-run interests in low production costs, there must also be a good balance between the interest of the enterprise in quick and uninterrupted deliveries to customers and its interest in efficient operating methods. In a few industries, market considerations or the strong technological position of the company make costs of production of secondary importance. In many other industries, costs of production are of less *immediate* importance than are uninterrupted deliveries to customers. But in most industries, success depends in the long run on costs being competitive, and management's success in achieving competitive costs depends in large measure on industrial relations policies.

A few firms are in a position to dictate the nature of their relationship with the union; many small firms must take what conditions the union offers and get along as best they can; most firms, however, are more or less an equal match for the union, and the quality of their relationship with the union depends on the skill shown in negotiating and administering the agreement. The best goal for most firms is a stable relationship with the union on terms that permit the firm to be competitive and to adapt itself to changing conditions.

How can this goal of a stable and competitive relationship be achieved? Through the manner in which the company negotiates and administers the union-management contract. Here is where top management plays a decisive role. Top management may not conduct negotiations, and it may not participate directly in very many administrative decisions, but the kind of policies pursued in negotiation and administration are its responsibility. For example, only top management can decide that customers must wait and that large profits must be temporarily sacrificed to resist efforts by the union to saddle the company with wasteful working rules or feather-bedding practices. Unless top management takes a firm position in advance against accepting uneconomic practices, subordinate officials will tolerate them rather than assume the responsibility of failing to meet production schedules.

A good job of negotiation and administration requires that a management representative be prepared to give almost unlimited time to these matters. Most managements are more interested in making and selling goods than in discussing grievances or the terms of contracts. Union representatives, however, often have almost unlimited time for these matters. Managements that are in a hurry to get back to making goods are likely to find that their haste is very expensive—that discussions are terminated only when management makes costly concessions. Hence, managements should be prepared, if possible, to negotiate with the unions through persons who are not responsible for day-to-day production. Large companies can afford to provide special personnel; small employers may need to economize the time of operating men by being represented by an association or a lawyer.

General Motors is an example of a top management that saw clearly from the start the importance of both good agreements and good administration of agreements. General Motors saw that the rise of unions threatened the freedom of management to run the plants and that this freedom would be gradually nibbled away

unless the company was willing, if necessary, to take long and expensive strikes to protect it. Hence, top management made it clear to subordinate management and to the union that the company was prepared at any time to take strikes over certain rights or procedures that top management regarded as essential to efficient operations.[1]

Another important question for the company is, "What kind of a man shall head the industrial relations staff?" If top management is aware of the important long-run effects of industrial relations on labor costs, it will see that the staff is headed by a man of stature and resourcefulness who commands enough confidence to argue for minority points of view within management if necessary and to recommend innovations in policies. Furthermore, men of perception, ingenuity, and insight are needed to work out the best industrial relations procedures. For example, management, while doing freely what it has a right to do under the union-management contract, should rely on persuasion rather than on the assertion of rights, lest it build up in the union a demand for changes in the contract. Another example is the decision of the management of a multiplant company to shift consideration of fourth-step grievances from the central personnel office to the plant where the grievance originated with those immediately involved, the complaining workmen and the foreman, present at the hearing. The reasoning was that the participation of the people immediately involved keeps the grievance concrete and helps them to see what the union-management contract is and what it means. A rep-

---

[1] Of course, the strong position of General Motors in the industry and the fact that it deals with millions of buyers rather than with two or three large customers helps the company treat industrial relations as important relative to sales, but in the main the success of General Motors in administering its contracts stems from top management's clear perception of the long-run importance of the issues involved.

resentative of management said: "If you are going to have people accepting something, you have to bring them into the process of putting meaning into the contract."

Should multiplant companies negotiate a master contract with the union for all their plants or separate contracts for each plant? Opinions differ on this. Some companies prefer the simplicity of master contracts.[2] Others have taken long strikes rather than sign master contracts. In several cases companies have gone through long strikes in order to get rid of master contracts. Particularly if a company is in several lines of business, with different plants making different products and facing different competitive conditions, there is a strong case for separate plant contracts rather than a master contract. There is also a case for separate plant contracts when plants are in labor markets with substantially differing wage scales. The important point, however, is that management should not make the decision without careful consideration of alternatives.

PROBLEMS OF ADJUSTING TO THE PRESENCE OF THE UNION

The coming of a union is almost bound to create uncertainty in the minds of many officials and technicians as to the effect on their duties, authority, and relations with employees. These uncertainties are particularly pronounced in plants where managements use supervisors to fight the efforts of the union to organize the employees. The foremen may wonder where they stand in relation to the union they opposed. Recognition of the union may

cause the foremen to feel that top management has let them down, in spite of the fact that recognition may be required by law. And recognition of the union may be interpreted by the foremen as evidence that top management is surrendering its right to run the plant.

As a general rule, foremen make the change from opposing the union to administering the union-management contract with surprising smoothness. But there are a few cases where the transition involves difficulties. There are plants where foremen fail to assert their authority in their own departments and allow many decisions pertaining to work assignments, rates, overtime, seniority questions that foremen usually make to be made by union stewards or committeemen. To avoid confusion in the minds of foremen and other superiors, top management at the beginning of its relationship with the union should make clear what it expects of subordinate and intermediate supervisors.[3]

The need to clarify what is expected of operating officers may persist in a few cases for years after the union has been recognized. An unusually astute and reflective management described the problem as follows:

The company came out of the war with an attitude on the part of second and third line management that you can't go forward and do things as long as you have unions. This raised a matter of delicate balance. Management mustn't try to defeat the unions and throw them out, but at the same time it must stand up for what is right and must sell lower management the idea that management must not pursue a policy of appeasement. This is a problem that has to be carefully handled because a lot of resentment against the union has been built up in the first line supervision. The first line supervision has to be brought back to the feeling that the union has to be accepted

---

[2] A study of 87 multiplant companies showed that 36 had master agreements, and 51 had individual plant agreements. Among the 36 companies with master contracts, 17 were with the United Automobile Workers. 8 with the United Steelworkers, 4 with the United Rubber Workers, 4 with the International Union of Electrical Workers, and the remainder with miscellaneous unions.

[3] Sometimes there is a case for appeasement or opportunism, as was pointed out above.

but not allowed to interfere with management.

Important in adjusting to the presence of a union is to inform intermediate and front-line supervision of the company's labor policies and the terms of the union-management contract. Some top managements have given out only incomplete information on these points, sometimes through oversight, but in a few cases deliberately. In a company manufacturing wire and cable· the vice president made secret agreements with the unions, which no one was allowed to see—apparently because he did not wish it to be generally known that he had consented to a union shop.

As a general rule, top managements have found it advantageous to have all levels of supervision well informed about the company's labor policies and know the essential provisions (as distinguished from the technical details) of the union-management contract, as well as the principal changes made in the contract as a result of negotiations with the union.

* * * * *

REORGANIZING MANAGEMENT TO DEAL WITH UNION

The rapid rise of unions after 1933 led to an increase in the number of industrial staffs and growth in those already established. . . . Frequently the growth of industrial relations staffs was unplanned, and their success depended in considerable measure on personalities rather than on a carefully planned division of duties between industrial relations staffs and operating officers. If the personnel manager was strong and aggressive, he often took over a large part of the decision making in the field of industrial relations. Frequently the operating people were glad to avoid the responsibility of handling labor matters. They did not know unions or the labor law and felt ill-prepared to decide labor issues, some of which were quite

technical. With the passage of time, however, these haphazard arrangements have given way to more carefully worked out divisions of responsibility between operating staffs and industrial relations staffs.

Although the arrangements vary from company to company, personnel is usually responsible for the various employee services not directly connected with production (such as worker training, handling workmen's compensation claims, processing arbitration cases, and often conducting negotiations), and both personnel and operations participate in handling various problems connected with the administration of the union-management contract, with personnel giving advice and the operating men making the final decision. However, in a company manufacturing automotive parts, the usual relationship between the foremen and the personnel officers in discipline cases is reversed. Instead of the foreman's seeking the advice of personnel and then making the decision himself, the foreman files a complaint against the worker with a recommendation for discipline to the personnel director. Personnel investigates the case and makes a decision—subject to the approval of the plant manager. It is claimed that this system has not taken prestige away from the foremen.

PROCEDURAL POLICIES IMPLEMENTING MANAGEMENT'S BASIC LABOR POLICIES

Implementing the general labor policies of an enterprise involves questions and procedures that call for policy decisions. A few of the principal issues are: (1) how far should management go in consulting with the union; (2) how far should management go in building up the prestige of union officers and giving them responsibilites; (3) how far should management go in acting jointly with the union; (4) how far should management go in acting independently of the union; (5) what should be the policy of management on submitting interpretation of the union-management contract to outsiders; and (6) what steps should management take to keep itself informed about what is happening in the administration of the union-management contract?

CONSULTING WITH THE UNION

Some managements have concluded that it is advisable to discuss plans rather freely with union representatives. They do not bargain with the union and do not feel any obligation to discuss plans with union representatives, but do so nevertheless. Some managements have set up regular weekly or monthly meetings between the plant manager or the personnel director and the union bargaining committee. A variety of problems are discussed—production schedules, technological changes, operating problems—with each side taking the initiative in bringing up matters for discussion.

Other managements fear that the practice of communicating their plans to the union will cause the latter to claim that management is obliged to consult it on innovations. They fear that the next step will be bargaining over management's right to make innovations. But there are advantages to management in discussing its plans with union representatives. Removing uncertainties in the minds of employees is often good for management as well as for the workers. Still another obvious advantage is that discussion of management's plans and problems sometimes evokes useful suggestions, and management may be led to modify its plans. Finally, such discussion is a good way of keeping union representatives informed about market conditions and the company's problems in meeting competition.

MANAGEMENT SUPPORT OF UNION OFFICERS

Most union committeemen like to be active, and enjoy having responsibilities.

Sometimes committeemen acquire responsibilities by stirring up grievances or by encouraging the appeal of grievances from department stewards to committeemen. But this kind of activity does not promote good administration of the labor-management contract. Some managements, therefore, go out of their way to give the committeemen work to do and responsibilities. In one company committeemen run the blood bank and administer the pension plan.

A company in the electrical equipment business makes an effort to support the local union leaders that the management likes. Two leaders who wanted to cause trouble were opposed by the company, but the needs of leaders who wanted recognition and status were satisfied. The policy of building up union leaders is obviously related closely to that of discussing management's plans and problems with them. Certainly if union leaders are able to report on management's plans to their members, their prestige with the rank and file is enhanced.

JOINT UNION-MANAGEMENT ACTION

Should management seek the help of the union in promoting safety, in reducing absenteeism, in getting shop rules observed, in cutting costs, and in improving technology?

The variation in managerial practice is wide. Some managements are opposed to seeking help from the union on the ground that such action would build up the prestige of the union. On the other hand, some weak managements go to great extremes in expecting the union to help them with their problems. The decision that best meets the needs of management depends on the general policy of the company toward the union, the nature of the problem, and the relative strength of the union and the employer. If it is the policy of the management to keep down the prestige of the union representatives, their help obviously should not be asked, but if management tries to help union leaders gain prestige and status, giving them jobs to do is a way of promoting their standing.

Much depends on the kind of help that is asked. Getting the union's help in promoting safety or a cleaner shop, in obtaining applicants for an apprenticeship course, or in reducing absenteeism is quite unobjectionable. Getting the union's help on matters of discipline raises more complicated issues. There is a difference between a union's refraining from obstructing management's efforts to impose proper discipline and aiding those efforts. Unions are often willing to refrain from protesting penalties that they believe have been justly imposed. They are often willing to warn members not to expect union help if they transgress shop rules, and unions may try to stop wildcat strikes that are preventing nonstriking members of the union from working. Some unions have been effective in breaking wildcat strikes against the employment or the promotion of Negroes. But managements that are so weak that they depend on union help to maintain discipline are likely to be in chronic trouble for many reasons, and they are not likely to get enough help from the union to get their shop rules well observed.[4] A few companies have embarked on a broad plan of union-management cooperation in which the help of the union is sought in developing ways of reducing costs and improving technology. To under-

take such a program (assuming that the union is willing) involves a major policy decision.

MANAGEMENT-EMPLOYEE
COMMUNICATIONS

Some unions believe that communications between management and employees should take place solely through the union. Efforts of management to communicate directly with the employees are regarded as "going over the head" of the union or its officers and are resented.

Managements cannot afford to accept as a matter of principle that they will communicate with their people only through the union. Managements should be in direct touch with employees and should not be dependent on intermediaries. But many managements never bothered to give their workers much information about the company and its affairs until unions became important. In recent years much more abundant information has been provided to employees, particularly information concerning the income statement and balance sheet (which has little interest to most workers), but little effort has been made to find out what questions the average employee would like to have answered and to answer them. For example, only a few companies give the employees an annual report on the industrial relations of the company. Most important of all, most managements lack arrangements for learning what the employees really think.

No two companies pursue the same policies on communicating with employees, but the policy in each case should deal with certain basic issues. It should include arrangements for determining the ever-changing subjects on which communication is needed—especially communication from employees to management. For example, changes in technology or prospective changes in technology or in production schedules create a demand for informa-

---

[4] Some managements report almost unbelievable lack of discipline among their employees. For example, an eastern railroad, which has been trying to build up rapid "piggy-back" service in competition with trucks, reports chronic lack of discipline among yard men. Yard men on the late night shift deliberately stall so as to create overtime work. From 2:30 to 4:30 or 5 a.m. they play cards, sleep, drink coffee, and swap stories, with the result that what little work is needed is pushed into the rush period around 5 a.m., when the incoming trains must be handled. In addition, the yard men will not work when it is raining or snowing, although they have proper apparel.

tion. So do negotiations, though the two parties often agree that offers or counteroffers will not be divulged. The making of a new union-management contract creates a demand for explanation of the changes that have been made.

A policy on communicating with employees should cover the means of communication. Some methods are far better than others. It is important that management see that the union leaders know the facts about the company and its business that management would like to have the employees know, since the union leaders are likely to pass some of this information on to their members. In communicating with the rank and file, word of mouth is usually better than the written word and responses to questions are more effective than speeches or broadcasts. Hence, supplying foremen and other supervisors with facts and reports so that they come to be regarded as rich and ready sources of information is probably under most circumstances the best way to communicate with employees.

CONTRACT INTERPRETATION BY OUTSIDERS

One of the most dramatic developments in industrial relations in recent years has been the almost universal acceptance of arbitration clauses in union-management contracts. Today about 9 out of 10 union-management contracts contain arbitration clauses. There remains, however, a hard core of unions and employers that are opposed to submitting the interpretation of contracts to arbitration.

If there is an arbitration clause, management must decide what policy it will pursue about letting cases go to arbitration. A few companies are willing to submit to arbitration cases that they are bound to lose. This is true of a large rubber company that has many arbitration cases. More usual is the policy of screening cases carefully and letting go to arbitration only those cases that management is confident

of winning. Settlements as a rule carry less weight as precedents than do decisions by the arbitrator. Management must balance the disadvantage of making some unfavorable settlements against that of getting some unfavorable precedents.

If management decides to keep out of arbitration all cases except those that it feels certain of winning, there must be some person or screening committee to review the grievances that the union is appealing to arbitration. The review should be made by someone who has not been involved in the cases at their earlier stages. In a multiplant company making automotive parts the review is made by the personnel manager at the corporation level. He recently sent back for settlement five cases that the plant manager was ready to let go to arbitration. The personnel manager felt that the company was bound to lose the cases.

SOURCES OF INFORMATION ON CONTRACT ADMINISTRATION

Planned stock taking should be a regular feature of every industrial relations program. An example of such a review is furnished by a large metalworking company that became concerned with the impact of unions on management—particularly on the attitudes of supervision and the ability of supervisors to put into effect the company programs. Surveys were made of several plants to find out whether some programs had been stopped by the unions. It was found that there had been no successful interference—that the planned changes in crew sizes, rates, and equipment had been executed. Some multiplant companies get a narrative industrial relations report from each plant each month. The emphasis is not on statistics (in fact, the inclusion of mere statistical information is discouraged) but on reports of significant events, developments, and attitudes.

CORPORATE ORGANIZATION OF LABOR RELATIONS*

Audrey Freedman†

Labor relations is highly centralized, with control of bargaining at the corporate level. The final economic choices are made by chief operating executives, with the analysis and advice of corporate-level executives specializing in labor relations functions.

Where the *cost of a factor of production* (such as investment capital or new production facilities, as well as labor) is at stake, decision making moves to the top of the corporation. The economic scope of the bargain brings wage terms and strike "options" to the chief executive officer's agenda. This pattern of organization is consistent with other survey evidence that labor relations concerns are primarily economic. The centralization of economic decision making is only slightly mitigated in divisionalized companies. And bargaining unit structure has only a very slight effect on the strong centralization of management decision making.

Specialization and staff analysis occur at the strategic point of developing the company's choices with regard to wage costs, and the possible sacrifice of production involved in strikes and other shutdowns. The lead is taken by corporate and division vice presidents of labor relations. These executives also are most concerned with the "institutional" aspects of labor relations, such as the extent of the union's representation rights and prerogatives; trend of changes in the structure of bargaining units; aspects of management rights that are critical to the direction of the work force; and other subjects on which the outside party—a union—may affect the scope of managerial control.

In the description of corporate management that follows, the function of *labor relations* is separated into more specific and narrow tasks and objectives. A questionnaire elicited responses in terms of *aspects* or emphases in the management of employee relations. In general, the picture emerges of a highly organized managerial structure, with little evidence of fragmentation, in which companies express a high level of satisfaction with their ability to coordinate policy and achieve management goals.

SETTING BARGAINING POLICY FOR THE COMPANY

Establishing wage and benefit terms that the company plans to pay is central to the work of labor relations. More specifically, this work includes:

1. Developing the company's initial proposals for wages and for benefits.

2. Establishing outside limits for the bargain.

3. Determining the issues on which the company will expect and/or opt for a strike.

* This analysis is based on a 1978 survey of labor relations practices in 668 private-sector unionized firms.

† Senior research associate, The Conference Board. Reprinted from *Managing Labor Relations* (New York: The Conference Board, 1979), pp. 7-34.

4. Evaluating and accepting the balanced total in the final, packaged agreement.

Also within this negotiating role lie the technical analyses attendant upon rate setting and cost analysis, and the detective work of evaluating external pressures—from national economic and political environment, to local labor market wage trends, to pressures on the union itself. The research and analysis that precedes the major cost decision of a large corporation is extensive. The actual mutual probing at the bargaining table is lengthy, detailed, painstaking—and spotlighted as *the* determinative forum. Finally, working out the exact terms of agreement, specifying these to the guidance (and satisfaction) of all levels of management, the union, and nonunion parts of the company, and interested publics such as insurers and stockholders—all of these bargaining steps may account for more labor relations staff time than any other activities.

WHO ESTABLISHES THE ECONOMIC TERMS OF THE CONTRACT?

The Chief Executive Officer has final authority over the labor-cost terms of bargaining—and also over the cost item of strikes—in over three fifths of the participating companies. Specifically, the Chief Executive—by his approval—decides how much the total wage and benefit package will be enlarged, and whether certain strike options would be worth their price, for major bargains in the company.

In many cases, the CEO's approval will represent a tighter guideline than a "total increase" figure, because of itemization and specificity: Particular items will have individual levels of acceptance, and some will be identified as trade-offs with separate trading terms attached. For example, a specific approval for one cost-of-living arrangement may be given—but only for one kind of formula, on one timetable, combined with only one amount of initial wage increase and specified deferred increases. The CEO may also set "policy" for bargaining by specifying some items on which the company will take a strike—for example, union shop demands or cost-of-living clauses. Again it is the economic impact of the strike that is the real basis for these specifications.

Primary responsibility for developing and recommending the cost decisions rests with the corporate vice president of labor relations (see Exhibit 1). Two themes can be seen at work in that chart: specialization and centralization. The "intelligence function" is clearly specialized; the foundation for the CEO's decision making is the analysis and recommendations of a *specialized* labor relations staff. Secondly, this specialized responsibility is still highly centralized at corporate levels. Involvement by plant-level management, either specialized or line, is minimal. In four fifths of the companies, plant-level management was not even mentioned as playing any role in making this basically economic decision.

THE EFFECT OF BARGAINING STRUCTURE

Bargaining theory suggests that the labor relations decision-making structure of *management* would vary according to the nature of the structure of *bargaining* (bargaining units). That is, where bargaining is done on a plant-by-plant basis, decision-making power on bargaining issues might also be vested in the management of the plant. Conversely, when the structure of bargaining is more corporatewide, there might be a corresponding centralization of decision-making power. Survey responses analyzed in this way do show differences in the expected direction. However, a high degree of centralization of management decision making is nearly as clear in plant-by-plant bargaining, as in broad-unit bargaining.

EXHIBIT 1   PRIMARY RESPONSIBILITY FOR THE ECONOMIC TERMS OF THE BARGAIN

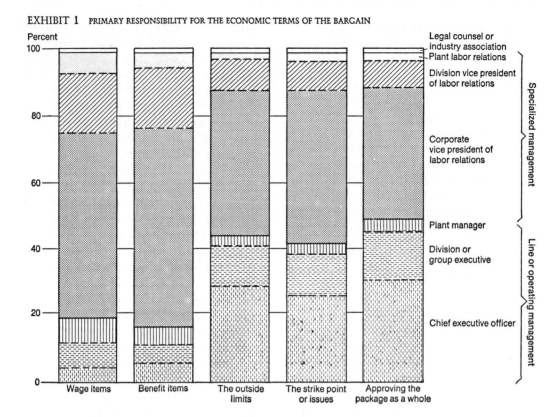

For example, only 18 percent of the firms with single-plant bargaining structures give plant-level management the primary responsibility for developing wage criteria. Only 14 percent in the single-plant structures give plant levels the primary responsibility for developing fringe benefit proposals. Fewer than 10 percent give plant management the responsibility for making the key strategic decisions on establishing the bargaining "limits," determining strike issues, and approving the final settlement package. Clearly, corporate management controls the key decisions in almost all firms, even when bargaining is done on a plant-by-plant basis.

* * * * *

THE COMPANY'S INSTITUTIONAL POSITION

What companies view as their overall "policy" vis-à-vis unions is evidently a differ-

ent matter from the economic decision making at bargaining time. The corporate head of labor relations—usually a vice president—is the final authority on policy toward unions and unionization according to *two out of three* companies. In the remaining *one third*, it is the chief executive. Directing union prevention activities, and dealing with a union organizing campaign are clearly in the vice president's hands. Company management officials who respond to a specific organizing campaign are vice presidents for labor relations, and group or division labor relations executives. About one of eight companies places plant management—both general and labor relations specialists—in charge of dealing with an organizing attempt. These proportions were not changed when predominant bargaining structure (single versus multiplant) was taken into account.

In nonunion companies on the other hand, overall policy toward unions is viewed as the province of the chief executive in over half of the cases. But managing the company's union prevention activities and dealing directly with an organizing campaign are specialized, usually at the corporate vice president level. Plant management is seldom in charge of responding to a union organizing initiative.

CARRYING OUT THE BROAD LABOR RELATIONS OPERATION IN COMPANIES

Basic economic decisions aside, *labor relations* amounts to implementation of corporate policy through a variety of activities largely carried out by specialized management and staff at the corporate or division level. For purposes of analysis, labor relations includes (as specified in the survey):

Union avoidance.

Contract administration.

Grievance and arbitration handling.

Unfair labor practice cases.

Representation elections.

Contract negotiation.

Strike preparation.

Communication on labor matters.

Research and other preparations for dealing with unions.

The questionnaire specified activities involved in contract negotiation and administration, and asked which manager has primary responsibility for:

General background research for bargaining.

Costing demands and proposals.

Advising the contract negotiating team.

Conducting contract negotiations.

Developing final language of agreement.

Monitoring operations to anticipate problems and/or carry out policy.

General administration of the contract—informing foremen, etc.

Handling grievances and arbitration.

Clearly, the corporate and division heads of labor relations and their staffs are heavily involved in all these functions. It is only in what might be called the operational aspects of labor relations—administration of contract, grievance handling, and monitoring—that the plant-level manager has a substantial role. When the company has a predominantly plant-by-plant bargaining structure, plant management and plant labor relations are also more heavily involved in preparation for bargaining. Multiplant, master contract bargaining, on the other hand, greatly suppresses the plant-level role in preparing for a new contract negotiation, and also in day-to-day monitoring, administration, and grievance handling.

* * * * *

LABOR RELATIONS STAFF: LEVELS AND REPORTING RELATIONSHIPS

The volume of work in labor relations gives rise not only to specialized staff, but also to staff at multiple levels in the organization. The significance of the work—the emphasis on centralized control—shows up in the extent to which labor relations staff work at the corporate level. More than 9 out of 10 companies have a corporate unit. Three out of five companies with division levels have labor relations staff in the division. Two thirds have labor relations staff within the plants.

These three levels—corporate, division, plant—are typical of most companies. The group level is characteristic of large multidivision companies, and even here labor relations staff sometimes makes its appearance.

In the majority of companies there is the usual functional or dotted-line relationship with counterpart staff at the next higher level. However, there are variations: About 31 percent of the plant labor-relations staffs report directly to a higher level labor-relations manager. The same phenomenon may occur at division level, that is, division labor relations staff reporting directly to group or corporate labor relations units. . . .

The most common ratio of labor relations staff to unionized employees in responding firms is about one staff member per 200 to 400 union-represented employees: 28 percent of firms are in this range. However, nearly a quarter of the companies (23 percent) have higher staffing levels—one for under 200 represented workers. One company in 10 (11 percent) has the "thin" staff ratio of one per 1,000 unionized employees. These were the larger employers, experiencing economies of scale in staffing. Perhaps, also, the actual number of contract negotiations and attendant planning activities is lower in very large, highly unionized, centralized-bargaining companies. Holding size of firm constant, the labor relations staff ratio in manufacturing companies is higher in firms that are more unionized; and that are in *industries* with higher strike incidence, higher labor cost to total costs, and more highly unionized.

EDUCATIONAL AND CAREER BACKGROUND OF LABOR RELATIONS EXECUTIVES

When it comes to labor relations, companies evidently put strong emphasis on specialized expertise. Experience in the specialty leads to the top spot. Fully four out of five top labor relations executives have spent their whole corporate life in the industrial relations or personnel function. The rest come from operations, or in 4 percent of the responding companies, law. Fifty-seven percent of the top labor relations executives in surveyed firms have degrees in either business or economics. Eighteen percent of the top labor relations executives received their training in law, while twenty-four percent received their training in other areas.

OUTSIDE ASSISTANCE

In addition to company staff, outside specialists may be hired to assist in bargaining, or in handling union organizing campaigns.

IN NEGOTIATIONS

In *preparation* for bargaining, companies also call upon the assistance of industry associations and, to a lesser extent, outside legal counsel. Nearly half of all companies reported using industry groups as part of the intelligence and data-gathering process that precedes developing a company wage target for bargaining. Two out of five companies consult law firms, whose analysis of contract language and arbitration history, and new labor law regulations, may lead to re-formation of terms in a new contract. A company is much less likely to hire an outside law firm if its highest ranking labor relations executive has a legal education. (However, less than one fifth of top labor relations executives had a law degree—most are trained in business management, economics, and other fields.) Consulting firms are used by only 11 percent of respondents.

In *actual negotiations*, outsiders take a backseat. Less than 4 percent of the companies employ consultants for this purpose. Some 14 percent use industry associations—these include most of the companies in industries where "association bargaining" on a group basis is the custom. Twenty-seven percent of the companies employ outside legal counsel at the bargaining table.

IN UNION AVOIDANCE

Outside assistance in countering a union organizing drive is used by a majority of the nonunion companies, and also by a majority of the companies that already have unions representing some of their employees. Unions frequently complain of "union-busting consultants" being hired.[1] Actually, only about one out of six unionized companies, and one out of three nonunion companies, use consultants for union avoidance of any sort. Industry associations assist in forestalling unionization in about half of the nonunion companies.

It is law firms that are frequently used by companies in the midst of union campaigns. In 70 percent of the companies with some of their work force already organized, and 95 percent of the nonunion companies, law firms are called upon. Legal counsel would be needed to guide the corporation in complying with National Labor Relations Board procedures for determining the appropriate employee unit, running an election to select the bargaining agent, and the mechanics of recognizing

that agent if elected. In fact, the minority of companies that do not require law firm assistance in the intricacies of NLRB election procedure are likely to have in-house counsel specializing in this subject.

INTERNATIONAL LABOR RELATIONS

About half of the surveyed unionized companies had branches, affiliates, or subsidiaries located outside of the United States. The most frequent practice was for labor relations policy to be determined by management in each country, individually, with an infrequent but periodic review by corporate headquarters in the United States. The second most frequent style of management is centered in the United States, with both policy and working involvement at the U.S. headquarters. This is likely to be true for companies with only a few international operations, according to interview comments. Occasionally, the extent of oversight will be mixed, with the countries most like the United States in custom, labor law, or labor unions receiving more U.S. direction. The nature of the work force and production facilities in another country, also, may account for diversity in management and policy oversight.

---

[1] Alan Kistler, Director of the Department of Organization and Field Services of the AFL–CIO, refers to "a new profession euphemistically called the labor-management consultant." He describes its role thus: "Members of this new professional group pursue the art of union-busting by attempting to choke off union growth at the initial stage: the organizing campaign. Their programs have evolved to the point that they no longer are merely reactive to individual situations but, rather, have become an institutionalized resource to management." Alan Kistler, "Trends in Union Growth." *Labor Law Journal*, August 1977, p. 540.

TOP MANAGEMENT: VALUES AND GOALS*

Fred Foulkes†

Interview data from this study suggest that historically there have been two primary types of top management motivation in large companies that are either entirely or predominantly nonunion. The evidence also suggests that all the companies in the sample have strong people-management concerns and objectives at the top of the organization, and as a logical consequence of these concerns devote substantial time, effort, and money to the management of human resources.

One primary type of motivation appears to stem from a set of values or from a philosophy on employees and how they are to be treated. The other primary type of motivation appears to stem from a fundamental purpose of remaining nonunion.

Companies with the first primary motivation may be described as *philosophy laden.* They have well thought out beliefs concerning the treatment of employees; their philosophy is usually in writing, and was generally first articulated by the company's founder. Their nonunion status seems, at least initially, to not be a goal but rather a result of the successful implementation of that philosophy. However, inherent in their thinking is the view that if management does its job well, the employees will feel that a union is not necessary—the nonunion status of these companies is then an essential by-product.

Companies with the second primary motivation may be described as *doctrinaire.* For certain reasons, top management has decided that the company, or perhaps just its new plants, are to be kept nonunion. In such companies, "union-avoidance programs" are implemented. . . .

Although it makes sense historically, the distinction today between the two types of management motivations is not clear-cut. The philosophy-laden companies are aware of unions and of union concerns. In fact, over time some have taken on the characteristics of doctrinaire companies. In addition, doctrinaire companies are not devoid of management values, philosophy, or policy statements about the treatment of their employees.

This chapter will examine both the philosophy-laden and the doctrinaire companies. While separate examples of each type will be offered, the motivation of most companies is mixed. The real question is one of relative emphasis. In examining the personnel programs and policies of these different companies, the distinction between motivational frameworks becomes less meaningful, because in certain fundamental respects the approaches of all the companies are very similar.

* [Foulkes' analysis is based on an exploratory field study of the personnel practices of 26 large companies that are either entirely or predominantly nonunion. The data are based on interviews with management representatives from various levels within each company.]

† Professor, Business School, Harvard University. Reprinted from Fred K. Foulkes, *Personnel Policies and Practices of the Large Nonunion Companies* (Englewood Cliffs, N.J.: Prentice-Hall, 1980), pp. 45–57. Adapted by permission of Prentice-Hall, Inc., © 1980.

PHILOSOPHY-LADEN COMPANIES

As indicated, there is a certain group of companies whose primary concern has not been to remain nonunion, but rather to implement a philosophy about people. When top managements were asked the reasons for their companies' nonunion status, many statements like this were given in reply:

> The men who started the company believed in fair treatment for employees and getting individuals involved in the business, listening to them, and being concerned with them.

COMPANY A

In commenting on company A's approach, the personnel director there said:

> The matter of trust or integrity of intention is fundamental. This means believing we are all equal as human beings in the sight of God and nature. A feeling of respect for the other fellow's dignity and an interest in listening to him because you want to know what he thinks and feels is part of this. An interest in an individual's potential capacities, and a concern and sympathy for his troubles and problems follow. He wants to be treated as a human being, especially by his supervisors. He will give and support increased productivity when he has faith in the worthiness of the common purpose, the honesty and competency of his leaders, and when he believes they care about him and other people and sincerely want to do the right thing.
>
> The kind of situation I have suggested as a way of living means there will be a more wholesome atmosphere at the work place. There will be less social distance during the working day. Innovations which are needed will be seen as confirmations of a feeling of mutual trust and good intent. The company receives the benefit of increased productivity, low turnover, flexibility in employee assignment, and employee responsiveness in time of production crisis or in other situations which require special efforts by all concerned.

> Of course, if management has not built this kind of atmosphere (which I think people hunger for), then naturally employees will not trust the administrative judgment because they don't feel that management really cares about them as human individuals—and they are probably right.

According to a retired personnel director of this company, "If the day comes when we do things only to keep unions out, then we will be in trouble."

COMPANY B

In company B, a basic principle is respect for and fairness to every individual. This principle was firmly laid down by the founder, who did not think or worry about unions, but was very concerned that it was too easy for people without power (that is, employees) to be controlled. Thus, it is said that the founder was sympathetic with employees, but autocratic with managers; he wanted employees to have opportunities to be heard and had a great concern for justice in the work place.

A person who had worked for the founder for three years said that only once did he hear him speak about unions, saying:

> I don't think we will ever have to worry about out company becoming unionized. Our people are treated well. We have what the unions want. That is our goal. Let them look to us.

The founder's son, later a chairman of the company, said that his father's philosophy was mainly a simple one:

> What I think is the most important is our respect for the individual. This is a simple concept, but in [our company] it occupies a major portion of management time. We devote more effort to it than anything else.
>
> This belief was bone-deep in my father. Some people who start out in modest circumstances have a certain contempt for the average man when they are able to rise above

him. Others, by the time they become leaders have built up a unique respect and understanding for the average man and a sympathy for his problems. They recognize that in a modern industrial nation the less fortunate often are victims of forces not wholly within their own control. This attitude forms the basis for many of the decisions they make having to do with people. [our company] was in the latter category.

* * * * *

How the philosophy is implemented is critical, of course. While some companies go further than others, in many there is either an absence or at least a minimum of double standards. Traditional status symbols between management and non-management people, and between blue- and white-collar workers, are either eliminated or minimized. For example, parking spaces may not be reserved and there may be a common cafeteria for everyone to use; whether an employee is a chairman or a janitor, he or she is covered by the same medical plan. As will be discussed in subsequent chapters, salary and profit sharing or other savings and investment plans for everyone are quite common in the large, nonunion company.

GROWING PAINS

It is important to remember that companies and their environments change over time, which can complicate the implementation of a company philosophy. In one of the philosophy-laden, entirely nonunion companies studied, the vice president of personnel, a former director of labor relations at a unionized company, in looking at the current situation, said:

> Change is coming so rapidly that it would drive a bulldog off a meat truck. The problem now is that the company is so big, the work force has changed, profit sharing is no longer a tonic, and the sophistication of the industry has changed.

* * * * *

The way in which the philosophy or the values of the founder become institutionalized as the company grows in size is critical. Over time, management frequently develops a real pride in the fact that the company is nonunion. This in turn seems to increase the motivation of management to stay nonunion. Having discussed the companies that either are or were philosophy laden in their primary motivation, let us turn to the group of companies whose primary motivation appeared to be a strong desire to stay nonunion.

DOCTRINAIRE COMPANIES

Of those companies put into the doctrinaire classification, there are two types. One type has had direct experience with unions, and based on that experience, decided to avoid unions in the future. The other type has not had any direct experience, although key individuals may have had some in other companies. Top-level managements of doctrinaire companies are opposed to third-party interference. . . .

DIRECT EXPERIENCE

One company's doctrinaire nonunion stance stems from an experience it suffered over 30 years ago, when several local unions coordinated their actions for a concerted strike against the company. At the time, the company had 12 operating sites, of which 10 were unionized. In all, over 90 percent of the company employees were union members. As a result of this strike, the president established a new policy toward unions. Briefly stated, it was to treat the present unions fairly, but to follow a policy of starting and keeping plants nonunion. The policy was to be pro-employee and pro-company, not anti-union.

The current situation is that out of 146 operating units, 115 are nonunion, and only 43 percent of the company's wage employees are union members. The increase in the number of union plants is predominantly due to acquisitions of already-unionized companies. Since 1946, the union has won only 7 out of 78 certification elections. This company considers its approach successful, and demonstrates it by citing higher productivity and morale and lower absenteeism in its nonunion plants. Management carefully selects and trains personnel administrators and foremen for the nonunion facilities, gives them a copy of a booklet entitled *The Supervisors Handbook on Maintaining Nonunion Status,* issues plant personnel superintendents a copy of *Confidential Guide to Nonunion Status,* and prescribes a rigorous role for corporate personnel in approving changes at the plant level and in auditing personnel activities.

In another large doctrinaire company, the percent of employees organized has decreased from 90 percent to 45 percent during the past 30 years. The history of this trend began long ago when management recognized the importance of employees' views and involvement, and therefore established work councils at several locations. When the National Labor Relations Act was enacted, such arrangements became of questionable legality because the employer had fostered their formation. Accordingly, company recognition of such councils was withdrawn. Thereafter, the employees formed independent unions at many locations. Upon proof of majority representation, the company recognized these unions according to law. However, during World War II experiences in expanded operations indicated to management that many new employees did not want unionization. At the time, the company's few nonunion plants were running well. Management then concluded that unions were not needed. Of the 50 plants built since World War II, only 4 are unionized.

One doctrinaire company arrived at its objective of being nonunion in a somewhat unusual manner. At this company, which had been unionized in the 1930s and 1940s, the union was decertified after World War II. Commenting on this, the director of personnel stated:

> The company's experience with the union brought a reappraisal of our climate and our management methods. We'd been to hell and back. Having gotten out, we decided it was not good for anyone. The long strike without pay, even most employees agreed, was no good. So, basically, we got the house in order, and we have determined to keep it so.

Putting the house in order, this person said, meant making substantial improvements in pay and benefits—but, more importantly, it meant "treating people as people." Since the institution of these and other significant personnel policy changes, there have been two union-organizational attempts, with the vote each time 2-to-1 against the union. The personnel director thinks that management can always depend on 25 percent of the employees being against the company. His view on union organizational drives is interesting: "No union organizes a company. You give it away. If an election is lost, it was lost prior to the campaign." This person's view appears to support the findings of Getman, Goldberg, and Herman, whose empirical study showed that neither the company nor the union is particularly successful in changing employees' minds during an election campaign.[1]

NO DIRECT EXPERIENCE

There is another group of doctrinaire companies that, for a variety of reasons, desire to remain nonunion even though they have not had any direct experience with

---

[1] See Julius G. Getman, Stephen B. Goldberg, and Jeanne B. Herman, *Union Representation Elections: Law and Reality* (New York: Russell Sage Foundation, 1976).

unionization. The vice president of personnel in a West Coast company who feels that unions are the result of "inept management" admits that management has done all it can to avoid unionization. When asked why the company opposed unionization, this person gave these two reasons:

> A union complicates matters. Without a union you are able to deal directly and quickly with the work force. With a union, this is not the case.
>
> A union creates a bad atmosphere. It creates an adversary kind of relationship. Where a union exists it pits people against the manager and this is not healthy for the company, for the manager, or for the people.

* * * * *

In another company, which was originally family oriented but is now managed by "professionals," an internal memorandum that was written by the vice president of personnel on raises and benefits stated the nonunion policy well:

> It is [our] policy to take all lawful steps necessary or desirable to operate on a nonunion basis. In effect, we have an implied, unwritten contract with our employees which says . . . that we will voluntarily take those steps which are necessary to ensure that . . . they will receive compensation and benefits which in their totality are competitive with the unionized companies in our field in this area.

In this company, the approach was recently questioned by a new president, who was brought in from the outside. There was a union-organizational drive going on at the time, and at a top management meeting at which the company's strategy was being reviewed, the new president asked:

> What's wrong if our employees want to join a union? It is their right under the law and I've managed in unionized companies before.

Needless to say, this statement "upset the apple cart," and the situation calmed down only after the vice presidents for administration and personnel were able to talk privately with the new president about the advantages of continuing the company's nonunion approach. The vice president of personnel was somewhat uncomfortable with the company's nonunion position: Earlier in his career, he had been a union organizer; now he was being paid to keep the union out. He could do it, he told the new president, because he had worked out the conflicts.

Top management at another company has a very explicit goal of staying nonunion for two reasons: (1) no outside third-party interference is desired and (2) the president wants to have something more innovative than a union. The "something" in this case is an employee committee, whose functions and responsibilities go far beyond the responsibilities of the employee committees of the 1920s. The company also has a profit-sharing plan and a pension plan, job posting, a formal grievance procedure with outside arbitration, much training and education, and a career-counseling system.

When this company experienced its first and only union-organizational drive, the president drew up a handwritten letter on personal stationery, which was reproduced and sent to each employee. The letter revealed much about the president, and about the president's philosophy and the nature of the company. A powerful document, the letter helped kill employee interest in the union.

* * * * *

In its effort to stay nonunion, one company adopted a harsh attitude toward an acquired plant that is unionized, located less than an hour away by car from one of the company's large nonunion plants. A close observer of this company stated that the unionized plant is used in a strategic and highly effective way as a scapegoat, to make it clear to the nonunion employees that they would not benefit from being unionized. Examination showed that wages and benefits *are* lower in the union-ized plant. When asked why this was so, the vice president of personnel defended the company's practices:

> The plants are in different communities and our philosophy is to pay in relation to community averages. Also, we're willing to take a strike there. We'd rather have 250 employees on strike than have 3,000 join a union. We don't, in any sense of the word, let the union plant dictate what we will do for our nonunion employees.

However, management maintains that it applies the same philosophy to all employ-ees. For example, another vice president said:

> We give merit increases to everyone twice a year, even in the unionized plant. Even in the unionized plant we approach things the same way—the philosophy is the same. We believe in sitting down and talking to our employees.

When asked how layoffs are handled at the unionized plant, the vice president of personnel said:

> We don't have layoffs at the unionized plant. They are sharing the work, too, be-cause people are still human beings and we try to treat them the same way.

CONCLUDING ANALYSIS AND COMMENTS

In this chapter, I have concentrated on the values and goals of predominantly and en-tirely nonunion companies. One group of companies was primarily philosophy laden in which the nonunion state seems to be a by-product of the successful diffusion of the management values or philosophy. For a variety of reasons, top managements in the other group, the doctrinaire compa-nies, have remaining nonunion as an ex-plicit goal. It needs to be recognized, how-ever, that the sources of motivation, even to a psychologist, are complicated. As sug-gested by the work of the late Raymond A. Bauer, the sources of motivation are so complicated that in more instances than not the individual may not well under-stand his or her own motives.[2] To the ex-tent that the motives are understood it is possible for the indivudual to rationalize his behavior in almost any terms he chooses.

Perhaps it is useful to think of top man-agement motivation as being on a contin-uum [shown at bottom of page] . . . At one extreme would be those companies which are militantly anti-union; at the other would be the companies described as philosophy laden. The continuum no-tion implies various shades or degrees of motivation with the word *reactive* associ-ated with the left side and the word *proac-tive* attached to the right side of the spec-trum. In addition to this notion of various degrees of motivation, it is also necessary to recognize that there is much fluidity as to where an organization lies on the continuum. For instance, the semi-saint-hood status that could be implied by the categorization of the term *philosophy laden* may cease if individual employees show an interest in joining a union. If a

Militantly Anti-union Doctrinaire Semiphilosophy-laden Philosophy-laden
anti-union

[2] *See* Raymond A. Bauer, "An Agenda for Re-search and Development on Corporate Responsive-ness," in *Soziale Daten Und Politische Planung*, ed. Meinoff Dierkes (Frankfurt/New York: Campus Pub-lishers, 1975), pp. 69, 70.

vigorous union drive began, the company's position on the continuum might shift to the left, toward the militantly anti-union side of the spectrum.

The top managements of many of the companies studied take pride in the fact that their organizations are nonunion. It seems to give them a certain status and prestige in the management community. Maintaining this source of self-respect also appears to be a powerful management motivation.

All this is to say that the distinction between philosophy laden and doctrinaire companies may be somewhat academic. Motivation is always complex, explanations can be rationalizations, and the values of managements may change over time. In fact, the motivation for most companies comes from a combination of sources, and is a question of relative emphasis. The reality is that the companies studied are very much motivated by a desire to stay nonunion because of efficiency, philosophy, pride, and anti-union bias, or all of these or some combination of these reasons. The motivation to stay nonunion is perhaps more clear-cut in those predominantly nonunion companies that have had experience with unions, and based on that experience, have decided to keep all of their new plants nonunion. Their goals are generally more explicit.

The basic finding is that, in all the companies in the study, there is a strong concern at the top about people management and the climate of the organization. Although the character of it varies, there is also strong top management motivation to remain nonunion. Consistent with this objective, all of the companies in the study devote substantial time, effort, and money to the management of human resources. An essential point, then, is that strong motivation is necessary, but is not a sufficient condition to stay nonunion—it is crucial; it is the basis for everything that follows.

PERCEIVED ADVANTAGES AND DISADVANTAGES OF BEING NONUNION*

Fred Foulkes†

I have been asked if it could be said that any of the companies I studied are non-union by chance or by luck. Frankly, no company in this study was nonunion by chance or by luck; in fact, each had been working hard to implement its philosophy or to achieve its goals. Since this is the case, it is important to understand *why* these companies work so hard to remain nonunion, and why it is so important to them to do so. In this chapter, we will take a look at the advantages and disadvantages of a nonunion operation, as perceived by the senior management and, in some cases, by the supervisors who must put company policy into practice.

PERCEIVED ADVANTAGES

The overwhelming majority of executives interviewed maintained that a nonunion operation is a more efficient one. They primarily attributed the greater efficiency to the flexibility that exists in the absence of the work rule restrictions that govern unionized plants.

The freedom to make changes in work

---

* [Foulkes' analysis is based on an exploratory field study of the personnel practices of 26 large companies that are either entirely or predominantly non-union. The data are based on interviews with management representatives from various levels within each company.]

† Professor, Business School, Harvard University. Reprinted from Fred K. Foulkes, *Personnel Policies and Practices of the Large Nonunion Company* (Englewood Cliffs, N.J.: Prentice-Hall, 1980), pp. 58–69. Adapted by permission of Prentice-Hall, Inc., © 1980.

assignments and shifts was probably most frequently cited to be the result of this greater flexibility. "People here do two jobs," said one executive, "and they can be asked to do three or four." Without work rule restrictions, cross-utilization of personnel is possible. According to many managers, the greater efficiency results in substantial savings. One executive said, "if we could not change peoples' jobs and shifts as easily as we do now, the company would be in great trouble." Some managers also felt that movement between work assignments reduces job boredom for employees.

Another major advantage of nonunion status, according to many executives, is low turnover rates. One company figured its turnover rate to be only about 40 percent of the industry average. Another company had such a low rate that it had not even kept records of turnover for the past two years. Still another company showed a turnover of 5.5 percent annually (only 3.5 percent when retirement losses are omitted). The combination of low turnover with a policy of promoting from within can, however, create a personnel problem, according to the senior vice president of a company with a turnover rate of 0.5 percent per month. At this company, its low turnover rate and its promotion policy led to difficulty in implementing affirmative action plans for women and minorities, particularly in higher-level jobs.

Some managers felt that they employ fewer people than union plants do in order to achieve the same levels of productivity. One company chairman, for instance, boasted of the superior productivity in his company compared to competitors. He cited a number of ratios in support of this point; for example, the company "mans lean" in the shipping department, with a volume comparable to the unionized competitors.

In some cases, managers felt that their approach to employee relations as a nonunion company gives them a distinct competitive advantage in hiring. Several statistics support this claim: One company, located in a city and known as the best employer in the area, receives an average of 8,000 to 10,000 applications for the 500 job openings it has in a normal year. Another company, which has been leading its industry in pay and benefits, had 23,000 applications on file for only 375 job openings. (This company also had fewer employees per sale dollar than any other company in its industry.) Many personnel officers were convinced that their employees are more loyal or hard-working and have higher morale than average workers. One vice president, although skeptical of others' claims of superior productivity in a nonunion plant, did believe that "being nonunion assures a fair day's work for a fair day's pay," something he seemed to imply does not occur in a unionized plant. Another executive reported that: "Our employees really put out in times of crisis; they'll work hard and won't even want to collect overtime."

Another advantage of nonunion status perceived by some members of management was that resistance to technological change is lower in a nonunion environment. Therefore, nonunion companies can make operational changes more easily than unionized companies can.

Due to the more efficient operation of the enterprise, then, the majority of executives believed a nonunion operation to be less costly. However, if it costs the compa-

nies in this sample less to operate on a nonunion basis, it is not because of lower wages. In general, wages and benefits are likely to be higher in the nonunion firms of an industry, with the exception of plants in southern and lower-wage communities. One executive did comment that the percentage of the sales dollar going to payroll was less at his company than at any unionized competitor, adding that "the company has saved millions of dollars over the years because our hiring wage rates are considerably lower than those offered by our unionized competitors." This company's management apparently believes it can attract enough capable people, in spite of its lower starting pay, by quickly advancing good performers to rates that are actually higher than those paid by its unionized competitors. Although a low starting wage is rare among the companies studied, it should be observed that the use of merit increases is widespread.

Another reason some managers thought that operating on a nonunion basis is less costly is that the expenses associated with strikes are avoided. One management official noted that his company had not lost one hour due to a labor problem in 47 years. He observed that this is undoubtedly a good selling point to customers. Another manager stated that his company "picked up business from a struck competitor that they never regained." Some managers felt that the reduced threat of employee unrest not only made them more attractive to customers, they expressed the belief that employees who have never paid union dues are also beneficiaries of the company's nonunion status.

Less managerial time spent on grievances and contract negotiations was another frequently cited cost-saving benefit of nonunion status. Several people, however, denied that there are any cost advantages at all associated with remaining nonunion. According to one official in a company with both union and nonunion plants, "it certainly doesn't cost less. It's about the same as a unionized organization, because we spend on training and communications instead of on negotiations, grievance administration, or arbitration." He felt that since pay scales are higher at the company's nonunion plants than the unionized ones, the nonunion ones probably cost slightly more. As a final word in the costs debate, the corporate director of employee relations at a different company with both union and nonunion plants said:

> The costs are hard to measure because many are intangible. One definite cost is the higher wages and better benefits package [at our nonunion plants]. However, the premium paid is not large and is more than offset by the productivity gain. The costs of specialized training of supervisors, attitude surveys, etc., are not relevant because they are used in both our union and nonunion plants.

Whether or not a nonunion plant is more economical, many of the managers interviewed maintained that time spent positively on human relations programs, rather than negatively on grievances, has a distinct effect on employee and management morale. Managers preferred to handle human relationships on a direct, individual basis rather than through an organization or a group characteristic of a union. In this way, they felt, employees' loyalty will then go to the company rather than to the union. Managers mentioned positive attitudes, high morale, and loyalty. . . .

In the view of many of those I interviewed, the freedom to experiment with employee-relations plans, the opportunity to deal directly with workers, and the avoidance of an adverse relationship between management and employees lead to improved company morale. In the course of our conversations, it also became clear that a further advantage of a nonunion status is the satisfaction of certain emotional needs of top management. Many managers took obvious pride in their personnel philosophies and accomplishments, and felt that their efforts had a direct and visible effect on the life of the company. With such belief in the perceived advantages of a nonunion environment, it is not surprising that some looked upon a union as a personal affront.

PERCEIVED DISADVANTAGES

The senior managers interviewed were almost unanimous in agreeing that there are no disadvantages associated with being nonunion. However, one possible disadvantage began to emerge by implication rather than by outright declaration, the apparent freedom to experiment claimed by so many personnel managers may be illusory. As will be shown in subsequent chapters, many managers deny themselves some of the flexibility advantages that their company's nonunion status gives them. Some companies, for example, have full-employment practices. Some companies give considerable weight to seniority even in promotion decisions. The practices of many companies are such that they refrain from using much of their cherished flexibility.

Occasionally—although examples are rare—employees who knew well that management wished to remain nonunion would exercise their power to unionize to their advantage. At one plant, for instance, there had been an election drive to unionize each year for 13 years, and each year the employees invited one of three unions to come in and organize the plant. Part of management's response had been to give a formal dinner dance for the employees. After this had gotten to be an annual affair, the three unions finally realized they were being used, and declined further invitations from the employees to organize the plant. (It should be noted, by the way, that this company's other nonunion plants were infrequently targets of organization attempts.)

At another company, the employees of one small, isolated unit threatened to unionize in order to obtain more recognition from its large parent company. According to the firm's vice president of personnel, these employees had argued that they had to say they wanted a union in order to get a management of their own. In yet another company, personnel managers felt that their annual attitude survey, which top management assessed very seriously, was abused by employees. The managers objected in particular to one question on the survey that asked the respondent to agree or disagree with the statement: "Most employees I know would like to see the union get in," their objection being that employees who did not actually want a union would agree with the statement simply to keep management on its toes and sensitive to employees.

Judging from these cases, it appears that the doctrinaire nonunion company can become the victim of what it perceives to be a blackmail routine. However, from the standpoint of workers, in the absence of union organization the *threat* of unionization is their only source of collective power. Whether this power is wielded frivolously or is reserved for serious complaints remains an unanswered question. The cases cited above appeared to be uncommon; they tended, moreover, to be associated with companies that were predominantly nonunion, and with those committed to avoiding unionization at almost any cost as a matter of doctrine rather than philosophy. For our purposes, we simply note that some members of management did feel that employees can exploit the knowledge that their company desires to remain nonunion.

The second disadvantage of a union operation was expressed most strongly by the supervisors and managers who actually implemented the policies of top manage-

ment. The only person, among all the top management people I interviewed, who directly expressed any doubt at all about the advantages of being nonunion, was a vice president of personnel who said:

> I frankly feel that there are substantial disadvantages to being nonunion if you have weak managers, especially at the first and second level, because it takes good judgment, honesty, integrity, and much hard work by each and every member of management to maintain a positive employee-relations climate. If you don't have strong supervision, a well-written, tightly managed union contract might be the best way to go. I believe some of the low-paying companies with poor supervision are a good example of this.

Many other executives did agree that the management job at a nonunion plant is more difficult than at a unionized one. One officer, who had held a variety of jobs in unionized plants, thought that the personnel manager's job is easier in a unionized plant because the decisions are not as far reaching there: "You have a contract to help you interpret various things."

*   *   *   *   *

Finally, with respect to the management job in a nonunion plant versus one in a unionized plant, a company chairman made this point:

> If the union were to come to our company, in some ways it would make things easier, for certain things would then be clearly left to the union. Some of our supervisors, in fact, think that it would be easier to manage with a union.

There was not complete consensus on this matter, however; one vice president of personnel said that any supervisor who says that working in a nonunion plant makes his job more difficult has probably never worked in a union plant. In his view, the supervisor in such a situation is always in the middle between the employee, the union steward, and management.

Many supervisors, however, agreed with the opinion that their function would be more difficult in a nonunion company. Indeed, it was not clear to me whether the top managements of some of the companies studied had given adequate consideration to the concerns of their supervisors. I uncovered some cases that were not only difficult from the supervisory point of view, but also appeared disadvantageous for the company, at least in the short run. Those supervisors who did agree had three general complaints. First, they believed that decisions were more difficult because of the flexibility of their companies' policies. Second, they felt that some employees abused certain policies, and that the risk of excessive tolerance was high. In addition to finding it difficult to discipline employees for poor attendance records, many supervisors found it virtually impossible to discipline for poor performance. Finally, some supervisors found the work environment to be too loose for high productivity. It should be observed before we explore these concerns that supervisors in unionized companies will voice the same or similar complaints, and that most of these problems may arise whether or not a company is nonunion.

The threat of employees abusing what is perceived to be the greater freedom of a nonunion plant particularly worries some supervisors. One, who formerly worked for a highly unionized firm, commented:

> This company is more ambiguous than any other company I am used to. One of its strengths is the fact that we treat people as individuals, but it is also a weakness. For example, the company has an extremely liberal short-term disability plan, and, as a result, the company suffers much absenteeism. Supervisors, moreover, have a lot of discretion. Instead of having a hard and fast rule, there is a lot of flexibility. The supervisor has to consider the reasons for the absence, and he can still recommend raises. You don't just look at the numbers.

A personnel administrator at the same company told of some of the frustrations of dealing with employee problems in a company that prides itself on individual treatment. She said that when difficult problems are taken to top management for solutions, guidance, or direction, the answer frequently received from the top is "do what is right."

* * * * *

In particular, some supervisors found discipline onerous in their companies. According to one manager:

> Discharge and discipline are almost impossible. If you become a permanent employee, your job is very secure. Dismissal is almost unheard of at this company. The company stresses attendance, and besides stealing, about the only way for a person to be discharged is for having a very bad attendance record. But it is extremely difficult to discharge an employee. You have to put an ironclad case together.

At another company, a supervisor made the highly dubious statement that:

> It is easier to fire an employee in a union shop. Here, it doesn't pay to rock the boat. Senior employees feel a lot of security. Unless you are a complete alcoholic, a rapist, or absent an awful lot, you are not going to get fired. After a person has been with the company 15 years, he cannot be fired without the president's approval.

One wonders if this supervisor has ever tried to fire anyone in a union shop!

* * * * *

In addition to the difficulties associated with disciplining employees for poor performance and attendance, supervisors also complained of other employee behavior that can make the supervisor's job more difficult. One company, for example, maintains a recreation room for employees. Equipped with pool tables, card tables, current magazines, and fresh coffee, this lounge is very attractive by any standard. Commenting on it, a supervisor of skilled maintenance people said:

> The company offers so many things for the employee to play with that it makes the supervisor's job harder. I'll have some employees shooting pool 15 to 20 minutes after their break time. I went up to one employee and he said, "Well, what are you going to do, fire me?" He knows I can't do that. It makes it bad for the supervisor. Nothing is said about half-hour breaks, two-hour lunches, or coming in late. Our hands are tied.

Illustrating the difference between a line view and a staff view concerning these problems, the personnel director at this company had this to say about the lounges:

> Some of this company's nicest facilities are the employee lounges. While some outsiders see this as a waste of money, it is this way because we think good working conditions and good resting conditions go hand in hand.

In one company, which had dispensed with time clocks as part of its decision to put all workers on salary, some supervisors felt that workers were taking excessively long lunch breaks and were working less overtime than they had been assigned. One supervisor said: "No one has the guts to address this problem. I don't either. The employees take turns on the machines, and without time clocks, they lie when they fill out their time cards." This supervisor would prefer an individual incentive system and a return of the time clocks. Another supervisor at this company, who also complained about the loss of the time clocks, mentioned that when the clocks were removed many of the supervisors were up in arms. However, a vice president had argued that if the supervisors pushed the issue, he would know that more time clocks were needed, and fewer supervisors.

This supervisor also said that the removal of time clocks was consistent with the liberal philosophy of the company: In his view, the company is run for people rather than for profits.

One additional complaint came from a supervisor who said that his company takes better care of its nonexempt employees than its exempt ones. In his view, the company overlooks and overworks its first-line managers; he supervises 90 employees, and some supervisors have as many as 120 people.

In sum, lower management may be the casualty in a nonunion firm. Some of their views of upper management and the personnel department sounded to me like the negative views supervisors generally take of unions. They felt that they were constrained by management philosophy, that those on-high sided with the employee, that they were persistently being examined and judged by the upper echelons, to be definite penalties for a supervisor known to have difficulty dealing with employees. In the words of several supervisors: "The manager here will not be promoted unless he is good in employee relations"; "it does not pay to make waves, and be labeled as someone who has people problems"; and "in this company it will stifle your career to get a reputation that you cannot get along with people."

CONCLUDING ANALYSIS AND COMMENTS

The most difficult question to answer is whether or not a nonunion operation is more efficient, and therefore more economical. The absence of hard data is the greatest obstacle to discovering the truth. Moreover, few companies in the sample had comparable competitors. During the course of my study, in fact, two persons asked if I could supply any evidence for them, as both wanted data with which to convince their top managements that the effort to remain nonunion was worthwhile. [Among executives, there is by no means any consensus on this issue that is based on hard data.]

Some consultants estimate that a union will raise labor costs 20 percent to 35 percent. One has broken it down to first-year and ongoing costs, and has included such items as legal and arbitration expenses. Also, the initial costs for a company wishing to remain nonunion may be high, but if a union comes in it would be easy for the costs to increase, as the experience of the consultants suggests. In his book, *Making Unions Unnecessary*, Charles L. Hughes wrote:

> Unions are expensive. A privately-conducted study of 83 companies shows that the payroll and benefits costs of unionized companies average 25 percent more than those of nonunion companies or the nonunion facilities of companies that have both labor organizations and union-free operations. This cost is not primarily in individual wages and benefits, but results from redundant employees, narrowly defined jobs, restrictive production, strikes, and slowdowns. The costs are the price of inefficiency and ineffectiveness. The tragedy is that the money does not go to the people. With few exceptions, employees within a given industry earn about the same rates of pay whether they are union members or not. Many nonunion companies keep their wages in line with unionized companies, and most partially unionized corporations match nonunion wages to their labor contracts. The additional costs that result from the presence of labor unions is mostly in lower productivity: union members lose, company management loses, and the consumer loses.[1]

Dr. Hughes informed me that his sample included about 300 companies with both union and nonunion operations. His statements were based on payroll and benefits as a percentage of billings. According to Hughes, it takes fewer people to run a nonunion company due to the absence of restrictive work practices.[2] However, the fact that the nonunion plants of many companies are the newer, more modern facilities that have younger work forces may help explain the ratio; indeed, unless the data is corrected for these variables as well as for many others, it is difficult to get a handle on the precise costs of operating a union company versus the costs of operating a nonunion one.

Although there is a remarkable absence of hard data for very understandable reasons, most senior executives did *think* that it costs less to operate on a nonunion basis. However, for a variety of reasons, there are major comparability problems even among companies in the same industry with respect to any independent analysis of this issue. Some of the companies in the sample, moreover, have relatively unique product–market situations. While this is changing, a few of the companies have, or at least have had, little effective competition. Of course, there are also difficult productivity measurement problems. If it does cost the companies in my sample less to operate on a nonunion basis, except for a few very unusual cases the savings for these companies are clearly not due to lower individual wage and benefit costs. The savings come from higher productivity, which in turn results from greater flexibility in the use of people, less resistance to technological change, a more favorable employee relations climate, and the savings associated with lower absenteeism and turnover.

Unless there are opportunities for the study of nonunion plants versus comparable union plants, companies should be very skeptical of the statements made about the costs and benefits of operating nonunion. Such statements need to be examined with caution. While costly and inefficient union plants may exist, this is

[1] Charles L. Hughes, *Making Unions Unnecessary* (New York: Executive Exterprises Publications, 1976),p. 2.

[2] Private correspondence.

not necessarily a result of their unionized status only. By the same token, the perceived lower costs of apparently efficient nonunion plants may be the motivation for, rather than the result of, their nonunion status. What seems particularly clear, in any case, is that investigation into the precise costs and benefits of being nonunion is needed.

In the absence of hard data, people are left to their subjective perceptions. In sum, the testimony of top management is that the productivity of the nonunion company is higher. The views of some supervisors, however, raise questions about the testimony regarding high productivity of some of the senior managers interviewed. Even if the perceptions of top management are faulty (and I am not prepared to say that they are), they do count: Myths can be significant.

The assertions of higher productivity of some of the predominantly nonunion companies would seem to have more merit, since some of these companies have comparable facilities that are unionized. Here too, however, the data is vague. For example, is productivity higher in a nonunion plant *because* it is nonunion, or is it due to a younger, more rural work force associated with the plant's location? Moreover, in some cases productivity in a unionized facility is below management's desires due to concessions erroneously made to the union over the years in order to avoid strikes.

Management at one large company not in the sample became increasingly frustrated by the work rule restrictions agreed to over the years. Under a new chairman, this company began to bargain more toughly (allowing several strikes) and to regain, via work rule changes, the money spent in wage and benefit increases. In fact, some people have said that some plants are managed in such a way as to encourage decertifications. Also, this company's management has actively worked to keep its new plants nonunion through the introduction of a merit-salary concept resulting in premium pay and job enrichment, and by (in the words of an executive of a competitor) "running its plants fairly." The motivation for the behavior of this management, to emphasize, springs from the unsatisfactory work rules and inefficiencies existing in its unionized plants. This being the case, and for other reasons as well, the productivity of its newer, nonunion plants is higher than at its unionized plants.

Viewed broadly, the economic motivation for staying nonunion seems stronger in the predominantly nonunion company and in some doctrinaire companies than in the companies I have termed philosophy laden. In the latter, lower costs seem more of a by-product of the successful implementation of the philosophy rather than its goal. But what is rationalization or myth, and what is fact or fiction, is not always clear.

Again, the distinction between philosophy laden and doctrinaire companies is not clear. The philosophy or values of managements may change over time. Companies do become unionized, even though their primary goal was to remain nonunion. Given the motivation of top management, the skill with which the management philosophy is applied is crucial if the desired consequences are to be realized and the undesirable consequences minimized.

Discussion and analysis of this larger task will occupy major parts of the subsequent chapters of this book. In addition to top management's commitment, the role of the personnel department is important, as is a number of basic personnel policies and practices including employment security, promotion from within, pay and benefits, and formal communications programs. However, geographic location, the company's technology, the size of plant, and the nature of the work force are also important.

MANAGEMENT OBJECTIVES IN BARGAINING*

Audrey Freedman†

For unionized companies, bargaining—the actual negotiation of a contract—is a crucial event. And while union security, management rights, and other institutional arrangements may once have been major issues, today the wage and benefit package gets the spotlight. Company managements usually negotiate with a specific wage and benefit objective and a set of objectives on nonwage items. Past history and development of the union contract in the individual company is the baseline for analysis of current objectives. The pivot point is where the individual company is, immediately prior to bargaining.

MEANING AND SUBTLETIES OF TARGET SETTING

For unionized companies, wage targets and nonwage goals specify the best deal the company expects to get. Not just a list of what management wants, they are actually an evaluation of what, given the situation, will occur when management's trade-off schedule meets the union's agenda. This interpretation suggests that attaining a target represents a realistic optimum exchange from management's point of view.

Thus, target setting includes the use of

good judgment about the union's ultimate settlement point and trade-offs—and the costs to each party of various strategies and maneuvers, including strikes and lockouts. These judgments temper "what management would ideally prefer" and produce what can be called a realistically planned outcome.

PATTERNS IN MANAGEMENT'S CRITERIA FOR WAGE SETTING

Local labor market comparisons are the primary wage criterion in nonunion companies (see Exhibit 1), and also in situations where the employer is the dominant party in collective bargaining. In the absence of unions, or where unions are weak, employers are free to offer wages only in the amount necessary to draw and retain the desired quality and quantity of workers from the local labor market. Companies in this position are also likely to give more weight to criteria specific to the firm, such as financial ability, and to internal comparisons of wages in the firm.

Where unions are present and strong, it becomes necessary for management to add criteria that reflect the union's demands. The influence of strong unions creates the effect of an industrywide wage level (as opposed to localized wages). One of the ways unions seek to "take wages out of competition" is to induce management to emphasize industry comparisons or "patterns," and to put less weight on differentiated local wage levels. Thus, in

---

*This analysis is based on a 1978 survey of labor relations practices in 668 private-sector unionized firms.

† Senior research associate, The Conference Board. Reprinted from *Managing Labor Relations* (New York: The Conference Board, 1979), pp. 35–46.

unionized firms, *industry patterns* are given priority over local wage levels as a wage targetting criterion (see Exhibit 1). This priority is even stronger in situations where the union is particularly powerful because of high unionization, a multiplant (or even companywide) bargaining structure, or where the costs of a strike are severe. The more powerful the union is relative to the firm, the more weight given to the union-preferred wage criteria and the less weight given to local labor market and firm-specific criteria.

To be more specific, within the unionized group of responding companies, those that gave greater weight to *local labor market conditions* were found to be (1) smaller; (2) in single-plant bargaining structures; (3) less unionized; (4) independent of any "pattern bargaining"; and (5) manufacturing firms in industries with higher labor-to-total-cost ratios. Conversely, firms that assigned greater weight to *industry comparisons* were (1) larger; (2) in more centralized bargaining structures; (3) in pattern bargaining relation-

EXHIBIT 1   SCALE OF COMPANY CONSIDERATIONS IN SETTING WAGE AND BENEFIT TARGETS

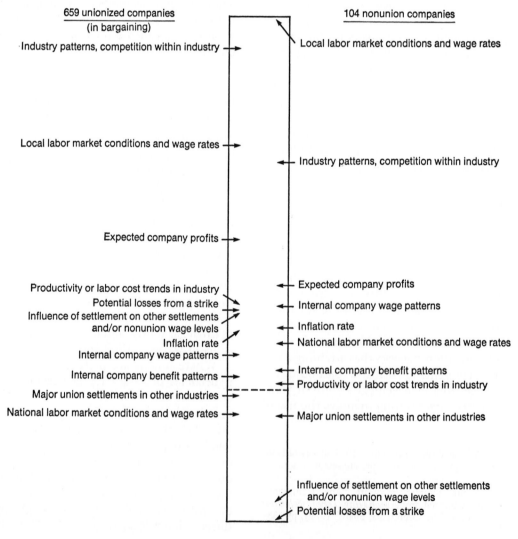

ships; (4) more likely to be found in the transportation, communications, or public utilities industries; and (5) in industries with lower labor-to-total-cost ratios.

Nevertheless, where unionization is present, an overall high priority was accorded to industrywide or bargaining-related criteria as opposed to local or firm-specific factors. This suggests that the majority of the firms have accommodated their wage policies to the "realities" of union agenda in collective bargaining. And, even in union-free companies, as Exhibit 1 shows, the industry comparison has secondary importance.

WAGE-TARGETTING CRITERIA IN DETAIL

Among the surveyed companies, as a whole, the wage criteria given priority are: industry patterns and competition; local labor market conditions and wage rates; and expected profits. However, after these top three, a variety of other points were considered. These are all shown on Exhibit 1, a ratio scale that depicts their respective importance.

Very few companies gave "national" labor markets first (or even second or third) mention. However, a very small but noticeable group of companies placed high importance on major union settlements in other industries. On closer examination, these companies are not "all of a kind," nor are they all major national companies with companywide bargaining units. Nine, in fact, are companies bargaining plant by plant, and four are single-plant companies.

Companies were also asked to indicate the factors considered in setting wage and benefit targets for their *largest bargaining unit* so that this could be compared with companywide factor rankings. Divergent rankings would suggest a degree of union power in major units (but only in major units) that forces the company to shift considerations. It could also imply that

management purposely makes exceptional policy for its biggest unionized group. The two sets of rankings, however, were almost completely parallel. At the major bargaining unit, there is slightly more relative weight given to the productivity or labor-cost factor—perhaps because it is more susceptible of exact quantification in a particular unit such as one plant.

NONUNION COMPANIES RANK THE CONSIDERATIONS

The most noticeable aspect of the nonunion companies' considerations is much more diffusion among the criteria that are taken into account in wage setting. The nonunion respondents cited such items as "internal company wage patterns" more often, and also national labor market conditions and wage rates. The citation of consumer price inflation suggests that, even without union pressure, managements incorporate some concepts of real-wage maintenance into their wage policies.

Without union pressure, nonunion companies more freely stress those comparisons that are particularly important to their individual situations. Withal, nonunion companies are most likely to base their wages on local area wage rates, as already noted.

BARGAINING STRUCTURE AND WAGE TARGET FACTORS

The unionized company's emphasis on industry patterns is even stronger in companies with a centralized, multiplant bargaining structure. Decentralized, plant-by-plant bargainers are somewhat more able to use local wage rates as a primary criterion. In this respect, plant-by-plant bargainers are more like nonunion companies. . . .

The effect of master contract bargaining units is particularly noticeable in the rating of local wage levels as *"not consid-*

ered" by one fifth or more of the multi-plant bargainers. These master contract companies are most clearly dealing with an "industry rate." However, there is no commensurately heavy downgrading of industry patterns by the single-plant bargainers. This is why industry patterns receive the highest rating for the unionized companies taken as an undifferentiated group.

* * * * *

NONWAGE GOALS

Companies often have "policies"—long-standing, companywide positions or traditions with respect to their unionized employee groups. On occasion, these may be specified as *bargaining objectives for a particular contract* negotiation. This could occur, for example, during negotiation of a first contract for a newly organized unit: Management might choose to initiate a policy stance on, for example, union security clauses. Another occasion when "policy" could become an objective or goal in a specific negotiation might occur if the company bargainers expected a union demand on an item that has long been implicit company policy or tradition. Historical examples in actual bargaining are numerous, covering subjects such as union security, cost-of-living clauses, supplemental unemployment benefits, companywide bargaining units, or other structure changes. Thus, a union drive to change some contract term that is *also* fundamental company policy, will very likely cause the company to identify the item as an "objective" in negotiations. In this case, the objective would be to maintain the status quo—the company policy—intact.

Bargaining goals or objectives outside the wage area will also include items that, while not part of company policy, complete management's agenda at each bargaining round. Eighty-seven percent of the companies in The Conference Board survey had a set of nonwage goals in their latest negotiation, in their largest bargaining unit. In terms of specific nonwage goals, companies reported objectives in eight to nine subjects per company, with the most frequent mentions: (1) paid time off; (2) flexibility on assignment of employees; (3) pensions; and (4) health benefits (see Exhibit 2).

The list derives from two sources: expected union initiatives as well as company goals. Respondents were asked to identify areas where (1) management expected a union initiative and its goal was *to keep the status quo;* (2) management had a goal of making the existing provision *more favorable to the company* by tightening or otherwise improving it; and (3) management was prepared *to give something in exchange* for, or in trade for, something else. . . . Thus, a lack of "mentions" in Exhibit 2 represents a lack of activity in that subject area—not necessarily any absence of the subject in the contracts, letters of agreement, or past practices of the employer. Even in the least frequently mentioned subjects—income security bargaining and union security arrangements—over half of the companies had a bargaining objective.

The frequency of mentions suggests relative "heat" in the subject area. *The source of the initiative,* however, is significant. For example, pension bargaining objectives were specified by more than four out of five companies. But the management plan was to tighten or take back some pension element in less than a tenth of the companies. [Examination of each] company's planned position on [cited bargaining] subject[s] for the 568 companies identifying goals and goal achievement shows that, in 61 percent of the 4,939 citations, the company expected a union demand and had specified its goal as maintaining the status quo. On average, companies expected to resist about five such union initiatives. On the other hand, companies were prepared to make favora-

EXHIBIT 2   MANAGEMENT NONWAGE GOALS *Percent of companies with a goal in area*

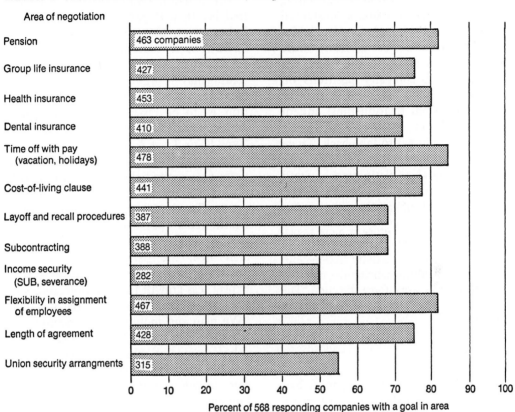

Percent of 568 responding companies with a goal in area

ble-to-the-union offers in over one fifth (21 percent) of all goal citations—nearly two per company. Lastly, a little over one sixth (18 percent) of the goals involved tightening up or obtaining an agreement that would be more favorable to the management.

The overall picture of company bargaining objectives in the mid-1970s is one of status quo or "stand pat" positions on the part of management. Newspaper stories about "take backs" characterizing management's stance in 1978 seem to have over-emphasized a few situations. The survey data show management anticipating union demands in many areas, willing to trade on a limited number of subjects (chiefly on funded benefits), and seeking favorable

exchanges from the union in one subject area: flexibility in assignment of employees.

. . . itemized nonwage objectives are discussed below.

COMPANY OBJECTIVES

Management negotiators are guided by company objectives that have been developed in advance. These objectives reflect (1) the reality of the company's current financial position; (2) the union's agenda and power; and (3) a variety of external trends and pressures that—to some extent—pattern the anticipations and analyses of both bargaining parties.

When analyzed by a yardstick internal

to each company individually, bargaining over *benefit items* contains a substantial potential for exchange: Companies planned to "give" almost as many times as they planned to "hold the line." On the other hand, company positions on those nonwage items that clearly might be called institutional relationships, and/or affect supervision of the work force, ranged from stand pat to take back. There was little room for exchange in this territory. The fairly clear distinction between trading and nontrading territories may bear a very light touch of rationale:

> The nontrading territory is more associated with incalculable (but potentially major) costs; with productivity-altering outcomes; with institutionalizing the union as a participant in work force direction. The trading territory, on the other hand, is simply "money."

FUNDED BENEFITS

A high proportion of all companies had specific bargaining goals in this area, many of them planning to offer benefit liberalization, or entirely new benefit items, in exchange for another goal that management was seeking. This was particularly true in the pension area, where 38 percent of responding companies planned to liberalize the program. In some cases, where bringing the plan into compliance with the Employee Retirement and Income Security Act (ERISA) may have required changes, the high response for "give" on this item may include some such liberalizations that were treated as bargaining chips for exchange in union negotiations.

Health benefits was a second area of give. A third of the companies reported plans to use added health benefits in exchange for some other item, and 30 percent planned to use life insurance in this way. The elements for trading may have been wage or other items and union demands in the benefit area. . . .

For each of the four benefit areas identified, less than 10 percent of the companies indicated an objective of tightening, or "getting back" something previously negotiated. Thus, within the benefit area the trading may be primarily a company-anticipated union demand for benefit liberalization A; to be resisted by the company, which planned to offer liberalization of Type B (or Type A-1) instead.

Company interviews, and the survey pretest, suggested the great sense of risk felt by management about its benefit programs. To some extent, the price of a health-benefit package, once negotiated, is out of management's control. In the pension area, the risks are seen as even greater—particularly by companies that expect less growth in their work forces in the future. One respondent flatly stated: "We plan and monitor the bargaining on benefits even more than on wages." Another company observed that benefit changes are pattern changes (because of companywide programs) *and* they are long-term commitments that are never rescinded. Therefore, even though that company bargains plant-by-plant, its bargaining objectives on benefits are set and reviewed at corporate headquarters.

TIME OFF WITH PAY

The most frequently mentioned goals involved paid-time-off practices such as vacations and holidays. Some union leaders have identified the reduction of work time as the major union initiative of the late 1970s, giving as the primary rationale an increase in employment and in membership that was expected to follow.[1] The sur-

---

[1] "Stimulating new job opportunities while increasing job security and providing workers with more leisure are the aims. We expect that thousands of additional workers will be put on the payroll" from page 1 of a United Auto Workers news release, October 2, 1977. See also "Slowing the Decline in the Auto Work Force," *Business Week,* October 25, 1976, p. 114.

vey data show that the highest proportion of companies expected to bargain on this subject and had a goal (Exhibit 2). About half (46 percent) planned to hold the line in the face of union pressure; but 28 percent had an offer they were prepared to make. Only 10 percent planned to reduce paid time off in some specific respect.

COST OF LIVING CLAUSES

"Escalator clauses" were once considered the concern of only a few industries and unions. But, by the late 1970s, they were the subject of specific bargaining objectives in nearly four out of five (78 percent) responding companies. Hold-the-line strategy is clearly very strong: Three out of five companies had a firm goal of keeping the status quo; that is, fending it off if they have no cost-of-living clause; and not enriching its formula if they already have COLA. A little over one third (37 percent) of the largest bargaining units already had COLA clauses.

Inflation, coupled with increasing duration of union contracts, has been accompanied by growth of COLA to its present level of 43 percent of *major* bargaining agreements (a Bureau of Labor Statistics grouping of contracts covering 1,000 workers or more).[2] However, escalators were present in only 38 percent of the smaller of these agreements (covering 1,000–4,999 workers), while 78 percent of the large contracts covering 50,000–99,999 had COLA, and it was present in *all* contracts covering 100,000 or more.[3] The median number of workers in the largest bargaining unit in companies surveyed by The Conference Board was 852, the average was 3,045.

[2] See U.S. Bureau of Labor Statistics, *Characteristics of Major Collective Bargaining Agreements*, July 1, 1976, Bulletin No. 2013, Table 1.4; also Victor Sheifer, "Collective Bargaining and the CPI: Escalation *vs.* Catch-up," *Proceedings* of the Thirty-first Annual Meeting, Industrial Relations Research Association, August 29–31, 1978, p. 260.

[3] Sheifer, p. 259.

LAYOFF AND RECALL PROCEDURES

Layoff and recall clauses in union contracts may have been "exercised" in depth during the 1974–1975 recession, the deepest since the 1930s. Bargaining objectives on layoff and recall terms in the contract were specified by 68 percent of the companies. Two out of five (39 percent) expected union demands for a more favorable clause, and planned to resist change. Nearly a quarter of all companies (23 percent) planned to tighten their existing provisions, or obtain one more favorable (to the company.) Thus, this subject was the second most likely to have a "takeback" goal. It is closely related to flexibility in assignment of employees—the subject most likely to have a management take-back objective.

The role of seniority in layoff and recall procedures is central, and the scope and arrangement of seniority units in the company or plant affect the efficiency with which a work force reduction can be accomplished—and the remaining workers be reassigned for maximum productivity. In a 1972 Bureau of Labor Statistics study analyzing the layoff and recall provisions of 364 contracts, all but one assigned seniority a part in governing the order of layoff.[4] The weight given seniority relative to other factors, the order and timing of successive displacements downward in the job scale (bumping), and other aspects of job-placement (and replacement) moves probably represent the bulk of bargaining substance on this subject.

SUBCONTRACTING

Layoff insecurites raised by the recession also caused some union demands for more restrictions on subcontracting, "to keep more work for our members." Companies,

[4] Bureau of Labor Statistics, *Layoff, Recall, and Worksharing Procedures*, Bulletin No. 1425–13, p. 31.

expecting this, had specific goals of maintaining existing contract clauses in 55 percent of the bargaining cases. This was the second highest "stand pat" position, after that on cost-of-living clauses. Subcontracting restrictions appear in about half (52 percent) of major contracts (those covering 1,000 or more workers).[5] If their incidence is the same or lower among The Conference Board respondents, then a large part of the bargaining goals in this group was avoidance of any *introduction* of restrictions on subcontracting.[6]

INCOME SECURITY

Half of the responding companies had an agenda on the subjects of severance pay, supplemental unemployment benefits, and similar income-security plans. This was the least often mentioned subject area for planned objectives.

A great majority of companies with objectives on this subject expected union demands for liberalizing benefits, and planned to retain the status quo. Some 5 percent of companies planned to liberalize—a course that was taken recently in the auto and steel industries.[7]

FLEXIBILITY IN ASSIGNMENT OF EMPLOYEES

This was the subject on which management planned to make gains. Eighty-two percent of all companies had a specific goal. In most cases, it was to obtain more favorable contract terms. This was the sole area in which management had a clearly

positive stance: In all other subjects, management's position was preservation of the status quo. The nature of the subject area (flexibility in assignment of employees) is relatively broad and unspecific (as opposed to, e.g., COLA). However, it would cover much of what in bargainers' shorthand would be called "management rights terms." Thus, the objective of getting more favorable terms may be interpreted as getting back management latitude and freedom that was eroded in earlier bargains, or by arbitration. It is also possible that, just as the 1974–75 recession sharpened union awareness of some contract job protections, it also sharpened the pressure on management to adjust and readjust work assignments, schedules, work force arrangements and the like, in ways and at speeds precluded by existing union agreements. . . . There are data strongly suggesting that flexibility in directing the workforce is *not* being sought for the purpose of removing *barriers to new technology:* major problems in that area are not reported.

LENGTH OF AGREEMENT

Half of the companies (49 percent) planned to hold the line in the face of a specific union demand on this subject. In the early 1960s, the proportion of major agreements of three years' duration or more was two out of five.[8] It is 70 percent at present.[9] The long-term trend toward lengthened contract terms may have been encouraged by NLRB rules that prevent replacement of existing union representation during contract terms of up to 3 years. Cost-of-living clauses have also helped, by making long-term wage contracts respon-

---

[5] *Characteristics of Major Collective Bargaining Agreements,* July 1, 1976, Table 7.3.

[6] An assumption that would best fit the smaller, plant-by-plant bargaining structure in the surveyed group.

[7] A fuller discussion of recent bargaining on this subject can be found in Audrey Freedman, *Security Bargains Reconsidered: SUB Severance Pay Guaranteed Work.* The Conference Board, Report No. 736, 1978.

[8] Marvin Friedman, "Discussion," *Proceedings* of the Thirty-first Annual Meeting, Industrial Relations Research Association, August, 1978, p. 278.

[9] *Characteristics of Major Collective Bargaining Agreements,* July 1, 1976, Table 1.4.

sive to inflation and thus less susceptible to bad guessing. Finally, the cost of bargaining and the attendant risks may have made short-term contracts unappealing to both parties. This mixture of causes and incentives to lengthen contract terms has not recently been interrupted by rapid inflation and the form of wage and price controls instituted in late 1978. In the first quarter of 1979, renegotiated contracts "had an average duration of 31.8 months, compared with 30.5 months when the same parties previously bargained."[10]

UNION SECURITY

In addition to recognizing the union as exclusive bargaining agent for the covered employee group, employers have been asked by unions to negotiate various forms of "union security" arrangements in the contract. Essentially, these clauses promote union membership either by requiring it, or by creating strong incentives to join and remain a member. Very generally, "union shop" clauses require all employees to join within a specified time after employment—and to remain members.

"Agency shop" clauses require payment of agency fees to the union, by all those who choose to remain nonmembers. "Maintenance of membership" clauses, less stringent, essentially restrict withdrawal from membership to a specified time period.

This subject was a battleground a generation ago, but by now union shop clauses are prevalent except for those 20 "right to work" states where they are prohibited. Some 71 percent of major contracts have varieties of union shop clauses, and another 7 percent have agency shops. Three percent have maintenance of membership and 18 percent have no specified union security other than recognition.[11]

Just under half (48 percent) of the companies had a goal of maintaining the status quo in the face of a union demand on this subject. Given the broad coverage of some kind of union security, it seems most likely that the demands expected were in the nature of a "tighter" security clause—perhaps reducing the time that a new employee can postpone joining to its legal minimum of 30 days.

---

[10] U.S. Department of Labor, News Release, April 27, 1979, p. 2.

[11] *Characteristics of Major Collective Bargaining Agreements*, July 1, 1976, Table 2.1.

PART FOUR

THE BARGAINING STRUCTURE AND BARGAINING POWER

CHAPTER 8

Bargaining Structure

The material presented in Part Three examined how unions and managements operate as organizations. It focused on the characteristics, functioning, and goals of each in the collective bargaining arena. What became readily apparent is that each party's organizational structure for bargaining is determined by what each thinks will maximize its outcomes from the bargaining process. Consequently, the internal needs of each as an organization are manifested in the type of bargaining structure adopted. Clearly, bargaining structure is a function of the needs of the parties, the constraints placed on these needs by their interaction with one another, and the environmental constraints in existence, e.g., legal mandates concerning unit determinations. It is also clear that the development of a bargaining structure represents an important struggle in industrial relations, resulting in a structural power balance between the parties that affects both the process and substance of collective bargaining.

OVERVIEW

Bargaining structure refers to whether bargaining occurs at a local, regional, industrial, or national level. On the union side it refers to the groups to be covered by a particular contract, e.g., a narrow group of skilled employees or a broad group of industrial employees in one location or in several. On the employer side it refers to the degree of centralization, e.g., one plant, multiplant, multiemployer in one industry, or multiindustry grouping.

While bargaining structures vary across bargaining relationships, the U.S. system of industrial relations is generally characterized by decentralized collective bargaining. This generalization is due to the predominance of single employer–single plant negotiations in manufacturing where unionization grew in the early years of the modern labor movement. However, multiemployer bargaining structures are predominant in nonmanufacturing, which was organized later, and the trend for much of the period following the 1930s has been towards centralization.

Why do bargaining structures change? The article by Weber defines bargaining structures and analyzes their determinants. The reader should consider how each of these determinants might explain why changes have occurred in the U.S. structure. Weber addresses these changes and analyzes why there has been pressure towards the consolidation of bargaining units.

In analyzing the Weber article, the reader should consider the possibility that instead of a trend toward either centralization or decentralization, bargaining may be proliferating at all significant levels of a bargaining relationship, due primarily to the organizational needs of both parties. For example, while a union may push for a centralized bargaining structure in order to maximize its bargaining power, it may then experience local dissension that requires the development of internal structures that extend participation to the local levels and resolve conflicting needs. The union may also experience pressure to allow negotiations of a subset of issues in supplemental contractual agreements at local levels.

The conflicts that arise due to the need for bargaining at all levels of a bargaining relationship result from the fact that there are advantages to both centralized and decentralized bargaining structures. From the union's perspective, a centralized structure may provide more economic power, more political clout, and a greater ability to insure equity in compensation rates across workers. A decentralized structure, however, allows the union to answer the immediate needs of employees, makes it easier to achieve consensus, and in instances where "whipsawing" is possible may also be the level where power is maximized. From the employer's perspective, a centralized structure may be an advantage in that all bargaining is concentrated into one period. A multiemployer structure may also limit competition in the product market. On the other hand a decentralized structure may be an advantage since it provides recognition of important distinctions between employers with regards to their financial picture; it reduces the potential for political grievances; and since unions have power at the local level, decentralization has a greater chance of insuring industrial relations stability.

The argument that pressures toward decentralization and centralization exist simultaneously in a given bargaining relationship gains credence by an examination of trends in European countries. Generally, bargaining structure in Europe is characterized by centralized bargaining, even to the extreme of economy–wide bargaining in Sweden. In the past 15 years, the pressure has been toward decentralization of the bargaining structure in order to address an increasing unrest among workers. At least one scholar has taken the position that the conflict over bargaining structure accounts for the tremendous increase in strike activity in these countries in the late 1960s and early 1970s.[1]

A final consideration regarding bargaining structure is the potential impact multinational corporations (MNCs) might have on bargaining structures. The Craypo article examines the characteristics of MNCs that

---

[1] See Solomon Barkin, ed., *Worker Militancy and Its Consequences* (New York: Praeger Publishers, 1975).

give them a tactical advantage in bargaining and what impact such an advantage may have on bargaining structure.

It should be noted that the special characteristics of MNCs that give them a bargaining advantage have been dealt with recently by several international organizations that have attempted to regulate various aspects of MNC operation.[2] In June 1976, the Organization for Economic Cooperation and Development adopted guidelines for regulation of MNCs. Included in these guidelines were regulations concerning labor relations. These required that MNCs not make threats of production transfers during bargaining, that MNCs observe prevailing wage standards and guarantee employment security, and that MNCs provide access to information necessary for bargaining. In 1977, the International Labor Organization went further in providing more explicit and detailed regulations. Although to date these regulations carry little weight, they represent a growing attempt on the part of international labor to limit the bargaining clout of MNCs. Ultimately, the expressed goal of this labor activity is international collective bargaining! The reader can easily imagine the problems such a bargaining structure would confront.

---

[2] For a review and analysis of efforts by international bodies to regulate multinational corporations, see John P. Windmuller and Jean A. Baderschneider, "International Guidelines for Industrial Relations: Impact and Outlook," *Proceedings of 33d Annual Meeting of the Industrial Relations Research Association*, New York, December 1977, pp. 81–89.

STABILITY AND CHANGE IN THE STRUCTURE OF COLLECTIVE BARGAINING

Arnold Weber*

Commentaries on the structure of collective bargaining have been broadly descriptive of the state of union-management relations in the United States. Initially, interest in bargaining structure focused on the establishment of decision-making units that would maintain an effective balance of power between unions and management. As collective bargaining has matured, attention has shifted to the need for bargaining structures that can accommodate the goals of specific employee and employer groups while preserving the essential power relationships in the bargaining process. These objectives cannot be achieved independently of other considerations that determine the course of collective bargaining developments. Although the structure of collective bargaining may be viewed in a narrow, technical framework, it is also a vital element in a chain of interdependence linking together the aspirations and demands of the parties, the bargaining process, and the external environment.

*   *   *   *   *

BARGAINING STRUCTURE DEFINED

The problem of defining *bargaining structure* is similar to that of arriving at an ac-

ceptable definition of love; both terms describe important phenomena, but it is not clear what the appropriate level of analysis should be. In fact, collective bargaining structure cannot be identified with any simple notion of the bargaining unit. Instead, a given bargaining structure is comprised of a *multiplicity of units* tied together in a complicated network of relationships by social, legal, administrative, and economic factors. The basic element of any bargaining structure is the *informal work group* whose members are unified by common aspirations and a common interpretation of their environment. The *election district* or "appropriate bargaining unit" is superimposed upon the structure of informal work groups by the National Labor Relations Board for purposes of employee self-determination in regard to union representation. The election districts, in turn, may constitute the building blocks for the *negotiation unit*, or the unit within which formal collective bargaining takes place. Beyond the negotiation unit, it may be possible to distinguish the *unit of direct impact*, a set of individual negotiating units whose decisions are directly affected by the terms of a bargaining agreement.

Since they reflect different factors, there may be considerable divergence in the scope of these four units in a specific bargaining situation. The informal work group may be founded on distinctions as varied as age, occupation, department, eth-

---

* President, University of Colorado. Reprinted from The American Assembly, *Challenges to Collective Bargaining*, ed. Lloyd Ulman (Englewood Cliffs, N.J.: Prentice-Hall, 1967) pp. 13–36.

nic or racial factors, sex, and shift assignment. The election district is largely the product of government determinations that have attempted to achieve a precarious balance between employees' rights of self-determination and the stability of collective bargaining. The negotiating unit has frequently been shaped by corporate and union structure, multiemployer organization, and alliances between unions. And the unit of direct impact may be circumscribed by the economics of the industry or by traditionally accepted relationships between pattern setters and pattern followers.

* * * * *

THE DETERMINANTS OF BARGAINING STRUCTURE

* * * * *

MARKET FACTORS

As the framework for economic decision making, bargaining structure will be strongly influenced by the market context within which negotiations take place. Unions generally have sought to devise bargaining structures that are coextensive with the specific market(s) encompassed by their jurisdictions. In building such structures unions may hope to attain their traditional goal of "taking wages out of competition" by insuring the uniformity of wage rates among producers who operate in the same market. At risk of oversimplification, industrial unions generally have pressed for bargaining structures that are related to the scope of the product market while craft unions have been most sensitive to labor market considerations.

Innumerable contemporary examples reveal the influence of market factors on bargaining structure. In the bituminous coal, ladies garment, and trucking industries, elaborate multiemployer negotiating units have been developed to blanket the product market. In automobiles, steel, and rubber tires, the unit of direct impact clearly encompasses all the major producers. Similarly, the bargaining structure in the construction industry has reflected variable market considerations. In commercial and residential construction, the negotiating units usually are highly localized. However, where labor and capital are mobile over a wide geographical area as in highway and pipeline construction, the bargaining structure will be enlarged to include statewide or national negotiating units.

Although trade unions generally have been most responsive to the relationship between market structure and bargaining structure, the employer also has an important stake in the reconciliation of these two elements. First, where there is severe competition among many firms in the product market, management generally will endorse multiemployer bargaining structures in order to impose some measure of regulation on market behavior. In retail trade, the large supermarkets have been concerned over the entrance of major discount houses, such as Korvette's, into the food retailing business. Consequently they have goaded the Retail Clerks to enlarge the unit of direct impact to include these new competitors.

Second, employers are concerned that they will be blanketed in bargaining structures that do not recognize real distinctions between union jurisdiction and market factors. In the automobile industry, the major independent parts producers have exerted considerable efforts to disentangle themselves from the automobile industry pattern on the grounds that competition among parts manufacturers is too keen to justify the application of the generous UAW–Big Three agreements to their situation.

Other, dynamic relationships may be distinguished between market structure and bargaining structure. Thus, the boundaries of bargaining structure will be readjusted to include employees engaged in manufacturing new products that serve as substitutes for extablished commodities whose markets are already subject to uniform collective bargaining determinations. In the economist's terminology, the bargaining structure will tend to embrace those product markets that are characterized by a significant measure of cross-elasticity of demand. If the substitutable products are produced by the same companies, few difficulties of adjustment are likely to arise.

* * * * *

THE NATURE OF BARGAINING ISSUES

In any market context, the type of issues emphasized will also have an influence on the development of bargaining structure. Some issues, like wages, have marketwide implications and must be handled within expanded bargaining structures to insure their effective resolution. Other issues, such as pensions and insurance plans, are best treated on a companywide basis because of the need for uniformity created by actuarial and administrative considerations. Finally, there are questions of work rules, safety, wash-up time, and other minutiae of industrial relations that are essentially local in nature and must be related to the conditions that prevail in a particular plant or department.

To some extent then, the structure of collective bargaining will reflect the substantive emphasis of negotiations at any point in time in a specific relationship. When the important issues are marketwide in nature, such as wages, there will be strong pressures for expanding the scope of the negotiating unit and centralizing decision-making power within the unit to avoid variations among plants or firms. Conversely, demands for decentralized or even "fractionalized" bargaining are likely

to develop when local problems are paramount. In fact, different negotiating units may be present in the same bargaining structure to consider various categories of issues. In this respect, distinctions are often made between "national" and "local" issues.

* * * * *

REPRESENTATIONAL FACTORS

Recognition of the structural implications of different categories of issues focuses attention on a related factor influencing the development of bargaining structures. As Neil W. Chamberlain has noted, a union is comprised of various work groups that may have divergent, and sometimes conflicting, goals in formulating the "common rule" governing a specific matter. These work groups are willing to form an alliance to augment their bargaining power. However, the formation of a common front inevitably involves a partial relinquishing of individual group goals. Each group will press for, or acquiesce in, the expansion of the worker alliance as long as the rate of substitution between the gains derived from the increment to bargaining power are greater than the perceived losses associated with the denial of autonomy in decision making. At some point, this rate of substitution will become negative, and tensions will develop within the union and the associated bargaining structures for the accommodation of special group interests or the fragmentation of the alliance. If this were not the case, there would be continued tendencies toward the development of "one big union" since extending the alliance to new work groups will make some positive contributions to bargaining power. Experience with the Knights of Labor, the Industrial Workers of the World, and other all-embracing labor organizations indicates that such limits do, in fact, exist.

The severity of the representational problem is determined by the degree of homogeneity of the union membership and the types of issues preeminent in the union-management relationship. Thus, representational problems are likely to arise where there is a substantial minority of craft workers in a large, industrial union. In the UAW, agitation by the skilled trades for the right of self-determination in collective bargaining has been a chronic problem since the early 1950s. In the pulp and paper industry, the dominant worker alliance has been maintained by preserving formal distinctions between two unions—the Pulp, Sulphite and Paper Workers, which represents most of the "production workers" and the Brotherhood of Papermakers, which speaks for the highly skilled paper machine operators. The unions have retained their separate identities, but for over 50 years have engaged in coordinated bargaining in common negotiating units.

The importance of representational factors is also determined by the nature of the substantive issues considered in different units of the bargaining structure. When general issues, such as wages, are the focus of negotiation, the problem of representation largely involves the development of decision-making procedures that will insure the equitable distribution of gains among the different work groups. The apparent absence of these procedures contributed to the "skilled trades revolt" in the UAW. However, other issues are significant only for particular work groups. In this case, the representational problem is one of assuming that such issues will be given adequate treatment in the established negotiating units. If specific work groups at the plant level believe their problems are not given sufficient attention they may press for new negotiating units. Under these circumstances, the leadership of the national union must decide to what extent the union's limited bargaining resources will be diverted from the achievement of national gains to an effort to satisfy the objectives of specific work groups.

The same calculus of anticipated gains and loss underlies the maintenance or fragmentation of employer alliances in collective bargaining. In the United States, the formation of employer associations for purposes of collective bargaining has been most widespread in the local service industries where the price of autonomy in labor negotiations often has been gross power deficiencies in dealing with large, comprehensive unions. Employer associations are generally found in retail trade, the hotel and restaurant industries, dry cleaning and laundries, building construction, and trucking. Other instances of long-term employer alliances are found in bituminous coal, men's and women's clothing, and shoes.

* * * * *

GOVERNMENT POLICIES

Although the parties have some discretion in adjusting bargaining structure to their preferences for autonomy and collective strength, government policies usually must be accepted as an external constraint on the direction and form of structural developments. Since the passage of the Railway Labor Act in 1926 and the Wagner Act in 1935, government policies have had a major impact upon bargaining structure.

Government influence has been wielded in both a direct and indirect manner. Initially, the designation of the "appropriate bargaining unit" by the National Labor Relations Board establishes the election unit for purposes of determining worker choice of union representation. If the union wins certification, the election unit may constitute an independent arena for collective bargaining, or it may be integrated with other election units to form a consolidated bargaining structure. Policies toward the scope of these units clearly have had a fundamental effect on the evolution of bargaining structure in specific industries. The plantwide determinations made by the NLRB in the mass producing industries during the 1930s helped to set the stage for the emergence of industrial unions and market-wide bargaining. More recently, the application of these same concepts to new industries, like atomic energy, have stimulated craft unions to create multicraft bargaining agents such as the Metal Trades Councils and the Atomic Trades and Labor Councils.

*   *   *   *   *

TACTICS AND POWER

Government policies define the *rules of the game* by which collective bargaining is carried out. Within the limits established by these rules, other tactical factors will help to shape the bargaining in a specific company or industry. Each party will seek to devise a structure that will maximize its capacity for inflicting real or expected costs on the other party in the course of the bargaining process.

Much of tactical maneuvering involves some variant of "whipsawing" by either the union or the employer. When a union bargains with a few large employers who operate in a well-defined product market, it will often try to maintain the individual firm as the negotiating unit while using the industry as the effective unit of direct impact. In the New York City newspaper industry, the various craft unions have sought to preserve collective bargaining on an individual company basis in order to negotiate a favorable agreement with the most vulnerable employer and then apply the "pattern" to the other firms. In response to this tactic the newspapers retreated to the protective confines of a city-wide publishers' association from which they may retaliate against whipsaw tactics

with a sympathetic lockout. In 1962, Local 6 of the International Typographical Union was able to splinter this common front by reaching a separate agreement with the *New York Post*. When a similar tactic was unsuccessful in 1964, the ITU sought to undermine the employers' defenses by an NLRB ruling nullifying the multiemployer arrangement.

Usually, the unions' desire to engage in whipsawing tactics is sharply reduced when many small employers are encompassed by its jurisdiction. Here, considerations of administrative efficiency and maintaining market-wide uniformity in wages and labor costs push in the direction of consolidated bargaining structures. Even in these cases, however, the unions may seek to retain enough flexibility to play off one group of employers against another. In Southern California, the Retail Clerks has developed an expanded structure covering all the supermarket chains in the Los Angeles area. Nevertheless, it has balked at including the smaller, independent food stores. In the event that a strike is called against the large supermarkets, the fact that the independents will continue to operate can have a moderating influence on potential employer resistance.

Tactical factors also help to explain the nature of bargaining structures in multiplant companies. When a firm has several plants engaged in the production of a homogeneous commodity, the union inevitably will seek to broaden the negotiating unit to encompass all the production facilities. If bargaining is carried out on a single plant basis, it is possible for the employer to blunt the effects of the strike in one plant by continuing production in another. For example, the maintenance of single-plant bargaining units has been a key factor in the ability of major oil refining firms to keep the OCAW at bay.

The employer is less likely to resist companywide bargaining where the multiplant firm is characterized by the vertical integration of production facilities, a situation in which different plants carry out separate phases of the overall production process. Under these circumstances, a union may be able to bring the company to its knees by a work stoppage in a single plant producing an essential part for the final product. Consequently, the employer may accept a companywide bargaining structure to avoid harassment by the union. In the agricultural implements industry, International Harvester moved to a master agreement shortly after the UAW had ousted the Farm Equipment Workers from the company. On the other hand, Allis-Chalmers strongly resisted the Automobile Workers' efforts to develop a master agreement covering all the plants where the union had representation. In the former case, there was a high degree of integration of production; in the latter, most of the company's production units were technologically independent of each other. Similarly, in the automobile industry itself, one of the virtues of a companywide agreement from management's point of view is the limitations it imposes on isolated union action in the key parts plants. Tactical factors usually are not determinate in the evolution of bargaining, but they may exercise an important influence in individual cases, especially in the early stage of the bargaining relationship.

THE CONSOLIDATION OF BARGAINING STRUCTURE

The trends in bargaining structure since the mid-1930s can be broadly interpreted in the light of the major variables discussed above. Between 1935 and the mid-1950s strong pressures were generated for expanding the size and scope of negotiating units and for moving the locus of decision making to higher levels. At the outset, considerations of bargaining structure were inextricably related to union efforts to or-

ganize the unorganized and to hold these gains in the face of employer counterattacks or incursions from competing unions. However, there short-term objectives reinforced the tendencies associated with other more fundamental factors.

As the trade unions were spurred to broad organizational campaigns in the 1930s, it was apparent that market factors required expanded structures in order to assure effective collective bargaining. From the union leaders' vantage point, the minimum structural requirements in industries like steel, automobile, and rubber tires called for company-wide negotiating units. In other industries, such as bituminous coal and men's and women's clothing, multiemployer negotiating units became an immediate objective so that the union might move expeditiously to "take wages out of competition."

Where it was not possible to establish a negotiating unit that was coextensive with the market, the objective of market-wide uniformity might be achieved by expanding the area of direct impact. Thus, the immediate post–World War II period was the heyday of "pattern" bargaining. The efficacy of such patterns probably was overstated at the time, but the emphasis on this tactic was an indication of the unions' rush to consolidate those bargaining structures which had taken shape during the 1930s and the World War II period.

The nature of the dominant issues in collective bargaining from 1935 to the mid-1950s also was conducive to the establishment of consolidated negotiating units and top-level decision making. Once fundamental institutional issues such as union recognition were resolved, the main thrust of negotiation was the improvement of wages and the formulation of minimum standards governing working conditions. Because the emphasis was on developing wage *uniformity* and raising the *level* of wages, the relevant framework for decision making was the product or labor market.

Little discretion could be given to particular groups within the union or, in some cases, in the employer's association. In steel, for example, the drive for wage uniformity resulted in the development of a common job evaluation system and wage structure covering all the major steel producers.

The pressure for expanded bargaining structures was sustained when the substantive emphasis of collective bargaining shifted from wages to fringe items in the early 1950s. In those cases in which the negotiating unit was still limited to the individual plant, the union suffered obvious disadvantages in bargaining over fringe items like pensions and insurance. Although a pension might be "negotiated" at the plant level, it was clear to union leaders that the details of the program were established at a top corporate level and left little room for modifications in local situations. Where unions could not establish companywide units for all bargaining issues, they attempted to create special negotiating units for pensions and other welfare items. In the chemicals industry, the Chemical Workers ultimately prevailed on management in American Cyanamid, Monsanto, and a few other large firms to enter into a master agreement covering pension, insurance and health plans. In other cases where small firms were involved, the emphasis on pensions was the occasion for devising special multiemployer negotiating units. In Connecticut, a statewide multicraft unit has been established to permit the negotiation of a single pension plan covering all organized construction workers in that state.

As this pattern of marketwide and corporate bargaining emerged, those government policies that impinged upon collective bargaining were generally neutral or tacitly supported increased consolidation. The basic element of bargaining structure subject to direct government influence, as indicated previously, is the "appropriate

bargaining unit." As such, the early NLRB unit determinations were largely irrelevant to the question of bargaining structure. That is, the bargaining unit was essentially an election district for purposes of selecting worker representatives. Incidentally, however, NLRB decisions in this area did affect the subsequent development of bargaining structure. The fact that the board endorsed plantwide, industrial units in the heavy, mass-producing industries laid the foundation for the subsequent erection of companywide and industrywide negotiating units.

Once the union had gained representation rights within the election district, the NLRB was generally indifferent to the form and scope of the actual negotiating unit that resulted from the interplay of market and institutional factors. In most cases, the board passively accepted the bargaining structures that took shape over time. Once these were established, a desire to "preserve the stability of collective bargaining" usually deterred the board from modifying existing arrangements. In this manner, NLRB policies severely limited the right of craft severance from larger plantwide units until 1954. In the case of multiplant bargaining structures that had been built from smaller election districts, the board usually endorsed the new boundaries of the negotiating unit as the basis for any subsequent representation election.

Government involvement in the development of bargaining structure, was most direct during World War II. At that time, the War Labor Board was given the responsibility for settling all labor disputes that threatened the national security. In its procedures, the WLB insisted on handling petitions for wage adjustments in particular firms and industries on a consolidated basis. The outcome of this approach in the basic steel industry was the "Little Steel Formula" which, in effect, made the entire industry the unit of direct impact for purposes of wage determination. A succession of similar cases in meat packing, cotton textiles, rubber, and other mass-producing sectors of the economy encouraged the unions to press for expanded bargaining structures. When the war was concluded, this process was irreversible in most cases.

Because many bargaining relationships were in a formative stage in the 1930s and immediate postwar period, tactical considerations also dictated an expansion of bargaining structure. Both organized labor and management sought to occupy the "high ground" in order to enjoy a tactical advantage over its adversary. Where the union attempted to whipsaw individual employers, management would often form defensive employer associations. Such a reaction took place in trucking, retail trade, and various service industries. Even in steel, the employers reluctantly concluded that closer coordination was necessary to counter the union's strategy of divide and conquer. On the other hand, when the union's bargaining power in a single plant was undermined by management's ability to maintain production in other units, the appropriate response was a strike against the entire firm. Through a series of maneuvers and countermaneuvers, the bargaining structure in many industries was expanded to include more units on each side of the table.

There is little direct evidence regarding the importance of representational factors in the development of bargaining structure through the post–World War II period. It is reasonable to assume, however, that at this stage many workers perceived greater potential gains from joining together in comprehensive units than from adhering to bargaining structures that would assume special interest representation. Indeed, John L. Lewis' program for leading labor out of the wilderness was founded on this assumption. In addition, the broad success of the CIO's organizing appeals and methods provided some verification of the belief that many workers were willing to trade narrow group interests for greater bargaining power.

* * * * *

BARGAINING STRUCTURE IN TRANSITION

Against this background, developments in bargaining structure since the mid-1950s have followed two divergent paths. On the one hand, there has been a continuation of historical tendencies toward the expansion of negotiating units and the centralization of decision making within these units. On the other hand, stresses have appeared in established bargaining structures indicating increased demands for decentralization and a greater measure of autonomy for local work groups.

CONSOLIDATING BARGAINING STRUCTURES

Recent trends toward the consolidation of bargaining structure shows the impact of normal market and tactical considerations. In the trucking industry, the Teamsters took a major step toward the creation of a national bargaining structure in 1964 when it negotiated a master over-the-road and cartage agreement covering approximately 450,000 workers employed by 1,000 trucking firms affiliated with 27 different employer associations. This change was another, crucial step in the dilution of local autonomy in collective bargaining, an attribute that had been fiercely defended by Teamster business agents in the past.

In the West Coast lumber and sawmill products industry, tactical factors have still dominated the development of bargaining structure. In 1963, the two unions with representation in the industry, the International Woodworkers of America and the Lumber and Sawmill Workers affiliated with the Carpenters Union, jointly struck two members of the six-firm Timber Operator's Council. The other four Council affiliates retaliated with a sympathetic lockout. The unions then attempted a flanking attack by reaching an agreement with the Simpson Company, a large firm that was outside the multiemployer negotiating unit. The agreement exceeded the original offer of the association; nevertheless, the employers refused to meet the "pattern." Ultimately, the unions called off the strike and settled for a wage gain that was slightly larger than the employers' original offer but less than the package agreed to by Simpson.

In other cases, unions have tried unsuccessfully to expand the scope of the negotiating unit when confronted with strong employer resistance. Although all the important cement firms are organized and produce a homogeneous commodity, the Cement Workers has continued to negotiate with management on an individual firm basis. Indeed, it was only following a multiemployer strike in 1958 that a semblance of a wage pattern appeared in the industry. The Communication Workers of America also has been thwarted in its effort to hold comprehensive negotiations for the units it represents in the Bell System. Instead, the negotiating unit is still the individual AT&T affiliate while a strong pattern influence has made the entire system the unit of direct impact.

A unique program for building coordinated negotiating units has been initiated by the Industrial Union Department of the AFL–CIO. Since 1961, the IUD has promoted collaboration in collective bargaining among locals of different international unions that represent workers at plants of the same company. As a matter of official dogma, the IUD declared that this drive for interunion coordination was a response to the increasing corporate diversification in the American economy. The more plausible explanation is that the IUD is acting as a supranational union agency to rationalize the historical incongruities or weaknesses of trade union structure and jurisdiction. That is, as a result of the AFL–CIO split, dual unionism in a given industry became a normal, acrimonious state of affairs. In addition, some international unions showed little restraint in accepting the membership of workers in firms outside of their formal jurisdictions. Because the AFL–CIO merger agreement recognized "established bargaining relations," many corporations are still characterized by two or more unions on the scene. Under these circumstances, the bargaining power of any individual union may be reduced by the fact that it can claim the allegiance of only a minority of the workers in a multiplant firm. In this context, the IUD has stepped forward and assumed major responsibility for the development of coordinated bargaining structures.

The general approach of the IUD has been to persuade the individual unions to formulate common bargaining demands and strategy. Once the attempt at coordination has been confirmed by the establishment of a "steering committee" or some other mechanism, the employer is asked to negotiate with the unions on a combined basis. The initial demands of the interunion combination generally have involved a single pension or insurance plan agreement. If this objective is achieved the unions presumably can move on to a master agreement covering other substantive issues. The IUD's program has been implemented with considerable vigor. By 1966, the IUD claimed that it had inspired or supported 76 instances of interunion activity in collective bargaining. The list of firms involved includes many large corporations such as Borg-Warner, Sperry Rand, Sylvania, Union Carbide, and the Armour Chemical and Fertilizer Company. The most ambitious program of interunion coordination was undertaken in 1966 when the IUD convened a committee bringing together representatives of seven international unions that bargainied for 160,000 employees of General Electric and Westinghouse.

The results of the IUD's campaign have been mixed. In 1965 the locals of four international unions tried to force the Wilson Sporting Goods Company to bargain with them on a joint basis. When management refused, the unions struck each of the four plants. This common front was broken when the Clothing Workers reached a separate agreement at the Kansas City plant. The other unions soon followed suit.

Despite these setbacks, the IUD can claim several modest triumphs. In 1961, the IUD successfully coordinated the demands of locals at eight international unions for improvements in the pension plan negotiated with the Minnesota Mining and Manufacturing Company. Another success was experienced in bargaining over pensions with the Revere Copper and Brass Company. It is significant to note that in this case only two unions, the IAM and UAW, were involved and that these unions had a previous record of successful coordination in the airframe and aerospace industries. Obviously, serious problems confront the IUD in its efforts to build new bargaining structures. In many instances interunion relations are plagued by past animosities and diverse policies, expiration dates may be widely distributed in time, and no formal sanctions are available to keep the individual locals in line. Moreover, the IUD can anticipate continued employer resistance. Nevertheless, if the gaps in existing bargaining structures are to be plugged, the IUD's program is an imaginative step toward that objective.

DEMOCRACY AND DECENTRALIZATION

While measures have been taken to shore up bargaining structures at their weak points, internal demands have been made for the modification of consolidated structures to provide more influence for narrow occupational and plant groups in collective bargaining. The pressure for decentralization has become sufficiently visible to cause concern among both industrial relations practitioners and the public. Although it would be an exaggeration to describe the situation as a "crisis," various signals indicate that significant changes will be, or should be, forthcoming.

Worker dissatisfaction with expanded bargaining structures appeared to arise first among the craftsmen. Normally, craft workers constitute a minority within industrial unions and the associated negotiating units. In this position, they cannot be certain that their special needs will be incorporated in the union's demands or the labor contract. As companywide and multiemployer negotiating units took shape few complaints were heard from the craft workers. Apparently, any loss of autonomy was overbalanced by the increase in bargaining power derived from participation in a broader worker alliance. However, with the solidification of expanded bargaining structures craft workers became increasingly dissatisfied with their minority status within these larger decision-making units. Rumblings were heard among craft workers throughout the late forties and early 1950s in major industrial unions such as the Automobile Workers, the Rubber Workers, and the IUE. The craft workers' grievance touched on various aspects of their position and rights in the plant, but wages was the most sensitive point of controversy. In many unionized industries there had been a steady compression of the wage differential between the skilled craftsmen and the unskilled and semiskilled workers. Although several economic factors contributed to this compression, the craftsmen were likely to attribute their plight to the belief that they did not exercise sufficient influence in union decision making or collective bargaining. The most dramatic instance of craft agitation took place in the automobile industry, as noted previously. Following the negotiation of the 1955 contract, the skilled tradesmen engaged in widespread wildcat strikes, formed their own union and petitioned the NLRB for an election to select their own bargaining agent. This campaign caused great concern to both the union and the automobile companies even though it was ultimately unsuccessful. Other instances of craft unrest have appeared in the rubber, communications, and steel industries.

The shift in the "terms of trade" between representational factors and aggregate bargaining power was generalized to other work groups by a significant change in the substantive emphasis of collective bargaining. Whereas union negotiators had been concerned primarily with wages and fringe benefits through the mid-1950s, the bargaining climate was drastically altered by the fears associated with automation and the existence of a chronic labor surplus in the economy. Now, the overriding short-term goals were job security and the equalization of economic opportunity. To achieve these objectives, it was necessary to focus on questions of seniority, employment guarantees, and the whole gamut of problems associated with the concept of "work rules." While the wage issue could be handled on a company-wide or multiemployer basis, the special problems of job security demanded a narrower framework.

In addition, in some large bargaining structures, such as steel, autos, and agricultural implements, the grievance procedure had become so clogged that commonplace problems of working conditions remained unresolved. Nor could these issues be handled effectively in consolidated negotiating units, especially when contract negotiations took place once every three years. The president of the Steel Workers might exact a generous wage offer from the eleven basic steel producers, but he could

not be expected to deal with manning requirements for an automated rolling mill or the question of wash-up time for workers in a plant in Aliquippa. Thus, the consideration of some issues would have to be displaced downward in the bargaining structure. Unless this shift took place these issues might not be resolved in a satisfactory manner to the particular groups affected, or might not be disposed of at all.

The tensions have been further accentuated by important changes in government policies. As indicated previously, government policies impinging on bargaining structure in the past were largely permissive or were consistent with the broad tendencies toward consolidation. In recent years, however, government policies have been modified. To further complicate the situation, the new policies have given conflicting cues to the various actors in the bargaining process. With the passage of the Labor-Management Reporting and Disclosure Act of 1959 the government strongly endorsed democratic practices in union government and administration. For the rank and file, "democracy" may mean greater autonomy in collective bargaining as well as the right of opposition candidates to demand space in the union newspaper. In addition, the *American Potash* decision in 1954 finally reaffirmed the conditional right of craft groups to sever from industrial bargaining units.[1] It is debatable whether LMRDA or the new craft severance rulings have had a direct effect on bargaining structure, but clearly they have changed the climate within which union decision making takes place.

The import of recent government policies has been different for the top union leaders than for the rank and file members.

---

[1] [Editor's note: The current standards for craft severance were established by the National Labor Relations Board in 1966 in the *Mallinckrodt Chemical Works* case. (162 NLRB 387)]

On the one hand, union leaders are under notice that the affairs of the organization must be conducted in a democratic manner. On the other hand, the enunciation of the "wage guidelines" by the President carries an admonition to be "responsible" in determining the outcome of collective bargaining. "Responsibility" is a concept that the rank and file trade union member is likely to limit to his family and creditors; for the president of a large national union, however, *responsibility* may be defined by a personal call from the White House. For a union leader to be responsible he must exercise firm control over the bargaining structure in order to guard against the potential "irresponsibility" of the rank and file members. Moreover, responsibility also means the avoidance of a strike to prevent harmful consequences for the national economy.

The dilemma created by these government policies was vividly illustrated by the negotiations between the five major airlines and the Machinists in 1966. Here, the union leadership demonstrated its responsibility by agreeing to a contract that was "consistent with the guidelines" and which would have ended a strike that was causing great public inconvenience. The rank and file union members, however, exercised their democratic rights and rejected the contract. Among other lessons, this case demonstrated the great difficulty of reconciling "democracy" with "responsibility" in expanded bargaining structures.

EVIDENCE OF DISCONTENT

Overall the changes in representational factors, the substantive emphasis of negotiations and government policies have engendered pressures for the decentralization of bargaining structures, especially from the rank and file union members. Evidence of these tendencies has taken various forms. First, rank and file workers dissatisfied with national agreements have, in some cases, "voted with their feet" and engaged in wildcat strikes. In the bituminous coal industry, miners in Illinois and Ohio struck to express their displeasure with the fact that the 1964 national agreement did not include provisions for enhancing job security. A contributing factor was the relaxation of the tight controls that had been kept on the membership for more than 20 years by the Lewis administration. Unauthorized walkouts also beset Ford and General Motors in 1961 and 1964. Although some have attributed these strikes to high-level union intrigue, the accepted explanation is the failure to resolve literally thousands of local problems that had accumulated during the contract term. In General Motors alone, an estimated 20,000 local issues were submitted for discussion during the 1964 negotiations.

Second, the rank and file members have shown a disposition to reject the contract agreed to by the union's negotiators. The 1965 annual report of the Federal Mediation and Conciliation Service indicated that "An increasing problem encountered is the situation where management and union negotiators reach tentative agreements on new contract terms only to have the proposed settlement rejected by rank and file members." The report goes on to state anxiously that, "no reversal of this unfortunate trend is now in sight."

Third, a concern over the centralization of decision making in collective bargaining appears to have been a factor in the ouster of the chief executives of several major unions. In the Steel Workers, an important element in I. W. Abel's campaign against incumbent president David McDonald was the charge that the latter had "lost touch with the rank and file steel worker." Ironically, the activities of the Human Relations Committee—which had been heralded as a major innovation in industrial relations—was used as evidence that undue influence on union decisions was exercised by persons who did not reflect rank and file interests.

Top level leaders also have failed to gain reelection in other major unions. James Carey was forced down from his position as long-time president of the IUE, and O. A. Knight decided not to run for reelection as president of the Oil Chemical and Atomic Workers when it was apparent that he would meet strong opposition. In the Rubber Workers, George Burdon was ousted from the presidency after a short time in office. Not all of these political upheavals can be attributed to rank and file demands for the decentralization of collective bargaining. Nonetheless, they do indicate a more intense desire on the part of the membership to have a leadership that is closely attuned to grass roots problems and sentiments.

Fourth, as a final resort, local discontent with the conduct of collective bargaining has resulted in defections from the parent union. In view of NLRB rulings protecting the integrity of companywide and multiemployer bargaining units, this path has not been easily or frequently used. For this reason, a successful schism is especially noteworthy. Such an occurrence took place in the West Coast pulp and paper industry in 1964. Collective bargaining in that sector is carried out in one large negotiating unit covering approximately 20,000 workers employed in 48 pulp and paper mills by 18 different companies. The employees were represented for many years by the Pulp, Sulphite and Paper Workers and The Brotherhood of Paper Makers. This arrangement had been lauded as a model of constructive industrial relations. Over the years, however, many frictions had developed between the local unions and the national leadership of the PSPW over the degree of autonomy that should be exercised by the locals in collective bargaining and other matters. The controversy became a crisis when the delegates from the West Coast locals insisted that they should have the right to elect the chairman of the union negotiating committee. The international's officers insisted that past practice should be followed and that the chairman should be appointed by an international vice president. Shortly thereafter, an independent union, the Association of Western Pulp and Paper Workers, was formed and petitioned the NLRB for a representation election on a multiemployer, coastwide basis. Despite bitter attacks on the rebels by the established unions, the independent won the NLRB election by a narrow margin. Once the new union was certified, it demonstrated its militancy by calling a strike. This was the first strike carried out in the multiemployer unit and the first general labor dispute in the West Coast pulp and paper industry since 1917.

Similar circumstances led to the breakaway of the American Airlines pilots from the Air Line Pilots Association in 1962. The American Airlines group had negotiated a contract governing the qualifications of the "third man" that did not meet international union standards on jet aircraft. In return for more permissive standards, the company had agreed to reduce the pilots' monthly flight schedules, a concession that promised greater security against possible displacement. When the international tried to block the contract, the American Airlines pilots formed an independent union, and like the West Coast paper workers, assured their autonomy by winning a representation election.

* * * * *

THE CHALLENGE

. . .Without a government prohibition on consolidated negotiating units, it is unlikely that there will be any drastic change in the nature of bargaining structure in the United States. For the unions, extreme decentralization would pose a threat to established gains. For many employers, the decentralization of collective bargaining would mean administrative chaos or guerilla warfare. In addition, it is important to note that in an international perspective, the structure of collective bargaining in the United States is still highly decentralized and affords relatively wide latitude for differences in labor agreements. In Western Europe, in contrast, bargaining structures typically span entire industries and in some cases, like Sweden and Denmark, the economy as a whole.

Although pressures for the decentralization of bargaining structures are real enough, it is probably an overstatement to conclude that American union members are entrapped or "alienated" in expanded bargaining structures. The very fact that workers have been able to express their discontents in one way or another provides some indication that these structures have not hardened into unyielding "monoliths." The paramount consideration is the maintenance of public and union policies that preserve the right of rank and file members to dissent against their leadership or, under extreme circumstances, to reassert a measure of autonomy in collective bargaining. If this approach appears to be untidy or sometimes disruptive, it is far superior to the application of any rigid formula to the determination of bargaining structures. Moreover, in various sectors, unions and management have shown a willingness to experiment with devices that will accommodate local needs without destroying existing structural arrangements. As with any form of government, the structure of collective bargaining in the United States must combine elements of stability and change. On the record of the past and current evidence there is some confidence that collective bargaining can respond effectively to the changing requirements of both its constituents and the external environment.

COLLECTIVE BARGAINING IN THE CONGLOMERATE, MULTINATIONAL FIRM: LITTON'S SHUTDOWN OF ROYAL TYPEWRITER

Charles Craypo*

A new corporate structure has emerged, which combines conglomerate diversification and multinational location, and several theoretical and practical issues have been raised regarding its impact on collective bargaining. Unions claim conglomerate structure permits top management to cross-subsidize funds between unrelated business activities and to keep subsidiary managers uninformed and powerless at the bargaining table; they claim that multinational operations enable an employer to undermine union bargaining strength by exploiting wage differentials among nation states. Managers of conglomerate companies, on the other hand, maintain that subsidiary divisions are managed on a decentralized basis and are financially self-sustaining; managers of multinational firms insist their national operations are managed autonomously and in conformity with national practices and procedures.

* * * * *

THE CONGLOMERATE, MULTINATIONAL EMPLOYER

Conglomeration is a recent and special type of corporate diversification in which a parent firm acquires companies that produce unrelated goods and services. Conglomerate firms superficially resemble highly diversified producers in some of the basic industries, such as electrical products, motor vehicles, and chemicals, but they differ in their type of diversification.

* * * * *

A business enterprise becomes a conglomerate firm as a result of diversification through merger, but there is no standard criterion for determining what degree of diversification is necessary to establish conglomerate status. The broadest definition of conglomerate merger is residual in approach; it defines as being conglomerate those business combinations which are neither horizontal nor vertical in content.[1] The more generally accepted definition is narrower; it includes only those acquisitions in which there is no discernible relationship in the nature of the business between the acquiring and the acquired firms.[2] The definition of a conglomerate company used here is a firm that does business in three or more unrelated product

* Professor at the NYSSILR, Cornell University. Reprinted in an abridged form, with permission, from the *Industrial and Labor Relations Review*, 29, no. 1 (October 1975), pp. 3–25. © 1975 by Cornell University. All rights reserved.

---

[1] John Blair, "The Conglomerate Merger in Economics and Law," *The Georgetown Law Journal*, 46 (1957–59), pp. 672–700.

[2] Reid, "The Conglomerate Merger: A Special Case," p. 141. For a discussion of the two approaches, see Lucile Keyes, "Proposals for the Control of Conglomerate Mergers," *The Southern Economic Journal*, July 1967, pp. 67–71.

groups and in which no single group accounts for more than two thirds of its total sales and earnings.

The multinational firm—like the conglomerate company—has become both prominent and controversial in recent years. Multinational structure poses a taxonomical problem because a business firm can be defined as multinational on the basis of structure, performance, or behavior.[3] In order to assess the impact of multinational location on collective bargaining, however, it is necessary to focus attention on the production process. Thus, the crucial factor here is the location of production within the firm. There is a potential impact on domestic collective bargaining whenever production occurs within horizontally integrated plants located both in the United States and abroad. This is true whether or not the integrated plants constitute a significant portion of the firm's total operations. For purposes of this analysis, therefore, a conglomerate, multinational employer is defined as a firm having a high degree of unrelated business activities and substantial multinational integration of production within particular product lines or groups.

On the basis of these criteria, a 1973 survey of the largest U.S. industrial corporations indicates that at least 15 percent of the leading 300 firms in American manufacturing are conglomerate, multinational employers, including at least 8 of the top 50: ITT, RCA, Tenneco, Union Carbide, Litton, Rockwell International, W. R. Grace, and Singer. The same proportion of the next largest 100 firms fit the definition, including 3-M, Bendix, TRW, Textron, Gulf & Western, U.S. Industries, FMC, American Home Products, Olin, and NL Industries, as do at least 28 of the next largest 150, such as AMF, SCM, Dresser, Dart, Studebaker-Worthington, Walter

Kidde, Colt, and Essex International. All of these companies were active in the merger wave of 1948–68, a period in which the largest 200 manufacturing corporations in 1968 acquired 3,900 companies having combined assets in excess of $50 billion.[4] Because so many of the largest American firms are conglomerate, multinational employers, it is important to understand the impact of this corporate form on collective bargaining.

LITTON'S GROWTH

Organized during the recent industrial merger wave, Litton Industries is one of the nation's leading conglomerate firms. It was incorporated in 1953 as a small electronics producer dependent on military contracts, but by 1960 it had acquired 15 related and unrelated companies and ranked 249th on the *Fortune* list of top industrial corporations; by 1972, after more than a hundred acquisitions, it ranked 35th, with annual sales exceeding $2.5 billion.[5]

Litton entered the typewriter business in 1965 with the acquisition of Royal Typewriter, the industry's second largest firm; Royal joined Litton's Business Systems and Equipment Group as the Royal Products Division. The following year a German company, Willy Feiler, was acquired because it had the electric portable typewriter technology Royal lacked, and a British company, Imperial Typewriter, was acquired because it gave Litton additional overseas production capacity and access to British markets. The foreign typewriter subsidiaries became ancillary units of Royal Products Division.

The typewriter division proved to be a profitable but not outstanding performer

[3] Yair Aharoni, "On the Definition of a Multinational Corporation," *Quarterly Review of Economics and Business,* Autumn 1971, pp. 27–37.

[4] Senate, *Hearings on Economic Concentration: Part 8, the Conglomerate Merger Problem,* p. 4558.

[5] *Fortune,* May 1973, p. 222. In 1973 Litton's dollar sales increased only slightly and the firm fell to 47th on the list. *Fortune,* May 1974, p. 232.

for Litton. In 1967, Royal met Litton's criterion for satisfactory earnings by its subsidiaries, earning nearly $7 million in pretax profits. Nevertheless, in January 1968, Litton reported the first decline in corporate earnings in its history, citing technical problems in the typewriter division as a major cause.[6] This was not the result of domestic typewriter production, though, which continued to be profitable in 1968; instead, as a subsequent investigation by the Federal Trade Commission discovered, losses in the portable typewriter operations were directly attributable "to the Willy Feiler acquisition fiasco."[7]

Acquisition, however, is the *modus operandi* of the conglomerate company, and operational mobility is the hallmark of the multinational enterprise. Litton chose to resolve the problem of inferior typewriter technology by making additional acquisitions and sought to improve efficiency by transferring manufacturing operations abroad. Faced with the same difficulties, a firm more committed to original research and engineering and to its existing production facilities might have built a new electric model and have tried to improve efficiency by reorganizing production methods.[8] In doing neither, Litton executives were perhaps only responding to the ease with which mobility and acquisition can be used to solve problems in multinational firms.

---

[6] *The Wall Street Journal,* January 23, 1968, p. 17.

[7] FTC, *Opinion, Litton Industries,* note 36, p. 49. The acquisition was described as a "fiasco" because the electric typewriter technology Litton obtained from it proved to be both costly and faulty; Litton eventually phased out Willy Feiler.

[8] Faced with problems similar to those at Litton-Royal, including high cost production and obsolete technology, the Olivetti Company, a worldwide producer and distributor of business machines including typewriters, updated its research facilities and reorganized its production processes. The latter included a 1971 labor agreement enabling Olivetti to implement a comprehensive work reorganization program in its main Italian plants. Francesco Novara, "Job Enrichment in the Olivetti Company," *International Labour Review,* October 1973, pp. 283–94.

In May 1968, Litton reached a merger agreement with Triumph-Adler, Germany's largest typewriter producer, a company that was about to introduce new electric typewriters on the U.S market. The acquisition was, according to a Federal Trade Commission complaint to enjoin the merger, "an alternative to original research and to developing a suitable machine based on the present state of the art." To accomplish it, Litton was required to subsidize Royal from intracorporate resources, which at the time reportedly amounted to a half-billion dollars in working capital and more than $140 million in annual cash flow. Royal itself could not have met the costs associated with the acquisition and relocation overseas. At that time the entire Business Systems and Equipment group perhaps could not have met them either if it had not had access to the revenues being generated in Litton's other product groups. . . . The Triumph-Adler acquisition required a $55 million outlay by Litton, mostly in cash, as well as substantial consolidation and relocation costs—a reported $2.3 million at Springfield and at least $17.2 million from the Hartford shutdown. By 1971, Litton's direct investment in Triumph-Adler was $69.5 million. Two years later, in March 1973, the FTC reversed a preliminary judgment and ordered Litton to divest itself of Triumph-Adler on grounds that in buying it "Litton again chose the acquisition route as the most economical, expeditious and less risky alternative to internal expansion." Litton asked for a reconsideration of the remedy, however, and in early 1975 the FTC rescinded the divestiture order on condition that Litton make no additional acquisitions in the typewriter field.

THE MOVE OVERSEAS

As noted, Litton also sought to resolve its problems by transferring manufacturing operations abroad. In fact, during 1969–73, Litton transferred all the manufacturing operations of its Royal Typewriter Company subsidiary to overseas facilities. The relocation occurred in three stages. First, during a strike in 1969 at Royal's portable typewriter plant in Springfield, Missouri, production of portable electric lines was transferred to the company's office typewriter plant in Hartford, Connecticut; later that year the struck plant was closed and production of Royal manual portable typewriters was consigned to a Portugese firm (not, however, owned by Litton). Second, in August 1970, the manufacture of office electric typewriters was moved from Hartford to the English plants of Litton's British subsidiary, Imperial Typewriter, and to those of the newly acquired German typewriter firm, Triumph-Adler. Finally, in January 1972, Royal disclosed plans to transfer production of its remaining models—manual office and electric portable typewriters—from the Hartford plant to its British facilities, and early the following year the move overseas was completed.

The impact on collective bargaining of this overseas move was shaped by two characteristics of the conglomerate employer: centralized management of decentralized production activities and operating and performance secrecy.[9] Centralized-

decentralization is a managerial system which enables a small group of headquarters managers to oversee and coordinate the activities of diversified or dispersed holdings. At Litton, an executive committee of the three top officers of the parent firm has ultimate financial and operational control; the executive committee members and group heads establish corporate goals applicable to each division, monitor individual division performance, and allocate managerial and financial resources within the enterprise.

In February 1969, Local 469 of the Allied Industrial Workers had struck the Springfield, Missouri plant when Royal refused to renegotiate the expiring contract on grounds the company could not legally bargain with the union pending the outcome of a motion filed with the NLRB by a dissident group inside the plant requesting that the union be decertified as bargaining agent. Also, the day before the contract expired, Royal made negotiations conditional on a 60-day extension of the agreement and union withdrawal of unfair labor practice charges it had filed against the company. The decertification attempt failed, and the plant shutdown announcement came exactly 60 days after the contract had expired (and the strike had begun). Royal had made its first comprehensive contract proposal the day before

---

[9] The following sources have been used to describe the collective bargaining events accompanying the shutdown of Royal's domestic typewriter plants: Royal Typewriter Company, 209 NLRB No. 174, 85 LRRM 1501 (1974); transcripts of testimony and the legal briefs and exhibits submitted by the NLRM General Counsel, the union, and the company in NLRB, *Hearing, In the Matter of Royal Typewriter Company, and Allied Industrial Workers of America, Local 469; Litton Business Systems, Inc., and Allied Industrial Workers of America, AFL-CIO*, Consolidated Cases Nos. 17-CA-3788, 17-CA-3922, and 17-CA-4023 (hereinafter referred to as NLRB, *Hearing, Royal Typewriter and AIW*); professionally prepared and jointly financed transcripts of contract negotiations between Royal Typewriter and Allied Industrial Workers, Local 496, at Springfield, Mo., from March 24, 1969 through October 7, 1969 (hereinafter referred to as *Transcript, Springfield Negotiations*), and between Royal Typewriter and United Auto Workers, Local 937, Hartford, Conn., from June 25, 1971 through February 10, 1972 (hereinafter re-

ferred to as *Transcript, Hartford Negotiations*); and correspondence between Royal and Litton officials and the unions obtained by the author from the AIW and UAW.

The author also interviewed Gordon Brehm, Assistant to the President, Allied Industrial Workers of America, on May 4, 1972 in Milwaukee, Wisc., and Stig Lindholtz, International Representative, United Auto Workers, November 2, 1972 in Hartford, Conn. Litton officials refused to furnish documentary information or to be interviewed. According to Frank Dee, an official of Litton Business Systems, a nonoperating subsidiary of Litton Industries, the company declined to cooperate initially because the unfair labor charges filed against the company by the AIW were still before the NLRB, and later, after the Board's decision, because appeals by both parties against the decision were awaiting disposition in federal court.

the shutdown announcement, offering the union a maintenance of membership clause in place of the union shop and a modest wage increase, but no job security provisions or fringe benefit improvements. The union membership unanimously rejected the offer later that day.

Union negotiators could neither penetrate Litton's decision-making system nor keep abreast of its operating options. They were told, for example, that Litton officials in Beverly Hills, California, where Litton headquarters is located, would make the decision whether to close the plant. Union proposals that might influence the decision were to be conveyed to Beverly Hills either by Royal officials or by Litton's director of industrial relations, who headed the management team in key talks preceding announcement of the plant shutdown. The union asked the Litton spokesman to specify the production problems that were causing Litton management to consider closing the plant and to furnish precise information on labor costs. Instead, he discussed Royal's general engineering and sales troubles: "What am I to do?" he asked when the union persisted. "Am I to go back to Beverly Hills and say you fellows will have to wait before you make a decision to close the plant? I think that would be unacceptable to them," he warned, because "there's a lot of money spent [here] daily."

The union's bargaining position was weak and therefore vulnerable to management stratagems. Its strike had no observable economic impact on Royal or Litton. Indeed, at one point in the proceedings, Litton's negotiator acknowledged that only the *Fibreboard* doctrine—which requires employers to bargain over decisions affecting the bargaining unit as well as the effects of such decisions—kept Royal at the bargaining table: "We are bringing this to you because we are required by law to do so," he said. This was just after he had informed the union that an antitrust objection raised by the Federal Trade Commission to Litton's Triumph-Adler acquisition was threatening a heretofore unannounced plan to produce Adler typewriters in Springfield. "I think if you could get the FTC to reverse itself, I think it would sure go a long way," he said, referring to the prospects of saving the Springfield plant. His offer was misleading, but the union had no way of knowing this—three weeks earlier Litton had signed a protective agreement with the FTC stipulating that no changes would be made in Triumph-Adler's physical facilities or operations in Germany pending outcome of the antitrust matter.

After the plant was officially closed,[10] the parties began bargaining over a termination agreement. A tentative settlement was reached covering vacation pay, health, and life insurance, and pension benefits, and also establishing limited preferential hiring rights for displaced workers. It was later turned down by union negotiators and the membership, however, because the company insisted the union drop all pending unfair labor practice charges as part of the settlement and a disagreement arose over disposition of the pension plan. Negotiations broke down when the union pursued legal remedies, and no termination contract was signed.

LITTON'S HARTFORD PLANT

At the Hartford, Connecticut plant, centralized-decentralization of control prevented United Auto Workers Union negotiators from confronting company policy makers. Litton's functional secrecy also added to the union's tactical disadvantage. By September 1971, when the company

---

[10] Royal tried unsuccessfully to maintain production during the first month of the walkout. The plant was closed March 27, 1969, the day after a shooting incident involving a union picket captain. Local 469 and the AIW were exonerated of any responsibility in the matter. Royal never reopened the plant.

gave the first indication that the plant would be closed, three months of contract renegotiations had produced an extension of the expired contract and agreement on funding of the pension plan. Both were advantageous to Litton. The first, made necessary by the August 1971 wage-price freeze, assured continuous production of medium-size electric typewriters during the relocation overseas; the second spared Litton a substantial cash payment during a period of financial difficulty.

Seven weeks before Royal announced that it might close the Hartford plant, company negotiators offered to delete from the contract a pension plan option they had taken a five-week strike to establish in 1968. The option allowed vested employees to receive a lump-sum payment of reduced benefits upon leaving the company in lieu of receiving full benefit payments upon reaching retirement age. Obviously the company's pension costs would have been reduced over the long run if vested workers chose to receive immediate payment of reduced benefits when they quit or were displaced.

In 1971 the situation had changed, however. If Litton had closed the plant with the lump-sum option still in effect, and all the eligible employees had selected that option, the company would have been liable for $5.6 million in lump-sum payments, an amount of cash it would not have wanted to pay at that time. . . . In 1971 Litton's interest and related expenses were running $70 million annually, and profits in the Industrial Systems and Equipment and the Defense and Marine Systems groups were down sharply; in addition, lagging production at Litton's Ingalls Shipyard, the company's largest operating subsidiary, was jeopardizing the substantial cash flow to Litton from a multibillion dollar contract it had with the U.S. Navy. Thus, costs associated with the reorganization of the typewriter division were not as easily subsidized in 1971–72

as they had been in 1969; in fact, the funds obligated under the pension option would have amounted to six times Litton's after-tax profits for its 1971–72 fiscal year.

To avoid that loss, Royal offered to guarantee future payment of the full amount of vested liabilities under the plan in exchange for immediate elimination of the lump-sum option, in this way assuming a (deferred) obligation of an estimated $8 million by which the Hartford pension plan was underfunded[11] but escaping imminent payment of the $5.6 million obligated under the option. When this offer was given to union negotiators, of course, they were unaware the plant would soon be closed. After lengthy discussions between the parties and their actuaries, during which Royal warned the union it would exercise its right under the contract to terminate the underfunded plan if the offer was not accepted,[12] the union agreed to the proposed change.

In January 1972, Royal officials confirmed the shutdown, indicating the Hartford plant would be empty within 18 months. Five weeks later agreement was reached on a termination contract. Under the contract each employee was to receive the 5.5 percent wage increase then in effect under Phase II of the wage-price control program until the point of layoff, but then would get no severance pay—the union's principal demand in the termination contract negotiations.

LITTON'S MULTINATIONAL ADVANTAGES

Litton's multinational organization complemented the tactical bargaining advantage its conglomerate structure gave it over the two unions. About one fifth of Litton's

---

[11] *Transcript, Hartford Negotiations,* August 25, 1971, p. 9.

[12] *Transcript, Hartford Negotiations,* August 25, 1971, p. 8, and August 27, 1971, pp. 11–12.

sales and one quarter of its manufacturing capacity are overseas, mostly in Europe, Canada, and Japan.[13] The Business Systems and Equipment group has had multinational locations since its establishment in 1959 with Litton's acquisition of Sweda, a Swedish data-register company. In 1971, according to the company, about 60 percent of the group's production and 35 percent of its sales were abroad.[14]

When the reorganization of typewriter production began in 1968, Royal had typewriter manufacturing plants in Leiden, Holland and in Leicester and Hull, England. Production of most Imperial models had been discontinued and the English plant capacity was then used to assemble and manufacture Royal typewriters and parts and to manufacture the electric portable typewriter developed by Willy Feiler, which was eventually discontinued because of design problems.[15] Royal also marketed portable typewriters produced by Royal Silver Company, a Japanese-based firm organized jointly in 1970 by Litton and a Japanese firm, Silver Seiko, which had previously supplied Litton with manual portable typewriters.[16]

Consummation of the Triumph-Adler acquisition in January 1969 opened the way for overseas production of all Royal typewriters. Foreign operations and capacity were being expanded as domestic facilities were being phased out. In 1969, the first stage of the domestic plant shutdowns, the Springfield portable typewriter works were closed. Part of the production was moved temporarily to Hartford and the rest was consigned to a Portuguese firm that purchased machinery from the Springfield plant. In 1970, during the second stage of the relocation, production and employment were expanded at Imperial Typewriter's Hull, England plant to accommodate the transfer of office electric typewriter assembly lines from Hartford. Triumph-Adler's manufacturing facilities in Germany were simultaneously expanded 25 percent in order to begin production of Royal's largest office electric typewriters, which had been made in Hartford, while the Triumph-Adler office electric lines were moved from Germany to Litton typewriter plants in Holland.[17] By 1971, which marked the beginning of the final stage, the German plants were capable of replacing Hartford as Litton's supply source for Royal office electric typewriters and the Hull, England plant of Imperial Typewriter was manufacturing parts for and assembling all of Royal's office manual and portable electric models.[18]

In this way Royal Typewriter became a worldwide distributor of typewriters manufactured in Litton's foreign subsidiaries and sold under the Royal and Adler brand names. Royal workers and their unions had no prior knowledge of these transfers of production (and jobs); on the contrary, they were often given press releases and other communications which proved to be inaccurate. Six weeks before the 1970 transfer of work from Hartford to England, for example, the president of Royal sent an encouraging letter to each member of the Hartford bargaining unit.

---

[13] SEC, *Litton 10K Report, 1972*, p. 6; and *Litton 10K Report, 1973*, p. 3.

[14] *The Wall Street Transcript*, August 9, 1971, p. 25.079.

[15] FTC, *Opinion, Litton Industries*, pp. 4–5.

[16] *Wall Street Journal*, March 9, 1970, p. 13.

[17] After the expansion of its Triumph-Adler facilities in Germany, Litton reported, employment would be increased from 8,700 to 10,000. (Litton Industries, *Annual Report, 1969*, p. 5.) Production movements involving Triumph-Adler plants are identified in FTC, *Initial Decision, Litton Industries*, p. 59.

[18] Substitution of foreign for domestic plants was extended to federal government typewriter contracts awarded Litton. Work on a 1970 contract for Royal electric typewriters was performed 60 percent in Hartford and 39 percent in Germany. The following year Litton sought amendment of a larger contract to permit complete production in England. (Letters from William Cotter, U.S. Congressman, Washington, D.C., to Jeremiah Driscoll, President, Royal Industrial Local 937, UAW, July 14, 1971, and to Roy Ash, Litton Industries, September 27, 1971.)

"We are entering an exciting era of new and better opportunities for the future," he wrote. "Our plans see Hartford continuing as our principal United States manufacturing facility and as our worldwide headquarters for technical, marketing, and administrative support to our expanding product lines and our growing operations around the world."[19]

Multinational plant locations gave the company a distinct advantage at the negotiating table by precluding meaningful bargaining over issues related to the work transfers. Overseas plants gave Litton alternative production capacity in the event of domestic work stoppages, and foreign wage levels discouraged purposeful discussion of economic issues. A few days before the Springfield employees met in February 1969 to take a strike vote over the company's refusal to renegotiate the expiring contract,[20] the plant manager delivered a cafeteria speech in which he advised against attending the union meeting. He warned that a strike would only invite relocation of production abroad. "Litton has typewriter plants at its disposal in Germany, Japan, Holland, England, Hartford, and in the Monroe system also here in the United States. The product line will not permit a loss of service to our customers because of a work interruption [here]," he said.[21]

The ability of the multinational employer to exploit national differences in wages at the bargaining table was demonstrated at both Springfield and Hartford. Asked by the Springfield union whether a voluntary wage cut might save the plant and provide the incentive for a contract settlement, Litton's director of Labor relations acknowledged that wages are always an important consideration in collective bargaining but in this instance a sufficient wage reduction was impractical. "I assume if your wages were down to an unrealistic level matching the Japanese or the Sicilians or some such thing, it might have a bearing," he said, "but that is totally unrealistic, we all know."[22] At Hartford, cost data provided by the company in connection with the 1970 transfer of heavy-duty electric typewriter production overseas showed average hourly earnings to be five times greater in Hartford than in Hull, England.[23] Union bargainers made no effort to negotiate wage cuts sufficient to keep the work in Hartford; 18 months later, when Royal disclosed plans to close the plant, the union did not broach the subject of economic concessions to offset the comparative wage advantages of foreign subsidiaries. In the absence of company overtures indicating possible areas where the union might cooperate with management to achieve economic savings sufficient to offset the considerable wage differential, union negotiators initiated no new proposals.

How does the loss of jobs in the multi-

---

[19] Letter from Ronald L. White, Hartford, Conn., to all Hartford employees, June 18, 1969. Also see *The Hartford (Conn.) Times*, June 21, 1970, p. 18F.

[20] The NLRB eventually ruled that this company action constituted an illegal refusal to bargain. Royal Typewriter Company, 209 NLRB No. 174, 85 LRRM 1501 (1974).

[21] Royal Typewriter Company, 209 NLRB No. 174, 85 LRRM 1506 (1974). The reference to Monroe was inaccurate because it has no typewriter manufacturing facilities.

[22] *Transcript, Springfield Negotiations,* April 15, 1969, p. 27.

[23] Letter from John Fairbrother, Industrial Relations Director, Royal Typewriter Company, Hartford, Conn., to William Zeman, Counsel, UAW Local 937, August 4, 1970. Company figures showed direct labor cost represented one third of unit cost of production in the United States, and therefore the wage differential between Hartford and Hull would have resulted in a unit cost saving of 26 percent (assuming no difference in nonlabor costs). The typewriter industry is of average labor intensity: wages as a percentage of value of shipments in the typewriter industry was 13.1 percent during 1970–71 compared to 14.0 percent for all manufacturing in those two years. (Figures derived from U.S. Bureau of the Census, *Annual Survey of Manufactures; 1971, General Statistics for Industry Groups and Industries,* M71 [AS]-1 [Washington, D.C.: G.P.O., 1973]).

national setting differ from that in which the domestic firm is driven out of business by foreign competition? In the former, workers are displaced by an administrative decision to transfer operations from one subsidiary to another *within* the firm; in the latter, they are displaced by direct price competition *among* firms that has forced a reallocation of production factors, including labor. In the second instance, the causal relationship is clear between production costs and market advantage; in the first, however, wages and other costs may not be the determining variable in the decision to relocate, for considerations involving taxation, market extensions, protective tariffs, and rationalization of multinational operations can be of equal or greater significance. Workers and their unions perhaps have a better chance of preserving their jobs when the threat is direct wage competition—and both they and the employer are in jeopardy—than when a production transfer is made among multinational subsidiaries to benefit the parent firm.

IMPACT ON COLLECTIVE BARGAINING

The bargaining events that accompanied Litton's transfer overseas of domestic typewriter production demonstrate the tactical bargaining advantage enjoyed by conglomerate, multinational employers. More than 80 separate negotiating sessions in two plant locations over a combined period of 18 months resulted in three contract extensions, agreement on a pension plan option, and conclusion of one termination agreement—all at the Hartford plant. Litton transferred overseas the jobs of about 2,500 unionized workers without having to incur severance or termination payments, improved pension benefits, worker relocation and retraining benefits, or any of the other compensations often obtained by unions in negotiations accompanying

plant relocations. The impact of conglomerate, multinational structure on collective bargaining is to give the employer, under certain conditions, the capacity to make the institutionalized bargaining system an ineffective method of resolving industrial disputes.

The sources of this impact are the changes effected in bargaining structure and procedure by four characteristics of conglomerate, multinational enterprise, two of which involve corporate organization and two corporate administration. The former are operational mobility and financial power, the latter managerial centralization and functional secrecy.

Conglomerate, multinational organization affects bargaining *structure* in two ways. First, growth through acquisition and the subsequent relocation of operations in response to environmental change are standard procedures for the conglomerate, multinational firm. Litton's repeated acquisition and reorganization of typewriter companies here and abroad made it impossible for the AIW to establish an effective bargaining relationship at Springfield or for the UAW to maintain its satisfactory relationship at Hartford. Second, multi-industry activities enable the parent firm to deploy financial resources from one division to another for strategic advantage against unions in any segment of the operations. Litton's demonstrated ability to cross-subsidize the Royal Typewriter division made it impractical for either union to try to bring sufficient economic pressure on its domestic plants to negotiate favorable terms in connection with the 1968 and 1970 job transfers; then, when Litton was in financial difficulty , it used the bargaining leverage derived from its global mobility to negotiate a settlement minimizing short-run financial costs to the company during the 1971–72 Hartford shutdown.

Conglomerate, multinational administration also affects bargaining *procedure* in two ways. First, centralization of authority allows overall coordination and direction of isolated production units on an interindustry, global basis. Litton's executive officers were made institutionally unaccountable both to their subsidiary managers[24] and to the unions with which local management bargained. Second, secrecy is endemic to the conglomerate, multinational structure. Conglomerate consolidation of the assets of previously independent companies prevents those outside the corporation from obtaining the information necessary to appraise the subsequent performance of subsidiaries. Also, multinational location of operations permits the firm to disguise subsidiary performance by, for example, locating profits in low-tax nations through intracorporate transfer pricing.[25] Union negotiators, for example, knew nothing of Royal's performance except for some aggregate figures produced in the Springfield talks to show Litton had been losing money in the typewriter division; neither did they know where the overseas plants were located nor what was being produced in them. In sum, Litton's

productive mobility and financial capacity removed the practical necessity to bargain and reach agreement with either union, and its administrative centralization and operational secrecy made it possible to initiate the shutdown without union awareness and then to accomplish the shutdown with a minimum of cost and union interference.

The full impact of the conglomerate, multinational firm on collective bargaining is shown by an analysis of its effect on the historic relationships among bargaining structures, economic markets, and industrial organization. Recent mergers have occurred largely in oligopolized product markets, as in the typewriter industy, where the top two firms, IBM and Royal, accounted for 50 percent of sales in 1968 and the four largest for 80 percent. In the product market, oligopolistic firms do not normally vie for increased shares of the market through price competition, but rather through product design, advertising, supply reliability, and other nonprice devices. In the labor market, no single firm in an oligopolized industry has an advantage if, as a result of industrywide contracts or strong bargaining patterns, each buys and uses labor under similar terms and conditions. But if one firm should negotiate labor agreements under more favorable terms than the others, or if it should obtain its labor outside the industry pattern, then that firm stands to reduce its labor costs relative to the others. Lower labor costs can either widen profit margins or offset cost disadvantages resulting from inferior engineering, production, and marketing performance—provided uniform, noncompetitive pricing practices prevail.

Conglomerate, multinational organization affords the best opportunity for the oligopolistic firm to obtain lower labor costs. It does not necessarily give the firm an advantage in product markets it shares with entrenched rivals when they are as large and wealthy as it is, but it does give

---

[24] Managers of Litton's Imperial Typewriter subsidiary in Hull, England, for example, reportedly knew nothing of the transfer of Royal production there from Hartford until it was reported in the American press. *Hull Daily Mail,* August 21, 1970, p. 1.

[25] A transfer price occurs between two subsidiaries of the multinational firm that transfer goods or services within the firm in a buyer-seller relationship; arbitrary pricing at a higher or lower figure than for actual value received is "frequently used to minimize the corporation's overall tax burden." Michael Z. Brooke and H. Lee Remmers, *The Strategy of Multinational Enterprise: Organization and Finance* (New York: American Elsevier Publishing 1970), p. 172. Litton has been shown to use intracorporate transfer pricing illegally. In 1974 five officers of Litton Systems, Inc. and its subsidiary, Litton Memory Products Division, pleaded no contest in federal district court to charges of defrauding the U.S. government of import duties by keeping two sets of financial records reflecting false and true production costs, having wired secret payments to Singapore and Mexican subsidiaries of Litton Business Systems, and submitting false and fraudulent information on invoices, all to understate the value of computer circuits imported by Litton's domestic plants. *The Wall Street Journal,* September 24, 1974, p. 48.

it an advantage in labor markets. Financial cross-subsidization invalidates the traditional balance-of-power premise of institutionalized collective bargaining, and international capital movements nullify established bargaining structures. A natural employer response under these conditions would be to specialize among world resource markets. It would be logical to transfer the manufacturing operations of acquired firms in industries where wages are an important part of production costs from higher to lower wage areas around the world and to consolidate the administrative and distributive operations of subsidiary groups in locations close to their major sales and financial markets. This is precisely what Litton did with its typewriter business.

The impact of the conglomerate, multinational firm on domestic industrial relations is to create pockets of bargaining imbalance reminiscent of the 1920s, when opportunities to obtain monopsony profits in labor markets peaked, undoubtedly because capital-intensive production under open shop conditions minimized real labor costs; such opportunities were probably eliminated by industrial unionism and the centralized bargaining systems established in the next decade. In the early post–World War II period, secure domestic markets enabled oligopolistic producers to pass on uniformly higher labor costs to consumers without reducing profit margins, but with increasing competition from abroad, some of it in international transfers by American-based multinational firms, pressure has been put upon domestic manufacturers to recoup diminished profit margins in their product markets by realizing cost savings in labor markets. Naturally the initial effect is greatest in labor-intensive industries where the potential cost reduction is largest for the firm that finds new, lower wage markets; nevertheless, where increased foreign competition has affected other, more highly capitalized industries— as it has in the auto industry—the response

has been similar: industrywide bargaining, wage patterns, and the union shop lose their effectiveness as protective devices for organized production workers. Thus, preunion exploitation of domestic industrial labor markets can be followed, after a lengthy interim, by conglomerate, multinational exploitation of world industrial labor markets.

What can organized labor do to offset this bargaining disadvantage? Its options lie in changing bargaining structures or in getting stricter government regulation of conglomerate, multinational firms. The first requires action at both the domestic and international levels. Domestically, unions must either coordinate their bargaining efforts or consolidate their bargaining units. The object of either would be to form an effective bargaining structure, but experience so far offers little encouragement to the unions. Their coordinated bargaining efforts have been least successful against conglomerate companies, and the NLRB generally refuses to consolidate existing bargaining units through unit clarification proceedings even in single-product situations. Self-help through collective bargaining is not out of the question, however, for unionists surely recognize that countervailing bargaining structures are most effective when they are based on mutuality of interests among workers. In the conglomerate setting this means confining coordinated bargaining activities initially to the individual product lines or industry groups where this identity of interests is most readily perceived. The *Phelps Dodge* decision makes it legally permissible for cooperating unions to bargain over common demands, settlements, expiration dates, and contract terms.[26]

At the international level this involves either coordinated bargaining among the

---

[26] AFL–CIO Joint Negotiating Committee, 184 NLRB, 976, enf den. *Phelps Dodge Corp.* v. *AFL-CIO Joint Negotiating Committee,* 459 F. 2d 374, 79 LRRM 2939 (1972), den cert. 409 U.S. 1059, 81 LRRM 2893.

affected unions in the various nation states or individual government action to restrict the mobility of the multinational corporation. Multinational bargaining is a reality in some instances, but to date only in firms strongly identified with specific product markets; there is no record of effective global bargaining among the unrelated operations of a conglomerate, multinational firm. In addition, American labor's legislative efforts to restrict capital movements abroad and the flow of imports into this country have been unsuccessful.

Unilateral restructuring of bargaining units by unions, if it can be done at all, is at best an evolutionary process, and statutory containment of corporate diversification and mobility is unlikely. For these reasons, certain changes in administrative law and legislation are in order; they would help to restore equality of bargaining power between conglomerate, multinational employers and unions without otherwise affecting the firm or its employees. First, to offset the advantage of cross-subsidization and centralized control of decentralized operations, the NLRB should permit consolidation of bargaining units through employee self-determination elections. Second, there should be legislation requiring sufficient public disclosure of the performance of individual product lines and industry groups within the multi-industry company for unions to assess the operating and financial condition of subsidiary employers with whom they bargain.

Third, adjustment assistance should be provided to workers who are displaced by foreign relocations. When workers are unable to prevent such movements, regardless of the motivation for them, or to negotiate termination agreements with their employers, they should be compensated financially in amounts approximating their individual lengths of service with the employer.

If this proposal is acceptable, then the remaining policy question is whether the multinational firm or the taxpayer should make the compensation. The answer depends largely on how one assesses the economic performance of multinational corporations. Using conventional comparative trade analysis, Kujawa concludes that it is the taxpayers' obligation. "If multinational enterprises and international trade provide general social benefits," he says, "society should attempt to relieve the burden of those left unemployed by foreign sourcing."[27] Private gain is thus equated with public welfare, in the tradition of neoclassical economic theory, and the public is asked to subsidize whatever social costs are incurred in the process. Subsidization of this kind rests, however, on the assumption that multinational firms do in fact offer us better products at lower prices. This is a debatable point. What is not questionable, however, is that plant relocation abroad represents a reduction in domestic capital stock and a corresponding increase in foreign means of production; this, by any calculation, represents a reduction in domestic productive capacity and, hence, a reduction in potential domestic standards of living. The dividend receipts of domestic investors offset neither directly nor entirely the nation's diminished ability to produce real goods and services. It is arguable, then, that the multinational employers—not the taxpayers—should make restitution for removing a portion of the capital stock from the economic system that created it. Of course workers are not the only ones affected by such removal, but they bear the most immediate, severe, and calculable cost.

Public policy in the matter, however, has apparently been decided in favor of public subsidy over private compensation, as in the Trade Act of 1974, which liberalizes the criteria under which workers who

---

[27] Duane Kujawa, "Foreign Sourcing Decisions and the Duty to Bargain Under the NLRA," *Law and Policy in International Business,* 4 (1972), p. 526.

are displaced by increases in imports may qualify for federal assistance.

In general, this is a desirable provision because it alleviates much of the human distress associated with job dislocation. But in the special case of job loss through multinational transfer of production within the same firm, should the workers be compensated by public funds? If they are, then the taxpayer bears part of the social cost of intracorporate reorganization when in fact the logic that equates private gain with public welfare in such reorganizations is questionable. It is understandable that spokesmen for multinational firms would have supported passage of the new trade act: apart from their interest in minimizing restrictions on multinational resource and product movements, they are reported to have been "hoping to head off pressure by labor groups for more restrictive measures" against job displacement.[28] Initial indications are that the 1974 Trade Act will be interpreted to provide relief denied workers under the old adjustment assistance programs.[29]

In any event, the proposals made here are conservative in effect. They try to remedy an emergent labor relations problem by using the traditional instruments of an established system of dispute resolution; they entail selected structural and procedural reforms to meet the new situation. Whether the established system is effective in this matter depends on whether unions and workers are able to match the organizational centralization and operational mobility of the conglomerate, multinational employer, if they wish to do so. The future depends in part upon the evidence gathered and reported by responsible parties. Students of industrial relations need to learn more about the institutional significance of what appears to be a permanent change in the structural foundations of collective bargaining.

[28] Mitchell "Recent Changes in the Labor Content of U.S. International Trade," *Industrial & Labor Relations Review*, 28, no. 3 (April 1975), p. 371.

[29] Announcing the first assistance program under the Act, a Labor Department official noted the expansive scope of the new provisions and predicted that about 100,000 workers a year will qualify for benefits compared with less than 54,000 during a twelve-year period under the old law. In the first month of the new program, 25 petitions covering some 7,500 displaced workers had been received by the Department. (Bureau of National Affairs, *Daily Labor Report*, May 14, 1975, pp. E1–E3).

CHAPTER 9

BARGAINING POWER

The bargaining power the parties bring to the table results from both the overall environment within which they operate and the bargaining structures the parties have created. Organizational characteristics such as internal union solidarity on the issues and management's financial condition also affect bargaining power. It should be remembered that according to our model bargaining power results from, and is a reaction to, the same pressures that determine bargaining structure.

OVERVIEW

The bargaining power quotient has long been recognized as the final determinant of bargaining outcomes. However, it is difficult to conceptualize bargaining power in a way that might provide insight into the nature of the bargaining process and its outcomes. Attempts to conceptualize bargaining power range from a decriptive overview of the factors that determine bargaining power to mathematical models of the bargaining process that predict bargaining behavior on the basis of utility functions. Our purpose here is to outline for the reader some of the considerations necessary to understand bargaining power and to summarize Chamberlain's classic approach to defining bargaining power.

BARGAINING POWER DEFINED

Bargaining power is a function of how economic, market, technological, interpersonal, socioemotional, and organizational factors are combined in a specific situation. The economic and market factors refer to the nature of the product and labor markets and the firm's position in its competitive market. Generally, the more inelastic the demand for a good and the more inelastic the resulting derived demand for labor, the more power the union has. Elasticity of demand refers to what happens to consumption of a good if its price changes. Demand is inelastic if a price change has little impact on the amount of the good purchased. If demand for a product fluctuates little in response to a price change, it is generally easier to pass wage increases along in the form of price increases. Brand preference and competitiveness within an industry are important factors in determining the elasticity of demand for a particular product.

In addition to the nature of the elasticity of demand, other market factors affect the degree to which a wage increase will reduce profits and therefore affect the relative power of labor and management. The degree of plant specialization (i.e., is the plant part of a vertically integrated production process that would be shut down if the workers in one plant strike) and the size of individual customers (i.e., does each account represent such a substantial proportion of a firm's sales volume that the loss of one account would seriously damage the firm's profit picture) are two such market factors. Labor market characteristics which improve the ability of an employer to replace its workers if a strike occurs are important power determinants as well.

The technological characteristics of the employer's production process also have an impact on the relative power of labor and management. When employers have technology that allows supervisors to run their operations during a strike, the employers have greater power because a strike does not necessarily mean a shutdown of operations. When technology is such that supervisors or other managerial personnel cannot take over production, the level of fixed costs associated with the production process determines the willingness of an employer to take a strike.

Other factors affecting bargaining power include the skill of the negotiators and the type of emotional response each elicits from the others. For example, a management negotiator that develops a high degree of trust among union negotiators is likely to be more powerful. Union organizational considerations, such as degree of unity, the level of the strike fund, the general level of worker savings, and the attitudes of outsiders—such as credit institutions, also affect bargaining power.

What is obvious from the laundry list above is that measuring general bargaining power is extremely difficult and quantifying bargaining power in a particular relationship is nearly impossible. Each of these factors as well as others the reader may add operate in varying degrees in any one relationship.

One of the most operational approaches to defining bargaining power was developed by Chamberlain.[1] He defined power in terms of the costs of agreeing and disagreeing. His model states that the

$$(1) \quad \frac{\text{Bargaining power of A}}{} = \frac{\text{Costs to B of disagreement with A's terms}}{\text{Costs to B of agreement with A's terms}}$$

and conversely, the

$$(2) \quad \frac{\text{Bargaining power of B}}{} = \frac{\text{Costs to A of disagreement with B's terms}}{\text{Costs to A of agreement with B's terms}}$$

---

[1] Neil W. Chamberlain, *Collective Bargaining* (New York: McGraw-Hill, 1951), chap. 10.

If the value of the first equation (1) is greater than one, B would prefer to settle and A would have more power. Conversely, if the value of equation (2) is greater than one, A would prefer to settle and B would have more power. Thus, the power of the union is greater where the costs to the employer of disagreement are larger than the costs of agreement. Chamberlain goes on to argue that during bargaining, each party formulates its demands based on its estimate of its own and its opponent's power functions. When the value of the bargaining power of both parties rises above one, an agreement is reached.

Chamberlain's conceptualization of bargaining power is one of the most widely read theories on the subject and has provided the analytical framework for discussions concerning both union and management tactics in bargaining. Generally these discussions conclude that tactics are chosen by a party in order to make the cost of disagreement on its terms higher to the other party. Hence, the reason for the use of the strike by a union is the degree of cost it inflicts on management. The complicated relationship between bargaining power and tactics is the topic of the Bacharach and Lawler article included in this chapter. They develop a theoretical conceptualization of bargaining tactics as a function of perceptions of bargaining power and the likelihood that power will be used. The Bacharach and Lawler piece is also of interest because it shows how simulation experiments can deal with problems confronted by practitioners, the choice of bargaining tactics being an important concern for both union and management practitioners as such tactics affect bargaining outcomes.

POWER AND TACTICS IN BARGAINING

Samuel B. Bacharach and Edward J. Lawler*

Bargaining behavior is typically preceded by an evaluation of the available tactics and of the power relationship between the bargainers. Indeed, it would be foolhardy to adopt a particular bargaining stance without a careful evaluation of the power and tactics available to oneself and to one's opponent. An analysis of this process, to have both theoretical and practical import, must therefore specify the dimensions of employee and employer power, classify the relevant tactics, and relate the power dimensions to the evaluation and selection of tactics. This research develops such an analytical framework and tests some major implications of the framework under highly controlled conditions.

The studies of Chamberlain and Kuhn, Stevens, and Walton and McKersie present theoretically illuminating and empirically insightful analyses of bargaining tactics.[1] These authors fail to relate the tactical aspects of bargaining, however, to an explicit theory of bargaining power. The link between bargaining power and bargaining tactics is simply assumed and left undeveloped on a theoretical and empirical level. The failure to articulate the connection between power and tactics is partly due to the fact that students of collective bargaining adopt a nonanalytic approach to power. As noted by many writers, power has remained a blurred analytic construct in the collective bargaining literature.

We have argued that a theory of bargaining tactics must be based on an explicit, multidimensional conceptualization of power and that the parties' selection of tactics is ultimately based on their evaluation of the dimensions of power.[2] The evaluative process that underlies tactical action in bargaining can be divided into three steps. First, bargainers evaluate their own power capability and that of their opponents. Second, given these perceptions of power, bargainers consider the likelihood that the power capability will actually be used. Third, in the context of their power situation, bargainers evaluate their own tactical options and attempt to anticipate their opponent's tactics. The first two issues were examined in prior research by the authors;[3] the third step is the key tactical dilemma confronting bargainers and the prime concern of this paper.

* Associate professor of industrial and labor relations at the New York State School of Industrial and Labor Relations at Cornell University and associate professor of sociology at The University of Iowa. Reprinted in an abridged form, with permission, from the *Industrial and Labor Relations Review*, 34, no. 2 (January 1981), pp. 219–33. © by Cornell University. All rights reserved.

[1] Neil W. Chamberlain and James W. Kuhn, *Collective Bargaining* (New York: McGraw-Hill, 1965), Carl M. Stevens, *Strategy and Collective Bargaining Negotiation* (New York: McGraw-Hill, 1963), and Richard E. Walton and Robert B. McKersie, *A Behavioral Theory of Labor Negotiations* (New York: McGraw-Hill, 1965).

[2] Samuel B. Bacharach and Edward J. Lawler, *Power and Politics in Organizations: The Social Psychology of Conflict, Coalitions, and Bargaining* (San Francisco: Jossey-Bass, 1980), and Edward J. Lawler and Samuel B. Bacharach, "Power Dependence in Individual Bargaining: The Expected Utility of Influence," *Industrial and Labor Relations Review*, January 1979, pp. 196–204.

[3] Samuel B. Bacharach and Edward J. Lawler, "The Perception of Power," *Social Forces*, September 1976, pp. 123–34; and Lawler and Bacharach, "Power Dependence in Individual Bargaining."

POWER AS DEPENDENCE

We have argued that the notion of power embedded in power-dependence theory provides a flexible and insightful backdrop for both researchers and practitioners to deal with the power and tactical aspects of bargaining. . . .[4]

Power-dependence theory stipulates that one party's power is a function of the other's dependence, which varies directly with the value the second party attributes to the outcomes at stake (outcome value) and inversely with the availability of the same or better outcomes from alternative sources (outcome alternatives).[5] Outcome value is viewed as the "importance of" or "need for" the outcomes in question, rather than outcome magnitude. Take an employee-employer conflict as an example. Power-dependence theory suggests that the employee is dependent on the employer to the extent that the employee has poor alternatives and values the outcomes at issue highly while the employer is dependent on the employee to the extent that the employer has poor alternatives and values the outcomes highly. Overall, the employees' dependence on employers is determined by their own situation (the employee's own alternatives and outcome value), and the employers' dependence is determined by their own situation (the employer's own alternatives and outcome value).

The power-dependence perspective implies a variable sum approach to power,

in contrast to the conventional zero-sum approaches that prevail in the bargaining field. A zero-sum approach stipulates that an increase in one party's power, by definition, implies a decrease in the other's power; this assumes that there is a finite, unchanging level of "total" power in the relationship. Zero-sum conceptualizations focus on *relative* power and assume constant *total* power. This is an important distinction, because if we apply the zero-sum assumption to the dependence relationship of parties, it leads us to conclude that any change in one party's dependence will have an equal and opposite effect on the other's dependence. On the other hand, a variable sum approach recognizes that total as well as relative power may vary and treats the relationship between the two parties' power (dependence) as an empirical question.

Total power refers to the sum total of dependence in the relationship: the dependence of A on B *plus* the dependence of B on A. Relative power is the ratio of one party's dependence to the other's dependence: A's relative power refers to the ratio of B's dependence on A to A's dependence on B, while B's relative power is the ratio of A's dependence on B to B's dependence on A. These ratios are the reciprocal of one another and, therefore, relative power is inherently zero sum. However, the fact that total power is analytically distinct from relative power means that there is no a priori connection or relationship between relative and total power. Total power can change with or without a change in relative power and vice versa.

*   *   *   *   *

Applied to power-dependence theory, a variable sum approach suggests that the interrelationships among the four dimensions of dependence—employee's outcome alternatives, employee's outcome value, employer's outcome alternatives, employ-

---

[4] Bacharach and Lawler, *Power and Politics in Organizations.*

[5] Richard M. Emerson, "Power-Dependence Relations," *American Sociological Review*, February 1962, pp. 31–40; Richard M. Emerson, "Exchange Theory Part I: A Psychological Basis for Social Change," in *Sociological Theories in Progress*, Vol. 2 ed. Joseph Berger, Morris Zelditch, Jr., and Bo Anderson (Boston: Houghton Mifflin, 1972); and H. Andrew Michener and Robert W. Suchner, "The Tactical Use of Social Power," in *Social Influence Processes*, ed. James T. Tedeschi (Chicago: Aldine-Atherton, 1972), pp. 239–86.

er's outcome value—are important tactical questions confronted by actors in a bargaining situation. On an "objective" level, there may be a zero-sum relationship among some aspects of the dimensions. For example, an increase in the wage rate may affect the employee's and employer's outcome value in an equal but opposite way; or a slack labor market may mean few alternatives for the employee and many for the employer. However, the relationships among these dimensions of dependence are not necessarily that simple. While an increase in the wage rate may be highly important to the employee, it may be irrelevant to an employer who can easily pass on the cost of the wage increase to customers; similarly, a tight labor market for the employer might make alternative jobs available to the employee while advances in technology might minimize the employer's need for the employees; or a slack labor market for the employer could decrease the employee's alternatives while high training costs could counterbalance the effects of the slack labor market on the employer's alternatives. The point is that the "objective" relationships among these dimensions of dependence are very complex and that point, combined with the fact that parties typically have only imperfect information on the pertinent social, economic, or political conditions, make the "subjective" or perceptual aspects of these relationships of prime concern to an analysis of tactics.

Overall, the dimensions of dependence provide actors a shorthand way to summarize and synthesize the power implications of the social, economic, and political conditions. In this sense, the dimensions of dependence are as much a perceptual phenomenon as they are objective features of the bargaining context. The interrelationship of the dimensions of dependence is primarily a matter of perception, especially as they relate to the tactical decisions in bargaining. It would not be appropriate to

assume that parties will treat the dimensions in a zero-sum manner even if that were the nature of the relationship on an objective level. It is just as reasonable, given our distinction between total and relative power, to assume that actors will treat the dimensions of their own dependence and of their opponents' dependence in a distinct and independent manner. We make neither assumption and suggest that this is an open question.

POWER AND TACTICAL ACTION

The tactical implications of the power-dependence theory vary somewhat with how one interprets the connection between dependence and power. The foregoing discussion represents a strict interpretation of the theory. It indicates that the power of a party is determined, not by the party's own dependence, but by his opponent's dependence. Consistent with the variable sum elements of the theory, each party's power is independently determined by the other's dependence on him, and a decrease in one party's dependence does not automatically increase the other's dependence. Our interpretation suggests a further distinction—between tactics that deal with one's own dependence and tactics that deal with the opponent's dependence, in other words, between the opponent's power over oneself and one's own power over the opponent. This distinction may be especially important in the evaluation of tactics, and we will return to it later.

This research will examine specifically the impact of the four dimensions of dependence on parties' evaluation and prediction of tactics. Two experiments are presented. The first experiment is concerned with three interrelated issues: (1) whether parties (employees and employers) use dimensions of their own or the other's dependence to evaluate their own tactical options, (2) whether parties use these same dimensions of dependence to predict the other's tactics, and (3) whether the role (employee, employer, or observer) of the parties alters their use of the dimensions of dependence to evaluate and predict the tactics of the employee and employer.

A second experiment in this paper carries the analysis of tactics one step further. The first experiment deals only with the *initial* or first tactic. The second deals with the question of how dependence affects the prediction of tactics at the next stage in the conflict, after one of the parties has adopted a given tactic. Specifically, experiment 2 is concerned with: (1) what dimensions of dependence will parties use to predict the other's countertactical response and (2) will the dimensions of dependence affect the extent to which employees and employers anticipate tactic reciprocation, that is, apply a "tactic matching" principle.

In an earlier study, we attempted to deal with the first issue specified above—whether parties use dimensions of their own or the other's dependence to evaluate their own tactical options.[6] The primary import of that study was that it established the empirical relevance of the tactics incorporated in the present research. As in that study, this research is concerned with an employee-employer situation in which the conflict is over a specific temporally bound issue (a pay raise). Within this context, the employee and employer have at least four options: (1) coalition (joint action with others in similar positions); (2) threat to leave the relationship (for employee, a threat to quit; for employer, a threat to replace the employee); (3) self-enhancement (persuading the other than one's inputs to the relationship warrant the outcomes at stake); and (4) conflict avoidance (resigning oneself to do without the outcomes at stake).

In line with our approach to power-dependence theory (discussed above), we will distinguish between those tactics that are based on a party's own dependence on the opponent (that relate to the other's power); and those tactics that are based on the opponent's dependence on self (that relate to one's own power). We will refer to the first set as "direct" tactics and the second set as "indirect" tactics. *Direct* tactics are grounded in a party's *own* dependence on the other. These tactics include a threat to leave the relationship and conflict avoidance. A threat to leave uses the party's own alternatives and conflict avoidance uses the party's own outcome value. In contrast, *indirect* tactics manipulate the opponent's ability to use direct tactics by altering the opponent's dependence (hence, the label, "indirect"). A coalition can reduce or blunt the alternatives available to the opponent and thereby alter the opponent's ability to use a threat-to-leave tactic. Self-enhancement, if successful, alters the value the other attributes to the outcomes at stake by emphasizing that one's own inputs to the relationship compensate for the other's loss of the outcomes at stake. In sum, two tactics use a party's own situation (threat to leave and conflict avoidance) and two tactics are directed at the opponent's situation (coalition and self-enhancement).

HYPOTHESES

We expect different dimensions of dependence to affect different tactics. This expectation is based on two assumptions. First, persons will use the level of alternatives and the value of the outcomes at stake to identify points of strength or weakness in each other's situations. Second, different tactics can deal with different sources of strength or weakness. An actor with good alternatives, for example, should perceive a threat to leave as a more viable strategy, and lower levels of out-

---

[6] Lawler and Bacharach, "Outcome Alternatives and Value as Criteria for Multitactic Evaluations."

come value should make conflict avoidance more palatable. The basic implication of the foregoing assumptions is that different tactics deal with different dimensions of dependence and, therefore, persons will use different dimensions of dependence to evaluate different tactics.

Our expectation can thus be defined in four basic hypotheses. (In each one, the dependent variable is a tactic available to an "actor," as distinguished from an "opponent"; the actor can refer to either the employee or employer.) (1) The better an *actor's* perceived alternatives, the greater the likelihood of a threat to leave by the *actor*; (2) The lower the value an *actor* ascribes to the outcomes at issue, the greater the likelihood of conflict avoidance by the *actor*; (3) The better the *opponent's* perceived alternatives, the greater the likelihood of a coalition tactic by the *actor*—since a coalition can reduce the opponent's ability to use his alternatives; and (4) The lower the *opponent's* outcome value, the greater the likelihood of self-enhancement by the *actor*—since a relatively soft strategy, such as self-enhancement, becomes more effective if the other attaches low value to the outcomes. Each hypothesis indicates that *one* tactic should be especially sensitive to variation in *one* of the dependence dimensions. The hypotheses suggest where we should find the *strongest* links between the dimensions of dependence and the tactics, but they do not preclude the possibility of other unpredicted effects.

EXPERIMENT ONE

METHOD

Subjects and procedures. . . . A total of 528 undergraduates from two Northeastern universities were randomly assigned in equal numbers to one of the 16 experimental treatments. The role (employee, employer, observer) adopted by

the subject was counterbalanced within each experimental condition to assure that the effects of dependence could not be attributed to the particular standpoint (role) of the subject and to permit an analysis by role.

Before responding to a questionnaire, subjects read a description of a situation in which the employer (manager-owner of a clothing store) was in the process of deciding whether to increase the pay of some or all salespersons.[7] The employer had told the employee that he is currently against giving pay raises but will make the final decision in about two weeks. In this context, the "description of the situation" stated:

> [The employee] is faced with deciding whether to try to influence [the employer] before he makes the final decision. [The employee] has the following options: 1) as an individual, [the employee] could threaten to find another job; 2) . . . try to persuade [the employer] . . . by pointing to his good sales performance; 3) . . . join with other sales personnel and, as a group, attempt to pressure [the employer] into giving pay raises; or 4) . . . accept present pay and not try to influence [the employer]. Your task is to predict what options [the employee] will select.

The description then indicated that the employer could respond to the action of the employee in a number of ways and listed the same set of options, adjusted, of course, for the employer role.

The description also contained information that manipulated the dimensions of dependence. The availability of alternative jobs for the employee and alternative sales

---

[7] We did not specify how much of a pay increase the employee was asking for in the study. While this is not a trivial issue, we felt that it was better to leave this ambiguous. The reason is that our outcome value manipulation deals with the importance of the outcomes at stake. If we had included some specific amount of pay, this could have weakened the outcome value manipulation and undermined our ability to test the effects of outcome value.

workers for the employer manipulated the two outcome-alternative variables. specifically, the manipulation of the employee's alternatives indicated that there was a 10 percent or a 90 percent chance that [the employee] could find a better job, while the manipulation of the employer's alternatives indicated that there was a 10 percent or a 90 percent chance that the employer could hire another person with the employee's qualifications. Outcome value was manipulated by varying the importance of getting a pay raise (for the employee) or avoiding a pay raise (for the employer). In brief, the manipulations stated the employee considered a pay raise as very important or not at all important (employee outcome value), and the employer considered it very important or not at all important to avoid pay raises (employer outcome value). Subjects were informed that both the employee and employer had this information on each other's outcome alternatives and value, that is, both parties had information on all four dimensions of dependence.

Dependent variables. Separate questionnaire items for each of the four tactics asked subjects to (*a*) estimate how likely the *employee* would be to adopt the tactic and (*b*) estimate how likely the employer would be to use each tactic *in response to an influence attempt by the employee.* Subjects responded on nine-point scales, labeled "not at all likely" at the low end and "highly likely" at the high end.

The four questionnaire items, measuring subjects' evaluation of the employee tactics, took the following form. "How likely is it that the employee would (*a*) "threaten to leave the store and find another job?" (*threat to quit*); (*b*) "try to persuade the employer . . . by pointing to his good sales performance?" (*self-enhancement*); (*c*) "organize with other sales personnel and, as a group, pressure the employer to give pay raises?" (*coalition*); (*d*) "decide to accept his current

pay and not try to influence the employer?" (*conflict avoidance*). Items on the tactical response of the employer asked subjects to estimate the employer's response to an influence attempt, in general, without specifying the specific type of employee action (tactic) taken: "If the employee tries to influence the employer, how likely is it that the employer will. . . ." The same items were included, with appropriate adjustments for the employer position.

RESULTS

There were two steps to the analysis. First, a multivariate analysis of variance (ANOVA) was used to determine whether dimensions of dependence significantly affect multitactic predictions. Second, multiple regression was used to test the hypothesized effects of outcome alternatives and value on particular tactics.

Multivariate ANOVA. Consider the multivariate ANOVA for the *employee's* tactics . . . first. The multivariate analysis of variance revealed significant main effects for employee's alternatives and employee's value . . . There was no main effect for employer's value or employer's alternatives. . . . None of the interaction effects between the dimensions of dependence were statistically significant.

. . . [An analysis] with the subject-role (employee, employer, observer) as a factor revealed that the role occupied by the perceiver did not interact with or specify the dependence effects. In sum, the multivariate ANOVA for the employee's tactics shows that individuals (regardless of role) use the employee's *own* dependence (employee's alternatives and value), and not the other's (employer's) dependence, to predict the multitactic inclinations of the employee.

Next, consider the multivariate ANOVA for the employer's response to the employee. . . . This analysis showed a main effect for employer's alternatives . . . and employer's value . . . but no effects for the employee's alternatives or employee's value. . . . None of the interactions were significant, and an analysis with role as a factor showed no interactions by role. These results are consistent with the findings for the employee's tactics. Just as persons use the employee's dependence to predict the employee's multitactic tendencies, they use the employer's dependence situation to predict the employer's response.[8]

. . . [The results of the regression analysis, where dimensions of dependence were regressed on the subjective likelihood of employees and employers using a particular tactic, indicate] that all hypotheses regarding power dependence effects on *direct* tactics (threat to leave and conflict avoidance) were supported. As hypothesized, *employee's alternatives* had the largest effect (compared to the other independent variables) on an employee threat to leave . . . and *employer's alternatives* had the largest effect on the threat to leave response by the employer. . . . *Employee's value* had the largest effect on conflict avoidance by the employee . . . and employer's value had the largest effect on the perceived likelihood that the employer would respond with conflict avoidance. . . .

The importance of these results is further documented by comparing the effects of each independent variable. . . . Across the various equations, . . . the employee's alternatives affected the employee's threat-to-leave tactic more than any other tactic, and the employer's alternatives affected the employee's threat-to-leave tactic more than any other tactic. The same patterns exist for the links between each party's outcome value and conflict avoidance. Fur-

thermore, the direction of all these effects (lower value, greater likelihood of conflict avoidance; higher alternatives, greater threat-to-leave likelihood) is in accord with the hypotheses. In sum, data on *direct* tactics consistently provide support for the hypotheses.

In contrast, the data on *indirect* tactics (self-enhancement and coalitions) do not support the hypotheses. . . . The opponent's (employer or employee) alternatives were not used to predict an actor's inclination toward coalitions, and the opponent's value was not used to make self-enhancement predictions. In fact, the opponent's dependence does not affect decisions regarding any of the specific tactics. All significant effects on specific strategies . . . involve the actor's (whether employee or employer) own dependence situation.

DISCUSSION

The findings can be understood in the context of our interpretation of power-dependence theory presented in the introduction. Recall that the dependence of the *employee* on the employer (in other words, the employer's power) is determined by the *employee's* own alternatives and outcome value; whereas, the dependence of the *employer* on the employee (or the employee's power) is determined by the *employer's* own alternatives and outcome value. The most general implication of the first experiment is that individuals will use the employee's own dependence (or employer's power) situation to evaluate and predict the *employee's* multitactic decisions, and the employer's own dependence situation (or employee's power) to evaluate and predict the *employer's* multitactic decisions. Given that the power is based on the other's dependence, this means that individuals perceive an actor's tactics (whether the employee or the

---

[8] It should be noted that the overall tactic rankings are consistent with an earlier study (Lawler and Bacharach, "Outcome Alternatives and Value as Criteria for Multitactic Evaluations").

employer) to be based primarily on the opponent's power.

Within the foregoing constraint posed by the dependence structure (and reflected in the multivariate ANOVAs), the results affirm the notion that different dimensions of dependence affect different tactics. A threat to leave is perceived as more likely when the actor (whether employee or employer) has high rather than low alternatives, and conflict avoidance is perceived as more likely when the actor attaches low rather than high value to the outcomes at issue. Tactics that are based on the actor's own dependence situation (direct tactics) are evaluated and predicted from different aspects of the actor's dependence (alternatives versus value). In contrast, tactics that attack the opponent's dependence situation (indirect tactics) are not consistently predicted from any of the dimensions of dependence. The data reveal a few other relationships as well, but these are minor. It is noteworthy that the role standpoint (employee, employer, observer) does not qualify the results for dependence. It appears that individuals use the same criteria to predict *others'* tactics (whether from an opponent or observer standpoint) as they do to develop their *own* action plans, to predict their own behavior.

* * * * *

EXPERIMENT TWO

The second experiment addresses two questions: First, will different employee tactics lead individuals to use different dimensions of dependence to predict the employer's multitactic response? Second, given that the employee has already adopted a specific tactic, does a "tactic-matching" principle enter into individuals' prediction of the employer's response?

Regarding the first question, we offer the following corollary to the basic as-

sumptions in the introduction: *if the employee uses an indirect tactic (self-enhancement or coalition), individuals will use the dependence dimension that the employee attacks to predict the employer's multitactic response.* The indirect tactics attack different aspects of employer's dependence: self-enhancement is directed at the employer's value, while a coalition is directed at the employer's alternatives. Therefore, if the employee adopts self-enhancement, individuals will predict the employer's multitactic response from the employer's own value; on the other hand, if the employee selects a coalition tactic, the employer's alternatives will be used to predict the employer's response. In sum, although the first experiment failed to observe any effects of dependence on indirect tactics, the second experiment determines whether the employee's use of these indirect tactics affects the employer's response. No hypotheses for the direct tactics are offered because these tactics do not attack the employer's dependence situation.

The second goal of this experiment is to determine whether and how individuals use a "tactic-matching" principle. Experimental research in a variety of contexts indicates that actors often match their opponent's tactics. Threats often lead to counter-threats, cooperation to cooperation, and concessions to concessions. Matching on a behavioral level is well documented, at least in bilateral-power contexts, but the present research is concerned with whether individuals cognitively use the "matching principle" to aid the subjective prediction of tactics.

The tactic-matching principle is a rather strict variant of the reciprocity notion. The reciprocity principle suggests that people benefit those who benefit them and harm those who harm them. The matching principle, more specifically, suggests a tit-for-tat form of reciprocity whereby parties engage in behavior that is as comparable as possible to the other party's behavior. The comparability of the behaviors may vary across different social contexts, and the potential for precise or exact matching requires that both parties have similar behavioral repertoires. The present study provides actors (employees and employers) with the same options and thereby permits the strictest possible application of the matching principle. In this context, support for the matching principle is suggested to the extent that individuals expect the employer to adopt the same behavioral option as the employee (such as a threat to replace by the employer in response to a threat to quit by the employee).

An application of the power-dependence notion further suggests that the dimensions of dependence will modify expectations of tactic matching. Individuals should perceive a greater tendency toward tactic matching when power-dependence conditions are favorable to the particular tactic. Specifically, they should expect the employer to match (1) a threat to quit with a threat to replace especially when the employer has good alternatives, (2) conflict avoidance with conflict avoidance when the employer attaches low value to the outcomes, (3) a coalition with a coalition when the employee has good alternatives, and (4) self-enhancement with self-enhancement when the employee attaches low value to the outcomes. In sum, the second experiment will determine whether individuals expect a matching response and whether the dimensions of dependence modify these expectations.

METHOD

The design and procedures were identical to the first experiment. The same number of subjects (528) were randomly assigned to conditions, but none of these subjects had participated in the first experiment. The questionnaire items (tactics) were identical except that the subjects esti-

mated the likelihood of the *employer* adopting the four options in response to *each* of the four employee tactics. That is, for each employee action, subjects estimated the likelihood of the employer responding with a threat to replace the employee, self-enhancement, coalition, and conflict avoidance (a total of 16 items, 4 in response to each employee tactic).

RESULTS . . .

Multivariate analyses of variance were run to determine which dependence dimensions are used to evaluate and predict the employer's multitactic response to each of the four employee tactics.

Employer's response to indirect tactics. The results support both hypotheses. A multivariate ANOVA on the employer's response to the employee's self-enhancement tactic revealed a main effect for employer's value. . . . and no effects for the other dimensions of dependence. Data on the employer's response to a coalition revealed a main effect for the employer's alternatives . . . and no effects for the other dependence dimensions. Consistent with the hypotheses, the dimension of dependence attacked by the employee's tactic was used to anticipate the employer's response.

Employer's response to direct tactics. Although no explicit hypotheses were presented for direct tactics, the results indicate that individuals use different dimensions of dependence to predict the employer's response to conflict avoidance and to a threat to leave. Subjects used only the employer's value in predicting the response to the employee's conflict avoidance. . . . In contrast, when the employer was confronted with a threat to leave by the employee, individuals used three dimensions of dependence to predict the employer's response: employer's alternatives, . . . employer's value, . . . and the employee's alternatives. . . . The employer's alternatives had the strongest effect. In sum, the employer's value is used to predict the employer's multitactic response to conflict avoidance, and the employer's alternatives are given the greatest weight when individuals predict the employer's reaction to a threat to leave.

Univariate effects. The links between specific dimensions of dependence and specific tactics replicate the effects of the first experiment.

RESULTS: TACTIC MATCHING

[By examining] the perceived likelihood of each employer response to each employee behavior . . . we find that individuals expect the employer to match threat-to-leave and coalition responses, but not conflict avoidance. The data for self-enhancement show only a weak tendency toward matching.

Although the perceived likelihood of matching varies for different responses, the tendency toward matching could be a function of the dimensions of dependence. To determine the effects of dependence, a matching score for each response was computed. As in the first experiment, hypotheses regarding *direct* tactics are confirmed and those concerned with *indirect* tactics are disconfirmed. Individuals perceive a greater tendency toward matching a threat-to-leave tactic when the employer has many rather than few alternatives, and they see the employee as more inclined to match conflict-avoidance when the employer attaches low rather than high value to the outcomes at issue. These data suggest that the overall matching trend for threats to leave is accentuated when the employer has many alternatives, while the negligible overall trend for matching conflict-avoidance increases slightly under the circumstances of low employer value.

DISCUSSION

The results indicate that the type of tactic used by the employee has a bearing on the anticipated tactical response of the employer. With regard to indirect tactics, individuals use the dependence dimension that the tactic attacks in order to anticipate the response of the employer. Specifically, individuals predict the employer's response to a self-enhancement tactic from the employer's outcome value, the dimension of dependence that the self-enhancement tactic attacks. They predict the employer response to a coalition solely on the basis of the employer's outcome alternatives, the dimension of dependence that coalition attacks. Thus, while the data from experiment one suggest that the selection of indirect tactics is not affected by the dependence dimensions, data from experiment two lead us to qualify this conclusion. Dependence criteria do affect the employer's selection of indirect tactics *in response* to the employee's use of indirect tactics.

The direct tactics also have a bearing on the dependence criteria that underlie countertactic predictions. Specifically, individuals use only the employer's outcome value to predict the employer's response to conflict avoidance; and the employer's alternatives, primarily, to predict the employer's response to a threat to leave. The overall implication is that individuals will identify the dependence dimension underlying the employee's direct tactic and use that same aspect of the employer's situation to predict the employer's response. For example, a threat to quit by an employee is grounded in the employee's own alternatives, and individuals will use an analogous aspect of the employer's dependence situation (outcome alternatives) to predict the employer's response. The reciprocal dependence dimension forms the foundation for predicting the employer's response to direct tactics.

The "tactic-matching" hypotheses are supported for the direct tactics but not for the indirect tactics. The employer is viewed as more likely to match a threat to leave when the employer has many rather than few alternatives and as more likely to opt for conflict avoidance in response to conflict avoidance when the employer's value is low rather than high. In contrast, individuals expect matching responses to coalitions regardless of the dependence conditions. The weak overall tendency toward matching self-enhancement is also not modified by dependence conditions.

SUMMARY AND CONCLUSIONS

Subjectively predicting tactics appears to be an integral element of most conflict situations. As in everyday life, parties in a conflict situation will adjust their actions not only to the situational or structural context but also to their expectations of how their opponent will respond to this context. Indeed, this appears to be a critical determinant of success in conflict settings just as it is a key to maintaining harmonious relations in everyday life. A recent book on intelligence gathering in World War II, in fact, suggests that the success of the Allies was not based simply on power or military force but also on their ability to predict the tactical moves of Germany and adjust their own moves accordingly.[9] It is clear that multiple tactic judgments and predictions are important. The present research addressed the issue of how people use information on power dependence to formulate multitactic decisions and predictions.

To summarize, the research has four implications. First, the most general implication is that individuals use an actor's (whether employee or employer) own dependence, but not the opponent's dependence, to predict the actor's multitactic behavior. Both experiments consistently affirm this notion. Second, different aspects of the actor's dependence are used to predict different actor tactics. Both experiments indicate that individuals use an actor's outcome alternatives to predict the likelihood of a threat to leave and the actor's outcome value to predict the likelihood of conflict avoidance. Third, the second experiment suggests, furthermore, that individuals use different aspects of dependence to predict the actor's response to different tactics used by the opponent. Specifically, they use an actor's alternatives to predict the actor's response to coalition and threat-to-leave tactics by the opponent, and they use an actor's value to predict the actor's response to self-enhancement and conflict avoidance. The fourth implication of the research is that the dimensions of dependence affect differentially the perceived likelihood of tactic matching. Individuals view an actor as more likely to match a threat to leave if he has good rather than poor outcome alternatives and conflict avoidance if he attaches low value to the outcomes at issue.

This paper reinforces our belief that power-dependence theory provides an appropriate framework for the understanding of the cognitive processes underlying bargaining. Combining the findings of this paper with those in previous research shows that a dependence approach to bargaining power allows us to understand three critical cognitive issues in the bargaining process: (1) how bargainers estimate each other's power capabilities;[10] (2) how bargainers assess the likelihood that each other will use his power;[11] and (3) how bargainers evaluate and select among available tactics and anticipate the likely response to available tactics.

These issues and their resolution should not be the exclusive domain of abstract theorizing; they must also be confronted on a day-to-day basis and applied to very specific contexts by practitioners. Our

---

[9] F. W. Winterbotham, *The Ultra Street* (New York: Dell Publishing, 1974).

[10] Bacharach and Lawler, "The Perception of Power."

[11] Lawler and Bacharach, "Power Dependence in Individual Bargaining."

methodology has admittedly been artificial and removed from the "real world." However, as George Strauss points out, there are few experimentally derived hypotheses about bargaining that might not also be tested in ongoing labor-management relations.[12] On the other hand, one of the primary problems of moving from laboratory experiments to field applications is the unit of analysis. This study, like most experimental analyses of bargaining, has focused on individual bargaining, and the relationships discovered herein may differ when analyzed in the context of bargaining between collectives.

The prime importance of this paper is that it presents and empirically examines a new framework for linking the analysis of power and tactics in bargaining. The research affirms the validity of the framework in a preliminary way, and this is the primary role of experimentation in the bargaining field. Field observation may modify our basic framework, suggesting new experiments that may then suggest new ways to organize field observations. In this sense, the experiments in this paper represent not an end point but an important step in the dialectic between experimentation and field studies.

---

[12] George Strauss, "Can Social Psychology Contribute to Industrial Relations?" in *Industrial Relations: A Social Psychological Approach* ed. Geoffrey M. Stephanson and Christopher J. Brotherton (New York: Wiley, 1979), pp. 365–93.

PART FIVE

THE COLLECTIVE BARGAINING PROCESS AND OUTCOMES

CHAPTER 10

The Process of Bargaining

The preceding chapters provide an overview of the environmental, organizational, and structural framework within which bargaining takes place. Each of these areas has been dealt with as an important determinant of the bargaining process. In this chapter the process will be examined from both a theoretical and descriptive viewpoint and information regarding the parties' preparation for negotiations will be presented.

OVERVIEW

Once a collective bargaining relationship is legally established, the parties must negotiate an agreement and learn to live under it. Collective bargaining is, therefore, a continuous process with the heaviest focus of management and union activities directed toward the period of actual bargaining. During bargaining for an initial contract, management and the union must move from the extreme winner-take-all position of the organizing campaign to the need to coexist in an ongoing relationship. During bargaining over the renewal of a contract the parties must overcome conflicts which occurred in implementing the previous contract. In both cases, the activities leading up to negotiations set the tone of the bargaining process. They determine whether the parties are open about their positions, whether they freely exchange proposals, whether they trust one another, and whether bargaining is characterized by hostility or friendship.

Contract negotiations embody the experiences management and the union share. They are probably the most concentrated and significant aspects of their relationship. Even though this is true, the actual process of bargaining, i.e., the behavior of the parties at the table, has been examined in only a few instances. The bargaining process has not been reported for a variety of reasons. First, negotiations take place in private. When outsiders are involved, bargaining takes on additional posturing that makes the achievement of a settlement more difficult. As a result, the parties do not like to involve the "public." Second, the existence of bluffing confounds any assessment of the compromising activity achieved or required for settlement. And, finally, once a contract is reached, attention focuses on the *implementation* of its contents.

While few scholars have attempted to examine actual bargaining behavior, numerous attempts have been made to conceptualize the collective bargaining process from a normative perspective.

THE BARGAINING PROCESS: THEORETICAL OVERVIEW

Over the years numerous theories have been developed to explain the bargaining process. These theories are diverse in their orientation, ranging from sophisticated mathematical models based on refined utility formulations to behavioral models based on the psychological aspects of negotiator behavior. While we cannot hope to capture the full range of theoretical models conceptualizing collective bargaining, our purpose here is to give the reader an idea of how difficult it is to conceptualize the bargaining process and include all of the various determinants of its operation.

Frederik Zeuthen has conceptualized the bargaining process as a series of compromises made by each side.[1] Concession behavior is based on each party's assessment of the potential cost associated with insisting on one's own demand, thereby risking disagreement, and the cost of settling on the other party's last offer. In other words, party A decides if it should compromise to avoid disagreement or maintain its position hoping the other side will move. Every time party A makes an offer, the value of disagreeing to the other side, party B, goes down (i.e., disagreeing costs more) because the new position represents a gain from party A's earlier position. When the gain from party A's latest offer is greater than the gain from pursuing party B's own demand given the probability of disagreement, party B will settle at party A's offer.

While the practical value of Zeuthen's theory is limited since it assumes that each party has perfect knowledge of the other party's risk-willingness as well as its own and that each can be quantified, it does provide one testable hypothesis: bargaining outcomes will split the difference between each party's initial position. This is due in part to the fact that Zeuthen assumes concessions will be based on symmetry in movement by parties with identical utility functions. The Hamermesh article included in this chapter tests this hypothesis with results that may shed light on the amount of bluffing behavior in bargaining.

Economic models of collective bargaining based on utilities and objective measures of costs, time, and risk, have been criticized for their assumptions that negotiators are rational and that they act to maximize utility. Behavioral models of collective bargaining have been developed to address this limitation by viewing bargaining as a socioemotional, nonrational aspect of human behavior. The classic behavioral theory of bargaining and one of the most widely read of any of the bargaining theories is

---

[1] F. Zeuthen, *Problems of Monopoly and Economic Welfare* (London: George Routledge and Sons, 1930).

that developed by Walton and McKersie.[2] Portions of their theory are presented in this chapter.

Walton and McKersie's theory is based on the assumption that different modes of bargaining behavior are required to reconcile differences between the parties. Distributive bargaining is designed to handle issues over which a clear conflict exists. Integrative bargaining occurs when issues can be resolved to the benefit of both parties. Different types of issues require that different modes of interaction exist—distributive issues being resolved through adversarial, confrontational actions and integrative issues being resolved through mutual problem-solving modes of action. Walton and McKersie also indicate that both intraorganizational bargaining and attitudinal structuring are important aspects of bargaining. Intraorganizational bargaining is necessary if the expectations of the constituencies of each organization are to be in line with the negotiators. The highly political nature of unions as organizations makes this process a very important factor in determining the nature of bargaining. The failure of either party to effectively reach an internal consensus could lead to bargaining impasses not necessarily attributable to the actual negotiation process. The attitudinal structuring process recognizes that bargaining is also a socioemotional, interpersonal process, whereby each party attempts to influence the attitudes of the participants. Walton and McKersie come the closest of any of the theorists to recognizing and conceptualizing the various systems of behaviors that have an impact on the bargaining process.

THE BARGAINING PROCESS: DESCRIPTIVE OVERVIEW

In addition to the development of models and theories attempting to conceptualize the bargaining process, the bargaining literature is filled with descriptive conceptions of bargaining. For example, bargaining has been viewed as a holdup where the union steals from management; as a poker game where the winner is the best bluffer; as a debate filled with rhetoric and name calling; as a horse trade based on a give and take atmosphere; as a ritual based on the assumption that the negotiations are only for show after the parties strike a secret bargain; as power politics were strength determines the outcomes; as a "rational process" where all the facts are laid out in an unemotional fashion and the appropriate answer appears. While these characterizations have marked negotiations at some time, it would be a mistake to conceptualize collective bargaining with just one of these characteristics. Instead it is likely that bargaining relationships evolve through several different stages over time as negotiators gain experience.

While the nature of actual negotiations is so personal and unique that generalizations are limited, some common characteristics have emerged. Early stages of bargaining are filled with excessive demands and theatrics.

---

[2] Richard E. Walton and Robert B. McKersie, *A Behavioral Theory of Labor Negotiations* (New York: McGraw-Hill, 1965).

This is due in large part to the fact that neither party knows the other's final bargaining position. Thus, in order to maximize the outcomes in their favor, each party engages in an excess of actions in an effort to pinpoint how far the other side is willing to go. The Hamermesh article indicates that the union may engage in more of this behavior than management. Essentially, bargaining becomes a finding-out process.

After the first few meetings, which are often friendly in tone, the parties begin the process of making counterproposals and compromises attempting to formulate trading points. While both parties attempt to avoid rigid positions, it becomes obvious that each party has its own interests which are likely to be in conflict with the interests of the other party.

While the progression from issue to issue can take a number of forms, it is common for the parties to go through each of the easier issues attempting to get "tentative agrees," and then move to progressively more difficult issues. The art of negotiating requires the ability to combine or package various elements of unsettled issues in different proportions. The final agreement may be the result of a lot of trading and compromise. This is why each side builds-in bargaining points and each side tries to ferret out vital demands.

As bargaining proceeds, the gaps begin to narrow but usually during the late stages of bargaining there are still unresolved issues. This is where the strike deadline becomes the impetus for settlement. The union costs out demands in terms of going out on strike and management costs its position in terms of taking a strike. Both parties may also engage in tactics to show their strength and convince the other that their threats are real. For example, the union might take a strike vote. Eventually, however, the negotiations run their course and the parties settle, strike, or form a joint labor-management committee to study a certain issue during the contractual period.

During negotiations, both the caucus and recess bargaining are important tools. The caucus is used by the parties to evaluate surprise demands and develop counterproposals. Most important, however, it is used to maintain cohesiveness by allowing the parties a chance to reestablish internal priorities. The use of the caucus is outlined in a very pragmatic way in the AFL–CIO article presented in this chapter. Recess bargaining is also an important tool providing periods during which the parties may cool down and engage in informal bargaining.

While the descriptive overview of the bargaining process outlined above applies to the private sector, the nature of the interaction process in the public sector differs. Kochan's article presented in this chapter defines the special nature of this interaction with particular attention to the "multilateral bargaining" required because more than two distinct parties are involved in the negotiating process. This multilateralism has implications for how the bargaining proceeds and the ability of the parties to ultimately strike a bargain.

BARGAINING PREPARATION

The success of collective bargaining is a direct function of the thoroughness of the preparations made by both parties. Preparation is second only to the actual negotiations in importance. It is necessary because each party must substantiate its position. This is done by supplying what has been called "factual ammunition."[3] The type of supportive data needed by the parties is outlined in this chapter in several articles written from both union and management perspectives. These articles present a prescription for bargaining preparation.

In addition to providing supporting data, bargaining preparation serves several additional purposes. First, preparation is necessary in order to understand complex issues and cost out innovative programs. Second, it creates confidence within a party and usually speeds negotiations. Finally, it sometimes serves an intraorganizational function if various levels of individuals are involved. This involvement may improve morale as a sense of participation develops and may have the positive side effect of making it easier to sell the final agreement and ultimately to implement the contract.

The final aspect of collective bargaining we wish to deal with here is the problem of costing out bargaining proposals and the final settlement. With the increasing complexity of collective agreements, costing has become more difficult. It has also become very important at the bargaining table. It is now common for both the union and management to go to the table armed with cost figures. The article by the Labor-Management Services Administration included in this chapter outlines techniques used in costing wage and/or salary and fringe benefits.

---

[3] Arthur A. Sloane and Fred Witney, *Labor Relations*, 3d ed. (Englewood Cliffs, N.J.: Prentice-Hall, 1977), pp. 190-95.

WHO 'WINS' IN WAGE BARGAINING?

Daniel S. Hamermesh*

Bargaining theory contains very few interesting propositions that can be tested empirically. Hicks's model suggests that the final outcome of the collective bargaining process will lie somewhere between the maximum the employer will offer to avoid a strike and the minimum the union will accept without a strike.[1] While its analysis of union and management resistance is useful, the indeterminacy of the wage settlement makes the model useless for predictive purposes.

Cross links uncertainty concerning the opponent's rate of concession to the bargainer's own rate of concession and thus explicitly introduces into the theory the possibility that mistaken expectations on either side can produce a strike or lockout.[2] He also implies that one bargainer's offers should be most responsive to his opponent's demands at that point in time when he realizes the seriousness of his opponent's intentions. In labor negotiations, this point in time is likely to be the period directly preceding the expiration of the old contract, so we should expect a flurry of bargaining at this time. This implication is verified by observing most collective negotiations, but beyond this it holds little interest for empirical research.

Only the models of Zeuthen and Nash contain an interesting and potentially verifiable empirical hypothesis.[3] Both imply that the union and management will settle at that point which maximizes the product of the increments to their utilities. If both sides in the negotiations have identical utility functions and there is no bluffing, the outcome of bargaining will be to "split the difference" between the extreme points of the core. If we construct data representing the initial union demand, the initial employer offer, and the final settlement and make some assumptions about the net amount of bluffing and the shape of the utility functions, we should be able to provide some evidence concerning whether the parties do "split the difference." The result of this test should be of interest even apart from its implications for bargaining theory, for it provides the first direct evidence on the relation of wage settlements to demands and offers.[4]

An alternative way of considering our test of the Nash result is to view it instead as a measure of the relative amount of bluffing by unions and management. If we accept the validity of the split-the-difference model, any deviation of the final settlement from the Nash point can be seen

* Professor of Economics, Michigan State University. Reprinted in an abridged form, with permission, from the *Industrial and Labor Relations Review*, 26, no. 4 (July 1973), pp. 1146–49. © 1973 by Cornell University. All rights reserved.

[1] John Hicks, *The Theory of Wages* (London: Macmillan, 1932), pp. 140–58.

[2] John Cross, *The Economics of Bargaining* (New York: Basic Books, 1969).

[3] John Nash, "The Bargaining Problem." *Econometrica* 18 (April 1950), pp. 155–62; and F. Zeuthen, *Problems of Monopoly and Economic Warfare* (London: G. Routledge and Sons, 1930).

[4] George de Menil, *Bargaining: Monopoly Power versus Union Power* (Cambridge, Mass.: MIT Press, 1971) attempts an indirect test of the Nash hypothesis using a model relating wage inflation to productivity per worker.

as a measure of differential bluffing. This interpretation is in a sense the complement of the other; either one assumes the absence of asymmetries in bluffing and tests the split-the-difference model, or one assumes the validity of that model and tests for differential bluffing. A simultaneous test of the Nash hypothesis and bluffing asymmetries cannot be conducted with data that reflect only offers and demands.

One difficulty with the Nash model is that its results are defined in the utility space, while the only data available measure compensation in money terms. In order to test the model, one must assume that both sides have identical utility functions whose sole content is compensation per employee and which are linear over the range of compensation discussed during bargaining. (These amount to the assumptions of the simplest model of Zeuthen.) We cannot, therefore, distinguish between a failure to verify the implications of the complete model due to its inapplicability to collective bargaining and a failure due to the inappropriateness of the assumption that each side has this unusual utility function. Whatever our results, they must be qualified by possibilities such as the employment effect of the wage increase entering the union leaders' utility function.

THE DATA

The data cover 43 negotiations concluded between September 1968 and December 1970.[5] Of these, 25 were teacher negotia-

tions, 9 involved firefighters or policemen, and 9 covered miscellaneous occupations. Data were constructed on the previous wage paid, the union's initial demand, the employer's initial offer, and the final settlement. Our data cover only wages; no attempt was made to reduce other forms of compensation and work rules to their monetary equivalents because of the difficulty of finding methods of calculation on which both sides agree.[6]

By necessity our data cover only negotiations in the public sector, for only there is the employer's offer a matter of public record. In the private sector, it is impossible, in all but a few cases, to find data on the employer's response to the union's initial demand. In any event, the public sector data are more easily analyzed, for there are few long-term contracts in this sector and thus it is not necessary to devise methods of compressing a number of deferred and cost-of-living increases into one figure representing the wage package. Furthermore, the demand for labor is likely to be relatively inelastic in this sector. Our failure to include the employment effect in the union leaders' utility function should bias our results less than it would in a test based on private sector data.

The raw data are used to compute $\dot{W}_D$, the percentage wage increase initially demanded; $\dot{W}_E$, the increase initially offered by the employer; and $\dot{W}_S$, the increase finally settled upon. All of these figures are calculated at an annual rate of increase, so that, for example, if a particular contract is to last two years, the percentage increase is divided by two. The following are the means and the standard errors of the means of the designated variables: $\dot{W}_D$ ($\bar{x} = 22.85$, $\sigma_{\bar{x}} = 2.10$); $\dot{W}_E$ ($\bar{x} = 8.28$, $\sigma_{\bar{x}} = .77$); $\dot{W}_S$ ($\bar{x} = 11.95$, $\sigma_{\bar{x}} = .94$).

---

[5] These data were all culled from issues of Bureau of National Affairs, *Government Employee Relations Report* (Washington: B.N.A., various years) and were the only ones available for this period which had all the required information. Great care was taken to ensure that the initial demands and offers used were actually the first made by each side, but there is the possibility that the basic material failed to report the earliest publicized demand (offer) in some cases. An appendix listing these data is available on request from the author.

---

[6] For a discussion of this problem, see Daniel Hamermesh, "Wage Bargains, Threshold Effects and the Phillips Curve," *Quarterly Journal of Economics*, August 1970, p. 507.

TESTING THE MODEL

To test the "split difference" model, we employ the null hypothesis:

$$Z = [\dot{W}_D - \dot{W}_S] - [\dot{W}_S - \dot{W}_E] = 0.$$

The mean of Z is 7.23, indicating that, on the average, the final settlement lies much closer to the employer's initial offer than to the union's initial demand. The t-value of the test of the null hypothesis is 3.83, so that we can reject the hypothesis that Z equals zero.[7] Our result thus implies either that (1) the two parties' utility functions are not identical and linear with respect to wage increases; or (2) the amount of bluffing by the union is greater than by the employer; or (3) the "split the difference" theory of bargaining is inapplicable.

The first of these possibilities cannot be rejected, but there is no reason to assume (as one must, to rationalize our results) that the public employer's utility decreases more in response to a given percentage wage increase than the union leader's utiity is increased by the same wage increase. For the reasons described previously, it is always difficult to distinguish between the second and third possibilities; this difficulty is especially severe in analyzing negotiations in the public sector, where the pressure of public opinion may force employers to offer an acceptable increase at the beginning of negotiations. There may thus be very little room for bluffing by state and local governments. Public employee unions, on the other hand, have an incentive to engage in bluffing in negotiating their first few contracts. After several rounds of negotiations, their relative bargaining power may force them to lower their demands as their threats become less credible. Since negotiations between public employers and unions have begun only quite recently, however, the unions may still be bluffing more than employers.[8] The third possibility is simply that the difference is not split equally.

On one level, our results show that public employee unions only receive approximately one fourth of the difference between their wage demands and the amounts public employers offer them. In this superficial sense, public management might be said to "win" in collective negotiations. On a deeper level, however, this conclusion cannot be supported, since we do not know the minimum increase for which union leaders are willing to settle, and since we expect more bluffing by unions than by employers in the public employment sector.

This study demonstrates the severe problems involved in using existing bargaining theory to derive and test propositions about behavior in nonexperimental situations. Any empirical test is likely to be confounded both by the existence of asymmetries in bluffing and by the possibility that the utility functions of the parties differ in makeup and are not linear with respect to observable monetary quantities. One must conclude that the likelihood that current theory can help us to reach concrete conclusions based on tests using data on the collective bargaining process is small indeed.

---

[7] The variable Z was regressed against dummies for occupation, for the type of public employee relations law, and for the occurrence of a strike. None of these could explain any significant degree of variation in Z.

[8] The fact that differential bluffing is sufficient in our sample to place one side beyond its threat point is demonstrated by the high proportion of cases (32 out of 43) in which some work stoppage occurred after the initial demand and offer were made.

[Note: See Mario F. Bognanno and James B. Dworkin, "Who 'Wins' in Wage Bargaining? Comment," *Industrial and Labor Relations Review*, 28, no. 4 (July 1975), pp. 570–72, for additional discussion of Hamermesh's analysis.]

A BEHAVIORAL THEORY OF LABOR NEGOTIATIONS

Richard E. Walton and Robert B. McKersie*

* * * * *

THE ANALYTICAL FRAMEWORK

Labor negotiations, as an instance of social negotiations, is comprised of four systems of activity, each with its own function for the interacting parties, its own internal logics, and its own identifiable set of instrumental acts or tactics.

We shall refer to each of the distinguishable systems of activities as a *subprocess*. The first subprocess is *distributive bargaining*; its function is to resolve pure conflicts of interest. The second, *integrative bargaining*; functions to find common or complementary interests and solve problems confronting both parties. The third subprocess is *attitudinal structuring*, and its functions are to influence the attitudes of the participants toward each other and to affect the basic bonds which relate the two parties they represent. A fourth subprocess, *intraorganizational bargaining*, has the function of achieving consensus within each of the interacting groups.

DISTRIBUTIVE BARGAINING. Distributive bargaining is a hypothetical construct referring to the complex system of activities instrumental to the attainment of one party's goals when they are in basic conflict with those of the other party. It is the type of activity most familiar to stu-

dents of negotiations; in fact, it is "bargaining" in the strictest sense of the word. In social negotiations, the goal conflict can relate to several values; it can involve allocation of any resources, e.g., economic, power, or status symbols. What game theorists refer to as fixed-sum games are the situations we have in mind: one person's gain is a loss to the other. The specific points at which the negotiating objectives of the two parties come in contact define the issues. Formally, an *issue* will refer to an area of common concern in which the objectives of the two parties are assumed to be in conflict. As such, it is the subject of distributive bargaining.

INTEGRATIVE BARGAINING. Integrative bargaining refers to the system of activities which is instrumental to the attainment of objectives which are *not* in fundamental conflict with those of the other party and which therefore can be integrated to some degree. Such objectives are said to define an area of common concern, a *problem*. Integrative bargaining and distributive bargaining are both joint decision-making processes. However, these processes are quite dissimilar and yet are rational responses to different situations. Integrative potential exists when the nature of a problem permits solutions which benefit both parties, or at least when the gains of one party do not represent equal sacrifices by the other. This is closely related to what game theorists call the varying-sum game.

ATTITUDINAL STRUCTURING. Distributive and integrative bargaining pertain to

* Professor, Harvard University and Professor, Massachusetts Institute of Technology. Reprinted from *A Behavioral Theory of Labor Negotiations* (New York: McGraw-Hill, 1967), pp. 4–45, 126–43, with permission from McGraw-Hill Book Company.

economic issues and the rights and obligations of the parties, which are the generally recognized content of labor negotiations. However, we postulate that an additional major function of negotiations is influencing the relationships between parties, in particular such attitudes as friendliness-hostility, trust, respect, and the motivational orientation of competitiveness-cooperativeness. Although the existing relationship pattern is acknowledged to be influenced by many more enduring forces (such as the technical and economic context, the basic personality dispositions of key participants, and the social belief systems which pervade the two parties), the negotiators can and do take advantage of the interaction system of negotiations to produce attitudinal change.

Attitudinal structuring is our term for the system of activities instrumental to the attainment of desired relationship patterns between the parties. Desired relationship patterns usually give content to this process in a way comparable to that of issues and problems in distributive and integrative processes. The distinction among the processes is that whereas the first two are joint decision-making processes, attitudinal structuring is a socioemotional interpersonal process designed to change attitudes and relationships.

INTRAORGANIZATIONAL BARGAINING. The three processes discussed thus far relate to the reconciliation process that takes place between the union and the company. During the course of negotiations another system of activities, designed to achieve consensus within the union and within the company, takes place. Intraorganizational bargaining refers to the system of activities which brings the expectations of principals into alignment with those of the chief negotiator.

The chief negotiators often play important but limited roles in formulating bargaining objectives. On the union side, the local membership exerts considerable influence in determining the nature and strength of aspirations, and the international union may dictate the inclusion of certain goals in the bargaining agenda. On the company side, top management and various staff groups exert their influence on bargaining objectives. In a sense the chief negotiator is the recipient of two sets of demands—one from across the table and one from his own organization. His dilemma stems from conflict at two levels; differing aspirations about issues and differing expectations about behavior.

Intraorganizational bargaining within the union is particularly interesting. While it is true that for both parties to labor negotiations many individuals not present in negotiations are vitally concerned about what transpires at the bargaining table, the union negotiator is probably subject to more organizational constraints than his company counterpart. The union is a political organization whose representatives are elected to office and in which contract terms must be ratified by an electorate.

* * * * *

THE PROPOSITIONS GENERATED

What kinds of propositions does our theoretical framework generate?

First, the most fundamental propositions of the study are those that link goals and tactical behavior. We assert that the behaviors which we call distributive bargaining are indexes for inferring goal conflict or perceived goal conflict. Conversely, the knowledge that goal structures are in conflict becomes the basis for predicting that class of behaviors we identify as distributive bargaining tactics.

Consider one other process, attitudinal structuring. The observable behaviors we designate as tactics for that process are proposed as an index of the degree of concern about the maintenance or changing of the basic relationship pattern between the parties and as an indicator of the direction of change desired. Of course, the association works in reverse: If you know the party's objectives in this area, you can predict that he will tend to engage in the class of behaviors we have identified as attitudinal structuring tactics. Inasmuch as we may actually identify as many as a hundred behaviors as tactical in a single subprocess, we would have a long list of propositions if we chose to formalize them. We shall not.

The second type of proposition represents a refinement of the first. Because there are often many specific behaviors that can perform any given tactical assignment, it is rather difficult to make precise predictions about behavior from a knowledge of goals or motivations alone. Thus, occasionally our framework and analysis lead to propositions indicating which specific strategies or tactics tend to be used to pursue given goals under given circumstances. This goes a step beyond starting with goal structures and predicting the class of behaviors and represents a step that must eventually be taken if we are to understand the negotiation process in general and tactical choice in particular. We assume that persons act purposefully, even in what they perceive as a fast-moving and fluid situation. Thus, for example, after analyzing the logic of the situation, we offer the hypothesis that the more prior knowledge a management has about the minimum acceptable package to the union, the more likely it is to use a final-offer-first strategy. The final-offer-first strategy is just one of several alternatives within distributive bargaining.

A third type of proposition deals with action-response relations rather than with complex-choice situations. These are explicit or implicit hypotheses that specify the several consequences (noting especially the unintended consequences) of a given type of action: a given tactic has X consequences for the distributive bargaining process, Y consequences for the integrative bargaining process, and Z consequences for the process of attitudinal structuring. For example, our analysis of the several processes suggests that the more management's commitments approximate the final-offer-first strategy, the less problem-solving activity will occur during negotiations, and the more negative will be the sentiments relating the parties. These are both descriptive statements and predictive hypotheses.

The multiple consequences of a single act—due to the simultaneous occurrence of the processes—is the fact which interrelates these processes. And it is this phenomenon that we want to examine closely. We shall be particularly interested in discovering and enlightening the most important dilemmas produced by the conflicting demands of the several subprocesses. How the subprocesses interact and how the dilemmas are resolved must be understood in theorizing about negotiations.

In short, the few propositions which we have made explicit and the other propositions which are implicit in the statement of the theory are about how people actually tend to behave and how elements of the process actually interact. They should lead, therefore, to predictive hypotheses about how people will tend to behave in various circumstances and under varying conditions.

"THE DISTRIBUTIVE BARGAINING MODEL"

Distributive bargaining is central to labor negotiations and is usually regarded as the dominant activity in the union-management relationship. Unions represent employees in the determination of wages, hours, and working conditions. Since these matters involve the allocation of scarce resources, there is assumed to be some conflict of interest between management and unions. The joint-decision process for resolving conflicts of interest is distributive bargaining. The term itself refers to the activity of dividing limited resources. It occurs in situations in which one party wins what the other party loses.

* * * * *

Before proceeding, a few clarifying remarks should be made. For the purposes of this [section] we are assuming that each negotiator behaves in the self-interest of his organization. He brings neither a generally competitive nor a generally cooperative orientation. Many negotiators do not behave "rationally." Some acts of behavior can be understood only in terms of the relationship objectives of the institution or the personal needs of the negotiator. . . .

For the present we are also assuming that a negotiator represents the consensus of his organization. For the most part, we shall not distinguish here among the wishes of the international union, the rank and file, etc., or among the desires of top management, staff groups, etc. This matter will be considered later when we take up the subject of intraorganizational bargaining. However, from time to time we shall need to relax this assumption in our discussion of distributive bargaining in order to examine certain behavior critically relevant to this process.

SETTLEMENT RANGE

AGENDA ITEMS: ISSUES AND PROBLEMS

The agenda item appropriate for distributive bargaining is an issue. Items appropriately handled by integrative bargaining are problems. When items contain important possibilities for both processes, they are said to be "mixed situations" or "mixed issues."

The agenda items and processes can be differentiated in terms of two dimensions of the underlying structure of payoffs: the

total value available to both parties and the *shares* of the total available to each party. Distributive bargaining is the process by which each party attempts to maximize his own share in the context of fixed-sum payoffs. Integrative bargaining is the process by which the parties attempt to increase the size of the joint gain without respect to the division of the payoffs. Mixed bargaining is the process that combines both an attempt to increase the size of the joint gain and a decision on how to allocate shares between the parties.

ISSUES AND DISTRIBUTIVE BARGAINING. The fixed-sum, variable-share payoff structure is our point of departure for defining an issue. It describes a situation in which there is some fixed value available to the parties but in which they may influence shares which go to each. As such there is fundamental and complete conflit of interests. In labor negotiations there is an attendant feature to the competitive payoff structure—the possibility of default. This modifies the extent of the conflict between the parties. If either party should insist upon a sum greater than the fixed amount available, or if their combined demands exceed this fixed amount, they suffer mutual losses.[1]

An issue can be represented as in Exhibit 1.

If one conceives of some spectrum of outcomes *C* through *I*, *C* allows Party[2] maximum satisfaction of 6 units and provides Opponent no satisfaction. Outcomes *C* through *I* represent the distribution of values to Party and Opponent 6,0; 5,1; 4,2;

---

[1] For the distributive bargaining issue treated here, we assume that the major bone of contention between the parties, and consequently a strike issue, is the size of the economic package. This is the justification for the assumption that a failure to make compatible demands regarding the issue results in losses and not merely no gain.

[2] We shall use Party and Opponent to differentiate the parties. The labels are intended to apply equally well to the union and company situations in negotiations. If a statement is not applicable to both, we shall use the terms *company* and *union*.

EXHIBIT 1   *C, D,* ETC., REFER TO OUTCOMES

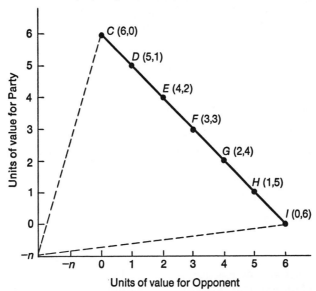

3,3; 2,4; 1,5; and 0,6. Outcomes *B* and *J*, which fall outside this series, are accompanied by zero units or losses for both parties. What we have in mind is a demand of 7 by either party or some combination of demands which totals 7 or more. This refers to the mutual losses associated with excessive demands which violate the bargaining range and result in a work stoppage.

Because we intend to make further use of both utility functions and game matrixes, we shall illustrate an issue in matrix form (see Exhibits 2 and 3).[3]

Exhibit 2 follows the conventional representation of payoff matrixes. Party chooses among rows 0 to 7 (here rows represent alternate demands), and Opponent chooses among columns 0 to 7 (his own demands). The units of measurement can be regarded as some objective value, such as money.[4] Coordinating the matrix to la-

bor negotiations, we assume some no-trade point as having less than zero utility and assume some positive range of mutually advantageous trades. (Thus the range might involve 6 cents, from $2.50 to $2.56, the limits to a mutually advantageous trade.)

If the two parties choose demands that add up to 6, they receive the amount of the demands. If their demands add up to less than 6, they receive their respective demands adjusted upward to bring their combined total to 6. If their demands total more than 6, they default and suffer mutual losses, arbitrarily set here at −6,−6.

The possibility of a default is an important aspect of distributive bargaining. In one sense it changes the game to a varying-sum game, in that both parties will be better off if they can avoid the default region of the payoff matrix. For the moment we shall not specify whether the default represents temporary costs incurred by a strike or a permanent breakdown of the relationship.

Exhibit 3 is a truncated version of the matrix in Exhibit 2, in that it allows for only two of the row and column choices.

---

[3] Following the convention of game theory, the first entry in each cell specifies the payoff to Party and the second entry the payoff to Opponent.

[4] It will be necessary to modify this later as we introduce and substitute subjective evaluations for objective value units.

EXHIBIT 2   ISSUE PAYOFFS IN MATRIX FORM

OPPONENT STRATEGIES
(DEMANDS)

	0	1	2	3	4	5	6	7
0	3,3	2½,3½	2,4	1½,4½	1,5	½,5½	0,6	
1	3½,2½	3,3	2½,3½	2,4	1½,4½	1,5		
2	4,2	3½,2½	3,3	2½,3½	2,4			
3	4½,1½	4,2	3½,2½	3,3				
4	5,1	4½,1½	4,2					
5	5½,½	5,1						
6	6,0							
7								

PARTY STRATEGIES (DEMANDS))

Mutual losses of −6,−6 associated with failure to agree

It is sufficient to illustrate the essence of the choice problem but represents a drastic oversimplification of the alternatives usually available in labor negotiations. However, the 2 × 2 or 3 × 3 matrices are most frequently used in illustrations of game theory or in experimental studies of game behavior, and we shall have occasion to employ them ourselves in discussing the relevance of this literature to labor negotiations.

EXHIBIT 3   A TWO-CHOICE ISSUE

PARTY STRATEGIES	OPPONENT STRATEGIES	
	SOFT (1)	HARD (5)
Soft (1)	3,3	1,5
Hard (5)	5,1	−6,−6

PROBLEMS AND INTEGRATIVE BARGAINING. This process applies to a variable-sum situation in which a wide range of possible total values is available to the pair of parties (depending, for example, on the quality and creativity of their joint decision making) and in which the parties need not be preoccupied at the same time with the question of allocation of the values between them.

They may be relieved from this preoccupation with "who gets how much" by any of several circumstances. For example, in its most fundamental form a problem is one which affects both parties in exactly the same way; each solution considered offers the same inherent benefit to both. ·Or the parties may have agreed in advance to share equally (or in some other specific proportion) whatever total value is realized by their efforts. This would require prior agreement to make side payments if the alternative outcome (selected because it has the highest joint gain) has disproportionately high inherent benefits for one side. Still another possibility is that, rather than agree in advance to their respective shares of the total value, the parties agree to make this allocation of the joint gain after the outcome. Under each of these arrangements the parties have maximum incentive to choose an outcome with the highest total value. Interests are identical or parallel throughout an array of potential outcomes, as depicted in Exhibit 4.

Exhibit 4 shows the parties as benefiting equally (although this particular basis for sharing is not essential) in outcomes *Q* to *U*, and total values are 0 to 8, respectively. Outcome *Q* is assumed to be the

EXHIBIT 4 Q, R, ETC., REFER TO OUTCOMES

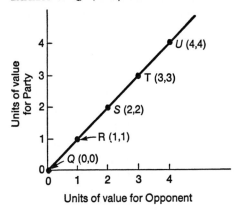

status quo, and only outcomes which improve the joint gain are considered. The possibilities of mutually beneficial outcomes *R, S, T,* and *U* are known to the parties only through the process of integrative bargaining.

* * * * *

THE CONTENT OF ISSUES. For an issue to arise there must be some dissimilarity between the value systems of the two parties, and the item in question must appear to require some choice between the value systems. Whether or not a party's position is in its own best interest, the fact that the party's current preferences are opposed to those of the other party is sufficient to create an issue.

Even though many situational factors strongly influence how agenda items are perceived and hence how they are resolved, we believe that there are some items which tend to involve more inherent conflict of interest than others do. We can distinguish three types of objectives: economic, rights and obligations, and relationship patterns. When economic objectives are involved, there is often basic conflict. Decisions about wage levels involve a choice between giving more of the "good life" to employees or to stockholders and managers. . . .

Basic conflict can also exist around rights and obligations. One class of issues, which in part reduces to a choice among basic values, is that concerned with union security. For example, privileges and freedom accorded union officials may enhance the status and effectiveness of the union at the expense of management status. A similar type of issue is that which pits employee job rights against management prerogatives and flexibility. . . . While these issues usually involve some inherent conflict, they almost invariably also contain some integrative potential. They best illustrate what we refer to as "mixed items."

Let us elaborate briefly here on the question of mixed items in order to explain what we mean by that term. An improvement in the layoff protection for employees usually entails some loss in management flexibility, but inasmuch as there may be several ways of increasing layoff protection, it should be apparent that the amount by which management's flexibility is compromised to provide a given amount of protection can vary considerably. To the extent that the matter is perceived as involving inherent conflict, it will be the subject of distributive bargaining. To the extent that the matter is seen as having some mutual interests or potential for integration, it will also be the subject of integrative bargaining and hence mixed bargaining.

Attitudes and relationship patterns also can be the focus of differing objectives. For example, one party may desire to foster a cooperative relationship, while the other party may desire to preserve an arm's-length relationship. . . .

Technological, economic, organizational, and other social forces shape the outlook which each side brings to the bargaining table. To explore the connections between these environmental forces and the objectives of the parties would take us beyond the scope of this study. We are less interested in why a particular objective is chosen by a company than in the fact that it conflicts with an objective of the union. We are interested in how these issues are handled and settled.

* * * * *

AREA OF INTERDEPENDENCY

Certain long-term limits define the basic area of interdependency and consequently describe the most fundamental limit to the two-party conflict. Beyond each of these outer limits one or the other party would terminate the potentially advantageous relationship.

It is the purpose of this section to discuss the nature of this joint dependency and indicate the factors which limit or prescribe this range.

As we have indicated, the distributive process occurs around many specific issues, both economic and noneconomic. For ease of exposition we shall confine ourselves to the wage issue. In this and the following sections "wage rate" should be taken to represent the overall remuneration from employment.

The area of dependency stems from two sources: market rigidities and jointly created gain. These two sources will be discussed in turn.

MARKET RIGIDITIES.   The two organizations engaged in social negotiations stand to benefit by dealing with each other. In the union-management relationship, the lower limit to this area of interdependency would be the point at which the employees would seek a new employer or bargaining agent. At some upper limit, where management would be forced to seek a new relationship, it would invoke its next-best alternative to remaining in the current relationship. Management might move, it might seek another union, or it might hire nonunion labor. If a bargain is to be made between the parties as currently constituted, it must occur within the limits.

We have referred to the limits as if each were the problem of one party or the other. In reality, because the very existence of the business and employment opportunities are at stake at either limit, the two prices are experienced as limits by both parties.[5] That is, neither party has an interest in knowingly going above the higher or below the lower of these prices. Within this range, exchange benefits both parties, but the higher the price, the more the gain goes to labor, and the lower the price, the more this gain goes to management.

Within this range both sides stand to benefit from a bargain, which presumably specifies both price and quantity. Siegel and Fouraker, who review how the price and quantity variables have been handled in the literature, note that quantity (employment) is set so as to maximize the joint gain; i.e., quantity can be considered fixed, and bargaining centers on the question of price.[6]

Thus, at either edge of the range a sharp discontinuity would occur in quantity as the relationship is terminated and employment falls to zero. In actual fact it is unlikely that employment remains constant throughout the range, rather it is likely to diminish steadily as the wage rate is pushed toward the upper limit. This is an important factor in defining utility curves; a negotiator may be hesitant to approach the outer limits of the opponent because of the effects on employment.

* * * * *

MUTUALLY CREATED GAIN.   Thus far we have considered only the area of interdependency that stems from market rigidities. Another source of interdependency

---

[5] For a good discussion of these limits and a review of the literature see N. W. Chamberlain, *Collective Bargaining* (New York: McGraw-Hill, 1951), pp. 213–15.

[6] Sidney Siegel and L. E. Fouraker, *Bargaining and Group Decision Making* (New York: McGraw-Hill, 1960), p. 9.

has been heretofore overlooked. It stems from the fact that collective bargaining is not just a process of dividing existing resources but is also a process sometimes used for creating additional values or mutual benefits.

The creation of additional benefits can take place over both the long and the short run. Over the long run, considerable joint gain can be produced by the attitudes of trust and confidence which exist among employees, union officials, and management. For example, through the mechanism of a union-management cooperation scheme such as the Scanlon Plan, unit labor costs might be reduced to the point at which management would be willing to pay a particular labor force represented by a particular union considerably more than otherwise might be available. The joint gain grows out of the relationship and is something not available to either side elsewhere. The employees could leave the establishment and go elsewhere, but their contributions would be less and their compensation less accordingly. In the given establishment their contributions are higher because of the unique collaboration which produces joint gain.

Another instance of the willingness of employees to accept less than the market rate because of compensations gained from a given plant might exist if the plant were close to their residence or if it provided many social satisfactions of an intangible sort. Again, these factors are not reflected in the market rate since they represent unique attributes of the given company. Thus, it is possible for joint gain to exist because of a unique matching of employee and employer attributes.

Another important source of enlargement of the area of interdependency is the negotiation process itself. As we shall see in the chapter on integrative bargaining, considerable joint gain can be created through the use of problem-solving and utility-matching techniques.

* * * * *

SUBJECTIVE UTILITIES ASSOCIATED WITH VARIOUS SETTLEMENTS

The bargaining spectrum as defined above would consist of all the possible proportions into which the scarce resources could be distributed, each represented by a point or a price. However, bargaining is normally confined to a narrower range than that delimited by the outer limits of interdependency. This occurs for several reasons relating to the utility functions and probability functions of the negotiators. The matter of subjective utilities will be explored in this section.

It is important to distinguish between objective values and subjective preferences or utilities. (In our earlier discussion of issues and their underlying fixed-sum payoff structures we referred only to objective units of value such as monetary units.) Here we do not assume that a party's satisfaction, i.e., utility, is linear with money. Each unit of money added does not add the same amount of subjective utility.

* * * * *

What we hope to show by our analysis of utility and probability functions is that parties enter negotiations with more limited expectations about where on the spectrum serious bargaining will take place.

THE UNION'S UTILITY FUNCTION. Let us consider the utility function that a union negotiator might have for possible wage levels within the bargaining spectrum. Certainly the union negotiator's preferences would be influenced by his appreciation of the membership's preferences. However, we can now point to an important distinction between the utility functions of the membership and those of the union official. The value which underlies the former is primarily purchasing power of the wages received. The value reflected by the official's preference curve is the security

EXHIBIT 5   THE ZERO POINT AND UNITS OF THE INTERVAL SCALE ARE ARBITRARY

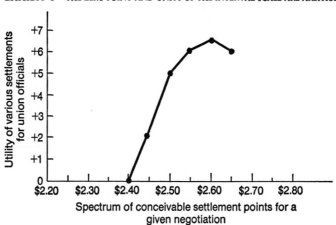

Spectrum of conceivable settlement points for a
given negotiation

of the institution he represents and the security he enjoys as an official in that institution at the various possible wage levels which he might gain and maintain.[7] It stands to reason that this security is affected by a series of evaluations of the official's specific performances. A union official is sensitive to how well he does in negotiations relative to the settlements negotiated elsewhere. Exhibits 5 presents a curve which reflects these ideas.

The following assumptions underlie Exhibit 5:

1.   Present wage rate is $2.40. The settlements reached elsewhere, which are the standards against which the union negotiator believes he will be evaluated, range from increases of 5 to 10 cents per hour. Any change from 5 to 10 cents would be of maximal value to him, since it would greatly influence his relative standing as a negotiator. The 5-cent increase to $2.45 would represent the threshold to this range.

2.   We assume that no wage increase represents another threshold—we have designated this point as the point of zero

utility on the diagram. Any increment in the settlement up to 5 cents would be valued positively but at a lower rate. Hence the added utility between 0 and 5 cents ($2.40 and $2.45) is shown as 2 utiles, contrasted with an addition of 3 utiles for the next 5-cent increment of 5 to 10 cents.

3.   We assume that increments above 10 cents will be valued less but still positively. The chart shows the 5-cent increment from $2.50 to $2.55 as adding one utile and the 5-cent increment from $2.55 to $2.60 as adding one-half utile.

4.   At some point, represented here as $2.60, the value of higher settlements to the union official actually becomes negative. This is based on the assumption that settlements can be so high as to make his life difficult in certain ways. Higher figures might raise the expectations of the membership to have similar settlements in the future or to influence the expectations of other groups he also represents.

What sorts of factors enter into the union negotiator's thinking to influence his preferences? It is not necessary to explain here why certain economic demands or provisions are valued positively, for example, why the union negotiator's utility curve for employees' wages is generally a rising one. The question is: What factors

---

[7] We assume that negotiating an adequate wage level is a necessary, but certainly not a sufficient, criterion for security as a bargaining agent.

explain the discontinuities in the utility curve? The discussion focuses on three points: zero utility, maximum marginal utility, and maximum total utility.

The *status quo* often represents the point at which a union negotiator begins to attach positive value to a settlement. A union official often feels that he must succeed in accomplishing some improvement through negotiations. The point at which the rate of increase in utility is at a maximum is usually associated with "coercive comparisons."[8] Coercive comparisons may stem from the precedent value of prior wage settlements in the given relationship or from the settlements in allied situations. Both precedent and patterns play an extremely important role in creating discontinuities in the utility curves.

The point at which utility starts to decrease absolutely is influenced by many factors. As suggested earlier, the utility of higher wage settlements may be decreased by the problems which the negotiator would encounter in subsequent negotiations with the same company or in concurrent negotiations with other companies.

However, another consideration serves to constrain the utility curve. This involves the subject of outer limits. Each negotiator places less utility on increments in position near the outer limit of the opponent. For example, union officials become progressively less interested in increasing the wage rate as wages reach the upper limit. Depending upon the slope of the company's demand curve, higher wage rates may provoke important employment effects for the union. Thus, to the extent that the company's demand for labor is elastic, there will be some restraining influences on the union's utility curve.

---

[8] A. M. Ross, *Trade Union Wage Policy* (Berkeley, Calif.: University of California Press, 1948). See also Leon Festinger, "A Theory of Social Comparison Process," *Human Relations* 7, no. 2 (1954), pp. 117–40.

* * * * *

THE COMPANY'S UTILITY FUNCTION.   Let us now consider the utility curve that a company negotiator might have under the same circumstances. In many respects the curve would be influenced (in a reciprocal way) by the same factors just enumerated (see Exhibit 6).

The following assumptions underlie Exhibit 6.

1.   The company has no desire to put through a wage reduction. The point of maximum utility is $2.40, the present wage.

2.   Settlements slightly above $2.40 bring some drop in utility but not a great deal. Between $2.45 and $2.50 there is a rapid drop in utility as the wage approaches the limit set by pattern settlements.

3.   The point of minimum effective ·utility represents the "maximum offer" which the negotiator can give without being replaced by top management.

Let us analyze the factors that shape the company's utility curve in terms of maximum total utility, maximum marginal utility, and zero utility.

Like the union, the company is not interested in pushing the wage rate to the opponent's outer limit. Certainly the company would not have any interest in pushing wages below the point at which it would have difficulty in retaining the desired work force, although it might not be deterred from pressing for a wage rate which would induce the employees to abandon the union. Note our assumption that management shares an interest in preventing wages from going below "the level necessary to attract and maintain the desired work force." This has buried within it many complications and prior assumptions. Moreover, there are some important exceptions to the statement itself.

First, look at the complications. The

EXHIBIT 6

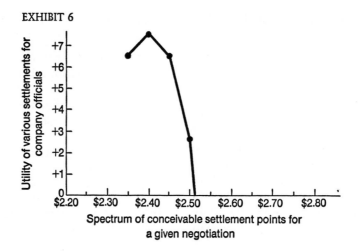

level required to "attract" a work force might be considerably higher than that required to "maintain" a work force. The level which would constitute the point of maximum utility would depend on whether the company needed to attract a new force or merely needed to maintain the present one. "Desired work force" is also a concept needing explanation. Presumably the higher the wage level, the more desirable the quality of the work force recruited. We assume an optimum point at which the marginal wage cost and the marginal productivity resulting from attracting a higher quality worker are equal.

Now, look at an exception. We have assumed a single economic criterion to the company's wage policy—it would want to spend only enough to keep its work force. This is undoubtedly more than an oversimplification; it is probably grossly contrary to the real world. Many business firms have established wage policies which contribute to their images as good employers, as progressive companies, etc. These policies have been internalized and are valued for their own sake. For many of these companies the point below which they would allow their wage level to fall is consider-

ably above the point at which they would begin to lose their work force.

The point of maximum change in utility would be fixed by settlements in other situations. As the wage rate approached the high side of the pattern, the company negotiator would experience sharply reduced satisfaction.

The company negotiator might tolerate a settlement slightly above competition. The company negotiator would experience zero utility in some sense at the point at which he would be in danger of being replaced.

How high a company negotiator would be willing to go depends upon a number of complex factors. If competitors could be required to sign the same contract (as is usual in industry or association bargaining), if the wage increase could be passed on in the form of a price increase, if labor costs represented a small percentage of total costs, or if profits were ample, then the point of zero utility for the company might be considerably higher.[9]

---

[9] All these conditions might also work to raise the company's outer limit. Whether they affect the utility curve directly or indirectly does not really matter for the purposes of this discussion.

SUBJECTIVE DISUTILITIES OF A FAILURE TO
AGREE: STRIKE COSTS

As previously stated, the purpose of this
analysis is to determine where, within the
long-term area of dependency, actual bargaining will take place in any particular
negotiation. Just as the negotiator's preferences for various possible settlements are
important, so too is his evaluation of the
costs associated with a failure to agree. The
negotiator understands that if a particular
position he adopts turns out to be unacceptable to the other party and the parties
fail to reach agreement, certain costs are
incurred. In collective bargaining the "certain costs" are typically strike costs.[10]

The possibility of a strike and the costs
of such a strike for the negotiator is always
the other side of the coin to the advantages
demanded. The prospect of incurring
strike costs encourages caution in a negotiator's thinking. The more costly the failure
to agree, the more conservative his expectations will be. In the next section we shall
learn more about why this is true when
we combine strike costs and utilities with
probabilities.

TYPES OF STRIKE COSTS. *Labor's
costs.* The following are various aspects
of labor's costs or potential costs involved
in striking:

1. Loss of wages by employees. Drain
on financial resources of union.

2. Loss of institutional security. A
strike may result in a loss of membership
and even threaten the status of the union
as bargaining agent. Many employees may
find other jobs during the strike and not
return after the strike ends. The employee

replacements may not be as likely to join
the union or may at least delay joining.
Other employees who went through the
strike may drop their membership. Rival
unions or rival factions within the union
may exploit a strike situation and acquire
employee support for themselves.

3. Loss of goodwill with management.
This leads to antagonisms which may not
disappear with termination of strike. Management may be more adamant in the future, retaliating in ways of its own. The
deterioration in plant relationships can result in a disadvantage to both parties, since
the informal accommodations worked out
to the mutual satisfaction of both parties
may be contingent upon continuing trust
and the elimination of trust threatens
these working arrangements.

4. Loss of public image. A strike may
give the appearance that the union is acting irresponsibly and ignoring the public's
interest in maintaining the flow of goods
and services.

Management's costs. The following
are the various aspects of management's
costs or potential costs involved in striking:

1. Loss of operating profits (short run)
and market position (longer run). Possible
damage to plant and equipment through
idleness.

2. Loss of management status with
higher management or stockholders. If the
strike does not seem necessary or if it appears to have been mishandled, the managers responsible for negotiations may suffer
a loss of prestige. Their careers may be adversely affected.

3. Loss of goodwill with labor. Both
the union-management relationship and
employee relations can suffer, resulting in
low morale, low productivity, and resistance to changes initiated by management,
etc.

---

[10] The strike, which is a mutual decision, represents the major alternative to agreement. Failure to
agree may provoke other forms of economic pressure
such as slowdowns or social pressure such as criticism, but our analysis will center on costs associated
with strike action.

4. Loss of public image. The strike can have an adverse effect on attitudes of customers, governmental agencies, or legislative bodies.

Positive by-products. Sometimes by striking, a party also receives some positive by-products apart from any immediate concessions it may achieve. What are these by-products?

First, the strike which fails to obtain any concessions in the immediate negotiations may nevertheless have some value as a long-term investment. The credibility of a strike threat will be enhanced in the future, whether it is used with the same adversary or with another who only knows of the strike. . . .

Second, the internal organization of the party may more likely be strengthened than weakened by a strike (of short duration). Identifying an external enemy usually increases the internal solidarity of a group. In addition, winning a strike may gain new members.

Third, sometimes the strike has a positive psychological impact rather than an adverse one. It may serve as an outlet for pent-up emotions of workers. It may even serve to clear the air between the parties and provide a foundation for building constructive relationships.

* * * * *

PROBABILITY FUNCTIONS AND SUBJECTIVELY EXPECTED UTILITIES

. . . One school of decision theory makes a definitive point of combining utilities and probabilities into a composite concept: The subjectively expected utility (*SEU*) of an alternative is the product of the subjective utility and the subjective probability of success associated with that alternative.[11] The theory holds that a person will choose the alternative which maximizes subjectively expected utility. Let us trace out the implications of this formulation without becoming committed to the precise significance of the figure it produces.

Inasmuch as there are both potential positive and potential negative consequences associated with a given demand, the *SEU* of an alternate demand (x) is its utility (U) times the probability (P) that it will be acceptable *plus* the strike costs (S) associated with a failure to agree times the probability $(1 - P)$ that the demand will not be acceptable.

$$SEU = P(x) \cdot U(x) + [1 - P(x)] \cdot S(x)$$

* * * * *

The union official's subjective probability function is constructed out of his assumptions about the responses of management under various circumstances. He might ask himself, "Suppose I absolutely refused to go below 20 cents ($2.60)? Would management be likely to agree without a strike?" First, the union official would need to make some assumption about the (negative) utility of the various settlements for management. The union would be especially interested in knowing the general shape of management's maximum marginal utility? To know this would be to improve the union's ideas about where along the spectrum management might offer the most resistance. Within this sensitive area of the spectrum (as viewed by management), the union might expect more rapid changes in the probabilities of success of alternate demands. *The more disutility involved for management, the lower would be the union's estimate of its probability of success.* Simply stated, management is more likely to fight for issues it thinks are important.

Second, the union official would be concerned about the strike costs the company would face. *The lower the compa-*

[11] Ward Edwards, "Behavioral Decision Theory," *Annual Review of Psychology* 12 (1961), pp. 473–98.

EXHIBIT 7

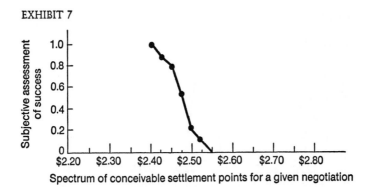

Spectrum of conceivable settlement points for a given negotiation

ny's strike costs, *the lower the union's estimate of the probability of success.* Essentially, management would be more willing to take a position which risked incurring a strike that would be less costly.

Third, the union official also would be concerned about his own strike costs. *The higher the union's strike costs, the lower the union's estimate of the probability of success.* In effect, the less a strike would cost the company and the more a strike would cost the union, then the more the union can expect the company to use coercion in furthering its objectives in the distributive bargain.

Let us assume that the union official's assessment of these factors led to a probability function like that in Exhibit 7.

The probability figures shown in Exhibit 7 can then be combined with the utility curve shown earlier. The results are the positive expectations associated with alternate demands (see Exhibit 8a).

EXHIBIT 8a   TABLE OF CALCULATIONS

INCREASE OF X	U(x)	×	P(x)	=	TOTAL
0¢	0		1.0	=	0
2½¢	1		.9	=	.9
5¢	2		.8	=	1.6
7½¢	3½		.5	=	1.75
10¢	5		.2	=	1.0
12½¢	5½		.1	=	.55
15¢	6		0	=	0

EXHIBIT 8b   TABLE OF CALCULATIONS

INCREASE OF X	S(x)	×	[1 − P(x)]	=	TOTAL
0¢	−2		.0	=	0
2½¢	−2		.1	=	−.2
5¢	−2		.2	=	−.4
7½¢	−2		.5	=	−1.0
10¢	−2		.8	=	−1.6
12¼¢	−2		.9	=	−1.8
15¢	−2		1.0	=	−2.0

Let us assume that the strike will have a disutility of 2 (coordinated with the positive utility scale of 0 to 7).[12] Using 1 − P(x) for the probability of a strike and −2 for the utility of a strike, we can calculate the expected costs associated with each demand (see Exhibit 8b). Exhibit 9 shows the net subjectively expected utili-

_____

[12] The calculation of this figure can be done as follows: The lump-sum costs represented by a strike can be converted into a stream of costs comparable to wages by a discount calculation. For the company the discount period would closely parallel the payout period used for any analysis of capital appropriations. For the union the payout period might be approximated by the length of the collective bargaining agreement. While this conversion from a lump sum to a stream of costs may not be operationally easy, it does not contain any conceptual problems. In his calculations, Cartter chooses a 20 percent discount rate for the union and a 10 percent discount rate for the company. See A. M. Cartter, *Theory of Wages and Employment* (Homewood, Ill.: Richard D. Irwin, 1959), p. 119. Reder also discusses how this calculation can be made. See M. W. Reder, "The Theory of Union Wage Policy," *The Review of Economics and Statistics,* February 1952, p. 38.

EXHIBIT 9

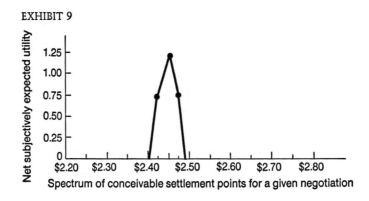

ties which result when one subtracts the subjective strike costs associated with each possible level of increase from the positive expectations.

The maximum *SEU* (1.2) is at 5 cents. What is the meaning of this figure? If the contest were one in which the union entered a single sealed bid without further haggling, this figure would be its optimum bid. But other points on the spectrum are important to the union negotiator. Between 2½ and 7½ cents subjectively expected utility is reasonably high (.7 and .75 respectively). Outside of these points expected utility drops sharply. The union negotiator would hope to approach 7½ cents, but he also recognizes that he may not do as well and the settlement may be closer to 2½ cents. This is suggestive of the idea of target and resistance points, concepts which will be introduced in the next section.

* * * * *

TARGET AND RESISTANCE POINTS

While our discussion of *SEU* was not developed in order to identify a single objective or decision choice for a negotiator, it did serve to focus attention on a portion of the bargaining spectrum where the alternatives involved relatively high expected utilities. We have termed the boundaries of that range as target and resistance points.

The need for distinguishing multiple points rather than a single objective results from the particular type of decision situation facing the negotiator. Inasmuch as a fixed deadline will terminate negotiations, a party is forced to a decision rule about settling or striking. Hence his need for a resistance point or a level of achievement below which he would choose to sustain a strike over the issues still unresolved. We assume that the negotiator anticipates the need for such a decision rule well in advance of the zero hour, formulating a tentative resistance point as one guide to his behavior at the bargaining table.

Another feature of labor negotiations explains why negotiators need an additional decision rule, a target. We have already said that negotiations are not one-shot decision-making situations, even though the ultimate exchange before a strike deadline might be so represented. Negotiations involve a series of decisions interspersed with performance activities—in short, they are situations involving complex goal strivings. The negotiator can do more than enter an "optimum bid"; he can influence the area in which final bids will be exchanged. If this is an achievement situation, the negotiator needs something to aim at, so to speak.

EXHIBIT 10

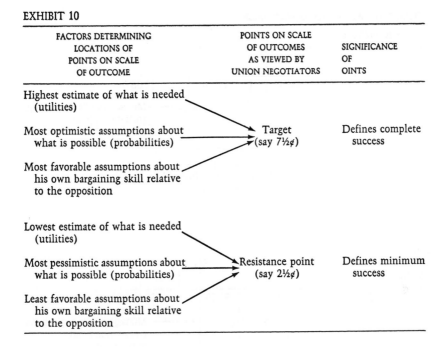

FACTORS DETERMINING LOCATIONS OF POINTS ON SCALE OF OUTCOME	POINTS ON SCALE OF OUTCOMES AS VIEWED BY UNION NEGOTIATORS	SIGNIFICANCE OF OINTS
Highest estimate of what is needed (utilities)		
Most optimistic assumptions about what is possible (probabilities)	Target (say 7½¢)	Defines complete success
Most favorable assumptions about his own bargaining skill relative to the opposition		
Lowest estimate of what is needed (utilities)		
Most pessimistic assumptions about what is possible (probabilities)	Resistance point (say 2½¢)	Defines minimum success
Least favorable assumptions about his own bargaining skill relative to the opposition		

There is additional anecdotal support for the idea that a negotiator identifies more than one intermediate position (in addition to his conception of the outer limits or the area of long-term dependency). Support for this assertion comes from the language used by negotiators. Consider the following statements: "I hope to get 7 cents, and must have at least 5 cents"; "I'd be happy with an 11-cent package, but we couldn't go below the pattern of 8 cents under any circumstances." The words or phrases such as "hope," "happy with," on the one hand, and "must have at least" and "couldn't go below," on the other hand, certainly refer to different points of prominence on the bargaining spectrum as conceived by a negotiator.

Exhibit 10 contains a graphic representation of these distinctions. The resistance and target points are aspirations. Aspiration level theory explains the process of goal formation by reference to the same variables of utility and probability. Although the theory usually prescribes a point, one can think of the range bounded by the target and resistance points as an aspiration zone.[13]

For the reasons mentioned earlier we believe that the latter view is more appropriate to bargaining activity (True, as negotiations unfold, this range narrows and approaches a point, but it is just this process by which a negotiator establishes a particular referent for his ultimate decision that we want to understand in all of its complexity.) For convenience we shall use the term "aspiration" when we want to refer to both target and resistance point. Whether the term describes a range or a point will depend upon the stage of negotiations.

SETTLEMENT RANGE. The area between the parties' respective resistance points is referred to as the settlement range. The range, however, can be positive or negative. In the positive range the resistance points are compatible. In the range

---

[13] W. H. Starbuck, "Level of Aspiration Theory and Economic Behavior," *Behavioral Science*, April 1963, pp. 128–36.

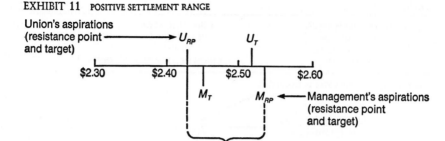

EXHIBIT 11   POSITIVE SETTLEMENT RANGE

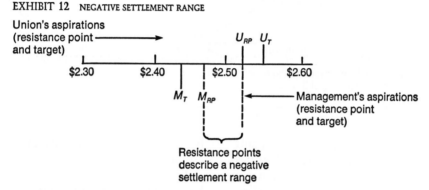

EXHIBIT 12   NEGATIVE SETTLEMENT RANGE

bounded by these two points both parties would settle in preference to sustaining a work stoppage (see Exhibit 11). The negative settlement range depicts the situation in which the resistance points are incompatible (see Exhibit 12). There is no settlement which would be minimally acceptable to both parties.

In practice, the target of one is usually selected in a way that represents the best estimate about the other's resistance point. Thus, for all intents and purposes a party usually behaves as if his own resistance point and target describe *the* settlement range. However, the settlement range as defined here is only determined objectively by combining the private aspirations of the two parties.

Perhaps the most common configuration is one in which both parties (1) prefer and entertain hopes for positions which

are incompatible but (2) are resigned to accept other less ambitious positions which are compatible. The targets are not compatible, but the resistance points are.

The resistance points of parties will tend to be compatible if each party has a relatively accurate picture of the other's utilities. Whether these resistance points are compatible at the outset of negotiations depends in part upon the existence of stereotype utility functions.[14] Of course, these stereotype functions need to be appropriate for the particular negotiator, i.e., to approximate his true utility function. When there are well-established traditions and role requirements for each of the negotiators and when the specific pressures

---

[14] J. C. Harsanyi, "Bargaining in Ignorance of the Opponent's Utility Function," *Journal of Conflict Resolution*, March 1962, pp. 28–38.

bearing on them are generally known, the negotiators tend to enter bargaining with more or less consistent expectations about each other's utility function.

Influence of patterns. Whether the resistance points describe a positive or a negative settlement range depends in more specific terms upon all the factors previously enumerated in this chapter. A few words need to be said about the influence of patterns, since their impact is usually to define a fairly narrow range, whether positive or negative. In some instances, the union views the pattern settlement as a floor from which to bargain upward, and the company views it as a ceiling from which to bargain downward (that is, both interpret the pattern in a way most favorable to themselves and then regard it as their resistance point). In this situation a small negative range will exist; but it may be hard to close, nevertheless.

When the parties are free to set their own pattern, the settlement range is likely to be large, although it cannot be said whether it will tend toward the negative or the positive direction. The willingness of a company to become a pattern setter in wages or benefits may create a positive range. By making a breakthrough, the company gives the union an important advantage over and above the substantive gain of the settlement. The new pattern strengthens the union's bargaining position in subsequent negotiations. In return for this advantage, the union may adopt a restrained position in other areas, even to the extent of giving the company concessions. But it is just as likely that the pattern-setting situation could produce a negative range. When uncertainty exists, the union and the company may well be overambitious in formulating their aspirations.

Some empirical work on strike activity is pertinent here. The frequency of strike activity can be one indicator of the prevalence of the negative range. In a study of strike activity, Albert Rees relates the business cycle and the tendency to develop incompatible expectations. The negative range is most likely to occur just prior to the peak of business activity.

Why does the strike peak consistently precede the reference peak (high point of the business cycle)? The strike peak is probably a maximum in the divergence of expectations between employers and unions. Unions pay close attention to employment, which generally does not lead at the peak. They are also influenced by previous wage increases received by other unions and by increases in the cost of living. The attention of employers is likely to be focused on some of the activities which do not lead at the peak, and they will thus resist demands for which the unions are still willing to fight.[15]

"INTEGRATIVE BARGAINING MODEL"

* * * * *

AGENDA ITEMS AND INTEGRATIVE POTENTIAL

ISSUES AND PROBLEMS.   We referred to the subject matter of distributive bargaining as issues. The subject matter of integrative bargaining is problems. The two subprocesses involve dramatically different activities because they deal with quite different potential payoff structures. . . . The contrasts can be summarized briefly. Issues involve a fixed total objective value which can be allocated between the parties in various shares or proportions. Problems, on the other hand, are agenda items which contain possibilities for greater or lesser amounts of value which can be made available to the two parties.

In its extreme, or pure, form as issue would require that whatever gains are

---

[15] Albert Rees, "Industrial Conflict and Business Fluctuations," *The Journal of Political Economy,* October 1952, p. 381.

available to one necessarily entails a corresponding and equal sacrifice by the other. Similarly a problem in its purest form would be an agenda item for which the parties would assign the same preference ordering to all possible outcomes and about which the two parties would be equally concerned. For an issue the interests of the two parties are diametrically opposed; for a problem the interests are identical or completely coincidental.

In actual fact, few items correspond to these pure types. Thus, we have tended to employ issues, problems, and mixed items in a somewhat more relaxed fashion. Issues are those items in which gains to one *tend* to involve corresponding sacrifices for the other. Our discussion and illustrations of distributive bargaining have applied to the broader conception of *predominantly* conflict situations. Distributive bargaining tactics were viewed as instrumental to the extent that the payoff structure approached the pure "issue" type.

Similarly, the concept of problem covers more than the situation in which gains available to one necessarily allow corresponding and equal gains by the other. It is applied to situations in which the total payoff is varying sum in a significant way, even though both parties may not share equally in the joint gain, and indeed one may even suffer minor inconveniences in order to provide substantial gains for the other. Presumably, when the direct results of a problem solution are high benefit–low sacrifice, the slightly inconvenienced party can receive some side payment or reciprocal treatment in another problem area. However, this gets ahead of the story— here we are interested in the fact that for certain agenda items some outcomes allow significantly larger joint payoffs than other outcomes do, without concerning ourselves with the allocation of these payoffs between the parties.

We complete the spectrum by defining a mixed agenda item as one in which there are both significant issue aspects and problem aspects and where there is more than token conflict potential and integrative potential. We shall treat the mixed items in detail in the next chapter as a part of the discussion of the dilemmas of distributive and integrative bargaining.

Issues, problems, and mixed items have different types of outcomes. Issues result in compromise solutions. Problems result in integrative solutions in some degree. Mixed items can result in either compromise or integrative outcomes, depending upon the orientation of the negotiators and their tactical approach to the agenda item.

* * * * *

INTEGRATIVE POTENTIAL.   The range of situations assumed by the integrative bargaining model and tactics includes agenda items of two types. In the first, one (or more) possible resolution(s) of the agenda item by itself offers both parties a gain in absolute terms over their respective positions in the status quo; for such a resolution neither party experiences any loss. This may mean that the utility functions of the two parties are identical or parallel, but this need not be the case. The necessary condition is that at least one arrangement different from the status quo would allow each to move to a more favorable position on his relevant utility curve. These absolutely integrative solutions to an agenda item may not be obvious to the parties, but if in an objective sense they exist, the situation is said to be of this first type.

The second type of integrative situation is less clear cut. None of the possible solutions of a given problem permit improvement upon the status quo for both parties. We have in mind a situation in which the many possible solutions represent widely varying sacrifice-benefit ratios, but where one solution involves no more than token sacrifice. Thus, the parties must determine the best of the partially integrative solutions.

We can illustrate situations that have high integrative potential by discussing some common problem areas and alternate solutions in collective bargaining. Agenda items involving strictly economic values are much less likely to contain integrative possibilities than are items referring to rights and obligations of the parties.

It is just a fact of economic life that "money is money." With money, one side's gain is the other side's loss. Money can only be divided into units; it cannot be reformulated into an arrangement that may be an improvement for both sides. Thus, inherent integrative potential is more apt to be found in qualitative issues—in matters that involve the rights and obligations of the parties. To quote a participant in the Human Relations Committee in steel: ". . . the joint study approach is least effective when applied to wages, very useful on fringes, and has its greatest future promise on 'job security' issues."[16] Consequently most of the following examples fall in the area of rights and obligations, and many pertain to job security. We have organized the examples around such collective bargaining matters.

Individual job security and management flexibility. Often the provisions of the contract achieve some measure of one of these values only at the expense of the other value. For every increment in employee job security provided by seniority rights, management has incurred a corresponding loss in flexibility in managing manpower or operations. In these cases the bargaining outcome is fundamentally and strictly a compromise between the two values. However, parties sometimes achieve considerable integration of these twin interests in job security and manage-

ment flexibility, in part because the unique circumstances allow for this possibility and in part because of imaginative and diligent problem solving. In the following discussion we shall analyze several facets of the situation and provide illustrations of solutions both of a relatively compromise and relatively integrative character.

One aspect of providing job security involves arrangements about "competitive" rights, namely, the rules for allocating jobs among competing employees. Consider the solution adopted by the parties to one negotiation in the meat-packing industry:

> Many plants were being closed. New plants were being opened at distant points. The union wanted employees from the old plants to be able to move to the new plants with full seniority. The company, which often established a new plant because of inducements provided by local officials, was anxious to hire employees from the adjoining area. In one situation it was proposed that the old employees carry one-half of their seniority. The arrangement seemed acceptable to both sides since it protected somewhat the vested interest of the older employees and at the same time did not give them an overwhelming edge on newer employees for whom management felt considerable responsibility.

The solution providing for old employees to carry one half of their accumulated seniority to new plants probably represented a good balancing of the interests of the parties. Nevertheless, it would appear to have been more of a compromise than an integrative answer to the underlying concerns of the parties.

A somewhat different problem arose in the agricultural equipment industry in this general area of competitive job rights and provides another illustrative solution.

> In the closing down of the McCormick Works of International Harvester, the following issue arose: As soon as the company announced the shutdown of the plant, the union wanted employees released so that

---

[16] Bureau of National Affairs, *Labor Relations Reporter* no. 198 (Washington, D.C., Oct. 10, 1963), p. 2.

they could apply for work at other International Harvester plants. For its part, the company desired to keep many of these employees since they were necessary in the phasing-out operation. The solution reached established a "pegged" seniority date at other plants, if at any point after the company announced its plans to shut down the plant a job opened at other plants which the given employee could fill. Thus, the employee continued on in the plant being terminated, all the time acquiring seniority at the plant to which he would be eventually transferred.

By the imaginative arrangement devised in this case both job security for employees and management efficiency were achieved. This solution apparently was more integrative than compromise.

*　*　*　*　*

In another case in which few senior employees were being promoted because of a lack of the requisite skills, the parties transformed an issue into a problem.

At first the company and the union were in dispute about why so few senior employees were being promoted. One solution offered by employees was that seniority be given more weight in promotions. After considerable discussion, it was agreed that the company would inaugurate a "self-help" program for employees. It would pay for outside education and do everything possible to help the employees improve their skills in advance of promotion opportunities.

By this solution the union achieved its objectives of improving the promotional opportunities of senior employees and management retained its preferred criteria for making promotion decisions. It is not clear whether the solution enabled both parties to gain over the status quo (that would depend on how management valued the improved opportunities for senior employees), but the solution appeared to be at least a high-benefit–low-sacrifice one.

An important matter which has produced a number of innovations is the question about the rights of displaced employees.[17] The Brookings study reports on the area-availability arrangement used in southern Michigan. This plan is used in the Ford Motor Company and enables a presently employed worker to have priority over a new worker. Often the company's interest is coincident with that of the union when the skills of the displaced employees are needed in the new plant. "The plan did not provide interplant bumping rights, but it established a preferential hiring policy and therefore it was a part of a system of enhancing seniority rights."[18]

A number of special retraining programs have been developed to help the employee who has been displaced from his former plant. An example is the work done under the Armour Automation Fund. The many efforts that the parties have pursued to meet the needs of displaced employees while keeping the financial liabilities of the employers within limits have been described and analyzed by Thomas Kennedy.[19]

Preserving jobs and management efficiency. Often the arrangements which serve the union's interest in preserving jobs entail a corresponding sacrifice to the company in terms of its operational effi-

---

[17] Several reviews have been published which summarize the innovations in this area: Derek Bok and Max D. Kossoris, *Methods of Adjusting to Automation and Technological Change* (Washington, D.C.: U.S. Department of Labor, no date); and *Recent Collective Bargaining and Technological Change*, BLS Report 266 (Washington, D.C.: U.S. Department of Labor, 1964).

[18] S. H. Slichter, J. J. Healy, and E. R. Livernash, *The Impact of Collective Bargaining on Management* (Washington, D.C.: The Brookings Institution, 1960), p. 166.

[19] Thomas Kennedy, *Automation Funds and Displaced Workers* (Boston: Division of Research, Graduate School of Business Administration, Harvard University, 1962).

ciency. Subcontracting is a matter which has important implications for these two interests.

The parties often invoke incompatible principles in the area of subcontracting.[20] The starting point for the union would be to prohibit subcontracting. The starting point for the company would be to claim unilateral and unfettered rights. Stated in this way, the matter is an issue and is subject only to compromise.

However, by exploring the various reasons which underlie the parties' interests in the issue, new possibilities may emerge. The union's reasons can include the following: (1) to protect normal employment opportunities for its members, (2) to preserve the particular union's jurisdiction and strength, (3) to enlarge work opportunities of its members, (4) to combat escaping from unionism, and (5) to protect union standards against competition. The reasons for the company's interest in subcontracting include some of the following: (6) more rapid completion, (7) more adequate skills, equipment, or plant, and (8) lower cost. Unless the company's reasons also include specifically antiunion objectives, such as to reduce employment opportunities for union members, to escape unionism, or to subvert union standards; and unless the union has comparable anticompany intentions, there is probably some integrative potential.

Let us turn to integrative potential. There are different ways in which either absolute prohibition of subcontracting or unfettered freedom can be modified. Management's rights could be qualified by procedures it must follow preliminary to a subcontracting decision, such as prior notification to the union, consultation, mutual agreement, etc., or they can be modified

by specifying conditions under which subcontracting is permitted, i.e., by indicating decision criteria. Whichever of these two general methods of limiting management's rights represents the most integrative solution will be the one which provides maximum protection to the union (in the terms 1 to 5 listed above) for the minimum sacrifice of flexibility and efficiency on the part of the company (in terms of 6 to 8 listed above).

Now suppose that the parties explore the second method, that is, the conditions under which management is permitted or it not permitted to subcontract. Several criteria are sometimes incorporated into contract clauses governing subcontracting: Are present employees working a short work week, a full work week, or are they working overtime? Do present employees possess or lack the requisite skills? Is work to be performed on or off the premises? Again, in order to achieve the best integration of interests, the parties must subject each criterion to the test of the particular utilities of the parties in the situation. Often a specific criterion carefully worded affords the workers precisely the protection they are most concerned about without any sacrifice of the flexibility wanted by management.

Other solutions to the conflict between jobs and efficiency can be found in a number of the cost-reduction or incentive plans that have been developed over the years. Under the West Coast Mechanization Fund the union agreed to let the shipping companies do away with work rules in return for an annual contribution of $5 million to a fund from which the union would pay for short work-week, early retirement, and other benefits that might be needed because of the increased mechanization. This solution gave the union an alternative to a blind and opportunistic opposition to management's attempts to automate, which would indeed have achieved a slow-

---

[20] Slichter, Healy, and Livernash, *Impact of Collective Bargaining*, pp. 280–316.

ing down of mechanization but at higher cost to the employers. Similarly, the solution contained obligations for management and benefits for displaced employees which were predictable and therefore could be planned for by both the firms and the worker households involved.

* * * * *

Institutional security. The area of union security provides the substance for many issues that occasionally can be converted into problems. Most unions press adamantly for union shop arrangements. Most companies resist requiring their employees to join the union as a condition of employment. Here is a conflict between the "free-ride" argument and the "right-to-work" argument. In some situations the agency shop, wherein the employee pays a fee to the union for the bargaining services provided, has been adopted and found satisfactory by both sides.

A study of collective bargaining by the National Industrial Conference Board illustrates another way in which a mutually beneficial arrangement was realized.

> The company recognizes that as exclusive bargaining agent in this bargaining unit the union is obligated to represent nonunion as well as union members and that in carrying the burden of contract administration, the union performs some service for all employees in the bargaining unit. Therefore, in recognition of these things, and in consideration for the pledge of the union that its officers or members will not intimidate or coerce employees into joining the union, and in the interest of harmony, the company agrees when new employees have completed their probationary period as provided in this contract, the personnel manager or his representative will place in the hands of such employee a copy of the union contract together with a letter from the company rec-

ommending that the new employee join the union.[21]

Occasionally important goals of the two negotiating parties are such that they can be accommodated by the same means. An instance of this is provided by the first postwar negotiations between the UAW and the Ford Motor Company. The years 1941 to 1946 had been marked by an extremely large number of wildcat strikes in Ford, a fact which had been experienced by the company as a considerable handicap to its production efforts. An important objective of the company in the 1946 negotiations was to establish a means for reducing the number of unauthorized work stoppages. The union officials, for their part, had been embarrassed and were less effective on several occasions because they had not been able to maintain internal discipline within their ranks. Although they objected to the company's early proposals for curtailing wildcat strikes and could not show open support for the company's intentions, these union officials were interested in establishing more central control in this area. Consequently, the parties were able to devise a set of procedures and penalties for unauthorized work stoppages which allowed both union and management to largely attain their respective objectives. The eventual means chosen represented for both an improvement over the status quo.

Other problem areas occasionally provide an opportunity for mutual improvement over the status quo if the parties can just find the right solution. Allocation of overtime, when it has been troublesome for both parties, might provide such potential. Absenteeism is another such area.

---

[21] J. J. Bambrick and M. P. Dorbandt, *Preparing for Collective Bargaining*, Studies in Personnel Policy no. 172 (New York: National Industrial Conference Board, 1959), pp. 14–15.

UNION CAUCUS: IMPORTANT BARGAINING TOOL

AFL–CIO Labor Studies Center*

To the uninitiated, collective bargaining is a process in which representatives of labor and management sit across the table from each other and work out an agreement. It is thought of as a give-and-take process across a table. Experienced negotiators know this description is far from the truth.

Most of the time what really takes place at the bargaining table is the announcement of a position by one side accompanied by some words of justification. The other side responds, sometimes with questions, sometimes with a general comment and questions. Often, particularly during the later stages of negotiations, one side will leave the room for a caucus. This is particularly true of the union side. During the caucus, the union reviews its positions and proposals. During the caucus, the union prepares its answers to a management proposal. It is in the caucus that the real give-and-take discussion takes place in bargaining. That's why caucusing is so important to the bargaining process.

The basic reason for many union caucuses is to evaluate a company proposal and decide how to respond. For the local union member on the bargaining committee, that is just what is going on at a caucus. For the experienced bargaining committee, much more is happening. The experienced negotiator is well aware that caucuses give the committee opportunities to do many other things beside deciding to accept or reject a proposal. Experienced bargainers use caucuses for a variety of reasons.

To consider the whys and uses of the caucus in bargaining, let's back up a bit and recall the whole structure of a bargaining committee from the union side. Because on a small scale, the bargaining team does not reflect the membership, its diversity of interests and concerns are reflected in their interests and responses to demands the union makes as well as to company proposals. Examples:

The long-service employee on the bargaining team is probably more concerned about pensions than improving the amount of vacation for the newer employees.

The newer employee is less interested in strict seniority than the older employee and is probably more concerned about getting ahead.

The married employee with a large family is more interested in expanding health and hospitalization benefits than the single worker.

The members of a bargaining team who are also elected union officers are more interested in changes that will strengthen the union as a whole (i.e., improved grievance procedure, right to call periodic membership meeting on company property, etc.) than the average member. And the skilled craft workers have less interest in speedup problems than assembly-line workers. And so it goes.

* Reprinted by permission of the AFL–CIO. "Union Caucus" was prepared in 1976.

Some members of the union bargaining committee consider themselves as having a constituency among the membership. Their behavior will be governed by what they perceive their constituency wants rather than the desires of the union as a whole. Hence, one of the major functions of the caucus is to keep the members of the bargaining committee together.

There are other uses of and reasons for a union caucus.

1. Make sure everybody understands the company proposal for each group.

2. Find out how each member of the committee "read" the company's latest position or proposal. Example: Was it a final position? Was it a bargaining position? Are they just playing games? Does it indicate a real change in the company attitude on a given issue? Is it evidence of a split on the company side?

3. Let the members of the committee react (explode) over what's happening at the table. This may be especially true if the committee is operating under a fairly tight one-spokesperson rule.

4. Pull the committee together. This may be especially necessary where suddenly everybody has started talking at the table and they are starting to disagree about the importance of an issue.

5. Cool off some of the committee members, particularly after a heated exchange at the table.

6. Slow down the pace of negotiations when things are moving too fast. (i.e., company counterproposals coming too fast to study properly.)

7. Change the subject. Decide on the next issue or proposals to be discussed.

8. Add emphasis to a point or proposal the union has just made and pressure the company to respond.

9. Plan strategy and tactics for the rest of that bargaining session as well as those

scheduled ahead.

10. Review how the union's basic bargaining game plan is proceeding and how it is working.

11. Deal with unexpected developments away from the bargaining table. Examples: Settlement of a major strike in the industry in a nearby community; rumor that the company is planning to subcontract part of work of another union in the plant, etc.

12. Keep the members of committee mutually apprised of what's going on at the table both in terms of what's being said and what's not being said.

13. Make sure the note-taker on the committee got that last company statement down accurately as it may be useful at the next membership meeting or in the next bulletin to the members.

14. Evaluate the hardness of the company's position on a union proposal and whether now is the time to think about modifying the union's proposal.

15. Re-assess the members' support on the issue under discussion at the table. This is particularly important toward the end of bargaining when questions like these get raised:

Do you think the members will strike over the difference between what's been offered and what we are asking for?

What do you think we need to settle this issue?

How long would we have to strike to get what we want in this area?

Do you think the members would buy the company's proposal if we can do something in this other area?

From the above list, it is clear that the union caucus can be an important and useful tool in the bargaining process.

For maximum usefulness, a couple of ground rules are useful to the caucus:

- The caucus should be conducted like any other small group meeting: in orderly but informal way with one member acting as chairperson.
- Everybody should be encouraged to present their views, but not hog the discussion.
- Every effort should be made to arrive at a consensus. Votes should be avoided as voting can be divisive, especially in small groups and can lead to splits in the committee which become apparent to the company at the table. Visible splits in committee weakens the union's position.

- Caucuses should take place in a comfortable, uncrowded place where everybody can see everybody else. Avoid the standing-in-a-telephone-booth type caucus.
- Time shouldn't be wasted in a caucus but take enough time so that everybody on the committee feels satisfied that his or her point of view has been expressed and considered. Skillful use of the caucus can be a great aid to the union bargaining committee in dealing with management at the table.

10–4

A THEORY OF MULTILATERAL COLLECTIVE BARGAINING IN CITY GOVERNMENTS

Thomas A. Kochan[*]

Although a vast descriptive and prescriptive literature concerning the nature of the collective bargaining process in the public sector has accumulated in recent years, little progress has been made toward developing theoretical models of these bargaining processes. This paper will address that issue by presenting a behavioral theory of the bargaining process in city governments.[1] In addition, the results of an empirical test of the theory based on data col-

[*] Professor, Massachusetts Institute of Technology. Reprinted in an abridged form, with permission, from the *Industrial and Labor Relations Review,* 27, no. 4, (July 1974), pp. 525–42. © 1974 by Cornell University. All rights reserved.

[1] The central concepts and propositions included in the model were derived from two earlier case studies of collective bargaining in Madison and Janesville, Wisconsin. The present study, therefore, is an effort to expand on, formalize, and test the hypotheses suggested by the results of these case studies. See Thomas A. Kochan, *City Employee Bargaining with a Divided Management* (Madison, Wis.: Industrial Relations Research Institute, 1971).

lected from 228 cities that bargain with locals of the International Association of Fire Fighters (IAFF) will also be presented.

THE INSTITUTIONAL CONTEXT

Collective bargaining in city government can be viewed as a special type of decision-making process that has both interorganizational and intraorganizational aspects. Traditionally, collective bargaining has been conceptualized as a bilateral process involving the interaction of representatives of employees on one side and management on the other.[2] With the growth of bargaining in the public sector, this traditional view of bargaining has come under serious attack. Since the organizational structures found in city governments have been designed to conform to the principle of separation of powers,[3] a number of semiautonomous management officials often share decision-making power over issues traditionally raised by unions in collective bargaining. Because power is shared by both administrative and elected officials, it has been argued that what often begins as a "variant of private sector bargaining" ends up by becoming an extension of machine politics.[4]

The basic thesis of the model tested in this paper is that these political and organizational characteristics of city government lead to the development of a multilateral bargaining process. Although others have discussed this type of bargaining in the public sector,[5] this paper is believed to be the first to present a formal theory of multilateral bargaining in which the concept is operationally defined and to test empirically several hypotheses concerning the determinants of this form of bargaining.

THE CONCEPT OF MULTILATERAL BARGAINING

Multilateral bargaining is defined as a process of negotiation in which more than two distinct parties are involved in such a way that a clear dichotomy between the employee and management organizations does not exist. In the language of game theory, the concepts of bilateral and multilateral bargaining corresponds to two-party and n-party games, respectively. As Caplow has demonstrated, the difference between a two-party and a three-party game reflects a basic qualitative difference between the types of processes that take place within each game.[6] The involvement of any more than three parties, however, is seen as merely an extension of a three-party process.

In this model, it will be the degree of multilateral bargaining experienced in a city that will serve as the dependent variable. The complete model of the bargaining process that was developed and tested in this research project consists of two stages. The first stage addresses the development

---

[2] See, for example, F. Y. Edgeworth, *Mathematical Physics* (London: Paul, 1881); Neil W. Chamberlain and James W. Kuhn, *Collective Bargaining*, 2d ed. (New York: McGraw-Hill, 1965); Richard E. Walton and Robert B. McKersie, *A Behavioral Theory of Labor Negotiations* (New York: McGraw-Hill, 1965); or Myron Joseph, "Collective Bargaining and Industrial Relations Theory," in *Essays in Industrial Relations Theory*, ed. Gerald G. Somers (Ames, Iowa: Iowa State University Press, 1969).

[3] Edward C. Banfield and James Q. Wilson, *City Politics* (New York: Vintage Books, 1963).

[4] George H. Hildebrand, "The Pubic Sector," in *Frontiers of Collective Bargaining*, ed. John T. Dunlop and Neil W. Chamberlain (New York: Harper and Row, 1967), pp. 125–54.

[5] For one of the earliest theoretical statements on this issue, see Kenneth McLennan and Michael H. Moskow, "Multilateral Bargaining in the Public Sector," *Proceedings of the Twenty-First Annual Winter Meeting* (Madison, Wis.: Industrial Relations Research Association, 1968), pp. 34–41. For a further discussion, see Michael H. Moskow, J. Joseph Loewenberg, and Edward J. Kozaria, *Collective Bargaining in Public Employment* (New York: Random House, 1970).

[6] Theodore Caplow, *Two Against One: Coalitions in Triads* (Englewood Cliffs, N.J.: Prentice-Hall, 1968).

of internal management conflict. It proposes that internal conflict is a function of the diversity of goals and the dispersion of power within the city management structure. The second stage then relates internal management conflict and a number of other management and union characteristics to the occurrence of multilateral bargaining. It is the second stage of the model that will be discussed in this paper.

A number of researchers have attempted to apply the general concept of multilateral bargaining to the context of local government labor relations and to refine its definition to fit this institutional context. The most basic problem in developing an operational measure of the concept is determining the identity of the parties to the process. McLennan and Moskow have defined a party in this context as any individual or collective body that is capable of imposing a cost on at least one of the other direct parties to the agreement.[7] Those authors were primarily concerned with the impact of interest groups in the community on the bargaining process, however, and thus they did not need to be concerned with identifying the "direct parties" to the process. Juris and Feuille point out that another type of multilateral bargaining is common in city governments—namely, the involvement of what they call "nonlabor-relations city officials" in the bargaining process.[8] Although these two descriptions suggest that the involvement of both community groups and certain city officials should be included in a definition and therefore a measure of multilateral bargaining, there is still the problem of distinguishing between labor relations and nonlabor relations city officials. In order to resolve this problem, character-

istics distinguishing bilateral from multilateral bargaining processes must be specified. Unfortunately, this in itself is a problem, since the collective bargaining literature does not provide a clearly defined set of behaviors that are consistent with a bilateral process. Consequently, some assumptions about bilateral bargaining need to be made in order to develop a measure of multilateral bargaining.

It is assumed that a bilateral bargaining process is one in which a formally designated negotiator or negotiating team represents the employer in direct negotiations with a corresponding negotiator or negotiating team representing the employee organization. The purpose of these two individuals or groups is to reach a tentative bargaining agreement. When an agreement is reached, the negotiating representatives take the package back to their respective principals for ratification. An extremely important assumption here is that all interactions between management officials and the employee organization are channeled through the formally designated negotiators. In addition, the negotiators are assumed to serve as the public spokesmen for the parties on bargaining issues.

This is obviously an oversimplification of the way collective bargaining works in any context, but this description is useful as a base line in testing any model that attempts to explain departures from the conventional bilateral pattern of behavior. Thus, the specific types of behavior used in this study to measure the extent of multilateral bargaining in a city are those that clearly violate this assumed pattern of bilateral behavior.[9] Because of the impor-

---

[7] McLennan and Moskow, "Multilateral Bargaining in the Public Sector," p. 31.

[8] Hervey A. Juris and Peter Feuille, *Police Unionism: Power and Impact in Public Sector Bargaining* (Lexington, Mass.: D.C. Heath, 1973).

[9] Juris and Feuille used this definition of multilateral bargaining in their study of police bargaining in 22 cities. They found that the concept provided a valid description of the union-management interactions in these cities and thus provided further empirical evidence for the construct validity of this characterization of the bargaining process. See Juris and Feuille, *Police Unionism*, pp. 45–51.

tance of this concept to the model and to bargaining theory in general, the specific types of behavior used to characterize it in this context are described in detail in a later section of the paper.

DETERMINANTS OF MULTILATERAL BARGAINING

Now that the concept of multilateral bargaining has been delineated, its major determinants can be hypothesized. The major proposition in the model is that *the greater the extent of internal conflict among management officials, the more likely that multilateral bargaining will take place.*

To understand why internal management conflict is proposed as the most important cause of multilateral bargaining, it is useful to think of the relationship among city management officials in terms of a coalition. In essence, for bargaining to be bilateral, the management officials who share decision-making authority must coalesce and act as a single unit vis à vis the union. If the management coalition does not form or breaks apart at some point during the internal decision-making process so that different officials openly favor different positions on bargaining-related issues, internal conflict occurs. When internal conflict occurs, management officials have two basic options: (1) to resolve their differences internally and then allow the designated management negotiators to represent their mutual interests in bargaining with the union or (2) to represent their interests separately, by directly intervening in the bargaining process. If they choose the latter option and internal conflicts are carried over into the bargaining arena, either because of tactics of the employee organization or on the initiative of management officials, the necessary condition for multilateral bargaining—the involvement of more than two distinct par-

ties—is fulfilled.[10] Typically, in this type of situation, factions can be identified within management that (1) advocate a position more favorable to the employee organization on an issue or (2) support a bargaining position that is inconsistent with the positions of either the employee organization or the designated management negotiators.

Although the model proposes that internal conflict is the basic determinant of multilateral bargaining, it also assigns a role of influence to several other variables. For example, it is plausible to assume that the degree of multilateral bargaining would be affected by the extent of management commitment to negotiations. Although most cities that have an established bargaining relationship with their employees have set up formal procedures that specify bilateral negotiations, not all city officials are likely to be equally committed to using these channels as a mechanism for decision making on employment relations matters.[11] Hildebrand suggests that a basic reason for this aversion is that

---

[10] In other words, the occurrence of internal conflicts within a city management provides the motivation for the various city officials to directly pursue their interests in the interorganizational bargaining process. On the other hand, if little or no disagreement exists among the management officials or if their disagreements are adequately resolved through the internal management decision-making process, there is no incentive for the various officials to intervene directly in the union-city negotiations process. As will be developed more fully below, one reason that this problem is far more prevalent in the public sector than in private industry is that there are multiple points of access to public officials that allow unions to apply pressures that further push the officials toward direct involvement. Also, because decision-making power is so often shared among public officials, they can usually intervene in the bargaining process (if they have the incentive to do so) far more easily and effectively than can management officials in a private company who are not designated negotiators.

[11] For an empirical assessment of differences in commitment to the bargaining process by local government officials, see George Fredrickson, "Role Occupancy and Attitudes toward Labor Relations in Government," *Administrative Science Quarterly,* December 1969, pp. 595–606.

elected officials experience role conflicts when faced with the task of representing the interests of their constituents and acting as a member of a management that is engaged in negotiations with a union.[12] Furthermore, the introduction of collective bargaining into an organization necessarily requires some shifting of the locus of decison making and is bound to be met with resistance from those who feel threatened by such shifts. This is especially true in city governments because of the strong role civil service commissions have traditionally played in making employment relations policy and the interest that those responsible for these functions have in maintaining their autonomy.[13]

Thus, city officials who are not committed to collective bargaining are likely to seek alternative mechanisms for policy-making and, by doing so, to reduce the likelihood that bargaining will remain within the formal bilateral channels. It is therefore proposed that *the weaker the commitment of management decision makers to collective bargaining, the more likely that multilateral bargaining will occur.*

Another variable that would influence the level of multilateral bargaining is the conflict resolution policies of management. Some cities have recognized the problems inherent in coordinating the roles of the various management officials in bargaining and have developed policies for achieving the commitment of all relevant decision makers prior to the beginning of negotiations. Hildebrand labeled

such policies as mechanisms for obtaining a "family understanding" concerning the procedural and substantive issues related to bargaining. For example, New York and Baltimore and a few other large cities have set up labor policy committees composed of city officials from the various decision-making units within the management structure, and a growing number of cities have established specialized labor relations departments. To the extent that such procedures are successful, a kind of co-opted commitment of the management officials is achieved, and the ability of the parties to influence decisions outside of the formal negotiation process is constrained. Consequently it is suggested that *the greater the number of internal conflict resolution procedures that exist, the less likely that multilateral bargaining will occur.*

UNION POLITICAL STRENGTH

Up to this point, only city management characteristics that lead to multilateral bargaining have been considered. A number of characteristics of the union involved, however, are also likely to have an important effect on the type of bargaining that occurs. Since multilateral bargaining is basically an outgrowth of the political relationships that exist among city officials, most of the union characteristics that are proposed as determinants of multilateral bargaining reflect some aspect of the union's political strength.

Political pressure tactics by unions, for instance, can produce situations of multilateral bargaining. Chamberlain and Kuhn have suggested that an alert union will be aware of differences among the decision preferences of management officials and will devise tactics to take advantage of these internal differences.[14] In the public

[12] Hildebrand, "The Public Sector."

[13] See, for example, Murial M. Morse, "Shall We Bargain Away the Merit System," *Public Personnel Review*, October 1963, pp. 239–43; Chester Newland, "Collective Bargaining Concepts: Applications in Government," *Public Administration Review*, March/April 1968, pp. 117–26; and Milton Derber, "Who Negotiates for the Public Employer," in Public Employee Relations Library, Special Issue, *Perspectives in Public Employee Negotiations* (Chicago: Public Personnel Association, 1969), pp. 52–58.

[14] Chamberlain and Kuhn, *Collective Bargaining,* p. 218.

sector, the high level of publicity given rivalries among city officials should increase this awareness of employee representatives. As an alternative to engaging in confrontation tactics such as a strike, union leaders might attempt to influence the outcome of bargaining by inducing officials with interests similar to their own to actively represent their position in the management policy-making process. The use of such tactics has been widely discussed in the public sector bargaining literature. Consequently, it is suggested that *the more frequently that employee organizations use political pressure tactics, the more likely that multilateral bargaining will occur.*

For a union to be successful in inducing city officials who are not part of the formal negotiation process to actively support its demands, it must possess sufficient political resources to influence these city officials, or it must feel that the constituency preferences of the officials are similar enough to the union's interests so that the officials will react favorably to the union demands. This type of a relationship has been thoroughly discussed in the political science literature, as the concept of "political access." [15] Thus, it is suggested that *the more political access the union has to city officials, the more likely that multilateral bargaining will occur.*

Not all of the political tactics that affect the nature of the bargaining process are employed during the actual period in which bargaining takes place. Employee groups realize that maintaining political access and being successful in the use of political pressure during negotiations require taking an active role in elective politics within the community. Thus, it is pro-

posed that *the more the local union is involved in city elections, the more likely that multilateral bargaining will occur.*

These three union variables are likely to be highly interrelated. A union is not likely to attempt to apply political pressure during negotiations if it does not have access to city officials, and if it has not been instrumental in putting and maintaining elected officials in office, it is not likely to enjoy access to them.[16] Since these are three distinct sets of union activities or characteristics that help one understand the *process* by which elected officials are motivated to become involved in the bargaining process, however, it will be useful to measure their separate impact on multilateral bargaining before assessing their combined effects.

One final union tactic that needs to be incorporated into the model of multilateral bargaining concerns the effects of pressures applied by a union when an impasse is reached in negotiations. It has already been suggested that if the union chooses to apply political pressure during negotiations, multilateral bargaining is more likely to result. The effects of tactics designed to apply pressures similar to those of a strike—such as a work slowdown, a "sickout," or picketing—are more difficult to predict. For example, city officials may perceive strike pressure to be an external threat and respond to it by resolving their differences. This type of behavior would be consistent with the Walton and McKersie model of intraorganizational bargaining.[17] McLennan and Moskow, however, suggest that exactly the opposite is likely to result.[18] They argue that multilateral bargaining is likely to increase as negotia-

---

[15] For discussion of the use of these strategies in other political decision-making processes, see Michael Lipsky, "Protest as a Political Resource," *American Political Science Review,* December 1968, pp. 1144–58; and Ralph H. Turner, "The Public Perception of Protest," *American Sociological Review,* December 1969, pp. 815–31.

[16] For examples of union election involvement, see James A. Craft, "Fire Fighter Strategy in Wage Negotiation," *Quarterly Review of Economics and Business,* Autumn 1971, pp. 65–75.

[17] Walton and McKersie, *A Behavioral Theory of Labor Negotiations,* pp. 281–351.

[18] McLennan and Moskow, "Multilateral Bargaining in the Public Sector," p. 34.

tions move from the initial discussion to the hard bargaining and impasse stages, since the disagreements become more visible to the public during these stages and interest groups become activated.

Throughout this discussion of the nature of the bargaining process in city government, the importance of the "politics" of the relationships both among city officials and with the union has been stressed. Consequently, it is expected in this study that the pressure to assume their roles as political leaders motivates city officials to respond by becoming active participants in bargaining when a visible impasse is reached in negotiations. It is thus proposed that *the greater the number of visible impasse pressure tactics that a union uses in negotiations, the more likely that multilateral bargaining will occur.*

SAMPLE AND METHODOLOGY

The research design employed in this analysis might best be described as a cross-sectional comparative field study or, in more formal terms, as an ex post facto correlation design. Because of the cross-sectional nature of the design, the data are not capable of providing a strict test of the causal propositions presented in the model. This limitation is dealt with by clearly specifying the theory tested and then analyzing the data accordingly. Thus, these data can only provide a test of the plausibility of the relationships posited in the model and can only disconfirm rather than confirm the theory.

Data were collected by means of a series of mailed questionnaires sent to all 380 cities (in 42 states) that had a formal bargaining relationship with the IAFF in 1971. Questionnaires were sent to the following sets of management officials in each city: (1) management negotiators, (2) city managers or mayors, (3) fire chiefs, (4) a random sample of three city council members, and (5) members of the civil service commission with jurisdiction over the

fire department. Data were solicited from all of these city officials in order to increase the reliability of the measures of the variables in the model for each city. The responses from officials in each city were then combined to obtain an overall city score for each variable. In addition, a questionnaire designed to measure union tactics and behavior was sent to a representative of the IAFF local in each city.

Usable questionnaires were returned by 65 percent of the management negotiators, 70 percent of the fire chiefs, 27 percent of the other city officials, and 59 percent of the union representatives. From these responses, enough data were obtained to include 228 cities in the analysis. (The criterion for including a city was responses from two or more management officials.) This provided an overall response rate of approximately 60 percent. A comparison of the characteristics of respondent and nonrespondent cities showed that the cities that responded are slightly smaller and pay slightly higher wages and fringe benefits than those that did not respond. In addition, a comparison of wages and working conditions in 1972 in the 228 cities used in this study and in 667 cities covered by an IAFF wage survey showed that mean wages and fringe benefits were significantly higher in the study sample than in the larger sample.

MEASURE OF MULTILATERAL BARGAINING

Table 1 presents the results of applying an index composed of five items that is used as an overall measure of the relative amount of multilateral bargaining that occurs in city governments bargaining with IAFF locals. The city officials who were surveyed in each city were asked to rate on a seven-point scale the extent to which a number of activities had occurred in the past, in the course of bargaining with the Fire Fighters. An overall index was obtained by summing the city responses on the five items.

TABLE 1   MEANS AND STANDARD DEVIATIONS OF MEASURES OF MULTILATERAL BARGAINING AND TOTAL INDEX*

$n = 228$

	MEAN	STANDARD DEVIATION
City officials took actions outside negotiations that affected the bargaining leverage of city negotiators	2.67	1.20
Employee representatives discussed bargaining demands with city officials who are not on the formal bargaining team ["end-runs"]	3.85	1.29
Interest groups in the community became involved in bargaining	2.20	1.00
City officials overturned or failed to apply agreements reached in negotiations	2.33	0.96
Elected officials intervened in an attempt to mediate an impasse	2.69	1.27
Total multilateral bargaining index	13.73	4.16

* Measures were constructed from ratings by city officials on a seven-point scale.

* * * * *

The data in Table 1 show that the type of multilateral bargaining that occurs most frequently in fire fighter bargaining in these cities is the end-run variety [where the union makes "end runs" around the city negotiators to other city officials to obtain concessions not granted in negs]. In addition, the involvement of elected officials at the time of impasse and actions by city officials that affect the bargaining leverage of management negotiators also seem to be relatively frequent phenomena. The failure to implement bargaining agreements and the involvement of community interest groups are less common.

* * * * *

MEASUREMENT OF INDEPENDENT VARIABLES

Internal management conflict.   Three measures of internal conflict were obtained. City officials were asked to rate on a seven-point scale (*a*) the amount of conflict they experienced with other city officials in general in making bargaining decisions; (*b*) the amount of conflict they experienced specifically with each set of other management officials (mayors or city managers, city council members, labor negotiators, fire chiefs, and civil service commissioners); and (*c*) the amount of conflict that they experienced over decision making on five sets of bargaining issues (wages and fringe benefits, departmental

work rules, grievance procedures, management rights, and discipline and discharge issues). From the data on conflict among officials and across issues, indices were constructed by summing the aggregated city responses for each of the five items. . . .

Management commitment to bargaining.   City officials were asked to rate on a seven-point scale the extent to which they felt collective bargaining is the most appropriate way to make decisions on the five sets of issues described above (wages, work rules, etc.). A total score for management commitment was obtained by summing the city score for each item. . . .

Internal management conflict resolution.   The chief management negotiator was asked to indicate whether the city had no policy, an informal policy, or a formal written policy for resolving intramanagement conflicts on (*a*) who participates in negotiations, (*b*) how agreements are ratified by the city, and (*c*) jurisdictional conflicts between the bargaining process and the civil service commission and conflicts over the substantive bargaining issues. Again, a total score for each city was obtained by summing the ratings assigned to each item. . . .

Union political pressure tactics.   City officials were asked to rate on a seven-point scale the extent to which the Fire Fighters (*a*) appealed directly to the mayor or city manager, (*b*) appealed directly to city council members, and (*c*) attempted to use publicity in the community in order to achieve their bargaining demands. An overall index of political pressure tactics was then obtained by summing the scores on these three items. . . .

Union election involvement. The union respondent in each city was asked to check whether or not the union engaged in the following activities: (*a*) endorsing candidates for mayor, (*b*) endorsing candidates for city council, (*c*) contributing to the campaigns of city officials, and (*d*) contributing manpower to city election campaigns. For each item, a score of one was assigned if the union reported that it engaged in the activity; zero was assigned otherwise. An overall election involvement index was obtained by summing the scores on the four items. . . .

Union impasse pressure tactics. Similarly, the union representatives were asked to indicate which of the following tactics the local had employed: (*a*) work slowdowns, (*b*) "sickouts," and (*c*) picketing. A score of one was assigned for each of these pressure tactics if the union had used it, and zero was assigned otherwise. An overall index was obtained by summing these values. . . .

Union political access. The city labor negotiator was asked to rate the degree to whch the IAFF local possessed political influence with the major or city manager, the city council, the fire chief, and the civil service commission. These influence scores were to be summed for each official in order to arrive at an overall access measure. The items, however, did not meet the criterion of internal homogeneity, and thus the overall index was not used in the analysis. Instead, union influence with the city council alone was used as the measure of access.

* * * * *

REGRESSION ANALYSIS

In order to assess the combined effects of these determinants of multilateral bargain-

ing, three regression equations were computed; each equation included one of the three measures of internal management conflict along with the other management and union variables. Table 2 presents the results of these regressions. The models presented were all linear regression models.

The data in Table 2 indicate that internal management conflict is probably the most important determinant of multilateral bargaining, since the regression coefficients for the internal conflict measures remain highly significant even when all the other management and union characteristics are entered into the equation. . . .

The addition of the other two management characteristics, commitment to bargaining and internal conflict resolution procedures, increases the amount of variance explained by only between 1 and 2 percent in the three models. By adding the union variables to the model, however, the amount of variance explained increases 13 percent for the model using general management conflict and conflict across issues and 15 percent for the model using conflict with specific groups of officials. Together, the union and management determinants of multilateral bargaining included in this model explained 37 percent of the variance using general conflict, 29 percent of the variance using conflict with specific officials, and 35 percent of the variance using conflict across issues.

Since there are high intercorrelations among the union variables included in the model, it is not surprising that some of the regression coefficients fail to remain significant when all these variables are entered. Those that do remain significant are political pressure and impasse pressure tactics. The results on the impasse pressure variable suggest that city officials are somewhat reluctant to become involved in bargaining—i.e., behavior by city officials that leads to multilateral bargaining seems to be more a *response* to union pressures

TABLE 2   STANDARDIZED REGRESSION COEFFICIENTS FOR THE HYPOTHESIZED DETERMINANTS
OF MULTILATERAL BARGAINING

| | *t-values in parentheses; n = 228* | | |
INDEPENDENT VARIABLE	EQUATIONS		
Conflict among city officials in general	.402		
	(7.03)‡		
Conflict with specific groups of city officials		.264	
		(4.43)‡	
Conflict across issues			.365
			(6.37)‡
Management commitment	.110	.124	.114
	(2.02)†	(2.17)†	(2.07)
Management internal conflict resolution	−.022	.056	−.085
	(0.40)	(−0.97)	(−1.52)
Union political pressure tactics	.189	.232	.208
	(3.28)‡	(3.87)‡	(3.58)‡
Union election involvement	.054	.042	.101
	(0.94)	(0.68)	(1.75)*
Union impasse pressure tactics	.168	.239	.197
	(.293)‡	(3.96)‡	(3.41)‡
Union political access	.039	.040	.001
	(0.70)	(0.68)	(0.20)
R^2	.37	.29	.35

* Significant at the .10 level.
† Significant at the.05 level.
‡ Significant at the .01 level.

than an autonomous desire to become actively involved in bargaining. The positive association between visible impasse tactics and multilateral bargaining supports the McLennan and Moskow contention that multilateral bargainng tends to reach a peak after an impasse in negotiations occurs.

CONTROL VARIABLES

In any empirical study that uses a nonexperimental design to test its hypotheses, questions arise over whether some alternative variable can account for the correlations observed between the independent and dependent variables. To resolve this question, a number of control variables were included in this study. Since none of these variables showed a strong relationship with multilateral bargaining, they were not entered in the regression analyses presented in the previous section. The cor-

relations between these control variables and the multilateral bargaining index are presented in Table 3.

These control variables were chosen in

TABLE 3   CORRELATIONS BETWEEN CONTROL VARIABLES
AND THE MULTILATERAL BARGAINING INDEX

| *n = 228* | |
CONTROL VARIABLE	CORRELATION
Comprehensiveness of bargaining law	−.05
Factfinding procedure in the law	−.02
Compulsory arbitration procedure in the law	.06
Age of the bargaining relationship	.13
Years of private sector experience of management negotiator	−.12
Years of public sector experience of management negotiator	.02
Professionalism of management negotiator	.01
City population	.11

$r \geq .13$ is significant at the .05 level.
$r \geq .18$ is significant at the .01 level.

order to test several aspects of the "conventional wisdom" that is presented in the literature on public sector bargaining. It should be noted that it has seldom, if ever, been explicitly argued that the factors discussed below are causes of multilateral bargaining. Implicit in much of the prescriptive literature, however, is the argument that public sector bargaining is an abnormal deviation from the way collective bargaining "ought to" work and that as soon as the parties gain experience with the process, or public policies formalize and regulate the bargaining process, negotiations will conform more closely to the private sector (presumably bilateral) model.

To test the argument that comprehensive legislation promoting collective bargaining for public employees will encourage negotiations to become more formalized and therefore conform more closely to a bilateral model, an index was developed to measure the comprehensiveness of the law governing bargaining between city governments and fire fighters in each state. Its correlation with multilateral bargaining in these cities is shown to be only −.05.

A few states have attempted to deal more directly with the problem of dispersion of power within management (on the assumption that dispersion of power is the key cause of multilateral bargaining) by spelling out in the state law who management is and further specifying how the bargaining process should operate. Specifically, New York and Connecticut have provisions in their laws identifying the executive as the management representative in bargaining. If these laws are having an effect on the bargaining process, there should be less multilateral bargaining in these states than in the country as a whole, and also the model should overpredict the extent of multilateral bargaining in these states because this provision in their laws is not accounted for in the regression equa-

tions. Neither of these results occurred. The average score on the multilateral bargaining index is 14.4 for all cities studied in New York State, 13.2 for all cities in Connecticutt, and 13.7 for all 228 cities studied, indicating that neither of these states deviates significantly from the national average. Furthermore, an examination of the residuals of the regression equations showed no tendency to overpredict multilateral bargaining in the cities in these two states.

It might also be argued that the existence of more formalized impasse resolution procedures in the state law should reduce the amount of multilateral bargaining. Again, however, this is not the case—the correlation between multilateral bargaining and the existence of the factfinding procedures is −.02, and between multilateral bargaining and the existence of compulsory arbitration procedures, it is .06. Consequently, the extent of multilateral bargaining is affected little by the nature of the laws governing public sector bargaining in each state.

Another argument often found in the literature is that one of the reasons for the lack of bilateralism in the public sector is the lack of "maturity" in the bargaining relationships. Those suggesting this argue that as soon as the parties learn how collective bargaining is "supposed to" work, public sector bargaining will conform to the bilateral pattern that characterizes private sector negotiations. To test this alternative explanation, a correlation was computed between the number of years the city and the union have been negotiating labor agreements and the city's score on the multilateral bargaining index. This correlation is .13 ($p < .05$), indicating that the more mature the bargaining relationship between the parties, the *more* multilateral bargaining that occurs. This finding not only rejects the "lack of maturity" hypothesis, it also reinforces the view that multilateralism is not a transitional phenomenon growing out of the parties' lack of expertise and is instead a natural outgrowth of the institutional context of city government decision making.

The same type of reasoning concerning the lack of expertise or understanding of how collective bargaining "ought to" operate led to the examination of the relationship between multilateral bargaining and the extent to which management is represented by professionals with prior experience in labor relations. Again, negative correlations with experience and professionalism variables would be expected if this argument is valid. Yet, Table 3 shows the correlations with the multilateral bargaining index to be .01 for a measure of professionalism (number of professional labor-relations associations to which the negotiator belongs), .02 for the number of years of experience the management negotiator has in public sector labor relations, and −.12 for the number of years of private sector experience that the management negotiator has. Thus, the only professionalism variable that seems to have any negative relation with multilatral bargaining is the amount of private sector experience the management negotiator brings to city government bargaining, and this effect is slight.

Another control variable that was examined was city size. Since the bargaining process is generally thought to be more formalized in larger cities and since the larger cities have been bargaining longer than smaller cities, it was felt that size of city might be negatively correlated with multilateral bargaining—again based on the "lack of maturity" argument. The correlation between size of city and multilateral bargaining is .11, however, and so again the evidence does not support the alternative explanation.

In summary, none of the control variables show strong enough correlations with multilateral bargaining to provide an alter-native explanation for the findings presented in Table 2.

CONCLUSIONS AND IMPLICATIONS

This analysis has demonstrated that variations in the extent of multilateral bargaining within a large sample of cities are systematically related to a number of union and management characteristics. These findings show quite clearly that the nature of the collective bargaining process in city governments is a natural outgrowth of the political context in which it operates. The close relationship hypothesized in the bargaining model between the political conflicts that occur within city governments and the nature of the union-city bargaining process received strong support. The importance of the political relationship among the parties was further reinforced by the correlation found between the political strength of the unions and multilateral bargaining.

Perhaps the model and empirical evidence presented here will put to rest the belief that the type of bargaining often found in city governments is an abnormal deviation from "normal collective bargaining" that will be eliminated as the parties and the laws under which they operate become more sophisticated. Such an argument simply ignores the underlying forces that influence the bargaining process in the public sector. As the evidence presented here suggests, the process responds to the nature of the relationships that exist among the diverse interests that share power over bargaining issues.

Finally, it is hoped that this exercise has shown the applicability of the techniques of theory construction, behavioral measurement strategies, and quantitative analysis to an area of collective bargaining theory. The strategy employed was first to develop an empirically based understanding of the process by means of case study research. This provided the foundation and the general framework for developing the propositions of the model. Then, by formally developing a behavioral model of the process and employing a comparative research design, the model was put to an empirical test.

Hopefully, others will join in similar efforts to expand and improve the model presented here as well as to develop models of the collective bargaining process along other dimensions of interest. By doing so, the overly descriptive and prescriptive orientation of collective bargaining research can be changed to one in which a balance is struck among theoretical, empirical, and prescriptive orientations.

10-5

COLLECTIVE BARGAINING: LINING UP THE FACTS

AFL–CIO Department of Research*

At one time, collective bargaining was largely a matter of unions pressing for such basic rights as recognition and acceptance. In that atmosphere, economic data usually played a limited role at the bargaining table. But today, *economic information* is a significant force in most bargaining and especially during the current period of wage controls, which demand more economic documentation.

Major U.S. unions, bargaining on behalf of large numbers of workers, have long since entered the sophisticated era of bargaining backed by economists or other specialized experts who handle data peculiar to their industry. But thousands of contracts are negotiated on the local level by part-time union officers or those whose pri-

mary responsibilities carry them into numerous other trade union activities.

For them, the importance of various types of economic data will vary widely from time to time, from union to union and from industry to industry, but the basic package of necessary information should include wage and fringe benefit levels; economic conditions, both nationally and in a particular industry or company; changes in the cost of living; family budgets for a reasonable standard of living and increases in productivity and profits.

While the economic facts may not point to specific answers in bargaining, they usually can help narrow the difference, reduce the area of controversy and indicate the general range of a reasonable settlement. But relying on such material too heavily may lead to an economic debate which strays far from the merits of the union position. Negotiations should not be con-

* Reprinted from *The American Federationist*, March 1972, by permission of the AFL–CIO. Prepared by AFL–CIO's Department of Research as an update of material published in 1961.

ducted on the basis of who can put together the most impressive-looking or greatest quantity of data.

Some further cautions are in order:

- Economic information need not be formal or exhaustive to be useful. Its value does not depend on quantity or the use of technical language.
- All data have limitations. They should not be accepted without question—and this applies both to material presented by management and to material selected for the union's own information. Being aware of the limitations includes knowing who is covered and who isn't, how old the material is, whether it's representative or specially selected, what is left out and the like.
- Selection and interpretation are important. Some types of information are pertinent or useful, others are not; much depends on the light in which it is put. It is not enough merely to put some facts on the table; the most appropriate ones must be chosen and they must be put in perspective.
- Inaccurate or weak data can easily be turned against the user. Similarly, unfavorable data cannot be ignored if the negotiator is to be able to respond.

Wage information is always among the most important material for the union representative in preparing for negotiations.

Wage statistics are not necessarily needed to justify wage demands and such demands need not be limited by comparison with wages negotiated elsewhere. Other facts aside from wage comparison often warrant wage increases. Nevertheless workers can make a better bargaining case if they are not offered as much as is negotiated elsewhere or if they are paid less then other workers in the industry, trade or area.

Useful wage data usually fall into the broad categories of (1) result of recent bargaining settlements across the nation, in the industry, trade or area or (2) current levels of wage rates for similar work nationally, in the same industry or in the area.

Information on recent major settlements is provided regularly by the labor press and to some extent by the daily press as well. A national union's newspaper, its bulletins on bargaining and other material usually provide reports on that union's own settlements.

The Industrial Union Department of the AFL–CIO annually publishes a comparative survey of major collective bargaining agreements and also does special analyses for its coordinated bargaining activities. Private firms such as the Bureau of National Affairs (BNA) publish special services which report collective bargaining settlements. And each year, the March issue of the AFL–CIO magazine, the *Federationist*, rounds up a general picture of wages and fringes bargained across the country in the previous year.

Another basic source is a monthly report called "Current Wage Developments," published by the U.S. Department of Labor's Bureau of Labor Statistics (BLS). This report lists, industry by industry, the results of each recent collective bargaining settlement covering 1,000 or more workers. It presents the name of the company and union involved, the location and number of workers affected, the amount of wage increase, changes in benefits and other major terms of the settlement.

Several months usually intervene between the date of a major settlement and its appearance in the published report. But despite this delay and despite the limitation to settlements involving 1,000 or more workers, these reports over the year are often useful as an index to adjustments negotiated in a particular industry in the preceding year and a handy guide to wage trends in general. These reports also include a tabulation of the average size of wage increases.

Union wage scales are reported once a year by the BLS for four industries: building trades, printing, local transit, and local trucking. These union wage scales are reported for 52 large cities.

In the case of the building trades, reports are also provided quarterly on union wage scales in each of 100 cities for seven major crafts: bricklayers, carpenters, electricians, painters, plasterers, plumbers, and laborers. The annual report presents data for additional crafts, almost two dozen in all.

Average hourly and weekly earnings in different manufacturing industries and major non-manufacturing industries are also published in the BLS.

The detailed breakdowns are published in a monthly bulletin called "Employment and Earnings." It can be purchased from the U.S. Government Printing Office, Superintendent of Documents, Washington, D.C. 20402, for $10 a year.

This report shows, for example, that average earnings of all production workers in manufacturing in December 1971 were $3.69 an hour and $150.18 a week. It also presents such data for manufacturing in each state and for major cities in many states. It reflects the overall movement of average earnings in an industry from year to year. Similar data for states and cities, often with finer industry breakdown and some information on nonmanufacturing as well, is available from most state labor departments.

In BLS figures, most earnings reported are gross earnings. They include overtime and shift premiums, so are somewhat higher than straight-time earnings and may increase or decrease with changes in the number of hours worked even though there is no change in wage rates.

The average earnings figures are also affected by the distribution of workers. Thus, an industry with a large number of skilled, relatively high-wage workers will have higher average earnings than an industry with mostly unskilled, relatively low-wage workers, even though its wage rates paid for the same job may be identical.

Similarly, if an industry increases the proportion of workers in its lowest-paid jobs, average earnings will decrease even though there is no actual decrease in wage rates. This is true, for example, in retail trade at Christmas time, when many low-paid sales clerks are hired and average hourly earnings show a drop. When these workers leave in January, the average earnings rise.

These average earnings for any given month suffer from a time lag before they are published. For all manufacturing, data for a month are published early in the following month. The breakdowns for individual industries are not available until two or three months later.

Industry wage surveys by the BLS are a good source of information on wages for specific jobs. These surveys present straight-time hourly earnings data for key occupations in that industry. Breakdowns are often provided for time as against incentive workers, by size of establishment, union versus nonunion establishments and by region or major city. The surveys usually also offer data on various fringe benefits.

The major limitation of this survey is that it studies too few industries each year and the available data are often quite out of date.

Area wage surveys are also undertaken by the BLS. These provide wage data for each of 89 major metropolitan areas. The data are not presented separately for individual industries but rather cover a combination of industries.

The occupations surveyed are those found in most industries—but unfortunately are not the key occupations in any specific industry. The occupations usually surveyed are office, maintenance, and custodial jobs.

Industry and the area wage surveys cover both union and nonunion workers, so allowance should be made since the nonunion workers usually pull down the average wage levels. Also, survey wage figures should be adjusted upward to take into account the time lag in publication.

In addition to wage information, at least every other year, the survey contains information on the prevalence of certain fringe benefits such as shift premium, holidays, vacations, and the like. The area survey results are published for each of the 89 cities in an "Area Wage Survey" bulletin, available usually for 35 to 50 cents, also from the Government Printing Office.

General considerations such as the state of the national economy also affect all workers. Such factors as the level and trend of business activity and consumer purchasing, employment and unemployment, and future prospects all have some bearing on wage negotiations—even if they are not discussed at length in the bargaining.

While more significant in negotiations with the largest employers, national economic information usually offers some helpful background for even the smallest bargaining units and is often valuable to the union membership in considering a contract for a ratification vote.

The basic trade union position is that the U.S. economy needs growing markets, particularly growing mass consumer markets, and that unions can best contribute to this objective by pressing for and achieving steady and sizable wage advances.

Various union publications report statements by the AFL–CIO Executive Council or AFL–CIO testimony before Congress on the national economy, which are often useful as bargaining background.

Developments in a particular industry or trade are especially relevant for collective bargaining. This includes not only profit and wage developments in a given industry or trade, but also its sales, production and new order trends, investment plans, new products and new methods, price increases of the company's products, and other economic changes.

The trade journals and industry association reports are usually the best continuing sources for such information. Periodic reports on many industries from the U.S. Department of Commerce also are useful source material.

Change in the cost of living is particularly important in periods when prices are rising rapidly, as they have in the last few years.

An increase in the cost of living is in effect a wage reduction, since existing wages buy less than before. To restore the lost wages, it is necessary to raise wages by an amount at least equal to the rise in the cost of living. If the cost of living increases 5 percent, each $1 in wages has to increase to $1.05 for the worker merely to be as well off as before—and this doesn't account for increased taxes on the higher wage.

While a wage increase to make up for higher living costs is important, it still only restores lost buying power and does not provide any improvement. Additional wage increases are necessary to provide a "real" increase that enables a worker to buy more than he could before.

Many long-term agreements include a cost-of-living escalator clause to protect wages against rises in the cost of living during the life of the agreement. Such clauses provide for automatic adjustments in wages, usually quarterly, to make up for changes in the cost of living.

Changes in the cost of living usually

are measured by use of the Consumer Price Index prepared by the Bureau of Labor Statistics. This index, published monthly, measures changes in prices of consumer goods and services.

It presents a national figure and separate figures on changes in 23 major cities. The national figure has come to be widely viewed by management and labor as the most acceptable yardstick of living-cost changes for wage negotiations.

Taking a recent full year, December 1970 to December 1971, the Consumer Price Index rose 3.4 percent. In the preceding year, December 1969 to December 1970, the rise was 5.5 percent.

How much it costs to live decently, however, is not measured by the Consumer Price Index. Information on how much is needed to support a family on at least a modest standard of living is available from the U.S. Department of Labor in its City Worker's Family Budget survey.

This survey showed an average annual income of $10,664 was needed by a worker to maintain a family, including a wife and two children, at a "modest but adequate" standard of living in major American cities at 1970 prices. This means $205 a week.

The survey also provides separate estimates for each of 40 major cities. They range from a low of $9,212 a year in Austin, Texas, to a high of $14,535 in Anchorage, Alaska.

Productivity is another basic, but important, consideration in bargaining. Productivity, the amount produced per hour of work, has been increasing steadily in this country and the increases warrant steady increases in wages.

While precise measurement of productivity is extremely difficult, there is wide agreement, substantiated by data published by the Bureau of Labor Statistics, that the rise in the nation's productivity since World War II has been at an annual rate of about 3 percent. Currently the

rate is most likely going up faster, as normally occurs in recoveries from a recession.

This is the amount at which real wages—wages after adjustments for changes in the cost of living—should be increased annually for workers to share minimally in the benefits of the nation's productivity gains.

Advances in productivity reduce labor costs of production per unit. They thereby permit corresponding increases in wages— without requiring increases in price levels. Indeed, wage increases not only are justified to keep pace with productivity increases but are necessary to assure sufficient consumer buying power to provide a market for the increased output of goods. If a worker's wages don't increase with productivity, workers will receive a smaller share of the firm's returns and a smaller share of the nation's income.

Productivity changes within individual industries or companies often play a prominent role in shaping wage settlements. For some industries, data are available from the Bureau of Labor Statistics. But most often they are calculated roughly by the negotiators themselves by comparing changes in employment with changes in output, usually production or sales, to show the increase in output per employee or per manhour.

Profits or "ability to pay" is often another important factor in bargaining. The general financial condition of the employer and the industry and apparent future prospects provide a general background guide on wage adjustments. This information is useful even if the union negotiators have no intention of getting bogged down in arguments about accounting or financial statement details.

Financial statements are technical documents subject to substantial manipulation. Profits can be understated in many ways. For instance, the recent tax changes dealing with accelerated depreciation allowances and the investment tax credit can cast an entirely different light on the company's projection of its status.

If a company is a corporation with public sale of stock, its financial statements to stockholders are usually readily available on request or in a financial reporting service such as Standard and Poor's or Moody's, available in any good public library. Standard and Poor's also publishes "industry surveys" which, although meant primarily for investors, may offer helpful background on trends in the industry.

For major manufacturing industries, the Federal Trade Commission and Securities and Exchange Commission publish quarterly reports presenting combined financial information.

10-6

BARGAINING OUTLINE FOR MANAGEMENT*

I. PREPARING FOR NEGOTIATIONS

The day to start preparations for negotiations on your *next* contract, is the day your *present* contract goes into effect.

Everything that happens under your present contract may become a factor in your next negotiations. Any clause that causes confusion, works unfairly, or proves unworkable probably should be revised at the next negotiations. But unless notes are made at the time the trouble occurs, it is apt to be forgotten by the time the next negotiations roll around. And where there is constant difficulty, it is well to have a record as to the seriousness of the difficulty.

---

* Reprinted from *Collective Bargaining Negotiations and Contracts*, BNA, 14, pp. 11–28, April 24, 1975. Initially prepared by a management consultant for CBNC in 1956.

SUPERVISORS MAKE NEGOTIATIONS AND RECOMMENDATIONS

To make it as easy as possible to record situations which indicate the need for revision of any contract clause, some companies have those copies of the contract that are provided for supervisors printed with a blank page between each page so that the supervisor can make simple notations of actual occurrences at the time they occurred on difficulties created by any particular contract clause. These negotiations, when reviewed immediately prior to contract negotiations, provide a wealth of material necessary to make practical revisions.

No one knows the operating faults in any labor contract as well as the supervisors who are required to bargain under it daily. They usually know what works and what does not work, so their opinions on needed revisions are among the most important you can get.

To obtain full benefit of their opinions, many companies, about one month before the start of actual negotiations, secure from each supervisor his practical suggestions. These suggestions should include three things: (1) what paragraphs need revision, (2) why that particular paragraph needs revision, and (3) how the clause could be revised.

When all of these suggestions have been collected they should be put in your contract negotiations file.

STUDY APPEALED GRIEVANCES

Another continuing process in the preparation for contract negotiations is a study of the grievance files. Appealed grievances, in particular, and especially those repeatedly arising under the same contract clause, give a clue to needed revisions.

If a study of the grievance records shows that the grievance was brought because of confusion as to the meaning or intent of the clause, either on the part of the employee, the union, or the supervisor, there probably is a need for revision of the language of the clause, so its purpose and intent will be clear to everyone.

STUDY OTHER CONTRACTS

Each set of contract negotiations is conducted under the shadow of a mass of practice and precedent reflected in the contract provisions of other employers in your community and in your industry. Industry or area "patterns" have a profound—but not necessarily controlling—effect on your negotiations. If the "pattern" is one with which you agree, knowledge that the pattern exists can be most helpful. If the pattern is one which you oppose, you must know the extent of the pattern in order to judge your chances of success in securing a deviation from that pattern.

To make sure that you have all the information you will need, both in support of the position you want to take and in defense against contract clauses you want to avoid, you will want to make sure that you develop a complete list of all the contracts that might have a bearing on your own negotiations. You can be sure that the union is fully equipped with samples of existing contract clauses to use to bolster its demands. In order to bargain on an equal basis, you will want to know where the contract clauses are that will bolster your position. And the time to find them is *before* you get so busy in other phases of your negotiations that you do not have time to do it.

MAKE LIST OF COMPANIES

So you will want to make a list of the names of the companies whose contracts might have a bearing on yours. These would include companies of various kinds in your own community and companies, wherever located, in your own industry. Both are important, for your employees are obtained normally from your own local labor market, yet you must sell your product in competition with companies outside of your local area within your own industry.

While both of your lists must include the "pattern setters," both locally and industrywide, they also should include *all* of the comparable companies—those of a comparable size, doing comparable work, and in a comparable type of community.

GET COPIES OF OTHER CONTRACTS

As soon as you have determined which contracts will have an effect on your negotiations, you will want to get copies of all of them. At the time copies are solicited it would be well to establish the type of contract that will permit full flow of information as such information might be needed at a later date.

ANALYZE THE OTHER CONTRACTS

Each clause in every contract studied should be appraised *as to its applicability to your own situation.* Many clauses would fit one situation perfectly, and yet be almost disastrous in another type of situation.

To help you in analyzing each contract, you might wish to mark each paragraph as you go through a contract with three different types of symbols: "OK" for those that would properly fit your situation; "NG" for those you would not want to agree to under any circumstances; and "?" for those that you would prefer not to have, but to which you might be able to agree to if you had to.

Those marked OK would then be your "most favorable clauses"; you will want to list all of them so you can use them during negotiations to prove that such clauses have been agreed to elsewhere. The union, of course, will have its own list of "most favorable clauses," most of which probably will be on your NG list.

Where you find an OK paragraph in one of the contracts negotiated by the same union you are dealing with, you will want to keep that paragraph particularly in mind. Make a note of it and keep it in your negotiations file.

CHECK YOUR OWN BARGAINING PRACTICES

Many contract provisions have their origin in difficulties arising in the shop which have not been handled satisfactorily. They normally reflect issues over which employees can be excited. They frequently are the issues that are used to stir up enthusiasm for a strike.

Failure of some employers to give adequate notice of impending layoffs, for example, has resulted in demands for contract provisions requiring notice far in advance. Arbitrary actions of other employers in promotions and transfers, have given rise to complicated seniority provisions. Failure to permit the use of voluntary arbitration procedures has created the demand for compulsory arbitration.

Favoritism toward some employees by some employers has resulted in demands for elimination of merit ranges, as well as "joint determination" provisions on many matters. Failure to give proper attention to safety has brought about demands for safety committees. And there are many other examples.

The fewer of these real issues that there are, the better it is for all parties concerned. And if there is no need for some particular (and usually restrictive) clause, a contract can usually be negotiated without such a restrictive clause being included.

REVIEW YOUR WAGE PICTURE

Despite the efforts on the part of some unions to negotiate uniform wage rates, wages are rarely uniform between companies either in the community or in an industry.

From the practical viewpoint you probably will want a set of wages which will permit you to recruit the proper type of workers in your community and at the same time permit you to be competitive within your industry. Both points are important.

To do this you will have to obtain accurate knowledge on the rates being paid by those companies which you have selected as representative for the purpose of your negotiations. As you did in selecting the companies for your contract study, you will make sure that they include representative and comparable companies in your own community, representative and comparable companies in your industry, and the "pattern setters," both locally and industrywide.

Most companies object to mailing their

rates promiscuously to companies where they do not know any individuals well. Most companies, however, will provide such information in a personal interview, at which time arrangements can be made for the exchange of information in case of revision of rates at a future date.

The information should contain two basic things: rates on key classifications and average earnings.

In developing each of these two, it is important that both types of figures show to what extent the rates actually are comparable. For example, on machine operator's rates, information such as the following should be obtained:

1. Is the operator merely a feeder, or is he required to make his own set-ups?

2. Is this a long run job, where the operator works on the same part most of the time, or is it a series of short run jobs where the operator must have considerable flexibility?

3. What tolerances are required?

4. Is it a light job, medium, or heavy?

5. What is the "scrap hazard" on the job? In other words, if the operator scraps a job would it entail a loss, in materials and labor, of 50¢ or $50.00?

And on the average earnings figure, you probably will want average *hourly* earnings, both straight time and overtime. Published wage surveys also can be most helpful.

At the time you get your comparative rate figures, be sure to find out and record the date of the next wage negotiations, as well as whether or not they are subject to automatic escalation. Few things can be as disturbing as to find that the figures on which you are basing your wage negotiations have become obsolete.

You now have collected most of the information and opinions you need to start negotiations.

II. ADOPTING NEGOTIATING POLICY

Each member of your negotiating team can do a better job if he knows in advance what he is expected to accomplish, and how he is expected to accomplish it.

The objective of most negotiations is to accomplish a satisfactory working agreement with your union. Obviously, in order to secure such an agreement, it will be necessary for you, eventually, to secure an agreement of the members of the union's negotiating committee. One method of doing this is to work *toward* the kind of agreement you feel is essential instead of being forced into the defensive position of working *against* the type of agreement the union might present. To do this, as I see it, you would want to *do* the specific things that would make the type of agreement you want possible, but would also *avoid* doing things that would prevent reaching an agreement on the type of contract you wish. One means of doing this would be to follow sound positive bargaining principles in all of your contract negotiations. These principles, basically, are the following:

1. *Assume a positive bargaining attitude.* For example, at the outset of the negotiations, management spokesmen could make a statement somewhat like this: "We are all here, both the company and the union, to do what is fair and right and in the best interests of the employees of the division. The company gives its assurances now that it will do its part; by the same token, it will expect the union to do its part." With this approach, we can start out by reaching *agreement* with the union at least on one point right at the outset. We want to get the union into the habit of agreeing with us, and a sound and positive bargaining attitude will help toward accomplishing that. On the other hand, if we should take the attitude, "I

won't do anything until you force me to," the union will be sure to generate enough pressure to force you to do a lot of things. That is a natural human reaction and the union representatives are just as subject to natural human reactions as anyone else.

2. *We must recognize the point of view of the union bargaining committee.* The local union bargaining committee is a group from which we eventually will have to secure an agreement. If we ignore them or if we take action which ignores or discredits their intelligence or which assumes dishonesty or lack of sincerity on their part, we will have a difficult time later when we try to get them to accept our point of view.

3. *If we are to get the union to agree with us, we have to get the members of the bargaining committee to change their original opinion.* In order to get the members of the bargaining committee to change their opinion, we must do three things: First, we must recognize their opinion and let them know that we do. This was covered in Item 2. Second, we must recognize the probable sincerity of their opinion and let them know that we do. This also was covered in Item 2. Third, *we must figure out a means satisfactory to them to have them accept another opinion in place of their original one.* To do this we have to provide the members of the union bargaining committee with sufficient information and sufficient ideas to permit the members to sell those ideas to the membership in general.

4. *As we conduct our negotiations we must keep in mind that what is perfectly logical to a person with a management background might not appear at all logical to a person with a union background.* We must use examples that the union can both understand and accept. We must use illustrations that are within its representatives' knowledge and experience. There are a number of fields in which the basic un-

ion training is the exact opposite of management training. One example is on the subject of corporate finance and the retention of a portion of profits for improvement and expansion. We must accept it as a fact that the union will not and is not permitted to agree with what we understand as sound principles on this subject. So, on this and any other subject where there would be basic disagreement or automatic lack of understanding, it would be well to switch the discussion by a statement similar to the following: "We could probably argue about that point all day and neither of us would convince the other, so let's agree that we disagree on that point and pass on to something else. The objective in this meeting is to reach agreement so let's talk about the things on which we can agree rather than waste our time where we know we cannot agree."

5 *On the points where we wish to reach agreement, point out the similar things.* If the point is one where it is important that an agreement be reached, it would be well to search the union's proposal and investigate the union's thinking in an effort to find some point or principle on which the union and the company can agree, at least in principle. Sometimes it can be pointed out: "Evidently we are practically in agreement on principle on this matter and our differences are only in matters of words. Now let's see if we can work out a set of words that expresses our agreement properly."

6. *On points where we wish to avoid agreement, point out the differences.* Agreement is impossible if the differences remain in the forefront of the discussions. If confusion results from the emphasis on differences, it would be well to keep in mind that this should not make us deviate from our positive bargaining attitude.

7. *On points where agreement is desired, bring about a clear understanding of the point involved.* In bargaining with

the union, clear logic can be an important factor. The clear logic should be established early in the negotiations and referred to time and time again as the negotiations continue. The repetitive value of restatements of the clear logic of the situation is of utmost importance.

8. *In bargaining attitudes we get in return exactly what we give.* If we "try to put something over" on the union committee we can expect the union committee to try to put something over on us. If we misrepresent a situation to the union committee we can expect the union committee to misrepresent situations to us. If we start indulging in personalities or abuse or name-calling, we can expect the union committee to likewise indulge in personalities or abuse, or name-calling. If we start shouting or get excited, we can expect the union committee to shout back and also get excited. By the same token, if we make sure that we are honest, sincere, fair and calm in all of our dealings with the union committee, we can expect that they will be more apt to respond by being more honest, sincere, fair and calm in their dealings with us.

9. *One method of laying the ground work for securing agreement and acceptance by the union of our points of view is to personalize the things that are good and depersonalize the things that are bad.* If the members of the union committee, either individually or collectively, take an attitude or an action that is constructive, sound, correct, or good, it would be well to give recognition personally to that fact. Statements like, "Joe was perfectly right when he said so and so," or, "the committee took a sound position on that point." On the other hand, if the action of the committee as a whole or any of its members individually was wrong or stupid or malicious or just plain silly and it is necessary to make reference to the subject matter of the action or discussion, make sure

that no individual nor the group as a whole is charged with dishonesty and insincerity, stupidity or silliness. We can point out that an idea is unsound or a statement is incorrect without inferring that the person who expressed the idea or statement is personally responsible for it.

10. *We must keep putting the burden of proof on the union.* In cases where the union is asking for a change in the contract, insist that the union prove its point. Point out that they have to convince us that the change is good, proper, is workable and fair from the viewpoint of all parties concerned. Unless and until the union has proven its point there is no basis for agreement with the union on it. If the union has a point that has merit, that must be acted on accordingly. If the point has little or no merit, the effort of the union to prove its point will provide, in many cases, the reasons why agreement should not be reached on the point. In many cases where the union is given a free opportunity to accept the burden of proof, the union representatives will eventually convince themselves that their ideas had little or no merit in the first place.

11. *Ask questions that cannot be answered by either yes or no.* Questions like, "why do you think this is so," or,"how do you think that would work out in practice," or, "what is the reason for making this request?" plus a whole variety of questions based on the "who, what, where, when, why and how" questioning technique can be helpful in developing discussion in a constructive way. In many cases it permits the union to make a statement which can later be quoted by the management group in summarizing position opposite from the union's original position.

12. *Keep negotiations moving and to the point.* When negotiations start to drag, the management negotiators can do a variety of things to keep them moving toward the eventual objective which is agreement.

If the negotiations strike a snag on some particular point, it might be well after sufficient discussion had been had on that point to say, "Let's agree that for the moment the union and the company are in disagreement on this particular point. We have discussed it fairly fully and it is apparent that we are not going to be able to reach an agreement on the point today, so let's pass that point temporarily and take up the next subject which is ——."

If during the negotiations the union starts going off on tangents or discussing unrelated subjects, it might be well to say, "That all may be interesting, but it does not seem to be helping us get any closer to an agreement on this subject. Our purpose in being here is to reach an agreement. Let's concentrate on the things that will help us reach agreements and save time by eliminating from the discussion all those things that will keep us from reaching an agreement."

III. PLANNING YOUR NEGOTIATION SESSIONS

In following the foregoing policy, your work can be more effective if you plan in advance a constructive program of action.

One of the most effective ways to do this is to list carefully the things you want to *accomplish* in the negotiations, and then follow through on your plan to make sure that as many of them as possible are actually accomplished.

A sample outline of an overall pattern that might be followed could be the following:

First negotiating session:
Purpose: To establish bargaining climate.
To establish foundation of principles.
To establish bargaining schedules.
To establish bargaining routines.
To receive union proposals.

Second negotiation session:
Purpose To clarify intent of specific union demands.
To establish basic principles of each demand.
To draw out, for the record, union arguments for each demand.
To avoid revelation of company position on any demand.

Third negotiation session:
Purpose: To lay foundation for company counter-proposal.
To switch discussion from union proposal to company counter-proposal.

Succeeding bargaining sessions;
A. Initial discussion of specific contract clauses.
Purpose: To lay foundation for company position.
To find points of agreement in principle.
To establish for the record agreements in principle.
To secure concurrence on idea of redrafting to reflect points of agreement.
To draw out union on points in disagreement to find basis for counter-arguments.
To secure agreement on acceptable clauses.

B. Second discussion of specific contract clauses.
Purpose: To secure agreement on counter-proposals.
To eliminate from negotiations items that are:
1. Impossible to agree on.
2. Unnecessary.
To defer discussion on items that might create an impasse, before impasse is reached.

To make sure that this overall outline is accomplished, you would want to prepare in advance a careful agenda for each negotiating session to make sure that each point you want established becomes firmly established. . . .

* * * * *

KEEP YOUR SUPERVISORS INFORMED

As you proceed with your negotiations, you will want to keep all of your supervisors currently informed on the negotiations. This is done for two specific purposes: (1) It gives them a better understanding of what each contract clause means and the reasons for its being in the union contract and (2) It gives them an opportunity to correct any misstatements that might be made by the union with respect to any condition or situation that might come into the discussions in support of or in opposition to any contract proposal.

One method of keeping the supervisor informed is to provide him with copies of the minutes of the negotiations. If the minutes are properly and accurately kept they can be of great value, not only during the negotiations but also at a later date when any question comes up as to what was intended to be covered by any contract clause.

To keep the minutes most effectively they should be concise, factual, and completely without expression of opinion of any sort. They should include the proposals and counterproposals of either side, the arguments for and against by either side, and the conclusions reached.

It should be reemphasized that the minutes must be completely unbiased and factual. They should be such that if the union asked for copies of them, the copies could

be provided and the union would have to agree as to their fairness and accuracy.

THE LAST DAY OF NEGOTIATIONS

Normally after agreement has been reached on practically all of the contract there are two or three paragraphs remaining for settlement.

What you probably want to do is to be able to secure the signatures of the union negotiating committee almost immediately after agreement has been reached. This requires some advance planning and some work. Many companies, at this point, type up signature copies of a final draft, leaving the date blank and leaving the unresolved portions of the agreement either blank or in the form that the company wants in the final agreement. Where the latter is done, all that is left is a selling job to sell the union on the contract as written. Where the pages are left blank in those spaces, all that is needed is to have the languge typed in after agreement has been reached. A typist should be kept nearby to do the physical typing.

Should the union object to signing the contract after negotiations have been concluded on the basis that the contract is subject to approval of the international and subject to ratification of the local union membership, provision can be made to have the following line included as the last line of the contract: "Signed subject to ratification by the employees."

Should the union again point out that approval of the international is needed, you can point out that if the union wishes to secure that approval before calling a ratification meeting, the union has that privilege; but the company would not attempt to interfere with internal union affairs.

CALCULATING SETTLEMENT COSTS*

As has already been mentioned, "compensation" consists of both salaries and/or wages and fringe benefits. It encompasses all forms of wage payments (including, for example, bonuses, commissions, and incentive payments) as well as the cost to the employer of all types of fringes.[1] Obviously, the higher paid, senior employees in the bargaining unit tend to enjoy higher compensation, while the compensation of those at the opposite end of the salary and seniority spectrums tends to be lower.

For bargaining purposes, the most relevant statistic is the unit's average compensation or, more specifically, its *weighted* average compensation. The weighted average compensation (hereafter "average compensation" or, simply, "compensation") is merely an expression of how much it costs the employer, on the average, for each person on the payroll. It is this figure which presumably will be increased through negotiations.[2]

Although precision in computing these compensation costs depends very much on detailed data usually available only in the employer's payroll records, it is possible to develop some reasonably accurate approximations even without such detailed information.

Indeed, the ability to do so may be quite important in making judgments as to whether a settlement proposal is or is not satisfactory. Moreover, an awareness of the concepts and techniques that are involved in these computations can prove invaluable in carrying on the bargaining dialogue or in dealing with a third-party neutral.

These computations, it must be remembered, are not performed simply to engage in a mathematical exercise. The reason for seeking out this type of information is its usefulness at the bargaining table.

The value of salaries and fringe benefits must be known so that the value of any bargaining offer or settlement can be judged. Logically, therefore, the base compensation costs as of the point in time of negotiations—or, more accurately, immediately prior to the receipt of any increase—must be known.

The information that is needed in most cases in order to compute compensation costs is (a) the salary scales and benefit programs, (b) the distribution of the employees in the unit according to pay steps, shifts, and length of service, and (c) for purposes of some medical care programs, the employees' coverage status. If this information is in hand, just about all but one item of compensation can be readily computed.

The sole exception is the cost of the overtime premium. Overtime is apt to vary widely from week-to-week or month-to-month. Consequently, the data for any one pay period are an inadequate gauge where overtime is concerned. Simply by chance, it may cost the employer more one week than the next. It is common practice, therefore, to cost-out the overtime premium by averaging the cost of that benefit over the prior 12 months.

---

* Reprinted from Labor-Management Services Administration, *The Use of Economic Data in Collective Bargaining*, 1978.

[1] Technically, employee compensation may also include the cost of legally-required employer payments for programs such as social security, unemployment compensation, and worker's compensation. These items are disregarded in this analysis.

[2] It is also referred to as the "base" compensation—that is, the compensation figure against which the cost of any settlement will be measured in order to determine the value of the settlement.

So far as the other elements of compensation are concerned, however, it is not necessary to study a full year's experience. With salaries, vacations, holidays, etc., the costs can be based on a snapshot taken at a fixed point in time on the basis of the provisions in the current collective bargaining agreement and the current distribution of the employees in the bargaining unit. That snapshot of compensation costs should be made as of the time the parties are at the bargaining table.

The purpose of this section is to provide guidance on how to perform those computations, as well as the computations to determine the cost—the value—of an *increase* in compensation. The development of such compensation information gives the parties a basis for weighing the value of any particular wage and fringe benefit package.

Before the value or cost impact of any

increase in compensation—whether in salaries, fringes, or both—can be gauged, the first step is to develop the base, or existing, compensation figure. A pay increase of $500 per employee, for example, means something different for a bargaining unit whose existing salary and fringe benefit cost per employee amount to $20,000 per year than for a unit whose compensation is $10,000. In the latter case, it represents an increase of 5 percent, but on a base of $20,000 it amounts to only 2.5 percent. Thus, the base compensation figure is essential in determining the percentage value of any increase in compensation.

In order to demonstrate the computation methods for arriving at the base compensation figure, a Sample Bargaining Unit has been constructed and certain levels of employment, salaries, fringe benefits and hours of work have been assumed:

Sample Bargaining Unit

(a) **Employment and Salaries**

Classification	Number of Firefighters	Salary
Probationary		
Step 1	5	$10,100
Step 2	10	11,100
Private	65	12,100
Lieutenant	15	13,500
Captain	5	14,500
	100	

(b) **Longevity Payments**

Longevity Step	Number of Firefighters	Longevity Pay
Step 1	20 Privates	$ 500
Step 2	10 Privates	1,000
Step 2	15 Lieutenants	1,000
Step 2	5 Captains	1,000

(c) **Hours of Work**

The scheduled hours consist of one 24-hour shift every three days (one on; two off), or an average of 56 hours per week and a total of 2,912 hours per year.

(d) **Overtime Premium**

All overtime hours are paid at the rate of time-and-one-half. The sample bargaining unit is assumed to have worked a total of 5,000 overtime hours during the preceding year.

(e) **Shift Differential**

The shift differential is 10 percent for all hours between 4 p.m. and 8 a.m. However, 10 members of the unit work exclusively on the day shift, from 8 a.m. to 4 p.m.

(f) **Vacations**

15 employees—(probationers) 5 shifts
35 employees—(privates) 10 shifts
50 employees—(all others) 15 shifts

(g) **Holidays**

Each firefighter is entitled to 10 paid holidays, and receives 8 hours pay for each holiday.

(h) **Clothing Allowance**

$150 per employee per year.

(i) **Hospitalization**

Type of Coverage	Number of Firefighters	Employer's Monthly Payment
Single Coverage	15	$20.00
Family Coverage	85	47.00

(j) **Pensions**

The employer contributes an amount equal to 6 percent of the payroll (including basic salaries, longevity, overtime and shift differentials).

1. COMPUTING BASE COMPENSATION

On the basis of the foregoing information on employment, salaries and benefits, we are now in a position to compute, for the Sample Bargaining Unit, its average base compensation—in essence, the cost of compensation for the average employee.

(a) Average Straight-time Salary			
(1)	(2) Number of Fire-	(3)	(4) Weighted Salaries
Classification	fighters	Salary	(2) × (3)
Probationary Step 1	5	$10,100	$ 50,500
Step 2	10	11,100	111,000
Private	65	12,100	786,500
Lieutenant	15	13,500	202,500
Captain	5	14,500	72,500
	100		$1,223,000

Average Annual Basic Salary =

$1,223,000 ÷ 100; or $12,230 per year

(b) Longevity Pay			
(1)	(2) Number of Fire-	(3)	(4) Total Lon-
Longevity Step	fighters	Longevity Pay	gevity Pay (2) × (3)
Step 1	20	$ 500	$10,000
Step 2	30	1,000	30,000
			$40,000

Average Annual Longevity Pay =
$40,000 ÷ 100;* or $400 per year

* Since the unit is trying to determine its average base compensation—that is, all the salary and fringe benefit items its members receive collectively—the total cost of longevity pay must be averaged over the entire unit of 100.

The combined average salary cost and average longevity cost amount to $12,630 per year. On an hourly basis, this comes to $4.337 ($12,630 ÷ 2,912 hours). This hourly rate is needed to compute the cost of some fringe benefits.

(c) Average Cost of Overtime			

Overtime work for the Sample Bargaining Unit is assumed to be paid for at the rate of time-and-one-half. This means that part of the total overtime costs is an amount paid for at straight-time rates and part is a premium payment.

	(1) Annual Cost	(2) Number of Firefighters	(3) Average Annual Cost (1) ÷ (2)
Straight-time cost ($4.337 × 5,000 overtime hours)	$21,685.00	100	$216.85
Half-time premium cost (½ × $21,685.00)	10,842.50	100	108.43
Total Overtime Cost	$32,527.50		$325.28

It can be seen from these overtime-cost calculations that the half-time premium is worth $108.43 per year on the average, while the straight-time portion is worth $216.85. This means, of course, that total pay at straight-time rates amounts to $12,846.85 ($12,630 plus $216.85) per firefighter.

(d) Average Cost of Shift Differential

The Sample Bargaining Unit receives a shift differential of 10 percent for all hours worked between 4 p.m. and 8 a.m. But 10 members of the unit who work in headquarters are assumed to work hours that are not subject to the differential. This leaves 90 employees who receive the differential.

Since the differential is paid for hours worked between 4 p.m. and 8 a.m., it is applicable to only two thirds of the normal 24-hour shift. It, therefore, only costs the employer two thirds of 10 percent for each 24 hours. That is the reason for column (5) in the following calculation. Each employee receives the differential for only two thirds of his 24-hour tour.

(1) Classification	(2) No. on Shift Pay	(3) Salary	(4) 10% of Col. (3)	(5) .667 of Col. (4)	(6) Total Cost (2) × (5)
Probatíonary					
Step 1	5	$10,100	$1,010	$ 674	$ 3,370
Step 2	10	11,100	1,110	740	7,400
Private					
Longevity-0	35	12,100	1,210	807	28,245
Longevity-1	17	12,600*	1,260	840	14,230
Longevity-2	7	13,100*	1,320	880	6,160
Lieutenant	12	14,500*	1,450	967	11,604
Captain	4	15,500*	1,550	1,034	4,136
	90				$75,195

Average Annual Cost of Shift Differential = $75,195 ÷ 100;† or $751.95 per year

* Basic salary plus longevity pay.

† Since the unit is trying to determine its average base compensation—that is, all the salary and fringe benefit items its members receive collectively—the total cost of the shift differential must be averaged over the entire unit of 100.

(e) Average Cost of Vacations

Vacation costs for the unit are influenced by (a) the amount of vacations received by the employees with differing lengths of service, and (b) the pay scales of those employees.

(1) Classification	(2) Number of Firefighters	(3) Hourly Rate*	(4) Hours of Vacation†	(5) Total Vacation Hours (2) × (4)	(6) Total Vacation Costs (3) × (5)
Probationary					
Step 1	5	$3.468	120	600	$ 2,080.80
Step 2	10	3.812	120	1,200	4,574.40
Private					
Longevity-0	35	4.155	240	8,400	34,902.00
Longevity-1	20	4.327	360	7,200	31,154.40
Longevity-2	10	4.499	360	3,600	16,196.40
Lieutenant	15	4.979	360	5,400	26,886.60
Captain	5	5.323	360	1,800	9,581.40
	100				$125,376.00

Average Annual Vacation Cost = $125,376 ÷ 100; or $1,253.76 per year

* Derived from annual salaries (including longevity pay), divided by 2,912 hours (56 hours × 52 weeks). The 10 firefighters who do not receive shift differential would be on a regular 40-hour week and would, therefore, have a different hourly rate and vacation entitlement. The impact on cost, however, would be minimal. It has, therefore, been disregarded in this computation.

† Since each firefighter works a 24 hour shift, the hours of vacation are arrived at by multiplying the number of work shifts of vacation entitlement by 24 hours. For example, the figure of 120 hours is obtained by multiplying 5 shifts of vacation × 24 hours (one work shift).

(f)   Average Cost of Paid Holidays

Unlike vacations, the number of holidays received by an employee is not typically tied to length of service. Where the level of benefits is uniform, as it is with paid holidays, the calculation to determine its average cost is less complex.

In the Sample Bargaining Unit, it is assumed that each firefighter receives 8 hours of pay for each of his 10 paid holidays, or a total of 80 hours of holiday pay:

(1)   Average Annual Cost of Paid Holidays = $346.96 (80 hours × $4.337 average straight-time hourly rate), or

(2)   Total Annual Cost of Paid Holiday hours per year = 8,000 (80 hours × 100 employees)

Total annual cost of paid holidays = $34,696.00 (the unit's average straight-time hourly rate of $4.337 × 8,000 hours)

Average annual cost of paid holidays = $346.96 (34,696.00 ÷ 100 employees)

(g)   Average Cost of Hospitalization

(1) Type of Coverage	(2) Number of Fire- fighters	(3) Yearly Premium Cost to Employer	(4) Total Cost to Employer (2) × (3)
Single	15	$240	$ 3,600
Family	85	564	47,940
	100		$51,540

Average Annual Cost of Hospitalization =
$51,540 ÷ 100; or $515.40 per year

(h)   Other Fringe Benefits

(1)   Pensions cost the employer 6 percent of payroll. The payroll amounts to $1,370,723 (salary cost—$1,223,000; longevity cost—$40,000; overtime cost—$32,528; and shift differential cost—$75,195). Six percent of this total is $82,243 which, when divided by 100, yields $822.43 as the average cost of pensions per firefighter, per year.

(2)   The yearly cost of the clothing allowance is $150 per firefighter.

As the recapitulation below indicates, total compensation—salary plus fringes—for each firefighter averages $16,795.78 per year.

Once having determined the base compensation costs, it is now possible to compute the value—or cost—of any increase in the items of compensation. The methods used to make these computations are essentially the same as those used to compute the base compensation data.

Before proceeding to that exercise, however, a general observation about the computation of base compensation should be made. Since the purpose is to produce an average *total* cost per employee—whether by the hour or by the year—it follows that the objective must be to capture and include in the computation, for each item of compensation, the full amount of the employer's expense. This is why accurately maintained payroll records are desirable. Among other things, such records can

help to resolve what might otherwise be protracted debates over approaches to the costing-out process on certain complicated benefit programs.

Average Annual Base Compensation for the Sample Bargaining Unit		
(a) Straight-time earnings		$12,846.85
Basic salary	$12,230.00	
Longevity pay	400.00	
Overtime	216.85*	
(b) Fringe benefits		$ 3,948.93
Overtime premium	$ 108.43	
Shift differential	751.95	
Vacations	1,253.76	
Holidays	346.96	
Hospitalization	515.40	
Clothing allowance	150.00	
Pension	822.43	
(c) Total		$16,795.78

* This is only the straight-time portion of overtime pay. The premium portion appears with the fringe benefits.

One such item that comes to mind is paid sick leave. Many paid sick leave programs permit the employee to accumulate unused sick leave. Suppose, for example, the employees are allowed five paid sick leave days each year, with the opportunity to "bank" the unused days and, upon separation or retirement, to receive pay for one half of the days in the "bank."

With such a program, it is likely that not all of the employees in the unit would use all five days each year. It would be incorrect, however, to cost out sick leave on the basis of the days actually taken each year since, at some subsequent point, there would be partial reimbursement for the unused days. Further complicating matters is the fact that the employee's rate of pay at the time the reimbursement takes place will very likely be higher than it is when the unused days are put in the "bank." Obviously, there is no way of knowing what that future rate of pay will be, so there is no way to determine now how much those "banked" days will be worth at the time of reimbursement.

One way to cost out the unit's paid sick leave in any year may be simply to charge everyone with five days. Needless to say, this may misstate the true cost and may generate controversy and debate.

Such disputes may be avoided if the actual total dollar cost of the sick leave program for the year can be derived. To do this, however, it would be necessary to have the dollar costs for each piece—that is, in our example, the cost of the days used in the year plus the cost of the reimbursements made in the year—in order to produce a total annual cost. That total, divided by the number of employees in the unit or by the number of hours worked by the unit during the year, would then yield the cost per employee or per hour for this particular benefit.

In a case such as the sick leave program cited above, the availability of dollar amounts reflecting total annual costs would, as mentioned earlier, help to forestall controversy over the procedure to be used for costing out the benefit. And this approach would be consistent with the basic concept that is involved in costing out the other elements of employee compensation. That approach, as was also mentioned earlier, seeks to capture and include in the computation the full amount of the employer's expense for each item of compensation.

2. COMPUTING THE COST OF INCREASES IN ITEMS OF COMPENSATION

In order to demonstrate how to cost-out any increases in compensation, it will be assumed that the Sample Bargaining Unit negotiates a settlement consisting of the following package:

An increase of 5 percent in basic salaries.

Two additional shifts of vacation for all those at the second step of longevity.

An improvement in the benefits provided by the hospitalization program, which will cost the employer an additional $4.00 per month for family coverage and $2.50 for single coverage.

The cost of this settlement—that is, the amount of the increase in compensation that it represents—would be computed in the manner presented below, starting first with the cost-impact of the salary increase. As will be noted, the objective of the computation is to find the *average* cost of the increase—that is, the cost per firefighter, per year.

A. INCREASE IN COST OF SALARIES. The increase in average annual basic salary (0.05 × $12,230) is $611.50. The cost of longevity pay does not increase. This is because longevity increments for the unit are fixed dollar amounts. If these payments were based on a percentage of salary—that is, if they were linked to the pay scales—then the cost of the longevity payments would also have risen by 5 percent. However, as a fixed dollar amount, these payments remain unaffected by the increase in basic salaries.

As a result, the increase in the unit's total average salary ($12,230 in basic salary plus $400 in longevity) is, in reality, not 5 percent, but only 4.8 percent ($611.50 ÷ $12,630).

This difference is important because of the way in which pay increases impact on the cost of fringe benefits. This is commonly referred to as the "roll up". . . . As salaries increase, so does the cost to the employer of such fringes as vacations, holidays, overtime premiums, etc. This increase in cost comes about even though the benefits are not improved.

Some fringes, however, are not subject to the roll up. This is the case with respect to those fringe benefits that are not linked to pay rates. Examples of this type of fringe benefit include shift differentials that are stated in cents-per-hour (in contrast to a percentage of salary), a flat dollar amount for clothing allowance, and most group insurance programs.

B. COST IMPACT OF THE "ROLL UP." The increase in average straight-time pay (basic salary plus longevity pay) of the Sample Bargaining Unit was shown to be 4.8 percent. This means that the average cost of every benefit linked to salary will likewise increase by 4.8 percent. In our example, therefore, the average cost of compensation will go up by $611.50 per year in salaries, *plus*, however much this adds to the costs of the fringe benefits as a result of the roll up.

But there is more. For our example, it is also to be assumed that the Sample Bargaining Unit will gain a vacation improvement—two additional shifts at the second step of longevity— and an improved hospitalization program.

The employer's contribution for the hospitalization program of the Sample Bargaining Unit is a fixed dollar amount and is, therefore, not subject to any roll up. Thus, we need in this instance be concerned only with the costing-out of the improvement in that benefit.

This is not the case with the vacations. Here the cost-increase is double-barreled— the cost of the improvement *and* the cost of the roll up.

None of the other fringe benefits of the Sample Bargaining Unit will be improved. Consequently, so far as they are concerned, we need only compute the increases in cost due to the roll up. The fringes which fit this category are overtime premiums, holidays, sick leave, shift differentials, and pensions.

(1) Fringe Benefit	(2) Base Average Annual Cost	(3) Roll up Factor	(4) Increased Cost (2) × (3)
Overtime			
Straight-time	$216.85	0.048	$ 10.41
Premium	108.43	0.048	5.20
Shift differential	751.95	0.048	36.09
Holidays	346.96	0.048	16.65
Pensions	822.43	0.048	39.48
			$107.83

As is indicated in the table [above], column (3)—the added cost due to the roll up—is obtained by multiplying the base (presettlement) cost by 0.048. Obviously, if shift differentials and/or pensions were based on a set dollar (or cents) amount (instead of a percentage of salary), there would be no roll up cost associated with them. The only increase in cost that would result in such a situation would be associated with an improvement in the benefit item.

Having performed this computation, we can now begin to see the impact of the roll up factor. As a result of the increase in pay, the four fringe benefit items will together cost the employer an additional $107.83 per firefighter, per year.

C. INCREASE IN COST OF VACATIONS. As noted earlier, the vacation improvement of two shifts—48 hours (2 shifts × 24 hours)—is to be limited to those whose length of service is equal to the time required to achieve the second step of longevity in the salary structure. Thus, it will be received by 30 members of the unit—10 privates, 15 lieutenants, and 5 captains.[3]

The first step in the computation is to determine the cost of the *new* benefit under the *existing* (old) salaries—that is, before the 4.8 percent pay increase:

(1) Number of Firefighters	(2) Hours of Increased Vacation	(3) Total Hours (1) × (2)	(4) Existing Hourly Rates	(5) Cost of Improvement (3) × (4)
10 Privates	48	480	$4.499	$2,159.52
15 Lieutenants	48	720	4.979	3,584.88
5 Captains	48	240	5.323	1,277.52
				$7,021.92

The calculation thus far reflects only the additional cost of the vacation improvement based on the salaries existing *prior* to the 4.8 percent pay raise. In other words, if there had been no pay increase, the vacation improvement would result in an added cost of $7,021.92. But there was a pay increase. As a result, the base year vacation costs—including now the added cost of the improvement—must be rolled up by the 4.8 percent factor. Every hour of vacation—the old and the new—will cost 4.8 percent more as a result of the pay increase:

(1) Classification	(2) Existing Vacation Costs	(3) Increase in Cost	(4) Adjusted Base Costs (2) + (3)	(5) Roll up Factor	(6) Increased Cost from Roll up (4) × (5)
Probationary					
Step 1	$ 2,080.80	—	$ 2,080.80	0.048	$ 99.88
Step 2	4,574.40	—	4,574.40	0.048	219.57
Private					
Longevity-0	34,902.00	—	34,902.00	0.048	1,675.30
Longevity-1	31,154.40	—	31,154.40	0.048	1,495.41
Longevity-2	16,196.40	$2,159.52	18,355.92	0.048	881.08
Lieutenant	26,886.60	3,584.88	30,471.48	0.048	1,462.63
Captain	9,581.40	1,277.52	10,858.92	0.048	521.23
	$125,376.00	$7,021.92	$132,397.92	0.048	$6,355.10

[3] In costing out an improvement in vacations, the computation should cover the cost impact in the first year *only*. There is no need to be concerned with the impact in subsequent years when, supposedly, more and more employees become eligible for the improved benefit. For computational purposes, it must be assumed that the average length of service in the unit remains constant. This constancy is caused by normal personnel flows. As the more senior staff leave because of retirement or death, the staff is replenished by new hires without any accumulated seniority. Thus, for this type of computation, it must be presumed that the proportion of the workforce which benefits from the improved vacation will be constant year after year.

It should be noted that an improvement in vacations (or any other form of paid leave) that is offset by corresponding reductions in on-duty manning does not represent any increase in cost to the employer.

By adding the two "new" pieces of cost—$7,021.92, which is the cost of the improvement, and $6,355.10, which is the cost due to the impact of the wage increase—we obtain the total increase in the cost of vacations. It amounts to $13,-377.02. In order to figure the *average* cost, this total must be divided by the number of firefighters in the Sample Bargaining Unit. The increase in the average cost of vacations, therefore; is

$$\$13,377 \div 100, \text{ or } \$133.77$$

Had the vacation improvement been granted across-the-board, to everyone in the unit, the calculation would have been different—and considerably easier. If the entire unit were to receive an additional 48 hours of vacation, the total additional hours would then be 4,800 (48 hours × 100 employees). These hours would then be multiplied by the unit's old average straight-time rate ($4.337), in order to arrive at the cost of the additional vacation improvement which, in this case, would have come to $20,817.60 (4,800 hours × $4.337). And, in that case, the total cost of vacations—that is the across-the-board improvement, plus the impact of the 4.8 percent salary increase—would have been computed as follows:

(*a*) Roll up of old vacation costs ($125,376 × 0.048)	= $	6,018.05
(*b*) Cost of vacation improvement	=	$20,817.60
(*c*) Roll up cost of improvement ($20,817.60 × 0.048)	= $	999.24

These pieces total to $27,834.89. When spread over the entire Sample Bargaining Unit, the increase in the average cost of vacations would have been $278.35 per year ($27,834.89 ÷ 100 employees).

This latter method of calculation does not apply only to vacations. It applies to any situation where a salary-related fringe benefit is to be improved equally for every member of the unit. An additional paid holiday would be another good example.

D. INCREASE IN COST OF HOSPITALIZATION. In this example, it has been assumed that the Sample Bargaining Unit has negotiated as part of its new package an improvement in its hospitalization plan. As with most hospitalization programs, the one covering this unit is not linked to salaries.

This improvement, it is assumed, will cost the employer an additional $4.00 per month ($48 per year) for family coverage, and $2.50 per month ($30 per year) for single coverage. Thus, based on this and previous information about the breakdown of employees receiving each type of coverage . . . , the calculation of the increase in hospitalization cost is as follows:

(1)	(2)	(3)	(4)
			Total
		Annual	New
Type of	Number	Cost of	Cost
Coverage	Covered	Improvement	(2) × (3)
Single	15	$30	$ 450
Family	85	48	4,080
			$4,530

The unit's average hospitalization cost will be increased by $45.30 per year ($4,530 ÷ 100 employees).

3. THE TOTAL INCREASE IN THE AVERAGE COST OF COMPENSATION

At this point, the increase in the costs of all the items of compensation which will change because of the Sample Bargaining Unit's newly-negotiated package have been calculated. All that is left is to combine these individual pieces in order to arrive at the total increase in the unit's average cost of compensation. This is done in the tabulation which appears below.

As the recapitulation shows, the average increase in salary costs amounts to $621.91 per year, while the average increase in the cost of the fringe benefits (including *new* benefit costs, as well as *roll up* costs) comes to $276.49, for a total increase in average annual compensation of $898.40 per firefighter, per *year*. That is the total annual cost of the settlement per firefighter.

Increase in Average Annual Cost of Compensation for Sample Bargaining Unit		
(a) Straight-time Earnings		$621.91
Basic salary	$611.50	
Longevity pay	—	
Overtime (straight-time portion)	10.41	
(b) Fringe Benefits		$276.49
Overtime premium	$ 5.20	
Shift differential	36.09	
Vacations	133.77	
Holidays	16.65	
Hospitalization	45.30	
Clothing allowance	—	
Pensions	39.48	
(c) Total Increase in Average Annual Cost of Annual Compensation		$898.40

There remains one final computation that is really the most significant—the *percent* increase that all of these figures represent. The unit's average base compensation per year was $16,796. The total dollar increase amounts to $898. The percent increase, therefore, is 5.3 percent ($898 ÷ $16,796), and that is the amount by which the unit's package increased the employer's average yearly cost per firefighter.

4. COMPUTING THE HOURLY COST OF COMPENSATION

The increase in the cost of compensation per *hour* will be the same. The approach to the computation, however, is different than that which was used in connection with the cost per year. In the case of the hourly computation, the goal is to obtain the cost per hour of *work*. This requires that a distinction be drawn between hours worked and hours paid for. The difference between the two is leave time.

In the Sample Bargaining Unit, for ex-

ample, the employee receives an annual salary which covers 2,912 regularly scheduled hours (56 hours per week, times 52). In addition, he works an average of 50 hours of overtime per year. The sum of these two—regularly scheduled hours and overtime hours, or 2,962—are the total hours paid for.

But they do not represent hours worked, because some of those hours are paid leave time. The Sample Bargaining Unit, for example, received paid leave time in the form of vacations and holidays. The number of hours actually worked by each employee is 2,600 (2,962 hours paid for, minus 362 hours of paid leave.)[4]

The paid leave hours are, in a sense, bonuses—hours paid for, above and beyond hours worked. Thus, in order to obtain the hourly cost represented by these bonuses—that is, the hours of paid leave—the annual dollar cost of these benefits is divided by the annual hours *worked*.

It is the same as if we were trying to compute the per-hour cost of a year-end bonus. The dollar amount of that bonus would simply be divided by the total number of hours worked during the year.

So it is with *all* fringe benefits, not only paid leave. In exchange for those benefits the employer receives hours of work (the straight-time hours and the overtime hours). Consequently, the hourly cost of any fringe benefit will be obtained by dividing the annual cost of the benefit by the annual number of hours *worked*. In

---

[4] Each firefighter receives 80 hours in paid holidays per year. The average number of hours of vacation per year was derived as follows:

15 firefighters × 120 hours (five 24-hours shifts)	= 1,800 hours
35 firefighters × 240 hours (ten 24-hour shifts)	= 8,400 hours
50 firefighters × 360 hours (fifteen 24-hour shifts)	= 18,000 hours
	28,200 hours

This averages out to 282 hours of vacation per firefighter (28,200 ÷ 100) which, together with 80 holiday hours, totals 362 paid leave hours).

some instances that cost is converted into money that ends up in the employee's pocket, as it does in the case of fringe benefits like shift differentials, overtime premiums and clothing allowances. In other instances—such as hospitalization and pensions—the employee is provided with benefits in the form of insurance programs. And in the case of paid leave time—holidays,[5] vacations, sick leave, etc.—the return to the employee is in terms of fewer hours of work.

The average annual costs of the fringe benefits of the Sample Bargaining Unit were developed earlier in this chapter in connection with the computations of the unit's average annual base compensation. They appear in column (2) below.

In order to convert the costs of those fringe benefits into an average hourly amount, they are divided by 2,600—the average hours worked during the year by each employee in the unit. As can be seen, the hourly cost of all fringe benefits amounts to $1.518.

($12,630 ÷ 2,912 hours). Even with the straight-time portion for the year's overtime included ($216.85), the average straight-time hourly rate of pay will, of course, still remain at $4.337 ($12,846.45 ÷ 2,962 hours).

A recapitulation of these salary and fringe benefit cost data produces both the average *annual* base compensation figure for the Sample Bargaining Unit and the average *hourly* figure.

	Hourly	Yearly
Earnings at		
Straight time	$12,846.85 ÷ 2,962 = $4.337	
Fringe Benefits	3,948.93 ÷ 2,600 = $1.519	
Total		
Compensation	$16,795.78	$5.856

As indicated, on an annual basis, the average compensation cost comes to $16,795.78, a figure that was also presented earlier in this chapter. And on an hourly basis, the average compensation of the unit amounts to $5.856.

(1) Fringe Benefit	(2) Average Annual Cost	(3) Average Hours Worked	(4) Average Hourly Cost (2) ÷ (3)
Overtime Premium*	$ 108.43	2,600	$0.042
Shift Differential	751.95	2,600	0.289
Vacations	1,253.76	2,600	0.482
Holidays	346.96	2,600	0.133
Hospitalization	515.40	2,600	0.198
Clothing Allowance	150.00	2,600	0.058
Pensions	822.43	2,600	0.316
	$3,948.93		$1.518
* Includes only the premium portion of the pay for overtime work.			

In addition to the fringe benefit costs, compensation includes the basic pay. For our Sample Bargaining Unit this is $12,630 per year (average salary plus average cost of longevity payments). On a straight-time hourly basis, this comes to $4.337

---

[5] Typically, of course, firefighters do not receive time off, but are paid an extra day's pay for working a holiday.

Essentially the same process is followed if the *increase* in compensation is to be measured on an hourly (instead of an annual) basis.

The five percent pay increase received by the Sample Bargaining Unit would be worth 21 cents ($12,230 × 0.05 = $611.50; $611.50 ÷ 2,912 = $0.21). The annual increase in the unit's fringe benefit costs per firefighter—$276.49 for all items

CALCULATING SETTLEMENT COSTS

combined—works out to 10.6 cents per hour (276.49 ÷ 2600 hours).

Together, these represent a gain in average compensation of 31.6 cents per hour, or 5.4 percent ($0.316 ÷ $5.856). This is one tenth of a percentage point off from the amount of increase (5.3 percent) reflected by the annual data—a difference due simply to the rounding of decimals during the computation process.

CHAPTER 11

Industrial Conflicts and Impasse Resolution

In the last chapter we discussed the nature of the bargaining process, viewing it as a function of environmental, organizational, and structural factors. From the readings, we were able to include interpersonal and attitudinal factors as additional determinants of the nature of that process. In this chapter we discuss what happens in collective bargaining when a settlement is not reached. By focusing on industrial conflicts and impasse procedures, the reader should gain a deeper understanding of the bargaining process, particularly the motivation for engaging in compromising behavior and the implications and risks associated with not reaching a settlement.

INDUSTRIAL CONFLICTS

Industrial conflict refers to work stoppages resulting from either a strike or a lockout. Simply stated, a strike occurs when employees refuse to work. While a complete shutdown of an employer's operation is the most common result of a strike, other levels of employee activity may also be used, e.g., slowdowns, working to rules, irregular attendance (note the "blue flu" suffered only by police officers), etc. The potential or actual use of a strike or any other economic weapon by workers gives them power at the bargaining table. The basic purpose of the strike or its threat is to provide an impetus to get the parties to settle since the consequences of settlement may seem less severe than the consequences of a strike.

The strike is not, however, without an employer counterpart. A lockout occurs when an employer shuts down its own operation and literally locks its workers out. The workers no longer perform their jobs and no longer get paid. By engaging in a lockout, usually in anticipation of a strike, employers gain the initiative by deciding themselves when the work stoppage begins. In some instances a lockout serves to discourage a strike and reduces union unity if the workers are caught off-guard by the action. An employer has the right to lockout his employees once an impasse occurs and the contract has expired.

The majority of industrial disputes do not involve lockouts since employers are usually very reluctant to stop production given that there is some uncertainty as to whether a union's strike threat is real and the union has the solidarity necessary to take all the workers out and keep them out on strike. Employers have preferred to wait for the strike and in some cases counteract its effect by replacing the strikers with other workers.

While the inconvenience and waste of strikes and/or lockouts often result in negative public reaction, it must be pointed out that national labor policy is premised on the possibility of economic action. The present statutory policy concerning collective bargaining emphasizes both "good faith" bargaining and the availability of economic devices that allow each party to make the other inclined to agree with its terms. Consequently, one of the basic functions of the strike or lockout is to produce an agreement.

The first article included in this chapter focuses on defining and analyzing more specifically the functions of a strike. Dunlop points out that while a strike or lockout designed to change the bargaining position of the other side is the most common, industrial conflicts may have other purposes. He also examines why the role of work stoppages may be changing in the U.S. system of industrial relations. The article by Brett and Goldberg focuses on causes of strikes in the bituminous coal industry, an industry that has been plagued by "wildcat strikes," i.e., strikes during the term of a contract which are not authorized by the agreement.

We refer to strikes and lockouts as economic weapons because both inflict costs on the parties. A strike or a lockout results in lost net earnings for the employer and lost wages to the employee. As we discussed in the chapter on bargaining power, the result of a dispute is dependent, in part, on which party has the greatest economic power and can hold out the longest. Consequently, both parties often attempt to emphasize during the bargaining process the costs associated with work stoppages. The "strike cost computer" included here is one device adopted by management to show employees the economic effect of a strike on employee finances.

IMPASSE RESOLUTION PROCEDURES

The development of impasse resolution procedures represents an evolution from less to more outside intervention. While the threat of a strike is viewed as the final impetus to get the parties to settle, recognition that strikes can occur when a settlement range exists led to the development of dispute mediation. Dispute mediation involves intervention by a neutral third party to help the parties involved in a negotiations dispute to reach a voluntary settlement. With dispute mediation as an accepted settlement technique, some parties questioned why such disputes should occur at all and began to use "preventive" mediation, in which the mediator becomes involved in the bargaining process prior to a dispute occurring. Such intervention has not been accepted generally by the parties. The

Stevens article included in this chapter examines the functions of mediation and analyzes the tactics used by mediators. The Brett, Goldberg, and Ury study examines a particular application of mediation strategies in the coal industry.

Since work stoppages in some sectors of our economy have been viewed as jeopardizing the health and safety of the entire economy, the process of factfinding developed as a more formal type of dispute intervention process.[1] Factfinding is a quasi-judicial process in which a neutral party examines the facts in a case and makes public recommendations that are designed first to mobilize public pressure on the parties that will then force them to settle and/or, second, to provide a neutral interpretation of the facts that may allow each party to reevaluate its bagaining position without losing face.

Unlike mediation and factfinding, arbitration of bargaining disputes represents intervention with results binding on the parties. It is designed not as a supplement to the right to strike but as a substitute for the use of the strike. The arbitrator, a neutral third party, renders a decision on how a particular dispute is to be resolved, i.e., the arbitrator determines the substance of the negotiated agreement and the decision binds both parties. Because of its binding nature, arbitration has not been widely accepted in the private sector.

With the exception of arbitration, impasse resolution procedures in the private sector developed as devices available in addition to the right to strike. Their use in the public sector, however, has been as substitutes for the right to strike. Since most state legislatures have viewed the strike as an inappropriate bargaining weapon in the hands of public sector employees, they have designed procedures adopting some or all (in varying forms) of the dispute resolution strategies outlined above. The Kochan article describes the various dispute-resolution systems that have emerged and focuses on the problems in implementing such systems. As the use of compulsory arbitration has emerged as the key public policy debate with respect to many of these dispute resolution systems, the Feuille article is included in this chapter to provide an analysis of the advantages and disadvantages of arbitration.

---

[1] In 1947 the "national-emergency strike provisions" were enacted as part of the Taft-Hartley Act. The act provides for the use of factfinding in threatened or actual strikes that affect "national health and safety."

THE FUNCTION OF THE STRIKE

John T. Dunlop*

The strike has had many meanings at different times and places. It has been seen by friend and foe alike as leading to an uprising by the working class against a capitalist society. Carleton Parker saw the strike as the pugnacity to be expected psychologically from economic suffering and social humiliation. The International Workers of the World sang:

> Tie 'em up! Tie 'em up; that's the way to win.
> Don't notify the bosses till hostilities begin.

In colonial areas of the world the strike was used to demonstrate against the foreigner and to promote independence. The strike has been represented as an expression of a fundamental constitutional right: to work or to refuse to work in concert with one's peers. The strike is also described as an extension of a free market, a normal development when buyers and sellers fail to agree. Still others envisage the strike as an amoral instrument in collective bargaining, to be used as a last resort to facilitate agreement; "it is a means by which each party may impose a cost of disagreement on the other." The social theory and social history of the strike, however, is beyond the scope of this chapter. The present concern is rather the function of the strike, or more precisely of a few types of strike, in the current industrial relations system of the United States.

---

*Lamont University Professor, Harvard University. Abridgement of chapter 4, "The Function of the Strike," from *Frontiers of Collective Bargaining*, edited by John T. Dunlop and Neil W. Chamberlain, pp. 103–20. Copyright © 1967 by J. Dunlop and N. Chamberlain. By permission of Harper and Row, Publishers, Inc.

* * * * *

STRIKES CLASSIFIED BY FUNCTION

The strike can play many roles even when our concern has been narrowed to disputes arising over the terms of reopened or expiring agreements. It is not sufficient to say that the strike (or lockout) is a means of imposing a cost of disagreement or a means of changing a position in negotiations and achieve a settlement. A review of a number of strikes over contract terms suggests that it may be useful to distinguish four types according to function or purpose. It is unfortunate that we do not have a body of detailed case studies of particular work stoppages in recent years to use in the analysis of strikes and in the study of mediation.

STRIKES TO CHANGE THE STRUCTURE OF BARGAINING

The central purpose of a number of significant strikes and lockouts in recent years appears to be the desire by one party to change the structure of bargaining: to change the organization holding the leadership role on one side or the other, the geographical scope of the negotiations, or the level of negotiations, national or local, at which various issues are settled. A traditional arrangement of bargaining is unsatisfactory to some party, and a strike is used to try to achieve a transformation. The objective is not to reach agreement within the existing structure of negotiations but rather to change that structure itself. Sometimes the purpose is achieved; sometimes the old resists change; and in other cases the old system is destroyed, but no stable new arrangement is found.

While a number of recent strikes were nominally directed against management, their major objective was to change relationships with other unions. A review of the major stoppages in each recent year, published by the Bureau of Labor Statistics, suggests that an attempt to change the structure of bargaining in some way was primarily involved in an appreciable number of these work stoppages. It is a significant category. These stoppages appear to arise frequently in the maritime, printing, and construction industries.

* * * * *

The National Labor Relations Board now has limited influence in disputes over the structure of bargaining. The certification of bargaining units, which I prefer to designate as election districts, has an influence on bargaining structure in multiplant firms and craft severance situations, particularly where rival unionism is acute. Multiple-employer bargaining units confront a confusion in the law with regard to the obligation to bargain and the use of the strike to compel a settlement against a single firm; the rules relating to withdrawal from a multiple-employer bargaining unit are also uncertain. The question may be raised whether the role of the National Labor Relations Board in disputes over the structure of bargaining should be strengthened as a means to reduce such stoppages. On the record to date, my judgment would be in the negative, in part because the Board has appeared to be concerned to develop generalized rules which have little place in structure of bargaining issues.

STRIKES TO CHANGE THE RELATIONS BETWEEN PRINCIPAL NEGOTIATOR AND CONSTITUENTS IN UNIONS OR MANAGEMENTS

The relations between union leadership and members, and company or association

negotiators and principals, are typically complex and vary from case to case. This is intimate and relatively unexplored terrain. There is a class of strikes that are aimed primarily at affecting these relations on one side or both.

In some cases a strike may be designed to solidify and to unite a union or an association, to strengthen the internal leadership both in dealing with the opposite side and in accommodating conflicting interests within the group. In rival union situations or where there are active competitors for internal power, a strike may demonstrate to external rivals strength, militancy, and virility, or it may arise because bargaining compromises with management are incompatible with internal political survival. It has been said, for example, that the racial composition of new employees of the Transit Authority in New York City and the problems of control they posed for Mike Quill significantly enhanced the need for a large settlement and even a strike on January 1, 1966. The basic steel interim settlement in the spring of 1965 involved an accommodation without a strike to internal political uncertainty in a union election year.

Other strikes may arise, despite the better judgment of the leader or top negotiator on either side, because there appears to be no other way to secure a change in view among the membership on the union side or among one's principals or association members in management. The strike serves to bring the constituents around after a period of the more realistic judgments of one or the other or both the principal negotiators.

STRIKES TO CHANGE THE BUDGETARY ALLOTMENT OR POLICY OF A GOVERNMENT AGENCY

Strikes among some government employees at times have been directed less against the immediate government employing agency than toward securing for that agency appropriations or grants from the politically responsible executive or legislative body—that is, funds that are outside the resources of the agency. The strikes in New York City of teachers and of transport workers involved this factor, compelling the mayor and the governor to develop resources to meet the requirements of an acceptable settlement. The timing of budget making and collective negotiations in government employment is central to settlement of disputes; indeed, the failure of such coordination has been a major factor in some strikes of government employees. "It is a fundamental principle in government employment that collective negotiations and the resort to procedures to resolve an impasse be appropriately related to the legislative and budget making process."

In cases of government procurement the direct employer is often a private contractor. A strike against such an employer may be directed primarily to change some of the procurement policies prescribed by the government contracting agency. The dispute may be less with the immediate employer than with the constraints imposed upon him by the agency. The government procurement agency, for instance, may divide a construction project into a number of separate contracts, which result in a mixed union and nonunion labor policy on the same site even at the same work stations. A strike against a contractor may be designed to secure policy commitments from the agency to preclude such a condition. As a member of the President's Missile Sites Labor Commission, I have elsewhere stated: "The fundamental fact is that the procurement policies in effect at Cape Kennedy are inconsistent with labor relations policies which would secure a higher degree of uninterrupted operations."

Some strikes may constitute a rejection of governmental stabilization policy. The parties might well be in disagreement about the government's policy of con-

straint. The Machinists' strike in 1966 against five airlines and the recommendations of an emergency board headed by Senator Morse involved this factor. As governments seek to develop and implement wage and price stabilization policies, this type of work stoppage may be expected to increase, at least in the absence of a no-strike pledge as in wartime.

STRIKES TO CHANGE A BARGAINING POSITION OF THE OTHER SIDE

The most frequent type of strike or lockout over the terms of reopened or expiring agreements is presumably one whose purpose is simply to change a bargaining position of the other side. There is no problem with the structure of bargaining; it continues as in the past. The negotiators and their constituency are as one, or at least their relations are not a factor. The government is not involved. In these circumstances the strike or the lockout is a means to compel a change in position of the other side, toward the position of the party exerting the pressure.

The issues separating the parties may be relatively simple and analogous to those faced in earlier negotiations, or they may be highly complex or novel. They may concern wages and fringe benefits, for example, or they may include methods of wage payment, seniority systems, subcontracting, manning schedules, wage differentials among job classifications, adjustments to significant technological changes, plant closings, training, grievances procedures and the arbitration system, and union security.

These four categories of work stoppage over the terms of reopened or expiring agreements are designed to encourage an analytical approach by facilitating common classification and comparative study. For the present purposes, such differences are significant to the development of procedures to facilitate the settlement of disputes over terms of agreements.

Since the types of strikes by function are specialized, even over the terms of expiring agreements, so should be procedures to prevent such work stoppages. Substitutes for a work stoppage need to be designed in accordance with the diverse functions and specialized purposes of the strike.

The use of joint study committees, for example, may be expected to be most significant to disputes that may result in strikes or lockouts to change the structure of bargaining, (type 1) or to change a bargaining position on a complex issue or range of problems, (type 4), or in some cases to assist in changing the relations between negotiators and constituents or principals, (type 2) particularly when issues are complex. Disputes of these types are most likely to lead to prolonged work stoppages, as they involve the most difficult problems of adaptation. A study committee would not ordinarily be effective in cases involving efforts to change the relations between the principal negotiator and constituents, (type 2) unless it was used as a long-term educational device; this problem is internal and political. A study committee in cases involving procurement policy (type 3) cannot be an effective alternative to the strike unless some continuing sessions include government agency representatives.

*   *   *   *   *

THE CONTROLLED USE OF THE STRIKE DURING THE AGREEMENT TERM

The function of the strike in disputes over the terms of an expiring agreement may be contrasted fruitfully with the deliberate and limited use of the strike to resolve certain disputes, after specified procedures have been utilized, during the term of the agreement. In the automobile industry, for example, collective bargaining agreements have explicitly excluded from arbitration certain disputes over production standards, health and safety, and wage rates on new jobs. The agreements provide for procedures for resolving such disputes to be followed at local plants and then by the national department of the union and the central industrial relations office of the company. If no agreement is reached, written notice permitting a strike, only within a 60-day period, may be filed with the central industrial relations office of the company. . . .

The strike, or the threat of strike, during the term of an agreement, is used in the automobile industry as a special-purpose instrument. The issues on which a strike may arise are narrowly specified; detailed procedures are prescribed for both local and national levels; the powers of arbitrators are expressly limited to exclude these items; the strike may take place only after notice and within a specified period; responsibility for the strike is controlled by the national negotiators of the agreement. It is said that the strike in these circumstances is a more appropriate instrument than arbitration for resolving a dispute and reaching agreement over a production standard established by management. The strike, or its threat, places pressure on local management to establish reasonable standards, on local union leaders to secure acceptance of these standards, and on both parties to reach an agreement. The same pressures operate at the national level. It would have to be a major question before the national union would authorize a strike involving a whole plant, or before company management would decide to shut down a whole plant. The strike, or its threat, has proved an effective pressure in the resolution of disputes over the past 25 years. As the contract language cited above indicates, there is danger that the possibility of the strike on a limited issue may be used for bargaining about other issues. It is not easy to isolate the strikable issue.

In the over-the-road trucking industry the strike or the lockout may apparently be used to resolve any grievance that is unresolved by the grievance procedure or by *ad hoc* agreement to arbitrate. . . . The system has the advantage that it compels the parties to resolve their own disputes; it results in better solutions, and it saves the costs and delays of arbitration; it avoids referring disputes to outsiders unfamiliar with the industry.

This "open end" grievance procedure, with resort to economic power, has been described as a tool of internal political control by Hoffa, as a means to discriminate and play favorites among companies and employees. The Jameses state: "Most labor leaders strongly favor arbitration as the final stage of the grievance procedure for it helps ensure that justice rather than power is the basis for settlement and relieves their obligation to call a work stoppage over a grievance involving only one individual." The Jameses appear not to be familiar with other "open end" grievance procedures in this country and with the absence of final steps for many plant-level problems in Great Britain and Western Europe. Their preoccupation with power has diverted them from a more dispassionate review of the function of the strike in this grievance procedure.

The national agreement between General Electric and the International Union of Electrical, Radio and Machine Workers provides another illustration of the possible use of economic power to resolve certain grievances arising during the term of an agreement. Article XV, paragraph 4b provides in part as follows:

(i) Some types of grievance disputes which may arise during the term of this Agreement shall be subject to arbitration as a matter of right, enforceable in court, at the demand of either party.

(ii) Other types of disputes shall be subject only to voluntary arbitration, i.e., can be arbitrated only if both parties agree in writing, in the case of each dispute, to do so.

The agreement then defines matters in each category. The strikes and lockout article precludes such action ". . . unless and until all of the respective provisions of the successive steps of the grievance procedure . . . shall have been complied with by the local and the Union, or if the matter is submitted to arbitration. . . ." Thus, if a matter is not a mandatory subject of arbitration and has not been submitted to voluntary arbitration, it becomes a subject for economic action after the grievance procedure has been utilized.

* * * * *

The significant point is that in the . . . collective bargaining agreements cited here, the parties have themselves designed a function for the strike during the term of the agreement. They have sought to prescribe a limited and special purpose for the strike; they have designed procedures and constraints specifically to meet their problems and circumstances, and these provisions are not transferrable or generally applicable elsewhere. These instances of the controlled use of the strike during the agreement suggest the possibility of greater control of the use of the strike or the lockout in disputes over the terms of expiring agreements.

WILDCAT STRIKES IN BITUMINOUS COAL MINING

Jeanne M. Brett and Stephen B. Goldberg*

Wildcat strikes have long been a problem in the unionized sector of the bituminous coal industry.[1] In the period from 1971 to 1974, there was an average of more than 1,500 wildcat strikes per year.[2] The rate doubled in the 1975–77 period to an average of more than 3,000 strikes.[3]

Previous research on wildcat strikes has assumed that strikes are born of shared frustration with working or living conditions,[4] but it is not clear why coal miners strike when they have a contractual procedure for resolving grievances. A 1972 study concluded that the strikes were due to excessive delay in the grievance procedure.[5] Changes in the 1974 National Bituminous Coal Wage Agreement were intended to reduce the delay and so lessen strikes,[6] but these changes accomplished neither goal.[7]

Kerr and Siegel, in their 1954 study, suggested that the coal mining industry has characteristics in common with other strike-prone industries.[8] First, the mining occurs in isolated locations in which it is the primary source of employment. Second, the work may attract or condition tough, combative workers, who would rather take the direct action of striking than wait out the grievance procedure. To the extent that frequent strikes are the product of features of the industry that

* Associate professor of organization behavior and professor of law at Northwestern University. Reprinted in an abridged form, with permission, from the *Industrial and Labor Relations Review*, 32, no. 4 (July 1979), pp. 465–83. © 1979 by Cornell University. All rights reserved.

[1] The term *wildcat strike* refers to a work stoppage during the term of a collective bargaining contract that is not authorized by that contract. Clark Kerr and A. Siegel, "The Interindustry Propensity to Strike—An International Comparison," in *Industrial Conflict*, ed. Arthur W. Kornhauser, Robert Dubin, and Arthur M. Ross (New York: McGraw-Hill, 1954), pp. 189–212. Keith Dix, Carol Fuller, Judy Linsky, and Craig Robinson, *Work Stoppages in the Appalachian Bituminous Coal Industry* (Morgantown, W. Virginia: Institute for Labor Studies, 1972).

[2] These data come from the files of the Bituminous Coal Operators Association and apply only to BCOA members.

[3] BCOA files.

[4] Kerr and Siegel conclude that wildcat strikes are spontaneous collective action (See "The Interindustry Propensity to Strike"), but Slichter, Healy, and Livernash treat strikes as calculated action. See Sumner Slichter, James J. Healy, and E. Robert Livernash, *The Impact of Collective Bargaining on Management* (Washington, D.C.: The Brookings Institution, 1960), p. 675.

[5] Dix, Fuller, Linsky, and Robinson, *Work Stoppages in the Appalachian Bituminous Coal Industry.*

[6] Comparing the National Bituminous Coal Wage Agreement of 1971, Article XXII, section (b), and National Bituminous Coal Wage Agreement of 1974, Article XXIII (in Appendix) indicates that the 1974 contract eliminated one step of the grievance procedure and reduced the time allowed in the remaining steps. In addition, the 1974 contract added a Tripartite Arbitration Review Board, designated to hear appeals from arbitrators' decisions. This unusual step was taken in an effort to achieve industrywide uniformity on contract interpretation.

[7] Data from the Arbitration Review Board (personal communication, July 25, 1978) show that during the term of the 1974 contract approximately 2,700 grievances were sent to arbitration each year. There were 750 appeals to the Arbitration Review Board during the last two years of the contract. The Review Board had a one-year backlog when the 1974 contract expired.

[8] Kerr and Siegel, "The Interindustry Propensity to Strike."

cannot be changed, such as isolation and, perhaps, the characteristics of its work force, little can be done to alleviate the strike problem.

Strike frequency may differ, however, among mines that are similar in such features as location and work force characteristics. If this is so, and the factors associated with this variation can be identified, at least some of them may prove susceptible to change.

This study tests several possible explanations of wildcat strikes in bituminous coal through an examination of questionnaire and related data covering 293 underground mines and interview data gathered at two high-strike and two low-strike mines.

DEFINING HYPOTHESES

In comparing the strike frequency of different mines, it is important to differentiate between two types of wildcat strikes: the "local" strike, which grows out of a dispute between the striking miners and their employer, and the "sympathy" strike in which the miners at one mine strike to aid miners at another mine in a dispute between the latter and their employer. Most sympathy strikes are initiated by the appearance of a picket. Because of the powerful tradition in the industry against crossing a picket line, the appearance of a single picket will nearly always result in a refusal to work, even though the miners at the picketed mine may know little or nothing about the underlying dispute.

This study focuses on local strikes, because we are primarily interested in the extent to which conditions at a particular mine contribute to strikes at that mine. Strikes caused by pickets from another mine or a desire to support employees on strike at another mine are the product of union tradition and loyalty, not of local conditions. Similarly, strikes over industrywide or companywide policies or ac-

tions are, by definition, not the product of local conditions.

The interrelationship between local strikes and the grievance procedure is [such that] each step in the grievance procedure is represented as a conflict episode.[9] Each episode begins with a problem, such as a miner's dissatisfaction with some condition of work. There are two behavioral responses possible: the miner can take his problem up with his foreman in step 1 of the grievance procedure or he can instigate a strike. If the problem remains unresolved, it generates a second conflict episode with the same alternatives: the next step of the grievance procedure or a strike.

. . . A problem can move through the stages of the grievance procedure without ever stimulating a strike and, alternatively, that a strike may occur during any stage of the process. The strike may occur in lieu of a discussion of the problem in the grievance procedure or as a result of the failure of such a discussion. The strike in turn may result in resolution of the problem or initiation of the grievance procedure to resolve the problem.

* * * * *

METHOD

Two separate studies were carried out. The first was a preliminary, archival, industrywide study, and the second was an intensive four-mine survey of miners, union leadership, and mine management.

INDUSTRYWIDE STUDY

The Bituminous Coal Operators Association (BCOA) compiles daily reports of wildcat strikes at mines operated by member companies. On the basis of these re-

---

[9] Kenneth Thomas, "Conflict and Conflict Management," in *Handbook of Industrial and Organizational Psychology*, ed. Marvin Dunnette (Chicago: Rand McNally, 1976), pp. 889–936.

ports, we built a 1975–76 profile of wildcat strikes, which included the number of strikes at each mine and the beginning date, duration, and reason for each strike (as reported by the employer).

In the course of constructing these profiles, we became aware of a number of gaps and inconsistencies in the BCOA records. Accordingly, the strike profile of each mine was sent to the company that operated that mine for verification. Each company was also asked to provide information about itself and about each mine it operated. At the company level, this information included the company's labor relations structure and policy for dealing with wildcat strikes. At the mine level, it included: location (county and UMW district); type of mining (surface or underground); average height of coal seam (if underground); mandays lost per million hours due to accidents; proportion of coal sold (1) to parent company, (2) under long-term contracts, and (3) on the spot market; average number of miners; turnover rate; average productivity per manday; total number of days (excluding weekends, holidays, and vacations) on which work was not available for all employees for any reason other than a wildcat strike.

Of the approximately 100 companies that were BCOA members at the time this study was conducted, completed responses were received from 35. The companies that responded included 7 of the top 15 operators, measured in terms of 1976 coal production. Five of the companies operated 20 or more mines, 10 operated 6 to 12 mines, and the remainder operated 5 mines or fewer. The total number of mines covered by this study is 336. Of these, 293 are underground mines and 43 are surface mines. All these mines are located in the eastern or midwestern coal fields (West Virginia, Virginia, Kentucky, Ohio, Indiana, Illinois, Tennessee, and Pennsylvania).

After receiving the completed mine-information questionnaires, we collected environmental data for the county in which each mine was located. These data included: population, unemployment rate, occupational distribution, family income, and quality of housing, schools, and public services.[10]

FOUR-MINE STUDY

Sampling. Of the 336 mines on which we had data, four mines were selected for further study. Two were operated by one company and two by another. (The two companies will hereafter be referred to as A and B. The two mines operated by A will be referred to as A_1 and A_2; the two mines operated by B will be referred to as B_1 and B_2). All the mines were located in West Virginia within UMW District 17.

In order to compare mines with many strikes against those with few strikes, we selected one of each type from each of the two companies. In determining whether a mine was high-strike or low-strike, we focused on those 1976 strikes that were local in nature, excluding those initiated in response to pickets from another mine or by sympathy for miners engaged in a strike at another mine. We also excluded strikes caused by industrywide or companywide policies or actions.

In 1976, there were 11 local strikes at A_2 and 1 at A_1; there were 15 local strikes at B_2 and 4 at B_1. The same pattern continued in 1977, albeit with a slightly reduced number of strikes ($A_1 = 2$, $A_2 = 8$, $B_1 = 1$,

---

[10] Housing quality was measured by the percent of owner-occupied units, the median value of owner-occupied single-family units, the percent of units lacking plumbing, and the percent of units occupied by more than one person per room. School quality was measured by the proportion of the county budget spent on education. Public service quality was measured by the proportion of the county labor force employed in government. Data came from the U.S. Bureau of the Census, *County and City Data Book* (Washington, D.C.: G.P.O., 1972).

$B_2 = 4$). This reduction was at least partially due to the fact that there were fewer days available for local strikes in 1977: an industrywide strike caused by the reduction in medical benefits idled all four mines from approximately June 21 to August 1 and on December 6 all mines went out on an economic strike at the termination of the 1974 Wage Agreement. Hence, there were only eight to nine months available for local strikes in 1977.

The four mines, having been chosen on the basis of strike frequency, are not representative of the population of all mines. Thus there may be chance relationships, based on peculiar circumstances at the four mines. We chose to run this risk in view of the limited number of mines that could be studied with the available funds and our desire to maximize the variance on the basic criterion, frequency of wildcat strikes.

The mines chosen for intensive study had the following numbers of employees: A_1—143; A_2—155; B_1—295; B_2—194. Of these, a sample of 25–34 was selected for personal interviewing at each mine. The sample consisted of all union officers and committeemen (four to seven employees), plus a random sample of rank-and-file employees, stratified by shift. In addition to these employees and union officials, we interviewed the superintendent and personnel coordinator at each of the B mines, the manager of mines, superintendent, and personnel coordinator at A_1, and the manager of mines and personnel coordinator at A_2. The B mines did not have managers of mines and the position of A_2 superintendent was vacant at the time the interviews were conducted.

Obtaining the interview. We used a variety of devices to demonstrate the legitimacy of the study and to maximize cooperation. Initially, we obtained approval of the study from UMW President Arnold Miller, BCOA President Joseph Brennan, UMW District 17 President Jack Perry, and officials of each of the companies involved. Approximately one month before interviewing began, we met with the mine committee at each of the four mines and with the union representatives servicing these mines. We described the study to them, answered their questions, and asked that they advise miners that the study was legitimate and that the union had no objection to the miners being interviewed. All the miners in the sample, as well as an additional 50 miners at each mine, were sent letters containing a brief description of the study. (The letters were sent to miners other than those in the sample in order to minimize the risk that the comparatively small sample size would lead to intense speculation about how and why those few miners had been chosen for interviews.)

Cooperation with the study by those persons we sought to interview was almost universal. All local union officials and management personnel agreed to be interviewed. Of the 124 miners whom we sought to interview, only two refused; these two were replaced by other miners from their mine and shift. The overall completion rate was 91.2 percent, the overall refusal rate 1.6 percent.

Content of the interview. The primary purpose of the interview with miners was to determine their attitudes toward those factors that might be related to strikes. In addition to demographic and employment history questions, each miner was asked for his views about working conditions, management, union officials, the quality of life in the area (housing, schools, and so forth), arbitrators, and the grievance procedure. Each miner was also asked a number of questions about wildcat strikes, both those based on local issues and those due to the presence of pickets.

Local officers and committeemen were asked all the questions that were asked of rank-and-file miners plus various questions related to their union duties—their training in grievance handling, the amount of time they spent in grievance handling and other interactions with management, their attitudes toward management, and their actions when a strike was imminent or actually taking place.

The questions asked of the mine superintendent and personnel director was similar to those asked union officials—the training received by management personnel in grievance handling, the amount of time spent in grievance handling and other interactions with union officers, their attitudes toward the union officers, and their actions when a strike was imminent or taking place. In addition, they were asked about the managerial structure at the mine, the extent to which advice on labor relations issues was sought from management personnel away from the mine, and the authority to settle grievances at various levels of management.

For the most part, we had to generate the interview questions; but we based the working-conditions questions on the Job Description Inventory, the quality-of-life questions on the Institute for Social Research survey, and the union-management attitude questions on those used by Stagner, Chalmers, and Derber.[11]

Interviewers. Three additional interviewers helped the researchers conduct the interviews with miners, but the interviews with union officials and management personnel were conducted exclusively by the researchers. Prior to the commencement of interviewing, the interviewers toured an

underground mine so that they would have some familiarity with mining operations.

RESULTS

Our basic assumption was that there are substantial differences in strike frequency among mines. One of the major purposes of the industrywide study was to test the validity of this assumption.

Initially, we found substantially fewer strikes at surface mines than at underground mines. In both 1975 and 1976, there was, on average, one strike per year at the surface mines but over three strikes per year at the underground mines. Because the strike problem was greatest at underground mines, we decided to focus our analysis exclusively on underground mines. (All the discussion that follows refers solely to underground mines.)

There were significant differences between companies in the average number of strikes per mine. In 1975 the average varied from 0 at some companies to 9 at others ($F = 3.84$; $p \leq .05$). In 1976 some companies again had no strikes while others averaged as many as 17 per mine ($F = 4.51$; $p \leq .05$). There was a significant correlaton between a company's strike record in 1975 and 1976 ($r = .61$; $p \leq .01$).

Even within the same company, there were some mines that had many more strikes than others. For example, in 1975 one company had an average of 3.2 strikes at the 38 mines it operated. The number of strikes at those mines, however, varied from 0 at 11 mines to 9 at 2 mines and 16 at another mine. Similar variations in strike frequency were found between the mines operated by many other companies in the industrywide sample, as well as between the mines in the four-mine study.

There were also significant differences between UMW districts in average number of strikes per mine. In 1975 the average

[11] Patricia C. Smith, Lorne M. Kendall and Charles L. Hulin, *The Measurement of Satisfaction in Work and Retirement* (Chicago: Rand McNally, 1969); Angus Campbell, Phillip E. Converse, and William L. Rogers, *The Quality of American Life: Perceptions, Evaluations and Satisfactions* (New York: Russell Sage Foundation, 1976); and Ross Stagner, W. Ellison Chalmers, and Milton L. Derber, "Guttman-Type Scales for Union-Management Attitudes Toward Each Other," *Journal of Applied Psychology,* October 1958, pp. 293–300.

varied from 1.5 in District 5 to 6.5 in District 12 ($F = 3.24$; $p \le .05$). In 1976 the average varied from 1.7 in District 5 to 6.3 in District 6 ($F = 3.29$; $p \le .05$). District strike frequency like company strike frequency, tended to be stable between 1975 and 1976 ($r = .86$; $p \le .01$).

Since most companies operate mines in only a few districts, it is possible that the difference in company strike frequency was primarily due to district differences rather than to differences in company practices or characteristics.[12] To determine which factor accounted for more of the differences in strike frequency between mines, they were grouped by district and by company.[13] Grouping the mines by company accounted for 23 percent of the differences in strike frequency in 1975 and 27 percent in 1976. Grouping them by district accounted for 8 percent of the differences between mines in strike frequency in 1975 and 9 percent in 1976. Thus, although a greater proportion of the differences in strike frequency can be attributed to company practices and characteristics than to district characteristics, there are still substantial differences in strike frequency per mine within both companies and districts.

In sum, the basic assumption of substantial differences in strike frequency among mines is borne out by the data. We turn next to the hypotheses that may explain these differences and consider the extent to which the data support them.

---

[12] Of the 32 companies in the sample, 21 operated mines in only 1 district, 2 operated mines in 2 districts, and 4 operated mines in 5 districts.

[13] The statistical index used was a measure of association called Omega squared (ω^2). When ω^2 is zero, knowing the group to which a mine belongs tells us nothing about that mine's strike frequency. When ω^2 is one, knowing the group to which a mine belongs tells us its strike frequency exactly. Omega squared can be expressed as a percentage. See William C. Hays, *Statistics* (New York: Holt, Rinehart & Winston, 1963), p. 325.

HYPOTHESIS 1

Low-strike mines may have fewer labor problems than high-strike mines because

a. Communities in which low-strike mines are located are less isolated, are less occupationally homogeneous, and have a better quality of life than communities in which high-strike mines are located.

We did not test the effects of community isolation or occupational homogeneity because we could not agree on how to measure those variables. We did test the relationships between strike frequency and county quality-of-life indicators (housing, schools, and public services), though we have no illusions that these indicators are precise measures of the constructs we wanted to test. There were no significant relationships between indicators of quality of life and strike frequency in the industrywide study.

In the four-mine study, we sought to determine whether employee perceptions, as distinguished from objective measures, of the quality of the community environment contribute to wildcat strikes, particularly when the miners attributed an unsatisfactory environment to the employer. Miners were asked for their views about local housing, public services, and pollution. Across all mines, the greatest dissatisfaction was expressed with housing: 73 percent of the miners indicated that there was not enough satisfactory housing in the area for them and their families, whereas only 53 to 57 percent were dissatisfied with the quality of the schools, public services, and pollution levels.

There were significant differences between the mines in the extent to which the miners were dissatisfied with housing, public services, and pollution levels, but none of these differences distinguished between high- and low-strike mines. Approximately half (46 percent) of the miners blamed their employer for high levels of air and water pollution; 36 percent blamed their employer for unsatisfactory housing, 9 percent for unsatisfactory public services, and 2 percent for unsatisfactory schools. There were no significant differences between the high-strike mines and the low-strike mines with respect to the attribution of unsatisfactory community services to the employer.

b.   There are fewer young miners at low-strike mines than at high-strike mines.

The employees at the B mines attributed a substantial proportion of their strikes to the younger miners who, as one miner said, "haven't any family, and don't care if they miss work and make everyone else miss." Indeed, this view was held by 65 percent of the B_2 miners and 58 percent of the B_1 miners. At the A mines, far fewer of the employees attributed strikes to the younger miners—only 28 percent at A_1 and 21 percent at A_2. These differences did not distinguish between high- and low-strike mines.

There were approximately 20 miners younger than 24 at each mine. There were also approximately 10 miners who had no dependents at each mine other than A_2, where there were none.[14] If the hypothesis that strikes are caused either by young miners or those with no dependents is sound, the data should show that such miners are more militant than are other miners. There was no relationship, however, between a miner's age or number of dependents and his attitudes toward working conditions, management practices, or the grievance procedure. Nor was there any relationship between a miner's age or number of dependents and either his ap-

proval of the goals of the strikes at his mine or his belief that strikes were likely to be successful in resolving disputes in favor of the miners.

c.   Low-strike mines are smaller (have fewer employees) than high-strike mines.

In both 1975 and 1976, large mines in the industrywide sample had significantly more strikes than did small mines. . . . While one cannot be certain of the reasons for the relationship between mine size and strike frequency, it is likely that dealings between management and miners are less frequent and more impersonal at large mines than at small ones. In addition, the resolution of grievances may take longer at large mines, either because there are more grievances or because managers at the larger mines have broader responsibilities and spend less time on employee relations.

d.   Low-strike mines have better working conditions than high-strike mines.

The data from the industrywide study showed that there were no significant relationships between a mine's average coal seam height, productivity, or accident rate and the frequency of wildcat strikes at the mine. The data from the four-mine study likewise showed no significant relationships between the miners' satisfaction with their working conditions and the frequency of strikes. Job satisfaction was high, with no differences between the mines that related to strike frequency: 90 percent of the miners said that they found their work satisfying, 84 percent said that it gave them a sense of accomplishment, and 72 percent said that it was challenging.

Management practices are sometimes alleged to generate conflict that leads to wildcat strikes. High levels of conflict may contribute to strikes because miners are frustrated and angry at management or be-

---

[14] These data are estimates from the proportions in the sample.

cause so many grievances are filed that they are not dealt with promptly.

We measured the level of conflict by asking miners in the four-mine study a series of questions about relations with their foremen. We asked if foremen treated the miners fairly, were consistent in discipline, kept promises, cared about the miners as individuals, and pressured miners for production. We also asked how much friction there was between miners and foremen, and how satisfied the miner was with his foreman. The miners at the low-strike mines consistently reported better relations with their foremen than did miners at the high-strike mines. While the differences were statistically significant only on the question about friction ($F = 5.98$; $p \leq .05$), the clear trend on all items toward more favorable foreman-miner relationships at low-strike mines than at high-strike mines lends some support to the hypothesis that a poor relationship between foremen and miners contributes to strike-generating conflict.

e. Management at low-strike mines acts to alleviate unsatisfactory conditions as they arise, whereas management at high-strike mines does not.

We did not ask any questions in the four-mine study that would indicate directly whether management at low-strike mines dealt with problems as they arose, thereby obviating the need for the miners to use the grievance procedure. We do know, however, that the superintendents at A_1 and B_1 did have regularly scheduled meetings with the mine committee, whereas the superintendents at A_2 and B_2 did not. In addition, it appeared that the superintendents at A_1 and B_1 spent substantially more time underground, where they would be accessible to miners, than did the superintendents at A_2 and B_2. Our questions about how superintendents spent their time, however, were not well formulated and did not capture this distinction empirically.

Summary. The hypothesis that there are fewer labor problems generated at low- than high-strike mines was not supported by the data. No evidence was found that the objective or perceived quality of living or working conditions was better at low-strike mines than at high-strike mines. Nor was there evidence that more young miners or miners with no dependents worked at high-strike mines than at low-strike mines, or that these miners were more critical of working conditions or more strike-prone than other miners. The evidence does indicate, however, that strikes may be associated with management's ability to deal promptly with problems. Low-strike mines employed fewer miners than high-strike mines; it may be that fewer miners generate fewer problems or that management at smaller mines may have time to deal with problems as they arise. Management at low-strike mines appears to be more accessible to miners than management at high-strike mines, and there is less friction between foremen and miners at low-strike mines than at high-strike mines.

HYPOTHESIS 2

Problems are resolved effectively at the local level (steps 1 and 2 of the grievance procedure) at low-strike mines but not at high-strike mines because

a. First level foremen at low-strike mines have the authority to resolve grievances whereas those at high-strike mines do not.

We asked miners in the four-mine study if they had ever gone to their foreman with a complaint or a grievance. Approximately half said that they had, with no significant differences between high- and low-strike mines. However, significantly more miners at the high-strike mines than at the low-strike mines said that their foreman could never resolve their complaints or grievances ($x^2 = 8.4$; $p \leq .05$).

b. Management and union at low-strike mines have a problem-solving relationship whereas at high-strike mines they do not.

There were substantial differences between the labor relations climates at the high- and the low-strike mines in the four-mine study. Both the mine committee and mine management had unfavorable attitudes toward each other at the high-strike mines and favorable attitudes toward each other at the low-strike mines ($F = 7.21$; $p \leq .01$). At the high-strike mines, for example, mine committee members reported that management was not generally cooperative with the union or willing to settle a dispute when the union had a good claim. Similarly, management at the high-strike mines reported that the mine committee was not cooperative with management and abused its power. Such reports were substantially less frequent at the low-strike mines.

Mine management and mine committee members' attitudes toward each other are a product of previous interactions, including discussions about wildcat strikes. It seems unlikely that unfavorable attitudes cause strikes directly, but they may limit the ability of the mine committee and mine management to resolve problems peacefully and thus contribute indirectly to strikes.

It was impossible to determine whether the mine committee and mine management at the low-strike mines were actually resolving a higher proportion of grievances than at the high-strike mines, since step 2 grievance resolution data were not available. We did, however, question mine management and the mine committee to determine how grievances were actually

dealt with. At all mines, the superintendent or mine manager asserted that he had the power to resolve grievances and that the basic procedure for dealing with grievances was that established by Article XXIII of the 1974 Wage Agreement. There seemed to be no difference in the frequency with which local management sought advice from the company labor relations staff or in the issues on which advice was sought. There were, however, differences in the way in which the contractual procedure was implemented. At A_1, the grievant was free to discuss his grievance informally with the superintendent before the regular step 2 meeting between the mine committee and the superintendent. In addition, any grievance not settled at step 2 was the subject of a further meeting of the grievant, the mine committee, the superintendent, and the manager of mines. At A_2, which had the same management structure as A_1 (including a superintendent and a mine manager), these additional meetings were not held. Furthermore, there was evidence that the step 2 meeting was somewhat perfunctory. According to the A_2 manager of mines, management regarded 80–90 percent of the grievances brought to step 2 as without any contractual basis. It was the superintendent's practice—rather than to discuss such grievances—to tell the mine committee to prepare a written grievance. When they had done so, he would write his position on the grievance form, and with no further discussion, send it to step 3.

This report of the step 2 procedure at A_2 was confirmed by one of the mine committee members, who reported "every time, they say 'well, we'll send it up to arbitration.' They don't want to settle at the mines where we're supposed to." So, while Company A had no formal policy of centralized grievance handling in the early stages of the procedure, the A_2 manager effectuated such a policy.

The personnel coordinators at both B_1

and B_2 indicated that a miner and the mine committee were free to discuss a grievance with them at any time. Neither had the power to resolve grievances, however. At B_1, the superintendent was also willing to discuss grievances with miners and the mine committee at any time. The B_2 superintendent had the personnel coordinator investigate the grievance and then schedule a step 2 meeting.

It has been hypothesized that large mining companies (companies that operate many mines) will have, on the average, more strikes per mine than small companies, because decision making about grievances has been centralized in order to promote standard company policies across mines. This centralization may cause strikes because it prevents serious negotiations at the mine site or because it delays the resolution of grievances.

In the course of the industrywide study, we asked about each company's labor relations structure and the responsibilities of each position therein. We did not attempt to measure the intervening variable—degree of centralized decision making—because we were only able to collect data from a single key informant. Even so, we were able to test the hypothesis that large mining companies have, on the average, more strikes per mine than small companies. The resulting correlation was not significant, indicating that large company size and its associated coordination problems do not necessarily result in wildcat strikes.

Future research needs to measure the intervening variable. It may be that those large companies with low-strike records were decentralized and that their grievances were dealt with at the mine site, or it may be that few of the grievances that stimulate strikes raise issues of company policy, so that even in centralized companies, the crucial issues are dealt with at the mine site. In any event, it is clear that mine size (number of employees) is related to strike frequency but company size (number of mines) is not.

Summary. The hypothesis that problems are resolved effectively at the local level at low-strike mines, but not a high-strike mines, is supported by the data. Significantly more miners at the high-strike mines than at the low-strike mines said that their foreman could never resolve their complaints. The mine committee and mine management appeared to have a problem-solving relationship at the low-strike mines, but not at the high-strike mines. Mine managers at low-strike mines were also making a stronger effort to resolve grievances locally than were those at high-strike mines.

HYPOTHESIS 3

Miners may have greater confidence in the nonlocal steps (3 and 4) of the grievance procedure at low-strike mines than high-strike mines because

 a. At high-strike mines, but not at low-strike mines, there is a perception that the grievance procedure is too slow.

There were many more grievances at the B mines than at the A mines that could not be settled at the mine level, and hence were referred to step 3 of the grievance procedure. The rate of step 3 grievances per 100 miners per year was: $A_1 = 4.5$; $A_2 = 11.0$; $B_1 = 13.0$; $B_2 = 27.3$. Of those grievances that reached step 3, an average of 30 percent were referred to arbitration.

The average time required to process a grievance from the date it was signed through step 3 varied from 39 days at B_2 to 81 days at B_1. The average time from signing to the arbitrator's decision varied from 138 days at B_1 to 204 days at A_2. None of these differences was associated with strike frequency.

Ninety percent of the miners believed that one reason for wildcat strikes was the existence of excessive delay in the grievance procedure. The proportion of miners attributing the delay to management, the union, and the arbitrator varied considerably, but none of these differences distinguished between those mines with a high-strike record and those with a low-strike record.

b. At high-strike mines, but not at low-strike mines, there is a perception that the arbitrators are unfair.

Distrust of arbitrators was great, perhaps as a result of the union's lack of success at arbitration. Only 31 percent of those grievances that went to arbitration from the four mines in 1975 and 1976 were sustained in whole or in part. Sixty-two percent of the miners thought that the union lost at least some grievances because the arbitrators were biased or unfair. Thirty-three percent thought that all or most arbitrators were biased or unfair, with more miners holding this view at A_2 (46 percent) and B_2 (34 percent), the high-strike mines, than at A_1 (21 percent) and B_1 (29 percent), the low-strike mines.

Of those miners who thought that arbitrators decided grievances unfairly, 63 percent (35/71) believed that the arbitrators were bribed by the employer. Fourteen percent attributed the arbitrators' unfairness to their unfamiliarity with the coal mining industry. The latter view was particularly prevalent at B_2, where, according to one of the miners, "the men couldn't get transportation inside the mine and grieved and the arbitrator went against the man and later we found out that the arbitrator didn't even know what a man trip was. The president said this. Most arbitrators never even seen the inside of a mine."

c. At low-strike mines, but not at high-strike mines, miners consider themselves to be well represented by the union in the grievance procedure.

Across all four mines, 30 percent of the miners reported that they were not satisfied with the way in which the union handled grievances, and 35 percent reported that they were not satisfied with the union's district field representative (the elected step 3 and 4 representative of the union in grievance handling). Fifty-three percent of the miners thought that they lost grievances because the union's district representatives were not as skilled as the management representatives. The proportion of employees holding this view differed at the four mines ($A_1 = 45$ percent; $A_2 = 76$ percent; $B_1 = 59$ percent; $B_2 = 56$ percent), but this difference was not related to strike frequency.

Summary. The hypothesis that miners have greater confidence in steps 3 and 4 of the grievance procedure at low-strike mines than at high-strike mines is not supported by the data. There is a widespread perception that the grievance procedure is too slow and that the union loses some grievances because the arbitrators are biased and others because the union representatives are not as skilled as the management representatives. These perceptions do not, however, distinguish between high- and low-strike mines.

HYPOTHESIS 4

Striking has a different value at low-strike mines than at high-strike mines, because

a. Union leaders at low-strike mines, but not at high-strike mines, are politically strong, and they use that strength to discourage strikes.

In the industrywide study, we found no relationship between the proportion of votes received by each district president in the most recent election and the average frequency of wildcat strikes in the mines in that district. There were, however, few district presidents who had a strong political base. The winning candidate for district president received over 50 percent of the vote in only three of the nine districts studied, and over 55 percent of the vote in only one district. It is possible that the susceptibility of nearly all district presidents to political challenge acts as a general deterrent to action on their part to discourage wildcat strikes.

* * * * *

In sum, the district presidents do not appear to have the political strength to take any measures against wildcat strikes. Some of the local presidents may have such strength, but they limit their efforts to persuasion, at least in part because they doubt their authority to take stronger action.

b. Miners at low-strike mines, but not at high-strike mines, perceive that they will be disciplined by management for striking.

Management policies for disciplining strikers were examined in both the four-mine and the industrywide study. Few (6/30) of the companies in the industrywide study followed a consistent policy of taking disciplinary action against strikers. Of those companies that did not take disciplinary action against strikers, two thirds reported that they had not done so because they could not prove which miners had instigated the strike, and that in the absence of such proof an arbitrator would not uphold discipline against strikers. The remainder said that disciplining strikers was likely to be counterproductive, since such discipline frequently served to prolong the original strike or trigger a new strike.

Mine managers at both A mines had taken disciplinary action against strikers. The superintendents at the B mines had not, as they were never able to single out the individuals who had instigated the strike.

c. Miners at low-strike mines, but not at high-strike mines, believe that striking will not effectuate the outcome they desire.

In the four-mine study, the miners at the high-strike mines, significantly more than those at the low-strike mines, believed that it was necessary for them to strike to get management to talk with them. More than 60 percent of the miners at A_2, and almost half of the miners at B_2, said that they had to strike "all the time" or "frequently" to get management to talk about something, while fewer than 25 percent of the miners at A_1 and B_1 held this view.

. . . Significantly more miners at A_1 and A_2 than at B_1 and B_2 believed that a wildcat strike helps to resolve a dispute in their favor. Within each company, however, more miners hold this belief at the high-strike mine than at the low-strike mine. While a substantial proportion of miners at A_1, a low-strike mine, believed that a strike would help to resolve a dispute in their favor, few of them believed that it was necessary to strike to get management to discuss grievances. The miners at A_1 appeared to be willing to use the grievance procedure, rather than strike, even though many thought a strike would be successful.

The beliefs that striking is necessary to get management to discuss a problem, and that a strike helps to resolve a dispute in the miners' favor, may well be based on previous experience. If the miners had a problem that mine management resolved only after a strike, that would tend to set up a contingency between striking and the resolution of problems. A belief in such a contingency is likely to increase the perceived value of future strikes.

Summary. The hypothesis that striking has different values at low- and high-strike mines is only partially supported by the data. The likelihood of either union pressure against strikes or management discipline for striking is uniformly low. Striking is considered to be effective in helping resolve a dispute in the miners' favor by miners at both high- and low-strike mines. However, at the high-strike mines, but not at the low-strike mines, getting management to discuss a problem is perceived to be contingent on striking.

HYPOTHESIS 5

At high-strike mines, but not at low-strike mines, there exists a strike-prone minority, which is followed, though not supported, by the majority.

At all mines in the four-mine study, particularly the B mines, a substantial proportion of the miners reported that their mine had struck very often for something that they did not personally think was worth striking for. There was, however, no relationship between a mine's strike frequency and the extent to which strikes at that mine were supported by a majority of the miners. This result indicates that minority-led strikes may not distinguish between high- and low-strike mines, but they may contribute to the generally high level of strikes in the industry.

* * * * *

CONCLUSION

This research is based on two studies of wildcat strikes, a preliminary, archival, industrywide study, and an intensive four-mine survey of miners, union leadership, and mine management. Neither of these studies provides definitive answers to the causes of wildcat strikes. The industrywide study lacks psychological depth, and the four-mine study lacks generalizability. To-

gether, however, the two provide considerable information about wildcat strikes in the coal mining industry.

Initially, it is clear from the industrywide study that it is possible to operate a coal mine under a UMW contract without frequent wildcat strikes. Although there are some mines at which strikes are commonplace, there are other mines at which strikes rarely, if ever, occur over local issues. Hence, there exists some basis for optimism that the factors that contribute to local strikes can be isolated and dealt with. To the extent that the number of local strikes can be reduced, the occasions on which local strikes lead to picketing and industrywide strikes can also be reduced. This research makes some progress in isolating those factors that contribute to the differential frequency of wildcat strikes in the coal mining industry.

The evidence bearing a hypotheses 1, 2, and 3—which test the relationship between wildcat strikes and the grievance procedure—suggests that the key to the wildcat strike problem lies at the local level. It appears that problems exist at both low- and high-strike mines but that at low-strike mines management is more accessible and able to deal promptly with those problems. This may be due, in part, to differences in the effectiveness of first-level foremen at high- and low-strike mines. Apparently, foremen at low-strike mines are able to resolve miners' complaints more frequently than foremen at high-strike mines. Another aspect of the ability to deal promptly with problems is the relationship between mine management and the mine committee At low-strike mines, but not at high-strike mines, management and the mine committee have a problem-solving relationship. Furthermore, management at low-strike mines appear to be making a particular effort to solve problems.

Miners at both high- and low-strike mines have so little confidence in the grievance procedure that it is not surprising that they strike if they believe that a grievance cannot be resolved locally. Another factor that probably contributes to strikes is the widespread belief that strikes help to resolve disputes in the miners' favor. Strikes have an instrumental value, particularly at high-strike mines, where miners believe that they have to strike to get management to talk about problems. On the other hand, the evidence does not support the widespread beliefs that high-strike mines are characterized by a higher proportion of young workers with no dependents and by a higher proportion of minority-led strikes.

These conclusions, identifying the factors that distinguish high- and low-strike mines, are based almost entirely on data from the four-mine study. Accordingly, they must be considered tentative until tested on a larger data base.

Evidence from the industrywide study also fails to support several hypotheses about the differences between high- and low-strike mines. The quality of life is not objectively worse in the areas in which high-strike mines are located than in the areas in which low-strike mines are located. Also, compared with low-strike mines, high-strike mines do not have less satisfactory working conditions, more accidents, or higher productivity. Thus, further research on these hypotheses seems unwarranted.

The conclusions from these studies, if supported by further research, suggest two possible courses of action—improve the ability of mine committees and local management to resolve problems at the mine site, and increase the confidence of the miners in the nonlocal steps of the grievance procedure.

Improving the effectiveness of problem solving at the mine site is a formidable but not insurmountable task. A problem-solving relationship between mine management and the mine committee cannot be built overnight. Such a relationship

evolves out of the experiences that the two parties have in working together. The question is how to change those experiences. The usual answer is training and, in fact, training programs that have been available to local union leadership and mine management for a number of years. Yet, while training may be useful to familiarize local officials with the Wage Agreement, it does not get to the heart of the matter of building a problem-solving relationship. We know of no research indicating that the relationship between union and management can be changed from conflictful to problem solving by training.

The most satisfactory means by which to encourage the growth of a problem-solving relationship is to reward the parties to that relationship for solving problems. On the management side, this means that mine managers must be rewarded for solving problems without strikes. At small mines, mine managers may be able to avoid strikes by dealing with problems as they arise. At larger mines, where mine managers are less accessible, structures can be developed to deal with problems quickly. Such structures might include giving foremen increased power to resolve grievances, and rewarding them for doing so. An industrial relations position could be created and the person in that position given the authority to act for the mine manager on labor relations problems.

It is more difficult to build a reward structure for problem solving on the union side. Local union members who want to work, not strike, will have to support the mine committee's attempts to solve problems with management. This will require that those miners who want to work put social pressure on the minority that wants to strike. It might be necessary to provide a procedure to ensure that the majority rules. The union could amend its constitution to provide, for example, that no miner should engage in a strike unless that strike had been authorized in a secret-ballot vote, by a majority of the miners employed at the mine involved. The amendment could also provide that any member who did engage in an unauthorized strike would be subject to discipline, including expulsion from the union.[15]

Although such a provision would represent a substantial change in UMW practice, it is entitled to serious consideration. For, whatever may be the consequences of frequent wildcat strikes for the future of the coal mining industry as a whole, it is clear that the destructive impact of such strikes will weaken the unionized portion of the coal mining industry and reduce the proportion of coal mined by UMW miners. The stakes, in short, are great, and the changes required to meet the problem may have to be equally great.[16]

Increasing miners' confidence in steps 3 and 4 of the grievance procedure may be a more difficult task. Decreasing the amount of time required to process grievances through steps 3 and 4 is certainly worth attempting, but the likelihood of obtaining significant improvement, in light of experience in other industries, does not appear to be great. The average time from the filing of a written grievance to the issuance of the arbitrator's decision at the four mines varied from 138 days to 240 days, and the average time in American industry in general that year was 268 days.[17]

Another alternative would be to reduce the number of grievances going to arbitration. The power of the union to settle grievances, even if the grieving individual objects to the terms of the settlement, is clear.[18] To be sure, there may be political pressures on an elected union representative to arbitrate any grievance supported by a powerful individual or faction within the union. One way to reduce these pressures, and to prevent clearly nonmeritorious grievances from going to arbitration, would be for the UMW to provide for the appointment, rather than the election, of its district representatives, who are responsible for deciding which grievances are to be arbitrated.

The widespread belief that many arbitrators are either dishonest or incompetent by reason of their unfamiliarity with coal mining, may, to some extent, be a product of the substantial influx of new arbitrators into the coal mining industry during the term of the 1974 Wage Agreement. It is possible that, as the arbitrators acquire more familiarity with the industry, their decisions will be perceived by the miners as more attuned to industry realities. Furthermore, if the number of grievances going to arbitration can be reduced, fewer arbitrators will be needed, and the parties can eliminate those who do not have the trust of the miners.

Many of the problems of the grievance procedure, which may contribute to strikes, can be reduced if management and the union can resolve more of their disputes at the mine site rather than through recourse to arbitration. Other employers

---

[15] At present, the UMW constitution contains no provision for local strike authorization. Nor does it provide for suspension or expulsion of members engaged in unauthorized strikes.

[16] It is possible that local strike authorization would render the local union liable in damages for breach of the implied no-strike provision contained in the BCOA–UMW contract. On the other hand, local treasuries are not often substantial, so that this potential risk may be outweighed by the certain financial harm to indivdual union members of continuing under the present system. Additionally, if the union were to adopt and enforce a provision barring minority strikes, it is possible that the employers would agree not to seek damages or disciplinary sanctions for those strikes authorized by majority vote.

---

[17] *30th Annual Report of the Federal Mediation and Conciliation Service,* 100 LRR 28 (January 8, 1979).

[18] See *Vaca* v. *Sipes,* 386 U.S. 171 (1967), 194–95: "[T]he individual employee has no absolute right to have his grievance arbitrated. . . ."

and unions have drastically reduced both the number of grievances going to arbitration and the amount of time required to resolve grievances.[19] It is possible that this could be accomplished in the coal mining industry if the various employers and local

unions with which they deal are willing to engage in a serious effort to do so.[20]

_____

[19] Arthur M. Ross, "Distressed Grievance Procedures and Their Rehabilitation," *Proceedings of the Sixteenth Annual Meeting*, National Academy of Arbitrators (Washington, D.C.: Bureau of National Affairs, 1963).

_____

[20] Efforts are being made to improve labor relations in the coal mining industry. The 1978 Wage Agreement provides for the establishment of a Joint UMW–Industry Development Committee, which is to investigate and report on means of improving both labor relations and productivity. Additionally, in March 1978 President Carter established a presidential commission on the coal industry. That commission, which is headed by West Virginia Governor John D. Rockefeller IV, has been directed to study and report on a range of coal industry problems, including labor relations.

11–3

MANAGEMENT TECHNIQUE: STRIKE COST COMPUTER*

The following "personal strike cost computer" was designed by the Bridgeport, Conn., Manufacturers Association "with the hope that it would help avert or shorten strikes by illustrating simply the economic effect on the employee and his family finances." The computer is intended to show how long it will take at

_____

* Reprinted from *Collective Bargaining Negotiations and Contracts* [CBNC], BNA, August 20, 1970, p. 501.

poststrike wages to recover earnings lost during a strike. The 1954 original edition of the computer covered weekly take-home pay ranging from $30 to $100; the second edition covers a weekly range from $80 to $150. Effects of strike costs on weekly pay at five dollar intervals between $80 and $150 are shown in the following tables for strikes of 1 [and] 5 . . . weeks' duration. The Association notes that information on the tables may be combined to find effects of strikes of other durations.

IF YOU STRIKE FOR 1 WEEK
And You Strike For

IF YOU TAKE HOME	YOU LOSE	0¢	1¢	2¢	3¢	4¢	5¢	6¢	7¢	8¢	9¢	10¢
						TO GET IT BACK IT WILL TAKE YOU						
$80.00–$81.00	$81.00	Never	3 yrs. 46 wks.	1 yr. 49 wks.	1 yr. 15 wks.	50 wks.	0 wks.	33 wks.	28 wks.	25 wks.	22 wks.	20 wks.
$85.00–$86.00	$86.00	Never	4 yrs. 7 wks.	2 yrs. 3 wks.	1 yr. 19 wks.	1 yr. 1 wk.	43 wks.	35 wks.	30 wks.	26 wks.	23 wks.	21 wks.
$90.00–$91.00	$91.00	Never	4 yrs. 19 wks.	2 yrs. 9 wks.	1 yr. 23 wks.	1 yr. 4 wks.	45 wks.	37 wks.	32 wks.	28 wks.	25 wks.	22 wks.
$95.00–$96.00	$96.00	Never	4 yrs. 32 wks.	2 yrs. 16 wks.	1 yr. 28 wks.	1 yr. 8 wks.	48 wks.	40 wks.	34 wks.	30 wks.	26 wks.	24 wks.
$100.00–$101.00	$101.00	Never	4 yrs. 44 wks.	2 yrs. 22 wks.	1 yr. 32 wks.	1 yr. 11 wks.	50 wks.	42 wks.	36 wks.	31 wks.	28 wks.	25 wks.
$105.00–$106.00	$106.00	Never	5 yrs. 5 wks.	2 yrs. 28 wks.	1 yr. 36 wks.	1 yr. 14 wks.	1 yr. 1 wk.	44 wks.	37 wks.	33 wks.	29 wks.	26 wks.
$110.00–$111.00	$111.00	Never	5 yrs. 17 wks.	2 yrs. 34 wks.	1 yr. 40 wks.	1 yr. 17 wks.	1 yr. 3 wks.	46 wks.	39 wks.	34 wks.	30 wks.	27 wks.
$115.00–$116.00	$116.00	Never	5 yrs. 30 wks.	2 yrs. 41 wks.	1 yr. 44 wks.	1 yr. 20 wks.	1 yr. 6 wks.	48 wks.	41 wks.	36 wks.	32 wks.	29 wks.
$120.00–$121.00	$121.00	Never	5 yrs. 42 wks.	2 yrs. 47 wks.	1 yr. 48 wks.	1 yr. 23 wks.	1 yr. 8 wks.	50 wks.	43 wks.	37 wks.	33 wks.	30 wks.
$125.00–$126.00	$126.00	Never	6 yrs. 3 wks.	3 yrs. 1 wk.	2 yrs. 1 wk.	1 yr. 26 wks.	1 yr. 11 wks.	1 yr.	45 wks.	39 wks.	35 wks.	31 wks.
$130.00–$131.00	$131.00	Never	6 yrs. 15 wks.	3 yrs. 7 wks.	2 yrs. 5 wks.	1 yr. 29 wks.	1 yr. 13 wks.	1 yr. 2 wks.	46 wks.	40 wks.	36 wks.	32 wks.
$135.00–$136.00	$136.00	Never	6 yrs. 28 wks.	3 yrs. 14 wks.	2 yrs. 9 wks.	1 yr. 33 wks.	1 yr. 16 wks.	1 yr. 4 wks.	48 wks.	42 wks.	37 wks.	34 wks.
$140.00–$141.00	$141.00	Never	6 yrs. 40 wks.	3 yrs. 20 wks.	2 yrs. 13 wks.	1 yr. 36 wks.	1 yr. 18 wks.	1 yr. 6 wks.	50 wks.	44 wks.	39 wks.	35 wks.
$145.00–$146.00	$146.00	Never	7 yrs. 1 wk.	3 yrs. 26 wks.	2 yrs. 17 wks.	1 yr. 39 wks.	1 yr. 21 wks.	1 yr. 8 wks.	1 yr.	45 wks.	40 wks.	36 wks.
$149.00–$150.00	$150.00	Never	7 yrs. 11 wks.	3 yrs. 31 wks.	2 yrs. 21 wks.	1 yr. 41 wks.	1 yr. 23 wks.	1 yr. 10 wks.	1 yr. 1 wk.	46 wks.	41 wks.	37 wks.

IF YOU STRIKE FOR 5 WEEKS
And You Strike For

TO GET IT BACK IT WILL TAKE YOU

IF YOU TAKE HOME	YOU LOSE	0¢	1¢	2¢	3¢	4¢	5¢	6¢	7¢	8¢	9¢	10¢
$80.00–$81.00	$405.00	Never	19 yrs. 24 wks.	9 yrs. 38 wks.	6 yrs. 25 wks.	4 yrs. 45 wks.	3 yrs. 46 wks.	3 yrs. 12 wks.	2 yrs. 40 wks.	2 yrs. 22 wks.	2 yrs. 8 wks.	1 yr. 49 wks.
$85.00–$86.00	$430.00	Never	20 yrs. 35 wks.	10 yrs. 17 wks.	6 yrs. 46 wks.	5 yrs. 8 wks.	4 yrs. 7 wks.	3 yrs. 23 wks.	2 yrs. 49 wks.	2 yrs. 30 wks.	2 yrs. 15 wks.	2 yrs. 3 wks.
$90.00–$91.00	$455.00	Never	21 yrs. 45 wks.	10 yrs. 48 wks.	7 yrs. 15 wks.	5 yrs. 24 wks.	4 yrs. 19 wks.	3 yrs. 33 wks.	3 yrs. 6 wks.	2 yrs. 38 wks.	2 yrs. 22 wks.	2 yrs. 9 wks.
$95.00–$96.00	$480.00	Never	23 yrs. 4 wks.	11 yrs. 28 wks.	7 yrs. 36 wks.	5 yrs. 40 wks.	4 yrs. 32 wks.	3 yrs. 44 wks.	3 yrs. 15 wks.	2 yrs. 46 wks.	2 yrs. 29 wks.	2 yrs. 16 wks.
$100.00–$101.00	$505.00	Never	24 yrs. 14 wks.	12 yrs. 7 wks.	8 yrs. 4 wks.	6 yrs. 3 wks.	4 yrs. 44 wks.	4 yrs. 2 wks.	3 yrs. 24 wks.	3 yrs. 1 wk.	2 yrs. 36 wks.	2 yrs. 22 wks.
$105.00–$106.00	$530.00	Never	25 yrs. 25 wks.	12 yrs. 38 wks.	8 yrs. 25 wks.	6 yrs. 19 wks.	5 yrs. 5 wks.	4 yrs. 12 wks.	3 yrs. 33 wks.	3 yrs. 9 wks.	2 yrs. 43 wks.	2 yrs. 28 wks.
$110.00–$111.00	$555.00	Never	26 yrs. 35 wks.	13 yrs. 17 wks.	8 yrs. 46 wks.	6 yrs. 34 wks.	5 yrs. 17 wks.	4 yrs. 23 wks.	3 yrs. 42 wks.	3 yrs. 17 wks.	2 yrs. 50 wks.	2 yrs. 34 wks.
$115.00–$116.00	$580.00	Never	27 yrs. 46 wks.	13 yrs. 49 wks.	9 yrs. 15 wks.	6 yrs. 50 wks.	5 yrs. 30 wks.	4 yrs. 33 wks.	3 yrs. 51 wks.	3 yrs. 25 wks.	3 yrs. 5 wks.	2 yrs. 41 wks.
$120.00–$121.00	$605.00	Never	29 yrs. 4 wks.	14 yrs. 28 wks.	9 yrs. 36 wks.	7 yrs. 14 wks.	5 yrs. 42 wks.	4 yrs. 44 wks.	4 yrs. 8 wks.	3 yrs. 33 wks.	3 yrs. 12 wks.	2 yrs. 47 wks.
$125.00–$126.00	$630.00	Never	30 yrs. 15 wks.	15 yrs. 7 wks.	10 yrs. 5 wks.	7 yrs. 29 wks.	6 yrs. 3 wks.	5 yrs. 2 wks.	4 yrs. 17 wks.	3 yrs. 40 wks.	3 yrs. 19 wks.	3 yrs. 1 wk.
$130.00–$131.00	$655.00	Never	31 yrs. 25 wks.	15 yrs. 38 wks.	10 yrs. 25 wks.	7 yrs. 45 wks.	6 yrs. 15 wks.	5 yrs. 12 wks.	4 yrs. 25 wks.	3 yrs. 48 wks.	3 yrs. 25 wks.	3 yrs. 7 wks.
$135.00–$136.00	$680.00	Never	32 yrs. 36 wks.	16 yrs. 18 wks.	10 yrs. 46 wks.	8 yrs. 9 wks.	6 yrs. 28 wks.	5 yrs. 23 wks.	4 yrs. 34 wks.	4 yrs. 4 wks.	3 yrs. 32 wks.	3 yrs. 14 wks.
$140.00–$141.00	$705.00	Never	33 yrs. 46 wks.	16 yrs. 49 wks.	11 yrs. 15 wks.	8 yrs. 24 wks.	6 yrs. 40 wks.	5 yrs. 33 wks.	4 yrs. 43 wks.	4 yrs. 12 wks.	3 yrs. 39 wks.	3 yrs. 20 wks.
$145.00–$146.00	$730.00	Never	35 yrs. 5 wks.	17 yrs. 28 wks.	11 yrs. 36 wks.	8 yrs. 40 wks.	7 yrs. 1 wk.	5 yrs. 44 wks.	5 yrs.	4 yrs. 20 wks.	3 yrs. 46 wks.	3 yrs. 26 wks.
$149.00–$150.00	$750.00	Never	36 yrs. 3 wks.	18 yrs. 1 wk.	12 yrs. 1 wk.	9 yrs.	7 yrs. 11 wks.	6 yrs.	5 yrs. 7 wks.	4 yrs. 26 wks.	4 yrs.	3 yrs. 31 wks.

11–4

MEDIATION: FUNCTIONS AND TACTICS

Carl Stevens*

WHAT INSTITUTIONAL ARRANGEMENTS CONSTITUTE MEDIATION?

William Leiserson has observed that there is some confusion in answer to this question. For example, is a third party who simply "observes" negotiations—sitting in on but not participating—properly said to be mediating? Also, as he observes, mediation agencies as often intervene after as before a strike or lockout, and whether they are settling strikes or disputes, both efforts are called mediation—as if a strike were the same thing as a dispute. Is the locked-door technique, whereby the parties are confined to a room for extended periods until through sheer ennui they can easily be brought to agreement without being too finicky about what they agree to, properly called mediation? Is a publicly constituted third party with the power to make public recommendations really mediating or arbitrating?

For the present, a simple definition of mediation which is silent on most questions such as the above will suffice. Mediation is the intervention (the institution of mediation includes the prospect of, as well as actual, intervention) of a third party in collective bargaining negotiation before or after a strike or lockout. The objective of this party is to secure agreement. He does not have the power to make a binding award, although he may be able to bring "pressure" to bear in favor of a

_____
* Professor, Reed College. Reprinted from *Strategy and Collective Bargaining Negotiation* (New York: McGraw Hill, 1963) pp. 124–52. Reprinted in 1978 by Greenwood Press, Inc.

recommended settlement. The interest is in the functions a third party so motivated might serve, what tactics he might employ. The efficiency of such functions and tactics is of interest, but the question of whether these are in some sense really mediation is not.

In the ensuing analysis, certain factors which may impede the agreement process, and the mediator functions associated with these factors, will be neglected. Some of these are involved with what Clark Kerr has termed *the case of awkwardness*—the case in which the mediator supplies the negotiation skills which the parties themselves lack. We might include here various kinds of "ludic" complications such as vindictiveness, bitterness, unreasoning obstinacy, and bad manners. These factors have been neglected in our decision to deal primarily with the "mature" collective bargaining relationship. This in no way implies that these factors are not frequently encountered in the mediation of industrial disputes. Indeed, Cole lists them as the principal problems of the mediator. Kerr includes the case of awkwardness as among the most common from a mediation point of view.

For the same reasons, we shall neglect the case in which two parties would prefer open economic warfare, parties who do not wish to mediate but have been constrained by public authority, or perhaps the demands of constituents to do so. Involved with this kind of situation are two more cases distinguished by Kerr, "The case of the hoodwinked membership": here the mediator helps the negotiators to fool the ignorant constituents into thinking that a real effort is being made to settle the dispute, whereas the leaders really want a strike for their own purposes. "The case of the impotent members": the members have no control over their leaders and hence nothing is to be gained by pretense to a real effort at settlement through mediation.

We also assume in this section that the mediator is essentially the servant of the parties rather than the servant of public or of political authority. Finally, we assume that although the mediator may bring pressure to bear upon the parties by manipulating pressures naturally present in the situation, he does not attempt to use essentially extrasituational pressures contrived by himself—a threat to "put the parties on the spot" by publicly attesting to their incompetence and lack of good faith, and so forth.

THE PERSONAL FACTOR IN MEDIATION

There has been frequent emphasis on the personal qualities of the mediator in discussions of the mediation process. In the extreme, this emphasis leads to "agnosticism" with respect to analysis of the mediation process. A less exaggerated view permits analysis of the process, but still gives considerable weight to the personal factor. Wilson, for example, makes clear at the outset of an analysis of mediation techniques, that such discussion cannot get very far without extensive reference to the "ideal mediator," his personal qualities, qualifications, personality, and so forth. He observes that: "While experts are not in agreement as to the weight of the personal factor, it cannot be denied, I think, that the process of mediation is largely a personal function of the mediator. . . ."

Emphasis upon the personal factor has produced some research upon and analysis of mediators themselves. A technically excellent and carefully done example of such a study is that of Landsberger. The main question he sets out to answer is whether psychological tests are capable of predicting the parties' reaction to a mediator, that is, of distinguishing those mediators who will be deemed "good" by the parties. On the basis of interviews with persons who had considerable first-hand experience with collective bargaining and mediation, Landsberger built up a set of 10 criteria—areas of mediator behavior—which seemed to be the ones to which the parties had most frequent reference when describing a mediator and attempting to evaluate him.

1. Originality of ideas.
2. A sense of appropriate humor.
3. Ability to act unobtrusively.
4. The mediator as "one of us."
5. The mediator as a respected authority.
6. Willingness to be a vigorous salesman when the situation requires it.
7. Control over feelings.
8. Attitudes toward, and persistence and patient effort invested in the work of mediation.
9. Ability to understand quickly the complexities of a dispute.
10. Accumulated knowledge of labor relations.

This list of *areas of mediator behavior* is of considerable interest. Even by itself it says a little, by inference, about the tactics of mediation. That is, the fact that a good mediator quickly understands the complexities of a dispute, has original ideas, and is willing to be a vigorous salesman when the situation requires, suggests that mediation is not, as is often supposed, essentially passive. Beyond this, scrutiny of the list suggests in a very definite way the permissive aspect of the personal factor. One can well imagine that a person with a low score in these terms would enjoy little success as a mediator (or in many other endeavors). Except in this permissive sense, no such study by itself casts light on the question of the "weight" of the personal factor (as opposed to tactical factors, for example) in mediation.

DISCUSSION ORGANIZED AROUND BARS TO AGREEMENT

An attempt has been made to organize this discussion around a number of different bars to agreement—the characteristics of the negotiation status confronted by the mediator which account for the inability of the parties to agree, or which describe the kind of tactical situation in which the failure to agree is manifest. There is no implied weighting of these bars with respect to relative importance. With respect to each, an attempt is made to emphasize those tactics and functions of mediation which are of primary importance in resolving that particular situation. This does not mean that other tactics and functions may not also be involved. For example, with respect to a particular bar, some aspect of the mediator's control over the communications structure in the negotiations may be of peculiar importance and in consequence will be emphasized. This does not imply that some other mediator function such as removing nonrationality from the situation may not also be efficacious vis-à-vis other aspects of the situation containing the bar in question.

NO CONTRACT ZONE THE MAJOR PROBLEM: THE STRAIGHTFORWARD CASE

No contract zone is the situation in which the least favorable terms upon which the parties are willing to settle do not overlap. . . .

Within this category it is helpful to distinguish two subcategories. One, the case in which the absence of a contract zone reflects the basic situation and the parties'

perception of that situation rather than being the result of tactical maneuver. We deal with this case in this section. Two, the case in which a contract zone was inherent in the situation (at least if it were perceived rationally by both parties), but now there is none by virtue of the tactical maneuvering of the parties. We deal with case two in the next section.

* * * * *

PERSUASION AND RATIONALIZATION

. . . Tactics of persuasion are B's attempts to control A's course of action by operations upon A's preferences and/or operations upon A's perception of the extra-negotiation environment. Just as the parties A and B may operate upon each other by persuasion, so may the mediator operate upon one or both of them by persuasion. The parties, particularly if they are relatively new to collective bargaining, may underestimate the cost of a strike or lockout, or overestimate the cost of agreement with the opponent upon the opponent's terms. In such a situation, the mediator may abet the agreement process by assisting them to see the realities of the situation. If the parties would agree in the light of this realistic appraisal of the costs and gains associated with alternative courses of action, the mediator may serve a real function, and this may be one of the more important functions served by mediators generally.

If a mediator is resorting to persuasive tactics in an effort to induce the parties to change position, he should bear in mind the important asymmetry in the effects of what were previously termed Class I and Class II tactics. For example, in an attempt to move A's equilibrium position toward that of B, the mediator may attempt to increase A's estimate of the cost of disagreement with B on B's terms. Or he may attempt to decrease A's estimate of the cost of agreement with B on B's terms. Both classes of tactics may be effective in moving A's position toward B. However, emphasis upon tactics of the first class will, in contrast with emphasis upon tactics of the second class, tend to increase the level of tension and anxiety in the negotiation situation, and hence increase the chances of a breakdown. To be more definite, suppose that the mediator is attempting to induce the parties to agree to a certain "package." He might emphasize to both that if a strike takes place it will be long and bitter, involving a major loss of markets and profits for the company and probably a destruction of the organizational integrity of the union. Conversely, he might emphasize to the company that the package in question will by no means put it at a competitive disadvantage vis-à-vis the firms in its market area. He might emphasize to the union that the package in question is "salable" to its constituency. It is an implication of conflict-choice theory that emphasis upon tactics of the first sort will increase the likelihood of a breakdown of the mediated negotiations, that is, it may precipitate attempts to "escape" from the negotiation situation. Of course, the mediator may have no option (if he is bent upon persuasion) but resort to tactics of the first sort. In this case, he had best contrive so far as possible to prevent the parties escaping from the mediated negotiation situation.

A delicate problem may arise if the mediator has resorted to persuasion. The mediator does not have a direct interest in bringing the parties to a realistic appraisal of the situation. His objective is to induce them to agree. Bringing them to a realistic appraisal of the situation may be a means to this end. However, bringing them to a nonrealistic appraisal may also be a means to this end. That is, it might be the case that a party could be brought to agreement if he overestimated the cost of a strike, underestimated the gains to be had

thereby, and underestimated the cost of agreement with his opponent upon his opponent's terms. In this case, the mediator might abet the agreement process by deliberate deception.

The possible utility of deceptive tactics may arise in ways rather more subtle. From an analytical point of view, one of the most important aspects of the mediation process is the mediator's control over the communications structure in the negotiation situation. Control of the communications structure generally facilitates attempts at persuasion and also coercion. The mediation tactic which has been described as one of "unselling" and "selling" is an example. Suppose that the mediator has separated the parties and is conveying offers between them. He may, in talking to the party making the offer, minimize the possibility that it will be accepted—in favor of something else—while a few minutes later "across the hall" he may be maximizing the desirability of accepting the offer. He may in this way draw forth further offers and counteroffers which will more nearly coincide.

Generally speaking, control of the communications structure may enable the mediator to bring pressures to bear upon the parties which involve an element of deception. An interesting case in point is an example given by Hugh G. Lovell. In this case, the union suspected that the company was involved in important defense contracts, and that this circumstance would create considerable difficulty in the event of a strike. The union asked the mediator to check this. Upon interrogation, the company testified with apparent sincerity that indeed this was the case, that there was much important and secret work in progress. The mediator suspected that the company's view might have stemmed from an exaggerated idea of the importance of the work on the part of the local defense authorities. A call to the Defense Department confirmed this, indicating that the department was not at all concerned about a strike in this company. The mediator so advised the company, thereby depriving it of what it had thought was a major defense weapon. The mediator did not, however, simultaneously inform the union. He let it continue for some days (until the next conference) under the pressure created by its suspicions.

We have been concerned with that aspect of persuasion as a mediation tactic involving operations upon the parties' perception of the negotiation environment. The mediator might also attempt by persuasion to alter their preferences, per se. One doubts, however, that this aspect of the persuasion tactic would be very effective in the typical bargaining context.

Closely related to persuasion are the tactics of rationalization. The implications of tactics of rationalization for mediation functions are quite straightforward. . . . For example, the mediator may supply a party with arguments which the party may in turn use to rationalize a position (or retreat from a position) vis-à-vis his own constituents. This may be a potentially important mediation tactic.

Beyond this, it should be recognized that the mere fact of a mediator's entrance into a dispute provides the parties with a means for rationalizing retreats from previously held positions, particularly if the mediator can be made to appear to take a part of the responsibility for any settlement.

COERCION

Tactics of coercion are B's attempts to control A's behavior by operating upon the range of outcomes available to A as these outcomes depend upon B's own course of action. Tactics of coercion are frequently based upon bluff, and mediation tactics may involve the relationship of the mediator to the bluff tactics of the parties.

If either party is bluffing about his own course of action, the mediator may be able to abet agreement by removing the ele-

ments of bluff from the situation. That is, suppose that agreement is impeded, for example, because A believes that his bluff about willingness to take a strike (or to continue a strike indefinitely) will prevail, will bring B to terms. He would make a concession if he did not believe in the strength of his bluff weapon. The mediator may be able to diagnose A's true intentions, so advise B, and then advise A that the bluff is no longer effective. It would seem, however, that a mediator involved in a bluff situation would have to be on guard against becoming an unwitting tool of either (or both) of the parties. A party may have only partially succeeded in an effort to make its bluff fully convincing to the opposite number. If, however, that party can successfully bluff the mediator, he may enlist the mediator as an unwitting ally in his deception. For example, A may not quite believe B's assertion that he will strike, but he might believe the mediator's assertion that B will strike. The mediator's assertion is apt to be much more creditable, for A has reason to believe that B may be attempting to fool him, whereas his presumption will be that the mediator is not. Further, he may have confidence in the mediator's ability to "see through" B—if there is anything to be seen.

At this juncture the problem of deception as a mediation tactic arises once more. The mediator does not have a direct interest in eliminating bluff from negotiations. His objective is agreement. Elimination of bluff may be a means to this end. However, it might be that conniving in a bluff will be a means to this end. Thus, for example, A might capitulate if he did not suspect that B was bluffing. The mediator, aware that B was bluffing, might nevertheless convince A that he was not. It would not be appropriate to become involved here in the issue of whether a mediator, in pursuit of his objective of bringing the parties to agreement, "should" use deceptive tactics in conjunction with the persuasive and coercive tactics of the parties. One point should be made in this connection, however.

Ann Douglas, in discussing the invention of "fictions" with respect to the mediation process has observed that the claim of neutrality enjoys such widespread credence among mediators that it could almost be said to be universal in the profession. In her view, the essential function of this fiction is to shield the mediator from responsibility for the outcome of mediated negotiations, to "purge the mediator of liability for the course of treatment, regardless whether the patient gets well or succumbs." This function is in turn necessitated by the ambiguous status in our culture of peace-making via the intervention of third parties into disputes. Whether the notion of the mediator's neutrality serves this social function is not critical in this context.

However, other aspects of the notion may be critical. If the claim to mediators' neutrality is read as a disclaim to any influence on the direction and shape of the outcome, then this claim is indeed a fiction. However, the concept of mediators' neutrality can be much more narrowly construed. It can imply that the mediator, in pursuit of his objective of bringing the parties to agreement, does not (even though it might be tactically efficacious in the light of his basic objective) connive in bluff and deception and/or deliberately distort the realities of the negotiation and extranegotiation environment as he sees them. Abjuring these tactics still leaves plenty of scope for him to be an active and inventive agent in the negotiations and to focus "pressures" upon the parties. One may inquire what the significance of neutrality is in this sense. One significance is the matter of acceptability of the institution of mediation by the parties. If the mediator were nonneutral in the sense that he connived in bluff tactics, he would in effect conspire with one party against the

other. It seems doubtful that both parties to a dispute would desire to admit a third known to include conspiracy in his kit of tools.

A second significance has to do with the mediator's neutral posture towards "nature"—the extranegotiation context of the dispute. Within some limits for variation, the basic determinants of the outcome of collective bargaining negotiation are the determinants of the basic power relationships which underlie the conflict in an industrial relations system. Negotiation is a social control technique for reflecting and transmuting these basic determinants, while at the same time containing the conflict short of overt trials of industrial warfare. The mediator's primary function is to abet the containment function of negotiation. In any particular case, there would be a kind of fortuitous conspiracy (distinguish systematic interparty discrimination) involved if the mediator were nonneutral in the sense that he deliberately distorted the realities of the negotiation and extranegotiation environment as he saw these. But the important nonneutrality here would be that vis-à-vis the "system," that is, it would involve a distortion of "legitimate" determinants of the outcome. In a continuing negotiation process such as collective bargaining, solutions achieved in this way would be spurious and transitory, would subsequently be undone, and would generally reduce the efficiency of mediated negotiation as a social control technique.

The final point to be considered under the straightforward case of no contract zone is the function of mediation as a substitute for the "information strike." As we discussed earlier, an important coercive tactic in negotiation is the notbluff. The principal tactical problem associated with notbluff is conveying the truth of the intended course of action. For example, how does A convince B that he will take a strike unless B makes a concession? One possibil-

ity is simply to let the deadline expire and
in consequence of that expiration to take
a strike. If, in such a case, B would have
conceded the position had he made a correct estimate of the probability (1.0) that
a strike would occur, only the information
content component of the strike has served
a legitimate function. Such a strike should
not, perhaps, be considered strictly "unnecessary," for the institutional arrangements may not have permitted A to lay
hold of a device (short of actually taking
the strike) which would get his point
across to B. Nevertheless, one may argue
that it is socially undesirable that strikes
should occur in circumstances such as
these. One function of mediation is as a
substitute for this kind of strike. That is,
the mediator is in a position to testify to
B regarding A's intentions, and this testimony may be compelling even though A's
own assertions regarding his intentions
were not.

* * * * *

MEDIATION AS A WAY TO "COME
CLEAN" WITHOUT PREJUDICE

Analysis of the later predeadline stages of
collective bargaining negotiation reveals
that there are a number of tactical bars
to full freedom of communication between
the parties. The tactical bars in question
give rise to the problem . . . of how to
"come clean" without prejudice. How may
a party announce his equilibrium position
without prejudice, that is, without, by the
very act of the announcement, making the
ultimately to be agreed-upon position less
favorable to himself than might otherwise
have been the case? We may briefly reca-
pitulate the reasons why such an announcement may be prejudicial.

1. Such an announcement involves retreat from the ostensible position, a retreat
which may be interpreted by the opposite
number as a sign of weakness, or even as

a sign of impending collapse and capitula-
tion.

2. Operating under the deadline rule,
the solution of the negotiation game is the
equilibrium position occupied by the party
who "gives" at 11:59. At 11:59 (the last
moment before a strike) the time has come
for last proposals. In the nature of the case,
one of these proposals is an offer, the
other, if there is a contract zone, is agreement. There is a tactical asymmetry in this
situation in the sense that the advantage
may well have gone to the one who waited.

3. Even though a party does not wish
to strike or to take a strike, it may be forced
upon him, and this consideration may
cause him to be concerned about the status
quo which strike negotiations will inherit
from the prestrike negotiations, therefore,
he may for these reasons be reluctant to
announce his true equilibrium position.

An implication of these tactical bars to
full freedom of communication is that the
parties may be in (covert) agreement in
the sense that their equilibrium positions
are consonant but may fail to reach overt
agreement. Thus, because of these bars,
a party's final prestrike proposal may not
state the least favorable terms (to himself)
upon which he is willing to settle but
terms more favorable to himself. In such
cases, if the parties would have settled had
each stated the least favorable terms upon
which he was (or would have been) willing
to settle, the intervention of a mediator
may be of real assistance.

Another aspect of these tactical problems is also relevant to mediation functions. They all have in common the fact
that each is an influence making for the
photofinish, making for delay in an announcement of equilibrium position—the
least favorable terms upon which one is
willing to settle. The approach of the deadline brings with it an 11:59, the last moment at which a change in ostensible position may be made, and a 12:01, the

moment beyond which a strike is inevitable. However, as we saw, the deadline is not a knife edge in time. Rather, it is a sort of zone in time, if only in consequence of the fact that if a strike is impending various preparations must be made. This means that under the influence of these forces for delay by the time one party has decided that 11:59 has arrived, it may already be 12:01. Thus, an inadvertent strike may take place, which might have been precluded by the intervention of a mediator.

It should be noted that the tactical problems adverted to here may constitute bars to agreement in cases in which there are also other bars to agreement. Hence, discussion of mediator's function in this context is also relevant to mediation in those other contexts. However, in what follows, we may proceed as if we were considering the "pure" cases of bars to agreement on the grounds suggested in this section. That is, in these cases, the parties are supposed to be in (covert) agreement in that their equilibrium positions are consonant. They have not achieved overt agreement because their ostensible positions have not, for the reasons adduced, incorporated the least favorable terms upon which each is willing to settle.

In these instances, the critical function of the mediator stems in large part from the role he plays as part of the communications structure of the negotiations. For example, he can receive information from each party without passing that information on to the opposite number. If, on the basis of such information, it turned out that the equilibrium positions of the parties were indeed consonant, he could simply announce to the parties that they were in agreement, and thereby resolve the dispute. That is, in such a case, even though the ostensible positions of the parties were divergent, they would not have to alter these positions at all—prior to the moment of actual agreement.

Even if the mediator enters the picture prior to a strike, resolution of the situation is not apt to be so simple as above suggested. The parties may hesitate, at least early in the game, to reveal their true positions to the mediator. There is no reason, for example, for A to suppose that because he has revealed his true position to the mediator that B has done likewise. If the mediator simply passes this information on to B, the difficulties discussed remain. However, the mediator may do much more than simply pass information along. Peculiarly appropriate to agreement difficulties of the sort here considered, he may appear to be the author of proposals which are in point of fact originated by (and even represent the true equilibrium positions of) the parties. Or each side may give the mediator something to use as he sees fit. The major advantage here is that a party need not (appear to have) become committed to a position (his own) since it appears to be the mediator's position. Indeed, if the tactical situation should demand it, he might denounce the mediator's position as stoutly as he does that of his opposite number. Thus the parties can make ostensible concessions via the mediator with much less hazard than would be the case in making such concessions directly, and we might expect such concession to be made. As the mediation progresses, the confidence of the parties in the mediator will become established. Especially if he has implied a deadline of his own (having been appropriately patient with what has gone before), the parties will be encouraged to reveal their true positions to him. This, in the nonmanifest contract zone cases here under consideration, will be sufficient to resolve the dispute.

The function of the mediator in suppressing information may also be important in these cases. An existing contract zone may be wiped out if, for example, A, learning of B's true equilibrium position (considerably less favorable to B than was his ostensible position), interprets this as a sign of B's collapse and promptly revises the terms upon which he is willing to settle. Thus the mediator may have to slow down the pace of B's retreat.

Particularly in cases of this kind, the timing of the mediator entering the dispute may be critical. In light of the possibility of negotiation failures of the non-manifest contract zone type, it may be argued that mediation (of a sort) should be a part of many negotiation proceedings from their inception. Thus it might be required that the parties continuously submit information regarding their true equilibrium positions to a neutral third party. It would be understood and agreed that the sole function of this third party would be to receive the information in question and announce the fact of conditions necessary for bilateral compromise—if and when such conditions should eventuate. The value of employing mediation of this sort from the outset is that it might prevent the parties from destroying a condition necessary for bilateral compromise in their unaided attempts to discover the fact of its existence.

In any event, whether or not mediation of this sort is employed from the outset, the mediator should enter the picture prior to the deadline and occurrence of a strike. Once the strike has begun, the picture changes. What may have begun as an "unnecessary" strike may not be as easy to terminate as this genesis would imply. Misunderstandings are easy, and tensions created by the uncertainty of the situation may lead to violent reactions. Once the strike has begun, the nonmanifest contract zone may evaporate, and the mediator's task will be complicated.

Leiserson has suggested that there should be a period between the end of collective bargaining and the beginning of a strike in which the mediator can work. Such an arrangement might be very helpful in some cases. It would not seem, however, that it should be generalized as a rule to apply to all cases. In some situations, mediation might be helpful during the pre-deadline negotiation. In other cases, where there is no contract zone and the parties appear quite intractable, perhaps only the actual experience of a strike will lead the parties to a correct estimate of the cost involved and the probable gains to be had thereby. In such instances, mediation may be more effective after the strike has run its course for awhile. In general, however, and particularly in the nonmanifest contract zone case, there is a case for the mediator's entering the picture prior to the beginning of a strike.

INTRAORGANIZATIONAL PROBLEMS

The negotiators are the representatives of organizations. Ultimately, whatever package they come up with must be sold by each to his own constituents. We have noted that these considerations might pose a bar to agreement. Thus it may be the case that, insofar as the negotiators as delegates are concerned, a manifest contract zone has emerged in the course of negotiation. However, difficulties may arise in the effort to tailor a package which is as "salable" as possible (salable at all, in the extreme case) to the respective constituencies. In such a case, the negotiators in a sense share a common problem. A mediator may be helpful in this situation. For one thing, he brings with him the fresh view of a disinterested third party and (if the parties are fortunate) a facility for the invention of alternative proposals. He may come up with an ingenious solution which, although it was inherent in the situation, neither party had seen. In this kind of situation, the mediator operates as a kind of maximizer of "total welfare." He must attempt to get more for A without getting less for B, and vice versa. Equally important in this kind of situation is the face-saving function discussed previously.

The negotiator may find it difficult to endorse a given package, which he is willing to accept, to his constituents because the package may appear to discriminate in an awkward way as among the various interest groups represented in his organization. In such a case, if the mediator can appear to shoulder some of the responsibility for the outcome, the negotiator's problems in relation to his constituents may be eased.

11–5

MEDIATION AND ORGANIZATIONAL DEVELOPMENT: MODELS FOR CONFLICT MANAGEMENT

Jeanne M. Brett, Stephen B. Goldberg, and William Ury*

The U.S. industrial relations system was designed to contain the endemic conflict between union and management. A wildcat strike, or unauthorized work stoppage during the term of a collective bargaining agreement, occurs when the industrial relations system fails to contain labor-management conflict. . . . [We are] going to discuss and contrast two models—mediation and organizational development—for third-party intervention when a union-management relationship is unable to avoid frequent wildcat strikes. . . .

A few years ago, Steve Goldberg and Jeanne Brett spent some time studying wildcat strikes in the bituminous coal industry.[1] We found that some mines had many more wildcat strikes than others. We concluded that mines with frequent wildcat strikes had qualitatively different union-management relations than mines with few wildcat strikes. We were not able to determine whether the quality of the union-management relationship was a cause or an effect of wildcat strikes, but we were able to rule out enough alternative hypotheses to be quite confident that the cause of wildcat strikes lies within the local union-management relationship.

This spring we were asked to act as third-party consultants at a mine that had experienced 27 wildcat strikes in the pre-

* Associate professor and professor, Graduate School of Management, Northwestern University, and assistant professor, Harvard Business School. Reprinted from *Proceedings of the 33rd Annual Meeting of the IRRA*, Denver, 1980, pp. 195–202.

[1] J. M. Brett and S. B. Goldberg, "Wildcat Strikes in the Bituminous Coal Mining Industry," *Industrial and Labor Relations Review*, July 1979, pp. 465–83.

ceding 23 months. The entire day-shift had been jailed the preceding summer for striking in defiance of a district court injunction; the union was under a "life of the contract" injunction against striking. The mine was losing money, one third of the workforce had been laid off, and serious consideration was being given to closing the mine due to low productivity and high costs believed to be due to the wildcats.

Conflict management via third-party intervention typically proceeds through three stages. First, the parties perceive that the level of conflict is unacceptable and that they need the assistance of an expert or a neutral. Second, the third party diagnoses the conflict situation, and finally the third party proposes strategies for change.[2] In discussing each of these stages of conflict management at the mine, . . . contrast the mediation and organizational development models for third-party intervention.

THE THIRD-PARTY ROLE

The stimulus to seek third-party assistance in this situation was line management's threat to close the mine. The threat, backed up by a layoff of one third of the workforce, was credible to both company labor relations officials and the district union officers. They jointly sought third-party assistance from us, because we were viewed as experts by virtue of our research on wildcat strikes and Steve had credibility as a neutral by virtue of his eight years as an arbitrator in the industry. Bill Ury, who joined us, provided process expertise by virtue of his background in international mediation.

The first point . . . in contrasting mediation and organizational development is that neither provided a proper third-party model for this situation. The situation called for a third-party role that was substantially larger than that of a typical mediator and rather different from that played by a typical OD consultant.

Mediators typically work with the parties after they reach a collective bargaining impasse. A mediator's goal is short term—to facilitate a collective bargaining agreement. While mediators use many of the same techniques as OD consultants, unlike OD consultants, they are not concerned with bringing about a permanent change in the parties' ability to manage conflict. The wildcat strike situation at this mine clearly called for a permanent change in the parties' ability to manage conflict.

OD consultants typically work with interpersonal or intergroup conflict within management. Their goal is to bring a permanent reduction in the amount of uncontrolled conflict in the system.[3] While this is an appropriate goal for this mine, the interorganizational context of union-

---

[2] R. H. Kilmann and K. W. Thomas, "Four Perspectives on Conflict Management: An Attributional Framework for Organizing Descriptive and Normative Theory," *Academy of Management Review* 3 (1978), pp. 59–68.

[3] This is perhaps an inappropriate characterization of most OD consultants' conflict-management goal. Kochan and Dyer and Strauss characterize OD consultants' conflict-management goal as the desire to reduce the total amount of conflict in the system. Strauss says OD consultants "assume the main impediments to agreement are misunderstandings, personality differences, and immature, nonauthentic relations"; that conflict when approached with trust and authenticity will yield a win-win solution. While this is a fair characterization of much of OD, it does fail to recognize the organization structure and design subfields within OD. Here conflict is viewed as structural, not psychological; it is not bad per se; and structural, not behavioral, interventions are needed to control conflict. T. A. Kochan and L. Dyer, "A Model of Organizational Change in the Context of Union-Management Relations," *Journal of Applied Behavioral Science*, January 1976, pp. 59–78; G. Strauss, "Can Social Psychology Contribute to Industrial Relations?" in *Industrial Relations: A Social Psychological Approach*, ed. G. M. Stephenson and C. J. Brotherton (New York: Wiley, 1979), p. 384. See also Kilmann and Thomas.

management conflict is very different from the intraorganizational context of conflict within management.

Kochan and Dyer and Strauss argue that OD models are inappropriate for the union-management context.[4] For example, because companies are structured hierarchically, the third-party consultant is usually brought in by a superior to deal with conflict between subordinates or subordinate groups. The consultant's relationship is with the superior. The consultant's diagnosis and recommendations for change are made to the superior who has the authority to implement the change.

In contrast, we were brought in jointly by the two parties to the conflict. While management had the authority to implement unilateral change in management practices, because the union is a democratic and not a hierarchical organization, the union leadership did not have the authority to implement unilateral change in union practices. Any recommendations which required change in the parties' interaction pattern required joint agreement. Whereas the OD consultant to management has to sell the change strategy to management, the third-party consultant in a union-management relationship has to sell unilateral changes and mediate bilateral change.

DIAGNOSIS

Both mediators and OD consultants attempt to diagnose the conflict by investigating the parties and the situation. The focus of a mediator's inquiry is much narrower than that of the OD consultant. The mediator seeks to understand each party's perceptions of the collective bargaining issues. He/she also attempts to determine if interpersonal relationships or the setting in which the negotiations occur is interfering with the parties' ability to reach an agreement.

The OD consultant's diagnostic orientation depends on his/her perspective on conflict management. Kilmann and Thomas describe four perspectives.[5] The first two perspectives focus on the situation. The second two on the parties.

The first perspective assumes that conflict develops in the interaction process between the parties. An OD consultant with this perspective would want to observe the parties' interacting. The second perspective assumes that conflict develops because of conditions in the interpersonal or intergroup environment which interfere with the parties' ability to resolve issues. An OD consultant with this perspective would interview the parties, probing to uncover rules, procedures, incentives, social pressures, and control mechanisms which might be stimulating the conflict. The third perspective assumes that conflict develops because of the underlying concerns or agendas of the parties. The fourth perspective assumes that conflict results because of unchangeable characteristics of the parties themselves. A consultant with the third or fourth perspective would interview the parties, probing to determine whether the parties' behavior in the conflict situation was or was not changeable.

The mediator's diagnostic focus reflects the first and third perspectives. These perspectives seek the cause of the conflict in the parties' interaction process and/or in the parties' perceptions. The mediator, however, because his/her goal is the short-term resolution of a collective bargaining impasse, is much more likely than the OD consultant to focus on particular issues.

Our wildcat strike situation called for a diagnosis more similar to that of a multi-perspective OD consultant than to a mediator. There were no specific issues to mediate at the time of the assessment. Our

[4] Kochan and Dyer, "A Model of Organizational Change."

[5] Kilmann and Thomas, "Four Perspectives."

previous research provided us with both a process model of the developmental phases preceding a wildcat strike and a structural model of environmental events associated with frequent wildcat strikes.[6] In our assessment, we were able to test the new situation against the research models. We found no evidence during the on-site assessment to reject these models. Interviews with the parties also indicated that conflict at the mine was tightly intertwined with the personalities of both union and management officials.

STRATEGIES FOR CHANGE

Mediators' change strategies are the same strategies used by most conflict management consultants. In OD, these techniques are called interpersonal peacemaking and process consultation.[7] In interpersonal peacemaking, the third party attempts to change the parties' perceptions and attitudes and, as a result, bring about a change in behavior. In process consultation, the third party attempts to change the parties' behavior directly by changing their interaction pattern.[8]

Two programs have applied interpersonal peacemaking techniques to union-management conflict. Blake and Mouton's program calls first for a period of perceptual and attitudinal restructuring, based on role-play techniques, and then joint devel-

opment of superordinate goals.[9] The program is based on Sherif's classic research on intergroup confict, known as the Robbers' Cave experiments.[10] In these experiments at a camp, Sherif divided boys into groups and generated intergroup conflict by having them compete in win-lose situations. Later, Sherif eliminated the conflict by having the teams cooperate to achieve a superordinate goal. Blake, Shepard, and Mouton's program has been implemented in at least one union-management situation, but no in-depth evaluation data are available.[11]

The second program is the Federal Mediation and Conciliation Service's Relations by Objectives or RBO program. This program uses the same techniques of attitudinal and perceptual restructuring and superordinate goal-setting that Blake and Mouton's program uses.[12] The program has been used in over 50 union-management situations and it has been submitted to outside evaluation.[13] Both programs use techniques, attitudinal and perceptual restructuring, and superordinate goal-setting, assumed to be useful in eliminating conflict. The assumption underlying these techniques is that conflict is bad and needs to be eliminated. We believe that both the

---

[6] J. M. Brett, "Conformity and Wildcat Strikes in the Coal Mining Industry" (Paper presented at the American Psychological Association, August 1977).

[7] R. Walton, *Interpersonal Peacemaking: Confrontations and Third-Party Consultation* (Reading, Mass.: Addison-Wesley, 1969); E. H. Schein, *Process Consultation: Its Role in Organization Development* (Reading, Mass.: Addison-Wesley, 1969). See also R. Fisher and W. Ury for a description of mediators' techniques, *International Mediation: A Working Guide* (New York: International Peace Academy, 1978).

[8] These are rather pure descriptions of the two techniques. Many practitioners mix the two techniques.

[9] R. Blake, H. Shepard, and J. S. Mouton, *Managing Intergroup Conflict in Industry* (Houston: Gulf Publishing, 1954).

[10] M. Sherif, O. J. Harvey, B. J. White, W. R. Wood, and C. W. Sherif, *Intergroup Conflict and Cooperation: The Robbers Cave Experiment* (Norman, Okla.: University Book Exchange, 1961).

[11] Blake, Shepard, and Mouton, *Managing Conflict.*

[12] T. A. Kochan, *Collective Bargaining and Industrial Relations* (Homewood, Ill.: Richard D. Irwin, 1980); J. J. Popular, "Labor Management Relations: U.S. Mediators Try to Build Common Objectives," *World of Work Report,* September 1976, pp. 1–3.

[13] One report was written by Professor Anthony Sinicropi, University of Iowa; it is not publicly available. The other is a doctoral dissertation—Denise Tanguay Hoyer, "A Program of Conflict Management: An Exploratory Approach," *Proceedings* of the Industrial Relations Research Association, 1979, pp. 334–35.

assumption and the techniques are inappropriate in a union-management setting.

The assumption is inappropriate for two reasons. Conflict may be bad—that is, cause ineffective intergroup and intragroup performance—but it may also be unavoidable. In the union-management situation, conflict is structural with respect to economics and power.[14] The more money and power for the union, the less for management. On the other hand, conflict, or at least controllable conflict, may be good—that is, cause effective intergroup and intragroup performance. The easiest way to see this is to consider again Sherif's experiments at the boys' camp. The boys were playing tug-of-war and baseball. Interteam rivalry stimulated high levels of intrateam performance. It was only when the rivalry spilled off the playing field into other camp activities—that is, when the conflict was uncontrolled—could one argue that the conflict was dysfunctional. In the union-management situation, Slichter, Healy, and Livernash argued and Freeman and Medoff are trying to show that controlled union-management conflict increases organizational functioning.[15]

The techniques of attitudinal and perceptual restructuring are inappropriate because there is no research evidence that attitude and perceptual change achieved in a training session effects a behavioral change.[16] Note that Sherif intentionally did not use these techniques. Sherif stimulated cooperation by providing superordinate goals. The Robbers' Cave Boys' Camp began to work together to achieve a common goal.

The superordinate goal-setting technique is inappropriate for union-management conflict because, while there are some potential superordinate goals in union-management settings, there are always many goals in conflict. In our situation, the day-to-day issues which were erupting into wildcat strikes were issues of economics and power. Interestingly, it was the joint realization that unless the strikes ended the mine would close which brought the parties together to try to control the conflict, but recognition of this superordinate goal neither eliminated the conflict nor showed the parties how to control it.

One strategy we recommended was process consultation. Bill Ury spent the summer working with both parties to try to improve their interaction pattern. His role was defined more like that of an OD consultant than a mediator in that he did not try to mediate particular issues, but made suggestions to improve the parties' negotiating behaviors when difficult issues arose.

A second change we recommended was in the makeup and responsibilities of the parties. It is only the naive consultant who comes in and says fire person X and your conflict will be resolved. This consultant ignores the possibility that it is forces exerted on X's role, not X himself or herself, which cause the conflict and that X's replacement, Y, will feel the same pressures and behave in the same manner as X. Obvi-

[14] T. Kochan, "Collective Bargaining and Organizational Behavior Research," in *Research in Organizational Behavior*, eds. B. M. Staw and L. L. Cummings (Greenwich, Conn.: JAI Press, 1980).

[15] S. H. Slichter, J. J. Healy, and E. R. Livernash, *The Impact of Collective Bargaining on Management* (Washington: Brookings Institution, 1960); R. B. Freeman and J. L. Medoff, "The Two Faces of Unionism," *The Public Interest* 57 (1979), pp. 69–93. Evolutionary models of social behavior as developed by Donald Campbell and applied to intragroup conflict by Karl Weick, if extended to intergroup conflict, would also argue that conflict is good because conflict preserves the groups' abilities to adapt to their joint environment better than does compromise. D. T. Campbell, "Ethnocentric and Other Altruistic Motives," in *Nebraska Symposium on Motivation*, ed. D. Levine (Lincoln: University of Nebraska Press, 1965), pp. 382–411; Karl Weick, *The Social Psychology of Organizations*, 2d ed. (Reading, Mass.: Addison-Wesley, 1979), pp. 119–43, 220.

[16] J. Campbell and M. Dunnette, "Effectiveness of T-Group Experiences in Managerial Training and Development," *Psychological Bulletin* 70 (1968), pp. 73–103.

ously, too, on the union side, one cannot recommend firing an elected official. We carefully did not recommend that management fire anyone, but that they add a labor relations expert whose role would absorb some, but not all, the labor relations responsibilities at the mine.

It is important to see the difference between adding a role and replacing a role incumbent. When you add a role, the forces exerting pressure on the new role need not be the same as the forces continuing to exert pressure on the old role. While this change strategy effectively altered the membership of one party, it was a change strategy stimulated by our belief that wildcat strikes are stimulated by conditions or forces in the local union-management environment which shape the parties' negotiating behavior. This strategy effectively altered environmental forces on the role which carried major management responsibility for labor relations.

The third change we recommended was a set of procedures designed to increase foremen's incentives to settle grievances. This change strategy was also designed to alter environmental forces, this time on the foreman's role. If this change were effective, it should reduce the amount of conflict moving upward in the system.

Our final recommendation was designed to control conflict that could not be contained within the grievance procedure. The key to controlling conflict that cannot be eliminated is to contain it within normative structures which channel the conflict to its resolution.[17] OD has much less experience than industrial relations with such structures. The collective bargaining system is a normative structure designed to contain the endemic conflict between union and management. We negotiated a new normative structure to channel the conflict at this mine which had previously erupted in wildcat strikes. This structure consisted of a pattern of behaviors to be engaged in by each party, if a strike threatened. This pattern of behaviors was worked out in some detail and cast as a formal written agreement, signed by local union leadership and mine management.

The introduction of a new normative system into a union-management relationship requires more than the agreement of union leadership and management. It requires the concurrence of the union members-employees. Because the union, unlike management, does not have an hierarchical authority system, an agreement between union leadership and management does not insure ratification of that agreement by the union membership.[18] In this situation the union membership failed to ratify the agreement. The reason the membership failed to ratify the agreement and an evaluation of whether or not we, as third parties, could have done more to facilitate its ratification are issues beyond the scope of this paper. I do not think, however, that the failure to ratify in any way diminishes the theoretical soundness of this intervention strategy.

CONCLUSION

In summary, neither mediation nor organizational development provides a complete model for third-party intervention when a union-management relationship is unable to control conflict during the term of the collective bargaining agreement. The third party's goal and diagnostic and intervention techniques are those of a sophisticated and versatile OD consultant. The third party's methods to facilitate in-

[17] P. Brickman, "Role Structures and Conflict Relationships," in *Social Conflict,* ed. P. Brickman (Lexington, Mass.: Heath, 1974).

[18] J. M. Brett, "Behavioral Research on Unions and Union-Management Systems," in *Research in Organizational Behavior,* vol. 2, ed. B. M. Staw and L. L. Cummings (Greenwich, Conn.: JAI Press, 1980), pp. 177–213.

tra- and interparty negotiations are those of mediation. Finally, this mine has not had a strike in the seven months since the interventions.

[For a detailed case analysis of the situation described in this article, see William Ury, *Talkout or Walkout*, Thesis, Harvard University, August 1982.]

11-6

DYNAMICS OF DISPUTE RESOLUTION IN THE PUBLIC SECTOR

Thomas A. Kochan*

INTRODUCTION

The central theme running throughout this chapter's analysis of the dynamics of dispute resolution in the public sector is that the challenges became greater as the majority of states moved through their first decade of experience under collective bargaining statutes. Thus, the transition to the second decade is characterized by (1) political and economic environments that produce disputes of greater intensity and complexity, (2) highly sophisticated bargaining representatives who are able to pursue aggressively the interests of their organizations through the various stages of dispute resolution, and (3) more assertive union members, management negotiators, politicians, and public interest groups. These developments follow the decade of experimentation with numerous dispute-resolution procedures designed to

substitute for the right to strike—procedures so varied and so often changed that by now we have had some experience with most of the commonly discussed alternative systems.

Two important assumptions underlie the analysis: (1) the factors causing collective bargaining impasses are diverse and (2) there is no "one best way" for resolving all types of disputes. Thus, after reviewing the record of the strike and its alternatives during this first decade of bargaining, the chapter will conclude with a description of the options available to policymakers holding different normative premises or assumptions regarding the appropriateness of alternative processes—fact-finding, arbitration, and the strike.

* * * * *

STRIKE ACTIVITY OVER THE FIRST DECADE

The variety of initial and subsequent approaches adapted in response to the pressures for bargaining rights provided an

* Professor, Massachusetts Institute of Technology. Reprinted from B. Aaron, Joseph Grodin, and James L. Stern, *Public Sector Bargaining*, IRRA Series (Washington, D.C.: BNA, 1979), pp. 150–90.

ideal laboratory for experimentation and learning about the performance of collective bargaining under alternative dispute-resolution systems. Throughout the remainder of this chapter, these experiences will be evaluated with the available empirical evidence. Data from the first decade of bargaining will be used to describe the current state of affairs as well as to illustrate the limitations of the research and data that have attempted to take advantage of the laboratory for research and experimentation.

AGGREGATE STRIKE EXPERIENCE, 1960–1976

The aggregate increase in public-sector strike activity between 1960 and 1975 is presented in Table 1. Strike activity accelerated most rapidly between 1966 and 1976. The relatively stable 1960–1966 period represents the final years in the pre-collective-bargaining era for most states. The number of strikes varied over these six years from a low of 28 to a high of 42.[1] In 1966, 132 strikes occurred, and the upward movement continued to a record 428 in 1975. The Bureau of Labor Statistics (BLS) reported that 2.2 percent of all public employees participated in a strike in 1975, a figure equal to the comparable rate for private-sector employees for that year. That year was somewhat atypical, however. In 1976, as in most previous years, all of the measures of strike impact, duration, and percentage of working-time lost ranged between one fourth and one half of the comparable private-sector figures. For example, the average duration of public-sector strikes (measured as average number of days workers were on strike) has been consistently less than half the duration of private-sector strikes. Since 1960, strikes by state employees averaged

5.6 days, and strikes by local employees averaged 7.4 days; the average duration of strikes for workers in all industries was 15.5 days. Similarly, the total percent of work-time lost due to strikes in the public sector remains considerably below the comparable private-sector rate. In 1976, 0.19 percent of total working time in the private sector was lost due to strikes, compared to 0.04 in the government sector. Even in 1975, a high year for governmental strikes, these same figures are 0.16 for the private sector an 0.06 for the government sector.

Ninety-two percent of all governmental strikes occurred at the local level between 1960 and 1975. State employees accounted for 7.5 percent of the strikes; federal employees accounted for only 0.5 percent. Thus, public-sector strikes are predominantly local and state government phenomena.

It is difficult to compare trends in strikes across occupational groups since the BLS only began reporting these data in 1971. The data show that between 1971 and 1975 approximately 55 percent of all strikes took place in public education. Strikes by fire fighters and law enforcement employees accounted for about 7 percent of the total. Sanitation workers accounted for approximately 6 percent, and no other occupation group accounted for more than 5 percent of the total number of strikes.

These aggregate figures tell us little about the performance of collective bargaining in avoiding strikes in the private and public sectors because the number of contract expirations in the public sector in a given year is unknown. The comparisons of the impact and the duration data do suggest, however, that the average public-sector strike is considerably shorter and has less impact than its private-sector counterpart, perhaps indicating that the sanctions against public-sector strikes, the essentiality of the services provided, and/

---

[1] The strike data are taken from the Bureau of Labor Statistics report, "Work Stoppages in Government," various years.

TABLE 1 WORK STOPPAGES BY LEVEL OF GOVERNMENT, 1960–1976

Workers involved and days idle in thousands

YEAR	TOTAL[a]			FEDERAL GOVERNMENT			STATE GOVERNMENT			LOCAL GOVERNMENT[b]		
	NUMBER OF STOPPAGES	WORKERS INVOLVED	DAYS IDLE DURING YEAR	NUMBER OF STOPPAGES	WORKERS INVOLVED	DAYS IDLE DURING YEAR	NUMBER OF STOPPAGES	WORKERS INVOLVED	DAYS IDLE DURING YEAR	NUMBER OF STOPPAGES	WORKERS INVOLVED	DAYS IDLE DURING YEAR
1960	36	28.6	58.4	—	—	—	3	1.0	1.2	33	27.6	67.7
1961	28	6.6	15.3						—	28	6.6	15.3
1962	28	31.1	79.1	5	4.2	33.8	2	1.7	2.3	21	25.3	43.1
1963	29	4.8	15.4	—	—	—	2	.3	2.2	27	4.6	67.7
1964	41	22.7	70.8	—	—	—	4	.3	3.2	37	22.5	57.7
1965	42	11.9	146.0	—	—	—		—	1.9[d]	42	11.9	145.0
1966	142	105.0	455.0	—	—	—	9	3.1	6.0	133	102.0	449.0
1967	181	132.0	1250.0	—	—	—	12	4.7	16.3	169	127.0	1230.0
1968	254	201.8	2545.2	3	1.7	9.6	16	9.3	42.8	235	190.9	2492.8
1969	411	160.0	745.7	2	.6	1.1	37	20.5	152.4	372	139.0	592.2
1970	412	333.5	2023.2	3	155.8	648.3	23	8.8	44.6	386	168.9	1330.5
1971	329	152.6	901.4	2	1.0	8.1	23	14.5	81.8	304	137.1	811.6
1972	375	142.1	1257.3	—	—	—	40	27.4	273.7	335	114.7	983.5
1973	387	196.4	2303.9	1	.5	4.6	29	12.3	133.0	357	183.7	2166.3
1974	384	160.7	1404.2	2	.5	1.4	34	24.7	86.4	348	135.4	1316.3
1975	478	318.5	2204.4				32	66.6	300.5	446	252.0	1903.9
1976	378	180.7	1690.7	1	—[c]	—[c]	25	33.8	148.2	352	146.8	1542.6

SOURCE: Bureau of Labor Statistics, Work Stoppages in Government 1975, Rep. No. 483, Table 1. 1976 data are preliminary.

Note: Because of rounding, sums of individual items may not equal totals.

[a] The Bureau of Labor Statistics has published data on strikes in government in its annual reports since 1942. Before that year, they had been included in a miscellaneous category—other nonmanufacturing industries. From 1942 through 1957, data refer only to strikes in administrative, protective, and sanitary services of government. Stoppages in establishments owned by governments were classified in their appropriate industry; for example, public schools and libraries were included in education services, not in government. Beginning in 1958, stoppages in such establishments were included under the government classifications. Stoppages in publicly owned utilities, transportation, and schools were reclassified back to 1947, but a complete reclassification was not attempted. After 1957, dashes denote zeros.

[b] Includes all stoppages at the county, city, and special-district levels.

[c] Fewer than 100.

[d] Idleness in 1965 resulted from two stoppages that began in 1964.

or the intense public and legal pressure brought to bear on striking workers and management have limited the duration and impact of strikes. The effects are similar to those of strike controls employed by the War Labor Board during World War II.[2] Whether the strike bans and procedures reduce the frequency of strikes cannot be determined from these aggregate data. To deal with this question we must turn to more disaggregated comparisons across policy alternatives within the public sector.

POLICY OPTIONS AND STRIKE FREQUENCY

A number of studies have attempted to examine the incidence of strikes for specific occupational groups in the public sector. Two central questions underlie all of these analyses: (1) Has the passage of collective bargaining laws increased or decreased the rate of strike activity? (2) How effective are alternative dispute-resolution procedures in deterring strikes? Before the impact of public-policy variables on strike activity can be estimated, it is necessary to control for differences in state and local economic and political environments, for the degree of public-sector unionization, and for other nonpolicy-related causes of strikes. After controlling for the environmental and unionization context of local governments, Burton and Krider found a "mild tendency" for 1968 and 1971 strike activity to be higher in states with laws requiring or permitting bargaining or establishing meet-and-confer procedures.[3] They also found that strikes were just as fre-

quent in states where bargaining was illegal. They concluded, therefore, that while statutes providing the right to bargain collectively or meet and confer perhaps have a "mild tendency to encourage strikes," laws that prohibit bargaining have little power to reduce the rate of strikes. Furthermore, their analysis showed no significant consistent effect for strike penalties or for policies providing fact-finding or mediation. Again, there was some evidence that a statutory provision for mediation or fact-finding tended to increase the rate of strike activity.

* * * * *

PERFORMANCE OF DISPUTE-RESOLUTION PROCEDURES

Since impasse procedures are designed to avoid strikes, the central criterion for evaluating their effectiveness revolves around . . . their relative effectiveness in deterring strike activity. In addition, however, the collective bargaining system in the United States has historically placed a premium on the process of "free" collective bargaining. That is, there is a deeply shared ethos among scholars, policymakers, and practitioners that values the ability of the parties to settle their own disputes without the intervention of an outside third party. Thus, one of the central objectives of any dispute-resolution procedure is to minimize the dependence of the parties on impasse procedures.[4] But some observers fear that the absence of an effective strike threat reduces the motivation to bargain and ultimately results in a process in which the parties become overdependent on the alternative procedures. This has been discussed in the litrature as the

---

[2] Herbert R. Northrup, *Compulsory Arbitration and Government Intervention in Labor Disputes* (Washington: Labor Policy Association, 1966), 21.

[3] John F. Burton, Jr., and Charles E. Krider, *The Incidence of Strikes in Public Employment,* in Labor in the Public and Nonprofit Sectors, ed. Daniel S. Hamermesh (Princeton, N.J.: Princeton University Press, 1975), 161–70.

[4] See, for example, the statement of the Taylor committee on this issue in Final Report, *supra* note 8, at 33.

"chilling" or the "narcotic" effects.[5] To the extent that these two problems occur in the bargaining system, we would expect over time to find (1) an increase in reliance on the procedures and (2) less meaningful bargaining taking place prior to the intervention of third parties.

The same problems exist in evaluating the impact of impasse procedures on the bargaining process as were present in attempting to make aggregate comparisons of strike activity across different types of laws and procedures. The absence of adequate controls for other factors affecting the use of impasse procedures limits the conclusiveness of most analyses. A number of studies of experiences in specific jurisdictions or states can be used, however, to reach a number of tentative conclusions regarding the performance of these alternatives over the first decade of bargaining.

DEPENDENCE ON PROCEDURES: A NARCOTIC EFFECT?

There are at least two points in the sequence of impasse-resolution efforts that are often used for comparing the degree of dependence on the procedures. The first point is the rate of initial impasses filed. Most impasse procedures start with an effort at mediation. This point of the procedure is analogous to the rate of reliance on mediation in the private sector. The second point is the percentage of negotia-

tions that require issuance of either a fact-finding report or an arbitration award.

Since the majority of jurisdictions outlaw the right to strike, it is not surprising that the rate of impasses is higher than the rate of reliance on mediation in the private sector. Similarly, the rates of going to either fact-finding or arbitration appear to be higher than the average rate of strikes in private-sector bargaining. For example, the Federal Mediation and Conciliation Service (FMCS) annual reports for the years 1967 through 1976 show that between 8 and 10 percent of all 30-day notifications of a contract expiration require a formal meeting with a mediator. Approximately 15 to 20 percent of the contracts in the private-sector covered by FMCS require either a formal mediation meeting or informal discussions with the parties over the telephone.[6] Of the 30-day notifications, only between 2 and 3 percent of the negotiations end up in a strike.[7]

Although the rates of initial impasses and the use of fact-finding and arbitration in the public sector vary widely, every study examined for this chapter shows a higher rate of intervention than do private-sector data. Consequently, the relevant question becomes not *whether* the absence of the right to strike will lead to greater intervention by third parties, but rather the *magnitude* of the difference that is associated with alternative forms of dispute-resolution procedures.

In a comparison of the rate of reliance on fact-finding versus arbitration in fire fighter cases during the 1971–1972 time period, Wheeler found that fact-finding was initiated 21.5 percent of the time. Arbitration was initiated in 37.3 percent of the cases operating under a conventional-arbitration statute. Similarly, 12.0 percent

---

[5] For a discussion, see Hoyt N. Wheeler, *Compulsory Arbitration: A Narcotic Effect*, 14 Ind. Rels. 117 (February 1975); Peter Feuille, *Final Offer Arbitration and the Chilling Effect*, 14 Ind. Rels. 302 (October 1975); Anderson and Kochan, "Impasse Procedures in The Canadian Federal Service: Effects on the Bargaining Process," *Ind. and L. Rels. Rev.*, April 1977, pp. 283–301; or Thomas A. Kochan, Mordehai Mironi, Ronald G. Ehrenberg, Jean Baderschneider, and Todd Jick, *Dispute Resolution under Factfindng and Arbitration: An Empirical Analysis* (New York: American Arbitration Association, 1978).

[6] Annual Reports of the Federal Mediation and Conciliation Service, 1967–1976.

[7] Ibid.

of the cases under fact-finding required a report, compared to 26.8 percent of the cases under arbitration that required an award.[8] (No final-offer-arbitration statutes were in effect during the period covered by this study.)

Feuille's study reviewed the performance of conventional arbitration and final-offer-arbitration procedures in a number of different settings.[9] No consistent difference was found in the percentage of cases initiating these different procedures; however, a lower percentage of arbitration awards was issued under the final-offer than under the conventional-arbitration procedures. Specifically, the median percentage of cases ending in an arbitration award under the 11 different conventional-arbitration statutes was 25 percent. The range varied from a low of 14 percent to a high of an estimated 40–50 percent. The median for the four final-offer statutes analyzed was between 10 and 12 percent, with a range from a low of 6 percent to a high of 33 percent.[10]

In a recent study, the impasse histories of police and fire fighters in New York State were compared with those of police and fire fighters in Wisconsin and Massachusetts.[11] The Wisconsin–New York comparisons provide the most complete information and the most instructive findings. Wisconsin had fact-finding as its basic impasse procedure for police and fire fighters until 1972 when the law was changed to final-offer arbitration on the total package. New York had fact-finding until 1974 when it changed to conventional arbitration. The results showed that (1) Wisconsin police and fire fighters went to impasse and received fact-finding reports in a far smaller percentage of cases

between 1968 and 1972 (6 percent compared to 26 percent) than did their counterparts in New York, and (2) both Wisconsin and New York experienced increases in impasses and in the number of cases going to the final step of their procedures after they changed to their respective forms of arbitration. For example, in Wisconsin during the first two years of the final-offer procedure, aproximately 34 percent of the negotiations went to impasse and approximately 10 percent were resolved by an arbitration award. These percentages increased in the second two years (1974–1976) under final-offer arbitration to an impasse rate of between 48 and 55 percent and an arbitration rate of between 12.7 and 14.6 percent of all negotiations. In contrast, after the arbitration amendments were passed in New York, approximately 76 percent of police negotiations and 53 percent of fire fighter negotiations went to impasse, while 32 percent of the police negotiations ended in an arbitration award compared to 26 percent of the fire fighter negotiations. Analysis of these data showed that both states experienced comparable increases in the number of impasses and of cases going to the final step of the procedures. Thus, even though large differences in the rate of impasses and arbitration awards exist across these two states, the differences appear to be due to something other than the difference between final-offer and coventional arbitration.

A similar effect appeared to occur as the Massachusetts police and fire fighter procedures changed from fact-finding to final-offer arbitration in 1974. Like Wisconsin and New York, Massachusetts experienced an increase in the percentage of cases going to an impasse after the change in the statute. A study by Somers showed that in the last year under fact-finding, an estimated 29.5 percent of police and fire negotiations reached an impasse, compared to 42.4 percent of negotiations during the

---

[8] Wheeler, *Compulsory Arbitration.*

[9] Feuille, *Final Offer Arbitration.*

[10] Ibid., p. 306.

[11] Kochan et al., *Dispute Resolution under Fact-finding.*

first year under the arbitration statute. Only 8.6 percent of all negotiations under the final-offer procedure required the issuance of an arbitration award.[12] Thus, here again final-offer arbitration did not appear to reduce the rate of initial impasses, but was more successful than conventional arbitration in achieving settlements prior to the imposition of an award.

In addition to the general increase in impasse rates over time, analysis of the New York data showed evidence of a narcotic effect. That is, those units that went to impasse in the first round had a higher probability than others of being repeat-users in the second and third rounds of bargaining. Thus, a pattern of repeated usage was clearly developing over time in this system. Similar analyses of bargaining histories of teachers in New York State and of federal employees in Canada have found repeated use of the procedures by the same units over successive rounds of bargaining.[13] Thus, at least three studies that have tracked the history of the same units over several rounds of bargaining have identified somewhat of a narcotic effect building up within the dispute-resolution systems over time.

The one characteristic that is most often found to be positively associated with dependence on impasse procedures is the size of the jurisdiction.[14] In their three-state study of final-offer arbitration, Stern et al. reported higher rates of impasse usage in the larger cities in all of the states.[15] In Michigan, for example, it was reported that while cities under 10,000 population make up 28 percent of all cities negotiating, they have received only 13 percent of all arbitration awards. On the other hand, the 7 percent of cities with more than 100,000 population have received 23 percent of all awards.[16] In Wisconsin, it was reported that the small rural municipalities were less dependent on the intervention of third parties than were either the larger cities or the suburban areas surrounding Milwaukee.[17]

The evidence of the repeated dependence on third-party intervention in the larger jurisdictions in New York State is even more striking. The five largest cities in the state (excluding New York City), that is, Buffalo, Yonkers, Rochester, Syracuse, and Albany, have reached an impasse with their police and fire fighters in about 90 percent of their negotiations between 1968 and 1976,[18] and have resorted to factfinding and beyond in more than 70 percent of all negotiations. Buffalo, the largest city and the one with the most severe financial problems and the most politicized bargaining environment, has gone to factfinding or beyond (or arbitration after the change in the law in 1974) with both police and fire fighters in *each* of the five times it negotiated with these groups during this time period. The record of the city with teachers and other occupational groups is similarly bleak. Over these years, sickouts, threatened slowdowns, court challenges of arbitration awards, and improper-practice charges have been common characteristics of bargaining in Buffalo.

While the systematic data from large cities in other states are not available, it

[12] Paul Somers, *An Evaluation of Final-Offer Arbitration in Massachusetts,* 6 J. Coll. Negotiations in the Pub. Sector 193 (1977).

[13] John E. Drotning and David B. Lipsky, *The Relations Between Teacher Salaries and the Use of Impasse Procedures Under New York's Taylor Law: 1968-1972,* 6 J. Coll. Negotiations in the Pub. Sector 229 (1977); Anderson and Kochan, "Impasse Procedures in the Canadian Federal Services."

[14] This is consistent with other studies that show size to be positively associated with other measures of industrial conflict. See, for example, Sherill Cleland, The Influence of Plant Size on Industrial Relations (Princeton, N.J.: Industrial Relations Section, Princeton University, 1955), 53.

[15] Stern et al., *supra* note 26.

[16] Ibid., pp. 52–53.

[17] Ibid., p. 95.

[18] These results are summarized in Kochan et al., *Dispute Resolution under Factfinding.*

is quite clear that cities such as Detroit, Milwaukee, Pittsburgh, Philadelphia,[19] San Francisco, and Boston as well as other major metropolitan centers have also been frequent users of impasse procedures. Clearly, these large cities have proven to be tough environments to instill effective bargaining without reliance on impasse procedures or the threat of a strike. These jurisdictions have more of the political, organizational, interpersonal, and personal characteristics that cause impasses— unions are more militant and willing to use political pressure and job actions, management is more politicized and subject to internal disputes and power struggles, negotiators are more experienced and skillful in utilizing pressure to achieve their goals in bargaining, and, finally, most of these cities have been experiencing severe financial difficulties in recent years.[20]

A number of very tentative conclusions can be drawn from the above analyses regarding the reliance on impasse procedures during the first decade of public-sector bargaining. First, a higher percentage of cases have reached impasses under both conventional and final-offer arbitration than under fact-finding procedures. It should be noted, however, that all of the states examined experienced an increase in the rate of cases going to impasse over time. Consequently, our comparisons of fact-finding with final-offer and conventional arbitration are confounded with time. To the extent that the increasing reliance on procedures is a function of time rather than a function of a change in the law, these comparisons overstate the differences between the two procedures. Second, no significant differences in the number of initial impasses were found in cases where final-offer arbitration was compared to conventional arbitration. However, fewer cases resulted in an arbitration award under final-offer arbitration than under conventional arbitration. Third, a narcotic effect has been observed in a number of jurisdictions operating under both fact-finding and arbitration. Fourth, large jurisdictions tend to rely heavily on whatever dispute-resolution procedure is available.

The Chilling Effect

Most theories of the bargaining process suggest that hard bargaining or movement will occur when the costs of continuing the dispute exceed the costs of making a compromise or a concession to settle the dispute.[21] In short, the parties are expected to make significant compromises toward an agreement only when under pressure to do so. This explains why most intensive bargaining appears to occur in the final days or hours prior to a strike deadline. In the public sector where the strike is constrained, we should expect it to be even more difficult to get hard bargaining in negotiations prior to an initial impasse. To the extent that multiple steps are built into the impasse procedures that proceed from milder to stronger forms of intervention (e.g., mediation followed by fact-finding and/or arbitration), the "final hour" or moment of truth is even farther removed from the initial bargaining process. Thus, while policymakers hope that the existence of impasse procedures will not "chill" bargaining, our theories of bargaining suggest that this is exactly what should happen.

A number of studies have attempted

---

[19] A recent study reported that the City of Philadelphia has gone to arbitration in each of its seven rounds of negotiations with its police and fire fighter bargaining units between 1970 and 1977. See Philadelphia's Experience Under the Pennsylvania Police and Fire Arbitration Law (Philadelphia: Pennsylvania Economy League, 1977).

[20] Kochan et al., *Dispute Resolution under Fact-finding.*

---

[21] See, for example, Neil W. Chamberlain and James W. Kuhn, *Collective Bargaining,* 3d ed. (New York: McGraw-Hill, 1965) pp. 171–73.

to assess the amount of hard bargaining or movement that takes place prior to impasses. Some of the early studies of this issue provided reasonably optimistic findings.[22] More recently, studies of the actual movement or compromising behavior have reported greater evidence of a chilling effect in negotiations. For example, a comparison of fact-finding in Wisconsin and New York in 1972 revealed that 80 percent of the parties rated bargaining prior to fact-finding as either slight or nonexistent,[23] and a multivariate study of fire fighter bargaining found a number of cases in which no movement off the initial positions took place prior to an impasse.[24] Similar results were obtained in an analysis of police and fire fighter bargaining in New York State: unions and employers held back concessions from their resistance points or bottom-line positions, and the parties reported that no or very little movement occurred prior to impasse under both fact-finding and arbitration statutes.[25] Even more disconcerting was the disclosure that less movement (and a higher probability of impasse) occurred in negotiations involving more experienced negotiators.

Thus, there is at least some direct evidence that as the parties gained more experience with bargaining, they became *less* willing to engage in meaningful negotiations prior to impasse. While these findings may not be generalizable to all of the public sector, they do suggest that the chilling phenomenon has become a significant problem in these jurisdictions. Furthermore, the studies reviewed above suggest that the chilling effect may have become more serious in the latter half of the first decade of bargaining, after the parties became more experienced with negotiating under dispute-resolution procedures.

DYNAMICS OF MEDIATION, FACT-FINDING, AND ARBITRATION

In this section some of the dynamics of the three major procedural mechanisms used to resolve public-sector impasses—mediation, fact-finding, and compulsory arbitration—will be described. The theories underlying each procedure will first be outlined in order to identify the expectations that scholars and policymakers had for each technique when they were first proposed, debated, and implemented. Then the performance of each technique in the public sector will be reviewed in order to illustrate the extent to which these a priori expectations were fulfilled in practice. Emphasis will be placed on the ways in which these procedures were modified and adapted over time to fit different situations and jurisdictions.

THE MEDIATION PROCESS

Mediation is perhaps the most widely used and least understood dispute-resolution procedure in collective bargaining. It is the first form of intervention in most disputes in both the private and public sectors. Yet there are few empirical studies of the mediation process. The few theoretical statements that can be drawn from studies of the private-sector mediation process suggest that mediation can be most successful when (1) the negotiations cycle has progressed to the point where the parties are under the greatest pressure to settle; (2)

---

[22] See, for example, James L. Stern, Edward B. Krinsky, and Jeffrey B. Tener, *Factfinding Under Wisconsin Law, 1966* (Madison: University of Wisconsin Extension, 1966); or Byron Yaffe and Howard Goldblatt, *Factfinding in New York State Public Employment: More Promise Than Illusion* (Ithaca: New York State School of Industrial and Labor Relations, Cornell University, 1971).

[23] William Word, *Factfinding in Public Employee Negotiations,* 95 Monthly Lab. Rev. 6 (February 1972).

[24] Hoyt N. Wheeler, *How Compulsory Arbitration Affects Compromise Activity* 17 Ind. Rels. 80 (February 1978).

[25] Kochan et al., *Dispute Resolution under Factfinding.*

the mediator is acceptable to and trusted by the parties; (3) the real bottom-line positions of the parties either overlap or are not far apart; and (4) the obstacles to a settlement reflect a breakdown in the communication process more than a real substantive difference on the economic or political issues involved.[26] The application of mediation as the initial step in impasse procedures in the public sector raises an additional important policy question: How effective is mediation when followed by fact-finding, conventional arbitration, final-offer arbitration, the right to strike, or some other form of dispute resolution?

The above hypotheses were formalized into a model of the mediation process and tested using the New York police and fire fighter sample.[27] Specifically, the effectiveness of mediation under fact-finding and conventional arbitration was compared, controlling for the effects of (1) different sources of impasse, (2) characteristics of the mediator, and (3) the strategies employed by the mediator. The sample was drawn from the last round of negotiations by police and fire fighters under New York State's fact-finding statute and the first round of bargaining under conventional arbitration. Approximately 30 percent of the impasses that went to mediation were resolved at this stage prior to passing the dispute on to the next stage of the procedure. After controlling for the other factors outlined above, it was estimated that the change in the law from fact-finding to arbitration increased the effectiveness of mediation, or the probability of settlement, between 13 and 18 percent. That is, there was a marginal increase in the number of settlements achieved under the arbitration statute as compared to what would have been expected had fact-finding remained in effect. This marginal increase, however, was limited to small jurisdictions that were experiencing a catch-up effect in their wage settlements. Management negotiators in these jurisdictions, because they recognized that arbitration would very likely impose a relatively high wage settlement, were under pressure to avoid it, and the mediators recognized that they could use the threat of arbitration to induce the management negotiators to make significant movement. Thus, the estimates of the effect of the change in the law probably suggest more about the impact of the threat of going to a procedure in which one party will be at a severe disadvantage than they imply about the inherent differences between mediation under fact-finding and under conventional arbitration.

The net effects of the change in the law were less important than the effects of some of the control variables examined. Specifically, the mediation process at this initial stage of the impasse procedure was *most* effective in resolving impasses where (1) the negotiators—especially the union negotiators—lacked experience; (2) the negotiations process broke down because one of the parties was overcommitted to a particular position; (3) a dispute was below average in intensity or difficulty, that is, the magnitude and number of sources of impasse were relatively small; (4) the parties were motivated to reach a settlement, and (5) an aggressive, experienced, and high-quality (as perceived by the parties) mediator was involved. On the other hand, mediation was *least* successful in situations (1) where the underlying dispute arose because of an employer's inability to pay; (2) where the parties had a history of going to impasse and to the later stages of the dispute-resolution procedure;

[26] See Carl M. Stevens, "Mediation and the Role of the Neutral," in *Frontiers of Collective Bargaining*, ed. John T. Dunlop and Neil W. Chamberlain (New York: Harper & Row, 1967), pp. 271–90. See also Carl M. Stevens, *Strategy and Collective Bargaining Negotiations* (New York: McGraw-Hill, 1963), pp. 122–46; and Kenneth Kressel, *Labor Mediation: Exploratory Survey* (Albany, N.Y.: Association of Labor Mediation Agencies, 1972).

[27] Kochan et al., *Dispute Resolution under Fact-finding*.

and (3) where the jurisdiction was among the largest. Some of the larger jurisdictions chose to skip the mediation process entirely since it was clear that any effort to resolve the dispute through mediation at the early stage of the impasse procedure was futile.

Other studies of the mediation process in the public sector have shown higher rates of settlement through mediation in the earlier stages of bargaining. For example, the early experience in Wisconsin under fact-finding was that more than 50 percent of the disputes were resolved through mediation. Under Wisconsin's final-offer statute, 70 percent of the cases going to mediation between 1973 and 1976 were settled at this step.[28] According to statistics published by the New York State Public Employment Relations Board, from 30 to 42 percent of all mediation cases involving teachers were settled at this initial stage of the procedure between 1968 and 1972. Furthermore, the same source reports that from 42 to 57 percent of all PERB cases were settled at the mediation stage over these five years. The data show a small drop in the percentage of cases settled by mediation in the later years and again reflect the tendency for the parties to go further into the procedures in this more recent time period.[29]

A group of mediators discussing the relative effectiveness of mediation under fact finding, conventional arbitration, and final-offer arbitration indicated that, in general, mediation appears to be more meaningful under final-offer arbitration than under either of the other alternatives. This perception is consistent with the finding noted above that the percentage of cases going on to an award under final-offer arbitration in Massachusetts, Wisconsin, and Michigan were all less than the percentage of cases going to conventional arbitration in New York State. Thus, there does appear to be a stronger incentive effect associated with mediation under final-offer than under conventional arbitration. This effect is weakened, however, the farther the mediation process is removed from the arbitration step of the procedure (e.g., compare mediation in Wisconsin where arbitration follows immediately with mediation in Massachusetts where fact-finding follows mediation before final-offer arbitration).[30] It is further weakened when mediation is an expected part of the arbitration process (e.g., compare Wisconsin and Massachusetts where few disputes are mediated at the arbitration stage with Michigan where mediation in arbitration settled 64 percent of arbitration cases in 1973 and 1974).[31]

It was reported that the conferees also felt that mediation was more effective under conventional arbitration than under fact-finding. This was contrary to the view of the Michigan mediators interviewed as part of that study. There it was reported that the parties felt that some of the life had gone out of mediation under arbitration that had been present in earlier years under fact-finding.[32]

As noted above, it would be a mistake to assume that mediation in the public sector takes place only at the initial stages of the impasse-resolution procedure. On the contrary, over time the distinctions between mediation, fact-finding, and arbitration have become blurred in the sense that mediation is often employed during, and sometimes even after, the fact-finding and arbitration processes have become initiated. A number of people have debated the wisdom and appropriateness of mixing the fact-finding and mediation processes or the mediation and arbitration pro-

---

[28] Ibid., Ch. 3.

[29] Annual Reports of the New York State Public Employment Relations Board, 1975.

[30] James L. Stern et al., *Final-Offer Arbitration* (Lexington, Mass., D. C. Heath, 1975), p. 32.

[31] Ibid., p. 54.

[32] Ibid., pp. 62–63.

cesses.[33] Some have argued that if we want to preserve the integrity of fact-finding and arbitration and provide a greater incentive to settle in mediation prior to going to these procedures, mediation should be discouraged or prohibited once these more formal impasse procedures are invoked. This position was adopted as the official policy of the Michigan Employment Relations Commission in the early years of bargaining in that state. Studies in Michigan, however, have shown that despite the official policy, fact-finders mediated in the majority of disputes.[34] In New York, the distinction between mediation and fact-finding not only has become blurred in practice, but has become institutionalized by a change in the way in which neutrals are assigned to cases. New York State's PERB no longer assigns a mediator at the first stage of the impasse procedure; instead a fact-finder is assigned under the assumption that he or she will attempt to mediate the dispute prior to conductng a formal hearing. Thus one additional step at which mediation traditionally occurs is eliminated, thereby not only saving time and money but also reducing the parties' incentive to delay and hold back concessions. The disadvantage of combining the two procedures is that the parties may hold back information from the mediator because they fear it will jeopardize their positions if the dispute goes to fact-finding. The more the parties hold back information and fail to put their strongest effort forward in mediation, the less likely the dispute will be settled prior to the fact-finding hearing. Although there has been considerable debate over whether media-

tion is more effective under this type of an arrangement or where the mediator will not be the fact-finder, there is little systematic evidence one way or the other.

In some cases mediation occurs after fact-finding. Again, in the State of New York it has become common for the parties to request and require postfact-finding mediation, or what has been labeled "super-conciliation." The term itself illustrates the difference between mediation at the initial stage of impasse and at the later stage of the negotiations where the process involves a much more aggressive intervention strategy by the neutral. In superconciliation the parties are at the final stage of bargaining and are faced with the threat of arbitration, a legislative hearing, a strike, or simply continued impasse. There is less room for delaying or holding back concessions because there is no next step in the procedure. Thus, the mediator can exert pressure on the parties to face reality, make concessions, or change their expectations.

Finally, there is "med-arb," a term that has been popularized as the public-sector bargaining process has evolved.[35] As the term implies, mediation occurs in the arbitration process itself—especially in tripartite arbitration. Some neutrals have argued for procedures in which the mediator serves as the arbitrator if the parties fail to reach an agreement through his mediation efforts. While we have few examples of this option built into the statutory impasse procedures (Wisconsin's new law provides for it), the strategy is widely used by arbitrators on an ad hoc basis. The dynamics of this process will be discussed in a later section.

THE FACT-FINDING PROCESS

Every discussion of fact-finding in the public sector has noted that the term is a mis-

---

[33] For a review of these debates, see Ralph T. Jones, *Public Sector Labor Relations: An Evaluation of Policy Related Research* (Belmont, Mass.: Contract Research Corp., 1975), pp. 162–67.

[34] Jack Stieber and Benjamin Wolkinson, *Fact-Finding Viewed by Factfinders: The Michigan Experience* (Paper presented to the 1975 meetings of the Society of Professionals in Dispute Resolution, 4).

[35] Sam Kagel and John Kagel, *Using Two New Arbitration Techniques,* 95 Monthly Lab. Rev. 11 (November 1972).

nomer. The fact-finding process involves more than the searching-out of the factual basis of the parties' positions; it also involves an effort to identify an acceptable compromise settlement. Most studies have found that fact-finders tend to give the greatest weight to some variant of comparability. The criteria of ability to pay, cost of living, interest and welfare of the public, and "good" labor relations practice tend to follow in mixed order as secondary factors.[36] Underlying the application of these criteria, however, is a search for an acceptable compromise. Thus, the effort to frame a recommendation that the parties will accept or use as the basis for negotiating an agreement captures the heart of the fact-finding process in the public sector. In a sense, when applied in this fashion, fact-finding is little more than mediation with written recommendations.

In a review of the early experience of bargaining under fact-finding, McKelvey found that most initial assessments of this process were quite favorable. She questioned, however, whether these early successes would prove illusory as the parties became more experienced and accustomed to bargaining under this procedure. In short, she feared that the fact-finding process would become less effective over time.[37]

Although the majority of states that have enacted bargaining legislation still have fact-finding as an important part of their impasse procedures for nonuniformed services, the bulk of the evidence suggests that its effectiveness, both in avoiding strikes and in achieving settle-

ments, has atrophied over time. For example, Gatewood's study of fact-finding in teacher disputes in Wisconsin found that of the 44 teachers' strikes between 1968 and 1974, only 11 were preceded by fact-finding, and in only two of 18 teacher strikes in 1974 was fact-finding used before the teachers turned to the strike as a tactic for reaching an agreement.[38] The data in the Gatewood study also documented an increased rate of rejection of fact-finding reports over time. The deterioration of the efficacy of the process was part of the motivation underlying Wisconsin's adoption of final-offer arbitration for fire fighters and police in 1972 and, more recently, of the final-offer/strike option for other state employees.[39] The move to arbitration in Wisconsin along with the adoption of arbitration for police and fire fighters in other states that had fact-finding procedures in the early years of bargaining provides perhaps the strongest evidence that the half-life of the fact-finding procedure in the public sector has been rather short.

Yet approximately half of the states with arbitration statutes covering police and fire fighters have kept fact-finding as an intermediate stage in their procedures. The question arises, therefore, what role does fact-finding play in an arbitration statute? Does it serve as an effective intermediate step with a unique function, or does arbitration simply become an instant replay of the fact-finding process? In New York State between 1974 and 1976, approximately 20 percent of the police and fire fighter cases that went to fact-finding were resolved at that stage.[40] For those cases that were not resolved, however,

[36] Howard S. Block, *Criteria in Public Sector Interest Disputes,* in Arbitration and the Public Interest, Proceedings of the 24th Annual Meeting, National Academy of Arbitrators (Washington: BNA Books, 1971), 165; or Richard Pegnetter, *Fact-Finding and the Teacher Salary Disputes: The 1969 Experience in New York State,* 24 Ind. & Lab. Rels. Rev. 165 (January 1971).

[37] Jean T. McKelvey, *Factfinding: Promise or Illusion,* 22 Ind. & Lab. Rels. Rev. 543 (July 1969).

[38] Lucian Gatewood, *Factfinding in Teacher Disputes: The Wisconsin Experience,* 97 Monthly Lab. Rev. 47 (October 1974).

[39] See "Report of the Wisconsin Study Commission on Public Employee Labor Relations" (Madison, Wis.: Legislative Reference Bureau, 1976).

[40] Kochan et al., *Dispute Resolution under Factfinding.*

the arbitration awards tended to follow the fact-finders' recommendations very closely. In 70 percent of the cases examined, the salary award was identical to the fact-finder's recommendation; where there were differences, the magnitude was relatively small. The major reasons indicated by arbitrators for deviating from a fact-finder's recommendation were that economic conditions had changed since the recommendation was issued, new information on comparable settlements was available to the arbitrator, or the parties found the fact-finder's recommendation to be unacceptable and therefore some modifications were necessary in order to increase the acceptability of the arbitration award.

The New York State PERB attempted to have the arbitrators use a "show cause" approach to the arbitration hearing, that is, they wanted the parties to identify what was wrong with the fact-finder's report. However, the parties objected to this approach and demanded the right to present their cases *de novo*. Yet in the executive sessions of tripartite arbitration panels, most of the arbitrators adopted a show-cause approach as a means of trying to either negotiate a settlement or resolve the disputed issues around the fact-finder's recommendations. Many of them were somewhat uncomfortable with having to second-guess the recommendations of another neutral, recognizing that in some future case *they* might be the fact-finder and someone else serving as an arbitrator might be second-guessing their opinions.

Thus, in New York State arbitration did look very much like an instant replay of fact-finding. Presumably, if the show-cause approach to arbitration following fact-finding could be effectively implemented, the role of fact-finding under an arbitration statute could be strengthened and improved. Fact-finding followed by final-offer arbitration might be still another way to strengthen its role in an interest-arbitration system. While the disadvantages of fact-finding in the New York procedure

were found to outweigh its contributions to the dispute-resolution system, there may be ways of designing an important role for this procedure under alternative arbitration schemes.

THE ARBITRATION PROCESS

One of the major questions facing designers of arbitration procedures centers on the pros and cons of tripartite versus single-arbitrator systems. Advocates of tripartite arbitration argue that it allows the parties greater control over the outcomes of the award, reduces the risk of obtaining an unworkable award, facilitates mediation in arbitration, and increases the commitment of the parties to the award. Opponents argue, on the other hand, that the public interest may be compromised by the involvement of the parties, bargaining and mediation in the earlier stages of the procedures will be less vigorous because mediation is available again, and the procedure is more time-consuming and cumbersome.

There is clear evidence that tripartite arbitration does become an extension of bargaining and mediation. Approximately 60 percent of all arbitration awards issued in the first two years under the New York statute were unanimous.[41] Furthermore, interviews with the parties to these arbitration panels clearly documented the heavy emphasis on negotiation and mediation in the executive sessions. The same has been true in tripartite arbitration under the Michigan final-offer statute since a high proportion of cases are settled in arbitration prior to an award. Thus, the med-arb process is a prominent component of tripartite arbitration structures in the public sector.

The pressure for negotiation in mediation and arbitration sessions is most evident in the larger jurisdictions when the economic and political stakes in the outcomes of the awards are the greatest and

---

[41] Ibid., ch. 8.

where the parties are militant enough to pose a threat to the "finality" of an award through strikes, refusals to implement the award, or court appeals. The 1976–1977 dispute between New York City and its police officers is a case in point. There the central issues were wages and a management proposal to change the number of hours worked and the deployment of personnel in patrol cars. The dispute went through several job actions, strike threats, mediation efforts, written mediation recommendations, court appeals, and an impasse-panel recommendation; ultimately it was placed before an arbitrator. After the arbitration award was written but before it was made public, the arbitrator gave the parties one more opportunity to negotiate a settlement. At this final stage, the parties were successful in reaching a negotiated accommodation. This case is instructive for a number of reasons. First, it shows that where the issues are complex, the stakes high, and the parties militant, negotiations continue through every stage of the impasse-resolution process. Second, it suggests that when the dispute involves a major change in operating procedures, arbitrators are reluctant to impose their own solutions. Third, it also illustrates the need to fashion an acceptable award when one (or both) of the parties is militant enough or seriously threaten to overturn or ignore the award. Fourth, it suggests the difficulty of adopting a "judicial" approach to complex interest disputes. There simply is no one best answer to these types of complex problems, nor is it very easy to identify what the "public interest" would dictate as the outcome of this type of dispute.[42]

A number of studies have examined how arbitrators use statutory criteria in framing an award. The most common finding is that comparability is used rather ex-

tensively, with cost of living or ability to pay taking top priority only in unusual circumstances.[43] As in fact-finding, however, the criteria are not applied in any consistent fashion. Instead of serving as uniform standards, these and other criteria, such as general labor relations practices, and interests and welfare of the public, appear to be used as general guides that are considered and applied on a case-by-case basis and used by the parties to rationalize their positions in arbitration. These findings again illustrate the premium that neutrals and partisans place on shaping an award that is acceptable to the parties.

Some commentators have expressed the fear that the arbitrators' stress on comparability as a decision criterion will make it difficult for either party to achieve a major innovation in arbitration. If this is true, arbitration may also have a limited half-life as the parties find that there are few gains left to achieve without breaking new ground. There is some evidence that this problem has emerged in the Canadian federal sector where a union has the option of arbitration or the right to strike.[44] In that system, the preference for arbitration declined among unions once they had achieved comparable contract provisions. The point of diminishing returns may have contributed to the decision of more units to shift to the strike route. As yet, there is little evidence of this problem arising in the U.S. systems. It is, however, an issue that merits attention in future studies.

BEYOND THE PROCEDURAL DEBATE

The design of a dispute-resolution system requires balancing the multiple objectives of avoiding strikes, minimizing third-party dependence and maximizing good-faith bargaining, protecting the public interest

---

[42] For an argument supporting a more judicial approach to arbitration, see Raymond D. Horton, *Arbitration, Arbitrators, and the Public Interest*, 27 Ind. & Lab. Rels. Rev. 497 (July 1975).

[43] See, for example, Kochan et al., *Dispute Resolutions under Factfinding*, ch. 8; or Jones, *Public Sector Labor Relations*.

[44] Anderson and Kochan, "Impasse Procedures in the Canadian Federal Services," pp. 292–93.

and the accountability of elected officials, and, in the long run, building the commitment of the parties and the public to a bargaining system that forces the parties to confront their problems effectively.

The record of various forms of dispute resolution that have been tried over the first decade of public-sector bargaining suggests that no "one best way" or optimal procedure for achieving all of these objectives has yet been identified. Thus, in this final section a number of comments will be made to interpret the results discussed earlier in this chapter in order to identify the tradeoffs that are associated with alternative systems.

Those wishing to provide as iron-clad a no-strike system as possible will probably need to embrace some form of compulsory arbitration. While no system can guarantee the complete absence of strikes, the record of strike avoidance, at least for police and fire fighters, so far has been better under arbitration than under fact-finding or in the absence of legislation. Whether this same experience will generalize to other occupational groups will be known only if more states extend these rights to a broader array of employee groups. There also is no way to determine at this point whether final-offer and conventional arbitration differ in their strike-avoidance potential.

For those concerned about the chilling effect of arbitration, the evidence from Massachusetts and Wisconsin suggests that the best choice is a system providing mediation followed closely by final-offer arbitration with a single arbitrator who is constrained from mediating at the arbitration stage. Under this type of system, a relatively high proportion of disputes will likely go to mediation; however, the mediation process should be relatively successful in reducing the number of cases that are passed on to arbitration. The mediation process, therefore, is the focal point of this system for resolving impasses.

A variant of this system—a tripartite arbitration structure—can be designed for those who wish to increase the parties' control over the final outcome. Even greater control can be imposed by using the issue-by-issue method of final-offer selection in a tripartite structure. This system builds the potential for further mediation into the arbitration stage of the procedure and would likely result in a similarly high percentage of negotiations reaching impasse, a lower settlement rate in mediation prior to arbitration, and a higher settlement rate in arbitration without an award. Another variant on this system for those who are opposed to final-offer arbitration—conventional arbitration with a tripartite structure—would be expected to have relatively similar effects, except that we might observe a higher rate of unanimous awards rather than mediated settlements without an award.

All of the above options assume that a high priority is placed on avoiding strikes. Relaxing this priority a bit relative to other objectives opens a wide array of additional options. For example, if one wishes to deal with the fear that arbitration stifles innovation or the ability to make major breakthroughs in collective bargaining, the dual impasse routes of arbitration or the right to strike can be built into the law. If the Canadian experience under this system generalizes to other jurisdictions, then we would expect that over time (1) the weak bargaining units lacking an effective strike threat will stay within the arbitration route as long as they can benefit from a "catch-up" argument, (2) the strong bargaining units with an ability and willingness to strike will prefer the strike option, (3) the rate of impasse will be relatively high in order to get to the critical pressure point in the procedure, and (4) the parties may switch from one option to the other over time as they grow dissatisfied with the outcomes from one route. A variant on this option, which makes it more difficult for the stronger party to dominate the choice of the routes, is found in the Wisconsin statute, where both parties must agree on the strike route or else the arbitration route becomes automatic.

A more liberal strike-based system might adopt the approach of Hawaii and several other states by allowing strikes after mediation and/or fact-finding have been exhausted, subject to a limitation in cases affecting public health and safety. Although experience under these statutes has not been very thoroughly analyzed, some evidence from Hawaii and Pennsylvania suggests that a reasonably high rate of impasses can be expected.[45] The number of strikes is likely to vary considerably depending on the nature of the economic and political environments and the characteristics of the relationships between the parties. For example, a higher strike rate might be expected in relationships involving strong, militant unions in complex political environments under a system of this type than under one where there was no statutory right to strike. Strikes that do occur might also tend to be of longer duration here than in jurisdictions where the strike is illegal.

Finally, those who are philosophically opposed both to the right to strike and to any form of compulsory arbitration can still rely on the most commonly used system—mediation followed by fact-finding. While it might be difficult, if not impossible, to return to this system once arbitration or the right to strike has been provided, this approach still may be useful as a first step in establishing bargaining rights in jurisdictions where the parties are unfamiliar with collective bargaining and dispute resolution. Since the states that have yet to establish bargaining rights are largely located in environments where

there is less reason to expect a rapid rise of militant unionism, the process of fact-finding with recommendations may have a longer half-life than it had in some of the states that adopted and then abandoned this system in the first decade of public-sector bargaining.

In summary, a variety of options are available to public policymakers, depending on the weights they assign to different policy objectives. Although each alternative offers a slightly different approach, in practice their similarities may outweigh their differences. As Rehmus recently noted, the parties have adapted the various dispute-settlement procedures in ways that suggest that the dispute-resolution process has come full circle.[46] Instead of the distinct steps envisioned by most states that start with negotiations, proceed to mediation, and then go to fact-finding and/or arbitration, the parties and neutrals have found ways to mix each of these processes together in combinations that fit the needs of their particular dispute. Thus, we have fact-finding followed by mediation, med-arb, arbitration followed by negotiations, strikes followed by fact-finding, mediation and/or arbitration, etc. Over time, as more experience is gained with these strategies and better data become available on their performance, we can understand more fully the potentials and limitations of all of the options. The more we learn, the more we are likely to be convinced of the futility of searching for the "one best way" or the "optimal" system for resolving all collective bargaining disputes. Instead, we should become better equipped to design alternative systems to meet different policy objectives or to adapt to changing circumstances.

---

[45] See Peter Feuille, *Symposium Introduction: Public Sector Impasses,* 16 Ind. Rels. 265 (October 1977).

[46] Charles Rehmus, *A Circular View of Government Intervention,* in Symposium on Police and Firefighter Arbitration in New York State (Albany, N.Y.: Public Employment Relations Board, 1977), pp. 165–78.

SELECTED BENEFITS AND COSTS OF COMPULSORY ARBITRATION

Peter Feuille*

In 1965, Wyoming became the first state to adopt compulsory arbitration[1] to resolve public employee bargaining disputes; by 1979, 20 states had implemented arbitration statutes covering various public employee groups. Our understanding of the potential impact of such arbitration, however, may not have kept pace with this rapid growth in coverage. Labor relations scholars, for instance, who have done the lion's share of the writing on the subject, have focused on the labor relations functions and effects of arbitration, while generally ignoring its political functions. Similarly, the analyses of these various functions have been shaped by some easily identifiable normative premises, but these premises have received little explicit attention. Furthermore, arbitration is most often viewed as an independent variable that affects such outcome variables as wages, strikes, or bargaining incentives; rarely is it seen as a dependent variable that might indicate the degree of interest group conflict or the distribution of political influence in a jurisdiction.

Accordingly, the following analysis considers three sets of benefits arbitration may provide and two sets of costs the process may impose. It does so by examining the normative premise and operational mechanisms associated with each of these five attributes and by discussing some tests (and accompanying research) that can be used to measure how well or poorly arbitration performs the various functions ascribed to it.

* * * * *

GUARDIAN OF THE PUBLIC INTEREST

Arbitration's most visible attribute is the ability of its binding award to guarantee (almost) the absence of strikes among covered employees and hence to prevent the interruption of covered public services. Arbitration proponents have used this strike prevention function more than any other to explain why arbitration is desirable, arguing that the prevention of such strikes protects the public's interest in continuously receiving such services. After all, few political slogans are as attractive (and vague) as "the public interest." Because strike prohibitions and arbitration tend to coexist, arbitration may at first seem superfluous as a device to prevent interruptions of public services. Yet policymakers have long recognized that prohibiting strikes merely makes illegal the strikes that do occur. Arbitration serves, therefore, as a no-strike insurance policy. This strike-prevention function ostensibly explains why public safety services—presumably the most "essential" of local government services—are most likely to be covered by ar-

---

* Professor, University of Illinois. Reprinted, in an abridged form, with permission, from the *Industrial and Labor Relations Review*, 33, no. 1 (Oct. 1979), pp. 64–76. © 1979 by Cornell University. All rights reserved.

[1] In pursuit of brevity and clarity "arbitration" shall henceforth be used in this analysis to refer only to compulsory and binding interest arbitration, except when specifically noted otherwise.

bitration states. Of the 20 arbitration
states, 12 require arbitration only for public safety personnel,[2] and the remaining
eight cover public safety as well as other
groups.

The usual test for whether arbitration
has protected the public is comparing
strike occurrences in jurisdictions with
and without arbitration. The available evidence shows that far fewer strikes occur
where arbitration is mandated.[3] Although
arbitration substantially reduces the probability of strikes compared to other impasse-
resolution procedures, it is not a perfect
form of no-strike insurance. It does not
protect against wildcats or against stoppages over issues outside the scope of bargaining and, as the Montreal police demonstrated in 1969, it may not always prevent
an unusually militant union from striking
in defiance of an unsatisfactory award (in
other words, there may be strikes authorized by the union leadership over issues
within the scope of bargaining).

The connections among the public's interests, strikes, and arbitration are more
complex, however, than the extent to
which strikes and arbitration are negatively correlated. Arbitration's public interest protection function assumes, first,
that some or all public employee strikes
are inappropriate and, second, that the
public's overriding interest in government
labor relations is "labor peace." . . .

The justification for denying public employees the right to strike is generally argued on the following bases: government
is sovereign, elected and selected to reflect
the collective desires of the citizenry, and
hence it should not be subject to adversarial pressure tactics on behalf of the few
at the expense of the many; because most
governmental services are offered on a
monopolistic basis, unions enjoy tremendous (and unfair) bargaining power when
they threaten to strike; and some or all
public employee strikes actually harm the
public (or will after a certain duration).[4]

In response to the first argument, an
appeal to popular sovereignty is an article
of faith, not capable of being empirically
tested; however, such an appeal ignores the
pluralist and selfish nature of the group
interests and pressures that pervade the
U.S. political system and that form the
basis for many (perhaps most) governmental actions.[5] Second, if the unfair bargaining power argument had merit, we should
see public employee unions negotiating
very favorable contracts. Yet, while there
is a substantial body of evidence that public unions have a positive impact on
wages,[6] the magnitude of this impact is
not large. In fact, it appears to be smaller
than in the private sector[7]—where the
unions presumably do not enjoy such
monopolistic protection. Furthermore, Kochan and Wheeler found that the presence

[2] Hawaii, Massachusetts, Michigan, Minnesota,
Montana, Nevada, New Jersey, New York, Oregon,
Pennsylvania, Washington, Wyoming.

[3] Hoyt N. Wheeler, "An Analysis of Fire Fighter
Strikes," *Labor Law Journal,* January 1975, pp. 17–
20; J. Joseph Loewenberg, Walter J. Gershenfeld,
H. J. Glasbeek, B. A. Hepple, and Kenneth F. Walker,
Compulsory Arbitration (Lexington, Mass.: D. C.
Heath, 1976), p. 165; James L. Stern, Charles M. Reh-
mus, J. Joseph Loewenberg, Hirschel Kasper, Barbara
D. Dennis, *Final-Offer Arbitration* (Lexington,
Mass.: D. C. Heath, 1975), p. 189; and Peter Feuille,
Final Offer Arbitration, Public Employee Relations
Library Series No. 50 (Chicago: International Person-
nel Management Association, 1975), pp. 10–11.

[4] This list borrows heavily from David Lewin,
"Collective Bargaining and the Right to Strike," in
Public Employee Unions, ed. A. Lawrence Chicker-
ing (San Francisco: Institute for Contemporary Studies, 1976), pp. 145–63.

[5] For instance, see David B. Truman, *The Govern-
mental Process* (New York: Knopf, 1951); Edward
C. Banfield, *Political Influence* (New York: Free
Press, 1961); Banfield and Wilson, *City Politics*
(New York: Vintage Books, 1963).

[6] For a review of these studies through 1976, see
David Lewin, "Public Sector Labor Relations: A Review Essay," *Labor History,* Winter 1977, pp. 133–
44.

[7] Sharon P. Smith, *Equal Pay in the Public Sector:
Fact or Fantasy* (Princeton: Industrial Relations Section, Princeton University, 1977), pp. 120–29.

of compulsory arbitration laws contributed much more to firefighter unions' ability to bargain favorable contracts than did the unions' use of militant tactics, such as slowdowns, sickouts, and picketing.[8] In addition, there is no evidence that the public unions in the seven right-to-strike states[9] have fared noticeably better at the bargaining table than their more constrained counterparts in other states. Thus, there is no systematic support for the belief that arbitration should or will serve as check upon public union monopoly power, nor is there any systematic evidence that supports the proposition that the unions possess such tremendous bargaining power in the first place.

In considering the third argument— that public employee strikes harm the public or will cause such harm after a certain duration—the observer wonders why this assertion never has been systematically documented. There certainly have been enough public employee strikes upon which to perform strike-impact research. Even police and fire strike impacts, which are supposed to be horrendous, have received rather cursory attention. In fact, the industrial relations research community so far has seemed content to rely primarily upon the commercial news media for "data" about the service-deprivation ef-

fects of government strikes. Furthermore, it is possible to interpret the public employee strike experience in this country as demonstrating that this strikes-will-cause-harm assertion contains more rhetoric than substance. The hundreds of public employee strikes since 1965 (including 338 protective service strikes during 1965–75), the relatively minor (or even nonexistent) strike penalties, and the slow growth of the legal right to strike strongly suggest that such strikes, including those by police officers and firefighters, are rather minor threats to the public interest (in other words, the public can tolerate such strikes better than conventional wisdom suggests). This *de facto* tolerance of strikes may have occurred because the government services are less "essential" to the short-run public welfare than is commonly believed and because government managers are better at providing short-run substitutes for struck services than the conventional wisdom has suggested.

The second assumption inherent in the notion of arbitration as the guardian of the public interest is that the public's only interest, or at least its primary interest, in public labor relations is "labor peace," and that any other interests are relatively unimportant.[10] Expressed another way, this assumption ignores the possibility that the public may actually consist of numerous "publics" with multiple interests in public labor relations processes and outcomes that go beyond a desire not to be inconvenienced by strikes. To take an obvious example, parents of school-age children and nonparents alike may prefer no teacher strikes; but the nonparents may be much more willing than the parents to have school district managements use strikes as a tool to support managerial demands for "less" relative to union de-

[8] Thomas A. Kochan and Hoyt N. Wheeler, "Municipal Collective Bargaining: A Model and Analysis of Bargaining Outcomes," *Industrial and Labor Relations Review*, October 1975, pp. 46–66. Gerhart found a positive relationship between favorable union contract provisions and a strike-activity index among local government employees, but this relationship was not statistically significant in the presence of other explanatory variables. See Paul F. Gerhart, "Determinants of Bargaining Outcomes in Local Government Labor Negotiations," *Industrial and Labor Relations Review*, April 1976, pp. 331–51.

[9] Alaska, Hawaii, Oregon, Montana, Minnesota, Pennsylvania, and Vermont. In 1978 Wisconsin started allowing municipal employees to strike if both the union and the employer refused to use final-offer arbitration to resolve their dipute.

[10] See Lewin, "Collective Bargaining and the Right to Strike," pp. 152–57.

mands for "more." Furthermore, there are public opinion poll data that suggest that the public may be more accepting of strike rights for some public employee groups than is commonly believed.[11] In addition, the conventional wisdom suggests that public management represents the interests of the public at the bargaining table and in the hearing room. If this suggestion has any merit, recent managerial behavior may also indicate changing public attitudes toward the strike (and certainly changing managerial attitudes). It still may be politically risky for candidates for public office to advocate public employee strike rights, but increasing numbers of public administrators seem to be more accepting of the right to strike, at least when the alternative is compulsory arbitration. Instead of assuming a unitary public with overriding interest in "labor peace," research might profitably focus on the extent to which different groups hold convergent or divergent views about the costs and benefits of various labor relations impasse arrangements.

The apparent normative premise underlying the public interest protection function of arbitration is that the public is a monolithic entity that is rather helpless in the face of a collective withdrawal of important public services and hence needs and wants to be protected from such withdrawals. The assertions that flow from this premise are either normative expressions of faith or empirically undocumented, and thus it is difficult to demonstrate systematically that the public needs to be protected from such strikes—even those involving "essential" services. Arbitration may substantially reduce the probability of public

employee strikes, but the case supporting the need for such a strike prevention device rests on empirically shaky ground.

GUARDIAN OF EMPLOYEE INTERESTS

Arbitration advocates argue that public employee strike prohibitions may make collective bargaining a one-sided process because employees have no readily available mechanism to manipulate management's costs of disagreeing with employee demands. Management can continue the status quo, ignore mediator or factfinder recommendations, or implement unilateral changes (at least after impasse), but the employees have no countervailing weapons; thus there is a serious imbalance of negotiating power in management's favor. Arbitration should correct this imbalance, for it eliminates management's ability to prolong the status quo indefinitely, ignore third party recommendations, or impose its own terms (it also eliminates union abilities to do these same things, but it is rare that the unions want or are able to do them). Arbitration, then, should increase the employees' negotiating strength until it is approximately equal with management's.

Some relevant tests of arbitration's effectiveness in fulfilling this function are the extent to which it promotes good-faith negotiations and the extent to which arbitrated and negotiated outcomes are distributed in a manner that balances union and management interests. There are reports from some jurisdictions that the introduction of arbitration promotes more genuine negotiating behavior by management,[12] but there is also evidence that in many instances arbitration inhibits the

[11] See Schick and Couturier, *The Public Interest in Government Labor Relations*, pp. 244–45; and Victor E. Flango and Robert Dudley, "Who Supports Public Employee Strikes?" *Journal of Collective Negotiations in the Pubic Sector*, 7, no. 1 (1978), pp. 1–10.

[12] See the reports on arbitration in Michigan, Pennsylvania, and Wisconsin in Stern, et al., *Final-Offer Arbitration.*

parties' ability or willingness to negotiate their own agreements.[13]

The distribution of outcomes could be measured by comparing the parties' bargaining goals with actual outcomes; by comparing bargained agreements with arbitrated awards; by comparing award winners and losers under final-offer arbitration; or by examining the parties' satisfaction (or lack of it) with the distributional nature of negotiation-arbitration processes. Some labor relations observers have concluded that arbitration outcomes are distributed in a balanced manner,[14] but many municipal managers object to arbitration, in large part because they perceive the process as more supportive of employee than employer interests.[15] Furthermore, the recurring line-up in state legislatures of union support for arbitration and managerial opposition to it[16] means that the unions perceive that arbitration is to their advantage in bargaining and managements perceive it is to their disadvantage. Some evidence suggests that these percep-

tions are accurate,[17] and so parties seem to be acting rationally. This lineup of support and opposition plus more rigorous research evidence suggest strongly that arbitration has worked effectively to enhance public employee negotiating interests.

Arbitration also may protect employee interests by acting as a labor market leveling mechanism. To the extent that Ross's "orbits of coercive comparisons" paradigm accurately specifies the process by which employee wage demands are formulated,[18] and to the extent that arbitration decisions are made primarily on labor market comparability criteria,[19] arbitration becomes "the visible hand" by which members of similar bargaining units seek to be treated similarly (at least within the same state). There is some evidence that on wages such an impact does occur, especially on behalf of covered employees in small bargaining units at the low end of the wage distribution.[20] This levelling or "regression to the mean" impact may cause some observers to conclude that arbitration is an efficient and effective method for ensuring equity and hence protecting employee interests, while others may question the need for such a mechanism in the absence of any persuasive reason why the covered employees should have such

---

[13] See Hoyt N. Wheeler, "How Compulsory Arbitration Affects Compromise Activity," *Industrial Relations*, February 1978, pp. 80–84; John C. Anderson and Thomas A. Kochan, "Impasse Procedures in the Canadian Federal Service," *Industrial and Labor Relations Review*, April 1977, pp. 283–301; and Peter Feuille, "Final Offer Arbitration and the Chilling Effect," *Industrial Relations*, October 1975, pp. 302–10. As would be expected, this (and other) research also suggests that negotiating incentives may vary with the shape of arbitration procedures and the nature of dispute-resolution alternatives available.

[14] Stern, et al., *Final-Offer Arbitration*.

[15] Thomas A. Kochan, Ronald G. Ehrenberg, Jean Baderschneider, Todd Jick, and Mordehai Mironi, *An Evaluation of Impasse Procedures for Police and Firefighters in New York State* (Ithaca: Cornell University, New York State School of Industrial and Labor Relations, 1977), ch. 10; and Hoyt N. Wheeler and Frank Owen, "Impasse Resolution Preferences of Fire Fighters and Municipal Negotiators," *Journal of Collective Negotiations in the Public Sector 5*, no. 3 (1978), pp. 215–24.

[16] Stern, et al., *Final-Offer Arbitration*; Thomas A. Kochan, "The Politics of Interest Arbitration," *The Arbitration Journal* (March 1978), pp. 5–9; Bureau of National Affairs, *Government Employee Relations Report*, July 11, 1977, pp.13–14.

[17] Kochan and Wheeler, "Municipal Collective Bargaining"; Stern, et al., *Final-Offer Arbitration*, ch. 6; Kochan, et al., *An Evaluation of Impasse Procedures*, ch. 6; Paul C. Somers, "An Evaluation of Final-Offer Arbitration in Massachusetts," *Journal of Collective Negotiations in the Public Sector 6*, no. 3 (1977), pp. 193–228.

[18] Arthur M. Ross, *Trade Union Wage Policy* (Berkeley: University of California Press, 1948).

[19] Charles J. Morris, "The Role of Interest Arbitration in a Collective Bargaining System," *Industrial Relations Law Journal*, Fall 1976, pp. 470 and 477; Irving Bernstein, *The Arbitration of Wages* (Berkeley: University of California Press, 1954), pp. 26–33; and David B. Ross, "The Arbitration of Public Employee Wage Disputes," *Industrial and Labor Relations Review*, October 1969, pp. 3–14.

[20] Stern, et al., *Final-Offer Arbitration*, pp. 144–45; Kochan, et al., *An Evaluation. . .* , pp. 216–17.

a protective device and other employees should not.

The normative premise upon which this arbitration function is based is that public employees with no right to strike should be protected against managerial domination of the bargaining process. The logical implication of this premise is that arbitration should be most prevalent in those situations in which the employees are on the short end of the largest power imbalances. As discussed earlier, however, arbitration laws apply disproportionately to those groups with the greatest withholding power and who typically have acquired considerable political influence—police officers, and firefighters. Thus, the two occupational groups who would be expected to negotiate most effectively without arbitration are the two groups with the highest incidence of arbitration coverage. This fact suggests that there are distinct limits to the policymakers' acceptance of the employee interest-protection function as a rationale for why arbitration statutes should be enacted: such a rationale applies only to those employees represented by unions who happen to have the ability to manipulate skillfully the legislative process to their own advantage. In short, the incidence of arbitration coverage seems to reflect less concern among policy makers for the general welfare and more concern for accommodating the requests of influential interest groups.

REGULATOR OF INTEREST-GROUP CONFLICT

From a broad political perspective (in contrast to the narrower labor relations perspectives just examined), arbitration may perform a useful conflict regulation function. The unionization of public employees brought out into the open a set of group interests (those of the various employees and their representatives) that represent claims upon public resources that were po-

tentially rather costly. Although such unionization did not create these claims, it certainly made them more visible, and it helped make overt the potential conflicts between public employees and the public. The widespread use of collective bargaining, with its militant posturing and strident rhetoric, and the increasingly frequent use of the strike became the visible manifestations of these interest-group conflicts. One policy response to this situation has been to provide third party impasse resolution procedures to regulate and contain the interorganizational and intraorganizational pressures that contribute to such overt conflict.

These impasse procedures, including arbitration, regulate public–public-employee conflict by institutionalizing trilateral decision mechanisms for the formation of public employment conditions and by absorbing the advocates' demands for particular outcomes. Arbitration performs this regulatory function primarily through the finality, impartiality, compromising, and face-saving features of the process. Supposedly, all the parties affected by an award will accept it because of legal requirements to do so and because of its issuance by a neutral third party who has attempted to balance employee and employer interests. Furthermore, managerial and union leaders can protect themselves from intraorganizational retaliation from their constituents by blaming the arbitrator for any unfavorable outcomes. As a result of these attributes, arbitration is said to absorb the interest group pressures that might cause strikes or other disruptions and, by absorbing them, to contribute to political and social stability. The normative premise underlying this arbitration function is that society needs such conflict-absorption mechanisms to contribute to societal stability.

Arbitration's effectiveness in performing this regulatory function can be measured by examining the legality of the process and the extent to which affected unions and managements comply with or accept the process and awards, strikes are prevented, arbitration reduces bargaining hostility, and the affected parties believe their legitimate interests have been adequately considered in the process. A review of relevant court decisions suggests that most of the time arbitration is constitutionally acceptable and hence its awards are legally enforceable.[21] The evidence also suggests that union and management compliance with the process is widespread, if not always enthusiastic, at least in those states with substantial bargaining and arbitration histories.[22] In addition, as noted previously, arbitration is associated with a general absence of strikes.

There is little systematic evidence about the extent to which arbitration has reduced bargaining hostility or fostered impasse-resolution legitimacy perceptions among the parties. To the extent that arbitration prevents strikes and strike threats it may reduce bargaining hostility, but these nonevents are very difficult to measure. There is a substantial body of evidence that union representatives believe arbitration legitimately considers employee interests, but this is not so for management representatives. And there simply are insufficient data to determine if citizens' views about arbitration are supportive, hostile, or apathetic.

The available evidence suggests, then, that arbitration effectively absorbs selected employer and employee pressures that might emerge as overt conflict and, in so doing, contributes to the institutionalized resolution of workplace conflict already begun by collective bargaining. However, the sharp divergence in enthusiasm for arbitration displayed by union and management representatives suggests that there are very different perceptions about the costs and benefits attached to arbitration's conflict-regulation function, and it appears unlikely that these perceptions will be reconciled. Furthermore, because empirical testing of this arbitration function may be difficult given its process (rather than outcome) focus, this function will win support primarily through a value judgment by those who place great importance on political pluralism and political stability.

INHIBITOR OF REPRESENTATIVE GOVERNMENT

The conclusion that arbitration performs a useful political function is contrary to the conclusion that arbitration is a decision process inimical to the tenets and operation of our system of representative democratic government. This latter conclusion is based on the normative premise that our political system should be structured to reflect the will of the governed, as expressed through a pluralistic diffusion of interests, by allowing for active and legitimate groups to make themselves heard during public decision processes.[23] However, compulsory arbitration contains two related elements that detract from this desired governmental system: a lack of accountability for public decisions and an intensification of the bureaucratic forces that insulate public decision processes from public influence.

Arbitration allows for authoritative public allocation decisions to be made in a relatively private manner by a nonelected

---

[21] For such a review, see Morris, "The Role of Interest Arbitration in a Collective Bargaining System," pp. 487–91. As Morris notes, a few state supreme courts have struck down arbitration statutes as unconstitutional, usually on the grounds that such statutes unlawfully delegate legislative authority. For reports on two such state supreme court decisions (in Colorado and Utah), see Bureau of National Affairs, *Government Employee Relations Report*, no. 708 (May 16, 1977), pp. 10–11, and no. 726 (September 19, 1977), pp. 12–13.

[22] Stern, et al., *Final-Offer Arbitration*.

[23] This premise is contained in Harry H. Wellington and Ralph K. Winter, Jr., *The Unions and the Cities* (Washington, D.C., The Brookings Institution, 1971), ch. 1, and appears to be based on Robert A. Dahl, *A Preface to Democratic Theory* (Chicago: University of Chicago Press, 1956).

third party who is not directly accountable for his or her decisions.[24] Regardless of whether this delegation of authority is constitutionally permissible, it is deemed politically undesirable because it reduces management's accountability for these allocations of scarce public resources and allows public officials (and union leaders) to evade their responsibilities for these allocations by using arbitrators as mechanisms to absorb any constituent dissatisfactions with these decisions. In other words, arbitration is a classic example of the delegation of public authority to private actors that has pervaded our post–New Deal political system.[25]

Similarly, arbitration represents an undesirable intensification of the bureaucratic-professional control over governmental employer-employee relations begun by civil service and carried forward by collective bargaining.[26] As civil service and collective bargaining have come to be administered by professionals in numerous state and local bureaucracies, so arbitration is administered in a similar manner by labor relations professionals. One of the procedural costs of such professionalization, however, may be to increase the proportion of allocative decisions that are made by labor relations professionals whose primary allegiances are to the arbitration process itself and to their immediate union and management clients and who are much less concerned with the interests of the larger groups (such as taxpayers and other employees) affected by arbitration

awards.[27] A second cost may be the development of arbitration constituencies among these professionals that act to ensure the continuation of arbitration legislation because of the tangible benefits (such as budget appropriations, income, and prestige) that arbitration provides to them.[28]

The major weakness of this critical view is that it tends to overlook the extent to which arbitration procedures can be "structured and limited in such a way as to preserve both the appearance and reality of the democratic process. . . ."[29] For instance, legislative bodies may restrict the scope of arbitrable subjects, limit the coverage of the arbitration legislation, specify exceedingly tight decision criteria, require that decisions be made by tripartite panels instead of single arbitrators, and mandate final-offer selection rather than conventional decision making. These and other procedural attempts to limit arbitral discretion may help make arbitration and the "democratic process" more compatible,

---

[24] For a more complete statement of this characterization of arbitration, see Raymond D. Horton, "Arbitration, Arbitrators, and the Public Interest," *Industrial and Labor Relations Review,* July 1975, pp. 497–507.

[25] Lowi refers to this phenomenon as "interest-group liberalism"; see Theodore J. Lowi, *The End of Liberalism* (New York: W. W. Norton, 1969), chap. 3.

[26] For a brief discussion of the professionalization of governmental collective bargaining, see Thomas M. Love and George T. Sulzner, "Political Implications of Public Employee Bargaining," *Industrial Relations,* February 1972, pp. 23–25.

[27] For instance, there is some evidence that advocate representatives, mediators, and factfinders pay little if any attention to the "public interest" during contract negotiations or impasse resolution. See Thomas A. Kochan, George P. Huber, and L. L. Cummings, "Determinants of Intraorganizational Conflict in Collective Bargaining in the Public Sector," *Administrative Science Quarterly,* March 1975, pp. 10–23, esp. Table 1; Kenneth Kressel, *Labor Mediation: An Exploratory Survey* (Albany: Association of Labor Mediation Agencies, 1972); and Jack Steiber and Benjamin W. Wolkinson, "Fact-Finding Viewed by Fact-Finders: The Michigan Experience," *Labor Law Journal,* February 1977, pp. 89–101.

[28] An interesting research effort would be to examine the actions or positions of state arbitration administrative agencies and arbitrators in those situations in which the renewal of an arbitration statute is being considered by the legislature. For a report on the position of the New York State Public Employment Relations Board during the 1977 arbitration renewal debate in that state, see Thomas A. Kochan, "The Politics of Interest Arbitration," *The Arbitration Journal,* March 1978, pp. 5–9.

[29] Joseph Grodin, "Political Aspects of Public Sector Interest Arbitration," *Industrial Relations Law Journal,* Spring 1976, p. 24. In this article Grodin explores how arbitration procedures can be made more compatible with the democratic process.

though it is likely that arbitration critics would argue that the search for these procedural characteristics is an explicit admission that arbitration is inimical to democratic government.

This critical view of arbitration is difficult to test empirically, for it is not addressed to substantive differences between arbitrated and negotiated outcomes but to the processes used to produce those outcomes. Similarly, it is difficult to demonstrate empirically that arbitration is or may be inimical to democratic government without first formulating an explicit and normative definition of democracy. Furthermore, even with such a formulation, it may not be possible to give operational and hence measurable meaning to such key [words] as *accountability* and *professionalization*. Instead, it is likely that this arbitration function will attract adherents and critics on the basis of its appeal to personal preference.[30]

INHIBITOR OF GENUINE BARGAINING

The belief that arbitration has a costly impact on bargaining incentives is often used to criticize the arbitral process. This conclusion is based upon the normative premise that collective bargaining is a valuable and desirable decision-making process that should be protected from inimical forces. Arbitration is cast as a villain because it does not have the voluntary and joint decision-making properties of bargaining and because it may lure unions and managements away from the bargaining process.

More precisely, arbitration may be a too-easily-used escape route from the difficult trade-off choices that must usually be made in order to negotiate an agreement. Arbitration will be invoked because one

or both sides believe that an arbitration award may be more favorable than a negotiated agreement *and* because one or both believe the costs of using arbitration are comparatively low (none of the trauma and costs of a work stoppage and none of the uncertainty of using other forms of political influence). As a result of this cost-benefit calculus, the availability of arbitration may have a "chilling effect" upon the parties' efforts to negotiate an agreement, and over time there may be a "narcotic effect" as the parties become arbitration addicts who habitually rely upon arbitrators to write their labor contracts. The logical conclusion of this reasoning is that arbitration will destroy and replace collective bargaining.

Researchers and practitioners have searched diligently for techniques to make arbitration and bargaining compatible, and this search has produced such proposals as final-offer arbitration (in all its permutations), closed-offer arbitration, and labor-management arbitration screening committees. In addition, there has been considerable research to measure this compatibility (or lack of it). The most widely used method seems to be the cross-sectional or longitudinal comparison of arbitration awards, as a proportion of all settlements, with other settlement techniques within or across one or more jurisdictions.[31] A sec-

---

[30] For an example, see Horton, "Arbitration, Arbitrators, and the Public Interest," and then see Joseph Krislov's "Comment" and Horton's "Reply" in *Industrial and Labor Relations Review*, October 1977, pp. 71–77.

[31] In addition to the sources cited in footnote 13, see Stern, et al., *Final-Offer Arbitration;* Peter Feuille, "Final-Offer Arbitration and Negotiating Incentives," *The Arbitration Journal*, September 1977, pp. 203–20; Thomas A. Kochan and Jean Baderschneider, "Dependence Upon Impasse Procedures: Police and Firefighters in New York State," *Industrial and Labor Relations Review*, July 1978, pp. 431–49; Hoyt N. Wheeler, "Compulsory Arbitration: A 'Narcotic Effect'?" *Industrial Relations*, February 1975, pp. 117–20; Daniel G. Gallagher, "Interest Arbitration Under the Iowa Public Employment Relations Act," *The Arbitration Journal*, September 1978, pp. 30–36; and David B. Lipsky and Thomas A. Barocci, "Final-Offer Arbitration and Public-Safety Employees: The Massachusetts Experience," Industrial Relations Research Association, *Proceedings of the Thirtieth Annual Winter Meeting* (Madison: IRRA, 1978), pp. 65–76.

ond method measures the number of issues taken to arbitration under different procedures.[32] A third method tracks the amount of movement, usually on wages, exhibited during negotiations under arbitration, compared with no arbitration, to see if the availability of a binding award affects compromising activity.[33] While most of this research gathers data from actual negotiations, recently some researchers have used laboratory simulations to test more carefully arbitration's impacts on negotiating behaviors.[34] Another method examines negotiator and arbitrator attitudes about various arbitral features.[35] In short, we probably have a larger body of research results on arbitration's impact on bargaining than on any other aspect of the process.

Generalizations are hazardous, but this research seems to support the following conclusions. First, the availability of arbitration has not destroyed bargaining, for in practically all arbitration jurisdictions a majority of agreements are negotiated. Second, in many cases the parties use the arbitration process as a forum for additional negotiations (or perhaps as a forum for their truly serious bargaining). Third, however, there are many union-management pairs who seem to have become quite dependent upon arbitration, with such dependency influenced by employer size, de-

gree of fiscal scarcity, prior use of impasse procedures, bargaining hostility, and so forth. Fourth, the shape of the impasse-arbitration procedure may affect the parties' use of such procedures, for negotiating behaviors seem to vary with the nature and extent of arbitral discretion (the presence of a final-offer selection requirement or the availability of factfinding recommendations, for example). In short, collective bargaining generally functions as a viable process in the presence of arbitration, but there is no doubt that arbitration has also increased union and management dependency upon third parties to resolve their disputes and in so doing has frequently sapped the vitality of the bargaining process.

Perhaps most important, there are no precise formulas with which to evaluate the research results. This means that a given body of data can be used to support differing and even opposing conclusions[36] and that personal preferences can play a strong role in the conclusions reached. Given that both collective bargaining and compulsory arbitration represent strongly held labor relations value judgments, the influence of personal preferences on these conclusions should not surprise anyone.

DISCUSSION

The major components of each of these arbitration functions are summarized in Table 1. The components include the impact that the procedure has (or is designed to have), the normative premise upon which each function is based, the operational mechanisms by which each impact occurs, and some of the measures that might be used to evaluate how well or

[32] Mollie H. Bowers, "A Study of Legislated Interest Arbitration and Collective Bargaining in the Public Safety Services in Michigan and Pennsylvania," Ph.D. dissertation, Cornell University, 1974; and Stern, et al., *Final-Offer Arbitration.*

[33] Wheeler, "How Compulsory Arbitration Affects Compromise Activity"; Kochan et al., *An Evaluation of Impasse Procedures.*

[34] William W. Notz and Frederick A. Starke, "Final Offer versus Conventional Arbitration as Means of Conflict Management." *Administrative Science Quarterly*, June 1978, pp. 189–203; A. V. Subbarao, "The Impact of Binding Interest Arbitration on Negotiation and Process Outcome: An Experimental Study," *The Journal of Conflict Resolution*, March 1978, pp. 79–104.

[35] Stern, et al., *Final-Offer Arbitration*; Kochan, et al., *An Evaluation of Impasse Procedures.*

[36] For instance, see Mark Thompson and James Cairnie, "Compulsory Arbitration: The Case of British Columbia Teachers," *Industrial and Labor Relations Review*, October 1973, pp. 3–17; Peter Feuille, "Analyzing Compulsory Arbitration Experiences: The Role of Personal Preferences—Comment," and Thompson and Cairnie, "Reply," *Industrial and Labor Relations Review*, April 1975, pp. 432–38.

TABLE 1 SELECTED COMPONENTS OF ARBITRATION FUNCTIONS

ARBITRATION'S PURPOSE OR IMPACT	NORMATIVE PREMISE	OPERATIONAL MECHANISMS	MEASUREMENT TESTS
Protector of the public interest	The public needs and wants to be protected from strikes.	A binding award prevents strikes.	Absence of strikes.
Protector of employee interests	Employees should bargain from position of equal strength with management.	Union can invoke arbitration over employer's objection and employer must accept award.	Comparison of awards with negotiated outcomes where arbitration is not available.
Regulator of interest-group conflict	There is a need for social and political stability.	Third party decision making absorbs and accommodates conflicting group pressures.	Comparison of the degree of overt labor relations conflict and hostility with and without arbitration.
Inhibitor of representative government	Public decision processes should be accessible and accountable.	Public authority is delegated to nonaccountable third parties.	Comparison of accessibility and accountability of labor relations decision processes with and without arbitration.
Inhibitor of genuine collective bargaining	Bargaining incentives should be protected and strengthened.	There exists a high probability of satisfactory award and low usage costs.	Comparison of bargaining behaviors with and without arbitration.

poorly arbitration performs these various functions. As the table suggests, arbitration advocates can point to three major benefits that arbitration might provide, while the skeptics can emphasize two sets of costs that these procedures may impose. The connecting thread among all these positive and negative functions is the set of premises upon which they are constructed, for each premise assumes that there is some group, process, or political condition that needs to be protected or enhanced. Much of the debate among students of arbitration seems to result from the different normative premises they hold; and since there is no formula for determining the relative importance of these premises, there is no reason to expect that there will emerge a single arbitration paradigm upon which everybody can, will,

or should agree. These same students, however, should agree that since arbitration has multiple impacts, it should be evaluated along several dimensions rather than simply looking at how well it prevents strikes.

This diversity of impact leads to a second point—that although arbitration is directed at government acting in its role as (unionized) employer, arbitration's more important long-run effects may be upon government as regulator of the polity. For instance, arbitration's most valuable long-run function may be the manner in which it quietly absorbs and accommodates conflicting interest group claims over scarce public resources. The price for this accommodation, however, may be the insulation of these allocative decisions from the direct influence of many individuals or groups with strong interests in these decisions. In addition, such insulation may be particularly unwelcome because it occurs primarily at the local level, which is the level of government supposedly most responsive to citizen influence.

Whatever arbitration's political impacts may be, they need to be discussed in tentative terms, for there seems to be a sort of Gresham's Law of Arbitration Research in which researchers' attention is drawn toward arbitration's labor relations impacts. With all its labor relations labels, though, public sector interest arbitration is established through the political rule-making process (primarily at the state level) and then operates as a surrogate for the political resource-allocation process (primarily at the local level).[37] Even though these political roles and impacts may be somewhat "messy" to study, they deserve more research attention than they have received to date. In particular, there needs to be a careful examination of the balance struck between the public-interest and private-interest impacts of arbitration.

As noted earlier, the most visible rationale for arbitration has been the perceived need to protect the public from the withdrawal of supposedly vital public services (though such perceptions seem to be based on little or no empirical foundation). However, the public interest appears to refer only to this strike-prevention objective, for once an arbitration system is implemented and working there seems to be little or no room for formal public participation in the arbitration proceedings. Furthermore, arbitration's availability reduces outcome uncertainty by eliminating the need for unions (or managements) to assume the risks of work stoppages or other forms of political-influence manipulation to press

their demands.[38] Even if arbitration is not used, its availability tends to ensure that over time the level of negotiated benefits in a jurisdiction will not diverge substantially from the level of benefits obtainable via arbitration.[39] In short, the passage of arbitration legislation is consistent with Downs's theory that producers will influence government action more than consumers "because most men earn their incomes in one area but spend them in many. . . ."[40]

The adoption of the view that arbitration is primarily a response to interest group pressures should have a salutary effect on public labor relations research and policy making. Such a view seems far more consistent with how arbitration legislation actually is passed and renewed than the suggestion that such legislation results from the policy makers' concern for the general welfare. Similarly, this view might provide a useful framework for investigating and explaining why different jurisdictions have adopted so many different arbitration procedures. Further, this view would explicitly allow for the use of arbitration as a dependent variable that measures the distribution of political influence necessary to shape public labor relations systems in a desired direction. In addition,

---

[37] A particularly useful research topic is whether arbitration alters the proportionate shares of government resources allocated to covered and uncovered employee groups.

[38] Arbitration may be particularly important to the unions as a risk-avoidance mechanism when they are faced with hostile environmental forces, such as "taxpayer revolts." During such periods, arbitration may be less important to the unions as a mechanism to get "more" and more important as a mechanism to protect against "less."

[39] One recent analysis demonstrated that within a single jurisdiction negotiated and arbitrated outcomes are quite interdependent. Henry S. Farber and Harry C. Katz, "Interest Arbitration, Outcomes, and the Incentive to Bargain: The Role of Risk Preference," *Industrial and Labor Relations Review* (October 1979). See Stern, et al., *Final-Offer Arbitration*, and Kochan, et al., *An Evaluation of Impasse Procedures*, for empirical results showing that the differences between negotiated and arbitrated wage increases are rather modest.

[40] Anthony Downs, *An Economic Theory of Democracy* (New York: Harper & Row, 1957), p. 254.

the interest group concept should focus more attention than has occurred to date on the political roles and effects of arbitration. Finally, thinking of arbitration as a response to interest-group pressures suggests the replacement of the unverified assumption that public employee strikes are inappropriate with empirical investigations of the comparative costs and benefits of strikes and arbitration. These investigations should produce much more informed debate about the desired shape of public dispute-resolution arrangements than has occurred so far.

CHAPTER 12

Bargaining Issues and Outcomes

For the parties to the industrial relations system, the most important components of that system are its outcomes. It is the outcomes of the system that determine the terms and conditions under which the workers in the system will be employed. It is the outcomes of the system that have a role in the determination of the employer's labor costs that, in turn, affect the profitability of the enterprise. For the workers, it is the outcomes of collective bargaining that may influence how they evaluate the leadership of the union.

This chapter examines bargaining outcomes with respect to wages, fringe benefits, and other terms and conditions of employment. Although wages may be the visible outcome of the system, they are not necessarily the most important for each party at all times. For example, in 1979 and 1980, the United Auto Workers made what it viewed as substantial wage concessions in order to insure that the Chrysler corporation would remain in business. In this instance, the UAW chose job security over wages.

WAGES

Recently, two well-known labor economists, after reviewing all of the research that has been done during the last 15 years on union wage effects, concluded that there was a wage premium of 10–20 percent associated with unionism.[1] As their review indicates, there has been a great deal of debate among researchers as to the effect of unions on wages. The question of the union effect on wages is more complex, and more difficult to answer, than might appear at first glance. The question often addressed is: "Do employees who are represented by a union receive a higher wage

---

[1] Richard B. Freeman and James L. Medoff, "The Impact of Collective Bargaining: Illusion or Reality," in *United States Industrial Relations, 1950–80: A Critical Assessment,* ed. Jack Stieber, Robert McKersie, and Daniel Quinn Mills (Madison, Wis.: Industrial Relations Research Association, forthcoming).

than they would receive if they were not represented by a union? In order to answer this question, it is necessary to have two items of information: (1) the wage rate received by the employees who are represented by a union and (2) the wage rate those employees would receive if they were not represented by a union. While the first item of information is easy to obtain by simple observation, the second item of information cannot be observed directly because there is no way of knowing, with certainty, what any unionized employee would be earning if he or she were not a member of a union. As a result, estimation of this second item becomes a difficult and complex task. Another way to address the question is by focusing on the average wage level of the firm rather than the wage rate paid to the employee.

A second problem in estimating the effects of unions on wages is attempting to determine the extent to which an individual's wage rate is due to unionism, and the extent to which it is due to other factors. The wage rate paid to any employee is determined by a host of factors, i.e., the education of the employee, work experience in the firm and prior to being hired, occupation, geographical location, industry, the efficiency of the employer's capital stock, and unionism.

Another question that may be asked is, "Are union wages too high?" Again, the question is more complex than would first appear. In 1978, the average hourly wage in the highly unionized automobile industry was $8.51 per hour, while in the less unionized retail trade industry, the average hourly wage was $4.19 per hour. Does this difference of $4.32 per hour indicate that wages in the auto industry are too high? It may be that the auto industry has a higher level of productivity than retail trade; if the workers in the auto industry are more productive than the workers in retail trade, one would expect auto workers to be paid more than retail workers. This does, not of course, answer the question of how much more?

In addition, it may also be asked, "If union wages are too high, do they contribute to increasing prices and to inflation?" This question can only be answered by examining the importance to pricing decisions of wage increases in the unionized sector, and the extent to which union wage increases lead price increases.

Finally, it may be observed that not all union wages are high and union effects may vary across unions. Unions such as the International Brotherhood of Teamsters and the United Mine Workers are thought to have more power, and the ability to obtain higher wages for their members, than such unions as the International Ladies Garment Workers Union or the Amalgamated Clothing and Textile Workers Union.

The readings that follow explore these issues. The first reading, by Harold Levinson, discusses the question of *union power* in terms of *employer power.* He examines the question of the relationship between the market power of the employer and the ability of a union to extract large wage increases.

The second reading, by Farrell Bloch and Mark Kuskin, addresses the question of whether or not unions affect the operation of other factors that might also affect wages. They conclude that other influences on wages operate to a lesser extent in the presence than in the absence of unions.

In the last reading, Daniel J.B. Mitchell examines the effect that unions and collective bargaining have on inflation. He concludes that unions do not appear to be a prime cause of inflation but can exacerbate ongoing inflation. They can, however, moderate it as well.

UNIONISM, CONCENTRATION, AND WAGE CHANGES: TOWARD A UNIFIED THEORY

Harold M. Levinson*

[This article examines the] issue of the relationship, if any, between the competitive character of the product market and the ability of a union to obtain wage increases. . . . [Several studies have indicated] that at least for certain time periods and industrial sectors, greater rates of increase in wages have been strongly [related to] three variables—relatively strong union strength (as measured by the proportion of production workers covered by collective agreements), relatively high "degrees of monopoly" (as measured by concentration ratios), and relatively high profit rates. Futhermore, attempts to isolate the separate effects of each [of these factors] on wages . . . have not been particularly helpful. . . . Consequently, these results have been interpreted by some writers as suggesting that the three variables do not act independently of each other, but rather that it is the combined result of strong union power facilitated by and functioning within, a "permissive" product market environment which *together* explain the more favorable wage movements. It should be noted that under this interpretation, strong unionism would still represent the primary or "initiating" force, since there is no reason to presume that more concentrated and more profitable industries would, on those accounts alone, continue to grant greater wage increases over time than would other industries. . . .

[Other researchers have questioned the basic notion of such a relationship. These researchers have noted that industries such as bituminous coal mining, trucking, and building construction are characterized by strong unions and strong product market competition. It has also been observed that these industries might be paying higher wages for higher quality labor; thus these firms would be paying higher wages even in the absence of unions. Moreover there is no reason why firms with market power could not use that power to resist unions rather than to give them high wage rates.]

TOWARD ANOTHER THEORY

* * * * *

In the remainder of this article, an attempt will be made to develop a more unified analysis of the forces affecting the wage change-degree of monopoly relationship, into which these various points of view may be fitted.

We have observed that in the manufacturing industries of the economy, a strong correlation has been found over fairly long periods of time between rates of increase in wages and two "explanatory" variables, union strength and concentration ratios. Rees has suggested, however, that "it just

* Professor of Economics, University of Michigan. Reprinted in an abridged form, with permission, from the *Industrial and Labor Relations Review*, 20, no. 2 (January 1967), pp. 198–205. © 1967 by Cornell University. All rights reserved.

so happens" that union strength and high concentration are correlated in manufacturing, but that such a relationship is not generally true in other sectors of the economy and indeed the opposite may well be the case.[1]

Segal's analysis, however, provides an explanation of the fact that the relationship between union collective bargaining coverage and an oligopolistic product market structure is not coincidental but follows rather from the relative ease of entry of new firms into production outside the jurisdictional control of the union.[2] Thus, industries having high concentration ratios are characterized by entry barriers imposed by the nature of the industry itself—high capital requirements, patent controls, established brand names, and so forth. Given these entry barriers, a union, once firmly established within all or a large proportion of the existing firms in the industry, is more able to maintain its jurisdictional control against the threat of erosion by the establishment of new nonunion firms and hence (other things equal) can press more aggressively for greater wage adjustments. By contrast, a competitive product market implies a much greater ease of entry of new firms as well as a much higher degree of plant mobility among existing concerns, both of which contribute to a gradual erosion of union jurisdictional control and to a lowered ability to obtain wage gains. The [strong relationship] observed in manufacturing between union strength and concentration is therefore not coincidental, but is systematically related by the structural interaction of entry barriers on the maintenance of union jurisdictional control.

---

[1] Albert Rees, "Union Wage Gains and Enterprise Monopoly," *Essays on Industrial Relations* (Ann Arbor and Detroit: University of Michigan, Wayne State University, Institute of Industrial Relations, 1961).

[2] M. Segal, "Union Wage Impact and Market Structure," *Quarterly Journal of Economics*, February 1964, pp. 96–114.

A CAUSE OF UNION STRENGTH

How then can the continuing presence—indeed in some cases the continuing expansion—of some of the strongest unions be explained, unions which are in industries characterized by large numbers of sellers, ease of entry, and strong competitive pricing pressures? Among the cases having these characteristics would be the Teamsters, the building tradesmen, the United Mine Workers, the offshore maritime seamen, the longshoremen, and some of the unions in the service industries.

The explanation suggested here lies in precisely the same logic as that relating to manufacturing, except that the protection against nonunion entrants which is provided by concentration in the manufacturing industries is provided by an alternative characteristic of production—the spatial limitations of the physical area within which new entrants can effectively produce. In every one of the industries mentioned, the technological or physical character of production requires that any new entrant into production must either locate his plant within a specific and relatively limited geographic area or must physically enter such a specific area at some important phase of the production process. Under this type of industrial structure, the union need only achieve a high degree of organizational strength within the limited strategic areas involved in order to be protected against the undermining effects of new nonunion entrants or of runaway shops, irrespective of how easy entry into the industry itself might be.

It should be noted that the point being made here regarding the importance of the spatial characteristics of the area of effective entry into production is not the same as the more commonly made point regarding the geographic area of the product market, though the two concepts are sometimes significantly related. In the construction and local service industries, for example, both the area of effective production and the product market area are local. In mining, however, the area of effective production is limited by the geographic location of the available mineral resources, but the product market is national in scope. Similarly, the important limitation in maritime is related to the requirements of production rather than to the extent of the product market, since the limited geographic availability of adequate port facilities requires that entrants into stevedoring or ocean shipping must be established or at some point must operate within the unions' jurisdictional control. Finally, in long-line trucking it is only necessary that the union be firmly established within a few key cities throughout a region in order to exert control over the great bulk of new entrants, since any entrant wishing to engage in important over-the-road operations almost invariably must function within the union's jurisdiction at some point in his operations. . . .

Once this key relationship is seen between the maintenance of union strength and the conditions of entry of new firms into effective production, the reason for the differing experience of the manufacturing and nonmanufacturing sectors with respect to the unionism-concentration relationship also becomes clear. This is because it is most commonly in manufacturing that concentration rather than spatial production limitations would be the dominant mechanism limiting the establishment of new firms outside the union's jurisdiction. For while it is true that the locational flexibility of some types of manufacturing operations is limited by high transportation costs, availability of raw materials, or other particular circumstances, the number of operations so limited is quite small relative to all manufacturing and even these few usually have a wide range of locational choices within broad regional limits. On the other hand, it is in mining, construction, transportation, and services where the spatial limitations on effective entry would most commonly

be found. Hence, . . . once the analysis is broadened to include nonmanufacturing, concentration is replaced by spatial characteristics as the primary mechanism for preventing entry outside the union's jurisdictional control, even in the face of a highly competitive product market structure.

EMPLOYER RESISTANCE TO UNIONIZATION

Up to this point, we have been concerned solely with the effect of product market structure on the strength of the union and on its ability to press aggressively for wage increases; we now suggest, however, that the competitive nature of the product market also has an important bearing on the employer's *ability to resist* such union pressure.

It is a commonplace observation that the history of the American labor movement indicated that oligopolistic industries have been more difficult to unionize than have competitive industries. With few exceptions, most of the earliest and strongest unions were to be found in such competitive industries as construction, printing, bituminous mining, men's and women's clothing, and a few local service industries such as local trucking and entertainment. Conversely, attempts to organize such oligopolistic industries as steel, automobiles, nonferrous mining, meatpacking, machinery, and shipbuilding were largely abortive except under the extremely favorable conditions of World War I.

While several other factors have undoubtedly also played a role in explaining the differing degrees of success in organizing different industries, one major consideration was the fact that the large oligopolistic employers had at their disposal substantial financial resources with which to resist union organizing efforts through such devices as the employment of spies and private police and the importation of strikebreakers; the funds available to smaller competitive employers for these purposes were usually much less. In addition, large financial reserves enable the oligopolist to more easily absorb losses attendant upon a shutdown of operations caused by a lockout or a strike involving a demand for union recognition; here again, the small individual competitor was in a much weaker position to withstand such a loss of current revenue. Hence, other things equal, the ability of a union to *organize* a new plant successfully was considerably greater if the employer were a small competitor rather than a large oligopolist.

The passage of the Wagner Act in 1935, by making anti-union practices unlawful, virtually eliminated the advantages previously held by oligopolistic employers with respect to their ability to resist the unionization of their employees. There is no reason to presume, however, that the relative bargaining advantages of the oligopolist are not still present insofar as the ability to resist union bargaining demands is concerned.

A closer analysis of the nature of employer bargaining strength is some of the most strongly unionized competitive industries provides much support for this point of view. In such industries as trucking, maritime, and construction, the great bulk of individual companies are small, with limited financial reserves with which to withstand a strike of any duration. Consequently, when faced with the threat of a work stoppage from such militant and organizationally strong unions as the Teamsters, the Longshoremen, the various seamen's unions, or the building trades, their ability to provide any significant resistance is very weak indeed.

EMPLOYER'S ASSOCIATIONS

As a result, employers in these industries and in others having similar characteristics have usually attempted to overcome this weakness by negotiating as a group through one or more employers' associations. An analysis of the actual bargaining policies of these associations in trucking, longshore, and maritime indicates, however, that they are often unable to maintain a "united front" in the face of a strike threat because of the large number of firms involved, the wide divergence of interests among them, and their generally poor financial resources. In trucking, for example, those firms whose operations are primarily intrastate are often subject to less stringent regulatory policies than those predominantly in interstate commerce; similarly, certain carriers are more affected than others by competitive modes of transportation, some handle types of freight more able to bear higher charges; and so forth. In maritime, there are strong internal differences between the subsidized and nonsubsidized carriers, between those engaged in freight versus passenger operations, etc. Similarly, in construction the varying importance of the different skilled trades in different types of construction and the varying time pressures under which different groups of contractors may be operating creates sharply different views regarding appropriate bargaining policy. Under these circumstances, a particular set of demands will be less burdensome to some employers than to others or the potential losses from a strike will be much greater to some than to others. And given the large number of employers involved and the limited financial reserves of many of them, one or another group will be anxious to avoid a strike and a settlement favorable to the union is usually forthcoming.

By contrast, the larger and financially much stronger firms in oligopolistic industries are in a relatively better position to withstand the potential losses from a strike, even when facing such formidable unions as the Automobile Workers or Steelworkers. In addition, the fewer firms involved in negotiations makes it easier to develop and maintain a unified policy in any joint negotiating endeavor, whether formal or informal. This is not meant to say, of course, that internal differences do not arise or that a "divide and conquer" technique may not sometimes be successful. Relatively, however, the seriousness of these problems is much less under oligopolistic than under competitive conditions.

The generalization is suggested, therefore, that *given a similarly high degree of union organizational strength, employers in a more concentrated industry will be able to resist union pressures more effectively than employers in a more competitive industry.* This proposition is quite consistent with the related hypothesis discussed earlier that (at least in manufacturing) *the greater the degree of concentration in an industry, the greater will be the union's ability to maintain a high degree of organizational strength and consequently the greater will be its rate of increase in wages.* Thus a high degree of concentration in the product market has a two-edged effect. On the one hand, it can provide the union with greater protection against the entry of nonunion competitors, and thus help to maintain the union's jurisdictional strength in the industry. Yet at the same time, it is also associated with fewer firms of larger size and greater financial reserves which are able more effectively to resist union pressures. But where the union is able to maintain complete jurisdictional control *despite* the competitive product market, because of spatial types of entry limitations—as in trucking, maritime, construction, or mining—its bargaining position would be made even stronger by the weaker "resistance power" of the competitive employers. This would suggest that, other things equal, this latter group of industries would experience as great or greater wage increases over time than would the strongly unionized and more concentrated industries.

CONCLUSION

The preceding discussion has attempted to provide an internally consistent explanation of the empirical results reported in the several studies noted at the beginning, including the positive correlation found in manufacturing between union strength and concentration and the negative coefficient associated with the interaction of unionism and concentration. It has also attempted to provide an underlying rationale for the observation—probably correct but as yet untested—that the unionism-concentration relationship is much less prevalent in the nonmanufacturing sectors of the economy and for the further observation—also still to be tested—that, other things equal, wage increases in strongly unionized, highly competitive, nonmanufacturing industries are at least as great as those in the strongly unionized, oligopolistic, manufacturing sectors.

WAGE DETERMINATION IN THE UNION AND NONUNION SECTORS

Farrell E. Bloch* and Mark S. Kuskin

Wage differences between the union and nonunion sectors result from sectoral variation in both worker characteristics, such as educational attainment and job experience, and labor market rewards to these characteristics. . . .

The first section of the paper contains estimates of separate wage equations for individuals in the union and nonunion sectors. The second focuses only on individuals in manufacturing industries for whom more details on the industry in which they work are available.

BASIC WAGE EQUATIONS

Our observations, taken from the May 1973 United States Current Population Survey, are limited to white, non-Spanish males between age 25 and 64 who are employed in the private sector. Focusing on white males circumvents complex interactions among wage rates, unionism, and discrimination. The age boundaries exclude most white males in school or with part-time jobs, for whom reported wage rates often do not reflect market values of accumulated human capital. Excluding public sector employees avoids complications due to the rather different wage structures for

* Professor, Center of International Studies, Princeton University. Kuskin was an undergraduate economics student at Princeton at the time of this study. Reprinted in an abridged form, with permission, from the *Industrial and Labor Relations Review*, 31, no. 2 (January 1978), pp. 183–92. © 1978 by Cornell University. All rights reserved.

private and government employees. However, although our restricted sample reduces wage variation that cannot be explained by our independent variables, it should be noted that results based on this sample may not be applicable to the remaining sectors of the work force.

The dependent variable in our wage equations is . . . each individual's usual weekly earnings divided by his usual weekly hours. This variable may include overtime work and thus should not be confused with individual . . . wage rates. The coefficients of the independent variables in our wage equations may be interpreted as the percentage change in the wage rate effected by unit changes in the explanatory variables.

Our most important independent variables are probably education, experience, and experience-squared. . . . Our education variable indicates years of formal schooling between zero and 18. One problem with this measurement is that individuals with more than 18 years of schooling cannot be differentiated from those with exactly 18 years of education. However, since only .13 percent of the union and 3.24 percent of the nonunion employees reported this maximum level of schooling, we assume that all such individuals have had exactly 18 years of education. . . .

The experience variable is defined as age minus education minus 6. This variable indicates potential work experience after the completion of formal schooling. It overstates work experience for those individuals who have not held jobs for their entire postschool careers, but this is much less likely to be the case for our sample than for a random sample of American workers. We expect that the [relationship between earnings, on one hand, and] the education and experience variables [on the other] will be positive, [since both education and experience would be expected to increase an employee's productivity on the job, other things equal, resulting in higher earnings for that employee. The relationship between] the experience-squared [variable and earnings is expected to] be negative, reflecting diminishing returns to work experience as experience itself increases. We also expect that the effect on wage rates of education and experience will be greater for nonunion employees than for unionized employees if employers in the nonunion sector are more responsive to market forces. This argument is perhaps stronger for the education than for the experience variable, given the importance of seniority and built-in pay increases for union members.

Other independent variables . . . include marital status, perhaps regarded by many employers as a proxy for such personality traits as stability and responsibility, and veteran status, indicating either training in a given skill or time lost in the civilian labor markert. The effect on wage rates of being married is expected to be positive, that of veteran status ambiguous, in both sectors.

Also included is a regional price index. . . . Although we expect the [relationship between the] price index [and earnings] to be positive in both the union and nonunion [sectors], we expect it to be [stronger] in the nonunion [sector], given the tendency for unions to attempt to eliminate wage differentials resulting from geographic differences, especially through centralized bargaining of unions in national product markets. Finally, we have included a set of . . . industry and occupa-

tion . . . variables to correct for varying labor demand across labor markets.

RESULTS

[The Appendix] contains the results from our estimated union and nonunion wage equations. . . .

Our predictions . . . are strongly supported by the results. The education, experience, and price level variables are all positively and significantly related to earnings. Furthermore, the corresponding effects in each equation are significantly greater in the nonunion equation than in the union equation.. . . . In addition, the coefficients of the variables indicating marital status are positive in each equation, with the effect stronger for married men with wife absent or deceased. The effect on the nonunion wage is significantly greater than that on the union wage . . . only for those men married with wife present. Veteran status does not appear to affect wages significantly in either sector.

In general, unions appear to have the effect of flattening out the wage equation. The union wage-experience profile peaks at about 27 years and, as noted above, is flatter than that of the nonunion sector, which peaks at about 28.5 years. Thus, an additional year of experience for a new worker raises the wage of union workers by about one percent and that of the nonunion workers by about 2.3 percent. For each additional 10 years of experience, the union effect declines by roughly .4 percent and the nonunion effect by .8 percent. The percentage increases in wage rates resulting from an additional year of formal education are 1.8 percent for union workers and 5.1 percent for nonunion workers. The effect on pay of a one percent increase in the price index is about one percent in the nonunion [sector] and roughly half that in the union [sector].

Johnson and Youmans also observe relatively flat union-education and union-age profiles, which they explain in terms of union seniority systems.[1] Under these systems, workers tend to be promoted if they remain with a firm, so there is little incentive for human capital investment. In addition, in unionized firms with seniority systems, employers are more likely to keep an older worker in a responsible position than to promote a younger worker.

The results also indicate that the union effect on laborers' wages is high relative to that for most occupational groups and that the effect on agricultural workers' wages is high relative to that for most industrial groups. No occupational union-nonunion differential is significantly higher . . . than that for the reference occupation, laborers; the differentials for managers and sales, clerical, and service workers are significantly lower. Only workers in welfare and other professional services industries have significantly higher industrial union-nonunion wage differentials than employees in the reference industry, agriculture; the differentials for workers in mining, manufacturing, railroads, and other utilities are significantly lower.

The above results must be qualified by the failure . . . to capture possible effects of the explanatory variables on forms of employee compensation other than money wage rates. If such effects are stronger for union members than others, then the effect of such variables as education and experience on *total* employee compensation will not necessarily be greater for nonunion workers.

UNION-NONUNION DIFFERENTIAL

In union-nonunion wage differential can be computed in many ways. [Depending on the method of estimation, we computed

---

[1] George C. Johnson and Kenwood C. Youmans, "Union Relative Wage Effects by Age and Education," *Industrial and Labor Relations Review*, January, 1971, pp. 171–80.

a differential that ranged from 9.29 percent to 15.87 percent.] . . . The union-nonunion differentials are generally greater in the lower skilled and highly unionized occupations.

WORKERS IN MANUFACTURING

We also estimated wage equations for workers in manufacturing industries. . . . Employers in concentrated [manufacturing] industries may pay higher wages than others if workers in these industries share the monopoly or oligopoly [return] obtained by these firms, a situation especially likely to occur when these workers are unionized and therefore have a relatively strong bargaining position. On the other hand, firms in concentrated industries may have substantial financial reserves with which to resist union wage demands, despite the fact that these firms originally may have been easier for unions to organize because of economics of scale.

[Manufacturing tends to be characterized by large establishments.] To the extent that establishment size indicates the ability to achieve economics of scale in providing fringe benefits, [establishment size may measure the extent to which employers are willing to provide employees with higher fringe benefits in lieu of higher monetary wages. Thus, establishment size may have a positive relationship with wages.] . . . To the extent that unions achieve relatively high percentages of fringe benefits in total employee compensation, the establishment size variable may be more strongly negative in the union equation than in the nonunion equation. [Although not presented here, generally the results for manufacturing are rather similar to those reported in the Appendix.]

The signs and relative magnitudes of the education, experience, and price level results are all the same as in [the Appendix]. The veteran-status [variable is] again [unrelated to earnings] and the marital-status variables are again positive, although not always [significantly related to wage rates] and in no case significantly different [between the union and nonunion sectors.]

The [estimates of] union-nonunion wage differentials [range from −3.43 percent to 6.97 percent for manufacturing only.] These relatively small differentials are consistent with the greater [effects] for manufacturing industry variables in the nonunion as compared with the union equation in [the Appendix]. The concentration ratio variable is negative in each equation, significantly so only in the union [sector] and not significantly different across [the two sectors]. These results provide mild support for the ability of firms in concentrated industries to withstand union wage demands and are also consistent with the hypothesis of concentrated firms' monopsony power. The establishment-size variable is negative in the union [sector] and positive in the nonunion [sector] although in neither case significant. . . . However, the nonunion establishment-size result is significantly greater than the union result. This is consistent with our hypothesis that both large firms and unions have relatively strong preferences for fringe benefits as compared with monetary wage payments.

CONCLUSIONS

The results of this paper clearly indicate differing structures of wage determination in the union and nonunion sectors. Nonunion sector wages are generally more responsive to individual worker levels of education and experience and to regional price-level variation. Despite the greater labor market rewards to these characteristics in the nonunion sector, union-nonunion wage differentials are positive for most occupations, especially so in those that are more highly unionized and less skilled.

Despite the different wage structures in the two sectors, estimated union-nonunion wage differentials . . . do not differ greatly [with different methods of computation].

Our estimates of these differentials from both separate and combined equations are generally slightly lower than those obtained by other investigators. Although there are important differences in the analysis and data used in other studies that render comparisons difficult, the most likely explanation for our relatively low estimates is the high unemployment and unanticipated inflation in 1973 relative to the late 60s, when the [other] studies were undertaken. One would expect union bargaining power to be weaker in periods of higher unemployment. In addition, contract-determined union wages are generally not as responsive to unanticipated inflation as are wages in the nonunion sector, although the increased use of cost-of-living escalators should reverse this trend.

As many authors have pointed out, these estimated union-nonunion differentials are imperfect measures of the extent to which unions have raised wages over levels that would have prevailed in the absence of unionism because nonunion wages themselves are affected by the presence of unionism. Nonunion employers may set higher wages in an attempt to prevent their firms from being unionized or simply to compete with union employers in recruiting labor. On the other hand, high union wages and possibly resultant high product prices will tend to reduce employment in the union sectors (and in those nonunion establishments where the threats of union organization and competing recruitment are effective) and to increase the supply of labor to the nonunion sector, thus depressing nonunion wages.

Union-nonunion wage differentials also allow union employers to ration the presumed excess supply of labor to union jobs by selecting especially well-qualified workers. Part of our estimated union-nonunion differentials may reflect sectoral differences in labor quality not accounted for by our independent variables.

APPENDIX

TABLE 1   SEPARATE WAGE EQUATIONS FOR UNION AND NONUNION EMPLOYEES

Standard errors are in parentheses

INDEPENDENT VARIABLES	DEPENDENT VARIABLE LOG (HOURLY WAGE)		T-STATISTIC OF DIFFERENCE
	UNION	NONUNION	
Education	.01771†	.05070†	−10.771†
	(.00222)	(.00211)	
Experience			
Experience	.00976†	.02272†	−5.587†
	(.00167)	(.00161)	
Experience-squared	−.00018†	−.00040†	5.185†
	(.00003)	(.00003)	
Price index	.00523	.01115	−6.247†
	(.00066)	(.00068)	
Marital status			
Spouse present	.09669†	.21582†	−4.454†
	(.01939)	(.01842)	
Spouse absent	.07578	.14859†	−1.276
	(.04037)	(.04032)	
Widowed	.06159†	.11524†	−1.351
	(.02781)	(.02834)	
Single, never married	—	—	—
Veteran status	−.00603	−.01058	.339
	(.00907)	(.00987)	
Occupation			
Professional workers	.29455†	.36544†	1.633
	(.03149)	(.02986)	
Managers	.16377†	.38286†	−5.517†
	(.02776)	(.02842)	
Sales workers	.06551	.25837†	−3.202†
	(.05175)	(.03080)	
Clerical workers	.05971*	.14681†	−2.115*
	(.02588)	(.03203)	
Craftsmen	.19981†	.21318†	−.414
	(.01735)	(.02728)	
Operatives	.07878†	.05103†	.790
	(.01816)	(.03007)	
Transport equipment workers	.05428†	−.00369	1.463
	(.02082)	(.03371)	
Service workers	−.10337†	−.00119	−2.202*
	(.02974)	(.03563)	
Laborers	—	—	—
Industry			
Mining	.36746†	.54119†	−1.721*
	(.08654)	(.05200)	
Construction	.61119†	.49830†	1.226
	(.08308)	(.03970)	
Manufacturing—nondurables	.23785†	.46514†	−2.475†
	(.08314)	(.03899)	
Manufacturing—durables	.23780†	.49688†	−2.842†
	(.08278)	(.03815)	

TABLE 1 (*concluded*)

Standard errors are in parentheses

	DEPENDENT VARIABLE LOG (HOURLY WAGE)		T-STATISTIC
INDEPENDENT VARIABLES	UNION	NONUNION	OF DIFFERENCE
Railroad	.36207†	.63607†	−2.319*
	(.08502)	(.08201)	
Other transportation	.45511†	.46091†	−.061
	(.08422)	(.04525)	
Other utilities	.28670†	.59577†	−3.219†
	(.08445)	(.04566)	
Wholesale	.28637†	.41775†	−1.374
	(.08666)	(.04039)	
Retail	.25799†	.20195†	.602
	(.08465)	(.03873)	
Finance	.29274†	.43634†	−1.341
	(.09878)	(.04144)	
Business—repair	.24169†	.33518†	−.929
	(.09103)	(.04302)	
Personal services	.26022†	.11579*	1.154
	(.11119)	(.05617)	
Entertainment	.31364†	.21384†	.870
	(.09925)	(.06340)	
Welfare	−.11910	−.47953†	2.349†
	(.14350)	(.05440)	
Hospitals	.11821	.22501†	−.814
	(.11819)	(.05520)	
Medical, except hospitals	.35951*	.33770†	.096
	(.21678)	(.07113)	
Education	.12998	.03052	.850
	(.10548)	(.05043)	
Other professional services	.43615†	.46666†	2.271*
	(.10238)	(.04716)	
Agriculture	—	—	—
Constant	4.84777	3.31053	
R²	.31042	.39709	
F	57.87279	157.52971	
N	4406	8167	
S.E.E.	.28251	.41935	

* Significant at the .05 level using a one-tailed test.
† Significant at the .01 level using a one-tailed test.

12-3

COLLECTIVE BARGAINING AND THE ECONOMY

Daniel J. B. Mitchell*

The economic impact of collective bargaining is potentially a huge topic. Many possible impacts might be considered, including some which are often considered to be beyond the scope of conventional economics. This chapter explores only some of the areas in which collective bargaining might be expected to have an influence, with an emphasis on macroeconomic concerns. It explores the impact of bargaining on wages, on wage determination and inflation, and on anti-inflation policy including guidelines and controls. . . .

KEY ECONOMIC IMPACTS

It will be argued below that unions and collective bargaining appreciably change the character of wage setting. Union wages can easily be shown to be higher than nonunion wages as a general rule. A more difficult question is causality. The wage gap could be the product of other influences which happen to be associated with unionization. Such other influences might include occupational, skill, and demographic differences between union and nonunion workers or differences in industrial characteristics (establishment size, capital intensity of production) between the union and nonunion sectors. Or, as some economists have argued recently, higher wage workers

* Professor and Director, Institute of Industrial Relations, UCLA. Reprinted from *U.S. Industrial Relations, 1950–1980: A Critical Assessment*, Jack Stieber, Robert B. McKersie, and D. Quinn Mills, eds. (Madison, Wis.: Industrial Relations Research Association, 1981), pp. 1–46.

might have a higher propensity to unionize, thus creating a statistical optical illusion.

A view on union impacts on wage differentials is an essential ingredient to research on the determination of wage *change*. If it is believed, for example, that unions have only a negligible impact on wage differentials, i.e., that they don't raise wages, then it is difficult to entertain theories that suggest that unions have much influence on wage change or inflation. . . . On the other hand, if it is believed that unions do create union/nonunion wage differentials, then it is worthwhile investigating whether unions create appreciable differences in wage-change responsiveness to business-cycle and other influences. Since wage-change and price-change determination are interconnected, it is further possible to consider questions of the union influence on inflation and on traditional anti-inflation policy. Views on union wage-change practices are also relevant to nontraditional anti-inflation policies such as controls and guidelines. Thus, the question on union/nonunion wage differentials is very much a starting point for other important concerns.

In the sections that follow, the issue of whether unions create wage differential relative to the nonunion sector will first be discussed. Rather than keep the reader in suspense, the conclusion will be that significant and sizable wage differentials are created. . . .

Second, evidence will be presented that wage-change determination outcomes in the union sector differ from those of the nonunion sector. Union wage change is less sensitive to real business conditions, a characteristic that has implications for macroeconomic policy. The union sector is also characterized by multiyear contracts and, in many cases, by escalator clauses. Implications of these special features for macroeconomic policy in the context of a simple macro-model will be explored. Also to be considered are implications of union wage-change determination for the occasional government forays into wage-price controls and guidelines. . . .

RELATIVE WAGES

Do Union Workers Earn More?

There is one question on union/nonunion wage differentials which can be readily answered. If it is simply asked whether union workers on average earn more than nonunion workers, the answer is emphatically yes.

In 1966, the Census Bureau published a report showing that private full-time wage and salary workers who were union members had a median annual earnings about 20 percent more than full-time nonunion workers. Differentials were especially marked for nonwhites and more pronounced for females than for males. A similar study, covering *both* public and private sector workers in 1970 provided additional support for these generalizations, although the union/nonunion differentials reported tended to be lower. A study covering *mean* usual weekly earnings in May 1977 reported wider differentials than in 1970. Unfortunately, changes in definition and coverage between the three surveys make judgment about trends difficult from these data. Both the 1970 and 1977 studies show relatively large earnings premiums for blue collar and service workers and small premiums for white collar workers.

The figures from the Current Popula-

tion Survey omit such fringe benefits as employer contributions to pension plans. However, union workers typically have more fringe compensation than nonunion workers and have a greater proportion of their compensation in fringe benefit form. In 1974, for example, the Bureau of Labor Statistics reported that straight-time earnings of nonoffice workers in union establishments were 49 percent higher than those received in nonunion establishments. But on a total compensation basis, the premium was 67 percent.

Unions typically ask for more in bargaining than management initially offers. There is some limited evidence that the outcome usually comes closer to the initial management offer than to the initial union demand. Nevertheless, the process will give the appearance of a union wage-raising effect. But without knowledge of what the wage outcome would have been under nonunion circumstances, the appearances of collective bargaining are not conclusive evidence of causality.

 . . . The presence of unionization is associated with various factors which might have an influence on earnings levels. . . . Based on a sample of 93 industries . . . [we can conclude that the more] heavily unionized industries can be seen to have lower proportions of female employees in their total work forces than lightly-unionized industries. They also tend to have lower quit rates, larger establishment sizes, and more capital-intensive methods of production (measured by depreciation per employee). And, of course, earnings levels are generally higher.

Female workers typically earn significantly less than males. While it would be inappropriate to explore the reasons for the sex differential in this chapter, it is evident that the lower proportion of females in the highly unionized sector could contribute to the sectoral earnings gap. Women are also more prone to be found in occupations and industries with shorter job tenures. Hence, their presence might be associated with higher quit rates, . . . Quit rates can be viewed as a measure of employee quality with "better" employees showing longer attachment to the employer. If so, the lower quit rate in the union sector could be a proxy for higher employee quality. Union agreements often contain seniority clauses dealing with layoff order, promotion opportunities, and other job-related matters. Such clauses reinforce and formalize employer-employee attachments, especially for long-service employees.

In theory, establishment size per se should not affect wage differentials. However, it has been argued that larger establishments require workers with greater ability for self-supervision. Thus, establishment size may be a proxy for a type of employee quality. Similarly, . . . physical-capital intensity may be a proxy for human-capital intensity. Since all these characteristics may have a bearing on wage differentials, some means for standardizing for their effects is needed.

DO UNIONS CAUSE WAGE DIFFERENTIALS?

. . . There are many problems inherent in [answering the question of whether unions cause wage differentials]. As pointed out in the oft-cited study . . . by H. G. Lewis in 1963, union wage impacts may affect both union and nonunion workers. Nonunion wages might be pulled up towards union levels if nonunion employers feel threatened by organization or if nonunion employees are substituted for union workers. On the other hand, some nonunion workers may be complementary to union workers and suffer a demand decline if demand for union workers decreases due to the wage impact. And workers from the union sector may be displaced by lessening employer demand into the nonunion sector, increasing supply and depressing nonunion wages.

Although there are definite . . . problems, . . . the weight of existing studies

points to substantial union-caused wage premiums. There is evidence, indeed, that these premiums have enlarged since the Lewis study, and that the trend to wider union/nonunion differentials has characterized much of the post-Korean War period. [Unreported data show that over] the entire period 1953–78, the annual rate of hourly earnings increase in the heavily unionized sector exceeded that of the lightly unionized sector by about 0.5 percentage points per year. This is a small discrepancy in a one-year period, but over a period of 25 years its continuous effect is substantial. Average union/nonunion pay differentials of 20–30 percent for production and nonsupervisory workers seem a reasonable estimate for the late 1970s.

COLLECTIVE BARGAINING AND INFLATION

Is collective bargaining "inflationary"? Some economists have asserted that wage-push theories of inflation are fallacious and that inflation has other causes. The division of views on this question is by no means delineated along a conservative-liberal spectrum. To Milton Friedman, for example, "inflation is always and everywhere a monetary phenomenom," that is, the result of improper monetary policy. Bargaining has nothing to do with it. Friedman has long been willing to concede that union wages may be characterized by a certain "rigidity" and even that collective bargaining "makes for a steady upward pressure on the wage rate." But he has seen this as a transitory problem which will eventually produce a "moderate amount of unemployment" sufficient to limit the wage pressure. . . .

In the late 1940s, economists who worried about wage-push inflation stemming from the union sector sometimes suggested government wage policy as a solution. By the 1950s, the language describing the process had changed. There was a tendency to speak more generally of "markup inflation," "wage-price spirals," and "administered inflation," language which has persisted. And there was also a tendency to look at price determination, along with wage determination, as a source of inflation.

Perhaps more significantly, federal government policy—under both Democrats and Republicans—at times has reflected a belief that direct intervention in wage and price decisions (and especially in wage decisions) was required to restrain inflation. This view can be seen in the Kennedy-Johnson guideposts, the Nixon controls, and the Carter guidelines. In all of these efforts, absolute numerical norms were established for wage increases, norms which were central elements of the programs. It is reasonable to suppose, therefore, that the concern of those establishing these programs was more on the wage side than on the price side. And since direct-intervention programs seem inevitably to focus on the larger, more visible units of wage determination, it is also reasonable to assume that cocerns about the collective bargaining sector were at the forefront of official thinking.

Before it is possible to discuss whether unions and collective bargaining are inflationary, the term itself must be defined. One possible definition of *inflationary* is an influence that causes inflation, i.e., an influence which by itself can transform a noninflationary situation into an inflationary one. An alternative definition, however, could be an influence which hinders the restraint of inflation by orthodox policies. In the latter case, the initial cause of inflation is not an issue. What matters is whether the influence (in this instance, collective bargaining) tends to perpetuate inflation, *once* it is underway.

There is little support among economists for the proposition that collective bargaining has been an initiating cause of any of the major inflations since World War II, that is, since unions became a sig-

nificant influence on wage determination. In particular, the era of inflation which began in the mid-1960s is generally viewed as having been initiated by traditional demand pressures emanating from monetary and fiscal policies surrounding the Vietnam War buildup and the Great Society social programs. If anything, . . . union wages tended to lag in their response to rising prices and aggregate demand during 1964–68. . . .

This conclusion suggests that the alternative definition of *inflationary*, i.e., a tendency to perpetuate ongoing inflation needs a further look. Before an analysis of this possibility can be made, however, certain characteristics of union wage-change determination need to be explored.

MAJOR CHARACTERISTICS OF UNION WAGE-CHANGE DETERMINATION

Wage agreements in the union sector differ from nonunion practices in that they are formalized (written and legally binding) and often multiyear. The one-year agreement in the "major" union sector (agreements covering 1,000 or more workers) has become a comparative rarity. Three years is the common duration for these larger settlements; according to BLS, 71 percent of the major private-sector agreements surveyed in 1976 had durations varying between 25 and 36 months. Although comparable data for contracts covering fewer than 1,000 workers are spotty, it appears that the duration pattern is roughly similar. The practice of negotiating formal multiyear agreements differentiates the union and nonunion sector. . . .

Because collective bargaining contracts tend to "lock in" wage decisions for comparatively long periods, contingencies are often built into the agreements. The major contingency provision is the escalator clause, which gears wage changes to changes in the consumer price index, and the use of such clauses is quite widespread.

Forty-four percent of the contracts covering 60 percent of the workers in the BLS survey had such clauses. Not surprisingly, the use of escalators was highly correlated with contract duration. Escalators are found mainly in longer-term agreements. And they are concentrated in contracts covering large numbers of workers. . . .

Escalator clauses mean that wage adjustments in the indexed component of the union sector will react very quickly to price changes. Thus, the institutional phenomenon of escalator clauses may decrease the lag between price changes and wage changes. In effect, union wage changes are subject to two, somewhat contradictory influences. The existence of long-term agreements suggests that at any moment in time, a component of the wage package is a product of past influences. But for escalated contracts, another component is sensitive to recent price movements.

Union wage changes tend to be less sensitive to labor-market conditions than nonunion. It appears, indeed, that the observed sensitivity of aggregate wage measures to indicators of labor-market tightness or looseness (or business-cycle ups and downs), such as the unemployment rate, comes mainly from the nonunion sector. . . . [An analysis of annual] changes in hourly earnings . . . for the period 1954–1976 . . . [indicated that] typically, industries with below-average unionization rates were more sensitive to labor-market conditions and those with high unionization rates were less sensitive.

One interpretation of this finding is that the lower sensitivity is merely the result of union use of long-term contracts. Even if unemployment were an important influence in union wage-change decisions, at any moment in time a large fraction of the union workforce is simply living under old agreements which cannot respond to current labor-market conditions. This factor alone would produce short-run insensitivity.

However, there may be more to the story. . . . The industries with below-average sensitivity to unemployment are also those with relatively fewer females, lower quit rates, larger establishment sizes, higher capitalization, and higher earnings. All of these characteristics fit neatly into the newer theories of "obligational" or "career" labor markets in which employer and employee are linked in long-term relationships, even in the nonunion sector. Under these theories, turnover costs produce wage behavior which departs from the textbook "auction" model. To employers, new hires involve screening, hiring, and specific training costs. Quits inflict these costs on the employer since departing employees must be replaced. . . . Wage premiums and fringe benefits are offered to valued employees to tie them to the employer. Wage structures become relatively inflexible and demand fluctuations are accommodated by variations in hours, employment, layoffs, and unfilled vacancies.

As noted, the industries which exhibit the lower wage-change sensitivity to unemployment also tended to have characteristics which suggest strong employer-employee linkages. . . . Moreover, observed quit rates are a direct measure of attachment. [Earlier], it was noted that larger establishment sizes and capital-per-worker ratios may suggest higher human capitalization which may involve more specific training. The wage differential between the less-sensitive industries and the more-sensitive may reflect premiums to reduce turnover as well as general skill, unionization, etc.

IMPLICATIONS FOR TRADITIONAL ANTI-INFLATION POLICY

The Traditional policy response to "excessive" inflation is demand restaint. Demand restraint, through such devices as a reduction in the rate of growth in the money supply, has empirically been associated with slowdowns or drops in real economic activity, a painful process which raises unemployment. That is, demand restraint has never been successful in producing only a reduction in the rate of inflation without adverse real consequences. The "soft landings" that government officials are prone to promise on the eve of such exercises have not been achieved.

* * * * *

Economists view control of the money supply as a key element of orthodox anti-inflation policy. The public's demand for money is viewed as determined by the price level, the amount of real economic activity, and the rate of interest that can be earned on other financial assets. A change in the growth of the supply of the money by the Federal Reserve, relative to the demand for money, sets in motion changes in prices, real economic activity, and interest rates, in order to restore a balance between demand and supply. If the growth of the money supply is constricted for anti-inflation reasons, the monetary authorities hope that the major impact of the restriction will be on price inflation.

* * * * *

Statistical studies of aggregate wage determination have generally found today's rate of wage change to be linked to past rates of wage and/or price change and some measure of real economic conditions such as the unemployment rate. Of course, those union workers who have escalator clauses will also have their wage change determined by current (or quite recent) changes in prices. It is through these relationships that the union impact on anti-inflation policy enters the economic system.

Unions appear to weaken the linkage between real economic conditions and the rate of change of wages. Put another way, when unemployment rises, the rate of increase of wages in the nonunion sector slows appreciably (although not dramatically). In the union sector, however, this effect is attenuated. The attenuation influence is shown on [Exhibit 1] as impact A. It occurs for reasons already discussed including the prevalance of long-term union contracts and the "career" labor market relationships associated with the union sector. . . . Impact A weakens the effectiveness of monetary policy in dealing with inflation. Essentially, if economic slack does not produce much reaction in the rate of wage inflation, then the effect of slack on price inflation will also be attenuated. If anti-inflation monetary policy works through the creation of economic slack, then its influence on price inflation is diminished.

The use of long-term contracts in the

EXHIBIT 1   THE VARIED UNION IMPACTS ON THE ANTI-INFLATION EFFECTIVENESS OF MONETARY POLICY

UNION IMPACTS	INFLUENCE ON EFFECTIVENESS OF MONETARY POLICY	IMPLICATIONS FOR INFLATION RESTRAINT
A–Attenuation of influence of labor-market conditions on wage change	Reduces effectiveness	If inflation has occurred in past, difficulty in slowing inflation through demand restraint is increased.
B–Linkage of wage change to past price and wage inflation through long-term contracts.	No change	If inflation has been high in the past, it will tend to be high in the present.
C–Linkage of wage change to current price inflation through introduction of escalator clauses	Increases effectiveness	Difficulty in slowing inflation though demand restraint is reduced. Exogenous price shocks will be more quickly reflected in wage and price inflation.

union sector elevates the importance of past inflation in the determination of today's rate of wage change. This influence—impact B of Exhibit 1—contributes to inflation momentum. Past inflation in wages and prices is reflected in current wage determination, which in turn is reflected in current price inflation. By itself, this linkage to the past does not reduce monetary policy effectiveness; a given amount of monetary constriction might still be capable of reducing the underlying inflation rate by a specified amount. But if inflation has been high in the past, the underlying rate—even after the reduction—will be that much higher today. That is, if inflation has been high in the past, a linkage between the past and the present ensures that there will be more inflation to reduce today. A monetary exercise that reduces the inflation rate by one percentage point will seem much more dramatic if the inflation rate that is reduced is initially 5 percent than if it is 15 percent.

Although impacts A and B of unions on monetary policy effectiveness are negative, the widespread use of escalator clauses in the union sector can have the opposite effect. Escalator clauses tie wage change to current (or slightly lagged) rates of price inflation, impact C on Exhibit 1. As long as there is *some* inflation responsiveness to economic slack in the economy, escalator clauses will amplify that effect. Consider the following sequence. A monetary restriction is imposed, which increases unemployment. The higher unemployment rate reduces wage inflation in the nonunion sector, an impact which is reflected by a slowing of price inflation. Union escalator clauses cause union wage changes to slow down in response to the price deceleration. This wage impact is again reflected in prices and again picked up through escalators and reflected in wages. And the process repeats.

Escalator clauses are not always good news, however. In the event of an upward external price shock, such as a large OPEC price increase, escalator clauses will quickly step up the rate of wage increase, thus spreading the initial shock. However, this impact is symmetric; a downward price shock, such as might be associated with bumper harvests in the world agricultural markets, will also be quickly diffused by escalator clauses.

It is evident from this review that the question of whether unions make it more or less difficult to halt ongoing inflation cannot be answered generally. The question can only be answered in the context of economic circumstances, a particular view (model) of the wage and price determination system, and a specific policy towards aggregate demand. In the analysis presented above, unions will tend to make achievement of a low inflation rate more difficult if past inflation has been high and if external price shocks are currently being felt. Under these circumstances, demand restraint will have only a small impact on inflation (impact A), nonescalated long-term contracts will tend to perpetuate past inflation (impact B), and external price shocks will quickly become part of the wage-price spiral via escalator clauses (impact C). Under other circumstances, however, union escalation practices could reinforce the impact of monetary restraint in reducing inflation.

The union impacts on monetary policy effectiveness can work in reverse. In the mid-1960s, for example, when demand policy became more stimulative, the presence of the union sector probably retarded the acceleration of inflation. Demand pressures reduced unemployment and economic slack. While the nonunion sector reacted quickly with an acceleration in wage increases, the union sector did not. The decline in unemployment had little initial impact on wage change in the union sector. Long-term union contracts tended to carry the momentum of *low* inflation from the early 1960s, into the future. Those union contracts with escalator clauses did amplify the acceleration of price inflation caused by increased demand. But in many cases, negotiators in the union sector had discontinued the use of escalators in the early 1960s, thus reducing the significance of the escalator effect.

Three provisos need to be added to the analysis. As previously noted, union wage change should not be viewed as a world apart from nonunion wage change. Rather, there is a spectrum of practices running from casual labor markets through career labor markets to formalized contractual unionized labor markets. There are areas of nonunion wage determination that tend to be "unionesque" and areas of union wage-change determination that are "nonunionesque." The influences summarized on Exhibit 1 will be the same whether they come from the union or the nonunion sector. But since the properties discussed are associated with formality (explicit contracts and written escalator formulas), they have been discussed in this chapter as union impacts. In any case, wage developments in the nonunion sector, because of its sheer size in the United States, will tend to dominate aggregate wage-change indexes. Hence, there is a definite limit on the ability of bargainers in the union sector to alter aggregate wage-change determination.

The second proviso is that the discussion has deliberately avoided an exploration of price-change determination. If there are elements of pricing which carry past inflation into the present (say, firms which set prices in advance based on expectations of rising costs extrapolated from past experience), the influence would be much like that of impact B in the labor market. If some influence reduces the responsiveness of price markups to product-market conditions (say, the presence of average cost pricers who tend to raise prices as demand falls because of the impact of

fixed costs on unit costs), the impact will be much like that of impact A in the labor market. And, of course, the influence of costs on prices has an escalator-like effect because price changes tend to reflect other price changes and—through input-output connections—ultimately reflect themselves. Such an effect is similar to impact C.

Proviso number three is that there may well be other aspects of union wage-change determination that have been neglected. There is, for example, a considerable literature on wage imitation, pattern bargaining, wage-wage inflation, and the like. The link between past and present wage inflation could be interpreted as such a wage-imitation phenomenon. To the extent that wage change in the union sector is influenced by the nonunion sector, impact A might be reduced. But, to the extent that the union sector influences the nonunion sector, impact A could be increased. There is considerable controversy, however, in the literature on the implications of wage-wage imitation and it seems best to withhold judgment on its impact based on the limited evidence presently available.

IMPLICATIONS FOR NONTRADITIONAL ANTI-INFLATION POLICY

Industrialized countries, including the United States, have been experimenting with "income policies," wage-price controls, and guidelines of various types since the end of World War II. Since the early 1960s, both Democratic and Republican administrations have dabbled with alternative forms of direct intervention into wage and price setting. . . .

At one extreme, mandatory controls may be imposed, which simply order wage and price setters to respond to the signal. At the other, a "voluntary" guideline is announced—usually with a great deal of hoopla—designed to convince wage and price setters that a new, less-inflationary era is at hand. If they believe it, i.e., if their inflationary expectations are altered, the beliefs will tend to be self-fulfilling.

Efforts at direct intervention in wage and price setting often end up with a special focus on union wage determination. This is partially because the union sector presents the potential for dramatic confrontations with the government, i.e., large-scale strikes in support of wage demands beyond the allowable limits. It is also because the union sector contains large groups of workers which tend to be highly visible. (Roughly half of the private union sector is covered by agreements involving 1,000 or more workers). And it is because the authorities are concerned about union impacts A and B, the attenuation of response to the signal and the tendency to reinforce inflation momentum. On the other hand, since impact C—the use of escalators—could reinforce the impact of the signal, it it not surprising that recent intervention efforts have adopted rules which favor the use of such clauses.

The difficulty with direct intervention in wage and price setting is more one of technique than rationale. What are the apporpriate rules in the labor market to deal with myriad complexities of wage determination? Merit plans, fringe benefits, productivity bargaining, spot labor shortages, and incentive systems all require treatment in the rules of the program. Apart from these technical issues, there is the delicate question of maintaining "credibility" for programs and in obtaining at least tacit support of organized labor. In the product market, where the linkages between buyer and seller are generally looser than in the labor market, the rules for pricing can easily result in shortages and distortions which try public patience.

Even the remedies for some of these difficulties tend to founder on practical application rather than theory. During the 1970s, various proposals for tax-based income policies (TIPs) were advanced. Un-

der these proposals the tax system would be used to reward "good" bahavior or penalize "bad" behavior of wage and/or price setters. The principle behind the proposal is a simple one; if wage and price setters have financial incentives to comply with whatever guidelines are in effect, obtaining compliance will be easier.

Originally, the Carter administration wage-price guidelines program was to have a variant of a labor-market TIP, known as real wage insurance. Under this proposal, workers in units which complied with the then prevailing 7 percent wage standard would have been eligible for tax rebates if prices rose by more than 7 percent. Thus, workers' real wages were to have been protected from unanticipated inflation, at least for the period that the proposal was in effect.

A major criticism of TIP plans has been their complexity. Even when confined only to wages, a TIP plan requires writing into the Internal Revenue Code all the intricacies of compensation determination. The same issues that pose problems for guidelines and controls rules—merit plans, fringe benefits, etc.—must be dealt with in a TIP plan. Moreover, there is little room for exceptions and flexibility, since the rules must be auditable by tax officials. . . . These complications led Congress—which must approve changes in the tax code—to reject the real wage insurance proposal shortly after it had been submitted.

In short, no one has yet divised an ideal strategy for obtaining labor cooperation with programs of direct intervention. Novel ideas such as real wage insurance have not developed to the point of practical application. Labor cooperation seems to be forthcoming mainly during efforts to phase out controls and guidelines. Phase III of the Nixon controls program—which was intended as a step toward decontrol—in 1973 attracted labor participation on an advisory committee. The second year of the Carter guidelines program included a social compact with organized labor involving labor participation on a Pay Advisory Committee. That committee recommended a substantial loosening of the wage standards, recommendations which were generally adopted.

Despite the ambiguous record of direct intervention programs, and the difficulty of obtaining labor support, the intractability of ongoing inflation remains a major economic problem. Periodic episodes of direct intervention are likely to occur in the future. Exploration of unorthodox approaches to inflation control is bound to continue.

CONCLUSIONS

Unions have significant economic impacts. They do create wage differentials between union and nonunion workers, possibly contributing at the margin of the relative decline of the overall unionization rate. And they do change the structure of wage-change determination, primarily by reducing the sensitivity of wage change to labor-market tightness and looseness, and—in the case of escalated contracts—by increasing sensitivity to recent price changes. Under some circumstances, these characteristics of union wage change can hinder anti-inflation efforts using traditional demand restraint. Under other circumstances, they may have the opposite effect. It is in those situations where demand restraint policy is frustrated in influencing wage movements that direct government intervention into wage determination is often suggested. . . .

The impact of unions depicted here is not a total revision of economic structure. In the U.S. case, the heavy majority status of the nonunion workforce must be recognized. And in the union sector, management plays an important role in wage decisions. On the other hand, unions cannot be simply incorporated into a simple demand/supply framework and neglected. They are not simply variants of monopoly firms which "mark up" wages of their members but otherwise have no dynamic consequences.

FRINGE BENEFITS

Since World War II fringe benefits have become increasingly important factors in the collective bargaining relationship. During the wage and price control period of World War II, the scope of fringe benefits expanded dramatically as unions and employers were forced to hold down basic wage increases. Such issues as pensions, vacations, health insurance, and sick leave quickly became central concerns in collective bargaining, and unions began to pursue strongly a wider range of benefits as well as higher levels of existing benefits. This trend has not abated. Throughout the 1960s and 70s, fringe benefit expenditures grew faster than wages. In manufacturing, they account for approximately 25 percent of total compensation paid per hour in unionized firms and 19.6 percent in nonunion firms. In all private sector firms, fringe benefits account for 22.7 percent of total compensation paid per hour in unionized firms and 17.4 percent in nonunion firms.[1] In the article that follows, Freeman examines the relationship between unionism and fringe benefits and analyzes the impact of unions on total fringe expenditures and on the fringe share of compensation.

Fringe benefits exist today in a wide variety of forms. From issues such as unemployment compensation to prepaid legal services, fringe benefits cover numerous employment concerns. While some benefits, most notably Social Security, are government mandated, others are voluntarily provided by employers. The second article included in this section outlines recent wage and fringe benefit trends. Table 2 in Reading 12–5 indicates the diversity of the benefits provisions presently provided in many negotiated agreements. Given the extensiveness and complexity of these fringe benefits, it is impossible to comment here on each one. However, because of its significance as an employment concern, pensions deserve special note.

As an area for bargaining, pensions could be one of the most volatile issues in the 1980s. A number of factors lead to this conclusion. The

---

[1] Richard B. Freeman, "The Effect of Unionism on Fringe Benefits," *Industrial and Labor Relations Review* (July 1981), pp. 489–509. These estimates are for the period 1967–72. See page 496.

first is the passage and implementation of the Employee Retirement Income Security Act of 1974. The second is the huge magnitude of assets accumulating in pension funds. The third is the possible future insolvency and/or reduction in benefits possible in the Social Security program. The interrelationship of these three factors presage important maneuvering in this decade.

The Employee Retirement Income Security Act (ERISA) requires employers with noncontributory pension programs to set aside money equal to the likely future benefits the program would be required to pay out. It also requires that employees be given the opportunity to have their benefits vest after accumulating a given length of service (as defined by the law) rather than having to wait until retirement. The law created the need for the establishment of trust funds and the accumulation of large funds for future payments.

These funds are administered by trustees independent of the employer. Most are banks, insurance companies, and other financial institutions. The accumulated funds are loaned or invested prudently with the aim that the assets will grow and be protected. While neither the union nor the management control the funds, at the national level unions are concerned about whether or not the funds are being loaned to, or invested in, organizations which are militantly antiunion. For example, in the J. P. Stevens campaign, the Clothing and Textile Workers put pressure on banks to avoid loans to the company and asked that officers of financial institutions investing pension money withdraw as directors from the Stevens' board. The pressure placed on Stevens helped lead to the company's ending some anti-union tactics used in its organizing campaign.

Possible problems in the future for the Social Security system may lead unions to bargain more strongly for future pension benefits—perhaps at the expense of present wage increases. This possibility could result in unions insisting on a joint voice in the choice of trustees and closely monitoring the investments made by the trustees.

THE EFFECT OF UNIONISM ON FRINGE BENEFITS

Richard B. Freeman*

Does collective bargaining alter the composition of the compensation package received by workers? Is the fraction of the labor cost spent on "fringe benefits" higher in union than in nonunion firms, and if so, why? How does the impact of unionism on fringes compare to its impact on wages, which is the focus of most studies of the union effect on pecuniary rewards?

Reviewing the evidence, Reynolds concluded that much of the increase in fringes in recent years was probably attributable to "voluntary employer action" and that "the specific influence of unionism is hard to determine."[1]

This study uses detailed and disaggregated data from individual establishments to show that . . . unionism does significantly raise the fringe share of compensation and, in fact, unionism raises fringes by a greater percentage amount than it raises wages. As a result, it is argued, the union impact on total compensation is noticeably understated by standard union wage equations.

The main source of data is the Expenditures for Employee Compensation (EEC) survey of the Bureau of Labor Statistics, which contains statistics on the compensation of office and nonoffice (production) workers in private nonfarm establishments.[2] By providing information on two types of workers within an establishment, one of whom (the office worker) is rarely organized, the EEC data permit some methodological advances in the estimation of union effects. *Within*-establishment differences in compensation can be used as units of observation, eliminating the potential effects of unobserved firm factors in much the same way as a comparison of brothers or twins eliminates family background effects in the analysis of earnings among individuals.[3] In addition, it is possible to exploit the establishment data to estimate models in which unionism of production workers induces firms to raise the fringes paid nonproduction workers within the establishment. These methodological innovations have a substantive effect on the magnitude of the estimated impact of unionism.

UNION IMPACT ON THE FRINGE SHARE

The division of a dollar of compensation per hour between fringe benefits and

* Professor of Economics, Harvard University. Reprinted in an abridged form, with permission, from the *Industrial and Labor Relations Review*, 34, no. 4 (July 1981), pp. 489–509. © 1981 by Cornell University. All rights reserved.

[1] Lloyd G. Reynolds, *Labor Economics and Labor Relations* (Englewood Cliffs, N.J.: Prentice-Hall, 1974). pp. 216–17.

[2] For a detailed discussion of the survey, see U.S. Bureau of Labor Statistics, *Handbook of Methods*. Bulletin 1910 (Washington, D.C.: G.P.O., 1976), pp. 175–83.

[3] Gary Chamberlain, "An Instrumental Variable Interpretation of Identification in Variance-Components and Mimic Models," in *Kinometrics: The Determinants of Socio-Economic Success Within and Between Families*, ed. Paul Taubman (Amsterdam: North Holland Publishing, 1971). p.197.

straight-time pay can be fruitfully analyzed in terms of the *supply price* of
fringes, defined as the wage workers would
forgo to obtain the benefit. The higher the
supply price facing an employer, the
greater is the probability that the employer
will provide the fringes, the greater is the
amount likely to be spent on the fringes
that are provided, and, as a consequence,
the greater is the fringe benefit share of
compensation.

There are several reasons for expecting
trade unionism to raise the effective supply price of fringes. The most important
one is that unions are political as well as
economic institutions; therefore their behavior must be consonant with the desires
of a majority of the workers. In a world
in which some workers can be viewed as
permanently attached to firms (for reasons
of transaction costs of mobility), while
others are more mobile or marginal, the
union will give greater weight to the preferences of the older, relatively permanent
employee than to the younger, more mobile one. This differs from a competitive
market in which the desires of the marginal employee set the supply price. In the
context of the median voter model, the
union would represent the tastes of the
median worker as opposed to the marginal
worker. If, then, as seem reasonable, older
presumably less mobile workers have
greater desires for fringes,[4] the supply price
of fringes will be greater under collective
than individual bargaining. Hence, firms
that engage in collective bargaining are
likely to allot a greater share of compensation to fringe benefits.

ADDITIONAL ROUTES OF THE UNION EFFECT

Trade unionism is likely to raise the supply
price of fringes in several other ways as
well. First, by increasing the length of the

attachment between workers and firms
(raising job tenure and lowering quit
rates),[5] unionism will increase the likelihood that workers will receive deferred
fringes such as nonvested pensions or life
insurance benefits. As a result, the value
of these fringes to workers will be greater
under unionism, raising the willingness of
workers to forgo wages to obtain these
fringes.

Second, in sectors of the economy in
which workers are attached to occupations
rather than employers (construction, for
example), or in which enterprises are short
lived (the garment trade), or in which
firms are relatively small (trucking),
unions provide the type of large permanent
market institution needed to operate most
fringe programs. Without unions (or some
comparable structure) the probability that
workers would receive deferred benefits
would be too small and the employer's
start-up costs too high for most benefits
to be economically sensible. What is
needed are multi-employer programs, of
the type initiated by unions in the afore-
mentioned industries, which vest benefits
across employers and provide the size to
reduce average set-up costs. In just such
a manner did unions operate as fraternal
benefit societies years ago.

Third, as argued by Freeman, Hirsch-
man, and Nelson, unions may elicit more
accurate information about workers' preferences for fringes than can be gained from
individual bargaining.[6] Conceptually, the

---

[4] For evidence see Stanley M. Nealey, "Pay and
Benefit Preference," *Industrial Relations* 3, no. 1
(October 1963), pp. 17–28.

[5] See Richare B. Freeman, "The Exit-Voice
Tradeoff in the Labor Market: Unionism, Job Tenure,
Quits and Separations," *Quarterly Journal of Economics*, June1980, pp. 613–73. Note that the estimates given are corrected for the likely impact of
fringes on attachment, so that the reduction in exit
can be taken as exogenous to the current problem.

[6] Richard B. Freeman, "Individual Mobility and
Union Voice in the Labor Market," *American Economic Review*, May 1976, pp. 361–68: Albert Hirsch-
man, "Some Uses of the Exit-Voice Approach-Discus-
sion," *American Economic Review*, May 1976, pp.
386–89, and Richard L. Nelson, "Some Uses of the
Exit-Voice—Discussion," *American Economic Review*, May 1976, pp. 389–91.

adversary relation between employers and employees—the fact that the level as well as allocation of the compensation package is at stake—argues for circumspection by workers in providing their employer with information about their preferences. If employers had complete knowledge of employee preference functions, they would seek to extract all of the worker surplus, striking a bargain that would leave workers at their minimum acceptance point.[7] This provides a motivation for nonunion employees to withold information about preferences. As the agent of workers, on the other hand, unions should obtain a more accurate revelation of preferences through their internal process of bargaining over the pay package that will be acceptable to the majority of members; in this way, unions may play an especially important role in eliciting employees' desire for fringes.

Empirically, there is some evidence that information factors are important in differentiating union and nonunion firms in the fringe area. Lester's 1967 review of surveys of managerial perceptions of worker preferences found "limited data . . . that workers value benefits more highly compared to wages than employers believe their workers do."[8] Lawler and Levin's study of union leaders concluded that they are generally good predictors of the members' preferences for various compensation packages, although they also seem to have understated the desire for fringes.[9] It is therefore reasonable to expect more accurate information on these employee prefer-

ences to emerge from collective negotiation, despite bargaining tactics, than from exit interviews, questioning of individual workers, and similar methods that provide workers little incentive to respond accurately.[10]

Fourth, the complexities involved in evaluating the costs and prospective benefits of modern fringe benefits may make workers more willing to accept fringes when they have a specialized agent, like a union, evaluating and monitoring employer claims and programs.[11] Significant investments in knowledge that lie beyond the purview of individual workers are needed to judge the true cost and future benefits of alternative compensation packages. Union lawyers, actuaries, and related experts are one institutional mechanism by which workers can obtain the expertise to bargain over these diverse benefits.

Finally, the fact that most fringe benefits have been ruled by the courts to be mandatory bargaining topics, whose lack of resolution can lead to impasses and strikes, is also likely to spur programs and expenditures in the union sector. Prior to the 1949 court rulings on pensions and group health insurance,[12] companies often

---

[7] Wassily W. Leontief, "The Pure Theory of the Guaranteed Annual Wage Contract," *Journal of Political Economy*, February 1946, pp. 76–79. This article on the guaranteed annual wage makes the argument using the standard Edgeworth box.

[8] Richard Lester, "Benefits on a Preferred Form of Compensation," *Southern Economics Journal*, April 1967, p. 494.

[9] Edward E. Lawler III and Edward Levin, "Union Officers' Perception of Members' Pay Preferences," *Industrial and Labor Relations Review*, July 1968, p. 517.

[10] The information argument can be investigated further by analyzing the extent to which, other factors fixed, union negotiated fringes spillover to nonunion firms. Since the nonunion firm will imitate the union employer only if workers prefer the allocation of the wage bill in the union sector, the existence of a positive spillover could be taken as evidence of a better information flow. If there were no additional information about preferences in the union package, nonunion firms would not be influenced by the *composition* of the union settlement.

[11] Armen Alchian and Harold Demsetz, "Production, Information Costs, and Economic Organization," *American Economic Review*, December 1972, pp. 777–95.

[12] In the Inland Steel Company case (1948), a National Labor Relations Board ruling that pensions were a mandatory subject was upheld by the Seventh Circuit. [*Inland Steel Co.* v. *NLRB*, 170F 2d 217, 22 LRRM 2505 (CA 7, 1948), *cert, denied*, 336 US 960, 24 LRRM 2019 (1949).]
In the W.W. Cross & Co. case (1949), group health insurance was ruled mandatory by the NLRB and upheld by the First Circuit. [*W.W. Cross & Co.* v *NLRB*, 174 F 2d 875, 24 LRRM 2068 (CA 1, 1949).]

argued that such benefits were "management gifts" and not subject to negotiation. Sice then fringes have become a major issue in almost all collective negotiations. While agreement need not be reached on these (or other) mandatory topics, the rulings have presumably impelled more serious negotiations and provisions than would have occurred if fringes had been ruled permissive topics.

In sum, unionism is likely to increase the number of fringes available to workers and the employer's expenditures on these programs. It is also likely to have sizeable effects on deferred benefits favored by older workers and benefits with high fixed costs, and to have especially sizeable effects on small firms in industries with unstable employer-worker relations.

OTHER DETERMINANTS OF FRINGES

The fringe share of the wage bill is likely to depend on several economic factors in addition to unionism, the influence of which must be held fixed in empirical work. Among the most important are:

Overall level of compensation. Fringes are likely to have a positive income elasticity and thus be correlated with total compensation per hour. If the elasticity exceeds one, the fringe share of the wage bill will also be related positively to total compensation.

Specific human capital. By creating an incentive for permanent employment relations, specific human capital will increase the fringe share of compensation. Workers will have a higher supply price for fringes because of the likelihood of remaining with the firm. Firms will use deferred fringes, notably pensions, to discourage quitting by the specifically trained.

Firm size. Two factors are likely to lead to greater fringe expenditures in larger than in smaller firms. First, given any fixed costs of instituting or operating a given program or any costs per worker that decline with number of workers covered, such as fees for managing a pension fund, larger firms will face lower costs per worker for purchasing fringes. Second, the greater tenure of workers with large firms, due to possibilities of within-firm mobility, will result in a larger proportion qualifying for benefits such as vested pensions and for higher benefits under plans linking size of benefits to length of service.

Demographic characteristics of workers. The supply price for fringes should vary among the population, depending on personal characteristics. Older workers, for example, tend to favor deferred fringes like retirement pay and medical and health insurance,[13] and women generally have less desire for fringes than men, in part because they are often covered by their husbands' pension and health plans.[14]

Tax benefits of deferred compensation are also important in determining expenditures for fringes. Because money placed into pension and related plans is not taxed when payment is first made, earns interest that is not taxed until paid out, is taxed at potentially favorable capital gains rates or as salary at lower income tax rates on retirement, the tax system raises the value of receiving income in the form of fringes as opposed to receiving income in the form of wages and thus encourages substitution of fringes for wages. Although we lack information of the precise effect of these tax benefits, they are related to the income of workers and therefore the control for the overall level of compensation also provides a rough control for tax benefits. As a result of the tax advantages, the income elasticity of fringes with respect to before-tax income will be biased upward since

---

[13] Nealey, "Pay and Benefit Preference."

[14] Nancy Herman, "Labor Union Participation and Compensation Preferences of Workers, undergraduate thesis (Harvard University, 1978). Herman shows that at the same level of wages women desire fringes less than men.

the true effect of income will be confounded with the price effect due to increasing tax rates and tax "savings" from fringes.

BASIC CROSS-ESTABLISHMENT ESTIMATES

. . . *With total compensation held fixed,* unionism significantly raises fringe spending, particularly on life, accident and health insurance, pensions, and vacation and holiday pay, and that it has its greatest impact on firms that are small or low-wage, or both. Since the calculations control for total compensation, the effect cannot be attributed to union monopoly wage gains but appears rather to represent the more complex aspects of union behavior discussed earlier. . . . The union coefficient indicates that in the period studied establishments that were organized paid nearly 10.1¢ more per hour for fringes.

With respect to other variables, both compensation and size of establishment also positively influence expenditures on fringes. The . . . estimate of the effect of an increase in compensation on fringes in all private industries is .133. [The effects of unions may] differ among firms with different levels of pay and size. . . . Union effects [are greater] on smaller and lower-paid establishments than on larger, higher-paid establishments. . . .

Specific Fringes

Which voluntary fringes are most affected by trade unionism? To what extent does the union effect operate by raising the likelihood that establishments will have a particular fringe program? To what extent does it operate by raising the amount spent by establishments with a particular program?

Table 1 presents calculations designed to answer these questions, Columns 1 and 2 record the cents per hour spent in 1967–

72 on the major fringes in the average establishment and the proportion of establishments that then provided the various fringes. They show that the most important fringes in terms of expenditures and availability were health, accident, and life insurance, vacation and holiday pay, overtime premiums, and pensions, with shift differentials, sick leave, and bonuses of nonnegligible but lesser significance.

Column 3 examines the impact of collective bargaining on expenditures for fringes using the linear model with straight-time pay plus required fringes as the measure of compensation. Because each fringe is too small to create a simultaneity problem, the column records the actual regression coefficients, rather than the simultaneity-corrected structural parameters. The regressions show that unions had their greatest positive effect on pensions, on life, accident, and health insurance, and on vacation and holiday pay, and had negative effects on overtime premiums, sick leave, and bonuses.

Column 4 reports estimates of the effect of collective bargaining on the provision of fringes, using a linear probability model and the same set of controls as in previous calculations. The estimates show that part of the union effect takes the form of changes in the probability that an enterprise will provide fringes. During the period studied, for example, trade unionism significantly raised the probability that pensions would be provided, by a striking .24 points in manufacturing and a .29 points overall. Unionism also raised the probability that an enterprise would provide life, accident, and health plans, overtime premiums, holiday pay, and shift differentials, while reducing the probability that sick leave and bonuses would be provided.

Column 5 turns to fringe expenditures by establishments *that had the specified fringe* in 1967–72. It records the estimated impact of unionism . . . [for] fringe spending on straight-time pay and required fringes, and the standard control variables. These calculations isolate the impact of collective bargaining on the level of spending, conditional on provision of the given fringe. The smallest fringe expenditures are ignored in the calculations as being too small to merit attention. The estimates

show that unionism affected the amount spent on most major fringes, with positive significant coefficients for all of the main fringes except pension plans and, in the all-industry sample, overtime. In all private industrial firms with life, accident, or health insurance programs, for example, expenditures per hour were 4¢ higher in

TABLE 1   ESTIMATES OF THE EFFECT OF COLLECTIVE BARGAINING ON SPECIFIC FRINGES, 1967–72[a]

SECTOR AND FRINGE	CENTS PER HOUR SPENT ON FRINGE, ALL ESTABLISHMENTS	PROPORTION OF ESTABLISHMENTS WITH FRINGE	COEFFICIENTS AND STANDARD ERRORS (IN PARENTHESES) FOR EFFECT OF BARGAINING ON		
			CENTS PER HOUR SPENT ON FRINGE, ALL ESTABLISHMENTS[b]	LINEAR PROBABILITY OF FRINGE[c]	CENTS PER HOUR SPENT ON FRINGE, ESTABLISHMENTS WITH FRINGES ONLY[d]
All Private Industry					
1. Life, accident, health	10.1	.850	4.8* (0.2)	.08* (.01)	3.9* (.03)
2. Vacation	8.3	.836	1.6* (0.2)	−.03* (.01)	1.9* (0.2)
3. Overtime premiums	10.1	.836	−.05 (0.4)	.03* (.01)	−0.7 (0.4)
4. Pension	9.4	.626	3.9* (0.4)	.29* (.01)	0.3 (0.5)
5. Holidays	5.2	.778	0.8* (0.1)	.01 (.01)	0.8* (0.1)
6. Shift differentials	1.1	.294	0.3* (0.1)	.17* (.01)	—
7. Sick leave	1.1	.351	−.05* (0.1)	−.10* (.01)	—
8. Bonuses	1.8	.271	−1.4* (0.3)	−.13* (0.2)	—
Manufacturing					
1. Life, accident, health	11.9	.952	4.5* (0.3)	.06* (.01)	4.0* (0.3)
2. Vacation	12.1	.960	2.8* (0.3)	−.01 (.01)	2.9* (0.3)
3. Overtime premiums	10.9	.955	−1.4* (0.4)	.05* (.01)	−2.0* (0.4)
4. Pension	9.3	.747	2.9* (0.5)	.24* (.02)	0.5 (0.6)
5. Holidays	7.3	.941	1.6* (0.1)	.03* (.01)	1.5* (0.1)
6. Shift differentials	2.1	.563	0.4* (0.1)	.23* (.02)	—
7. Sick leave	1.0	.314	−0.4* (0.1)	−.12* (.02)	—
8. Bonuses	1.4	.292	−1.7* (0.3)	−.19* (.02)	—

[a] Estimates in columns 3–5 are based on regressions with the following controls. For all private industry: 50 industry dummies, 3 region dummies, 1 SMSA dummy, 5 year dummies, ratio of office to nonoffice workers, and 5 measures of average characteristics of workers: years of schooling, % white, % male, % less than 30, and % more than 50 years of age; straight-time pay plus required fringes per hour; nonoffice employment. For manufacturing industry: 20 industry dummies and all of the other controls used for the total private sector.

[b] Based on regression of cents per hour spent on fringe on collective bargaining coverage and all control variables described in footnote a.

[c] Coefficient and standard error (in parentheses) based on linear probability regression of dichotomous measure of presence of fringes on collective bargaining coverage and all of the control variables described in footnote a.

[d] Based on regression of dollars per hour on fringe on collective bargaining coverage and all control variables described in footnote a with sample limited to establishments having the relevant fringe. Number of establishments = total number fringe group × proportion given in column 1.

* Significant at .01 level.

SOURCE: Calculated from Bureau of Labor Statistics, *Expenditures for Employee Compensation Survey*, tapes for 1967–68, 1969–70, and 1971–72.

the union sector; among firms with vacation programs expenditures were 2¢ higher, and so forth.

What factors explain the differential effect of unionism on the fringes distinguished in Table 1? Is the fact that unionism has its most sizeable positive effect on pensions, insurance, and vacation fringes, while having a negative effect on overtime spending, sick leave, and bonuses, consistent with the model presented earlier?

While a full explanation of the differential effects of unionism on the specific fringes lies beyond the scope of this article, the findings in Table 1 at least appear to be consistent with both models of the union given earlier. Those models suggested that unionism would raise fringes that involved deferred compensation and that were likely to be favored by older workers. Pensions fit both categories; health and life insurance are likely to be especially desired by older workers; and vacation pay has a strong seniority component, which should also make it favored by the more senior employees. As for the fringes that fare less well under unionism, the negative impact of unionism on bonuses is presumably attributable to standard-rate wage policies, which reduce managerial discretion in awarding pay. Such a policy is consistent with the median voter model but not necessarily with the optimizing cartel model.[15] The negative impact of unionism on overtime premiums can be attributed to the higher rates at unionized establishments, which should discourage management from using overtime. The negative impact of unionism on sick leave is somewhat more difficult ot explain, but may reflect the greater policing of sick leave in organized plants, which

tend to operate more "by the book" than nonorganized plants. Since the models presented earlier relate to worker preferences, what is needed to check further their ability to explain the pattern of fringes paid in organized as opposed to unorganized plants is detailed information about worker preferences and actual union behavior at bargaining tables. Such information is not available in our establishment data set.

THE UNION EFFECT ON TOTAL COMPENSATION

If unionism raises fringe benefits by substantial amounts, standard estimates of the union pay effect, which for reasons of data availability are generally limited to wages, understate the full impact of collective bargaining on compensation per hour. How large might this understatement be?

In all private industry, the impact of unionism on total compensation in 1967–72 was 17 percent above the impact of unionism on straight-time pay. In manufacturing, the union coefficient rises by 25 percent. . . . The union impact on fringes is therefore important not only in changing the composition of the wage bill but also in increasing the magnitude of the union effect on total pay.

THE UNION EFFECT ON TOTAL FRINGE EXPENDITURES

. . . It appears that unions raise *total* spending on fringes about equally through raising the fringe share of compensation and through raising the level of compensation. The union effect on fringe spending far exceeds the union effect on straight-time pay.

CONCLUSION

The analysis and findings of this paper can be summarized briefly. First, because

---

[15] For a discussion of how the median voter model is consistent with the standard-rate policies, see Richard B. Freeman, "Unionism and the Dispersion of Wages," *Industrial and Labor Relations Review*, October 1980, pp. 3–23.

of the political nature of unionism, which makes unions more representative of average than of marginal worker preferences and more sensitive to intensities of preference, and because of the role of unions as stable market institutions, and possibly because unions provide more accurate information about worker preferences for fringes than can be garnered from individual bargaining, unionism can be expected to raise the fringe share of the compensation package.

Second, estimates of the impact of unionism on the fringes of blue-collar workers show the expected positive effect, with the magnitude depending on the particular statistical model used for estimation. The estimated effect of unionism is sizeable in regressions that compare organized and nonorganized establishments; it is reduced when omitted firm factors are taken into account, but it is raised when allowance is made for the possible effect of blue-collar unions on the fringes paid white-collar workers in the same firm.

Third, the effect of unionism on fringes is especially large for deferred compensation plans favoring senior workers, such as pensions, insurance, and vacation pay, in accord with a priori expectations. This effect is greater for low-wage and small firms than for others.

Finally, because of the sizeable impact of unionism on fringes and the importance of fringes in the wage bill, standard estimates of the union wage effect understate the differential between unionized and otherwise comparable nonunion workers.

WAGES AND FRINGES: 1981*

The all-industries first-year wage increase negotiated in 1981 was 9.6 percent—up slightly from 9.5 percent in 1980. . . . In cents per hour, the 1981 median wage increase was 73.4 cents, compared to 70.1 cents for 1980. The survey is based on 1,463 contract settlements covering 50 or more workers.

Following is a comparison of first-year median wage gains negotiated in 1980 and 1981. The figures do not include cost-of-living adjustments.

	1980		1981	
All industries	70.1¢	9.5%	73.4¢	9.6%
All industries excluding construction	65.0¢	9.2%	66.1¢	9.0%
Manufacturing	61.2¢	9.0%	65.8¢	9.0%
Nonmanufacturing excluding construction	68.9¢	9.5%	66.6¢	9.5%
Construction	$1.25	11.3%	$1.55	11.8%

The highest first-year median wage gains in 1981 were in construction, 11.8 percent; and mining, 11.7 percent. The lowest first-year median wage increases were in railroads, 3.5 percent; and in primary metals, 4.6 percent.

Deferred increases were included in 89 percent of settlements reported in 1981, 89 percent of manufacturing, 86 percent of nonmanufacturing-excluding-construction, and 94 percent of construction agreements. Deferred increases are those effective ten or more months after the initial increase.

The following table shows median deferred wage increases due in 1982 and 1983 provided by contracts collectively bargained in 1981. In construction, the medians are based primarily on wage-fringe packages.

	1982		1983	
All industries	65.0¢	8.0%	60.0¢	7.5%
All industries excluding construction	60.0¢	7.9%	56.0¢	7.0%
Manufacturing	60.0¢	7.7%	56.3¢	7.0%
Nonmanufacturing excluding construction	60.0¢	8.0%	56.0¢	7.1%
Construction	$1.60	11.3%	$1.553	9.2%

Cost-of-living provisions were contained in 21 percent of contracts reported in 1981, compared to 29 percent in 1980. C-o-l clauses were included in 24 percent of manufacturing, 23 percent of nonmanufacturing-excluding-construction, and 5 percent of construction agreements.

Quarterly COLAs were most common in manufacturing contracts in 1981; annual adjustments predominated in nonmanufacturing-excluding-construction agreements.

Geographical analysis shows that the highest median first-year wage advance—10 percent—was negotiated in the Eastern regions and in the Western region. The Rocky Mountain and North Central regions had the lowest median—9 percent. In cents per hour, the high median was in the Middle Atlantic States, 78.5 cents; the low median first-year wage gain was in the North Central states, 68.2 cents.

Contract duration was three years in 57 percent of 1981 settlements mentioning the term, compared to 58 percent in 1980. Two-year terms were found in

* Reprinted from *Collective Bargaining Negotiations and Contracts,* The Bureau of National Affairs, no. 956, 18:977–980.

30 percent of contracts negotiated in each 1980 and 1981. One-year terms were reported in 6 percent of 1981 agreements, compared to 7 percent of 1980 contracts.

Fringe benefits were initiated or revised in 77 percent of agreements surveyed in 1981, compared to 81 percent in 1980. Changes or innovations in insurance benefits continued to be the most often negotiated, appearing in 75 percent of 1981 settlements breaking down fringe revisions.

Of settlement reports specifying changes in health-welfare, the most frequently changed or established benefits in 1981 were dental and life insurance—each 34 percent, compared to 38 and 32 percent, respectively, in 1980. Sickness and accident benefits were provided for in 28 percent of the agreements (down from 30 percent in 1980), major medical in 23 percent (up from 22 percent in 1980), and hospitalization in 16 percent (up from 9 percent in 1980).

Of 1981 settlement reports itemizing insurance changes, 11 percent revised or established optical plans, compared to 17 percent in 1980. In addition, changes were made in 1981 in the following benefits: accidental death and dismemberment (9 percent), surgical (8 percent), disability (7 percent), and prescription drugs (5 percent).

Of 1981 settlements spelling out fringe revisions, 59 percent revised pension plans compared to 66 percent in 1980. New monthly benefits in manufacturing industry plans averaged $12.49 per year of service, the same as in 1980. In the nonmanufacturing-excluding-construction sector, new benefits averaged $16.78 a month for each year of service, up from $14.24 in 1980.

Vacations were revised in 33 percent of contract reports containing fringe information; holidays were changed in 32 percent. Holidays averaged 11 a year in manufacturing, and 10 per year in nonmanufacturing-excluding-construction agreements.

Income maintenance provisions (severance pay and supplemental unemployment plans) were revised in 3 percent of 1981 agreement reports specifying changed fringes. Legal plans were added in 1 percent of contracts, the majority in the wholesale and retail and service industries.

TABLE 1   MEDIAN FIRST-YEAR WAGE INCREASES, 1981

	1ST-QUARTER 1981		2ND-QUARTER 1981		3RD-QUARTER 1981		4TH-QUARTER 1981		YEAR 1981	
All industries	64.0¢	9.3%	77.8¢	10.0%	77.6¢	9.8%	65.5¢	9.1%	73.4¢	9.6%
All industries, excluding construction	63.1¢	9.2%	69.0¢	9.0%	67.1¢	9.0%	65.5¢	9.1%	66.1¢	9.0%
Manufacturing	60.2¢	9.0%	69.3¢	9.0%	66.0¢	9.0%	65.5¢	9.0%	65.8¢	9.0%
Nonmanufacturing, excluding construction	67.7¢	9.8%	65.0¢	9.0%	69.5¢	9.2%	65.6¢	9.6%	66.6¢	9.5%
Construction	(*)	(*)	$1.585	11.6%	$1.545	11.8%	(*)	(*)	$1.55	11.8%

(*) Insufficient data

TABLE 2 FIRST-YEAR MEDIAN WAGE INCREASES AND REVISED FRINGE PROVISIONS[1] BY INDUSTRY, 1981

	TOTAL CONTRACTS[2]	MEDIAN INCREASE (CENTS PER HOUR)	MEDIAN INCREASE (PERCENTAGE)	DEFERRED INCREASES	COST-OF-LIVING CLAUSES	VACATIONS	HOLIDAYS	PENSION PLAN	INCOME MAINTENANCE	LEGAL SERVICES	INSURANCE[3]	LIFE INSURANCE	ACCIDENTAL DEATH & DISMEMBERMENT	SICKNESS & ACCIDENT	DISABILITY INSURANCE	HOSPITAL INSURANCE	SURGICAL INSURANCE	MAJOR MEDICAL	MATERNITY BENEFITS	DRUG PLAN	DENTAL PLAN	OPTICAL PLAN
Manufacturing																						
Apparel & other finished textiles	20	39.2	8.8	17	1	8	12	10	—	—	12	3	1	3	—	—	—	2	—	—	1	1
Chemicals & allied products	163	78.9	9.9	148	15	47	54	78	6	—	110	45	12	32	10	31	14	28	4	3	37	9
Electrical machinery & equipment	33	67.3	9.8	32	13	13	15	19	—	—	25	9	4	9	—	3	2	7	—	1	11	2
Fabricated metals	43	54.1	8.0	41	14	11	13	26	8	—	34	13	4	17	9	2	2	5	8	3	20	9
Foods & beverages	55	68.9	10.0	47	8	22	20	29	1	—	36	13	5	13	4	9	6	9	1	2	14	2
Furniture	19	57.5	9.4	18	1	6	6	9	—	—	14	3	—	3	—	2	—	—	—	—	1	—
Leather & leather products	9	—	—	9	—	4	2	5	—	—	7	4	—	4	—	—	1	2	—	1	—	2
Lumber & wood products	26	53.5	8.6	20	5	13	7	18	—	—	18	8	4	7	—	2	1	6	—	—	5	—
Machinery (except electrical)	45	67.8	8.0	40	20	16	14	27	2	—	26	16	7	19	4	4	3	12	—	2	11	6
Miscellaneous manufacturing	15	55.3	9.2	11	2	5	4	6	—	—	13	5	—	1	—	3	2	4	—	2	5	—
Ordnance	4	—	—	2	1	1	—	1	—	—	2	1	1	1	—	2	—	1	—	—	—	—
Paper & allied products	67	68.0	9.0	64	1	28	24	50	2	—	54	37	9	36	1	7	7	20	2	6	14	3
Petroleum & allied products	13	—	—	11	—	5	4	2	—	—	4	1	—	1	—	2	1	2	—	—	2	—
Primary metals	25	35.5	4.6	23	16	9	5	15	2	—	15	7	1	7	—	2	—	2	—	—	6	2
Printing & publishing	87	74.2	8.9	70	25	27	19	36	2	—	42	8	—	7	1	2	—	4	2	2	10	5
Professional, scientific & controlling instruments	8	—	—	8	3	3	3	5	—	—	5	3	—	—	—	—	1	2	—	1	3	—
Rubber products	10	—	—	10	1	4	3	5	—	—	6	2	1	5	1	1	1	2	—	—	3	—
Stone, clay & glass	67	70.0	9.5	60	22	13	18	38	1	—	48	22	18	25	2	8	9	21	7	—	15	2
Textile mill products	23	46.4	9.0	17	2	5	9	12	—	—	18	3	—	8	3	4	2	2	—	2	2	1

Tobacco	2	—	—	2	—	1	1	1	—	—	1	—	—	—	—	—	—	1	—	—	1	—
Transportation equipment	57	60.0	7.7	52	38	11	18	38	1	—	47	18	1	9	9	15	3	12	—	3	20	8
Total manufacturing	791	65.8	9.0	702	188	252	251	430	25	—	537	221	68	207	44	99	54	144	24	28	181	52
Nonmanufacturing (Excluding construction)																						
Agriculture	5	—	—	4	2	1	—	3	—	—	1	—	—	—	—	—	—	—	—	—	—	—
Communications	19	84.5	10.0	19	5	10	12	7	2	—	17	3	—	—	—	4	5	7	1	—	8	—
Insurance	16	57.3	8.8	81	9	3	3	6	—	—	8	3	—	—	1	—	—	2	—	—	5	2
Mining	15	120.0	11.7	11	3	4	5	9	1	—	13	7	1	5	—	—	—	—	—	1	8	5
Services																						
Except health care	82	52.8	9.5	12	8	18	13	34	2	2	46	9	—	8	3	8	1	4	—	4	15	8
Health care	95	68.7	10.0	72	10	20	17	12	—	2	43	9	—	2	3	3	—	3	1	1	13	6
Transportation services	1	—	—	1	1	1	1	1	—	—	1	—	—	—	—	—	—	—	—	—	—	—
Transportation (combined)	66	48.5	7.6	52	27	25	21	31	—	1	36	16	7	3	2	12	7	16	—	3	20	2
Airline	22	—	—	15	3	9	5	9	—	1	10	2	—	1	1	1	—	3	—	—	5	1
Railroad	8	34.2	3.5	8	7	7	7	1	—	—	7	7	7	—	—	7	7	7	—	—	7	—
Streetcar, bus & taxi	15	50.0	7.0	12	5	3	4	7	—	—	11	7	—	2	1	2	—	3	—	3	5	1
Water & other	21	48.5	8.0	17	12	6	5	14	—	—	8	—	—	—	—	2	—	3	—	—	3	1
Trucking & warehousing	5	—	—	5	1	4	3	3	—	—	3	1	—	1	—	—	—	—	—	—	1	1
Utilities (light, power, gas & water)	39	88.6	9.8	26	4	11	4	18	—	—	22	3	—	—	—	3	1	7	—	2	13	3
Wholesale & retail trade	110	64.7	8.8	105	33	24	29	65	3	5	71	13	2	8	5	10	—	10	—	3	21	13
Total nonmanufacturing-excluding construction	453	66.6	9.5	388	103	121	108	189	8	11	261	64	10	27	14	40	14	49	2	14	104	40
Total all industries excluding construction	1,244	66.1	9.0	1,090	291	373	359	619	33	11	798	285	78	234	58	139	68	193	26	42	285	92
Construction	219	155.0	11.8	205	12	1	—	52	—	—	53	1	—	1	1	—	—	—	1	—	2	—
Total all-industries	1,463	73.4	9.6	1,295	303	374	359	671	33	11	851	286	78	235	59	139	68	193	27	42	287	92

[1] Figures pertain to new or revised fringe provisions.
[2] Includes some contracts carrying wage increases of unspecified amounts; not included in tabulations of medians.
[3] Includes some contracts with unspecified insurance innovations or revisions.
— Sufficient data to compute median increase unavailable.

OTHER BARGAINING ISSUES

While wages and fringe benefits are central concerns in collective bargaining, numerous other topics have become important to the total bargain struck between the parties. Three of these topics are addressed here. They include: safety and health, quality of worklife (QWL), and income maintenance. The article by Wallace and Driscoll outlines collective bargaining activities concerning job safety and health issues. The papers by Fuller and Bluestone examine QWL programs involving General Motors and the United Auto Workers. Finally, the article by Millen focuses on the role unions and collective bargaining play in protecting the welfare of workers who lose their jobs.

SOCIAL ISSUES IN COLLECTIVE BARGAINING: OCCUPATIONAL SAFETY AND HEALTH

Phyllis A. Wallace* and James W. Driscoll

[A] major social issue . . . to confront collective bargaining in the 1960s was . . . heralded by federal legislation: the Coal Mine Health and Safety Act of 1969 and the Occupational Safety and Health Act of 1970 (OSHAct). These laws, according to Ashford, resulted from an increased injury rate (up 29 percent in the decade), the discovery of new occupational diseases (coal miners' black lung and cancers caused by asbestos and vinyl chloride), rapid technological change especially in chemical processing, the environmental movement's concern over toxins and pollution in general, and a better-educated, more affluent workforce.[1]

THE SCOPE OF THE PROBLEM

Whatever the cause of recent legislation, safety and health pose a major problem in the workplace. Accidents killed 13,100 people at work in 1980, according to the National Safety Council (NSC). Workers also die from diseases caused by working conditions. The then Department of Health, Education, and Welfare (HEW) estimated as many as 100,000 deaths each year from such occupational diseases. While the magnitude of such disease-related deaths due to cancer, respiratory ailments, and heart disease is in dispute, there is little disagreement about the growing problem of occupational disease.

In addition to deaths, the NSC estimated 2.2 million disabling accidents in 1979 at a cost to the economy of $23 billion.

Subjective reports by workers confirm the magnitude of the problem. Forty-six percent of all blue-collar workers in the 1977 Quality of Employment Survey reported unpleasant working conditions; 40 percent of all workers are exposed to air pollution at work, 29 percent to dangerous equipment and 29 percent to dangerous chemicals. Fifteen percent reported an injury or illness made more severe by conditions at work. Seventy-six percent of all workers surveyed felt workers should have complete, or a lot of, say over safety equipment and practices as opposed to 30 percent desiring such influence over wages and salaries.

Despite their importance, safety and health issues have been slow in calling forth significant legislative or bargaining activity.

* Alfred P. Sloan School of Management, Massachusetts Institute of Technology. Driscoll, formerly with MIT, is now with The Freeze Organization. Reprinted from *U.S. Industrial Relations, 1950–1980: A Critical Assessment,* ed. Jack Stieber, Robert B. McKersie, and D. Quinn Mills (Madison, Wis.: Industrial Relations Research Association, 1981), pp. 199–254.

[1] Nicholas Askounes Ashford, *Crisis in the Workplace: Occupational Disease and Injury, A Report to the Ford Foundation* (Cambridge, Mass.: MIT, 1976).

HISTORY OF REGULATION

Early industrialization in the United States left safety and health to the play of market mechanisms. Workers either accepted the risk of hazards or quit. Employers could be sued for negligence, but common law defenses of contributory negligence limited employer exposure. After the turn of the century, President Theodore Roosevelt urged the states to pass workingmen's compensation laws. In return for guaranteed (and limited) payments for injuries from an employer fund, workers gave up their right to sue under these laws. Finally in 1970, the federal government shifted the emphasis from compensation after the fact, to prevention.

The OSHAct, as it will be abbreviated, imposed a general duty on employers to provide a "place of employment . . . free from recognized hazards . . . causing death or physical harm." The National Institute of Occupational Safety and Health was set up in HEW to do research on hazards; the Occupational Safety and Health Administration to issue and enforce standards; and an Occupational Safety and Health Review Commission to monitor enforcement. Each worker in the United States was granted certain rights, namely to: (1) complain about violations of specific standards of the employer's general duty; (2) retain anonymity; (3) have a representative accompany the government official on any subsequent inspection; and (4) be protected against reprisals.

Implementation of this fundamental shift in employment relations has sparked controversy. According to the AFL–CIO, the Nixon administration provided lax enforcement, appointed a weak staff, and used the agency for political fund raising. Only under Labor Secretary Ray Marshall, according to AFL–CIO President Lane Kirkland, "have our unions been able to work with a Labor Department which believes in OSHA and is doing its best to make it work." On the other hand, according to management representatives, the law from the beginning has meant petty harassment, costly wasted investment, and distraction from effective safety and health programs.

Secretary Marshall initiated several reforms to meet management criticism: dropping some 1,000 standards, targeting inspections on high-hazard industries, and emphasizing consultation with employers. Nonetheless, Congress found such reforms insufficient and exempted small businesses in low injury industries from most inspections. The Reagan administration brings to OSHA a general determination to "get the government off the backs of industry."

Given the different interests of the two parties, no objective assessment of the OSHAct is possible. While the Supreme Court ruled that the economic cost of one specific standard for exposure to benzene was too great, the labor movement cites an overall decrease of 10 percent in fatalities and 15 percent in injuries due to the Act. Academic evaluations of a single standard have ranged from net negative to net positive and reflect the assumptions of the authors.

Against this larger societal debate, the question addressed here is how collective bargaining responded on safety and health.

COLLECTIVE BARGAINING ACTIVITIES

Contract negotiations. Although no empirical evidence exists, it is our experience that union and management representatives spend relatively little time in negotiations discussing safety and health and rarely, if ever, do negotiations go to impasse solely or primarily over these issues. A rare example is, according to Ashford, the 1973 negotiations between the Oil, Chemical, and Atomic Workers and Shell Oil, which resulted in a work stoppage in part over safety.

Local walkouts are undoubtedly more

TABLE 1 COLLECTIVE BARGAINING PROVISIONS ON SAFETY AND HEALTH

	PERCENT IN ALL CONTRACTS	PERCENT IN MANUFACTURING INDUSTRY CONTRACTS	PERCENT IN MINING INDUSTRY CONTRACTS
Some provision on safety	82	87	100
General statement of responsibility	50	58	75
Company to comply with laws	29	29	50
Company to provide safety equipment	42	46	92
Company to provide first aid	21	26	50
Physical examinations	30	30	75
Hazardous work provisions	22	19	67
Accident investigations	18	24	58
Safety committees	43	55	92
Dissemination of safety information to employees	16	18	38
Dissemination of safety issues to union	19	21	44
Employees to comply with safety rules	47	50	67
Right of inspection by union or employees safety committees	20	30	56
Wage differentials for hazardous work	15	6	6

SOURCES: First nine items, "Safety and Health Patterns in Union Contracts," Daily Labor Report #178, September 13, 1978, p. E-1. Last five items, "Major Collective Bargaining Agreements: Safety and Health Provisions," BLS Bulletin #1425–16 (Washington, D.C., 1976). Reproduced from Thomas A. Kochan, *Collective Bargaining and Industrial Relations* (Homewood, Ill.: Richard D. Irwin, 1980).

frequent in some unions such as the United Mine Workers or in extreme conditions such as the highly publicized sterlization of seven workers in the production of DBCP.

Kochan has assembled reports from several sources to describe the results of these negotiations in actual contract language (Table 1). Most contracts have some provision dealing with safety and health, and the frequency of such provisions has increased since the passage of the OSHAct. Also such provisions are concentrated in manufacturing and in specific industries such as mining where the hazards are greatest. However, the rights and benefits conferred on workers are relatively limited, most generally taking the form of a general statement of responsibility. Less frequently do contracts guarantee the workers' right to refuse hazardous work. Rarely do they impose more stringent standards for exposure than does the law.

The right to refuse hazardous work. Under the National Labor Relations Act

workers in the United States have a general right to strike as a "protected concerted activity."[2] A union can strike to win contract provisions on safety and health. However, based on the Supreme Court's *Gateway Coal* decision, if a contract provides for the arbitration of grievances, safety and health complaints must be brought to that forum[3] and strikes are prohibited.

There are two exceptions to this prohibition on work stoppages during the contract. Paragraph 502 of the National Labor Relations Act defines the quitting of labor in good faith because of abnormally dangerous conditions *not* to be a strike. In *Redwing Carriers*, the NLRB interpreted

---

[2] The following section relies heavily on Nicholas A. Ashford and Judith I. Katz, "Unsafe Working Conditions: Employee Rights under the Labor-Management Relations Act and the Occupational Safety and Health Act," *Notre Dame Lawyer*, June 1977, pp. 802–36.

[3] *Gateway Coal* v. *UMW*, 414 U.S. 368 (1974).

this exception narrowly.[4] The conditions must be *unusually* dangerous (even in a usually dangerous job) and supported by *objective* evidence (not beliefs). In 1980, the Supreme Court added a second exception when it upheld a controversial regulation from the Secretary of Labor in its *Whirlpool* decision.[5] If a worker reasonably believes a threat of death or serious bodily harm exists, *and* if there is no time to call for a government inspection, *and* if the employer has been notified and refuses to change the condition, then the worker may refuse to work.

The legal implication of this tangled web is paradoxical. Nonunion workers have the full protection of the NLRA to protect a work stoppage over any threat to safety and health, even if only subjectively perceived. Union workers covered by an arbitration clause have the right to quit work over safety and health only under the two exceptional conditions mentioned. Of course, the union workers have the more general political and economic protection of the union as well.

Arbitration. Grievances over safety and health are relatively rare. Nonetheless, they form an exception to the general arbitral principle that the union member should "follow orders first and grieve later." How much protection arbitration provides depends on the language of the contract and the beliefs of the arbitrator. Generally, arbitrators have *not* held the subjective belief of the worker to be an adequate justification for refusing work. Where a contract specifies such subjective fear as adequate, the arbitrators have ruled more frequently in favor of the grievant. A serious problem with arbitration of safety and health disputes was highlighted by a review of published cases. The median

time from discipline action for refusing hazardous work until the arbitrator's decision was over six months. Such delays, all too typical of arbitration, leave the discipline or discharge in place pending resolution with a chilling effect on other potential complaints.

Labor-management committees. As indicated in Table 1, 43 percent of the major contracts provide for a joint committee on safety and/or health, again more frequently in manufacturing and high-hazard industries, and again more frequently since the passage of the OSHAct. However, some committees, for example in the mining industry, long predate the 1970 act. The typical committee is composed of 50 percent union and 50 percent management, meets monthly, and has advisory power. The committee can inspect accidents, tour the facilities, and make recommendations to management. To bind management to action, however, the union has to resort to a grievance, a work stoppage, or calling for a government inspection.

The effectiveness of such committees is a matter of debate and some skepticism. Kochan, Dyer, and Lipsky, in a survey of International Association of Machinists locals in upstate New York, found that only a half of the joint committees had met as often as once a month; they also found wide variation in levels of committee activity.[6] Those committees which were active and involved in problem-solving behavior were associated with a lower issuance of citations following an OSHA inspection, thus indicating greater enforcement between inspections. High levels of committee continuity and activity were found where OSHA pressure was perceived as strong, where the local union was perceived to be vigorous, where rank and file

---

[4] *Redwing Carriers,* 130 NLRB 1208, 1209, 47 LRRM, 1470 (1961).

[5] *Whirlpool Corporation, Petitioner* v. *Ray Marshall, Secretary of Labor,* 48 LW 4189.

[6] Thomas A. Kochan, Lee Dyer, and David B. Lipsky, *The Effectiveness of Union-Management Safety and Health Committee* (Kalamazoo, Mich.: W. E. Upjohn Institute for Employment Research, 1977).

involvement was substantial, and where management approached safety issues in a problem-solving manner. The researchers also emphasized the importance of separating the committee from other bargaining activity.

INNOVATIVE JOINT EFFORTS

A similar pattern of forces for success emerges when overall joint programs are examined in detail. For example, in 1973 United Auto Workers and General Motors agreed on one full-time union health and safety representative in each plant. Picked by the International, the representative is trained and paid by the company. The jointly acknowledged success of the program depends in large part on the ability of the representatives to work effectively with management counterparts.

Likewise, the contract between the United Rubber Workers and B. F. Goodrich also calls for a full-time safety and health representative for the union in each plant, paid for by the company. Plant-level, union-management committees also meet monthly, tour the plant, and identify hazards for high-priority correction by the company maintenance department. What is unique in this relationship is an independent study of safety and health in the company's working environment funded with a contribution of 1¢ an hour and conducted by the Harvard School of Public Health.

In addition to strong local unions, a committed management and specialized staff, the existence of problem-solving forums appears helpful. For example, the Joint Labor-Management Committee of the Retail Food Industry worked together on a safety problem. One of the consensus standards for the retail food industry required meatcutters to wear protective mesh gloves when cutting meat. If the meatcutter is using a knife, the glove protects fingers from amputation. However,

if the same meatcutter is using a power saw, he or she is liable to lose an *arm*, because the mesh glove catches in the saw where a piece of flesh would not.

The industry-wide, general-purpose committee recognized this shortcoming, undertook a national survey of local experience and obtained a clarification of the standard from OSHA (not a change which would have triggered an elaborate rule-making process).

INNOVATIONS BY THE LABOR MOVEMENT

Education. A major problem facing the unions is the lack of skilled people in health and safety. In 1975, Ralph Nader's Health Research Group found only a handful of union experts. Even today, one high-level union official estimates only 65 safety and health professionals are working for unions, and these include only 40 industrial hygienists. The New Directions program of the Occupational Safety and Health Administration is supporting, in one way or another, practically every safety and health professional now working for the labor movement. . . . Both the Oil, Chemical, and Atomic Workers and the United Steelworkers, among other international unions, are seeking to identify hazards in local workplaces around the country and to educate members on hazard recognition. Likewise, the Building and Trades Department of the AFL–CIO has established a national safety and health resources center in Washington and is organizing sixteen regional centers for intensive training in high-hazard construction. The Labor Department has also made grants to university-based labor education programs to develop training on safety and health.

Coalition for Occupational Safety and Health (COSH). In 1972, activists in the Chicago area came together to form a local coalition for occupational safety and health, the first of what are now about a dozen across the nation. Typical of such efforts, the Massachusetts COSH is funded by dues from unions and individuals and a grant from . . . OSHA. Massachusetts' COSH provides education, training, and technical assistance to unions and workers including, in 1979, answers to over 300 telephone requests for information, typically questioning the impact of some chemical on humans.

MANAGEMENT PROGRAMS

The primary legal and practical responsibility for occupational health and safety rests with management. . . . Not only is management the classic initiator of action in industrial relations; but action on occupations diseases, in particular, requires such information as types of substances used in production, potential health hazards, and worker health records.

The elements of a successful management program all emphasize commitment: top level support, assignment of a specialized representative, delegation of significant decision-making power to that representative, formulation of written procedures, taining for managers and first-level supervisors, and inclusion of safety and health in formal performance evaluations. In addition, management must train individual workers in hazard and accident prevention. Unless individual workers have the knowledge and motivation to avoid hazards, then efforts to provide safe, healthy working conditions are limited. It is a truism in accident prevention that both the environment and the worker are potential causes.

Lack of management commitment to safety and health poses a potential problem, given the relatively limited collective bargaining and union initiatives described above. The petrochemical industry provides the most discouraging example. Epstein virtually accused the industry of criminal conspiracy and neglect in conceal-

ing health hazards from its workers.[7] Yet, even today, informed observers of the industry cite no management programs to identify worker risks, such as a review of company medical records for clusters or patterns of disease.

In the U.S. industrial relations system, significant improvement in safety and health will depend largely on management action. Nonetheless, within that context, it is possible to offer an assessment of collective bargaining's contribution to that end.

ASSESSMENT OF COLLECTIVE BARGAINING AND OCCUPATIONAL SAFETY AND HEALTH

No direct comparisons have as yet been made between union and nonunion organizations in safety and health performance. According to Kochan, union members report more serious problems with hazards on their jobs, but no significant differences in injuries.[8] He also cites suggestive evidence that union workers receive higher compensating wage differentials for hazardous work. Subjectively, union members report reasonable levels of satisfaction with their union's efforts on safety and health. They are less satisfied with safety and health performance of the union than with traditional bread-and-butter issues, but more satisfied than with nontraditional quality of work issues such as providing "interesting jobs."

Some high-level union officials say that future success lies not in collective bargaining, but in stricter legislation and grassroots education of workers regarding hazards. Indeed, when asked in the Quality of Employment Survey "To whom do you report health and safety hazards?,"

---

[7] Samuel S. Epstein, *The Politics of Cancer* (Garden City, N.Y.: Anchor Books, 1974).

[8] Thomas A. Kochan, *Collective Bargaining and Industrial Relations* (Homewood, Ill.: Richard D. Irwin, 1980).

only one union member in 20 cited a union representative. Likewise, unorganized workers in the same survey did not see collective bargaining as a way to improve safety and health at work. Only 1 percent of nonunion workers who would vote for a union if given the opportunity gave improved safety and health as a reason for their vote.

Despite the objective magnitude of the safety and health problem at work and the strong desire of workers for influence over its resolution, safety and health takes a distinct second place to traditional economic concerns such as wages, fringe benefits, and job security in both collective bargaining activity and impact. Safety and health are middle range issues in collective bargaining.

The reasons for this subordination are many and interrelated.

1. The problem is ambiguous. Even the number of deaths is uncertain and the causes of occupational disease are difficult to disentangle. It may be that bargaining is ill-suited to deal with such an amorphous issue.

2. Bargainers have other priorities. Since the OSHAct, stagflation has highlighted wage increases and job security.

3. The median voter is often assumed to determine priorities in an elected leadership, and most safety and health problems only affect a minority.

4. Unions fear liability for negligence damages if they take responsibility for safety and health. In *Helton* v. *Hake* (1978), the Missouri Court of Appeals held an Ironworkers local liable for $150,000 for a steward's failure to enforce a contractual safety rule. That particular contract had unusual language absolving the employer from responsibility for the rule in question. Based on other cases, unions appear to have no liability in the safety and health area beyond the usual duty to fair representation. However, the possibility raised by the Helton case has led some national unions to instruct their locals to avoid *any* safety and health language.

5. Negotiators, especially on the union side, lack access to relevant expertise and information.

6. Much of the labor movement's activity has taken place at the central level, testifying at OSHA hearings and challenging standards in the courts, while bargaining is decentralized.

7. The federal government has preempted union action by setting standards and providing an alternative complaint mechanism to the union hierarchy.

8. The Administrative Procedures Act of 1946 encourages an adversarial rather than a cooperative approach to solving safety and health problems. Both labor and management usually present the most extreme possible arguments about each hazard and almost never have a forum to explore creative solutions and compromises.

9. Because of the costs involved, aggravated by this adversarial process, management has resisted most of the legislative and bargaining initiatives on safety and health.

10. Collective bargaining, according to Ashford, could have allowed union and management jointly to develop specific solutions to particular industry and local conditions. However, based on our review of negotiations, contracts, arbitration and committees, most parties have not felt sufficient pressure on safety and health to develop effective mechanisms to solve these problems.

HOW QUALITY-OF-WORKLIFE PROJECTS WORK FOR GENERAL MOTORS

Stephen H. Fuller*

Quality of worklife is not a happiness program, although happy employees may certainly be a byproduct. It is not a personnel department program, although quality of worklife has important implications for personnel management. It is not a subtle employee incentive program, although employees motivated to achieving the goals of the organization certainly ought to be one of the outcomes. And, it is not another productivity program, although better productivity is certainly one of the important results.

Quality of worklife *is* all of these things and more:

- A continuing process, not something that can be turned on today and turned off tomorrow.
- Using all resources, especially human resources, better today than yesterday . . . and even better tomorrow.
- Developing among all members of an organization an awareness and understanding of the concerns and needs of others, and a willingness to be more responsive to those concerns and needs.
- Improving the way things get done to assure the long-term effectiveness and success of organizations.

General Motors is making a concerted effort to improve the quality of worklife for its employees. Projects are underway in most North American operations and in many overseas operations as well. The approach was not developed overnight. It evolved from a philosophy of management, shaped by events and experiences occurring over a considerable period of time.

A key component of our quality-of-worklife process is union participation. Quality of worklife became a joint effort of General Motors and the United Auto Workers in 1973, when a National Committee to Improve the Quality of Work Life was established. Representing the UAW on the committee are two officials of the international union. The corporation is represented by two personnel officers. The committee meets periodically to discuss activities underway in the corporation. One of its chief functions is to educate executives of the union and the corporation in order to encourage cooperative quality-of-worklife ventures at the local level.

The committee adopted minimum standards to assure that every GM plant has the basics of a quality-of-worklife effort. Each operation is expected to have:

- A group to oversee the quality of worklife process.
- A statement of long-term objectives incorporating quality of worklife along with other desirable business targets.

---

* At the time of this article, Mr. Fuller was vice president, General Motors Corporation. Reprinted from *Monthly Labor Review*, BLS July 1980, pp. 37–39, by permission of Stephen H. Fuller.

- Regular measurement of quality of worklife.
- Seminars and other activities to make the organization more knowledgeable about quality-of-worklife concepts and techniques.
- Adequate internal resources and skills to assure the developmental process is moving ahead and accomplishing its objectives.

APPROACHES VARY

A quality-of-worklife improvement program is mandatory at GM, however, specific approaches are optional. Following are some examples of approaches being applied at existing and new plants.

A decade ago, one of our assembly plants could have been characterized as a problem plant. There was an air of hostility between management and the union. Costs were high. Performance was poor. Something had to be done. Fortunately, the local management and union were willing to undertake some initiatives. As both sides explored and discussed their mutual problems and concerns, an atmosphere of understanding and mutual respect began to emerge. In 1972, the plant faced a major rearrangement which provided an opportunity for management to involve employees in planning the change, something that had not been done before. The rearrangement went well, due, in part, to the employees' suggestions.

Then, following the lead set by the GM–UAW National Quality of Work Life Committee, plant management and the union established their own committee. In 1977, management and the union initiated a 3-day training program providing employees at the plant training in team problem-solving. Although the program was voluntary, nearly all of the 3,600 employees participated. Today, employee morale at that plant is high, grievances are only

a fraction of what they were a decade ago, and the plant has become one of the best-performing assembly plant at General Motors.

Another GM plant abandoned the traditional organizational structure a few years ago. Today, the plant is organized into six business teams, each consisting of the necessary production activities and support elements: engineering, scheduling, material handling, quality control, maintenance, and accounting. The system has made support employees an integral part of the plant's business operations. The quality-control circle concept, which has flourished in Japan and is being introduced by a growing number of firms in this country, has been incorporated into the business-team structure. The circle concept gives employees the opportunity to meet regularly to discuss problems affecting their work environment and the plant's performance.

These are only two of many approaches underway in established GM plants. New plants provide a unique opportunity to design an organization from a blank sheet of paper. Free from the constraints of past practice and stereotyped roles, each plant is an opportunity to introduce new approaches.

There are three important considerations underlying quality-of-worklife initiatives in new plants: (1) there is no best system or organizational design, (2) there is an ongoing interaction among the parts of the system—a change in one part of the system can have a significant impact on the entire system, and (3) each part of the system must reinforce consistency of operations and facilitate employee involvement.

To achieve an organizational system in which each part is congruent with the rest, careful consideration is given to the basic values, principles, and objectives held by local management. The development of a philosophy and goals is viewed as a necessary first step in the planning process. (The philosophy and goals are statements reflecting the local management's beliefs about people and work and the relationship between those beliefs and the plant's objectives.)

A team concept is a major feature of many new GM plants. Job rotation within the team is encouraged. Employees thus acquire broader skills which, in turn, allows for greater flexibility in performing all of the tasks within the team. This concept tends to promote employee involvement and satisfaction, and to minimize the disruptive effects of occasional absenteeism and turnover. Employees are encouraged to move from one team to another once they have learned all of the jobs in the team. This further adds to the fulfillment of employee interests and to the expansion of experiences and achievements.

The team concept encourages employee responsibility and involvement. For example, employees may have responsibility for training team members; assessing individual team members' progress in satisfactorily performing job assignments; forecasting efficiency, scrap, and manpower requirements in their operating areas; recommending corrective action for improper conduct of team members; contributing to the selection of new employees; selecting team leaders; and maintaining operation of tools and equipment within process standards.

Employee-management communications essential. In our plants, emphasis is placed on effective communication, particularly face-to-face communication. It begins with the orientation, which includes, in addition to traditional topics, a thorough review of the plant's philosophy and goals. Periodic plant meetings and team meetings are used to discuss aspects of the business—for example, quality, schedules, scrap and rework, housekeeping, safety, employee facilities, production facilities, and customer orders. There also

is ample opportunity for employees to discuss their concerns with management.

The role of the personnel department at General Motors is to facilitate the development of the quality-of-worklife process by consulting with management, with employees, and with their elected representatives. Well-conceived and effectively administered personnel programs are absolutely essential for a strong quality-of-worklife effort.

One such program is a system of redress for those employees not represented by a union. A formal "open door policy" is one approach, but it must have the support of all levels of management. An effective appraisal system for all employees, including managers and executives, also is essential. The appraisal also should evaluate managers' support and implementation of quality-of-worklife principles.

Training for all employees is an absolute necessity. If employees are to be involved in the decision-making process, if they are to grow and develop, they must have the opportunity to acquire the necessary knowledge and skills.

Finally, it is necessary to have a statement of philosophy that spells out the general role workers have in the organization and how they are to be treated. A statement of philosophy that represents the consensus of senior management provides a basis for encouraging managerial behavior consistent across plants and functions. The philosophy also lets employees know how they can expect to be treated.

All efforts at General Motors require a firm commitment at the top levels of the corporation. Such support, combined with a variety of successful projects has led to the creation of a quality-of-worklife program in nearly all plants. This does not mean that GM has all the answers or that quality of worklife is fully developed in General Motors. There is much to be done, but the corporation is on the right track and making progress.

FUTURE OF THE PROJECTS

An important shift in union-management relations began in the decade of the 1970s. Unions and management showed a willingness to explore new alternatives and, in some instances, levels of cooperation once thought impossible produced dramatic results. What about the decade of the 1980s? What is the future of quality of worklife in America?

Two critical forces will have a significant impact on the future of quality-of-worklife projects. One is the changing values of workers. Increased sense of entitlement, disregard for authority, and a general low esteem of our institutions have been major factors in the developmental years of quality of worklife. Today's workers place less emphasis on material achievement and more on personal fulfillment. The value shift of Americans will significantly impact the future of quality of worklife.

The second force is economic. While business is being challenged to respond to dramatically changing values, our country is facing economic problems. The fact is, the United States is locked in a fiercely competitive economic struggle which could have either a positive or negative impact on quality of worklife—positive if it leads to innovative solutions and negative if it results in simply greater emphasis on traditional approaches.

Our nation's poor productivity improvement rate is a major factor contributing to our economic ills. The problem has not come about overnight. Between 1947 and 1967, output per hour of work in the United States nearly doubled. Since 1967, output per hour worked has risen only about one fifth. And in 1978, the U.S. productivity growth rate was an alarming one half of 1 percent, a dismal performance compared to the rate of growth of other major industrial nations, particularly Japan.

In the past, America has been able to compete with cheap overseas labor because of our capital investment. In 1978, however, capital investment per worker in this country amounted to less than $3,700, compared with nearly $5,000 per Japanese worker. There are many factors in addition to capital investment which contribute to Japan's envious productivity growth rate. Among them are government policies and programs that actively support economic expansion, technological innovation, harmonious union-management relations, and a totally dedicated work force. Group goals are far more important than individual successes in the Japanese structure.

I do not think we can ignore the traits present in the Japanese system. In this country, we have been overly loyal to organizational tradition. But, today, we cannot afford not to take new risks. The joint efforts of business, government, and labor are essential if we are to respond to the needs of a changing workforce and resolve our economic problems.

Stumbling blocks. As we push forward the frontiers of quality of worklife there are some formidable obstacles to overcome. One is the issue of control. Should control be viewed as external to the individual, as provided for through a supervisor and shop rules? Or should it lie within the individual's self-regulating ability and value system and based upon mutual influence and interest that leads to "win-win" rather than "win-lose" relationships? Moving from external to self-regulating sources of control would seem to be consistent with the quality-of-worklife viewpoint. How much training and how much information is management willing to provide if employees are to be self-regulating? Many organizations in the past have been cautious about sharing information, particularly financial information, for fear employees will use this knowledge to make "unfair" claims on the enterprise.

12-8

HOW QUALITY-OF-WORKLIFE PROJECTS WORK FOR THE UNITED AUTO WORKERS

Irving Bluestone*

In 1973, in bargaining with General Motors Corp. for a new national agreement, the United Auto Workers (UAW) proposed the establishment of a National Joint Committee to Improve the Quality of Worklife. The parties agreed to a document which set forth their general understanding on the subject and pledged to urge their respective local managements and local unions to cooperate "in (quality-of-worklife) experiments and projects."

How, where, and when to go about the task were left open for the parties to consider. Over time, certain generalized concepts have become accepted. However, the approach varies in each situation because the program is not imposed from the top down, but must be cooperatively and voluntarily developed and implemented from the bottom up—at the local union-management level.

Today, there are approximately 50 quality-of-worklife programs in UAW–GM bargaining units. Most are still in the early stages—an indication that such programs are not "instant utopias" but rather follow a slow, cautious, deliberate pace.

How did the UAW and GM go about

setting up a quality-of-worklife program? What were the "nuts and bolts" steps taken and how were they implemented? While no two projects are identical, the following describes in concrete terms what happened.

The fact that the National Joint Committee to Improve the Quality of Worklife exists and urges the local parties to consider undertaking a project supplies the initiative to create interest in the subject. A local management may contact the local union shop committee (or vice versa) suggesting the local parties discuss the possibility of initiating a quality-of-worklife project. The local union as a rule will contact the international union and ask for a thorough explanation of the concept, how it works, what it entails, and its advantages and disadvantages.

An international union representative will meet with the local union official and describe in detail the meaning and purpose of the concept and what has been done elsewhere and why. The representative will set forth certain guiding principles which are usually agreed upon as a basis for proceeding:

- There must be no increase in production standards as a result of the quality-of-worklife program—an assurance against speed-up. (Naturally, increased production due to technological change is another matter.)
- There must be no loss of jobs as a result of the program—an assurance

* Recently retired as vice president of the United Auto Workers and director of the union's GM department; presently University Professor of Labor Studies, Wayne State University. December 1981 speech given at the Conference on "Critical Economic and Work Force Issues Facing Western Nations"sponsored by the Work in America Institute and the International Institute of Labor Studies in Washington, D.C., and published in *Monthly Labor Review*, BLS, July 1980, pp. 39–41. Reprinted by permission of the Work in America Institute and Irving Bluestone.

of job security. (Obviously, layoffs due to business cycles are another matter.)

- The provisions of the national agreement and of the local agreements and practices remain inviolable.
- The program will be voluntary. No worker will be compelled to participate.
- The union representatives will be involved in all aspects of the program—sharing with management equally in the development and implementation of the program.
- Either party may cancel the program at any time—an assurance against either being tied to a project in which it has lost faith.

The local, after full discussion, will decide whether to proceed. It is advised to "go slow," to experiment with a pilot project at first and approach the program on a "cut and try" basis. The local understands that normal collective bargaining continues, that a quality-of-worklife program will not solve all the plant problems.

In the UAW–GM approach, no separate quality-of-worklife committee is formed. The local union shop committee—the elected representatives of the workers for purposes of handling grievances and bargaining—is the union counterpart in the program. This avoids any conflict in determining which subjects fall within the purview of adversarial collective bargaining and which are subject to the cooperative effort of quality of worklife.

A quality-of-worklife program cannot succeed unless the local parties develop a collective bargaining climate of mutual respect, a climate in which solving problems supersedes beating the other party down. Therefore, the first phase, before the parties can move significantly toward worker participation programs, entails fostering a mutually respectful relationship as the groundwork for a program which will involve the workers directly.

This is no overnight task. It may take months of getting together and talking things through. Essentially the problem is attitudinal, and breaking down distrust and cynicism on both sides is a slow but extremely rewarding process.

Once phase one is well underway, the road is paved for the local parties to embark on pilot projects in which workers on a volunteer basis become involved in problem solving and participate in making decisions regarding the workplace which, heretofore, have been denied them. By now, the parties have learned to work together more cooperatively. Without pervasive rancor and suspicion beclouding their efforts, they can join mutually in analyzing the problems which trouble the workers and create the opportunity for workers to help resolve them.

The overriding consideration is that all decisions are by mutual desire and consent at the local level. Neither the corporation nor the international union instructs the local parties; each is merely a catalyst (to advise and consult) when called upon.

There is ample evidence that the introduction of a quality-of-worklife program has a salubrious effect upon the adversarial collective bargaining system. For example, simultaneously with national negotiations between the UAW and GM, the local parties negotiate on local issues, including seniority, transfer, shift preference, equalization of overtime agreements, and other proposals to improve working conditions and health and safety, grievances, and other issues. Of the first 90 local settlements in 1979, all of which were accomplished without a strike threat, 44 were engaged in some stage of a quality-of-worklife program. Considering there are about 50 programs at GM, this represents a noteworthy achievement.

Studies at locations where a quality-of-worklife program has existed long enough to be meaningful indicate a more constructive collective bargaining relationship; a more satisfied work force; improved product quality; a reduction in grievance handling, absenteeism, labor turnover, and disciplinary layoffs and discharges.

These are all mutually desirable objectives; they represent benefits for the workers and advantages for both the union and the management. But above all, from the workers' point of view, they add up to one of the most fundamental objectives of unionism: the enhancement of human dignity and self-fulfillment at work.

For decades, we have heard corporation executives exclaim: "Our workers are our most valuable resource." Quality-of-work-life programs are designed to make that slogan a reality. How? By altering the autocratic climate of the workplace and providing workers, through their union, with the opportunity to participate meaningfully in the decision-making process at the workplace; by focusing management's orientation toward concern for the needs and aspiration of the workers; and by creating an atmosphere of cooperative effort between union and management to achieve the above noted objective.

12-9

PROVIDING ASSISTANCE TO DISPLACED WORKERS

Bruce H. Millen*

How can workers be protected against job loss caused by changing technology, economic structure, or public policy? Since the 1930s, trade unions have helped to safeguard workers through strategies of collective bargaining. In recent years, Congress has devoted increasing attention to the issue of alleviating the distress of job loss caused, or induced, by public policy. Several new or amended statutes, including the Regional Rail Reorganization Act of 1973, the Trade Adjustment Assistance Amendments of 1974, and the Redwood National Park Act Amendments of 1978, have provided job protection or adjustment assistance or both to certain classes of workers.

This article offers a brief review of both the collective bargaining and the statutory response to the threat of job loss. The programs described (whether collectively bargained or government initiated) are "reactive"; they are designed to protect workers against dislocation based on decisions already made or, at best, on decisions as they are being formulated.

* Director of the Office of Wage and Labor Relations in the Office of the Assistant Secretary of Policy, Evaluation, and Research, U.S. Department of Labor. Reprinted from *Monthly Labor Review*, BLS, May 1979, pp. 17–22.

COLLECTIVE BARGAINING APPROACHES

Unions always have played a key role in protecting workers from job loss resulting from technological or other change. They have succeeded through obtaining a wide variety of contractual clauses, including work rules, exclusive jurisdiction over certain work, transfer rights, reduction in jobs through attrition, and protection of long-service workers through seniority.

Union concern over job security has heightened recently because of an acceleration in the rate of change—the increased government effort to bring about structural change or to achieve socioeconomic goals associated with health, safety, and clean air.

WORK RULES.   One example of preserving jobs, most common in the printing, railroad, and longshoring industries, is the negotiaion of work rules often designed to increase, or at least to hold constant, the level of employment by specifying standard crew sizes. Data from a Bureau of Labor Statistics survey show that in 1975 approximately 23 percent of workers studied were covered by contracts with a provision for limiting or regulating crew size.[1] Many of these rules are based on safety factors or on reasonable workload factors such as weight. In some industries—printing, mining, transportation, construction, utilities—as many as 50 percent of the workers were covered by agreements that included a provision on crew size restrictions.

Longstanding work rules may become dysfunctional if they place the industry in a noncompetitive position. This situation occurred on the West Coast, when an elaborate set of restrictive work rules on longshoring placed severe limitations on employers' freedom to assign longshore-

men or on management's right to introduce new equipment.

To help the industry remain competitive, the union changed its approach to job security. Instead of resisting change, the union offered employers an opportunity to "buy out" the most restrictive work rules in exchange for a worker trust fund which would provide for an employer-financed, guaranteed workweek and early retirement rights.

Similarly, in May 1978, the National Constructors Association and eight craft unions affiliated with the AFL–CIO Building and Construction Trades Department signed an agreement that standardized work rules on major industrial construction projects in 11 States and gave management considerable latitude in assigning work and in the use of tools and prefabricated materials.

SLACK-WORK PROVISIONS.   Slack-work provisions are designed to keep all employees at work when operations are curtailed. Most of these provisions have limitations on the periods during which they are operative; therefore, they alone are not sufficient solutions to permanent displacement problems caused by plant shutdowns.

Worksharing is often part of a slack-work provision. Thirty-six percent of the organized workers examined by the Bureau of Labor Statistics in 1975 were covered by contracts providing for worksharing. Of these provisions, 75 percent provided for a reduction in hours. Other approaches to worksharing include division of work and rotation of employment.

Nine percent of the workers were covered by slack-work clauses that provided for restrictions on overtime. Clauses covering 27 percent included restrictions on subcontracting during periods of slack work.[2]

EMPLOYEE TRANSFER. Provision for transfer of employees among plant facili-

[1] *Characteristics of Major Collective Bargaining Statistics, July 1, 1975,* Bulletin 1957 (Bureau of Labor Statistics, 1975), p. 99.

[2] *Ibid.,* p. 85.

ties also can preclude displacement, if employees are willing to relocate to continue their employment. According to 1975 BLS figures, 47 percent of the workers studied were covered by contracts providing for interplant transfers under varying conditions. Thirty-two percent of these workers were under contracts providing transfer in the event of impending layoffs, and 20 percent were under contracts providing transfer in the event of plant closure, consolidation, or mergers.[3]

UNION JURISDICTION CLAUSES. Yet another method of protecting jobs through collective bargaining is the union jurisdiction clause, which establishes exclusive rights over certain kinds of work for members of specific unions, typically the more skilled tradesmen. These contract clauses reflect provisions for assuring job security, which are found in union constitutions or bylaws and which have been accepted by employers. Unions also may establish jurisdictional rights to certain operations through agreements requiring that workers operating new machinery remain within the bargaining unit.

Historically, jurisdictional disputes and strikes have presented serious difficulties. However, jurisdictional problems have been reduced greatly in recent years with the development of a mechanism by the AFL–CIO nationally for the peaceful settlement of internal interunion disputes.

ATTRITION PLANS. If the number of employees affected is a small percentage of the total work force, it is sometimes possible to avoid worker displacement by relying on normal attrition to achieve planned reductions in the work force. Through a combination of hiring suspension, voluntary quits, retirements, discharges for cause, transfers, and deaths, a work force can be reduced gradually to the required size. While attrition clauses are relatively common in the railroad indus-

try, according to BLS, only 0.5 percent of all collective bargaining agreements studied in 1972 (excluding railroads) provided this means for reducing the work force.[4] Attrition provisions most often are limited to specific situations and are applied only on a one-time basis.

Since 1971, the contract between the U.S. Postal Service and the Letter Carriers and American Postal unions has specified that reductions of full-time postal workers be achieved solely through attrition. To date, attrition has reduced the postal work force by approximately 80,000.

SENIORITY AND ADJUSTMENT ASSISTANCE. Because full protection from layoff or displacement cannot be achieved, most collective bargaining agreements provide greater job security to employees with longer service. Most agreements assign relatively more weight to seniority than to ability and other factors in determining the order in which employees are laid off. A 1971 BLS study found that all but 1 of the 364 contracts studied made seniority a criterion in layoff procedures.[5]

Plant shutdowns or large-scale layoffs, however, cannot be accommodated by rear-guard actions. Therefore, adjustment assistance or income maintenance programs have been negotiated.

The most common type of assistance is the severance pay allowance. According to 1975 BLS figures, 38 percent of workers studied were covered by agreements providing severance pay.[6] Such pay was provided most commonly in the event of permanent plant or departmental shutdown, technological displacement, and layoffs expected to last more than two years. The benefits received are related to length of service, with one-week's pay typically pre-

---

[3] *Ibid.*, p. 86.

[4] *Layoffs, Recalls, and Worksharing Procedures, 1972*, Bulletin 1425-13 (Bureau of Labor Statistics, 1972), p. 18.

[5] Ibid., p. 31.

[6] *Characteristics*, p. 90.

scribed for each year of service, up to a specified maximum.

Supplemental unemployment benefits (SUB) grant weekly payments from an employer-financed fund over and above State unemployment insurance benefits. In 1975, 28 percent of the workers studied by BLS were under SUB provisions.[7] While designed to provide relief against cyclical unemployment, SUB benefits can be an imperfect adjustment assistance program when plant closures occur. In recent years, the plans have been extended to provide weekly benefits to partially unemployed workers and severance pay and moving allowances to released workers.

EARLY RETIREMENT AND ADVANCE NOTICE. To reduce the size or the makeup of their work forces, an increasing number of companies have been encouraging their employees to retire early. According to BLS figures for 1974, more than 96 percent of those workers covered by defined benefit plans of more than 100 employees were eligible for early retirement benefits. The vast majority of these workers retire at their own option.[8]

Advance notice of layoff also can provide modest assistance to help employees in danger of job loss provide for financial contingencies and to find work elsewhere. Forty-four percent of workers studied by BLS in 1975 were covered by contracts with provisions requiring advance notice of layoff; a week or less (sometimes less than 24 hours) was the typical length of notice required.[9] In addition, 9 percent of the workers were covered by contracts requiring advance notice of plant closure and 17 percent by contracts requiring advance notice of technological change. In view of the limited nature of the typical warning, this device is little more than a palliative.

SPECIAL NEGOTIATED AGREEMENTS. In several cases, special agreements have been negotiated to protect specific groups of workers from the impact of displacement or technological change.

In 1936, the railroad unions and 141 carriers negotiated the "Washington Agreement of May 1936" to lessen the employment impact of railroad consolidations. Under the agreement, a railroad employee losing his job as a result of consolidation was awarded an allowance equal to 60 percent of his earnings in the year prior to loss of employment, for up to five years. Relocation expenses and losses on sales of homes were paid by the railroads, and benefits such as free transportation, pensions, and hospitalization continued during the period of protection. The Washington Agreement provided the model for virtually all subsequent protective agreements and legislation in the transportation sector.

In 1959, the Armour Company and the two unions representing its employees established the Automation Fund Committee in response to worker displacement from shifts in production caused by market changes and the replacement of obsolete plants. This tripartite committee was a comprehensive effort to cope with mass layoffs within the framework of collective bargaining. The committee's activities were supported initially by a $500,000 fund created under the 1959 agreement and financed through company contributions.

METHODS EFFECTIVE YET LIMITED. The array of methods developed by labor and management have been useful devices to protect workers in a single location or, as on the railroads, in a given industry. Some costs are incurred, of course, in following orderly processes of job and income protection to permit change to take place; but these costs must be balanced against the potential and actual economic, social, and political costs derived from unregulated job dislocation.

---

[7] *Characteristics*, p. 90.

[8] Unpublished Bureau of Labor Statistics data.

[9] *Characteristics*, p. 89.

Labor and management, however, are limited in their capacity to manage change in today's interdependent economy and in the face of what are often social policy decisions imposed by the body politic. Moreover, only roughly 25 percent of the work force are covered by union contracts, so that the protections offered fail to protect a majority of workers and place greater costs on specific union employers than on their nonunion counterparts.

LEGISLATED PROTECTION

Structural changes in the economy are taking place alongside of demands for such social imperatives as a cleaner and safer environment. The dual thrust of private and public policy has raised the spectre of job loss to a wide range of workers. They, as well as their unions, have been in the forefront of those urging adoption of various forms of protection and assistance in conjunction with the passage of legislation involving economic and social change. Many believe the Unemployment Insurance program is sufficient protection and workers dislocated by reason of government policy have no greater claim for assistance than do workers made jobless by regular market forces.

Others, including workers affected by such government decisions as the encouragement of trade or the consolidation of the railroads, perceive the problem differently. They view a worker's career as an investment deserving of a return when affected adversely by new national policies. The recent record indicates that the Congress is sympathetic to the special needs of the claimants for extraordinary relief as the quid pro quo to gain support for necessary legislation.

Statutory provisions protecting special groups of workers against the adverse effects of government actions first appeared in transportation industry legislation in the 1930s. Initially introduced into railroad industry statutes, protective provisions subsequently were incorporated into laws dealing with the airlines and urban mass transportation. Outside of the transportation sector, such statutory requirements were relatively rare until recent years, when Congress appended job protection provisions to legislation in fields other than transportation.

RAILROAD INDUSTRY. Federal legislation providing employment protection to railroad workers was first enacted in 1933 with the passage of the Emergency Railroad Transportation Act, a law that facilitated railroad consolidations. This statute, which expired in 1936, imposed a job freeze for all railroad workers. Soon after formulation of the Washington Agreement, the Interstate Commerce Commission (ICC), acting without an explicit statutory mandate, began to condition its approval of consolidation actions upon carrier acceptance of employee protection arrangements. Then, in the Transportation Act of 1940 (Sec. 5(2)(f)), Congress amended the Interstate Commerce Act to impose such a legal requirement on the Commission.

In 1970, Congress passed the Rail Passenger Service Act to preserve intercity rail passenger service by creating a private profitmaking corporation, the National Railroad Passenger Corporation, (Amtrak). Section 405 of the act provides protection for those employees who might be adversely affected by the corporation's takeover of intercity passenger operations. This section, modeled after Section 13(c) of the Urban Mass Transportation Act, requires a railroad to provide fair and equitable arrangements to protect the interests of employees affected by discontinuance of intercity rail passenger services. These arrangements include the following: (1) preservation of rights, privileges, and benefits under existing collective bargaining arrangements or otherwise; (2) continuation of collective bargaining rights; (3) protection of individual employees against a worsening of their positions with respect to their employment; (4) reemployment priority for employees terminated or laid off; and (5) paid training or retraining.

In addition, it became apparent early in the 1970s that additional Federal assistance to the railroad industry was needed when several rail carriers were involved in a series of bankruptcies that threatened liquidation and cessation of service. The Regional Rail Reorganization Act of 1973 attempted to deal with this problem by providing for the restructing of the rail system in the Northeast and Midwest and for the establishment of a profitmaking corporation, the Consolidated Rail Corp. (Conrail), to operate the restructured system.

Unlike earlier statutes that required employee protection but set forth only guidelines toward that end, Title V of this act specified the protective conditions that apply to adversely affected workers. Title V requires that protected employees who are dismissed or displaced to lower paying jobs receive a monthly allowance equal to their average monthly railroad earnings over the 12 months prior to the adverse action.

Employees with five years service or more on the effective date of the act are eligible to receive the allowance until they reach age 65 and become covered by the retirement system.

Under the title, laid-off employees may be required to transfer to vacancies for which they are qualified. If such transfers require a change in residence, the employees are reimbursed for all moving and traveling expenses for themselves and their families. The employees also may be reimbursed for any loss suffered in sale of their homes or for any loss incurred in securing cancellation of a lease.

All allowances, expenses, and costs provided employees pursuant to these protective arrangements are to be reimbursed ultimately by the Railroad Retirement Board from a $250-million authorization fund, known as the Northeast Rail Transportation Protective Account, maintained in the U.S. Treasury.

Payment of benefits under the various rail programs is made by the employer to the affected worker. In the case of Amtrak, the moneys are derived from general income, including Federal subsidies. In the case of Conrail, payments are derived from a U.S. Treasury account via the Railroad Retirement Board. As of December 1977, $90 million out of a total $250 million authorization had been used.

THE TRANSIT AND AIRLINE INDUSTRIES. The award of any grant or loan by the Department of Transportation in support of urban mass transit is contingent upon the certification by the Secretary of Labor that fair and equitable arrangements including collective bargaining rights have been made to protect the interests of mass transit employees within the project service area. Section 13(c) of the statute provides that such arrangements shall include essentially the same protections as those under the Rail Passenger Service Act noted earlier in this article.

Protective arrangements similar to those provided by the Urban Mass Transportation Act also are required under the High Speed Ground Transportation Act of 1965, which authorizes research and demonstration projects involving high speed ground transportation. Payments to employees are made by the operating entities, some of that money being derived from Federal subsidies.

Since 1950, the Civil Aeronautics Board (CAB) has approved mergers and related actions only when carriers accept arrangements for protection of employees. The CAB instituted this policy during a period of instability in the industry which was marked by a number of transactions among carriers.

The next important step in what is, essentially, a line of progression was the establishment of conditions by the CAB in 1972, called the Allegheny-Mohawk decision, which provided a wide range of protections, including wage retention for those downgraded, five-years' income maintenance at 60 percent of earnings for those dismissed, relocation allowances, and maintenance of fringe benefits.

Most recent has been the passage of the Airline Deregulation Act of 1978. Employees with more than four-years' service with a certified carrier (one suffering a reduction in force of 7.5 percent over a 12-month period) are entitled to a number of cash and service benefits. Assistance payments will be paid for a maximum of six years. Unlike other legislation of this type, the Secretary of Labor is authorized to determine benefit levels for each class and craft of employee. While these benefits have not yet been determined, the secretary undoubtedly will rely on precedents established in both the rail and air sectors of the transportation industry. Eligible employees have first right of hire with other carriers, are entitled to training and other employment services, and receive relocation allowances.

It is not yet clear whether payments to airline employees will ever be required. Should it be necessary, a special fund has been authorized by Congress, but no money has been appropriated.

TRADE ADJUSTMENT ASSISTANCE. Special programs of assistance have been created for workers adversely affected by increased imports. The first were established under the Trade Expansion Act of 1962. Then benefits were liberalized in the Trade Act of 1974. This act attempted to improve access to the program and to speed up the certification of impact and benefit delivery process. The qualifying criteria were eased substantially, and responsibility for worker adjustment assistance was assigned solely to the U.S. Department of Labor.

A worker certified by the Department of Labor as eligible to receive benefits un-

der the 1974 Trade Act may receive the following: (1) a basic Trade Readjustment Allowance for up to 52 weeks, equal to 70 percent of the average weekly wage earned before employment was disrupted by import competition when added to State unemployment insurance payments (older workers and workers in approved training programs are eligible for 26 additional weeks); and (2) full range of employment assistance services offered by State employment security agencies, including skills training and an allowance for job search and relocation.

Certification for eligibility for program benefits is a complex process. In recent months, the Bureau of International Labor Affairs has succeeded in reducing the time from application through investigation to certification of an adversely affected group to the 60-day statutory requirement in a high percentage of cases. Possibly another two or three weeks pass before the individual worker is certified for benefits by the individual State employment agency. Cash benefits are paid from the Federal Unemployment Benefits Account, and cost of training and other employment services is borne by CETA funds.

REDWOOD NATIONAL PARK ACT AMENDMENTS Legislation enacted in March 1978 provides protection to workers displaced by the expansion of the Redwood National Parks, established under a 1968 act. The Department of Labor began paying benefits under this program on September 13, 1978.

The act specifies benefit payments from the Federal Government to covered workers, including (1) supplemental layoff benefits for each week of total and partial layoff, equal to their level of earnings prior to the park expansion; (2) maintenance of fringe benefits, such as seniority, health insurance, and pension rights, which affected employees would otherwise have had; (3) severance pay equal to 1-week's layoff benefit for each month of service, up to a maximum of 72 weeks for workers with less than five years of service and for other workers who choose this option; (4) retraining; (5) job search allowance; (6) relocation allowance; and (7) preferential hiring for jobs in the expanded park. These benefits may be received for a six-year period.

An important aspect of this legislation is that the total or partial layoff of a covered employee between May 31, 1977, and September 30, 1980, is "conclusively presumed" to be attributable to the expansion of Redwood National Park. In other protective legislation, such as Trade Adjustment Assistance, the Department of Labor must certify the eligibility for coverage after the fact.

Benefit levels are high—$350 per week is not unusual. Many have suggested that disincentives to job search have come into play. It must be kept in mind, however, that the lumber industry is a high-paying sector in this area and that benefits are tied to previous earnings.

Cash benefit payments (weekly or severance) are paid out of the Federal Unemployment Benefits Account, and cost for employment services are supplied under CETA.

ECONOMIC ISSUES: EQUITY AND EFFICIENCY

No one can question the importance of the programs described in this article to individual workers caught in the shifts in public policy. And in many cases, desired public policy, whether it be maintaining free trade or revitalizing urban transit, could not have been achieved were it not for the existence of these specialized programs. Thus, the programs can be supported on the grounds that gains made by the society, or the economy as a whole, justify payments to individuals who suffer private losses.

Often, of course, it is difficult—as in the case of the expansion of the Redwood National Park—to quantify the gains to the public welfare and to compare them again with the benefits paid out to a specific group of workers. This means that in most instances—in the absence of generally accepted standards of what is "fair" in the society—the ultimate justification for a program, and for the redistributive function it represents, is a political one.

Political decisions or not, certain economic questions concerning both equity and efficiency must be addressed. On the equity side, every attempt must be made to treat people in similar economic situations in equal fashion. This is one of the arguments used by those who favor the exclusive use of unemployment insurance for all types of unemployment. If there are to be special assistance programs for certain classes of workers, then an attempt should be made to assure that horizontal equity across programs and within each program exists.

Economic efficiency demands that benefit levels and duration of benefits should be structured to encourage workers to seek new jobs. Or, under certain circumstances, lump-sum payments to discharged workers would spur earlier job search than would weekly benefits.

Care must be exercised in designing economically efficient programs. Job protection programs in inefficient industries promote less efficient utilization of labor and result in a misallocation of labor and resources not only domestically, but within the international economy.

This last element is at the base of the present effort by the Organization for Economic and Cooperative Development to develop "positive adjustment policies." The statement of such a goal, however, is a far cry from achieving it. As long as one person's definition of "efficiency" means another's job, the way is fraught with difficulties.

CHAPTER 13

Contract Administration

Grievance procedures culminating in final and binding arbitration are the dominant method used by unions and employers to settle disputes over the interpretation of collective bargaining agreements. While, in general, the parties to collective bargaining are unwilling to provide an outsider with authority to dictate all of the terms and conditions of employment contained in a collective agreement, such authority is generally provided to outsiders for the settlement of disputes over the individual terms in an agreement. The alternative would be for the union to strike each time it disagreed with a decision of the employer. A practice such as this would be unnecessarily disruptive to production and result in a substantial loss of income to employees.

The grievance procedure in most collective agreements is structured so that the parties to the collective agreement can have every opportunity to settle the dispute themselves, without the intervention of an outside arbitrator. Generally, the procedure is broken down into steps, so that at each step successively higher officials of the union and the employer discuss the problem and try to resolve it. The theory behind this is that the further the negotiators are from the dispute, the more dispassionate their analysis, since they are less likely to have been involved in the original decision. The process it seems, works. It is generally agreed that well over 90 percent of all grievances filed are settled prior to arbitration.

The arbitration process, when invoked, has the outward appearance of a judicial proceeding. Each side makes a statement to the arbitrator, calls and directly examines witnesses, cross-examines the witnesses of the other party, and enters evidence for the consideration of the arbitrator. Yet the arbitration hearing is much less formal than a judicial proceeding. The arbitrator will generally be extremely liberal in the admission of evidence, both documentary and from testimony, with the option of giving it the weight the arbitrator believes it merits. Also, there is often a great deal of on-the-record discussion between the advocates, as such discussion can often enlighten the arbitrator as to what actually happens or what the parties intended with a particular contract clause.

This section reprints five arbitration decisions on four issues that commonly occur in grievances. The first case presents the question of whether the employer had "just cause" to discharge an employee. The second case outlines the tests for determining "just cause." The third case presents the question of whether the less senior employee was more qualified for a promotion than the more senior employee. The fourth case involves the employer's right to subcontract work, thereby not providing its own employees with jobs and/or premium pay. The fifth case addresses two issues: the right of the employer to promulgate rules for the operation of the plant and the role of past practice in determining agreements between the parties.

CAPITAL DISTRICT TRANSPORTATION AUTHORITY

Arbitrator: S. Oley Cutler*

72 LA 1313 June 1, 1979

MISCONDUCT

Cutler, Arbitrator:—The issue in dispute between the parties hereto is agreed to by term:

> Did the Capital District Transit Authority rightfully discharge Employee M___?

PERTINENT CONTRACT PROVISIONS

ARTICLE 10—EMPLOYMENT

(a) Subject to the provisions of this Agreement, the printed rules of conduct governing employees as promulgated by the Company, as the same now or hereafter may exist, shall govern the conduct of all employees.

(b) The Company will, through its proper officers, meet and treat with the accredited representatives of the Union on all matters concerning employees covered by this Agreement.

(c) Subject to the provisions of this Agreement, the Union recognizes that the management of the Company and the direction and control of the work forces, including the full right to hire, discipline, suspend, discharge for proper cause, promote, demote or transfer, and to relieve employees from duty because of lack of work or for other proper and legitimate reason, is vested in and reserved by the Company. However, the Company recognizes the right of the Union

to negotiate on any of these matters involving working conditions, hours, wages, and benefits normally within the purview of collective bargaining. It is mutually agreed that the grievance procedure as herein provided will be followed in the event any grievance arising hereunder cannot be satisfactorily adjusted by and between the parties hereto.

(d) In case where Union has negotiated for an adjustment of wages, working conditions or any grievance and Company has made a decision thereon, should it change its decision, it will first notify the Union.

(e) When new employees are required in any of the groups represented by the Union, the Company will first consider the reemployment of any men previously laid off due to lack of work, according to seniority, providing they are qualified, in the judgment of the Company to fill the vacancies.

(f) It is specifically agreed between the parties hereto that there shall be no lockout of any kind or for any cause on the part of the Company, and there shall be no strike or other cessation of work of any kind, by any of the employees on account of sympathy or otherwise, which shall be participated in by any members of the Union, during the existence of this Agreement or any extension thereof.

ARTICLE 30—DISCIPLINE

(a) When an employee violates the rules of the Company, he will be called in by his immediate superior and advised of the violation and the amount of discipline. If the employee feels that he has been unfairly dealt with, he may call for a hearing in the presence of his Union Grievance Represen-

* Arbitrator selected by parties through procedures of Federal Mediation & Conciliation Service. Reprinted from *Labor Arbitration Reports* by permission of BNA, Inc.

tative, at which time the matter will be discussed and adjusted if possible. If no agreement is reached, the matter will then be taken up in accordance with the grievance procedure outlined herein.

(b) During grievance hearings, either side may call witnesses to appear in their behalf.

(c) Members of the Union are not to be reprimanded within the hearing of other employees or the public.

(d) Both the Union and the Company agree that grievances will be disposed of as speedily as possible.

ARTICLE 31—ARBITRATION

(a) Notice of demand for submitting any controversy or grievance to arbitration shall be given by either party hereto, in writing, stating the subject in dispute and shall be sent by registered mail to the office of the other party hereto.

(b) In the event any dispute cannot be settled in accordance with the provisions of Article 29, the matter shall promptly be submitted to a Board of Arbitration, consisting of two (2) members who reside in the Capital District, one to be selected by the Company and the other to be selected by the Union. If said board cannot reach an agreement in the matter in dispute within thirty (30) days, then a third member shall be selected by them from a panel of *seven* (7) arbitrators' names to be obtained from the Federal Conciliation Service.

(c) The majority decision of the Board shall be final and binding upon the parties. Each party shall bear the expense of preparing and presenting its own case and the expense of its own arbitrator. The expense of the third arbitrator and incidental expenses mutually agreed to in advance shall be borne equally by the parties to this Agreement.

BACKGROUND OF THE DISPUTE

The facts leading to the present arbitration are in dispute between the parties. Yet, as charged against the grievant, the following emerges: The grievant, M——, an employee of the company for 17 years, was driving the early morning shift from Albany to Nassau. At about 6:30 a.m. on or about December 11, 1978, a Miss Susan Thomas boarded the bus and gave the driver a dollar bill. Since his fare box was full, the driver allowed her to board without paying the exact fare and promised to give her the change on the same run on the following day. As she was about to depart the bus, she placed one of her hands on one of the bars surrounding the cab front section of the vehicle. Then, she asserts, M—— put his one hand over her hand and with his other hand, grabbed her about the neck to pull her forward as if to kiss her. She then left the bus and returned to her living quarters. She delayed notifying the company by telephone to complain of this incident for about two days when she had the opportunity to use her boy friend's telephone to make a complaint to the company.

Her call was received by a Mr. Louis Williams, Night Dispatcher for the company, who wrote up the complaint in the form indicated on the accompanying record. (Appendix B.[1]) The complaint was then processed through Mr. A. Kallner. M——'s suspension form his job was then ordered while the employer attempted to locate the complainant, Miss Thomas, to interview her. In his filed notice of grievance, (Appendix C.[2]), M—— upon being summoned to Mr. Kallner's office, demanded to know the reason for his suspension and was told nothing save that a serious charge was involved. This lack of notice to him is referred to in M——'s filed grievance. Business Agent Guire was apprised of the situation by Mr. James Griffin, Superintendent of Transportation. A hearing on this suspension was subsequently held by Mr. Griffin on December 19, 1978, at which Grievant attempted to give his own version of the "incident,"

---

[1] Editor's note: Appendix B is omitted.

[2] Editor's note: Appendix C is omitted.

namely, that he had not sufficient change for Miss Thomas' dollar and told her that he would give her the change the following day on the same run. He also absolutely denied touching her hand or attempting to kiss her.

On January 11, 1979, at a hearing chaired by Mr. Thomas Sharkey, Manager of Transportation, the company charged that on the basis of interviews with Miss Thomas conducted by a Mr. Wildzunas, Supervisor for the company, and also on the written accounts of the charge as placed already in the record in this case, the suspension order was converted into a permanent discharge. The grievant then pursued his case through the grievance process allowed by the contract, leading to the current arbitration.

POSITIONS OF THE PARTIES

The company. The employer advances three arguments in favor of its position. The first, and the principal one, is based on the testimony of Miss Thomas as to the incident of December 11, 1978. To this is added a second procedural argument that this "incident," coupled with M——'s work record as presented at the arbitration hearing, negates his credibility as a witness. The question is posed as procedural because it asks whether documentation presented to the arbitrator herein, upon whose admissibility he has not yet ruled, could possibly be so construed as to deny the employer the opportunity to introduce unfavorable aspects of M——'s work record so as to make linkage of them with the proof of the "incident" to constitute just cause for discharge under the contract.

The third argument challenges grievant's right at this time as a matter of procedure to raise the issue of fairness and equity in that he was not informed of the seriousness of the charges against him at the time of his suspension which led to his ultimate discharge. Such a claim, the company maintains, is made impossible since the grievant has waived it by not raising it at the lower grievance steps; and further that to sustain such a charge now would be in effect to constitute an application to stay arbitration—which at this point of the proceeding would be contrary to both the intent and case interpretation of Section 7503 (b) of the CPLR. As well, to accept this procedural move at this time would be to deny the validity of the parties' collective bargaining agreement which insures his right to arbitrate—that to deny the validity of one necessarily negates the validity of the other as well.

The union. The central, basic argument of the union here is the consistent and unimpeachable testimony of the grievant himself—the absolute denial of the "incident" as reported by Miss Thomas; namely, that he did not touch the girl with either hand at any time. Indeed he asserts that even if he had desired to do so, his position at the driver's seat, with the particular construction of the bars, etc., around the driver's section of the bus, made it impossible for him to have used his two hands in the way charged by Miss Thomas.

While admitting to the mistakes reported in the past upon his work record, grievant maintains that he accepted and paid the penalties for any possible misconduct in the past and that some incident of a decade ago of a contrary nature has no relevance as to constitute linkage here with the "incident" so as to constitute just cause for his discharge.

The union also charges the company with unfair delay in acquainting grievant with the nature of the charges against him—that this has not been raised before, and that this goes to show how his suspension was unjustly arrived at as a matter of company discipline over its work force. This point, the union urges, shows how the delay and the compiling of unsupported interviews tended to make grievant's suspension inevitable and then to make the discharge a logical, unavoidable next step. This, the union maintains, is the weight of its unfairness objection—it is not an attempt at a stay of arbitration as company counsel interprets it.

Further the union argues that the Arbitrator here has to weigh the credibility of a hard-working bus driver with a family to support and with 17 years of loyal service to his company, against the charges of a 17-year old girl of no known address or known occupation, whose testimony indeed was confused and at variance depending on the occasions she reported it.

DISCUSSION AND OPINION

There is no doubt that the conflicting views as expressed by the chief witnesses of both parties to this dispute contribute to make this a very difficult case to adjudge. However, a number of points do emerge quite clearly. First, the language of the collective bargaining agreement as to employee discipline and the procedures for addressing grievances under the grievance procedure leading to arbitration are very clear mandates agreed to by the parties. Second, a whole series of facts and a clear picture of the circumstances surrounding the incident of December 11, 1978, do emerge clearly as well. The correct judgment and conclusion of these facts and circumstances together with the past conduct of the grievant are part of the evaluation of facts that is intrinsic to the arbitration process, so as to lead to a reasonable and sustainable judgment on the arbitrator's part that the stringent demands of proper (or just) cause are met in order to justify a rightful and equitable discharge under the terms of the contract.

The burden of proof in a discharge case, such as this, rests upon the employer. As one well-recognized and highly-respected national authority once put it:

Discharge is recognized to be the extreme industrial penalty, since the employee's job, his seniority and other contractual benefits, and probably his reputation are at stake. Because of the seriousness of this penalty, the burden is held to be on the employer as to proof of wrongdoing.[3]

Any discharge is serious, of course; however, the more serious the grounds charged for the imposition of this penalty, the higher degree of proof that is required to sustain it. This sense of the situation is very well and strongly expressed in a recent arbitration decision:

In the area of discharge, it is incumbent upon the employer to prove guilt of wrongdoing and particularly so when the contract . . . for discharge requires just cause. Furthermore, the degree of proof in a discharge case is generally the "preponderance of evidence" rule. Proof beyond a reasonable doubt is normally required in those disciplinary cases where an employee is charged with "moral turpitude."

The opinion continues:

The employee's past record is often a factor in determination of the proper penalty for the offense. It is a further recognized principle in arbitration that there may be reasonable rules which are uniformly applied and adequately disseminated. 'Just cause' requires that employees be informed of the rules, the infraction of which may result in suspension or discharge . . . Furthermore, failure to conduct a fair investigation or interrogate the grievant before reaching a decision to discharge him violates the principle of industrial due process . . .

"Evidence concerning the giving of warnings of unsatisfactory conduct prior to discharge is germane in deciding if the penalty is justified. When an employee continues prohibited conduct after having been warned, the fact that he was warned will stand against him.

---

[3] Frank Elkouri and Edna Asper Elkouri, *How Arbitration Works,* 1952, Washington, D.C., Bureau of National Affairs, Inc., p. 166.

"In the area of burden of proof or burden of the affirmative the employer has the initial burden to justify his action. If the employer properly shoulders this burden or the grievant admits that he has performed the act for which he was discharged (or disciplined) the affirmative of the issue generally moves to the grievant. The grievant must then prove that there was good reason or excuse for his actions. Should the grievant successfully establish his reason or excuse for having committed the act or acts, the burden shifts back to the employer.

"The normal criteria for a discharge to meet the usual 'just cause' are:

1. The employee was forewarned.
2. Employer's position with respect to employee's conduct was reasonable.
3. Employer investigated before discharge.
4. Investigation was fair.
5. Substantial evidence supports the charge against the employee.
6. There was no discrimination.
7. The degree of discipline was reasonably related to the nature of the offense and the employee's past record.[4]

These quotations of traditional and current arbitration are especially applicable as can be seen, to the present case before us.

There is no denial that the company, as a public carrier, has a most serious obligation, a duty, of care for the health, welfare, and safety of its passengers. To effect this, it likewise must depend upon a work force, its employees, which is likewise obligated by the contract, the work rules, and the nature of the job to a high degree of professional conduct. It is not the arbitrator or the tenor of the preceding quotations that sets forth as almost a tort or criminal law evidentiary standards. Indeed, the parties to the contract here accept the concept of discipline, penalties for breach of discipline, and a grievance procedure for disputed disciplinary action upon the part of management.

Yet in our present case, despite the grave language quoted above about traditional disciplinary practice in discharge cases, we see as the foundation of its case, the employer relying upon the testimony of a 17-year-old girl, who although understandably nervous amid such proceedings, gave a confused description of the so-called incident of December 11, was unable to give dates or the description of the passengers on the vehicle, but was sure in the early morning darkness only of the identity of the grievant and the attempt to touch her which in her arbitration hearing testimony, she did not characterize as a kiss, but a movement to bring her towards him. Likewise in the available documentary evidence reporting the incident as recorded by company supervisory personnel, we find the above "incident" made more concrete and even the insinuating phrase "molesting" appearing in the report. Based upon these reports added to the grievant's file, the company compounded indefiniteness by unsupported opinion which is very serious in that it was initially kept secret from the grievant, yet led to his summary suspension, and all these weak links in turn joined together to "justify proper cause" for discharge in January 1979.

This is hardly the highest degree of proof to remove the shadow of a doubt in reaching such a conclusion.

Against such evidence is the word of the grievant, attempting to give his own version of the December 11 events, namely, that the girl did indeed board his bus, offered him a dollar bill for which he had no change because of a full fare box and offered in the seemingly casual operation of a suburban-semicountry bus run. He offered to give her her change the following day. This was technically a violation of company rules, a point on which he had once before been reprimanded and indeed warned, albeit under different fac-

---

[4] Atlantic Richfield Co. and Oil, Chemical and Atomic Workers Intl. Union, 70 LA 707, 715–716 (1978).

tual circumstances. M—— asserts that he was in good faith adherence to company rules on the fare collective issue, that when the fare box was filled as it was on that morning he was to call for a new bus to be sent out or wait until he returned to the garage with his box as it was. It is certainly an understandable solution to a perplexing question in this exact fare era.

Of greatest weight is the grievant's testimony that he did not touch the girl's hand or attempt to pull her toward him with his other hand. This seems to be strengthened by his own evidence that because of the unique construction of bars and railings around the cab and driver's seat section in the front of the bus, and with his preoccupation with the operation of the vehicle, his two hands were tied up in his work and it would have been physically impossible to have done all this hand work charged against him. A visual inspection of a like model bus by the arbitrator certainly confirms this interpretation.

Again, there is an unaccountable delay in Miss Thomas' report of the incident. In fact, the company admits its own difficulty in locating the lady to have her testify to one of its supervisors.

Over against this is grievant's absolute denial of the Susan Thomas version of the incident. His denial would perhaps be puzzling unless he happens to be telling the truth.

Absent other witnesses than Miss Thomas, and absent reliable documentary evidence on the part of the employer, one cannot but conclude that the balance of M——'s denial and reasonable explanation of the events of December 11 tend to favor the union's position in this dispute— which is to say that the company's evidence does not extend to remove any reasonable doubt such as is demanded in a case involving a very serious just cause for rightful dismissal.

As to the procedural argument offered by counsel for the employer herein, the claim is made that by raising the issue of unfair treatment of his case in that he was not made aware in a timely fashion of the charges against him prior to his summary suspension, grievant in effect made application for a stay of arbitration, obviously the grievant has a right to raise this issue at any time because it goes to the *gravamen* of any grievance as can be easily seen. The union never made any formal request for a stay of arbitration. By submitting to the lower steps of the grievance procedure and to the arbitration herein, grievant has not waived the substantial rights he has under the contract to protection from dismissal except for proper cause. What is most apparent in the unfairness issue is the bias that prevailed in the interrogatory stages as recorded by the company's supervisory personnel and compounded by the loose use of words such as "molestation," the withholding of the reasons for his suspension at the time of actual suspension—all these led to the suspension's taking effect and almost inexorably led to a discharge hearing that led to grievant's dismissal. These points are not "niceties of the law" as counsel characterized them, but essential safeguards to a worker's job security which today for the majority of Americans amounts to economic survival in a very inflationary, competitive economic national situation.

The company also points to M——'s overall work record, claiming that such record, together with the occurrence of the incident herein, surely conclusively established the groundwork for justifiable cause for this employee's discharge.

Let us examine the work record for certainly it does constitute a part of the overall evaluation necessary for proof of just cause in a discharge case.

The most serious of these reports is attached (Appendix D[5]). There is no doubt here of a serious offense and indeed of a

---

[5] Editor's note: Appendix D is omitted.

very serious warning. Although other records were offered at this time to refute grievant's case, such exhibits were not unaccepted but were seriously considered by us. What was lacking was a substantial proof of direct linkage of any prior incident to the present one here charged against the grievant.

In point of fact, there is no aspect of arbitration law and practice—including numerous court decisions—that more preoccupies serious students of arbitration law and practice, as was evidenced at the 1976 National Academy of Arbitrators conference.[6]

What is overlooked by the arguments on the grievant's work record is that his testimony has been consistent and reasonable. As to his past conduct, it is also an undeniable fact that we have here a man with 17 years of work for this company loyally and professionally performed.

Of especial note, of course, is the question of prior warning given the grievant as evidence of the company's legitimate exercise of discipline over its workers. What is the weight to be given this or any warning? It should be given weight commensurate to the infraction complained of. A warning coupled with a specific act of misconduct is most serious if the specific offense is repeated. We do not observe the pattern of the employee's conduct, of which the company here complains, to be

of such a nature as to compel a reasonable man to conclude that there is a direct linkage established so as to justify proper cause for the employee's discharge.

As was recently stated in a discharge case:

> Arbitrators are not required to apply constitutional law in dealing with employer-employee relations. Yet a discharge is often felt to be the industrial equivalent of a criminal penalty. Arbitrators therefore have thought it appropriate to discuss such questions as 'double jeopardy' and due process in considering the validity of a termination.[7]

Finally, in the balance here is the word of a hard-working bus operator over against the confused report of a young girl of no known occupation or address. Putting all of the factors together, it is impossible to say the employer has sustained to the degree required that amount of proof by proffered evidence against grievant to sustain just cause for a rightful discharge.

AWARD

1. The employer has not rightfully discharged grievant M——.

2. The grievance is upheld.

3. The employer is ordered to reinstate grievant to his former position, including back pay from the date of suspension to the present date with restoration of seniority rights.

---

[6] Feller, The Coming Trend of Arbitration's Golden Age, 1976 Conference Report, p. 97, at 110–112 especially.

[7] Filtrol Corp. and Oil, Chemical and Atomic Workers Local 1–128 (1975) AAA Arbitration Awards Summary, at p. 8.

ENTERPRISE WIRE CO.

Arbitrator: Carroll R. Daugherty*

46 LA 359   March 28, 1966

TESTS APPLICABLE FOR LEARNING
WHETHER EMPLOYER HAD JUST AND
PROPER CAUSE FOR DISCIPLINING AN
EMPLOYEE

Few if any union-management agreements
contain a definition of "just cause." Nevertheless, over the years the opinions of
arbitrators in innumerable discipline cases
have developed a sort of "common law"
definition thereof. This definition consists
of a set of guide lines or criteria that are
to be applied to the facts of any one case,
and said criteria are set forth below in the
form of questions.

A "no" answer to any one or more of
the following questions normally signifies
that just and proper cause did not exist.
In other words, such "no" means that the
employer's disciplinary decision contained
one or more elements of arbitrary, capricious, unreasonable, or discriminatory action to such an extent that said decision
constituted an abuse of managerial discretion warranting the arbitrator to substitute
his judgment for that of the employer.

The answers to the questions in any particular case are to be found in the evidence
presented to the arbitrator at the hearing
thereon. Frequently, of course, the facts
are such that the guide lines cannot be
applied with precision. Moreover, occasionally, in some particular case an arbitrator may find one or more "no" answers

* Reprinted from *Labor Arbitration Reports* by
permission of BNA, Inc.

so weak and the other, "yes" answers so
strong that he may properly, without any
"political" or spineless intent to "split the
difference" between the opposing positions of the parties, find that the correct
decision is to "chastize" both the company
and the disciplined employee by decreasing but not nullifying the degree of discipline imposed by the company—e.g., by
reinstating a discharged employee without
back pay.

It should be clearly understood also that
the criteria set forth below are to be applied
to the employer's conduct in making his
disciplinary decision *before* same has been
processed through the grievance procedure
to arbitration. Any question as to whether
the employer has properly fulfilled the
contractual requirements of said procedure
is entirely separate from the question of
whether he fulfilled the "common law"
requirements of just cause before the discipline was "grieved."

Sometimes, although very rarely, a
union-management agreement contains a
provision limiting the scope of the arbitrator's inquiry into the question of just
cause. For example, one such provision
seen by this arbitrator says that "the only
question the arbitrator is to determine
shall be whether the employee is, or is not,
guilty of the act or acts resulting in his
discharge." Under the latter contractual
statement an arbitrator might well have
to confine his attention to Question No.
5 below—or at most to Questions Nos. 3,
4, and 5. But absent any such restriction

in an agreement, a consideration of the evidence on all seven Questions (and their accompanying Notes) is not only proper but necessary.

THE QUESTIONS

1. Did the company give to the employee forewarning or foreknowledge of the possible or probable disciplinary consequences of the employee's conduct?

Note 1: Said forewarning or foreknowledge may properly have been given orally by management or in writing through the medium of typed or printed sheets or books of shop rules and of penalties for violation thereof.

Note 2: there must have been actual oral or written communication of the rules and penalties to the employee.

Note 3: A finding of lack of such communication does not in all cases require a "no" answer to Question No. 1. This is because certain offenses such as insubordination, coming to work intoxicated, drinking intoxicating beverages on the job, or theft of the property of the company or of fellow employees are so serious that any employee in the industrial society may properly be expected to know already that such conduct is offensive and heavily punishable.

Note 4: Absent any contractual prohibition or restriction, the company has the right unilaterally to promulgate reasonable rules and give reasonable orders; and same need not have been negotiated with the union.

2. Was the company's rule or managerial order reasonably related to (*a*) the orderly, efficient, and safe operation of the company's business and (*b*) the performance that the company might properly expect of the employee?

Note: If an employee believes that said rule or order is unreasonable, he must nevertheless obey same (in which case he may file a grievance thereover) unless he sincerely feels that to obey the rule or order would seriously and immediately jeopardize his personal safety and/or integrity. Given a firm finding to the latter effect, the employee may properly be said to have had justification for his disobedience.

3. Did the company, before administering discipline to an employee, make an effort to discover whether the employee did in fact violate or disobey a rule or order of management?

Note 1: This is the employee's "day in court" principle. An employee has the right to know with reasonable precision the offense with which he is being charged and to defend his behavior.

Note 2: The company's investigation must normally be made *before* its disciplinary decision is made. If the company fails to do so, its failure may not normally be excused on the ground that the employee will get his day in court through the grievance procedure after the exaction of discipline. By that time there has usually been too much hardening of positions. In a very real sense the company is obligated to conduct itself like a trial court.

Note 3: There may of course be circumstances under which management must react immediately to the employee's behavior. In such cases the normally proper action is to suspend the employee pending investigation, with the understanding that (*a*) the final disciplinary decision will be made after the investigation and (*b*) if the employee is found innocent after the investigation, he will be restored to his job with full pay for time lost.

Note 4: The company's investigation should include an inquiry into possible justification for the employee's alleged rule violation.

4. Was the company's investigation conducted fairly and objectively?

Note 1: At said investigation the management official may be both "prosecutor" and "judge," but he may not also be a witness against the employee.

Note 2: It is essential for some higher, detached management official to assume and conscientiously perform the judicial role, giving the commonly accepted meaning to that term in his attitude and conduct.

Note 3: In some disputes between an employee and a management person there are not witnesses to an incident other than the two immediate participants. In such cases it is particularly important that the management "judge" question the management participant rigorously and thoroughly, just as an actual third party would.

5. At the investigation did the "judge" obtain substantial evidence or proof that the employee was guilty as charged?

Note 1: It is not required that the evidence be conclusive or "beyond all reasonable doubt." But the evidence must be truly substantial and not flimsy.

Note 2: The management "judge" should actively search out witnesses and evidence, not just passively take what participants or "volunteer" witnesses tell him.

Note 3: When the testimony of opposing witnesses at the arbitration hearing is irreconcilably in conflict, an arbitrator seldom has any means for resolving the contradictions. His task is then to determine whether the management "judge" originally had reasonable grounds for believing the evidence presented to him by his own people.

6. Has the company applied its rules, orders, and penalties evenhandedly and without discrimination to all employees?

Note 1: A "no" answer to this question requires a finding of discrimination and warrants negation or modification of the discipline imposed.

Note 2: If the company has been lax in enforcing its rules and orders and decides henceforth to apply them rigorously, the company may avoid a finding of discrimination by telling all employees beforehand of its intent to enforce hereafter all rules as written.

7. Was the degree of discipline administered by the company in a particular case reasonably related to (*a*) the seriousness of the employee's proven offense and (*b*) the record of the employee in his service with the company?

Note 1: A trivial proven offense does not merit harsh discipline unless the employee has properly been found guilty of the same or other offenses a number of times in the past. (There is no rule as to what number of previous offenses constitutes a "good," a "fair," or a "bad" record. Reasonable judgment thereon must be used.)

Note 2: An employee's record of previous offenses may never be used to discover whether he was guilty of the immediate or latest one. The only proper use of his record is to help determine the severity of discipline once he has properly been found guilty of the immediate offense.

Note 3: Given the same proven offense for two or more employees, their respective records provide the only proper basis for "discriminating" among them in the administration of discipline for said offense. Thus, if employee A's record is significantly better than those of employees B, C, and D, the company may properly give A a lighter punishment than it gives the others for the same offense; and this does not constitute true discrimination.

Note 4: Suppose that the record of the arbitration hearing establishes firm "Yes" answers to all the first six questions. Suppose further that the proven offense of the accused employee was a serious one, such as drunkenness on the job; but the employee's record had been previously unblemished over a long, continuous period of employment with the company. Should the company be held arbitrary and unreasonable if it decided to discharge such an employee? The answer depends of course on all the circumstances. But, as one of the country's oldest arbitration agencies, the National Railroad Adjustment Board, has pointed out repeatedly in innumerable decisions on discharge cases, leniency is the prerogative of the employer rather than of the arbitrator; and the latter is not supposed to substitute his judgment in this area for that of the company unless there is compelling evidence that the company abused its discretion. This is the rule, even though an arbitrator, if he had been the original "trial judge," might have imposed a lesser penalty. Actually the arbitrator may be said in an important sense to act as an appellate tribunal whose function is to discover whether the decision of the trial tribunal (the employer) was within the bounds of reasonableness above set forth.—In general, the penalty of dismissal for a really serious first offense does not in itself warrant a finding of company unreasonableness.

ERIE MINING CO.

Arbitrator: Harry J. Dworkin*

49 LA 390   August 21, 1967

"RELATIVELY EQUAL" ABILITY

FACTUAL BACKGROUND

Dworkin, Arbitrator:—The instant arbitration appeal involves the rights and responsibilities of the parties in the selection of applicants for available jobs. The job vacancy arose in the Vehicle-Loader-Unloader job classification, Labor Grade 6. The company awarded the job to a junior applicant, thereby giving rise to a grievance on behalf of a senior applicant who, the union maintains, possessed the requisite qualifications for the job. The union urges that by virtue of his greater length of service, the grievant was contractually entitled to be awarded the available job. The company maintains that the grievant, the senior applicant, did not have the necessary qualifications; that the junior employee, who was the successful bidder, was significantly more qualified and that under such circumstances, the contract permitted the award of the job to a junior and relatively better qualified employee.

The job of Vehicle-Loader-Unloader, Labor Grade 6, is in the Agglomerating Department. The primary function of the job is to unload and load materials, equipment, and supplies from the trucks of independent carriers, and from company-owned vehicles and various other types of equipment. In the unloading operation, the employee utilizes a pendant-controlled crane within an enclosed area of the shop. The crane is 10 tons in capacity and has existed in the Agglomerating Department since 1957. The job of Vehicle-Loader-Unloader was established as a full time job

---

* Reprinted from *Labor Arbitration Reports* by permission of BNA, Inc.

in 1963 and has continued as an established job during the intervening four years. It is estimated that the job occupant spends approximately two hours per shift in the operation of the PCC; the balance of his shift is spent on other related duties.

The job description for VLU, dated April 7, 1961, includes the following:

TOOLS AND EQUIPMENT: Two and four-wheeled hand trucks, pendant controlled O.E.T. cranes, slings, chains, pinch bar, hook scissor tongs, spreader bar, fork lift attachment, etc.

* * * * *

WORKING PROCEDURES: Receives order from supervisor. Operates pendant-controlled crane with hook and auxiliary lifting fixtures while transferring equipment and supplies on and off of vehicles and railroad cars. Rigs loads using slings, chains and rope. Changes hooks, jigs and supplies from floor to floor using portable carts and elevator. Inspects tools and equipment and reports obvious defects to supervision. Makes required reports. Keeps working area in clean and orderly condition.

The grievant, the senior employee, has had 9½ years of continuous service with the company. He is presently classified as a Laborer, Job Class 2. During his several years with the company, he has held a variety of jobs, both on a permanent and temporary assignment basis. The grievant held the Pumpman Bay Job, Job Class 8, for a period of two years until the job was eliminated. He had a good record of service while on this job. The grievant held the job of Sample Grinder on a temporary basis, for two weeks, Job Class 5. He also served as Tripper Car Operator, Job Class 5, for three years with a good record of service. This assignment was discontinued when the job was eliminated. He also worked on temporary assignments on the jobs of Ball Mill Reject Attendant, Pipe Changer Job, and Ball Maker. The grievant states that he used a pendant controlled

crane for one month while assigned to Ball Maker. The grievant also held the job of Equipment Cleaner, Class 5, for a period of two years. While assigned to this job, he operated a steamer which included a boiler gauged at 80# pressure. The grievant also held the job of Filler Bag Washer, Class 4, for a period of four months. He voluntarily elected to leave this job and join the Labor Classification.

The company denied the grievance claiming that the junior applicant was properly awarded the job in accordance with the provisions of the Basic Labor Agreement and the Seniority and Post Agreement. The union maintained that the selection of job applicants should have been made on the basis of seniority "without regard to the ability factor," (Second Step Hearing). In the foreman's answer to the grievance, he stated that, "The successful applicant on the Posting was selected on the basis of ability, in accordance with (the) contract language."

POSITION OF UNION

The union maintains that the grievant acquired experience while temporarily assigned to the job of Vehicle-Loader-Unloader. In addition he had ample opportunity to observe the operator while the grievant was assigned to various jobs in the Agglomerating Department. The union represents that the grievant, the senior employee, has acquired experience on the job of Vehicle-Loader-Unloader, through assignment on various jobs in the department. In the course of these assignments he was able to observe the duties of the operator and the manner he performed his duties. The grievant has had occasion to use a pendant-controlled crane for the purpose of removing material and supplies from trucks in the course of loading operations while assigned to various jobs and tasks in the Agglomerating Department. The grievant has never previously held this job, however he has helped out on the job on a temporary basis. The grievant states that he is confident that he could handle the duties of the job in question in a satisfactory and safe manner.

By way of summary, the union urges that the nature of the job, its duties, responsibilities, and functions, are not of a highly technical character, and do not involve any significant skills or specialized duties. The job incumbent performs his duties without any close relationship with other groups. The job is referred to as being "relatively simple." The union feels that the job is such that it could be satisfactorily performed by the grievant in light of his past record, experience, and demonstrated ability on various other job assignments. The union reasons that the job of VLU should be filled on the basis of "straight seniority" from among those applying for the job through the bidding procedure. The grievant is deemed to be qualified under the contract. He possesses the ability to perform the work and physical fitness as specified in the contract; his skills and qualifications are deemed by the union to be at least "relatively equal" to those possessed by the successful applicant, a junior employee.

The union maintains that the grievant has demonstrated his ability to handle the Vehicle-Loader-Unloader job through his record of satisfactory performance on a variety of other jobs during his 9½ years of employment with the company. He is regarded as thoroughly familiar with the job, its functions, requirements, and responsibilities. In view of the foregoing, the union maintains under the language of Article X of the Basic Labor Agreement, seniority must be accorded "full consideration" and that the grievant's "length of continuous service" entitles him to the job.

POSITION OF COMPANY

The company has at the outset acknowledged that the grievant is regarded as a satisfactory employee, that he has performed his various job assignments during his 9½ years employment with the company in an acceptable manner; he has not been the subject of any disciplinary action or charges of unsafe practices; by reason of all of the foregoing he is rated by management as a "good employee."

Notwithstanding the foregoing appraisal of the grievant's general qualifications, and his background and experience, the company maintains that his seniority does not under the contract require that he be assigned to the job vacancy of Vehicle-Loader-Unloader. The company maintains that the grievant is not qualified by experience and ability to perform the duties of the job in question; further, a fair and objective evaluation of the abilities of the two employees in question, as regard the duties of the job, conclusively establishes that the junior employee's qualifications and ability are significantly greater than those possessed by the grievant, the senior applicant. Under these circumstances, the company maintains that it is contractually authorized to award the job to the junior applicant.

The company points out that the grievant has not had any sustained experience on the VLU job other than his observations of the performance of the job by others. In all probability, were he to be awarded the job, he would require training and instruction. The company urges that under the contract and the Seniority and Posting Agreement, the employee with relative greater ability is entitled to the job. In the instant case, the grievant lacked the basic qualifications for the job and was not considered to be qualified by management. The company points out that a major part of the work and duties of VLU involves the use of a pendant-control crane in moving parts, equipment, and material under varying conditions. The grievant has had but limited experience in the use of a pendant-controlled crane, and in the related duties and functions, other than the experience he acquired while serving as an Equipment Cleaner, Class 5 job, in the General Shop.

On the other hand, the junior employee is relatively and substantially better qualified to fill this job. The job is one which is not subject to being filled on the basis of straight seniority.

The company adduced testimony as regards the issue before the arbitrator, including the testimony of Mr. John Holst, superintendent of maintenance. He testified that the grievant, while assigned to other jobs, had experienced various problems and difficulties greater than normal. However, his general job performance was regarded as satisfactory and his deficiencies did not require or warrant disciplinary action. In the judgment of supervision, the grievant's performance while assigned to other jobs suggested that he lacked the ability to function without close supervision; at times he encountered difficulty in learning and performing various duties of his jobs. On some occasions he used poor judgment in positioning equipment; at times he did not exercise proper care in transporting equipment and material using a crane which was incidental to his job. Members of supervision testified that the grievant experienced some difficulty in adapting himself to the movement and positioning of material and supplies of varying shapes, weights, and textures. He frequently required instruction as to the proper method and procedure; he is said to have received "more than normal supervision and instruction."

The company maintains that a fair and objective evaluation of the backgrounds, abilities and qualifications of the junior and senior job applicants warrants the conclusion that the junior employee's "ability to perform the work" is substantially above that of the senior applicant; that their qualifications as prescribed by the contract cannot fairly be regarded as "relatively equal." Under these circumstances, the company maintains that it acted in ac-

cordance with its contractual right in awarding the VLU job to the junior employee, and that no contract violation resulted in the selection of the junior employee.

PERTINENT PROVISIONS OF CONTRACT

The September 10, 1965 Basic Labor Agreement provides as follows governing the selection of applicants for promotion to higher rated jobs:

ARTICLE X. SENIORITY

SECTION 1. FACTORS AND WHEN APPLICABLE

The parties recognize that promotional opportunity and job security in event of promotions, decrease of forces, and recalls after layoffs should increase in proportion to length of continuous service, and that in the administration of this Section the intent will be that wherever practicable full consideration shall be given continuous service in such cases. In recognition, however, of the responsibility of Management for the efficient operation of the mine, it is understood and agreed that in all cases of promotions, except promotions to positions excluded under the definition of "employee" in the agreement adopting this basic labor agreement and for the purpose of layoffs in connection with the decreasing of the working force and the recalling to work of men so laid off, the following factors shall be considered, and if factors *a* and *b* are relatively equal, the length of continuous service shall govern:

   a. Ability to perform the work;
   b. Physical fitness; ***

In addition to the Basic Labor Agreement, there is in effect a Seniority and Posting Agreement which substantially embodies the principles set forth in Article X, Seniority:

   C. In filling permanent vacancies, if ability to perform the work of the job to which the promotion is to be made and physical fitness are relatively equal, the following procedures shall apply: ***

OPINION OF ARBITRATOR

The instant dispute concerns the factors entering into the award of available jobs which have been posted for bid. The two applicants who are the real parties in interest, are the junior and senior employee respectively, who duly bid for the job vacancy of Vehicle-Loader-Unloader. The job was awarded to the junior employee, thereby giving rise to a grievance on the part of the senior employee that the company failed to accord proper consideration to his greater length of service. The company maintains that the junior employee's ability to perform the work was significantly and measurably greater, and that therefore the junior applicant was entitled to prevail in the award of the job over the grievant who had greater length of service.

The dispute is the traditional one of the relative value which should be accorded to seniority and ability in the award of available jobs to employees who have indicated their desire to be considered for a job vacancy through the bidding procedure. As is frequently the case, the union places greater emphasis upon seniority, or length of service, whereas the company stresses relative ability and maintains that the junior employee is entitled to be accorded the job under the contract where his demonstrated ability is appreciably greater. The company has urged that in the instant case, the facts support the conclusion that the junior applicant had relatively greater ability to perform the work involved, particularly as to an essential function of the job, the operation of the pendant controlled crane.

As a threshold matter, the arbitrator is duty-bound in a dispute of this type to look to the negotiated terms and conditions of employment as incorporated in the collective bargaining agreement, designed to govern the selection of employees who bid for available jobs. Where such provisions are clear and unambiguous, and the

meaning and intent of the parties are manifest, the arbitrator is required to accord such language contractual effect. Article X of the Basic Labor Agreement sets forth the fundamental principles which the parties regard as relevant in the selection of employees to fill available vacancies. The parties have stated in their labor agreement that promotional opportunity "should increase in proportion to length of continuous service" and that "wherever practicable full consideration shall be given continuous service in such cases." The contract states that in addition to giving practical consideration to seniority, the company is required and empowered to give consideration to qualifying factors, to wit, "ability to perform the work" and "physical fitness." Seniority or length of service is the controlling and determining factor in awarding an available job if ability to perform the work and physical fitness are "relatively equal."

In the instant case there is no dispute as to "physical fitness"; it must therefore be considered that both employees qualify as regards this factor. The remaining factor, ability to perform the work, is to be evaluated and assessed on the basis of the evidence submitted to the arbitrator bearing upon this issue. The language of the contract requires that where ability to perform the work is "relatively equal," that length of service shall govern; in such case seniority is the determining factor in the award of the job. Conversely, where it is demonstrated that ability as between one or more employees is not a relatively equal quality, in such case length of continuous service is not the governing factor. By way of construction of the contract language, it would be reasonable to conclude that where the demonstrated abilities as between two employees are not comparable, corresponding to or proportionate to, under such circumstances the ability to perform the work would *not* be regarded as relatively equal, and seniority would not then be the determining factor in the award of the job. While the phrase "relatively equal" does not connote an absolute equality, nevertheless, it does suggest a substantial, pertinent and comparable quality or degree; the language must be construed as indicating a meaningful relationship as disclosed by the assessment of ability with reference to the duties and functions involved, and as related to the job and the ability of other employees.

The evidence adduced in this case, relating to the relative abilities of the two employees to perform the work in question, indicates that the senior employee, the grievant, during his 9½ years of employment with the company has held a variety of jobs involving various classifications, labor grades, skills and responsibilities. An examination of the testimony and records reveals that the senior employee has held ten such jobs, however, he has not previously held the job of Vehicle-Loader-Unloader, other than on a brief, temporary assignment. The grievant's testimony was to the effect that he believed that he could handle the duties and functions of the job in a safe and satisfactory manner; that his ability was acquired through his observation of the performance of the job during periods of assignment to other jobs in the Agglomerating Department. The grievant has had no sustained experience as related to the duties and functions of this job, other than his observations of the manner in which the job was performed by other job incumbents.

The job of VLU is in Job Class 6. Included in the working procedure is the operation by the employee of a pendant-controlled crane with hook and auxiliary lifting fixtures for use in transferring equipment and supplies from vehicles and railroad cars, (Job Description, Vehicle-Loader-Unloader). These functions involve an estimated 25 percent of the employee's working time. The grievant's deficiencies as regard the skills required by the job in question are mainly concerned with the operation of the pendant-controlled crane, and certain incidental duties including adjustments which the operator is required to perform. The pendant-controlled crane is a 10-ton crane which has existed in the plant since 1957. A wide variety of material and equipment is normally loaded and unloaded with the use of the pendant-controlled crane. The evidence establishes that the junior employee had acquired experience on this job, including the operation of the pendant-controlled crane, by reason of having been assigned to this job on a temporary basis for a period of some seven weeks. During this assignment, he performed the duties in a highly satisfactory manner; his work was so regarded by members of supervision who observed his performance and who had the responsibility of evaluating his services.

The Basic Labor Agreement prescribes in clear and unambiguous language the requirement that jobs be awarded on the basis of specific criteria and qualifications. There is no warrant for suspending the application of the contract language in the instant case, and as regard such jobs which the union characterizes as "simple," requiring a minimum of skill and responsibility. The contract makes no distinction in awarding vacancies in classified jobs on the basis of the job requirements; it is sufficient that the job be one classified in a specific labor grade, in which case the contract regulates the promotion of job applicants to fill the vacancies. Relative ability remains a contractual requirement in filling such vacancies arising in classified jobs; the job in question, Vehicle-Loader-Unloader, is such a classified job.

The contract does *not* establish length of continuous service as the sole and determining qualification in filling classified jobs. In the instant case, the junior applicant had had some seven weeks of actual experience on the job and was deemed by management to be a relatively better qualified employee. There is no suggestion in the evidence before the arbitrator that the company acted arbitrarily, capriciously, or in a discriminatory manner in selecting the junior employee.

The evidence establishes that the grievant has generally been regarded as a satisfactory employee and has performed the duties of his job in a reasonably safe manner; he is not accident prone and there is no evidence of his having been involved in any disciplinary incidents. The evidence would reasonably support the finding that the grievant possessed the minimum qualifications for the job of Vehicle-Loader-Unloader, however, this would not ipso facto require that seniority be the determining factor in the award of the job. Under the contract, the company is accorded the right to evaluate the relative qualifications of job applicants as they related to their "ability to perform the work," and physical fitness, the latter factor not being of any moment in the present dispute. The foregoing contract requirement necessarily involves a comparison of qualifications. In the judgment of the arbitrator, so long as the company appraises the qualification in an objective manner, and its judgment is supported by the evidence, is fair and reasonable and free from bias or discrimination, its judgment may not be disturbed.

Under the contract, the company is authorized to compare the ability and physical fitness, with seniority prescribed as the controlling factor where the other factors are relatively equal. Where the evidence warrants the conclusion that a fair comparison of relative ability as related to the job reveals that the junior employee's ability to perform the work is significantly, measurably, and demonstrably greater, or "relatively" greater, the company is justified under the contract in awarding the job to such junior employee.

AWARD

The arbitrator finds from the evidence that the job vacancy existing in Vehicle-Loader-Unloader, Job Class 6, was properly awarded to the junior employee, for the reason that the evidence establishes that the ability of the junior employee to perform the duties and functions of the job in question, and relating particularly to the duties and responsibilities of operating a 10-ton pendant-controlled crane, was relatively greater than the ability demonstrated by the senior job applicant;

Under the circumstances, the company acted consistent with the language of the basic agreement, Article X (Seniority) and the Seniority and Posting Agreement, Article IV, Section C, in awarding the job to the junior employee.

HUBINGER CO.

Arbitrator: Anthony V. Sinicropi*

75 LA 742   September 12, 1980

TEMPORARY INTAKE LINE

I. BACKGROUND AND FACTS

Sinicropi, Arbitrator:—The facts of this case are not in dispute. On Saturday, January 28, 1978, the company experienced a stoppage of water flowing into the plant. As a result of this stoppage it was necessary to conduct an investigation as to the cause of the malfunction. After finding that some concrete blocks had clogged a water pumping system, and that removal of the concrete did not solve the pumping difficulties, a diver was hired to inspect the water intake line. In addition, the company hired Seither and Cherry (S.&C.) Contractors, a local construction company, to fabricate and install a new temporary river intake line and pump system to by-pass the broken system. The record further indicates that four S.&C. pipefitters and one S.&C. crane operator completed the task in approximately one and one-half days. After the temporary water intake line was installed, the S.&C. employees departed and the company assigned its own unit employees, including pipefitters, to repair the "old" broken river line.

As a result of the subcontracting the work in question to S.&C., a grievance was filed on February 3, 1978 by two of the company's pipefitters. Unable to resolve the matter at the lower steps of the grievance procedure, the matter was submitted for final and binding arbitration under the Collective Bargaining Agreement.

II. THE ISSUE

The issue in this case may be stated as follows:

> Did the Company violate the Agreement when it subcontracted the fabrication and installation of a new temporary river water intake line and pump system to Seither and Cherry Contractors on January 28 and 29, 1978? If so, what shall the remedy be?

III. RELEVANT CONTRACT PROVISIONS AND EXHIBITS[1]

(A) Contract Provisions

ARTICLE I

* * * * *

SECTION 3.   MANAGEMENT FUNCTIONS

1. The Management of the Plant and all Company operations shall be vested exclusively in the Company, including the direction of the work forces; the right to modernize and install new equipment and to rearrange production schedules; the right to hire; the right to suspend or discharge employees for just cause; the right to relieve employees from duty because of lack of work or for other reasonable cause; subject to the provisions of this Agreement.

---

* Reprinted from *Labor Arbitration Reports* by permission of BNA, Inc.

1 Editor's note: Exhibits are omitted.

2. The Company's "General Qualifications" for all employees are a part of the "Job Evaluation" agreement.

ARTICLE VIII

SECTION 1. MAINTENANCE
DEPARTMENTS WORK WEEK

*   *   *   *   *

4. When overtime work is required, a sufficient number of workers may be required to stay and complete the work. Refusal may result in disciplinary action.

ARTICLE XI

SECTION 1. JOB EVALUATION—JOB
DESCRIPTION—STEP-UP SCHEDULE

1. All jobs in the Plant with the exception of Limited Service jobs and those considered to be Extra Work, shall have job descriptions. These job descriptions shall be strictly followed and shall be so written that they will not conflict with other job descriptions.

*   *   *   *   *

ARTICLE XIII

SECTION 1. SUBCONTRACTING

1. On projects requiring the services of outside contractors, the Company will, except in emergencies, give the Union seven (7) days prior written notice, giving the scope of work, etc.

2. Assignments of work in the Maintenance Crafts will be on the basis of past practices, job descriptions, training, and classification and work regularly and customarily performed by such crafts. The Hubinger Company pipefitters will make provisions for tie-ins, and all tie-ins to pipe lines that have been in regular operation. In assignment of work where outside contractors are involved, jurisdictional awards or area practices between unions will be considered in assignment of such work. Nothing, in the above, shall prevent the Company from modernizing, using new equipment or directing the work force.

3. Hubinger Craft jobs will not be permanently discontinued during the life of this contract while subcontracting is being done in their craft.

SUMMARY
OF JOB CLASSIFICATION
—and—
JOB EVALUATION PLAN
THE HUBINGER COMPANY
—for all—
PRODUCTION AND MAINTENANCE
JOBS
—Coming Under—

The Jurisdiction of the Bargaining Unit

Preface

The Management of The Hubinger Company in collaboration with American Federation of Grain Millers, No. 48, AFL–CIO, Iowa State Federation of Labor, and The Keokuk Trades and Labor Assembly, Keokuk, Iowa, have agreed to establish job classifications and rates covering the jobs as they exist in the Plant.

Jointly the Company and Union feel evaluation is desirable for good labor relations and from an operating standpoint for the following reasons:

1. To provide the basis for a systematic Management and Union review of the duties and classifications of jobs.

2. To provide the basis for an effective, equitable and systematic measurement or evaluation of each job in terms of its relative contribution to the total production results of the Company's operation. The Management and the Union propose to make this material of value for wage adjustments, promotions, negotiations and other similar matters. A plan of wage rates is submitted in the form of a wage-rate evaluation chart and table.

3. To provide a useful guide in rating of the employees' performance and means of familiarizing supervision with the work expected of subordinates so as to establish a proper division of responsibility and authority.

IV. POSITION OF THE UNION

The union asserts that while the river-line failure partially disrupted plant operations, parts of the plant remained in operation. Moreover, in its judgment, there was sufficient starch slurry to run the starch and drum drier departments and also the high fructose end of the plant. Accordingly, the union argues that the situation created by the failure of the line is one that is no different than any other maintenance problem and thus no emergency existed.

In further support of its position, the union contends that the job descriptions contained in the collective bargaining agreement effectively guarantee that the company will not contract out maintenance work that would ordinarily be performed by unit employees. In this respect the union offers the award of Arbitrator J. V. McKenna, dated June 24, 1968 as support for this position.

The union also argues that the overtime section of the contract, Article VIII, §1, par. 4, requires the company to assign the work at issue to the Pipefitters. The union notes that Arbitrator John Gradwhol, in FMCS No. 77K/01773, found that the company is under an obligation to make an effort to determine whether the employees would be willing to work overtime in order to perform required tasks. In the present case the union contends that the company made no attempt to ascertain whether the unit employees involved (the pipefitters) would be willing to work the additional time to make the needed repairs. This failure, argues the union, was a violation of the Agreement.

The union has also argued that the company has violated Article XII, §1, par. 1 and 2 (subcontracting provision.). The union contends that work assignments, pursuant to this provision, should be made on the basis of past practice, job descrip-

tions, training and classification, and work customarily performed by such crafts. All the work performed on the day in question, argues the union, was "protected" by Article XII. This conclusion, the union points out, was also reached by Arbitrator Traynor in FMCS Case No. 79K/26526.

Finally the union notes that over the past five years the company has expanded its operations by 60 percent, yet the maintenance journeyman classification has not expanded by one person since 1964. The union contends that this factor alone raises questions concerning the "anti-union" bias of the company. The company's subcontracting decision, argues the union, has an adverse effect upon the bargaining unit and for this reason, and the reasons cited above, the present grievance should be resolved in favor of the union. As a remedy the union asks that the affected employees be paid for the hours improperly worked by the subcontractor's employees.

V. POSITION OF THE COMPANY

The company initially argues that it has the inherent and contractual right to subcontract unless it is established that such right is expressly limited by the Agreement. The company points out that it retains the inherent right to operate and manage its business except to the extent that this right is expressly limited by the terms of the Agreement. Moreover, the company notes that the parties had expressly incorporated this management right provision (scheduling of work) into their contract.

The company also asserts that the union failed to prove that the Agreement contains restrictions on the company's right to subcontract. The union, contends the company, bears the burden of establishing its claims and, with respect to the present case, it must show that the company has expressly surrendered its right to contract out. In this regard, the company notes that the job description of the Pipefitters (Article XI, Section 1) does not require the company to give work covered by this description exclusively to bargaining unit employees. Indeed, the company offers a recent decision by Arbitrator Lewis—. Solomon expressly holding that the job description provisions of the Agreement do not place any restrictions on subcontracting (FMCS Case No. 79K/26528 (1980)).

With respect to the overtime provisions, the company argues that merely because Article VIII, §1, par. 4 allows the company to require maintenance employees to stay and complete overtime work, it does not follow that the company must require maintenance employees to work where there is arguably overtime work. The company further asserts that a study of arbitral authority in this area demonstrates why this provision was inserted into the parties' agreement. Specifically, arbitrators generally hold that an employer may require a reasonable amount of overtime, however some restrictions may be imposed. Thus, Article VIII, §1, par. 4 was added to allow the company to require overtime without restriction.

Recent decisions, notes the company, have also upheld the company's decision to subcontract. Moreover, the company points out that this particular decision was prompted by an emergency—the malfunction of the water pumping operation. The company contends it did not know how long the repair operation would take. At any rate, the company points out that no maintenance employees were laid off, nor did any employee lose any work opportunity.

Finally, the company argues that the subcontracting of the disputed work was done in good faith, was not arbitrary, capricious, or unreasonable, and did not adversely affect the union or any bargaining unit employees. In this regard the company recognizes that its right to subcon-

tract must be balanced against the concerns of the union. Applying the criteria outlined by this Arbitrator at the 32d Annual Meeting of the National Academy of Arbitrators, the company urges that when the facts of this case are examined in view of these considerations, the arbitrator must conclude that the subcontracting was indeed proper.

VI. DISCUSSION

While this arbitrator accepts the proposition that an employer retains the inherent right to operate and manage its business except to the extent that this right is expressly limited by the terms of a collective bargaining agreement, it does not necessarily follow that an employer has the inherent right to subcontract under any and all conditions in absence of a specific contractual limitation. Arbitrators have generally held that where the agreement is silent on the subject of contracting out, management has an implied obligation to act reasonably when subcontracting [See, e.g., Wallen, "How Issues of Subcontracting and Plant Removal are Handled by Arbitrators," 19 Ind. & Lab. Rel. Rev. 265 (1966)].

In the present case, however, the Agreement is not silent. Article XII, §1, par. 1 provides that:

> On projects requiring the services of outside contractors, the Company will, except in emergencies, give the Union seven (7) days prior written notice, giving the scope of work, etc.

Par. 2 of that same Article provides in relevant part:

> Assignments of work in the Maintenance Crafts will be on the basis of past practice, job descriptions, training, and classification and work regularly and customarily performed by such crafts. The Hubinger Company pipefitters will make provisions for tie-ins, and all tie-ins to pipe lines that have

been in regular operation. In assignment of work where outside contractors are involved, jurisdictional awards or area practices between unions will be considered in assignment of such work . . .

It is clear that the company did not provide seven days notice when the particular subcontract was effectuated. There is, however, no serious contention that the work contracted was not of an emergency nature. An unexplained stoppage of water flowing into a corn processing plant is a serious condition calling for prompt measures. The record in this case indicates that evaporators in the refineries and steep water areas were shut down. Moreover, the entire corn grinding operations were inoperative. Nearly all jobs in the Refinery and the Mill and By-Products Departments were shut down for the 4:00 to 12:00 and the 12:00 to 8:00 shifts on January 28 and for the 8:00 to 4:00 shift on January 29. Indeed, even the Union, in its *Brief*, concedes that "it represents a crises and action must be taken. . . ." Under these conditions, this arbitrator cannot conclude that the notice provision of Article XII, §1, par. 1 was violated.

In this same regard, the arbitrator cannot accept the contention that par. 2 of Article XII was violated. There is no evidence of any past practice of the pipefitters performing work of this nature since such a situation like the present emergency never arose before. In addition, the arbitrator takes note that neither the company nor the union could anticipate how long the repair task would take at the time the emergency was discovered.

It must also be stated that the company, in making this specific contract, did not violate Article XI, Section 1, the Job Description provision. This arbitrator, similar to numerous others, is of the view that job descriptions do not limit the employer's right to enter into a subcontract. This same proposition has been noted by this arbitrator in a recent address before the

National Academy of Arbitrators. See, Sinicropi, "Revisiting an Old Battle Ground: The Subcontracting Dispute" in *Arbitration of Subcontracting and Wage Incentive Disputes*, Proceedings of the Thirty-Second Meeting, National Academy of Arbitrators (Washington, D.C.: BNA Books, 1980) (Stern & Dennis, eds.) at 147–48.

Similarly, this arbitrator cannot conclude that the overtime provisions of the Collective Bargaining Agreement, Article VIII, §1, par. 4, has been violated in the present case. An examination of that provision only mandates that "when overtime work is required, a sufficient number of workers may be required to stay and complete the work." The union is effectively asserting that because the contract provides that employees *may* be required to work overtime it is therefore mandated that employees *must*, if the circumstances warrant, be given overtime. While in certain circumstances the company may be required to offer employees an opportunity to work overtime before subcontracting, it is not because of anything in Article VIII, §1, par. 4. In this regard the arbitrator finds the citation of Arbitrator Gradwall's award misplaced. In that case it is clear that there was no emergency situation similar to the one at issue in the present case, and this arbitrator cannot equate the replacement with a burned-out motor (the factual situation in Arbitrator Gradwall's case) with the stoppage of water flow. Moreover, one could reasonably estimate the time required to replace a motor, whereas it was virtually impossible to estimate the time required to repair the water pumping system. Under these facts, it cannot be concluded that the company was obligated to offer pipefitters overtime.

It must also be stressed that there is no evidence, at the time the contract was made, that the pipefitters could perform all the functions required to make the necessary repairs. Even though the employees may have been able to perform *some* of the tasks, the employer, under this agreement, was not compelled or mandated to offer the employees the work. This conclusion is supported by examining a decision by Arbitrator Clair Duff in Joseph S. Finch, 29 LA 609 (1957), a decision cited by the company in its *Brief*. In that case the arbitrator held that the company's use of outside bricklayers was proper when its purpose was to fix a collapsed wall within a two-day period, even though the company had bricklayers who could have performed the task with the help of others. Noteworthy in that decision is the arbitrator's comments that the emergency nature of the particular job justified the unusual decision of the contracting out. Again, in the present case, there is no question that the situation presented an emergency which had to be remedied immediately.

Finally, and as noted by the company in its Brief at 27–33, this arbitrator, in a recent paper presented to the National Academy of Arbitrators, has enumerated the factors most frequently considered by arbitrators in reviewing the merits of a subcontracting decision where the collective bargaining agreement does not contain an express prohibition on subcontracting. Applying the cited factors to the facts of the present case, the arbitrator cannot conclude that the subcontracting in this case was prohibited by the agreement. Nothing concerning prior contract negotiations would lead one to conclude that this type of work could not be the subject of a contract with another firm. This is especially supported when it is realized that the work was of an emergency nature and not normally performed by the unit employees. Moreover, the work was of a temporary, one-shot nature where specialized equipment and material was necessary. Neither during the hearing nor at any time throughout the grievance procedure did the union allege that the company's sub-

contracting of the work was motivated by anti-union hostility or an effort to dismantle the bargaining unit. Indeed, the record indicates that the affected employees all worked between 48 and 59 hours during the week in question. In addition, the work contracted was sufficiently specialized so that the unit employees, while apparently capable of performing *some* tasks, could not complete the entire job, especially when it is realized that the S. & C. employees did possess the necessary skills. Furthermore, as evidence of the company's good faith, those portions of the tasks that could be performed by available employees with little trouble were, in fact, assigned such tasks (e.g., craft employees in the unit were assigned fabrication of repair boxes after the S. & C. employees completed the difficult work).

Both parties have introduced decisions by other arbitrators in support of their respective positions. While each arbitration case must stand on its own particular facts and circumstances, it is of note that Arbitrator Stephen Goldberg, in a decision involving this same Company under the *current* agreement (FMCS Case File No. 78K/23494, dated July 13, 1979), found that Article XII does not prohibit the company from contracting out, at least under the facts where notice was given to the union as required in the agreement. As indicated above, since the work was of an emergency nature, no advance notice of seven days could reasonably be given. Moreover, and as noted by Arbitrator Traynor in another subcontracting case at Hubinger, "subcontracting has been a way of life at this plant for over 30 years." In that decision, the arbitrator found that Article XII was not violated merely because the unit employees could perform "bits and pieces" of the contested work. Finally, in yet another decision (FMCS File No. 79K/26528), Arbitrator L. Solomon ruled that the job descriptions which may encompass the work at issue could not be used as a limitation on the company's right to subcontract.

The present case is not dissimilar to many of the issues presented in the above cited cases. On the basis of the facts developed at the hearing, the particular contractual provisions, and the emergency nature of the work at issue, this arbitrator can only deny the grievance of the union.

VII. AWARD

For the reasons set forth above the grievance is denied.

METAL SPECIALTY CO.

Arbitrator: Marlin M. Volz*

39 LA 1265   December 14, 1962

USE OF VENDING MACHINES

ISSUE

Volz, Arbitrator:—Was the disciplinary action taken against the grievants on September 4 and 5, 1962, for alleged violation of the coffee-break rule for just cause? If not, to what remedy are they entitled?

CONTRACT PROVISION

Section 1 of Article II of the Agreement states in part:

> Nothing in this Agreement shall limit the Company in the exercise of its functions of Management, among which are the right to hire new employees and to direct the working force, to transfer, discipline, suspend, discharge for cause, lay off employees be-

cause of lack of work, require employees to observe Company rules and regulations not inconsistent with the provisions of this agreement.

COMPANY RULES AND REGULATIONS

The addition made by the Company on August 14, 1962, to its Rule 9 is crucial to the decision of this grievance. It provides in part:

> We have been studying the problems created by the absence of a formal rule covering work breaks, and have decided to add the following provision to Rule 9:
> Effective September 4, and until further notice, hours of work will be as follows:

1st Shift
Start 7:00 a.m.
Break 9:00 to 9:10
Lunch 11:00 to 11:30
Break 1:30 to 1:40
Quit 3:30 p.m.
2d Shift

* Arbitrator selected in accordance with procedures of Federal Mediation & Conciliation Service. Reprinted from *Labor Arbitration Reports* by permission of BNA, Inc.

Start 3:30 p.m.
Break 5:30 to 5:40
Supper 7:30 to 8:00
Break 10:00 to 10:10
Quit 12:00 p.m.

We do not expect anyone to stay at his bench or machine constantly. He may leave whenever necessary to get a drink or take care of personal needs. We do expect him, however, after going for a drink or to the rest room, to promptly return to his job. He is not to visit, go to soft drink machines, eat sandwiches, etc. These activities will be confined to the break periods and lunch periods, and vending machines are not to be patronized except during breaks or lunch periods. . . .

This addition to Rule 9 will assure regular and equitable work breaks for all employees, as well as assist your Company in maintaining uniform production. We request your full cooperation.

Because of the importance of this change, we felt it desirable to send a copy of this notice to each employee at his home.

The union referred to Rule 3 on page 10 stating:

Empty bottles or containers must not be left at machines, on benches or in yard, but must be returned to the place provided for them.

It also mentioned Rule 20 on page 17 prohibiting gambling in any form on company property.

The company mentioned Rule 22 on page 17, which states:

Killing time during working hours in toilets or on any Company property is not permissable.

STATEMENT OF FACTS

On September 4 and 5, 1962, the grievants were given written warnings and suspensions for violating the formal coffee-break rule which the company adopted and posted on August 14, 1962, after a meeting of the shop committee, and which became effective September 4. Prior to the adoption of the rule, most of the men were in the habit of breaking every hour and, where desired, of going to the vending machines for coffee, coke, sandwiches, etc. The vending machines were first installed during World War II and were gradually added to until a complete assortment was provided. Much of the work is heavy, and the company has condoned the practice of breaking at the end of every hour, although it placed the formal rule into effect because it thought the men were abusing the privilege and loafing and idling around the vending machines.

The men work on incentive with a base rate. On November 13, 14, and 15, 1961, daily production averaged 112 percent of standard. It dropped steadily until it fell below 100 percent in February 1962 and has fallen gradually since until for the past few months it has averaged rather constantly between 96 and 97 percent. Before November of last year, production for several years averaged between 106 and 107 percent.

In meetings of supervision held last February, it was thought that the fall in production was caused by more and more men taking longer and longer breaks, particularly at the vending machines. Between Feb. 19 and March 2, 1962, a spot check was made, and it was found that the break taken by the men each hour averaged 13.42 minutes per man. Some were taking as long as 20 to 25 minutes. After several meetings of top management and at least one with union representatives, it was decided to post a notice on each vending machine stating that the area of the vending machines would have to be closed off and opened only at stated periods "if the present practices of many employees is not stopped and confined to reasonable visits to the machines." The situation improved temporarily, but another spot check taken for the period April 3 to April 20 showed that it had worsened and that the men were now averaging 14.8 minutes each hour on breaks. On April 23, 1962, another notice was posted calling attention to the need of complying with the company rules and that "Continued abuse of the company rules may be cause for disciplinary action."

Top management continued to hold discussions as the situation did not improve. Among the solutions proposed was to take out the vending machines or to close off the area and open it only at stated times, but these were rejected in favor of a formal coffee-break rule which was to be issued after the vacation season.

The matter came to a head somewhat earlier when the union filed two grievances in July questioning the method and the ordering by the plant superintendent of some of the employees off the bench at the vending machines and back to work. The plant superintendent apologized for the language used, but the company insisted upon its authority to order the men to work and denied the grievances.

On or about August 14, 1962, the company met with the shop committee and the business representative of the union and for about an hour and a half explained the new coffee-break rule which the company was instituting and which was to be effective beginning September 4, 1962. In addition to posting, a copy of the rule was mailed to each employee. It provided a definite 10-minute period in each half of the shift when the vending machines could be used. The rule permitted an employee at other times to "leave whenever necessary to get a drink or take care of personal needs." It added, "We do expect him, however, after going for a drink or to the rest room, to promptly return to his job." A grievance challenging the new rule was filed on August 17, 1962, and was denied by the company.

At 8 a.m. on September 4, 1962, seven employees took a work break at the vending machines in violation of the rule and were given written warnings. At 4:30 p.m. on the same day, another employee was given a warning. During the night shift almost all of the employees tested the enforcement of the rule. First, they thought of going en masse with their two committeemen to the union hall. The company denied permission to the group but permitted the two committeemen, Bays and Satterfield, to go. As they walked out at about 4:30 p.m., Meschke, plant manager, told the committeemen in substance: "You know the cause of this—because of all the grievances you filed." At 9 p.m. on September 4, 36 of the night-shift employees took a work break in the area of the vending machines and were given either written or oral warnings. The general foreman was home ill, and the foreman was unable to issue written warnings to all. The plant superintendent was called to be present, and he arrived a few minutes before 11 p.m. when 35 employees took a break at the vending machines and were given either a written warning for a first violation or a three-day suspension. At the time no one protested his innocence or accused someone of not being disciplined who was a participant. At the hearing, union witnesses testified that no die setter was disciplined.

At 8:00 a.m. on September 5, 1962, seven employees violated the rule, and those who had been warned the previous day were suspended three days. At 10 a.m. 28 employees took a break at the vending machines and were given either warnings for a first offense or three-day suspensions. At about 9:00 a.m. company and union representatives met, and the company offered to revoke the three-day suspensions and agree to arbitration; but the union committee would agree only if the men were made whole who were suspended at 8:00 a.m. and those who could not be contacted.

In a four-page mimeographed letter mailed to each employee on September 6,

1962, the company explained its position and the background of the rule. "There are three basic misconceptions," the letter stated, "which seem to need clearing up:

1. The belief that this rule was introduced to "show up" or punish the committee.

2. The belief that the Company does not have the right, under the Contract, to introduce this rule.

3. The belief that the Company would not discipline or discharge employees if as many as 50 or 60 were involved.

After reviewing the findings of the spot checks, the plant superintendent's ordering the men to work, and the filing of a grievance, the latter continued:

No Company can operate if its employees can stop work whenever and for as long a period as they choose. The Company felt that the only solution to the abuse, confusion and misunderstanding that was being caused by the absence of an exact rule covering work breaks was to put in a rule spelling out exactly what the breaks should be.

Since the suspensions the men have observed the rule except that they are taking breaks at their machines of about the same duration as formerly so that production has not improved. In setting production standards a 20 percent allowance has been included for personal relief, fatigue, unavoidable delays, etc. The men seem to feel that this should allow them a break every hour of up to 12 minutes. Their committeemen testified that the men were discouraged from working above standard since the company might then revise the rate. In their opinion the percentage drop in production as against standard was due to setting rates too tight on new jobs. Union testimony also suggested that the rule was enacted as a result of a disagreement as to Credit Union hours and that the personnel manager threatened to get the employees on the back of a member of the shop committee, Mr. Fore.

The company showed by a chart the location of drinking fountains and rest rooms. It was also shown that formerly for a period there were relief men and that now more of the production is on the line.

The grievance charges that the company discriminated against the shop committee and wants the practice stopped and the employees paid for all lost time.

DISCUSSION

The company took the disciplinary action in question against the grievants pursuant to its unnegotiated additions to its Rule 9, which restricted the use of vending machines to two 10-minute periods, one in the middle of each half day, and to the lunch and supper periods. In order to prevail, the union must show that the Amendment of Rule 9 was invalid. It may do this by establishing (1) that it violates an express provision in the contract, (2) that it materially changes a past practice or working condition which through mutual acceptance has acquired the status of a contractually-protected right, or (3) that the amendment is unreasonable either on its face or in its administration.

With regard to the first point, the Management Rights Clause (Article II, Section 1) reserves to the company the right to "require employees to observe company rules and regulations not inconsistent with the provisions of this Agreement." This clause does not restrict the usual authority of a company to make reasonable rules and regulations governing the internal operation of the plant and the conduct of the employees, including the establishment of formal periods for breaks. In fact, recognition of authority to compel observance of rules implies power to make rules; otherwise there might not be rules to observe. The clause does not require new rules to be negotiated. Its only limitation is that they may not be inconsistent with other provisions of the Agreement. The arbitrator's attention was not called to any such provision, and an examination of the Agreement discloses none. It is not necessary that rule-making power be affirmatively granted by the contract; it is enough that none of its provisions is inconsistent with the rule in question. As was observed by Arbitrator McIntosh in Dover Corp., 33 LA 861 (1959), a case very similar to this one:

> The basic rule of labor management relations is that management has all rights except those which it has bargained away in the Contract. Among the prerogatives of Management has always been the right to make reasonable rules for the governing of the conduct of the plant and its employees.

This inherent authority was also recognized in Detroit Gasket and Mfg. Co., 27 LA 717 (1956), a case cited by the union, wherein the arbitrator stated:

> Analysis of the Agreement itself fails to disclose any provision which can fairly be said to impose a limitation or a qualication upon the rights of the Company to prescribe machinery deemed necessary by it to prevent unnecessary and excessive time away from the job. Accordingly, the challenge of the Union is centered on what it contends is the inherently unreasonable character of the program which the Company has seen fit to adopt.

Therefore, the Amendment to Rule 9 establishing formal break periods for the use of the vending machines did not violate any of the express clauses in the contract.

PAST PRACTICE

However, this does not end the matter since it is well recognized that the contractual relationship between the parties normally consists of more than the written word. Day-to-day practices mutually accepted by the parties may attain the status of contractual rights and duties, particu-larly where they are not at variance with any written provision negotiated into the contract by the parties and where they are of long standing and were not changed during contract negotiations. Here, the Agreement is silent on the question of work breaks or the use of vending machines, thus leaving the matter open for determination by practice or by the adoption of reasonable plant rules. The company admits that before the effective date of the new rule, employees were generally free to leave their work stations at any time and to go to the vending machines for food or beverages. The union describes the practice as one which permitted employees to take breaks of different amounts of time each hour and to visit the vending machines as desired. It also stated that the men were under the impression from the 20 percent allowance in the incentive standard that they were allowed 12 minutes each hour to use as they saw fit. This long-continued practice certainly is entitled to recognition and, except through negotiation, cannot be abrogated. However, inherent in every practice is the principle that it is not to be abused and that, if it is, reasonable corrective action may be taken. It can not be inferred that the other party has accepted or acquiesced in the excesses constituting the abuse so as to make them binding. The employees, no less than management, are under a duty to act reasonably. Both must cooperate and meet the other halfway in following sound industrial practices which will enable the plant to be operated efficiently for the ultimate benefit of the men as well as the company. From the evidence it seems apparent that the men themselves changed the practice by more of them taking breaks and for longer and longer times. Company survey findings were not seriously disputed that time spent by each man on breaks in March averaged 14.8 minutes each hour and that much of this time was spent at the vending machines. While other reasons were offered by the union, it seems apparent that the increased use which the men were making of the vending machines contributed substantially to the sizable decline in production from 112 percent of standard to below 97 percent. While the practice recognized the right of the men to break every hour, it must have contemplated one which was reasonable under the circumstances. Certainly, from the evidence it does not appear that the company accepted a practice of allowing each hour from 13 to 14 minutes for breaks, or even for 12 minutes which the union contends the incentive standards permit for personal time. Without such mutual acceptance there can be no binding past practice or working condition. It must be noted that the 20 percent allowance added into the standard includes time for delay and fatigue allowances as well as time for personal needs, such as getting a drink, visiting the washroom, or taking a moment or two for relaxation. The purpose of these allowances is not to give the men a 12-minute break each hour but to permit the inclusion into the standard of variable items which affect productivity and which are virtually impossible to measure by time study. By the nature of the incentive system, the men cannot claim as break-time the allowances included in the standard for these immeasurable items unless agreed to or accepted by the company, which was not established by the evidence. What the evidence does show is that the parties accepted the principle of breaking on the hour, and the question is whether the Amendment to Rule 9 adequately reflects this principle as established by long-continued practice and custom.

The amendment formalizes the practice by recognizing a 10-minute break in the middle of each half day when vending machines may be used, and at other times it permits an employee "to leave whenever necessary to get a drink or take care of personal needs." However, he is expected

"after going for a drink or to the rest room to promptly return to his job." It seems to the arbitrator that to the extent that the amended rule officially sanctions two 10-minute breaks, which are not included in the contract, the men have gained; but apparently at other times the rule restricts them to shorter breaks than those to which they were accustomed. On balance, the question is whether the rule materially changes the former practice as it existed prior to the time that abuses crept into it.

The practice of breaking each hour has apparently been in existence longer than the widespread, indiscriminate use of vending machines. The restriction of the use of the machines to the two 10-minute periods and the lunch hour would therefore not appear to be a prejudicial deviation from the original, mutually accepted practice, especially in view of the problems which normally develop from the unrestricted use of such machines. However, the rule seems to change materially the practice and to be too restrictive regarding nonvending-machine breaks at other times. Each hour, in accordance with the previous custom, the men should be allowed, if they elect to take them, a few moments for rest in addition to personal relief time. However, the present practice of the men of taking at their machines as long a break as they formerly took at the vending machines is an abuse of the practice. The allowance of four minutes in the incentive standard for personal time should normally be adequate. All men working on a line should, so far as practicable, break at the same time. If so interpreted and applied, the Amendment to Rule 9 should not materially change the substance and the spirit of the practice as it originally developed and was accepted by the company.

This leaves the final contention of the union that amended Rule 9 is unreasonable in that it discriminates against the

Shop Committee and was vindictive. While there were incidents between members of the Shop Committee and supervision, particularly with reference to Credit Union hours and the filing of grievances over ordering the men from the vending machine area back to work, a preponderance of the evidence discloses that the Amendment to Rule 9 was under consideration for several months before the incidents and that at most only the effective date of the new rule was moved forward because of them. The arbitrator is satisfied that embarrassment to the Shop Committee was not a dominant motive in its promulgation, which was to correct the problems resulting from the use of the vending machines.

The final questions are whether the penalty imposed of a written warning followed by a three-day suspension for a violation of the rule was too severe and whether the company unjustly discriminated in its enforcement. In view of the advance notice given the men and their deliberate violation of the rule, such disciplinary action cannot be said to be unreasonable. The grievance and arbitration procedures of the contract, and not self-help, should have been used to test the validity of the new rule. The evidence does not disclose that the company knowingly discriminated in favor of or against any employee in enforcing the rule against the grievants.

AWARD

The grievances must be and are denied.

PART SIX

THE POLICY FORMATION/CHANGE PROCESS

CHAPTER 14

Collective Bargaining and Public Policy in the 1980s

THE POLICY FORMATION PROCESS

Up to this point we have examined four of the subsystems of industrial relations: the environment, the parties to bargaining, bargaining structure and power, and the bargaining process and its outcomes. We now turn our attention to understanding why and how the system of industrial relations changes. The key to understanding how change occurs is in what we call the policy formation or policy change process. This process refers to (1) society's (or its legislators') response to both the bargaining process and its outcomes and (2) management and union abilities to use or counter this response and be effective in the debate process. For example, public opinion toward labor immediately following World War II was shaped to a great degree by the tremendous level of strike activity occurring during 1945 and 1946. The negative public response led to legislative debate concerning policies that might limit the power of American labor. The result was the passage of the Taft-Hartley Act in 1947. Labor was unable to defeat its passage and the environment of industrial relations was changed.

Generally, the policy formation process has served as a mechanism through which to institutionalize change. History indicates that changes in labor relations and collective bargaining policy have been cyclical attempts to equalize power between competing groups. Hence the antilabor Taft-Hartley Act was preceded by the prolabor Wagner Act (1935). It is this change process that institutionalizes conflict and ensures that the system does not self-destruct; the change process is the safety valve that allows steam to be vented and keeps all the parties committed generally to the overall system. Of course, the type of change that occurs is constrained by the ideology of business unionism.

History also indicates that the formal groups involved in this change/policy formation process are broadening. Jack Barbash's article on "positive public policy" defines more clearly the involvement of various representatives of society in the policy formation process and assesses the impact of such involvement on the overall nature of labor policy. The article by Kau and Rubin examines the effectiveness of unions as an interest group in society by assessing the degree unions influence the passage of economic legislation.

LABOR POLICY IN THE 1980s

Given that labor relations policy continues to change, what are the signs for change in collective bargaining policies during this decade? We have identified several areas of concern:

1. There will be continued pressure for labor law reform. Included in this debate is concern over the lack of effective remedies that the NLRB can use against employers who refuse to bargain in good faith. Labor contends that the use of bargaining orders without the availability of punitive damages simply does not effectively deal with companies that repeatedly ignore the bargaining requirements of the law. Since the NLRB has already adopted the concept of "extra-remedial" relief, we may see more discussion concerning the use of punitive sanctions to get the parties to at least participate in the process.

2. Because of increasing concern for the economic waste associated with work stoppages and the view among some policymakers that binding arbitration has been relatively successful in the public sector, there is likely to be more intensified discussion concerning the role compulsory arbitration should play in the resolution of disputes over the terms and conditions of employment in the private sector.

3. Consistent with a concern for the waste associated with industrial disputes is an increasing concern over the effectiveness of adversarily-based collective bargaining. This concern calls into question the fundamental principle upon which collective bargaining is based. Certainly, any change in the adherence to this principle would result in dramatically changed public policy regarding collective bargaining.

4. During the early years of this decade, the federal government is expected to take a less activist role in the employment relationship. To the degree that this occurs, collective bargainers may more vigorously pursue contractual means for attaining employment ends that are thought to be embodied in employment law.

5. Recent evidence suggests that the judiciary is becoming increasingly concerned with individual rights in employment, beyond those that are guaranteed by legislation. In the past several years rights of union members regarding the obligation of their unions to process their grievances have been spelled out and expanded. Initial activity has begun in the area of challenging "at will" employment contracts, which at common law have allowed employers to discharge at any time and for any reason that is not governed by another law. Judicial activism, however, is at odds with the conservative approach represented by the 1980 election results. Clashes between the largely liberal judicial branch (reinforced by the huge numbers of federal district court appointments made by President Carter) and the increasingly conservative direction of legislatures could lead to restrictive legislation in the middle 1980s.

TRADE UNIONISM AND THE GENERAL INTEREST: A THEORY OF POSITIVE PUBLIC POLICY TOWARD LABOR

Jack Barbash*

Historically, public policy toward labor has reflected mainly the legislative and political pressures exerted by employers and unions for the reenforcement of their bargaining positions toward one another. This commentary undertakes to mark a shift in public policy orientation from a pressure group response towarrd the assertion of a more autonomous interest, neutral as between the claims of business and unions. Positive public policy is the shorthand term employed to designate this new orientation.

I

The Great Depression marks the divide in the direction of public policy toward labor from "pro-business" to "pro-union" . . .

There were some countertrends during this period. The declaration in section 6 of the Clayton Act (1914), "that the labor of a human being is not a commodity or article of commerce," was initially understood by the labor movement as the *magna charta* which would free it from the bitter affliction of the labor injunction in federal courts. This did not in fact happen until the Norris-LaGuardia Act was passed in 1932. President Wilson's policy for disputes settlement during World War I embodied an unprecedented support for

union organization to a degree that the union membership would not be surpassed until after the New Deal era. Although the Railway Labor Act of 1926 established procedures for disputes settlement and protected the railroad workers' right to collective bargaining, it permitted the company union in effect to coexist with the free union. Finally, after years of agitation in union and liberal legal circles, the Norris-LaGuardia anti-injunction act of 1932 ushered in a pro-union period—pro-union in the sense of rectifying procedural inequities weakening the union collective bargaining position.)

Norris-LaGuardia was followed in 1933 by section 7a of the National Industrial Recovery Act (NIRA), pressed for by the unions as the price for their support of the NIRA as a whole. The high point of pro-unionism came with the enactment of the Wagner Act (National Labor Relations Act) in 1935 and particularly with its constitutional validation in 1937.[1] The Wagner Act was probably the single most important influence in the ascendance of union power in mass production collective bargaining.

The ebb of union influence and the rise of business influence on public policy to-

---

* J. P. Bascom, professor of economics and industrial relations, University of Wisconsin. Reprinted from 1970 *Wisconsin Law Review*, 1134–44. © The University of Wisconsin, 1970.

[1] *NLRB* v. *Jones & Laughlin Steel Corp.*, 301 U.S. 1 (1937); *NLRB* v. *Fruehauf Trailer Co.*, 301 U.S. 49 (1937); *NLRB* v. *Friedman-Harry Marks Clothing Co.*, 301 U.S. 58 (1937); *Associated Press* v. *NLRB*, 301 U.S. 103 (1937); *Washington, Virginia, & Maryland Coach Co.* v. *NLRB*, 301 U.S. 142 (1937).

ward labor came with the Taft-Hartley Act (the Labor-Management Relations Act of 1947). Taft-Hartley took over most of the pro-union provisions of Wagner but reinstated protections for the employer in the collective bargaining process, thereby reflecting the heavy pressure from business on the first Republican majority in the Congress since 1930. The 8(b) provisions of Taft-Harley dealing with union unfair labor practices implemented a new legislative finding that "experience has further demonstrated that certain practices by some labor organizations, their officers, and members" can also "impair the interest of the public."

The Labor-Management Reporting and Disclosure Act of 1959 (Landrum-Griffin) represented a mixed bag of interests: on the one hand, the amendments to Taft-Hartley in title VII strengthened employer protections against union secondary boycott practices; on the other, a new order of interests emerged—the protection of individual rights of union members vis-à-vis union officers. For the most part the AFL–CIO supported the principle and much of the detail in this title of the law, as did many members of Congress commonly identified with pro-union voting records. There was, to be sure, support from employers who were perhaps less interested in union democracy as such than they were in what the institution of union democracy would presumably bring about, *i.e.*, the weakening of union power from below. The wave of rank and file discontent of the late 1960s proved to employers, however, that that which weakens the union does not necessarily help management. In fact, a weakening of union leadership lowers union capacity to come to agreement with the employer, thereby also weakening management. The Landrum-Griffin law in seeking to correct the power imbalance between union leadership and membership cut across the conventional union versus management alignment. This

aspect of the law, it argued here, signals the emergence of a new public policy toward labor.

II

Resolution of manpower, inflation and civil rights issues represent the fuller development of this new bent of public policy which displaces the traditional union versus management questions in the center of the policy arena. Manpower policy as embodied in the series of manpower acts since 1961[2] traverses the traditional union versus management alignment because it enhances the protective interests of both by increasing worker productivity and mobility through education, training, retraining and guidance, and, further, by strengthening the institutions of the labor market to achieve a better fit between the structure of supply and the structure of demand. In its reactive phase manpower policy responded to the immediate urgencies of depressed areas, youth unemployment, technological unemployment and the "competitively disadvantaged-unemployed, underemployed, low income earners, youth, older workers, nonwhites, those with low educational levels, etc."[3] . . .

Wage-price policy does not offer as clear-cut a case of neutrality between the relative claims of unions and employers. The union view is that the wage-price policy is likely to be more wage repression than price control. There is further, nothing like a consensus as to whether the wage-price program should rely on deflation, "jawboning," "guidelines," or a "freeze," to list the remedies currently in vogue. However, corroborating the thesis that wage-price policy is value free in re-

---

[2] U.S. Department of Labor: *Manpower Report of the President 193–97* (March 1970).

[3] Studies by the staff of the Cabinet Committee on Price Stability, January 1969, p. 26.

spect to the relative claims of unions and management are the strong support which wage-price policy has in "pro-union" intellectual circles,[4] and the willingness of the AFL–CIO to accept a wage price policy in principle, even if the severity of requisite conditions is hardly distinguishable from outright rejection.

The conditions upon which the AFL–CIO would appear to condition acceptance of wage-price policy appear to be that:

1. The wage policy must be part of a general incomes policy also enforceable against nonlabor incomes.

2. The standards for wage policy cannot, as under CEA guideposts be tied solely to productivity, as this perpetuates the inequities and injustices of the existing wage structure.

3. The quid pro quo for wage restraint has to be the achievement of a measure of price stability without substantial unemployment.

4. Wage restraint has to be temporary because rank and file opposition cannot be checked for more than a brief period.

5. Scapegoating of the unions as the flagrant inflationary influence must be avoided.

6. Economy must be exercised in the use of compulsion and restraint.

7. The tendency of the economic experts to show a systematic bias toward wage repression must be restrained if the supporting analysis is to be credible.

8. The wage price norms should be subject to negotiation or effective consultation.

Public policy regarding the protection of civil rights in the context of employment situations is embodied in title VI of the Civil Rights Act of 1964[5] and in the president's authority to prescribe standards for federal procurement. The policy enforced against both management and unions speaks for the existence and ascendancy of a new pressure group, *i.e.*, civil rights activists. It should be noted that although the Civil Rights Law was aimed in part against the unions, nevertheless "without the help and day-to-day work of the [union] legislative representatives . . . no civil rights legislation could have passed in any session of Congress."[6] The AFL–CIO, "keenly and painfully aware of the limitations imposed upon it by its structure" in applying sanctions against unions violating its own civil rights provisions, "turned to federal legislation as its primary instrument for wiping out discrimination. It is now an open secret that the fair employment practices section of the Civil Rights Act of 1961 was written into the law because of the bullheaded insistence of the AFL–CIO."

Civil rights public policy has also undergone a shift from pure reactivism. In the earlier reactive stage, civil rights policy moved to prohibit discrimination in employment. But the reactive policy of no discrimination has proved not to be sufficient in actually bringing together the black worker and the job. The initiating or positive posture of civil rights policy is demonstrated in the concepts of "outreach" and "affirmative action." These concepts recognize that policy objectives are not fulfilled simply by creating normal market incentives. Incentives alone have, in fact, proved to be inadequate to bring blacks to the job because they have lived so long out of the range of the conventional market incentive system.

[4] For example, the Kennedy "new economist," who in fact initiated in 1962 the first peacetime wage-price policy in the form of the Council of Economic Adviser's guideposts.

[5] 78 STAT, 253, 42 U.S.C. §2000(c) (1964).

[6] Clarence Mitchell, chief lobbyist of the NAACP in Washington, Excerpts from Speech at 14th Annual AFL–CIO National Conference on Community Services, AFL–CIO Release, May 20, 1969, p. 1.

In contrast, outreach and affirmative action therefore go beyond the incentive system to establish, first, the right of black workers as a class to an equitable share in the full range of job opportunities and, second, the obligation of management and unions to implement that right on their own initiative. The Chicago and Philadelphia Plans and their variants amount to a multilateral undertaking among unions, employers, civil rights groups and/or federal government to provide construction jobs to black workers proportionate to their numbers. Sanctions for noncompliance consist of litigation, disruption, and loss of federal contracts.

The above summary recital suggests two distinctive aspects of the theory of positive public policy. First, positive public policy seems to unfold in two stages. In the early reactive stage, public policy intervention, although neutral, is nevertheless determined by the frame of reference set by the union-management disputants. In the subsequent initiating stage, intervention is based on new ground, relying less on the contentions of the parties and more on a presumed objective or "scientific" interest usually advanced by a government spokesman.

Second, positive public policy appears to assert an unprecedented concern with the *results* of collective bargaining and trade unionism. The expressions of public policy in the Norris-LaGuardia, Wagner, Taft-Hartley and Landrum-Griffin Acts reflect the theory that the regulation of the *processes* of collective bargaining and unionism would be sufficient to achieve the intended effects. In contrast, wage-price policy, civil rights and manpower undertake to define publicly acceptable *results* of collective bargaining and unionism. The underlying assumption of wage-price policy is that to allow even balanced collective bargaining to go its own way is likely to yield economic results incompatible with a stable price level, strong balance

of trade and economic growth, and that some kind of external intervention is essential to achieve results compatible with economic policy objectives. Similarly, civil rights policy raises the question whether social peace does not require public intervention to protect the interests of Negro workers from the results negotiated by the white bargaining partners. Manpower policy gets at the results of the union-management relationship at the points of apprenticeship and other training periods which are deemed inconsistent with public policy interests in freer mobility.

The underlying economic theory is that the negotiations between the private parties do not sufficiently take into account the social costs of their bargaining results and that intervention is essential to make adjustments congruent with positive public policy.

The AFL–CIO and the National Association of Manufacturers both rejected an asserting and defining role for government with equal firmness.

Positive public policy has by no means displaced the pressure group interests; rather the two coexist. Republican appointees to the National Labor Relations Board are more likely to come down on the side of the employer in their decisions than are Democratic appointments and vice versa. It is unlikely that President Nixon as a Republican president would say as President Johnson did: "I have met with Mr. Meany and his assistants many times but with Mr. Meany 49 times, in personal meetings either in my office, the Oval Room or in the mansion. In addition . . . he has called me, or I have called him 82 additional times."[7] Unions engaged in national strikes are not unlikely to seek intervention to get themselves off the hook. Policymakers are, in short, still responsive to the demands of pressure groups but mainly in respect to short-run tactical

---

[7] *AFL–CIO News*, January 18, 1969, p.7.

needs. The key public policies toward labor, such as full employment, civil rights, manpower and wages and prices, are, however, now more likely to reflect an autonomous positive line than pressure group demands. Allowing for differences in pace and rhetoric, these key public policies are not likely to vary fundamentally in direction as between Republican and Democratic administrations.

III

The context in which positive public policy emerges may be termed the "post full employment economy" of the 1960s. Full employment[8] has displaced "slack demand, relative overproduction [and] insufficient investment" as the major economic problem because of the "ungovernable tendency of demand to outrun the economy's capacity to meet it without inflation and price rise[9] —hence, the focus on wage-price policy. In turn, the achievement of around 96 percent employment has highlighted the plight of the 4 percent unemployed, or the uncounted-"nonemployed," who have not shared in the general affluence because of ethnic attachment, geographic location, lack of education and training, or some combination of these, and whose condition has been made all the more intolerable by the general affluence—hence, the importance of a manpower policy to alleviate he structural obstructions to full participation by these groups.

The civil rights movement gave force, meaning, and organization to the previously inchoate resentment of the blacks. The rising political and social awareness of the Negro masses and the resultant threat of disruption moved the civil rights strategy from the reactive goal of nondiscrimination to the initiating goal of asserting the right to work of blacks as a class— hence, the importance of a civil rights policy.

The full employment condition has moderated class divisiveness which characterized earlier issues. As the mainstream of American business came to accept collective bargaining and to view unionism as a positive force in modern management, it moved from class struggle to problem solving. Management's new comprehension was facilitated by the profitability of enterprise in the era of full employment. Full employment by minority groups also made American business and unionism more amenable to the initiating role of public policy in the area of civil rights.

* * * * *

The broader based public policy toward labor has come about because the pressure groups themselves have begun to take a broader and more long-range view of their interests. The pressure groups have not, however, abandoned their protectivism but perceive more clearly now the relevance of protection to national policy and the longer run costs of intransigent protectivism. In economic terms the trade unions may be "superimposing upon their traditional, sectional direct bargaining with employers for money wages a new type of indirect bargaining through government for redistribution of real income."[10] In a generation the trade union movement has accordingly moved away from preoccupation with defensive reactions to antiunion measures such as the labor injunction, toward major emphasis on full employment and social welfare. For example, during the

---

[8] Full employment is used as a term of art here because full employment has not been achieved in any literal sense. High level employment is more accurate, but also more cumbersome.

[9] M. M. Postan, *An Economic History of Western Europe, 1945–1964* (London: Methuen, 1967), p.19.

[10] Forsy, "Trade Union Policy under Full Employment," in Richard A. Lester and Joseph Shister, *Insights into Labor Issues* (New York: Macmillan, 1948), p. 312.

1970 session of Congress, the AFL–CIO put the highest priority on "rising unemployment, occupational safety, environmental pollution, expanded health education, manpower training, antipoverty programs, skyrocketing interest rates and monetary policy reform, true bargaining rights for farm workers, and situs picketing rights for the building trades."[11] Only the last item represents a conventional "pure" trade union issue.

Responsibility for the enlargement of trade union policy perspectives can be attributed largely to:

1. The achievement of something like a stable balance of power with business so that the trade union movement is able to perceive its security needs more broadly.

2. The demonstration since the era of the New Deal that public policy can serve as ally as well as adversary.

3. The emerging union awareness that the condition of the nation's economy has much to do with the effectiveness of the trade union performance.

4. The ascendancy of the more expansive industrial union interest.

5. The growing public concern with unionism's power to inflict damage on the economy, a concern understandably less relevant to the underdeveloped unionism of a generation earlier.

Similar factors have been at work in broadening perspectives of modern business enterprise management. Having come to terms, more or less, with unions and collective bargaining, management need no longer view unions as a threat to the free enterprise system. Business has also come to terms with "aggregate demand" as essential for the effective planning of the industrial system.[12] A combination of

a sense of social responsibility and the threat of disruption has brought businessmen into the center of the minority employment problem. Here again, business has not abandoned its profit maximizing behavior but has gradually widened its perspectives to take account of the longer run and the urgent need for social as well as economic viability.

Finally, to pull together the diverse strands of this section: The origins of positive public policy stem from the achievement of full employment in the 1960s; full employment gave credibility to economics as science; full employment brought the wage inflation issue to the fore; full employment dramatized, by contrast, the plight of the disadvantaged; the profitability of enterprise which resulted from full employment produced a relaxation of business opposition to the union's economic demands; in turn full employment brought the unions relief from the insistent pressures of antiunionism and unemployment and made possible a broadening of union sights. Ultimately, full employment transformed the public image of the union from an underprivileged mass to "big labor."

IV

Some caveats need to be entered against possible misinterpretation of the argument that public policy toward labor is moving from pressure group protectivism toward objective or positive public policy. First, it is no part of the argument that positive public policy necessarily yields results ultimately more genuinely in the public interest. The positive public policy model relates only to the attitudes of policymakers, not to whether, in fact, a better result will necessarily follow. Nor should it be inferred that pressure group public policy is by its nature incapable of yielding results which ultimately prove to be in the "true" public interest. The Wagner Act, for exam-

[11] AFL–CIO, *Labor Looks at Congress, 1970* (Washington, D.C.: The Federation, 1970), p.iii.

[12] J. Galbraith, *The New Industrial State* (Boston: Houghton Mifflin, 1967), p. 31.

ple, a response to a pressure group interest, nevertheless served a "true"public interest by redressing a grave imbalance of power favoring management. Further, the possibility cannot be disregarded that what now purports to be "objective" or "neutral" public policy as between one alignment of classes may over the long run evolve into a class-serving ideology and form the basis for a bid for power by a "new class" of economic technocrats.

Finally, I do not intend to imply that conflict over labor problems is obsolete. What has happened, rather, is what might be called the rationalization of the labor problem, *i.e.*, traditional trial by struggle, rigid ideology, and trial-and-error behavior are giving way to rules, organization and expertise. Divergent interests inherent in labor disputes have not been eliminated— rather the methods of asserting those interests have simply been civilized. Similarly, labor and management are beginning to understand that not only do they have divergent interests, but that they also have interests in common.

Certainly, an assertion is not intended, nor are the above arguments to be construed as asserting the inherent superiority of the positive public policy approach over pressure group public policy. There are indeed many legitimate differences of interest among the pressure groups who have to do with the labor problem. These divergent interests should not be forced into synthetically "positive" molds. The evidence is far from clear that economics is yet sophisticated enough to displace pressure groups in wage determinations, and further, whether such a move would be worth the costs.

The advanced industrial nations of Western Europe came to positive public policy earlier than the United States. The need to repair the war-ravaged economies of Europe, the high priority placed on full employment and the more recent need to correct the inflationary effects of their post

full-employment era which began earlier than in the United States caused positive public policy to ripen earlier in Europe. The special character of the Western European approaches to positive public policy, most notably in incomes policy, manpower, planning and industrial relations reform, was demonstrated by the unique manner in which a consensus was negotiated directly by the trade unions and employers with the government.

The features of the post war West European environment which made varying degrees of negotiated consensus possible in the various nations were:

1. The spirit of unity engendered by the devastation of war and the sufferings of reconstruction.

2. The decline of ideologies which rejected consensus.

3. The widespread acceptance of the "export or die" principle.

4. The feasibility of planning in the relatively small scale of most of the national economies of western Europe.

5. The ingrained habit of pressure group consultation.

6. The availability of mechanisms for centralized negotiations, *e.g.*, economy-wide collective bargaining, powerful union and employer federations, tripartite social and economic councils and close trade union-political party alliances.

The European experience, nevertheless, does not easily lend itself to adaptation in the United States. This country has not experienced the kind of common ordeal which unifies divergent interests. Moreover, the vastness and complexity of the American economy raise real questions as to the practical manageability of negotiating economic policy. Even if negotiation of national economic policy were feasible, the question remains whether it would be desirable or wise to vest such great power in the hands of pressure groups.

THE IMPACT OF LABOR UNIONS ON THE PASSAGE OF ECONOMIC LEGISLATION

James B. Kau and Paul H. Rubin*

I. INTRODUCTION

In studying unions, economists have generally been concerned with the effects of unions as agents in market transactions (see, e.g., Lewis, 1963). However, in addition to these direct effects, unions can also affect market outcomes indirectly by changing the legal climate in which transactions occur. Thus, for example, both Silberman and Durden (1976) and Kau and Rubin (1978) have shown that unions are influential in affecting the voting behavior of Congressmen on minimum wage legislation and, as is well known, minimum wages have important influences on certain aspects of labor market equilibria. In this paper, the effects of labor unions in influencing economic legislation are examined in detail; thus, this is in a sense an investigation of some of the indirect economic effects of labor unions, as these effects are filtered through the political process.

There have been several studies of the political impact of unions (e.g., Barbash, 1972, Ch. 9; Bok and Dunlop, 1970, Ch. 14). However, these studies have largely been impressionistic and have considered the intent rather than the actual impact of union political activity. In this paper, empirical methods are used to assess the effects of certain forms of union political activity. The basic methodology, an exten-sion of our earlier research (Kau and Rubin, 1978, 1979d, 1979a) will be to focus on the influence of unions in determining the voting of Congressmen on particular bills with significant economic impact. There have been two studies directly concerned with union impact on the issue of minimum wages. Silberman and Durden found that Congressmen who had received contributions from unions were significantly more likely to vote in favor of minimum wage bills in 1973. Kau and Rubin found that Congressmen from states with many union members were also significantly more likely to vote for minimum wage legislation, and that this tendency has persisted from 1938 to 1974. Here, the results of these studies are generalized in two important ways. First, both the effects of union membership and political contributions paid by unions on the voting behavior of Congressmen are investigated. Second, the determinants of union contributions—that is, the factors which make it more likely that a particular Congressman will receive campaign contributions from unions—are evaluated.

The paper is organized as follows. In Section II, the determinants of campaign contributions are examined theoretically and empirically. Section III contains a set of equations which indicates the effects of both contributions and of union membership on Congressional voting, and reveals the issues on which unions seem to be influential. The last section is a summary.

* University of Georgia. Reprinted from the *Journal of Labor Research*, Spring 1981, pp. 133–45.

II. DETERMINANTS OF CAMPAIGN CONTRIBUTIONS

Labor unions are significant contributors to campaigns. In 1974, Common Cause published figures based on all contributions to political campaigns in 1972. The total amount contributed by economic interest groups was $8.5 million; unions contributed $3.6 million, while business contributed $1.7 million. (Business contributions were underreported since contributions from private individuals who were associated with business were not counted as being interest group contributions.) . . .

The central focus is the decision making process of an interest group which is contemplating making a contribution to a Congressman. There are two possible effects of this contribution: it can affect the probability that the Congressman will be elected, or it can affect the probability that he will vote as the interest group desires. For each representative, let P be the probability of election and let Q be the probability that he will vote as the interest group desires. Contributions can be used to elect a favorable representative (to increase P) or to secure the vote of a Congressman (to increase Q). Other factors will also affect P and Q. P will be related to the seniority of the representative (more senior representatives are more likely to be reelected). Likewise, for interest groups which have significant numbers of voting members in the representative's district (such as unions), Q will be affected by the number of members. Defining terms:

P = Probability that the representative will be elected
Q = Probability that the representative will vote as the group desires
S = Seniority of the representative
N = Number of members of the interest group in the representative's district

C = Contribution made by the interest group to the representative
V = Expected value to the group of the vote of the Congressman on relevant bills.

Then

$$V = P(C,S) \cdot Q(C,N) \qquad (1)$$

That is, the expected value of the vote of the Congressman to the interest group is the product of the probability of reelection of the Congressman (which is determined by seniority and contributions received) and the probability that his vote will be favorable (which is determined by the number of members of the group in his district and by contributions). There are 435 Congressmen; the interest group is concerned with maximizing [the sum of the expected values to the group of the votes of the 435 Congressmen on relevant bills.] . . .

Consider now the $Q(C,N)$ term, the probability that a particular representative will vote as the interest group desires. In any election, the winning candidate must put together a majority coalition. As N increases, the value to a candidate of having members of the group in his coalition increases. Thus, for interest groups with significant numbers of members (such as unions) one would expect that contributions would be relatively insignificant in changing votes; for such groups, the purpose of contributions would be to influence P, the probability that the desired candidate (that is, the candidate with union members in his coalition) wins. Since P is positively related to seniority, it is anticipated that, for interest groups with significant numbers of members, contributions could be negatively related to seniority of the representative.

Conversely, for interest groups with few members, the main method of accumulating political power is through campaign contributions. Such groups would not be concerned with who wins the election, since in any case their members would not be a significant fraction of the winning co-alition; rather, they would be interested in changing the future voting behavior of the probable winner. Thus, one would ex-pect contributions of business-oriented groups to be positively related to seniority.

Consider again the behavior of unions as contributors to campaigns. Though much of the contribution may be aimed at electing desired representatives, unions will also want to change the voting behav-ior of some representatives. Representa-tives from districts with few union mem-bers will probably not vote as the union wishes anyway, and representatives from districts with many union members will probably vote as the union desires inde-pendently of contributions. Representa-tives from marginal districts are those most likely to be swayed by contributions from unions, or from business.[1] . . .

In order to test these hypotheses, data were gathered on constituent characteris-tics: Central city residents; education of constituents; government spending in the district (HEW, DOD, other); average age of voters; farm population; blacks; oil and coal production in the state; union mem-bers in the state; subscribers to *Consumer Reports* in the state; number voting for each candidate in the Nixon-McGovern election in 1972 in the district; income of constituents . . . ; party of the repre-sentative; seniority of the representative; and aircraft and automobile manufactur-ing employment in the state.[2] Data were

---

[1] This point is due to Tom Borcherding.

[2] These data were found useful in other research, particularly Kau and Rubin, 1979b. Sources: Income, central city, blacks, education, age, farm, government spending, seniority, party, and electoral margin from *Almanac of American Politics,* 1974. The data are by Congressional districts; the remainder are state data. Union membership: Department of Labor, 1975; oil production, American Petroleum Institute, 1975; coal production, U.S. Bureau of Mines, 1975. Auto and air employment, U.S. Department of Commerce. (Air employment is actually nonautomotive transpor-tation employment; approximately two-thirds of this is aircraft related employment.)

also collected from Common Cause (1974) on contributions received from interest groups. These contribution data were disaggregated into about 60 categories, though in this paper only some of the fig-ures were used. The electoral margin re-ceived by the representative in the 1972 election is the dependent variable. The re-sults of the reduced form estimation are . . . [summarized below.]

First, . . . as predicted, seniority is posi-tively related to margin: more senior repre-sentatives are more likely to be reelected. It is also shown that business groups (gen-eral business contributions and an aggre-gate defined as contributions from real es-tate groups) are positively related to seniority, indicating that these groups are concerned with changing the voting be-havior of likely winners. Union contribu-tions, contributions from ideological groups (liberal, conservative) and contri-butions from political parties are nega-tively related to seniority: these groups are concerned with electing desired candi-dates, rather than with changing positions of candidates. It is also evident . . . that contributions are partly aimed at changing positions of representatives from marginal union districts, as predicted. There are some other results which are puzzling: oil production is often statistically significant. The significance of political party is not surprising: business groups largely contrib-ute to Republicans and unions to Demo-crats.

Political contributions can be made to elect favorable representatives or to change policies of likely winners. There is evi-dence that contributions are in fact made for both purposes. Unions and other groups which have large numbers of mem-bers seem to concentrate their contribu-tions in such a way as to elect certain repre-sentatives; those groups which do not have much voting power seem to use their con-tributions to change the position of likely winners.

III. EFFECTS OF UNIONS ON CONGRESSIONAL VOTING

In an earlier paper, the authors examined the role of union membership in determining the voting behavior of Congressmen (Kau and Rubin, 1979b) and found that union membership was significant in affecting voting on almost all issues. Moreover, unions seemed to be part of a "liberal" coalition in Congress, made up of union members, residents of central cities, and those with an interest in consumer affairs. This coalition represented economic and ideological issues; in addition, membership in the coalition seemed also to imply some logrolling. Empirically, it seems impossible to determine the extent to which union support for a position is due to the interests of the union and the extent to which it is due to logrolling. Thus, in this paper union behavior and influence is examined in connection with a set of issues on which, for theoretical reasons, one would expect unions to have some interest. The effects of both union membership and union contributions on voting are assessed to provide a better specification than has been used in previous research where either membership or contributions, but not both, have been employed. Consideration is given to votes dealing with minimum wages; food stamp benefits for strikers; wage-price controls; and CETA and OSHA appropriations. Theoretical expectations are specified for each issue. (A description of each bill named is in the Appendix.)

Minimum wages generally impact low-wage workers whereas union members are typically high-wage workers. However, union members are substitutes for low-wage workers. Hence, anything which served to increase the price of low-paid workers should serve to increase the demand (and thus the wage) of union members. One would therefore expect unions to support high minimum wages. More-

over, the rhetoric of union leaders indicates support for minimum wages, and past research indicates that unions do indeed support minimum wage increases. Two minimum wage bills are considered: one is a bill which would have permitted employers to hire persons under 18 for wages below the minimum; another is the final passage of the minimum wage bill. It is anticipated that unions would oppose the former and favor the latter.

The next bills deals with the issue of food stamps for strikers. By allowing strikers to obtain food stamps, the cost to workers of a strike is substantially lowered. This serves to increase the bargaining power of workers and serves to improve for workers the terms on which agreements will be reached. Thus, it is expected that unions would favor this provision. Since the bill under consideration would have prohibited food stamps for strikers, unions should oppose this bill.

Wage and price controls provide something of a puzzle to economists. It is generally believed that these do not work and serve merely to conceal inflation. Moreover, by freezing prices significant deadweight losses are imposed on the economy. Thus, the imposition of such controls is a negative-sum game; yet, during periods of inflation, there are often political pressures to impose such controls. It is not clear who benefits from such controls, and it is thus not clear who would favor them. (Such programs may be passed for primarily ideological reasons.) Thus, part of the purpose in examining wage price controls is to ascertain which interests support such controls. However, given that such controls are to be passed, it is clear that interest groups would be concerned with the actual form of the controls; in the limit, the optimum might be for everyone's income but one's own to be controlled. Thus, one would hypothesize that unions would favor measures which would limit the control over wages relative to prices. One of the bills proposed would require the Cost of Living Council to provide hearings before reducing wages. Unions could be expected to support this measure. The other bill extends the power of the President to propose wage and price controls. The direction of union sentiment on this bill cannot be predicted a priori.

With regard to program funding, one bill would have increased funds for CETA, a manpower training program. Because union members might be involved in providing training for the unemployed, unions would favor this bill. Alternatively, as mentioned above, unions seem to belong to a coalition which includes (sometimes) the disadvantaged, and for this reason might also be expected to favor this bill.

OSHA regulates workplace safety which rhetoric indicates that unions advocate. The reasons are not clear. One possibility is that the support of this program is ideological. An alternative hypothesis has been proposed by Posner (1977) who argued that OSHA increases costs of low paying (and hence non-union) firms and thus increases demand for union labor. One would thus expect unions to favor OSHA.

In addition to the two variables measuring union power (union contributions to the Congressman and union members in the state) several other variables were included in the model. These variables include demographic characteristics of constituents (central city, farm, black, educations); government spending in the Congressional district, divided into two types (DOD, HEW); and other contributions received by the Congressman (business, agriculture, coal, gas, environmental). Also included was a variable measuring the electoral margin of the Congressman in the last election (margin) and the percentage of the district voting for Nixon in the 1972 presidential election as an ideological measure. In previous research, ratings given to the Congressman

by the Americans for Democratic Action (ADA), a liberal pressure group, were used as a measure of ideology. However, that variable (which is based on voting behavior by the Congressman) may reflect either the Congressman's own ideology or the ideology of his constituents. The vote for Nixon in the district more clearly indicates the characteristics of constituents are accounted for in the model, the Nixon vote is a measure of ideology. Also, the correlation between the vote for Nixon and the ADA rating earned by Congressmen is $-.69$, which indicates that much of the ideological component of Congressional voting is due to constituent ideology, rather than choice by the Congressman.

* * * * *

[Empirical estimation[3] using the Congressional district as the unit of observation indicates that] in all cases, union contributions are significant in explaining voting and have the predicted sign. Union membership in the Congressman's district is significant twice. Thus, it appears that unions do in fact influence Congressional voting and that this influence occurs largely, but not entirely, as a result of the political contributions of unions rather than as a result of the voting behavior of union members.

It is also apparent that HEW (a measure of spending by the Department of Health, Education, and Welfare in the district) is significant six times and always has the same sign as Union Contributions. This indicates the existence of a coalition be-

---

[3] The statistical tool used is logit analysis, with a vote for a bill assigned a weight of one and a vote against assigned a weight of zero. All voting Congressmen were counted, as were those paired for or against the bill. Statistical procedures were greatly simplified by having the same sample size for all votes; therefore, all abstaining on a vote were assigned either for or against the bill in accordance with the vote of the majority of voting representatives from their respective states. Where this was impossible due to a tie, a random process was used.

tween unions and welfare recipients in influencing voting, at least on the issues considered here. The only other variable which is always significant is Nixon and it always has the opposite sign from union contributions. This finding is entirely consistent with the earlier results, where it was also found that ideological variables were important in explaining voting. Moreover, one again detects the liberal and conservative political coalitions that exist in Congress: The liberal element in this analysis is made of union members and HEW recipients; conservatives are represented through ideological interests.

IV. SUMMARY AND IMPLICATIONS

This paper reveals that unions have significant amounts of political power which is obtained both through the power of union members as voters and through campaign contributions made by unions to representatives. Moreover, unions seem to use contributions and membership in a controlled fashion; contributions seem to be given to representatives which the union wants elected who need assistance (i.e., those with little seniority) and to representatives from districts which have about the average number of union members, so that without union contributions the vote of the Congressman would be uncertain. Moreover, the evidence indicates that this strategy seems to be effective, for both union membership and contributions received from unions are significant in explaining the voting behavior of representatives; contributions are particularly important in explaining this behavior.

In analyzing the effects of unions, economists generally consider issues such as collective bargaining and effects on relative wages. It is generally acknowledged that unions also have some political power (e.g., Reynolds, 1974, p. 580). In this paper, the political effects of labor unions have been empirically documented. More-

over, these effects may be as important as the other effects of unions. Thus, unions have been important in explaining minimum wage legislation and, perhaps more importantly, the existence of wage-price controls, issues generally considered as more or less independent of union power. In a complete model of the economic influence of unions, it is necessary to consider also the ways in which the political behavior of unions influences the economic environment.

APPENDIX: BILLS USED IN THIS STUDY (DESCRIPTION FROM *CONGRESSIONAL QUARTERLY*)

1. **HR 7935. Minimum Wage.** Anderson (R Ill.) amendment to permit employers to hire youths under 18 or full-time students at $1.60 an hour ($1.30 for agricultural labor) or 80 percent of the applicable adult minimum wage (whichever is higher), for a period not to exceed 20 work weeks. Rejected by recorded teller vote 199–215: R 160–24; D 39–191 (ND 10–142; SD 29–49)[4] June 6, 1973. A "yea" vote supported the President's position.

2. **HR 7935. Minimum Wage.** Passage of the bill to increase the hourly minimum wage, to extend coverage to about 6 million workers and to extend overtime pay coverage to certain employees previously exempted. Passed 287–130: R 79–104; D 208–26; (ND 151–2; SD 57–24), June 1973. A "nay" vote supported the President's position.

3. **HR 8860. Farm Program Extension.** Dickinson (R Ala.) amendment to second Foley (D Wash.) substitute amendment (see vote 255(T), below), to prohibit food stamps for strikers and their families under the existing food stamp program, due to expire Sept. 30, 1973. Adopted by recorded teller vote 208–207: R 160–25; D 18–182 (ND 5–146; SD 43–36), July 19, 1973. The President did not take a position on the amendment.

4. **HR 6168. Wage-Price Controls Extension.** St Germain (D R.I.) amendment to

_____
[4] ND, SD. Northern Democrat, Southern Democrat.

the Widnall substitute amendment to require the Cost of Living Council to offer the opportunity of hearings before issuing an order reducing wages and to publish an explanation of such an order within 30 days after it was issued. Adopted by recorded teller vote 271–132: R 71–110; D 200–22; (ND 139–3; SD 61–19), April 16, 1973. The President did not take a position on the amendment.

5. HR 6168. Wage-Price Controls Extension. Gonzalez (D Texas) amendment to the Widnall substitute amendment to extend the President's controls authority for 60 days and direct him to develop and report to Congress by May 15, 1973, a comprehensive controls program. Rejected by recorded teller vote 151–253: R 5–177; D 146–76 (ND 115–27; SD 31–49), April 16, 1973. A "nay" vote supported the President's position.

6. HR 6168. Wage Price Controls Extension. Rousselot (R Calif.) motion to recommit the bill extending the President's wage price controls authority to the Banking and Currency Committee. Rejected 161–243: R 42–111; D 122–102 (ND 105–39; SD 17–63), April 16, 1973. The President did not take a position on the motion.

7. HR 15580. Labor-HEW Appropriations, Fiscal 1975. Obey (D Wis.) amendment to increase appropriations for the Comprehensive Employment and Training Act by $300-million, to $2,450,000,000. Adopted 231–171: R 47–130; D 184–41 (ND 144–6; DS 40–35), June 27, 1974. The President did not take a position on the amendment.

8. HR 15580. Labor-HEW Appropriations, Fiscal 1975. Symms (R Idaho) amendment to reduce appropriations for the Occupational Safety and Health Administration by $30,416,000, from $100,816,000 to $70,400,000. Rejected 179–218: R 126–49; D 53–169 (ND 6–141; SD 47–28), June 27, 1974. The President did not take a position on the amendment.

Glossary of Statistical Terms

ANALYSIS OF VARIANCE—ANOVA

Analysis-of-variance methods are used to compare the means of several sampled populations. For example, a firm, trying different methods of production in different plants, may wish to know if the observed differences in employee satisfaction are a result of the different methods of production or are attributable to chance variation. In other words, the firm wishes to know if the observed differences are significantly related to the method of production. ANOVA is one technique that may be used to examine this relationship. The analysis is based on a separation of the variance of all the observations into parts, each of which measures the variability attributable to a particular source (such as the production method). Whether the differences in employee satisfaction are significant depends on the overall variability among all the employees and on the variability within each group of employees.

CORRELATION ANALYSIS

Correlation analysis is used to examine the degree of relation between two variables by giving a measure of the extent to which variation (change) in one variable is associated with variation in the other.

Graphically, correlation is described as a linear relationship because the extent to which two variables are correlated is determined by the degree to which a straight line describes the points representing cases in a population. The figure below describes an example of perfect correlation between seniority and wages.

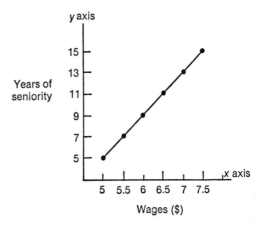

Only in the ideal situation of perfect correlation does a straight line describe all the points. Generally there is merely some degree of correlation. The closer the dots cluster around a central regression line, the higher the correlation. Since correlation refers to the degree to which two variables move simultaneously, two variables may show some correlation even when their relationship is not perfectly linear.

527

CORRELATION COEFFICIENT

Pearson product-moment correlation coefficient signified by r is a number which indicates the direction and magnitude (strength) of a relationship between two variables. The correlation may be direct or positive, indicating that high values of one variable tend to be associated with high values of another variable; or it may be negative, indicating that high values of one variable tend to be associated with low values of another. The maximum value possible for the correlation coefficient is +1.0 which is the value of a perfect positive correlation. A value of −1.0 is the most extreme negative value for a coefficient. Thus the range of values of the correlation coefficient is +1.0 (perfect positive correlation) $\rightarrow 0 \rightarrow -1.0$ (perfect negative correlation) with zero indicating no correlation.

DEPENDENT VARIABLE

A dependent variable is the factor or outcome the researcher is trying to explain or predict. It is caused by one or more of the explanatory variables. In regression analysis it is the variable to be predicted and is referred to as Y. It is also referred to as a criterion variable in ANOVA.

DUMMY VARIABLE

A dummy variable is a dichotomous variable that indicates the presence or absence of a particular characteristic or event. Observations with a particular characteristic (e.g., a college degree) are assigned an arbitrary number (usually 1) while all others are assigned another number (usually 0). This dummy variable measures the presence = 1 or absence = 0 of the particular characteristic being examined.

ESTIMATION EQUATION

An estimation equation often refers to the regression equation used to analyze (esti-mate) the relationship between the dependent and independent variables.

F-TEST

See STATISTICAL SIGNIFICANCE.

INDEPENDENT VARIABLE

Independent variables are the factors used to explain or predict changes in a dependent variable. They are also referred to as explanatory variables.

INTERACTION TERM

An interaction term is used in regression analysis to examine the joint effect of two variables on the dependent variable. The product of two or more terms is included in the regression equation as a new predictor variable. This multiplicative term is an interaction term. For example, in the following equation

$$Y = a + bx_1 + bx_2 + bx_1x_2$$

the term x_1x_2 is the interaction term.

MEAN

The mean is the average of a number of terms computed by adding the terms and then dividing by the number of terms.

MULTICOLINEARITY

Multicolinearity exists when two or more independent variables used in a regression equation are highly correlated. When a perfect correlation exists, regression becomes impossible. To the extent predictor variables are correlated, problems may arise in the regression analysis that affect the statistical results. Consequently, researchers attempt to minimize intercorrelations between independent variables.

N

N refers to the number of terms in each sample. It is the size of the sample.

NULL HYPOTHESIS

A testable hypothesis is stated as the alternative to what is believed to be true so that it can be rejected. For example, a researcher who wants to empirically test the belief that employees with 20 years seniority have higher salaries than employees with 15 years seniority would test the null hypothesis that there is no difference in salary between the groups.

REGRESSION ANALYSIS

BIVARIATE REGRESSION

While correlation generally describes the relationship between two variables, a researcher often wishes to use one variable to predict or control the other variable. A technique for prediction is called regression analysis. The variable to be predicted is referred to as Y, the dependent variable. The predicting variable is referred to as X, the independent variable. The dependent variable is expressed as a function of the independent variable. The basic equation for linear regression is $Y' = a + bx$ where Y' is the predicted value of Y, a is the value of Y at the Y-intercept (or y axis) when $X = 0$, and b is the slope of the regression line which measures the increase in Y for each unit increase in X. The slope b is the regression coefficient. When a straight line is used to relate two variables, the regression equation is linear.

MULTIPLE REGRESSION

Multiple regression is an extension of the principles of bivariate regression. It involves cases with two or more independent variables. The general equation for multiple regression is $Y' = a + b_1x_1 + b_2x_2 + \ldots \ldots + b_nx_n$. In this equation, b_1 and b_2 are regression coefficients; b_1 stands for the expected difference in Y between two groups which differ by one unit in x_1, when x_2 is held constant. Thus, b_1 measures the relationship between x_1 and Y, holding all other independent variables constant.

RELATED STATISTICS

BETA WEIGHT (β). A beta weight is a standardized regression coefficient expressed in standard units. This allows the researcher to examine the relative contribution of different variables which otherwise may be obscured by the different scale ranges of the predictor variables.

CONSTANT. The value of Y at the y axis when $X = 0$ is the constant. In the basic equation for linear regression $(Y = a + bx)$, it is represented by a.

MULTIPLE R. The multiple R is the multiple correlation coefficient which measures the predictive accuracy and strength of the linear association. It is the square root of the coefficient of determination. It varies from zero to ± 1. The coefficient of determination is preferred to the coefficient of correlation because it is a more clear-cut way of stating the proportion of variance in Y associated with X.

COEFFICIENT OF DETERMINATION (R^2). R^2 expresses the proportion of variation in a dependent variable explained or accounted for by an independent variable.

REGRESSION COEFFICIENT. Graphically this represents the slope of the regression line. It measures the increase in the dependent variable Y for each unit increase in the independent variable X. It is represented by b in the equation for regression. It is the unstandardized regression coefficient.

STANDARD ERROR OF THE ESTIMATE (SEE). SEE is used to evaluate the accuracy of the prediction equation. It is a means of determining the amount of error associated with a prediction. It is a measure of the standard deviation of actual Y values from predicted Y values, indicating the average error in predicting Y from the regression equation.

STANDARD SCORE (Z-SCORE)

A variable is standardized by relating it to its own standard deviation. A standardized variable has a mean $= 0$ and variance $= 1$.

STANDARD DEVIATION

Standard deviation measures the dispersion about the mean of a variable.

STATISTICAL SIGNIFICANCE

Before rejecting a null hypothesis, a researcher desires a sample value that has a very small probability of arising if the hypothesis is true. Researchers often reject a hypothesis only if the sample value has a liklihood of coming from the hypothesized population 5/100 of the time or less. This probability fraction is the statistical significance level of the test. The 5/100 is referred to as *.05 significance level*. A more strict significance level of 1/100 or .01 is sometimes used, making it more difficult to reject the null hypothesis.

The F-test is used as a measure of statistical significance. In regression analysis, it is a test of the null hypothesis that the regression coefficients are zero. An F-ratio of the variation explained by regression to that unexplained is computed. The results, compared to the probabilities associated with the F-distribution, determine the significance level. If the F-value is greater than the value for a given level of significance, the null hypothesis that $b = 0$ is rejected.

T-TEST FOR THE DIFFERENCE BETWEEN MEANS

The T-test is used by researchers to compare two groups of subjects to determine if the difference between the two groups is significant. For example, a researcher might be interested in examining the statistical significance of the difference in salaries between union and nonunion employees in a given company. The group means are used as the basis for comparison. A T-value is computed by dividing the difference between the means of each group by the standard deviation of the difference between the means.